FOODSERVICE AND HOTEL PURCHASING

For Laura, Teddy, Kathy, Pati, Roy, and Mark
who mean more to me than I've ever told them

CONTENTS

FOREWORD

Of all the activities that produce success in the operation of a foodservice establishment, the purchasing function provides the greatest challenge. The vast range of variables in supply, quality, variety, model, content, warranty, and adaptability of the thousands of items needed poses formidable decisions for even the most informed and the most experienced purchasers.

Foodservice and Hotel Purchasing looks at the array of purchasing problems and offers a management-of-materials approach to their solution. Its guidance can help you bring order from what too often approaches chaos. It provides a great deal of information, and thus is an excellent resource for purchase decision-making. But *Foodservice and Hotel Purchasing* is far more than just another collection of data. Its philosophy of purchasing guides you in the development of standards, specifications, procedures, and controls. Furthermore, mixed into this book's clarifying pages are glimpses of history that both explain the industry's purchasing dilemmas and offer enjoyable anecdotes.

Few subjects that have an impact on the purchasing function and an influence on successful operation are missing from the contents of this volume. Whether it be laws of contracts and warranties or the ethics involved in purchasing, the understanding of grades and their uses or the differences between coffees and teas, the purchase and conservation of energy or the right chemicals for the cleaning jobs, judging the flavor of food or how to buy the correct equipment—there is a great deal in this volume for you. When decisions are crucial and your choice can affect the very existence of the foodservice operation, this book is for you.

Ray Peddersen not only draws from his own experience in successful purchasing for foodservice establishments, but also includes some of the excellent information from the industry press and related publications. You will find special value in this book's treatment of energy conservation on a cost and benefit basis and its emphasis on development of sound, consistent economic criteria for making the needed limitations. Included is a valuable list of things that you can do in a foodservice installation to reduce energy use and cost.

For those concerned with good purchasing practices in a hospitality industry firm—and that means more than just the person with the formal purchaser title—this book is a veritable gold mine of information, principles, practices, and recommendations. You will find the following pages of tremendous value in the management-of-materials approach to purchasing.

Charles E. Eshbach
University of Massachusetts

PREFACE

The objective of this book is two-fold. The first goal is to provide an explanatory text for knowledge-seeking readers of *SPECS: The Comprehensive Foodservice Purchasing & Specification Manual* (Boston: CBI Publishing Company, Inc., 1977). I hope foodservice operators will find the commodities information and the new materials on wines and non-food supplies offered here useful.

The second and more important objective of this book is to provide a textbook for college programs. This book reflects my recent work as a member of a team of educational and technical experts who developed a university level course in Food Procurement under a USDA grant (Section 19, PL 95–166) to the California State Department of Education. The teaching strategy was designed by Douglas L. Minnis, Ed.D., Associate Dean of the Graduate Division, University of California at Davis. I am presenting Doug's thinking and strategy here, with his permission, in order that the adult student, along with the instructor, will know what is going on through the course of study.

A teaching strategy is a long-range plan, systematically using a series of teaching methods and curriculum materials so as to establish a situation in which students are most likely to learn. The choice of a teaching strategy depends on the curriculum content and characteristics of the students. In addition, the teaching style of the instructor makes the selection of one strategy more natural than another; an instructor should use a strategy with which he or she is comfortable.

All teaching strategies should involve a variety of teaching methodologies. This is desirable not only because different students learn best in different ways but also because a variety of approaches helps to reinforce learning for all students. A teaching methodology is used not because of a preferred value, but because the method is appropriate for the particular teaching task. Lecture, discussion, or role playing should not be judged good or bad but appropriate or inappropriate for a particular teaching task.

This textbook is designed to help the students prepare for the challenges of the marketplace and needs of the customers. To do this, it requires the student to think on three levels: recall, processing, and application. Subsequent steps require reflection on the process and evaluation of lesson content.

The course of study in this book is made up of a series of modules, each of which has a central theme or concept. A module usually will require several days to complete. The amount of material covered in one class period is referred to as a lesson. Each module includes an estimate of the number of class hours required for completion. This estimate cannot be taken too literally, because the needs of the students and the style of the instructor will make modifications of these estimates necessary. They are important, however, in helping the instructor maintain a pace sufficient for completing the course in time.

The central goal of this course is to help students master certain concepts well enough to be able to apply them in their professional positions. This strategy of teaching for transfer places emphasis on a series of intellectual tasks that help the student acquire and learn data, solve problems in a familiar setting with the data, and use the data in solving new problems. To facilitate this process of abstraction and generalization, the modules provide an opportunity for the instructor to help students study the intellectual process so that they can better understand what they have learned.

Each module includes three elements that serve as a preface to instruction: (1) goals, (2) objectives, and (3) background information necessary for the teaching of the module. The modules are written in such a way that the evaluation of student progress is based on the factors stated in the objectives at the beginning of the module. These statements give both the instructor and the student a clear definition of what learning is expected to take place during the study of the module. The goal statement gives the student some understanding of why the module is important; it should be dealt with in a class discussion. The major purpose of providing these elements at the beginning of the module is to provide orientation on what is to follow. Students who know clearly what is expected of them learn more than those who are uncertain of where they are going.

The first step in instruction is data collection and organization. The student needs a good set of data as the basis for problem-solving later in the module, and the student needs to learn to gather and organize data under the careful monitoring of an instructor. This step allows for a wide variety of teaching methodologies, and a wide variety of methods should be used. Lectures, films, field trips, observations, and readings are traditional and effective ways of gathering data. Careful instruction on how to gather data is also helpful to the student. Often, this means structuring the observation so that the student looks for the right thing. This structuring is so important that the instructor should provide for it in the use of each methodology. For example, in a lecture it is helpful if the instructor tells the students at the beginning of the lecture what key idea will be presented. In reading, the instructor should give the student an outline guide to the reading. Before seeing a film, students should know the purpose of the film, and they should have some specific things to look for while watching. Similarly, when students are sent to the school cafeteria to observe, they should have a checklist of specific things to look for.

Gathering data is a skill students have practiced since their early school experiences. Unfortunately, the skill of organizing data for usefulness has been neglected. This course of study is designed to help students organize data in each module. Charts, graphs, and summaries are helpful. Categorization of filing systems makes organization possible. Developing groups of related data items that can be retrieved by providing a descriptive name or label to the group is essential.

Instructors can help by carefully monitoring how students organize their data. If students have difficulty organizing data, it may be helpful to give instruction in the skill. The concept can be illustrated by providing participants with a number of items and asking that they put the items into two or three groups. They are then asked to label the groups and to justify the placement of each item in its group. An example of data organization is a chart with rows representing names of several categories (e.g., various foods) and columns that represent specific categories (e.g., calories, vitamins, cost, ease of preparation). Such an organization of data makes it easy to display and retrieve information.

The importance of careful, disciplined collection and organization of data cannot be overemphasized. The validity of solutions to problems depends on a solid data base. The discipline learned in this type of lesson can serve the student well in professional practice.

The analysis step requires the student to use the acquired data in solving a problem. Cause and effect relationships, similarities and differences, explanations, and other systematic relationships are considered. The module is designed to use higher thinking skills. Because this problem-solving involves high emotional risk, the instructor has to establish conditions that facilitate learning at this level. In the data collection and organization part of the curriculum, the students learn that there is usually a right answer (e.g., $2 \times 4 = 8$) and a wrong answer (e.g., $2 \times 4 = 6$) and that the teacher will "grade" the students' responses. When the student is asked to identify ways in which two items are similar or different, no clear-cut right or wrong answers are involved. To support student effort in this higher-risk learning, the teacher establishes a good learning environment by being more accepting of student responses. The teacher is more probing, more accepting, and less declarative.

The analysis step usually takes longer to complete than the data collection and organization step, and there is more need for students to share their thoughts. Group work and discussions are an essential part of the analysis step. Clear instructions, statements of expectations, careful instructor monitoring, and a specific and regular reporting procedure are prerequisites for good group work. A group chair and recorder are helpful and will be even more beneficial if the instructor spells out the specifics of their roles to all participants.

Discussions must be goal-oriented to be a successful part of the analysis step. If they are not, discussions tend to drift from one topic to another. To provide for goal orientation, the instructor should use a planned set of questions and should have ready a variety of ways of responding to students. Questions such as "How are these two alike?" "How are they different?" "Why does this item function this way?" and "Do you see a relationship between these items, and can you find a system of how things work?" all provide specific structure for the student. Responses to student answers can profitably include simple acceptance, probes for more information or clarification, or short informational statements from the instructor (a technique sometimes called responsive lecturing). To keep the discussion moving in the desired direction, the instructor can summarize what has been said and then start on a new subject.

Discussion is an extremely valuable learning tool in the analysis step because it gives students an opportunity to hear what others are thinking and, perhaps equally important, to understand how they are thinking.

The third instructional step is called application because the student is asked to apply what he or she has learned in the first two steps to a new but related problem. The step is a deliberate bridge between the lessons being studied and real-life situations. This attempt to improve transfer of learning is enhanced by asking the student to make predictions on the basis of the data and problem-solving done earlier in the module. In some cases such a prediction can be the suggested answer to a planned experiment, such as "What would happen to your long-range menu planning if you were no longer able to get peanut butter?" At times the learner is asked to develop a theory or an overall generalization that gives perspective to the material learned. This perspective will enable the learner to see how the principle can be applied in a wide variety of situations.

At times the application step is developed as a simulation or game in which the student is given a realistic problem similar enough to the problem solved in the analysis step to allow the use of principles learned. However, the new problem must also be different enough to require the student to generalize concepts learned before principles can be used.

The ideal learning conditions for the application step are similar to those of the analysis step. The student is asked to do some high-level thinking and to provide answers not clearly right or wrong. Instructor supportiveness and helpfulness are essential if the student is to succeed.

The fourth instructional step is reflection. This is a teaching situation in which the instructor deliberately attempts to help the students integrate their new learning and understanding with what they already know. It is at this time that the students and instructor deal with the question "What did I learn?"

During the reflection step the instructor makes the learning process explicit. The students need to be aware of the process, to understand the steps, and to recognize the higher levels of thinking they have been using. They need to understand the strategy and purpose for each step. Discussions of the relative productivity of various activities in each instructional step make the students more thoughtful during the study of the next module. Each module involves a style of thinking that can be used in other settings.

During the reflection step, the instructor has many opportunities to point out the dynamic nature of knowledge. Students may consider the knowledge base of a module to be static. It is not, of course, and some instructors find that the reflection stage is a good time to introduce students to both the dynamics of knowledge acquisition and the cyclical nature of inquiry. Questions such as, "How could we do this study differently now that we know . . .?" or "How does our theory, solution, or generalization relate to the new findings of the Department of Nutrition at UC, Davis?" Clearly both types of questions raise the student's understanding of the process to an explicit level.

Each module involves two kinds of evaluation. The first is formal in nature. A pretest determines how much students know when they enter the course; a post-test determines how much they know when they complete the course. This summative evaluation provides specific scores for each student and allows for a measurement of achievement in the course.

The second type of evaluation is for the benefit of both the instructor and the students as the course is being conducted. Formative evaluation allows the instructor and students to get feedback on progress in the course while there is still time to do something about disappointing performance and capitalize on those aspects that are going well.

In addition to the summative and formative evaluations, each module includes a checklist for evaluating the module itself. Each module was planned and written to provide for the best possible chance of learning. From the literature on how students learn and from experiences related to how instructor behavior affects student learning, a set of goals for the modules was developed. They are also included with each module. The checklist includes nine key considerations, broken down into four major groups: (1) effective teacher behavior; (2) effective lesson organization; (3) knowledge of students; and (4) appropriate teaching materials and ways of evaluating students.

Clarity, organization, and knowledge of the subject matter are essential for effective teaching. The modules can be structured to encourage these characteristics. Acceptance and probing are important, but it is necessary to learn these behaviors outside the module structure.

Experience has shown that students learn best when they are told the concept they are to learn; have an opportunity to see a demonstration of the concept; have a chance to practice and receive feedback from the instructor who has monitored the practice; and, finally, have an opportunity to reflect on what has happened and to integrate the new knowledge with the old.

Knowledge of students is essential, and the modules are planned so that the instructor can diagnose the level of student skill and adjust the level of instruction accordingly. This is one of the more sophisticated skills an instructor can have, and it is probably in this area that the greatest need for instructor modification exists because it is difficult to imagine the variety of skills students will have.

Instruction cannot be complete or adequate without a specific system of evaluation that informs the instructor and students of progress and problems. Thus, each module includes specific ways for the instructor to determine this progress, and the course of study includes a pretest and post-test to give more specific information.

Each course of study and each module in the course of study were planned to work the content of the course into an overall teaching strategy that would increase the opportunities of students learning the content. This integrated content/teaching strategy can be a helpful addition to the curriculum. Modifications can be made in the course of study to meet the needs of students without changing the basic structure of the modules.

Now that this is understood let us move on to the text. Have a wonderful new learning experience!

R. B. P.

ACKNOWLEDGMENTS

The preparation of any text is a herculean task; the preparation of so highly technical a text as *Hotel and Foodservice Purchasing* was even tougher. This work would not have been possible without the cooperation of many helpful professionals and friends. My thanks go to all those who urged the writing of this book, an outgrowth of *SPECS: The Comprehensive Foodservice Purchasing and Specification Manual,* and to Mike Tucker and Phil Mason of CBI Publishing Company, Inc. for their faith in the project. I would also like to express thanks to Linda Dunn McCue for providing a fine editing job and seeing this book through the maze of production problems. My gratitude also goes to Diane Halford for the months of typing various drafts of manuscript. Brother Herman, Marilyn Trownsell, Paul Diegnan, Sandra Hotchkin, Sandra Fuller, Donna Boss, Ed Sanders, Laura Falk, and Elisabeth Ream with their faith have all played a part in pushing this book out of my head and onto the printed page.

The source material for this book has been provided in large part through the generosity of the following, whose participation is gratefully acknowledged:

- *The Almanac of the Canning, Freezing, and Preserving Industries*
- American Hotel & Motel Association, for the use of materials from ''The Selection and Maintenance of Commercial Carpet.''
- American Spice Trade Association and Marshall Neale
- AVI Publishing Company, for the use of material from *Quality Control in Food Service* by Thorner and Manning
- *Bakery Production and Marketing Magazine*
- Jaques Bloch, CFE, and the Montefiore Hospital
- Blue Goose, Inc., for extensive use of material from their *Buying Guide*
- *Cereal Foods World*
- The Coffee Brewing Institute
- *Cooking for Profit*
- Corning Glass Works
- Crescent Metal Products, Inc.

- Crimsco Inc.
- *Financial Times*
- *Food Engineering*
- *Food Management*
- Christen George, R.D., for preparing the legal information
- Hastings House, Publishers, Inc., for material from Frank Schoonmaker's *Encyclopedia of Wine*
- Hobart Corporation
- Hollymatic Corporation
- *Institutions,* for various charts, reprints of articles, and convenience foods information
- Michael Joseph LTD, for information from George Rainbird's *The Wine Handbook*
- King Arthur, Inc.
- Klopman Mills (a division of Burlington Industries)
- Koch Supplies
- Libbey Glass (a division of Owens-Illinois)
- National Association of Institutional Laundry Managers, for broad use of material from their *Certification Manual*
- National Dairy Council, for milk and cheese information
- National Fisheries Institute, Inc.
- National Institutional Food Distributors Association (NIFDA)
- National Live Stock and Meat Board, for information from their publications and use of photographs
- National Marine Fisheries Service
- National Restaurant Association
- NCR Corporation
- *NOAA Magazine*
- Quadrangle, for the use of material from Terry Robards' *Wine Cellar Journal*
- *Restaurant Business*
- Jackson E. Scott of the H. W. Baker Linen Company, for use of material from their *Institutional Textile Manual*
- Sheraton Corporation
- Sparta Brush Company
- Stewart-Tucker Inc.
- Syracuse China Corporation
- United Fresh Fruit and Vegetable Association, for data from their publications, especially *Fruit and Vegetable Facts and Pointers*
- Utah State Board of Education, for the use of materials from *Planning the School Foodservice Facilities*
- Wear-Ever Food Service Equipment
- Wine Institute and Wine Advisory Board

Last, but far from least, let me pay tribute to my dear friend Peggy Cronin and my daughter Shaari Ann for the time away from them that this work caused. My most sincere apologies to anyone who contributed who has been inadvertently overlooked in these acknowledgments.

Raymond B. Peddersen
Salt Lake City, Utah
October, 1980

1

AN OVERVIEW OF MATERIALS PROCUREMENT AND SELECTION

INTRODUCTION

Purchasing is a function common to most organizations. Effective standards and controls need to be established and thoroughly understood in order to purchase economically. The purchasing function impacts upon the entire organization and, therefore, must be carefully integrated.

Chapter 1 presents a complete picture of the elements that comprise an effective purchasing system. These elements include consideration of unique properties within a given organization. Specific forms for food quotations, specifications, and delivery are presented, as well as a number of printed resources that will be helpful to food purchasers. The laws of contracts and warranties present food purchasers with information regarding governmental regulations. Perhaps one of the most critical responsibilities of buyers is to inspect the goods they are purchasing. Caveat emptor—"let the buyer beware"—still prevails. The legality of contracts requires four prerequisites: (1) mutual consent, (2) consideration, (3) the object must be legal, and (4) capacity of the parties. The Uniform Commercial Code was designed to ascertain the intention between the two parties and to enforce that contract.

Regulations of warranties, packaging, composition, identity, and labeling are described with a brief history of the laws and amendments that have occurred since the 1800s. Most notable of these laws are the Federal Food and Drug Law and the Fair Packaging and Labeling Act.

Emphasis on knowing and identifying differences in quality, the necessity for written specifications, common operator buying mistakes, and causes of high food costs are also stressed in this chapter.

This is a text that is written for students and foodservice operators who are interested in understanding the management of the materials used in the foodservice industry. The "materials manager" must understand the marketplace, purchasing, ethics and techniques, receiving, storage and handling, as well as specifications and utilization of foodservice materials. Thus, the concept of "materials manager" is far more broad than the concept of "food buyer." That which follows in the next few hundred pages is intended to serve the dual purpose of educating and referencing. If the information provided here is not exhaustive enough, the references provided with each chapter certainly provide the bulk of human knowledge in the discipline.

Purchasing food is an art, a science, and a business. There is an art involved in judging just the right ripeness of a melon, the qualities of a wine, the consistency of a potato. There is a science to the objective measurements of quality as well as the procurement of the correct use-level of an item at its best market price. The business is the management of materials, money, and time in the most economical way.

In many industries the purchasing function stands alone. But in foodservice the quality and the quantity of materials purchased are both the beginning and the end of the circle of total operation. Purchasing must be tightly interrelated. To put it another way, it is *not* possible to prepare high quality food from low quality ingredients, but it *is* possible to prepare low quality food from high quality ingredients.

Items purchased for industrial use, such as nuts and bolts, carry exacting specifications. There are, of course, definite measures that can be applied to nuts and bolts—percentages of different metals in the alloy, physical size, type and depth of threads, and so on. It is commonly believed that equally definite measures cannot be applied to foods. That belief is wrong.

Various agencies and departments of the federal government have established detailed specifications for virtually any type of raw product in the marketplace. The mass of these specifications runs to many thousands of printed pages, with the specification for an individual product often requiring eight or more pages.

These standards and the controls were established by the government to protect citizens from hazardous practices on the part of food processors, and to generally assure disease-free and unadulterated products. As foodservice operators, we do not need to know all the details about every product, but we do need to know the most important ones to do the best job in purchasing food for preparation. To that end, the author has included only the most pertinent details on the very broad range of food and food products available in the United States.

THE PURCHASING FUNCTION: WHAT IS IT?

Purchasing food and supplies is somewhat unique in that it goes beyond specifying products and placing orders. In foodservice the functions related to purchasing are generally done by the same people who do the purchasing. While a large volume operation might be an exception, most foodservice operations are not large volume. This section discusses those related functions.

Forecasting

If you do not know how many you are going to serve, you cannot know how much to buy. Therefore, you must predict how much will be served.

A CBI Book
(CBI is an imprint of Van Nostrand Reinhold Company Inc.)

Copyright © 1981 by Van Nostrand Reinhold Company

Library of Congress Catalog Card Number
ISBN 0-8436-2192-3

Designed by Debra L. Syrotchen

Van Nostrand Reinhold Company Inc.
135 West 50th Street
New York, New York 10020

Van Nostrand Reinhold Company Limited
Molly Millars Lane
Wokingham, Berkshire RG11 2PY, England

Van Nostrand Reinhold
480 La Trobe Street
Melbourne, Victoria 3000, Australia

Macmillan of Canada
Division of Canada Publishing Corporation
164 Commander Boulevard
Agincourt, Ontario M1S 3C7, Canada

16 15 14 13 12 11 10 9 8 7 6 5 4

Library of Congress Cataloging in Publication Data

Peddersen, Raymond B
    Foodservice and hotel purchasing.

    Bibliography: p.
    Includes index.
    1. Food service. 2. Purchasing. I. Title.
TX911.3.P8P39   642'.5'0687   80-20961
ISBN 0-8436-2192-3

FOODSERVICE AND HOTEL PURCHASING

RAYMOND B. PEDDERSEN, CFE, FHCFA

CBI

A CBI Book
Published by Van Nostrand Reinhold Company

Foodservice operators who make accurate predictions enjoy good controls, fewer headaches, and predictable operating expenses. Those who are inaccurate in their predictions spend a lot of time figuring out what to serve when they run out, or how to reuse leftovers. Bad forecasting is bad business.

A card that gives a history of food portions served can be used as a record to indicate the percentage of sales on one item compared to competing menu items. In almost every operation the consumption pattern of one item of a class (entrees, desserts, etc.), as opposed to any number of competing menu items of that class, will be fairly consistent.

Also, in most operations there is a pattern as to the total number of customers served. In a restaurant this may be a function of the day of the week, or the season of the year, or both; in an institution, it may reflect many factors.

By keeping careful sales records with customer count patterns, operators will usually be able to closely estimate (forecast) the number of customers expected on any given day. When this figure is multiplied by the usual consumption percentage of any given menu item, the result is an estimate of the number of portions needed.

In practice it is applied like this. Assume a standardized recipe for 100 portions of roast beef that calls for 30 lb. of IMPS No. 167-Knuckle. If the forecast is for 357 portions, then the buyer will know to purchase 3.57 $\times$ 30 lb. or 107 lb. (+ 1.6 oz.) of IMPS No. 167-Knuckle.

A more sophisticated system is to use these records to calculate a moving average. A moving average is simply the average number of portions served over a certain period of time. The simplest to calculate is one based on 10 serving times. To calculate the moving average:

1. Add the number of portions served the last 10 consecutive times the item was served.
2. Divide the total by 10.
3. Next time the item is served, subtract from the total (1) the number of portions served 11 times ago, and add the number of portions served this time.
4. Divide the new total (3) by 10.
5. Repeat (3) and (4) each time the item is served.

The moving average may then be used as your forecast.

Purchasing Systems

The relationship between the buyer and the purveyor must be one of trust and confidence. There are shady practices to be avoided on both sides. Some purveyors deliver supplies that are inferior to those ordered. This will continue until the buyer stops the practice by rejecting shipments that do not meet the specifications.

To be sure, purveyors who attempt this should be condemned for failing to keep faith with the buyer. On the other hand, the buyer should be condemned for failure to verify that the product received is the product that was ordered.

Specifications are of no use if they are applied only to the buying and no further. The person(s) responsible for receiving food must be as thoroughly familiar with the buying specifications as the buyer. The receiving person(s) must have reference materials readily available in the receiving area. These materials should include the two volumes of the *Meat Buyers Guide* (National Assn. of Meat Purveyors), this book, and any other references that contain clear and concise descriptions and pictures of foods.

Single Source Buying.   This occurs frequently when the buyer simply orders what is needed from one purveyor and is billed at a rate over which the buyer has no control. The products received may be of acceptable quality or better, but the buyer has no means of determining the price paid is a fair market price.

Competitive Buying.   This process means taking bids from two or more purveyors for any given item. The taking of bids may be done by telephone, by mail, or in person. All these methods require copies of the specifications to be in the hands of the purveyor.

When taking bids by telephone, the buyer must have a means of recording these bids. Commercial forms may be used or the buyer can construct one. Telephone bids are common in foodservice because of the short life span of products. Most operators prefer to order quantities close to their needs as often as they can, and so will take telephone bids and place orders for following day delivery. The financial pitfalls of this practice are discussed later in the section on financial controls.

Mail bidding takes place when the buyer can forecast needs far enough ahead to allow the sending and receipt of bids by mail. Included is a sample cover sheet to a bid which gives instructions to the purveyor in preparing the bid. Also shown is one page of a mail bid for groceries. Note that the instruction sheet is very clear about the cut-off time on receipt of the completed bids.

Selecting Sources

Telephone or mail bids may also be compiled on a form such as shown in this chapter. The most straightforward method is to assign the order for each product to the purveyor who has submitted the lowest bid on the item. When there are enough of these going to each purveyor, this is possible.

Note, however, that it costs a purveyor a lot of money to deliver. The delivery expenses (drivers, trucks, fuel, etc.) divided by the number of deliveries typically reveals a cost-per-stop of at least $10, and sometimes as much as $50. It is unfair to expect a purveyor to deliver orders of a dollar amount less than enough to make a *fair* profit. Thus, in the interest of good business relations, the buyer should not place a very small order with a purveyor but should, instead, award those items to the next lowest bidder.

Whatever the mode of taking bids, there must be a means of placing the order. Throughout the foodservice industry, it is common practice to place orders by telephone. There is no argument that this is efficient. What is wrong with this practice is that telephone orders give no written record (or confirmation) of orders against which

RETURN TO:
Raymond B. Peddersen
Director of Food Services
The Jewish Hospital
Cincinnati, Ohio 45229

THE JEWISH HOSPITAL FOOD QUOTATIONS—BID PREPARATION

PAGE 1   _____ COMPANY

PACK	ITEM	ESTIMATED ORDER QUANTITY	JEWISH HOSPITAL FOOD ITEMS FILE NO.	YOUR BID
6/10	ASPARAGUS SPEARS FCY. 54/80 CT	0	33035	
6/10	BEAN GREEN STD. 4/5 SVE 61/ZD/WT	3	33095	
6/10	BEAN DARK RED KIDNEY/SAUCE FCY.	0	33185	
6/10	BEAN SPROUTS	3	33215	
6/10	BEETS SLD. FCY. 2.5 IN. MAX	7	33245	
6/10	CABBAGE RED	3	33299	
6/10	CORN CREAM STYLE FCY. GLON	0	33335	
6/10	MUSHROOM PIECES	2	33395	
6/10	PEPPERS GREEN DICED	4	33560	
6/10	PEPPERS RED DICED	0	33562	
6/10	PEPPERS GREEN HALVES	3	33565	
24/2½ lb.	PIMENTOS BROKEN FCY.	2	33575	
6/10	SAUERKRAUT FCY. 2.5 PCT SALT MAX	4	33725	
6/10	TOMATO PUREE FCY. 12 PCT SDS	9	33780	
6/10	TOMATO PASTE FCY. 33 PCT SDS	2	33782	
6/10	TOMATO WHOLE X STD 68/ZD/WT	0	33785	

MAIL BID FOR GROCERIES

PRODUCT	PACK	USDA GRADE MIN. SCORE	MIN. NET MIN. DRAINED WT.	SIZE OR COUNT	REMARKS
ASPARAGUS, Spears	6/#5	Fancy 92/103 oz net	50½ oz.	54/80	All Green, Mammoth.
BEANS, BAKED Vegetarian	6/#10	Fancy 85			White beans, in tomato sauce.
BEANS, GREEN N. West Blue Lake	6/#10	XStd. 82/101 oz net	61 oz.	4 or 5 sieve	Pound. Variety.
BEETS Sliced	6/#10	Fancy 90/104 oz net	68 oz.	2½" Max. Diam.	
BEETS Whole	6/#10	Fancy 90/104 oz net	68 oz.	74/124	No softness, peel or black spots.
CARROTS, WHOLE "Belgian"	6/#10	Fancy 90/105 oz net	69 oz.	290/350	Orange-Yellow; no green
CORN, WHOLE Kernel	6/#10	Fancy 90/106 oz net	70 oz.		Golden. Brine pack.
MUSHROOMS, Whole, Button	24/#8Z	Fancy 85/16 oz net	8 oz.		Formosa; cream colored.
OKRA, CUT	6/#10	XSTD. 85/99 oz net	60 oz.		½" to 1" pods.
PEAS, Sweet	6/#10	XSTD. 82/105 oz net	71 oz.	4 or 5 sieve	
PEPPERS, Green Diced	6/#10				
PEPPERS, Red Diced	6/#10				
POTATOES, DEHY. Pearls.	6/#10				Without milk, vit. C added. Packed by Amer. Potato Comp. only. (Whip brand)
POTATOES, DEHY Sliced	6/4#				
POTATOES, INST. w/o milk, Vit. C added	6/#10				Packed by the Amer. Potato comp. only.
POTATOES, Sweet Mashed	6/#10	A 85	72 oz.		Golden type Brix 25°

TELEPHONE OR MAIL BID FORM

ITEM	QUAN	COMPANY		COMPANY		COMPANY	
QUOTATION SHEET — DAY ORDERED: ___ HILLSIDE HOSPITAL FOOD SERVICE — FOR DELIVERY ON:		UNIT PR	AMOUNT	UNIT PR	AMOUNT	UNIT PR	AMOUNT

food received can be checked for quantity and quality. When telephone orders are given, the purveyor should write on the invoice the specification that was bid on.

Also, it is essential that the invoice, or a substantial copy of the invoice, called a shipping ticket, accompany the delivery. The invoice must be checked against the buyer's quotation sheet to verify quantity and price. The food received must be checked against the invoice, the quotation sheet, and the specification book to verify that the quantity billed is the quantity received, and that the quality received is identical to that specified. *Never accept a delivery without verifying weight, quality, and price.*

A better method of placing orders is with a purchase order. The purchase order names the product, gives the specification or a reference to its number in the buyer's specification manual, and includes the price that has been agreed upon. A good purchase order will have at least three parts: a copy for the purveyor, a receiving copy to be used by the buyer in receiving the order, and a copy which is attached to the invoice and used to pay the purveyor.

Systems Contracting

It is the buyer's duty to obtain the specified product at the best possible price from purveyors that can be relied upon. Food passes through many hands before it reaches the foodservice operator. The different owners of the product, at one time or another, might include the farmer, the pre-processor (slaughterhouse), the processor (butcher, canner), the regional or national distributor, and the local distributor.

Each time the food changes hands, the new handler (owner) must make a profit. The further back on this line the food buyer can purchase, the less add-on costs will be reflected in the price.

Buying "closer to the farm" usually means having to buy very large quantities of a single item either immediately or over a predetermined period of time. In many areas, there are individual operators who have formed buying organizations to purchase for the group.

Frequently, individual buyers can buy in quantities larger than they can stock, at guaranteed prices by soliciting bids from several local purveyors, or by making a purchase from a national distributor and then making financial arrangements with a local distributor to warehouse and ship the product on a routine as-needed basis.

Many processing companies maintain warehouses and also sell to local distributors. It often takes no more than a phone call to eliminate one layer of handling costs. The difference can be 10 to 20 percent in buying price.

Such items as milk, ice cream, and bread are not easily bought on day-to-day or week-to-week bids. In selecting purveyors for these daily delivery products the buyer should solicit fixed price bids for a period of six months or a year, and award "sole-purveyor" contracts. Such contracts should be in writing and should specify any procedure for raising or lowering the contracted prices.

Other dairy products, such as cheese, butter, and eggs, can also be contracted for longer periods than week-to-week bids. Most major marketing areas have a publication that gives the wholesale prices being quoted on these items. In the New York City area, such a market guide is published by Urner Barry. A contract for cheese, butter, eggs, and even poultry, may be bid for and taken on a basis of a percentage above the prices quoted on the sheet.

Such a contract might specify that the eggs purchased would be priced 6 cents per dozen higher than the highest price quoted for the particular grade and size on the market sheet. The contract might also allow for cheaper prices for larger quantity purchases, such as 6 cents over market price when 10 cases or less are purchased, dropping to 5 cents over market price for 11 cases or more, and so forth.

Contracts like this simplify an operator's business because they guarantee the source of supply, fix the buy-price to the wholesale market, and limit the number of purveyors. For the purveyor, such a contract guarantees receiving a price which includes purchase and handling costs, and a fair profit.

The *Meat Service Report* is published weekly in Chicago. It is possible to write a systems contract with meat purveyors based on such reports as this.

There are several market reports which wholesale purveyors use as supply and pricing guidelines. Some, such as the USDA's are free; others, such as those mentioned earlier, are available only by subscription. The volume food buyer should learn which publications local purveyors use as market guides and obtain subscriptions.

One-Stop Shopping

One-stop shopping means purchasing all food and supply needs from one purveyor. The advantages of such an arrangement are several: (1) one order to place, (2) one

WEST COAST EDITION
PRODUCERS PRICE — CURRENT
ESTABLISHED 1858 – MORE THAN A CENTURY OF MARKET REPORTING SERVICE

Tuesday, February 7, 1978   Vol. 5, No. 46

EDITOR: PATRICK HARRINGTON
Associate Editors: PAUL B. BROWN
JOSEPH MANFREDI

PUBLISHED TUESDAYS AND THURSDAYS
by URNER BARRY PUBLICATIONS, INC.
4340 Redwood Hwy, Suite 237, San Rafael, CA 94903
Phone: (415) 472 - 2090
One Year's Subscription: $63.50 (postage included)
Copyright 1977 by Urner Barry Publications, Inc.

(+) or (-) indicates change from previous report

TURKEYS
*Does not include basting, netting or Timer
Ready to Cook (R.T.C.) Frozen
Grade A or Comparable Quality*

YOUNG HENS* heavy breeds	Truck Loads & Similar Quantities	L.C.L. 25 box min. Ex Dock
8 to 16 lbs.	59.0 +	61.0-63.0 +
YOUNG TOMS* heavy breeds		
14 to 22 lbs.	59.0	61.0-63.0
22 to 24 lbs.	59.0	61.0-63.0
24 to 26 lbs.	61.0 +	63.0-65.0 +
26 to 28 lbs.	63.0 +	65.0-67.0 +
28 to 30 lbs.	65.0	67.0-69.0
30 to 32 lbs.	67.0	69.0-71.0
32 to 34 lbs.	69.0	71.0-73.0
34 lbs. & over	70.0	72.0-74.0
FRYER-ROASTERS**		
3 to 9 lbs.	60.0	62.0-64.0

*Some nationally advertised marks of Hens,
Fryer-Roasters, and Consumer - Sized Toms
sell at three to five cents premium.
**Special pack sized in ½ lb. wt. range
sell at 2 to 3 cent premium.

CANNER PACKED TURKEYS
*Carlot or Trucklot – no neck – no giblets,
delivered Midwest area.
LINE RUN
(% A, balance may be B's, C's or P.M.'s)*

YOUNG TOMS
14 - 17 lbs.	Unquoted
17 - 20 lbs.	Unquoted
20 lbs. and up	Unquoted

YOUNG HENS
10 - 14 lbs. avg.	Unquoted

REGULAR PACK (B's, C's or P.M.'s)
YOUNG TOMS
14 - 17 lbs.	Unquoted
17 - 20 lbs.	Unquoted
20 lbs. and up	Unquoted
Breeder Hens	Unquoted

YOUNG HENS
10 - 14 lbs. avg.	Unquoted

– MARKETING SITUATION –

EGGS
Supplies adequate but clearing. Market
steady to firm.

TURKEYS
Fair interest developing for fresh hen
turkeys for Washington's Birthday.
Frozen hens and institutional toms
are firm.

CHICKENS
Market about steady in moderately active
trading. Undertone is unsettled as Southern
packers unable to ship loads into the snow-
bound Northeast.

TURKEY BREASTS
*BREAST - first portion of wing meat, back partially
removed, ribs in, some neck skin attached.*

	T/L	L.C.L. 25 box min. Ex Dock
4-6 lbs., per lb.	.99	1.00-1.03
6-8 lbs., per lb.	.95	.97-1.00
8-10 lbs., per lb.	.92	.94- .96
10-12 lbs., per lb.	.98	1.00-1.02
12-14 lbs., per lb.	1.08	1.10-1.12
14-16 lbs. & up, per lb.	1.10	1.12-1.14

BREAST - ribs & some neck
4-6 lbs., per lb.	–	–
6-8 lbs., per lb.	–	–
8-10 lbs., per lb.	.97	.99-1.01
10-12 lbs., per lb.	1.05	1.07-1.09
12-14 lbs., per lb.	1.13	1.15-1.17
14-16 lbs., per lb.	1.15	1.17-1.20

– BASTED & NETTED –
*BREAST - first portion of wing meat, back out,
ribs in, small portion neck skin*
4-6 lbs., per lb.	1.00	1.02-1.04
6-8 lbs., per lb.	1.00	1.02-1.04

RAW TURKEY PARTS

	T/L Bulk Pack Frozen	L.C.L. Bulk Pack Frozen	Fresh Tray Pack Warehouse Delivery
Half Breasts			1.09
Tenderloins			1.60
Thighs	.51	.53-.55	.75
Drums	.23	.24-.26	.42
Wings - whole	.25	.26-.28	.48
Wings - V	.21	.23-.25	.38
Wingettes			.59
Necks-Toms	.13	.14-.16	.34
Necks-Hens	.11	.13-.15	–
Tails	.18	.20-.21	.33
★ Hind Quarters			
(w/part gibs, toms)	.34 -	.36-.37	.42
(w/part gibs, hens)	.34 -	.36-.37	.42
Livers	.21	.23-.24	–
Hearts	.18	.20-.21	–
Gizzards-Natural	.20	.22-.23	–

★ Consumer pack

* RAW TURKEY MEAT T/L
BREAST -
Boneless & Skinless, per lb.	1.50

THIGH -
Boneless, per lb.	.65
Boneless & Skinless, per lb.	.77
White Meat (w/scapula), per lb.	1.10
White Trim, per lb.	1.04
Dark Trim, per lb.	.54
Body Skin, per lb.	.12

FRESH TURKEYS *(includes timer)*

	Truck Load	L.C.L.
YOUNG HENS		
8 to 14 lbs.	61.5 -	63.5-65.5 -
14 to 16 lbs.	63.0	65.0-67.0
YOUNG TOMS		
14 to 24 lbs.		
24 to 26 lbs.		
26 to 28 lbs.		
28 to 30 lbs.		
30 and up		

ICED CHICKENS T/L

Truck lot prices delivered warehouse Southern
Metropolitan California area - based on current
negotiations. (Deliveries: 3-7 days).

TODAY'S QUOTATIONS:
U.S. Grade A, Sized 2-3 lbs.	.42
U.S. Grade A, Size - Seller's Option	.42
California Grown, Sized 2-3 lbs.	.45

COMMINUTED MEAT T/L
(Mechanically deboned)

TURKEY –	
Low fat, no skin	.17
Higher fat, some skin	.16
CHICKEN –	
Under 15% fat	.19
Over 15% fat	.16
BEEF –	
18% fat or less	–
Over 18% fat	–
PORK –	
30% fat or less	–
Fatty tissue	–

FURTHER PROCESSED ITEMS
*Various fillers, including skin, cereal
and dry milk available at discounts.*

READY - TO - EAT
(3 - 5000 lb. min., Ex-Dock or T/L delivered)

OVEN ROASTED BREAST –	
Natural - with skin	1.80-1.85
Skinless	1.82-1.87
Skinless formed	–
OVEN ROASTED THIGH –	
Natural - with skin	1.24-1.35
WATER COOKED TURKEY ROLLS –	
White Meat	1.10-1.20
White & Dark Meat	1.05-1.15
Dark Meat	.89
WATER COOKED & DICED TURKEY –	
White Meat	1.15-1.20
White & Dark Meat	1.05-1.10
CURED –	
Turkey Ham	1.25-1.35
Turkey Franks	.50- .55
Turkey Bologna	.55- .61
Turkey Salami	.69- .75
Turkey Pastrami	1.25-1.33

SHELL EGGS
(Warehouse Del. So. Calif. Met. Area)

TOP GRADE-CARTONED PACK	
Large Whites	58.00-59.00 +
Mediums	57.00-58.00 +
Pullets	42.00-43.00 +
GRADED LOOSE PACK-TRACK	
Large Whites	52.00-53.00 +
Mediums	50.00-51.00 +
Pullets	35.00-36.00 +
LIQUID EGGS – West Coast-Tank Lot	
Whole, per lb., track	29.50-30.00
Pasteurized, per lb., track	30.50-31.00
Whites, per lb., track	18.50-19.00
Pasteurized, per lb., track	19.50-20.00

FROZEN EGGS   TRACK WEST COAST

CENTS PER POUND	T/L
Whole, no color	34.00-36.00
Whites	26.00-28.00
Yolks, 45% solids	
Actual 4	84.00-86.00
Nepa 4	83.00-84.00
Actual 3	80.00-81.00
Nepa 3	76.00-77.00
No color	70.00-71.00
Yolks, sugar 43% solids	
No color	56.00-57.00
Yolks, salt 43% solids	
No color	54.00-55.00
Blend	
30-32% egg solids	40.00-43.00
27-29% egg solids	39.00-42.00

delivery to receive, and (3) one bill to pay. One-stop shopping can reduce the purchasing, receiving, and accounting functions enough to generate substantial savings.

On the other hand, buying from a one-stop purveyor also has disadvantages: (1) no source of supply if the one-stop purveyor has a disaster or labor difficulties, (2) no alternative source should goods delivered be other than specified, and (3) no price competition.

Despite these disadvantages, many operators have found that the advantages financially outweigh the disadvantages.

It is my opinion that one-stop food shopping will be the accepted and prevailing mode of purchasing before the end of the twentieth century. One-stop companies are likely to develop from the merger of several small purveyors. This trend can be seen in the merger of fresh produce with frozen produce houses who then pick up distribution of frozen entrees, baked goods, and meat lines, and then merge with a general groceries and canned goods purveyor.

In almost any city of over 250,000 people, it is possible to purchase 75 percent or more of your needs from any of several large general variety purveyors. We are but a few short steps away from the time when these companies will realize the potential of one-stop shopping and, learning from the mistakes of the pioneers in the field, develop competitive one-stop shopping services in cities across the country.

Cooperative Buying

A cooperative is an association of persons who have voluntarily joined together to achieve a common economic end through the formation of a democratically controlled business organization, making equitable contributions to the capital required, and accepting a fair share of the risks and benefits of the undertaking.

Is buying through a central agency a practical possibility? Should you wish to consider such a proposition, it is well to ask the following questions: (1) What is a central agency? (2) Is it a possibility? (3) Is it practical?

First, a central agency is a source through (or from) which many or most of the items you purchase may be obtained, be they perishable or durable. Second, the context of possibility here suggests something that can or may exist or happen, or is in our power to do. This assertion of possibility should come before the third question of practicability. If it is possible to have a central agency, it is then wise to consider whether or not it is practical to operate such an agency.

Having defined the premises, let us now turn to how such an agency should be run, to better gauge if it is a "practical possibility."

Research. Setting up a central agency entails a great deal of research and organization to achieve the most suitable type of agency through which member institutions can purchase their requirements. The appointment of a subcommittee to investigate all aspects of such an agency appears to be the logical approach. It needs to be stressed that the most important ingredient necessary to achieve the most efficient and profitable results is *loyalty*.

If the agency is to function in the best interests of all, then every constituent member must, at all times, give the highest degree of loyalty to the aims and objects of the agency. Otherwise, its future could be jeopardized.

The agency should be set up as a cooperative. The desire to see a central agency brought into existence is only the first step. Beyond that, there are fundamental requirements to achieve this end.

The first and most important of these is *finance*. A cooperative trading agency requires substantial initial capital. Consider, for instance:

- Premises have to be acquired, whether purchased, leased, or rented.
- Warehousing, showrooms, and office areas have to be created.
- Goods have to be purchased for resale, and these goods have to be paid for.
- Wages have to be paid.
- Vehicles have to be purchased or leased, with subsequent delivery costs to be incurred.
- Ongoing operating expenses must be met.

All these items require initial capital. Therefore, the first consideration, is the financial structure. Under the cooperative system, all those interested would become shareholders and subscribe for an agreed number of shares. If 30 members subscribed for one $5,000 share each, then the actual initial capital would be $150,000 to get the project off the ground.

A preliminary formation meeting would then be held. Here the name of the agency could be decided upon, rules adopted, directors elected, and the various other officers appointed.

Subject to trading only with its own members, the net profits of such an agency would be subject to federal income tax only on the amount remaining after deducting the rebates on purchases.

The directors decide the basis of mark-up on the goods purchased for resale. Obviously the difference between the purchase price and the selling price must be sufficient to pay wages, all operating expenses, and leave "something over." If the margin between buying and selling is steady, the agency should prosper. As sales rise, the proportion for overhead should grow less, which brings us back to the question of loyalty. The members of the agency must insure that the largest possible share of their requirements are purchased through their own agency for it to be effective.

LAWS OF CONTRACTS AND WARRANTIES

A contract involves one person's offer, another's acceptance, and the giving of consideration. Whether made orally or in writing, a contract is legally binding on buyer and seller alike, as long as a law has not been broken and all parties to the contract are competent.

A written contract is more easily enforced than an oral one. The written purchase order is a contract that tells not only the specifications for food or equipment, but also the means of shipment, the responsibility for delivery and insurance, the price, and the method and timing of payment.

When placing an order for goods or services, the burden of being specific is on the buyer. Generally speaking, the courts will hold for that which is ordinary and customary practice unless a quite specific documentation of particulars was made with the order. What are some of the particulars to list?

1. Who is responsible for payment?
2. When is payment due? What are the penalties for late payment or rewards (discounts) for early payment?
3. Who has possession at what time? FOB? FAS? CIF?
4. Who pays insurance costs?
5. Who pays storage fees?
6. What is the expected condition of the merchandise upon delivery?

Procurement of foodservice goods is controlled by laws. Law is the prophecy and prediction of the probable outcome of a specific legal situation. It developed from English common law.

Common law grew from ideas, principles, customs, and commonly accepted practices in the community. Greek laws and Roman civil laws strongly affected common law, in addition to natural law, which states that humans endeavor to do good and avoid evil. English common law became evident in 1066 when William the Conqueror invaded England at the Battle of Hastings. In 1154 common law became even stronger when Henry II instituted the use of the jury system. This was the first time that twelve persons from the community were gathered together to decide the outcome of a case. Previously, kings were allowed to hand down decisions according to their whim, which could vary with each person. With common law, the king no longer was all powerful. Decisions were fair and predictable for the same cases.

English common law turned into New World law when the immigrants from England came to America. Common law was adopted and is now the basis for much of today's law.

There are still some persons who are limited, through common law, in their ability to make contracts. Minors, the insane, and intoxicated persons are not allowed to make a contract because they do not have the ability. The different states vary, but aliens are limited to contracting ability because they cannot contract for land. Convicts are not allowed to sue on a contract. Married people are limited in contracting with their spouses. Private corporations, such as companies, are limited in their ability to contract by federal laws. Public corporations, such as cities, are limited by the states.

Caveat emptor, "let the buyer beware," still exists from common law. The responsibility for inspecting goods rests on the buyer's shoulders. A buyer who fails to inspect goods must suffer the consequences. This also applies to customers of a foodservice. In *Webster* v. *Blue Chip Tea Room,* plaintiff Webster purchased a bowl of fish chowder and got a bone caught in her throat. She sued the defendant because the fish bone was not fit for human consumption. The decision was awarded to the defendant because the bones are natural to fish. Plaintiff Webster was told caveat emptor; she should have been aware of the possibility of fish bones being in the chowder.

Privity of Contract developed in the nineteenth century from common law. It means that a contractual relationship between buyer and seller must have occurred for a buyer to seek remedy for goods with which he or she is dissatisfied.

There are two types of law: criminal law (a violation of a public duty) and tort law (a violation of a private duty). An act can violate both criminal law and tort law; stealing an automobile would be an example. Tort law is seen in the foodservice industry through product liability. Privity of contract is not necessary in tort law. In *Smith* v. *Coca Cola Bottling Company of Pennsylvania,* plaintiff Smith sued for damages when he suffered injuries from a bottle of Coca Cola containing a spider. Even though the spider in the beverage did not cause the injuries, the decision was eventually awarded to Smith because spiders should not be found in bottles of Coca Cola.

The Uniform Commercial Code was developed from common law and serves the same purpose as common law, that of standardizing the probable outcome of a specific legal situation. It was designed to ascertain the intention between two parties, to determine if a contract is desired, and to enforce that contract. Under the code, the seller promises that the title of the goods is right and free from lien. This would mean the goods had to belong to the seller/agent and no hidden money was owed on the goods. Article Two, Sales, of the code covers most transactions in the foodservice industry. It does not cover the sale of a restaurant, which ordinarily would be covered by Article Six, Bulk Transfers. Under the code, restaurants sell services rather than merchandise, hence, they are not covered by the Uniform Commercial Code. Four states—California, Oregon, Washington, and Idaho—have added clauses to their state's code stating that Article Six, Bulk Transfers, does cover the sale of restaurants. All of the states have adopted the code except Louisiana. The code imposes time element or Statute of Limitations for remedy.

A contract is a promise or understanding that something will or will not occur. There are four prerequisites for a contract to be considered legal. They are:

1. Manifestation of mutual consent must occur. Both parties must be aware of all terms and agree on them.
2. Consideration must take place. Payment in money must happen.
3. The object must be legal. If the goods are stolen or not allowed in the United States, then contract cannot occur.
4. Capacity of the parties must also be present. Both contracting parties must be able to legally fulfill all terms of the contract.

A contract serves the purpose of notifying both parties of each other's expectations. Complete contracts will state who the agreement is with, the price, the quantity of goods, and the length of time the contract will last. It will describe payment, who bears risk of loss and when, what constitutes a discharged contract, an inspection clause, and the responsibility of each party. Total specifications for the goods should also be given. Buyer satisfaction is only as good as the specifications given. Stated also should be terms of delivery, such as:

1. FOB (free on board). The buyer takes total responsibility for the goods once they are on the carrier.
2. FAS (free along ship). The buyer has responsibility for the goods after they have left the ship. The seller has the responsibility for the goods while they are being transported to the ship and on the ship.
3. CIF (cash, insurance, freight). The seller has the responsibility of the goods until they are on the buyer's dock.

Voidable contracts are those in which all of the terms are not considered legal, or they have not met all of the criteria essential for a contract. Executory contracts are those in which one party has fulfilled their terms of the contract, but the other party has not fulfilled their terms. An example of this would be a purveyor who has delivered goods as per terms of the contract, but has not received consideration or payment for them. An executed contract is one which has had all the terms met by both parties. Unconscionable contracts are agreements that are not fair to a party. One party has had to agree to the terms of the contract even though it was felt the terms were unfair. The Uniform Commercial Code protects a person against these types of contracts. If one of the parties feels they have been subjected to an unconscionable contract, they can petition for it to be reviewed by a court.

Types of Contracts

There are four types of contracts. The type A contract is a total exclusive contract. Both parties agree upon a set price. The buyer agrees to buy goods only from that purveyor. The purveyor agrees to deliver the goods specified by the buyer. Type B contracts are partially exclusive. The price is agreed upon and if the seller carries the goods that are specified by the buyer, the buyer agrees to purchase only from this purveyor. Type C contracts are those which only have an agreed upon price. Buyers are not required to buy from that purveyor. The purpose behind such a contract is to have a standard price. Dual A contracts exist between two purveyors and one buyer. Prices have been standardized between the buyer and purveyors. The buyer is obligated to purchase from either of the two purveyors, but not from a third party. Buyers have the option to purchase goods from either one of the merchants by personal likes of a specific product.

Oral contracts are frequent in the foodservice industry. It is easy and convenient to pick up a phone and order the goods needed. This type of purchasing provides no written record of what has been ordered, and it puts the buyer at the mercy of the seller, who can deliver any quality available. Specifications are extremely important because they provide a written record of what the buyer expects. There is much less chance of the seller misinterpreting what the buyer means when the goods are ordered. Oral contracts are considered legal if:

1. There is written confirmation within 10 days.
2. There is judicial admission of a contract occurring.
3. The goods are special items or nonresellable goods.
4. The goods have been received and accepted.
5. The goods have been paid for.

The generally recognized statute of limitations for contracts is 5 years for an oral contract and 10 years for a written contract. The statute of limitations is the legally allowed amount of time to correct a wrong.

Goods delivery entitles buyers to accept all of the goods, reject all of the goods, or accept some fungible amount of the goods. Fungible goods are those which can be measured or weighed. If a merchant delivers more than has been ordered, buyers have the right to accept all of the goods, none of the goods, or only that which was ordered.

After Delivery

Upon delivery, buyers have the obligation to inspect goods to ascertain that they conform to certain specifications. Buyers must inspect the goods within a reasonable time. This is determined by the nature of the goods. Fresh produce must be inspected much sooner than canned goods.

Buyers also have the opportunity to test a small portion of the goods to assure that the goods meet specifications. If they test more than what would be considered normal, buyers lose the right to reject the goods. If a certain buyer claims that the goods do not conform to specifications, the seller must be allowed the same opportunity to test the goods. The expense of testing is usually born by the seller unless the buyer takes more time or goods than is considered normal.

A legal defect is an unanticipated object in goods. Centipedes in tomato soup, pebbles or fingers of gloves in canned vegetables, or glass in rolls are not expected objects in received goods. If these unanticipated objects were removed from the goods, and the products were still edible, they would not conform to the buyer's specifications. The buyer could reject these goods for this reason.

If goods are rejected by a buyer, he or she has the obligation to store, reship, or resell them. The seller should be notified that the goods are not acceptable and information requested as to disbursement of the goods. If the seller does not provide disbursement information, the seller should try to resell the goods to reduce money lost and ill feelings incurred through rejection. When the buyer is able to resell the goods, or merely store them for the merchant, the seller is obligated to reimburse the buyer for expenses. The buyer loses the right to reject goods if too much time has been taken to inspect or reject the goods.

A contract is considered discharged when there is a termination of duties. The most common discharge of contract is performance. If a term such as price cannot be agreed upon, then the contract is discharged. Conditions are not promises. They are a happening which will affect the discharge of a contract. The inability to deliver goods because there is too much snow to safely navigate the road is a condition which will affect the discharge of a contract.

Types of Warranties

There are three types of warranties: Warranty of Title, Express Warranty, and Implied Warranty. Warranties of Title mean that an object is what was ordered. When oranges are ordered, oranges should be delivered, rather than apples.

Express warranties are statements of facts or promises, descriptions, samples, or models. These facts affect the buyer and may determine whether the product is purchased. If these facts are made after the contract has been agreed upon, they are considered modifications of the contract and not an express warranty. Statements by salespersons that their product is the best is only opinion if not backed up with facts, and is not considered an express warranty. When the merchant inspects the goods and notices an obvious defect, such as a large crack in a table, and accepts the table anyway, the express warranty by description and model does not apply.

Disclaimers of warranty are clauses added to a guarantee by merchants. These clauses are express warranties and limit implied warranties. Phrases that frequently appear in a warranty disclaimer are: *as is* and *with all defects*. Warranty disclaimers will give a short statute of limitations; the usual span is ninety days. Disclaimers will also state that the merchant will perform repairs without cost, but it is the burden of the owner to transport equipment to and from the repair site, and to reinstall equipment. Damages are direct costs, if implied warranties are limited by a disclaimer, and the owner must bear the burden of repair cost after the statute of limitation expires. The most severe damages result in closure.

An implied warranty of merchantability does not mean that the goods are resellable, only that they are of fair and average quality. The Dallas Court of Civil Appeals says that even though an express warranty on secondhand goods may be inconsistent, it does not raise an implied warranty.

Implied warranties of fitness for a particular purpose are in effect when a specific need has been stated. The delivery of regular fruit cocktail when the buyer has stated the need for fruit cocktail for diabetics would be a violation of an implied warranty of fitness for a particular purpose.

Other methods for incurring liability are through fraudulent misrepresentation. The seller deliberately alters the product to get a higher price. Altering the grades on meat would be fraudulent misrepresentation, when the meat was held out to be and sold at the better grade price.

Nonfraudulent misrepresentation is when the seller unknowingly sells a product that has been altered. The merchant who sells meat that has had grade alteration and does not know of the alteration is guilty of nonfraudulent misrepresentation.

Another reason for liability is negligence. Negligence is incurred most frequently by a merchant who fails to inspect goods before selling them. Liability is also incurred through violation of statutory duty. This would be violating Food and Drug laws. Mislabeling cans is a violation of statutory duty.

Strict liability in tort is similar to implied warranties. The difference is that implied warranties cover all goods, whereas strict liability in tort covers only those goods that are normally sold by the merchant. The selling of a truck by a foodservice catering business would not be covered, but the food sold would be. A retailer who is being sued by a customer should have the aid of the manufacturer. If the manufacturer does not help clear the retailer's name, the retailer usually sues the manufacturer.

FOOD AND PACKAGING REGULATIONS

Regulations[1] regarding food and packaging (indirectly) go back to antiquity. Archeological discoveries from the Hittite period (3,500–1,200 B.C.) have proven that even then there was a fairly comprehensive system available dealing with foods. Egyptian pictographs have also been unearthed showing various officials measuring and weighing grain. But perhaps the earliest civilizations that food regulations can be directly traced are the Roman and Greek.

In its prime, the Roman Empire ruled almost all of modern-day Europe. Intrinsic to ancient Roman values was not only cleanliness, but the value of good commercial practice. For the former, the Romans built baths and concerned themselves with the purity of body as well as food. And for the latter, an elaborate system of weights and measures was devised.

In later centuries, Islamic civilization (600–1,000 A.D.) contained regulations regarding a weights and measure system which certified various containers as to their proper fill.

These very early regulations, however, were not directed toward providing a safe and wholesale supply of food for the common man. Rather, they were solely intended to protect each merchant from the other, and they were used for tax purposes by the ruler. This carried right through into the Middle Ages when Europe was fragmented into small fiefs or city states. At the end of the Middle Ages and right up into the late 1800s, bread was mixed with alum, beer adulterated by various narcotics, and tea leaves colored with carbonate of copper.

In the United States, the climate for proper and meaningful food legislation started to evolve after the Civil War (1860–1865). Spurred on by the conservation and human rights movements, it reached its climax during the Spanish-American War (1898–1901). When the battleship *Maine* exploded in Havana, Cuba, U.S. soldiers were subsequently rushed to the battlefront. Feeding these soldiers was as important as clothing them. One type of provision supplied to the U.S. Army was canned beef. The beef was purchased by the army and even before the U.S. soldiers arrived in Cuba, many died in Tampa, Florida, from the tainted product. Investigation showed that the

[1]*Food Engineering* (September 1977).

beef was pickled in formaldehyde, and that it was canned 30 years before during the Civil War. This outraged the American public. A group of concerned citizens, led by Dr. Harvey Wiley, pressed hard for regulations capable of stopping such practices. They did not succeed in capturing general consent until the early nineteenth century and the publication of Upton Sinclair's book *The Jungle.* It was then that the unsanitary conditions prevailing in some meat-packing plants first became known to the public. Theodore Roosevelt recognized the need for improving conditions of these meat plants and pushed for the adoption of food and drug laws. All this culminated in the passage of the first federal Food and Drug Law in 1906.

Food and Drug Law—1906

This was the first federal Food and Drug law established in the United States. It was not all encompassing, and it did contain many loopholes. Various regulatory Standards of Identity were written for some foods, and even today some still exist; for example, ketchup. An important aspect of this new regulation was that the government had to prove that there was unsanitary or poisonous property in the food that was dangerous to health. But a start had been made in the right direction. Administered by the newly formed Bureau of Chemistry under Dr. Wiley, many food processors saw the necessity for this regulation. They supported the act and backed up the Bureau of Chemistry. This was the first time that both government and industry joined to enforce a law.

Between 1907 and 1912, the law only referred to statements on composition or identity. With the passage of the Sherley Amendment in 1912, violators became subject to persecution. Even though the government had to prove harmfulness, more than 6,000 violators were brought to trial during the first ten years of the law. This was in spite of the Supreme Court which refused to consider these cases because the Court believed them to be in the realm of business and not public health.

In 1930, the McNary-Mapes Amendment was passed. This codified the quantity of contents in packaged foods. Exceptions were usually found in packaging of meat or milk products due to agricultural pressures. An interesting point is that both meats and poultry were not covered in the 1906 Act. Both meat and poultry were covered in the 1906 Meat Inspection Act and its later amendment. Because of this initial omission, and also the fact that the Bureau of Chemistry was relatively underfinanced, responsibility for the enforcement of regulations on meats and poultry was given to the USDA.

Other regulations soon followed. In 1914, the Federal Trade Commission (FTC) was given the responsibility for the enforcing of textile labeling. Wool was covered in 1941, while fur labeling followed later in 1952. In general, the existing food regulations up until the late 1930s were considered too weak to enforce a good wholesome food supply. As so often in the past, it took a new calamity to force the enactment of improved regulations. This occurred in 1937 with the "Elixir Sulfanilamide" event. When almost 70 people died as a result of taking this new drug, the public became incensed. The net result was the passage of more improved legislation in 1938.

Federal Food, Drug and Cosmetic Act—1938

Often referred to as a "patchwork cathedral to which is added new chapels continually in which to worship new deities," the 1938 measure was nonetheless truly revolutionary legislation. It has served as a model for other food and drug legislation on a worldwide basis. There are many aspects of this new law that set the pace for future activities. A new agency was set up called the Food and Drug Administration (FDA), and it was made responsible for all administrative decisions. Food additives were not controlled except where such additives were known to be poisonous substances. Even this was a significant improvement over the 1907 law since between 1907 to 1938 classification and regulatory laws regarding toxic additives were handled piecemeal as the problems arose, and chemicals prohibited for use in edibles or in materials coming in contact with them were mainly those which had a well-established history of toxicity.

The Second World War interfered with the full application of the 1938 Act, but several specific details of the Act are important. Standards of identity and a reasonable standard of quality and of fill for various foods were specified. Traffic in injurious foods was prohibited. More requirements about ingredients on labels were specified. Slack filling was brought under review, and the use of deceptive containers was prohibited. Penalties were invoked to control fraud or deliberate intent to violate the act.

The 1938 legislation designed to "provide (food) safe and wholesome to the people, honestly labelled and properly packaged" was the basic law relative to food packaging until the later 1950s. It was then that external events again caused a new stirring in the public's awareness of packaging safety.

In 1956, a convention of physicians meeting in Milan, Italy, devoted their seminars to a comprehensive study of cancer and its occurrence. They arrived at several rather startling conclusions. One issue was that cancer may be caused by the use of various chemical additives in food. There were not too many people that paid attention to the convention's conclusions at the time except for one U.S. Congressman, Rep. James J. Delaney (D.-N.Y.), who thought that the findings of the Milan convention were quite important and highly significant in the battle for public health. He managed to convince Sen. Estes Kefauver (D.-Tenn.), and they both pushed for the drafting of an amendment to the 1938 Act. Consumerism had just begun to become a vital factor in the public's minds. The net result was new legislation that directly concerned the packaging industry.

Food Additives Amendment—1958

This was the second most revolutionary concept in food legislation for the common man. The amendment deals with food supply in the United States, and takes cognizance of all chemical components of this supply, whether these components enter the food by direct addition or by indirect means, for example, by virtue of migration from a food packaging material.

When the 1958 Food Additives Amendment was passed, the FDA was faced with a great deal of work. It had to find a way to administer the new law as well as bring under control, by scientific evaluation, the many thousands of substances involved in foods and in packaging materials for foods.

One provision of the 1958 Amendment has turned out to be of great importance to the packaging industry (as well as the food industry) of the 1970s. This clause—commonly known as the Delaney Clause—bars the use of any additive in food that is found "to induce cancer in man or animal." At the time of its inclusion into the 1958 Amendment, the test methods used to detect carcinogenic substances were valid to about 20 parts per million. Advances in testing procedures have now brought these analytical methods to quantitative accuracies of about a few parts per trillion. Testing tolerances have been drastically narrowed since 1959, and researchers are now finding almost everything present everywhere. And yet the Delaney Clause specifically outlaws any additive in any amount found to be carcinogenic. How to cope with this provision is of great concern to the packaging industry at the present time.

While there was all this fervent activity between 1938 to 1958 in the food and drug areas, other legislation was not ignored.

The legislative measures in the agricultural area included the Federal Insecticide, Fungicide, and Rodenticide Act of 1947 which controls these type compounds in foods as well as in other commodities. These substances are under FDA jurisdiction and are not covered under the provisions of food legislation.

Consumer Age

In the 1960s, the age of consumerism came into full maturity. More and more people wanted to know more about what was in a product and how much it really weighed. One of the first packaging activities in the early 1960s that was directly influenced by the consumer movement was weights and measures. Important as far back as Roman times, the concept of weights and measures is intrinsic to good packaging. Local statutes controlled the various weights and measures on packaging in the states. The net result was total confusion since laws differed considerably between various states. An attempt to coordinate all these many state laws was made by the National Bureau of Standards (NBS). In 1965, a model law was drafted by the NBS, but it was really too late. All provisions in state laws that "are less stringent or require different information from the Labeling Act of 1966 are now invalid." This was due to the passage of the Fair Packaging and Labeling Act (FPLA) in 1966.

Fair Packaging and Labeling Act

Under the provisions of the FPLA of 1966 (effective July 1, 1967), responsibility was given to the FDA for the administration of the law. The part of the FPLA dealing with weights and measures is different from the NBS's model law of 1965 and is obviously binding on all states. In addition, the Department of Commerce (DOC) was given the responsibility of helping industry eliminate superfluous packaging. This is under the "proliferation of sizes" statement. The DOC did succeed in eliminating the production of one travel-sized toothpaste, as well as examining the various packages commonly used for potato chips. The vast importance of such acts cannot be overemphasized to the packaging industry. Basic to this provision is the question as to whether the government has the right to dictate the sizes of packages to be sold in the marketplace.

In recent years, there have been laws introduced to the nutritional labeling of foods. Various consumer groups have also demanded a new FPLA which would improve upon the provisions of the 1966 Act.

With the tightening of money in the United States, states and local municipalities have started to carefully examine both their overall profits as well as garbage disposability. Even though packaging wastes have been carefully documented to be a very minor part of the waste problem, many localities have focused in on packaging as the prime culprit in their battle for proper waste disposal. Over 1,000 bills have been introduced, on various levels, to "ban packaging." To date, only 4 on the state level have passed, but future activity is unknown.

In legislation relative to shipping, more careful coordination between the rail, air, and motor freight bodies is essential. This has occurred in recent years, and activity will probably increase.

ETHICS—MORALITY—MONEY

Food purveyors operate on a small profit margin. They are selling merchandise that is perishable; if the stock is not sold while it is fresh, it will (1) deteriorate and have to be sold at a discount, or (2) spoil and have to be discarded. Such conditions tend to make food purveyors fiercely competitive.

Food buyers are purchasing merchandise that can vary considerably in quality and therefore in price. The price difference between grades is often as great as 20 percent.

The avenue to dishonesty in food purchasing and purveying is paved with temptation. It is not difficult for a purveyor to arrange kickbacks to food buyers in exchange for an operation's exclusive business. The food buyer who accepts such an arrangement has no choice but to accept whatever is shipped to the operation, without complaint. More seriously, the food buyer has committed a felony by accepting a bribe.

There is no excuse for purveyors who offer bribes; they should be reported to their trade association and to the attorney general of the state. Likewise, there is no excuse for food buyers who solicit bribes; they should be reported to their employers and drummed out of the foodservice industry. This is a direct form of theft.

There are other, more subtle forms of theft. Consider these possibilities:

1. All the major food purveyors of any given type of product (such as fresh fruits and vegetables) may agree to set a floor, or minimum, price on certain products or all products. Except on floor prices set by manufacturers of certain products in states having Fair Trade Practice laws, such price fixing is illegal.

2. The purveyors of a given type of product establish territories. Each company gets a section which the other companies agree to respect. Such arrangements may or may

not be illegal, but they restrict the food buyer's ability to buy the best product at the best possible price.

Bribes can take forms other than money. For instance:

1. The premium offer. The buyer selects a gift from a sales incentive catalog in exchange for points earned. This perfectly honest marketing technique is ethical if (1) the price or the price plus the value of the premium is the best available on the specified product, and (2) the premium is to be owned and used exclusively by the operation that is paying for the food purchased. The problem with premium programs is that the catalogs usually contain 90 percent or more consumer products which would seem to tempt the buyer to use his or her position to obtain premiums for personal use. The cost of these premium programs, of course, is reflected in the price of the food products purchased.

2. The offer to purchase foods for personal use at discount prices. If all purveyors of a class extend this privilege, then there is nothing wrong in this. If the buyer's ability to make such purchases is limited to one or two purveyors of a class, then the buyer may be tempted to play "favorites."

3. Christmas and/or birthday presents. In some areas this is a common practice from purveyors to food buyers. Such presents usually take the form of liquor, perfume, clocks, and other inexpensive items. The acceptance of such gifts may not influence the buyer, but the cost is inevitably passed on. Acceptance of such gifts is bad policy.

4. The donation. Restaurants and institutions that ask purveyors to donate food or money to employee parties, annual picnics, favorite charities, or to the institution itself are, in essence, making such contributions a condition of doing business with them. The cost of such donations is inevitably passed on in purchase prices. A request for such contribution is a form of asking for a kickback and should be discouraged.

A listing of all the possible shady practices in the industry would be longer than this text. There are many ways that an operation can be taken. Consider, for example, the quality argument: The purveyor and the operator differ on the definition of quality (probably easy to do if there are no exacting specifications).

A recent "action line" test by a Salt Lake City television station revealed that most brands of ice cream sold in that city had less than the legally required 10 percent butterfat. An improper butterfat content of milk, with the various kinds of "cream" is easily slipped into an operation. Lettuce may be short weight and the lower layers of tomatoes may be of sizes other than ordered. Can the operator tell the difference between Grade A and Grade B eggs? 90 score and 92 score butter? A U.S. Choice steak and a U.S. Good steak? Grade A chickens vs. Grade B chickens? Southern poultry and northern? Repacked for fresh? Thawed frozen fish or fresh? Cod or pollack? Sole or flounder? Can the operator distinguish between types of tea or regions of coffee? Stale coffee dated fresh? Does the "pound " of coffee weigh 14 ounces? Is the count on the box of apples the same as the count *in* the box? Or steaks? Is that two-inch tail on a prime rib really three inches?

WORK SIMPLIFICATION

Work simplification is the key to most effective day-to-day operation for a foodservice organization.[2] The logic is simple: the more details to be handled and the more people there are, the greater are the opportunities for things to go wrong. Every job should be reduced to its basic components. Once reduced, tasks should be eliminated from the job, where possible, through the use of disposables, convenience foods, and automated equipment.

CONVENIENCE FOODS DEFINED

Convenience foods is a relatively recent term in foodservice. As with all new broad-based terms, its meaning is not always precise. A commonly accepted definition is: Convenience foods are those items to which some or all of the labor of preparation has been added at the time of purchase. Clearly, while this definition is accurate, it is broad enough to cover almost every food item an operator purchases, whether canned, dried, fresh, or frozen; whether meat, poultry, fish, fruits, or vegetables; whether baked goods, dairy products, and so on.

For purposes of this chapter, the term *convenience foods* generally means prepared entrees, customarily frozen, usually packed in multiple portions.

There is a vast range of such convenience food products now being packed for foodservice operations. Moreover, there is no longer a problem anywhere in the United States in acquiring them. There are, at this writing, in excess of 100 companies in national distribution of frozen foods.

The problem in setting up for use of convenience products comes with the short-term shelf-life refrigerated foods, such as prepared salads and desserts. However, a good convenience program will utilize prepared foods for all aspects of service.

Operators need convenience products for different reasons. Those in large cities have abundant potential labor, but it tends to be expensive. The small city and rural operator has the opposite problem, a lower wage scale, but a small pool of potential workers. Thus, the metropolitan operator needs convenience foods to reduce labor costs, while the nonmetropolitan operator needs them to fill the gap between labor supply and production needs.

In evaluating a convenience food program, there are three options to consider.

Option 1: Tailored Convenience Foods

Begin by standardizing all recipe cards for premise-prepared items, not only as to products but also as to procedures. Where possible, you specify quality and type of ingredients per USDA specifications.

---

[2]Raymond B. Peddersen et al., *Increasing Productivity in Foodservice* (Chicago: Cahners Books, 1973), pp. 181–86.

Then calculate, from production records, the annual number of portions needed and the maximum number of portions for which storage is available. Take these requirements to the nearest 2 or 3 producers of convenience foods and ask for bids—using your processing method—for these products. This eliminates many problems that occur when convenience foods are purchased without reference to storage limitations.

One common problem is packaging size. Companies in national distribution package their products in different packages. Even foodservice operators disagree on standard packaging size. A commercial cafeteria or public restaurant may well prefer the few portions that can be packed in a quarter- or half-size steamtable plan because their individual orders come along slowly. But the non-commercial high volume operator—such as a hospital, college, airline, or in-plant caterer—may well want the added portions in a full-size pan.

By specifying each package, the operator can tailor the best method and time of reheating for the specific product with his or her facilities, be they conventional or modern. A hospital with microwave ovens on each floor station will find frozen convenience products perfectly acceptable (so long as the containers are not metallic, of course), however, where high volume must be served in a short period, a more shallow package would be required for a convection oven.

If there is enough refrigeration, and conventional ovens are to be used, a bulk pack that can be reheated from the refrigerated state after a long defrost cycle may be preferred. Having the product packaged to your specification guarantees a product consistent with your tastes.

Among the minimum standards for user agreement for convenience products should be freedom from disease-producing organisms, nutritional content, shelf-life, and accuracy of the manufacturer's claims as to the number of portions per container. These standards should be applied also to the new frozen, dehydro-frozen, freeze-dried, chilled, or concentrated items that appear on the market almost daily.

Manufacturers and purveyors have special problems. For instance, chicken cordon bleu, veal marsala, stuffed cabbage, or codfish cakes are prepared differently in various regions of the country. What passes for good clam chowder in San Diego may not pass muster anywhere near the Charles River in Boston.

Option 2: General Marketplace

When an operation is not big enough to have its own convenience foods manufactured, the operator may enter the general marketplace.

The major shortcoming of convenience food packaging, besides varying sizes, is the failure of the container to communicate information about the contents and their use to the average unskilled kitchen employee. There are usually no receiving specifications on boxes to guide the receiver in examining the product for damage. There is no mention of dangerous temperature zones or shelf-life.

Sometimes instructions are on the bottom of the box, which means the worker may have to damage the product to read them. Instruction copy is confusing. Few companies provide line drawings. Those manufacturers who do publish product description sheets or merchandising brochures or, more importantly, nutritional data, generally make them available "upon request only." Such sheets should be included with each case.

Instructions should cover the following subjects: storage, including specific and numerical temperature figures, not simply the words "room temperature" or "freezing"; the method of removal from the master container; the number and size of portions; alternate uses of product and handling of leftovers; alternate preparation methods and service equipment that can be used; and any other appropriate warnings.

The instruction language should be clearly organized. It should be short and simple, bilingual, with illustrated instructions.

Option 3: Make Your Own

In this option, often termed a "ready-foods" system, an operation manufactures and freezes its own convenience products on premise. This system uses off-hour time periods to prepare, package, and freeze bulk quantities of foods.

TEMPERING IS CRUCIAL

Regardless of the option chosen, every operator is left with the complicated business of reheating. When food is removed from the freezer it must be carefully handled. Various types of food must be reheated differently. The only rule that always applies is, "Never defrost at room temperature." Instead, defrosting should be done under controlled conditions, either by heating or controlled refrigeration. If your volume is large enough to warrant it, several manufacturers now offer tempering refrigerators. These apply heat or refrigeration, as necessary, to maintain any size load within a limited, safe temperature range.

Whatever is done about tempering (bringing product from frozen to refrigerated) foods, it must be done carefully. Foods thawed slowly over 2 or 3 days generally retain more stability and "eat" better than those thawed quickly.

If the product permits, there is no doubt that a properly adjusted, forced-air convection oven does an effective job in terms of load, efficiency, and cost in reheating frozen convenience foods.

If microwave ovens are used, heating times must be adjusted to the thickness or shape of the products. Improper timing can produce mushiness, and a steamed or ozone flavor in meat. Microwave ovens make their greatest contribution in bringing refrigerated foods to serving temperatures. Combination convection-microwave ovens, properly used, should offer an answer to many problems.

Ovens—deck, convection, revolving, and microwave—are referred to as dry heat. Steamers (high pressure, low pressure, and atmospheric) and conventional and pressure fryers provide moist heat. Even if slower, they are effective methods of reheating and/or cooking.

Here, too, serving temperature is crucial. What holds true for freshly prepared foods applies equally to convenience foods. Hot food must be served hot, and cold food must be served cold. Any variance from this rule may prove disastrous for the palatability, pathogenicity, and nutritional value of the food. While the facts of heat loss for liquids are generally known, new data is needed for most other foods on time requirements, as related to specific states and mass, in order to set standards for reheating and holding during service.

The possibilities convenience foods offer for increasing productivity are almost limitless. A kitchen planned for total convenience food use may take perhaps half as much space and capital as a conventional kitchen. Labor requirements may be reduced by as much as 80 percent, although 40 percent to 60 percent is more common.

Today, almost any conceivable entree is available in a full convenience form. These items range in quality from unsatisfactory to the finest of haute cuisine. In addition, soups and sauces, sauced and seasoned vegetables, and cakes, pies, and fancy pastries abound in the marketplace.

While it is difficult to purchase pre-prepared salad plates, it is possible to buy fresh vegetables and fruits already peeled, chopped, diced, sliced, or in any form needed for salad preparation. Salad mixtures, including potato salad, coleslaw, macaroni salad, lobster salad, and tunafish salad, are readily available. Puddings and gelatins of high quality are also available.

GRADUAL MODIFICATION OFTEN BEST

Most foodservice operations are not in a position to adopt a total convenience system with requisite new equipment. Thus, it becomes advisable to gradually modify conventional systems when and where possible. If an operation still butchers meat, labor can be effectively reduced by purchasing cuts prefabricated to the specifications of the ''Meat Buyers Guides'' of the National Association of Meat Purveyors. Instead of operating a bake shop, labor can be eliminated by purchasing commercial fresh or frozen goods.

Hillside Hospital (Queens, N.Y.) Foodservice devised a three-part objective scale for rating convenience food products on subjective values. Included here is an individual product rating chart. Commercial pre-prepared products are rated against an in-house prepared product on six interrelated, yet individual, quality factors. The closer to 0 a commercial product scores, the greater its potential for replacing the house-prepared product. The goal is to equal the house product, not necessarily replace it.

Also shown in this chapter is a form that measures the cost, in labor dollars, of the on-premise product as compared with the tested convenience product. These cards are kept for future reference. The important data on these cards is transferred to a card which records similar data on various manufacturer's samples of a particular product. When an adequate number of samples have been tested, a decision based on comparative quality versus cost- and time-savings can be made. In this manner it is possible to test products over an extended period of time without a sophisticated research staff in the kitchen.

OBJECTIVE RATING FORM

Convenience Product Rating against   Date: _____
Hillside Hospital Product

Product _____ Packed by _____

Portion Size _____ Cost per portion _____

	−2 N.G.	−1 OK−	0 Same	+1 OK+	+2 Better	Comment
Color						
Sauce (Aroma)						
Sauce (Taste)						
Filler (Aroma)						
Filler (Taste)						
Seasoning (General)						
Total						
÷ 6=						

MEASURING COST LABOR DOLLARS

Cost per 100 portions Man Minutes	Hillside Hospital Product	_____ Product
Rec. and Storage		
Preparation		
Garnish and Display		
Difference x $.10		
Food Cost	$	$
Recipe No. _____ as of / /		
Diff.		
+ or −		

CONVENIENCE COMPARISON RATING CHART

Product _____

CO.	Qual. Points	100 Portion Cost	Man/Minute Savings	Test Date

Selection
Date _____

Comments
New Recipe Card No. _____

A list of man-minutes saved by using a selected product should be kept by the labor task analyst. Such lists should be categorized into cold products used by salad personnel and hot items prepared by cooks, and the minutes that can be saved through purchase rather than preparation of each product should be recorded. Then, when a position becomes vacant, and the time saved by using convenience foods in that work area is determined to be roughly equal in man-minutes to the output of the newly vacated position, the operator should leave the job empty and begin using the convenience products on the list.

These three simple forms can be quickly and easily filled in and maintained. Their use can prevent costly mistakes in customer satisfaction as well as money. This system, if used as outlined, can keep budget-oriented operations from cost overruns.

CUT IT OR BUY IT CUT?

The decision to buy carcasses, sides, or quarters and butcher them in the house, or to buy fabricated cuts of meat is not a difficult one to make. The procedures involved in making the decision are simple, but the time consumed may be substantial.

The information needed to make the decision is as follows:

1. Do you have a butcher? Not every operation has a qualified butcher; that is, one who has been through a lengthy training and apprenticeship. If the butcher does not know exactly how to cut meat, then a large amount of the meat dollar may be wasted due to cutting meat in a way that provides too few of the expensive cuts and too many

**COST-COMPARISON
CONVERSION TABLE**

BASE	STEAKS		
Primal Cut	N.Y. Steak	Fillets	Top Sirloin
90	147	146	144
95	155	155	153
100	163	165	162
105	171	174	171
110	179	183	180
115	187	193	189
120	196	202	198
125	204	211	207
130	212	221	216
135	220	230	225
140	228	239	234
145	236	249	243
150	245	258	252
155	253	267	261
160	261	277	270
165	269	286	279
170	277	295	288
175	285	305	297
180	293	314	306
185	302	324	315
190	310	333	324
195	318	342	333
200	326	352	342
205	334	361	351
210	342	370	360
215	350	379	369
220	359	389	378
225	367	398	387
230	375	407	396
235	383	416	406
240	391	426	415
245	399	436	424
250	407	445	433

Reprinted with permission from *The
Cornell Hotel and Restaurant Quarterly*
(November 1968), p. 87.

of the cheap cuts. If an operation does not have a good butcher, then it should buy only fabricated and portion cut meats.

2. Is your operation equipped to butcher meat? A butcher shop needs hard and mechanical saws, specialized cleavers and knives, special types of tables, proper refrigeration, and receiving facilities.

RELATIONSHIP BETWEEN MARBLING, MATURITY, AND QUALITY

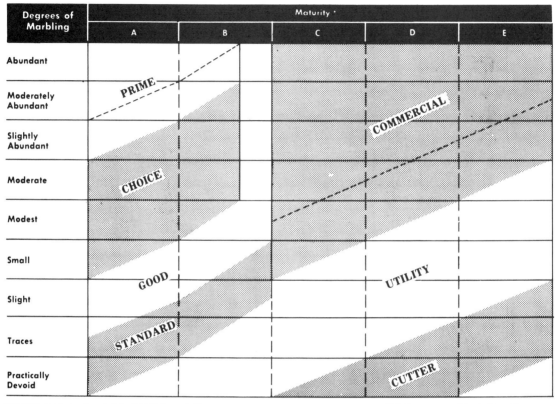

° Maturity increases from left to right (A through E)
· · · · · Represents midpoint of Prime and Commercial grades
° ° The A maturity portion of the figure is the only portion applicable to bullock carcasses.

U.S. Department of Agriculture, Consumer and Marketing Service, Livestock Division.

Official U.S. Standards for Grades of Carcass Beef SRA 99.

Courtesy of National Live Stock and Meat Board.

3. Can you afford the butcher's salary? If the butcher's salary, including taxes and fringe benefits, is $250 per week (or $13,000 per year), and if the operation saves an average of $.10 per lb. of meat through self-butchering, then the operation must use *more than* 2,500 lb. of meat per week to break even with buying fabricated or portion controlled meat cuts. Since 20 percent of the butcher's time is spent in set-up and clean up, this means he must be able to butcher almost 70 lb. of meat per hour. If the operation uses a lot of roasts, this will be possible, but if the operation uses mostly steaks, chops, ground meat, and diced meat, this level of productivity may well not be possible. Also, an institution that uses 2,500 lb. of butchered meat per week must feed an average of over 700 people per meal.

4. What is the cost per pound of meat butchered in the house? This determination is made by using a Yield Test Card. In the example, a hindquarter has been broken down using the New York cutting method which yields a good institutional mixture of cuts. The $__.____ per pound for the hindquarter is the *actual price paid.* The "market

YIELD TEST CARD

Item: Hindquarter of Beef — Grade: Choice — Date:
No. 155 — Y 6.2
Pieces: 1 — Weight: 150 lb.,   oz.
Total Cost: $ at   per 16.

Item	No.	Weight lb.	Weight oz.	% of Total Weight	Market Value per lb.	Total Market Value	Cost per
Knuckle	167	10	14		.98		
Round, Inside	168	19	11		1.24		
Round, Gooseneck, Bnls	170	23	14		1.07		
Strip Loin, bnls	180	10	15		1.92		
Top Sirloin Butt, bnls	184	9	12		1.65		
Bttm Sirloin Butt, bnls	185	5	2		.55		
Full Tenderloin, reglr	189	5	6		2.04		
Flank Steak	193	1	9		1.60		
Beef for Stewing	1195	21	14		.68		
Hanging Tender		1	9		N/V		
Fat and Bone		39	7		N/V		

Fabrication Multiplier

value per lb.'' figures are obtained either from the National Provisioner ''Yellow Sheet'' or from market quotations on the date of fabrication.

Note that there is a figure called fabrication multiplier at the bottom of the card. This is the ratio of the in-house fabricated cost to the market value. When this figure is known, it may be used to calculate future costs of in-house fabrication as the price of hindquarters changes.

5. What are the other implications of butchering at the operation? The biggest drawback is the possible nonusage of the cuts that are obtained by butchering. In order for butchering to be beneficial, the menu must call for the use of *all* the cuts obtained and in the *amounts* obtained. Close coordination of menu and butchering planning is needed to make butchering pay off.

Another drawback is that all the cuts obtained by butchering will be of the same grade. It is generally accepted that an operation will need U.S. Choice for broiling and dry roasting, but that U.S. Good is sufficient for pot roasting and stewing.

6. If I buy fabricated meat, how can I be sure it will be cut the way I want it?

The United States Department of Agriculture maintains an inspection service which verifies that the packer has prepared the meat to your specifications. This USDA Acceptance Service (stamp shown) is available, for a fee, to any operator using substantial quantities of meat as an aid in the meat purchasing program.

USDA STAMP

Constructive Procedures

Following are some constructive factors that should be part of the food buyer's policies.

Sales Representatives.   It is usually a sign of ignorance if a buyer is inconsiderate, harsh, ill-mannered, or suspicious of sales representatives in general. Most sales representatives are honest, hardworking, knowledgeable, and capable.

Sales personnel are in a position to help food buyers in many ways. There is always the possibility that they may have a money-saving proposition. Selling is highly competitive, and companies constantly generate new inducements to increase sales. Such advantages will never be realized unless the buyer's policy is to try to see every sales representative if possible.

Quality.   Needless to say, the more the food buyer knows, the more he or she will get out of every dollar spent because price is directly related to quality and quantity.

Price.   Likewise, the food buyer must keep abreast of current prices for specific grades and quality. It is impossible to study all the market reports and government and consumer bulletins, but at least some kind of a record should be kept so that prices can be readily compared when necessary, particularly items that are purchased frequently. For purchases made at rare intervals, such as equipment, the buyer should shop around until he or she is satisfied the best combination of price and service has been found.

Average Consumption.   The food buyer should always strive to purchase in accordance with need. Before making any purchase, the buyer should compute the average consumption of the item over a definite period. The amount to order then follows logically.

Competitive Buying.   The food buyer who fails to capitalize on the competition between companies loses financially. Instead of being a buyer, he or she is solely an "order giver." On the other hand, the buyer who capitalizes on competition will avoid such pitfalls as satisfied, one-house, sentiment, and friendship buying.

Quantity Buying.   In general, buying in quantity means lower costs. Usually a distributor is willing to reduce the cost per unit if it can get volume business. The cost difference may amount to only 25 to 35 cents a case, but in lots of 10, 20, or more cases, even small savings add up to a considerable amount. This is why it is so important for the buyer to know the average consumption of each item over a definite period.

Because there is the element of chance in most quantity buying, the food buyer must consider all factors before making such a purchase. What is the predicted supply of the item? If the supply is above normal, the price is likely to drop after a short time. Conversely, if there is a shortage, the price will no doubt rise as the supply dwindles. A normal supply means the price will remain stationary, barring something unforeseen.

In normal times, many food distributors contract for future delivery over a period of time. Suppose the food buyer wants 75 cases of an item. After getting the best price for the quality desired, he or she arranges to take delivery in 10-, 15- or 25-case lots and to pay as delivered. This procedure is called ''futures''—order it now, take it out as needed.

Seasonal buying. Even with modern transportation and frozen foods, seasonal buying has not been eliminated completely. In fact, the food buyer can make costly mistakes simply because many fresh foods cannot be purchased year around, in or out of the regular season. Seasons directly affect canned and frozen foods, so the buyer must be alert and familiar with the terms ''old'' and ''new'' pack and all that they signify.

Supply and Demand. Fundamentally the price of all merchandise is controlled by the demand for it. Here, a smart buyer's knowledge can pay high dividends. Some items are more affected than others, with perishables of all kinds heading the list.

At times, for instance, excellent buys of wholesale cuts of meat are available. The food buyer is far more likely to reap such an advantage from a jobber than directly from a packer. When a packer is overstocked on an item he calls the jobber to take it off his hands at a greatly reduced price. The jobber can pass this savings along because he wants a quick turnover.

Service. A buyer pays not only for merchandise but for service. To the experienced buyer, service includes such things as timely deliveries, an occasional emergency delivery, exactness in filling orders without padding or substitution, merchandise delivered in perfect condition, willingness to make adjustments or take back items for credit if necessary, procuring articles not in stock, efficient billing, and congenial relations.

In return, the buyer should be reasonable in demands or complaints. A practical way of avoiding unreasonable demands is to obtain all the facts before pushing a complaint. Even though a vendor is obligated, patience pays higher dividends than a harsh or threatening attitude.

Deliveries. The responsibility of the food buyer does not end when the order has been placed. Unless the receiving clerk is vigilant, considerable loss is inevitable, particularly in transporting foodstuffs, shortages, breakage, and delivery of the wrong merchandise. Certain merchandise ought to be weighed, so a large floor scale and a small table scale are indispensable.

To insure routine adjustments, delivery personnel should list mistakes and sign the slip. The same applies to anything picked up for return and credit. Any faults on the part of the delivery personnel must be brought to the attention of the main office. If the condition persists, more drastic action should be considered.

FOOD COSTS AND THE 40 THIEVES[3]

When you realize that foodservice products have two *perishable* time tables—*perishable* in the raw state, and *perishable* again in the processed state—you begin to understand some of the complexities. Here is a list of "40 Thieves" or causes of high food costs. There are many more, though some will not apply to all units because of operating differences.

Purchasing
1. Purchasing too much.
2. Purchasing for too high a cost.
3. No detailed specifications—quality, weight, type.
4. No competitive purchasing policy.
5. No cost budget for purchasing.
6. No audit of invoices and payments.

Receiving
7. Theft by receiving personnel.
8. No system of credits for low quality, damaged merchandise, or goods not received.
9. Lack of facilities and/or scales.
10. Perishable foods left out of proper storage.

Storage
11. Foods improperly placed in storage (e.g., fats, eggs, milk near strong cheese and fish).
12. Storage at wrong temperature and humidity.
13. No daily inspection of stored goods.
14. Poor sanitation in dry and refrigerated storage areas.
15. Prices not marked in storeroom.
16. No physical or perpetual inventory policy.
17. Lack of single responsibility for food storage and issues.

Issuing
18. No control or record of foods issued from storeroom.
19. Permitting forced or automatic issues.

Preparation
20. Excessive trim of vegetables and meats.
21. No check on raw yields.
22. No use of end products for production of low cost meals.

Production
23. Overproduction, Overproduction, Overproduction!
24. Wrong methods of cooking.
25. Cooking at wrong temperatures.
26. Cooking too long.
27. No scheduling of foods to be processed (too early, too late).

---

[3]Robert C. Petrie, "Food Costs and the 40 Thieves," *Cooking for profit,* November 1972. Reprinted with permission.

28. Not using standard recipes.
29. Not cooking in small batches.

Service

30. No standard portion sizes.
31. No standard size utensils for serving.
32. No care of leftovers.
33. No record of food produced and leaving production area.
34. Carelessness (spillage, waste, cold food).

Sales

35. Food taken out of building.
36. Unrecorded sales and incorrect pricing; "not charges" or cash not turned in.
37. No food popularity index or comparison of sales and inventory consumption.
38. No sales records to detect trends.
39. Poor pricing of menu items.
40. Employee meal costs—overproduction or unauthorized meals.

HOW TO WRITE A PURCHASING MANUAL[4]

A purchasing manual is not a frill or window dressing, it is an aid to better management. The *Guide to Purchasing,* of the National Association of Purchasing Management, declares that no purchasing manager has an excuse for not having at least an informal statement of purchasing policy and a collection of purchasing procedures.

A good manual can provide continuity and consistency which are otherwise hard to maintain. It can help to train and integrate new employees quickly. If purchasing is being centralized for the first time, a manual serves to clarify the value and authority of the function and its relations to other departments.

Much has been written about constructing purchasing manuals. Most of the advice deals with massive and elaborate manuals requiring time and manpower. In fact, many instructions on writing purchasing manuals are longer than the manual itself needs to be.

This section is a practical guide to the purposes, contents, and preparation of purchasing manuals. It emphasizes the "how," and then backs it up with some of the "why." The approach is based on the classic management formula: Plan—Do—Control.

Planning a purchasing manual means, essentially, deciding on its contents. These fall in two basic categories:

Policies are broad statements of purchasing's major objectives and relationships, often intended as much for the information of an outside audience—top administration, department heads, suppliers—as for purchasing itself.

Procedures, by contrast, are rather detailed outlines of the methods and routines that purchasing uses to achieve its objectives. They concern internal operations almost entirely.

---

[4]Substantially reprinted by permission of *Health Institutions Purchasing.*

This distinction is not always perfectly clear in manuals. Because there are two different audiences, there should ideally be two purchasing manuals, allowing for flexibility in preparation and circulation. The most realistic way to attack the problem is to consider policies and procedures as two separate parts of one manual.

The Policy Section

The policy section should contain essentially a foreword-endorsement from top administration, expressing its support for the authority of the purchasing function, and as many specific policies as are appropriate.

Endorsement by the administration gives you the one element crucial to the success of any program: management commitment. The endorsement is evidence that the policies in the manual are not being forced for purchasing's convenience, but to further the overall policies and objectives of the operation. By adding the administration's authority, the endorsement makes observance of the policies, and general acceptance of purchasing's role, far more likely.

The objectives, scope, and responsibility of purchasing can be stated briefly or in some detail, in a single section or several. I recommend these be treated briefly and generally in one section—perhaps titled ''The Role of the Purchasing Department'' with separate, subtitled paragraphs for each topic. The topics are related. None can be totally understood without some reference to the other aspects of purchasing's role. Therefore, keep them together.

If you start going into detail here, you inevitably slip over into consideration of specific policies. You can avoid duplication and confusion, and make the manual easier to use, if you save the details for the sections on specific policies.

Two other helpful, although not essential, items frequently appear in policy manuals. If they are used, they should be placed near the beginning.

One is an organization chart. It should show at least the reporting relationship of the purchasing manager to the administration and the basic organization. Larger segments of the total organization should be included only if they help clarify purchasing's role.

The second popular option is a code of ethics. Ethical questions arise frequently in purchasing, and few manuals ignore them completely. Many deal with them under specific policies, such as acceptance of gifts, conflict of interest, and the like.

To determine what specific policies a manual should cover, keep in mind what a policy is supposed to do. It represents a solution or a decision involving a problem or question that is so common as to require action repeatedly. By framing a policy, you provide a generalized solution and thus avoid a long process every time the problem comes up. Therefore, identifying such problems is the first step in formulating policy.

Every purchasing function has its own special problems. However, some are so common that they should be dealt with in every manual. Most of these deal with three basic kinds of questions: authority, supplier relations, and ethics. (Because of the nature of purchasing, some of the questions might be in one or more categories.) There are also a few miscellaneous questions.

Perhaps the best way to deal with them here is simply to list the questions that ought to be resolved by specific policy statements, if they are not settled by the general statement of policy. For example:

1. Which signature is required on a requisition?
2. What are purchasing's responsibilities and authority to challenge need or specifications?
3. Who may initiate or maintain contacts with suppliers or potential suppliers?
4. What are the criteria of supplier selection?
5. When is competitive bidding required?
6. Who takes part in negotiation?
7. Who may commit funds for supplies and equipment? What limits, if any, are there to this authority?
8. What authority or responsibilities does purchasing share with other departments?
9. What is the policy on cooperative purchasing arrangements?
10. Are there limits on sales calls?
11. Who handles requests for samples or literature?
12. What are the limits on accepting gifts or entertainment from suppliers?
13. What rules govern potential conflicts of interest?
14. Will the purchasing department make personal purchases for employees and staff members?
15. In what committees or organizations, inside or outside, is purchasing represented?

This list is by no means complete, but it indicates the general type of problems that can be settled by policy.

It is reasonable, but not essential, to formulate policy before procedures. In some cases, however, a newly hired purchasing manager may find it necessary to straighten out systems and procedures first and be content for a while with just the sketchiest statement of policy. Treating the two areas as separate, although related, permits this flexibility.

The Procedures Section

The procedures section of a manual can also be prepared according to the Plan—Do—Control formula. We will begin with the planning phase.

Once again, keep in mind the way the manual will be used. Ideally, it should enable an intelligent stranger to perform the routines necessary to keep the supply cycle going—at least competently.

Some purchasing managers begin a procedures manual with job descriptions. If your operation requires these, or if preparing them will help clarify your thinking, go ahead. However, it takes a lot of time to make up a really true and helpful job description. If systems and procedures are described accurately and completely, the roles of all purchasing employees should be clear enough to make job descriptions a luxury.

Perhaps more useful is a simple calendar of each employee's typical work week. It should highlight recurring events that are assigned specific time slots: supplier calls, meetings of committees, supply distribution days, inventory report deadlines, and the like. Such a calendar is easier both to prepare and to grasp than a job description. It simplifies employment and insures that no important task will be overlooked because the employee is sick or on vacation.

The heart of the procedures manual is the detailed descriptions of systems and routines. A good way to plan this section is to think through the procurement cycle, jotting down each major action. Then write a description, in sequence, of sub-events.

Many of these actions can be coordinated with forms or records. A copy of each should be included. Events in the procurement cycle, and forms involved, might include:

1. *Determination of Need.* Requisition or other request to purchase; reorder point on inventory records.
2. *Supplier Selection.* Supplier, product, or buy-history file; invitation-to-bid form.
3. *Ordering.* Purchase order; list or file of blanket orders in force; special forms for lease, rental, trial, or other nonpurchase procurement; inventory file; outstanding order file.
4. *Delivery.* Receiving report; inventory records.

In cataloging these events, be conscious of the questions of who, what, when, where, and how. Play down the "why" aspects unless they emphasize or clarify something that otherwise might be overlooked.

Instructions for purchase orders should specify: Who actually prepares them? Who signs them? Do some require more than one signature? What data is required, and where is it to be found? When are the purchase orders prepared—under what circumstances, at what time of day or week, and about how long before expected need? Where—to what offices or files—do copies go?

Some purchases are exceptional. They may be one-time, small-value orders, paid from petty cash; rush orders taking special attention; emergency orders placed outside normal office hours; orders for capital items. Special procedures for handling these situations should be included.

The arrangement of this material could follow any of several patterns. Perhaps the best is first to cover fully the most standard procedure. Then, for exceptions, give instructions only to cover differences in procedure. For steps that are the same for all types of purchase, refer the user to the standard procedure by page and numbered paragraph.

Here is a sample statement of purchasing objectives, scope, and responsibility that might be found in a purchasing manual.

The Role of Purchasing

1. Objectives. The primary objective of the purchasing department is to assure availability of supplies and equipment in quantity and quality consistent with set standards,

at the most favorable prices consistent with those standards. The secondary objective is to assure that the supply cycle is accomplished at minimum administrative cost.

2. Scope. The policies and procedures established by the purchasing department for procurement shall be standard.

3. Authority and limitations. Consistent with Item 2, only Purchasing has the authority to commit the organization spending of funds for supplies and equipment. In the case of high cost or capital items, this authority is subject to approval by the chief administrator. Purchasing has the authority to question any and all aspects of a requisition, including need and specifications.

4. Responsibility. Purchasing shall maintain systems, procedures, and records adequate to meet its objectives. It shall evaluate these, and its overall performance, periodically, in the interests of improvement. It shall prepare such reports and other data as the administration directors.

5. Relationships with other departments. Purchasing shall cooperate fully in filling the procurement needs of all departments. To this end it shall seek all information relevant to good procurement, and share it as dictated by the best interests of the organization. It shall exercise its authority in those interests, and shall not infringe on the authority of other departments.

6. Relations with suppliers. In dealing with suppliers, purchasing shall pursue the good of the organization vigorously, within the bounds of fairness, courtesy, and good commercial practice.

QUESTIONS

1. Define the following terms:

contract	tort law
warranty	FOB
law	FAS
common law	CIF
natural law	disclaimers of warranty effective
criminal law	

2. Discuss the important components of an effective purchasing system.
3. How does competitive buying differ from single source buying?
4. What are the advantages of systems contracting?
5. Discuss the four prerequisites for a contract to be considered legal.
6. Give an example of an executing contract.
7. What is the difference between a type A and type C contract?
8. How can a buyer protect him- or herself against unsatisfactory merchandise when employing oral contracts?
9. Briefly discuss the provisions of the fair packaging and labeling act; the Food Additives Amendment.
10. What is the sigificance of the buyer accepting a bottle of wine as a Christmas gift from a purveyor?

11. Give examples of three purchasing policies.
12. Define the meaning and implications of the phrase *Caveat emptor*.
13. Describe the purchaser's function.
14. Name some disadvantages of buying solely according to price.
15. What are some faulty criteria buyers frequently use?
16. Can the buyer be consistently assured of high quality at the best price?
17. What criteria will the receiving clerk use to determine which products need to be weighed upon delivery?

EXHIBITS

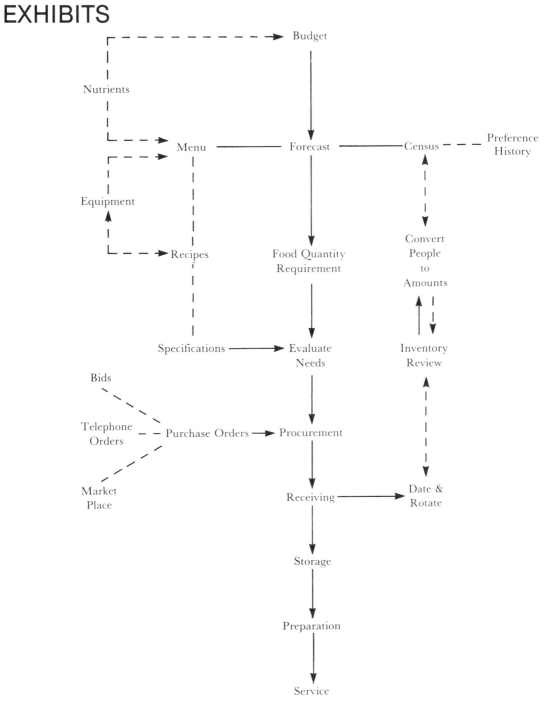

THE INSTITUTIONAL SUPPLY FUNCTION

2

QUALITY CONTROLS

INTRODUCTION

Each quality grade has its best use in an operation. It is important to remember that no one grade, even the top or most expensive product, is always the best for all purposes. Examples of the various uses of different grades are shown in picture form in this chapter.

Operators should be well aware of the factors that affect the scoring of products and ultimate grades. Some of these factors include: texture, maturity, flavor, uniformity of size, and type. These factors are thoroughly defined.

Quality standards are included in this chapter for meat (i.e., beef, pork, veal, lamb), fish and shellfish, eggs (fresh and processed), milk, cheese, butter, and poultry. Each product group includes information on processing, governmental regulations, charts and pictures, as well as descriptive and distinguishing characteristics of various products.

Quality *is* measurable on objective grounds even though there are many varied subjective attributes. Quality is measured in terms of a product's chemical and physical attributes which are: flavor, texture, color, appearance, consistency, palatability, nutritional values, safety, ease of handling, convenience, storage stability, and packaging.

USING YOUR SENSES

The five senses are invaluable. The average layperson can identify about 2,000 odors and tastes; the trained technician can identify some 5,000.

Smell is not really a function of the nose. It is a function of the olfactory bulb which is located way back in the nasal cavity. The rest of your nose picks up only the sensations of touch: heat, pain, and the like.

Taste is the most complex of the senses because flavor is a combination of taste, smell, and feelings. The tongue is the receptor of flavor. It registers only four responses: sweet, salty, sour, and bitter. It is the taste buds that pick up these sensations, and the intensity of these sensations is directly affected by the temperature of the food. Sweet tastes are picked up only at the front of the tongue; saltiness is determined at the sides of the back of the tongue; and bitterness is registered in the main body of the tongue.

The temperature of food tasted greatly affects the ability to judge flavor. Never, never, never sample food for taste that is below 40°F or above 100°F. The tongue will not register accurate sensations of sourness or subtle flavor detections in any temperature range except 40°F to 100°F. Those sensations of food being tough, mushy, gristly, or hard are really the qualities of firmness, softness, juiciness, chewiness, and grittiness.

How does one instruct a taste panel in order to get a valid judgment of the product? According to Marvin Thorner, Ch.E. and food technologist:

"Prior to the actual testing, an inexperienced taster should perform a series of examinations using solutions of foods having the four basic tastes. Dilute solutions of pure substances exhibiting the effects of sweetness, sourness, bitterness, and saltiness should be prepared. As each solution is tested, a mental note should be made of the reaction and the location of the stimulus on the tongue.

Before actual testing, the mouth should be rinsed with warm water. This preliminary step will freshen the mouth cavity and the taste buds for sharper perception.

The sample should be drawn into the mouth with a "slurp" or whirling action, so that all areas of the cavity are moistened. Immediately after the mouth is fully moistened and the sense registered, the liquid must be expelled. If the impression was not clear, a second or third test should be made. Between tests of the same or different substances, the mouth should be flushed with warm water.

The sense of touch plays an important role in taste evaluation. The temperature of the material must be noted, and if not in the proper range, it must be adjusted to meet its physical character.

Tasting should be done early in the morning because tasting senses become dulled later in the day. Limit the number of samples to no more than 6, as the taster's perception is rarely accurate after that point. Use 2 identical samples and 1 different sample—all blind coded—to weed out faulty perception. Use definitive words for judging, such as "like definitely," "like mildly," "neither like nor dislike, definitely."

Now what about the equipment that is used in the determination of quality? The first piece of equipment is the scale. Scales are needed to check the portion weights, not only as a receiving control but also as a cooking control. Microwave ovens will cook or reheat properly only when the timings are set in accordance with the product weights.

Thermometers are essential in the receiving function of convenience foods as a minimal check against product damage. For testing the temperature of plated or plate-ready foods, use only the cup-type thermometer because it brings up some of the food with it, which prevents the temperature from changing before the reading is made.

Another valuable tool is the Abbe Refractometer. This tool measures the density of liquids through the refraction or bending of light. For most operations the operator will want a hand refractometer. Tables supplied with USDA Standards enable the operator to measure such things as the amount of sugar in fountain syrups; the amount of total solids in sauces, gravies, and tomato products; and the purity of the fats and oils used in the operation.

Another helpful tool is the Brix Hydrometer. This instrument measures the sugar concentration in liquids. It is something like the hydrometer that the fellow down at the gas station uses to measure the amount of anti-freeze in automobile radiators. All the syrups of canned goods have USDA Specified Brix points. Only a Brix Hydrometer or a Hand Refractometer will enable buyers to know if they got what they ordered.

A fat analyzer is basic to a quality assurance program. This is a little machine about the size of a briefcase and just as portable. The fat analyzer will, in a 15-minute period, give an accurate reading as to the percentage of fat in ground beef. Not only is this essential to measuring the quality of fresh meat, but it is invaluable in determining the quality of frozen foods such as stuffed cabbage and stuffed peppers.

STANDARDS AND SPECIFICATIONS

The United States Department of Agriculture has determined standards and specifications for virtually every food product on the market. It is important that buyers use these specifications in the purchase of all foodstuffs.

Purchasing should be done on quotations, and since the reading of the detailed specifications is very involved, buyers should try this method: Prepare a typewritten list of all your specifications for your operation, and bind them into a booklet. Make divisions for the obvious purchase categories like milk, butter, eggs and cheese, fresh and frozen vegetables, meats, etc. Send each purveyor a copy of the appropriate section with the instructions that these are the detailed specifications on which future quotations will be taken. These specifications will mean *nothing* if the buyer does not have a receiving program which assures the quality of the goods received.

It is difficult to know just what quality level is needed in each product. Wherever there is a USDA A, B, and C Grade on canned fruits and vegetables, most operations should find USDA Grade B quite satisfactory. Grade A is just too much extra money for the difference in quality. Grade C generally allows an excess of defects which will affect the plate-worthiness of the foods. If the choice is between Grade A and Grade C—as an example, with jams and jellies, where there is no USDA Grade B—then take Grade A. On canned goods buyers must insist, at a minimum, that the cans or cases bear the mark of the Federal Inspector. If the operation is not large enough to take advantage of having the local USDA office run a grading inspection on a sample of the lot bought, buyers can, at least, cut their own cans and determine the appropriateness of the drained weight, sieve, or count, defects, and Brix of the syrup. The higher the Brix point, the more sugar in the syrup. For canned fruits which will be served in the juice, buyers will want a heavy syrup of 21°, or maybe extra heavy at 25°. Fruits for salads need only have a 16° Brix, which is called slightly sweetened water.

Frozen vegetables that are to be cooked need only be Grade B, but buyers must assure that each bears the USDA shield and the grade. Fresh vegetables and fruits, generally served in the raw state, should be Grade No. 1. On some products certification on the case is available. Local foodservice people should form a cartel of sorts to force the local fresh produce purveyors to keep a federal inspector on the premises to certify the grade of the products as shipped.

In meat, buyers should use the *Institutional Meat Purchase Specifications* (IMPS) or the *Meat Buyers Guide* (MBG) published by the National Association of Meat Purveyors. The MBG specs are the same as the IMPS but slightly shortened and accompanied by photographs which are a great aid in making receiving checks. The meat business can be very risky—the only way buyers can assure that they are getting a fair deal is to insist on the specs being followed. For all meats that are cooked by dry heat methods —roasting, broiling, pan-frying—USDA Choice should be used, as the fat in the muscle walls is needed for tenderness. For moist heat cooking—boiling, stewing, etc.,—USDA Good or Standard can be used, as the slow cooking process will break down the long muscle tissues and create a tender product.

Note that in the case of all foods buyers *must* require the Federal Grading. Not everything is graded.

During a recent year the following products were certified: 80 percent of the poultry, 69 percent of the butter, 67 percent of the lamb and mutton, 64 percent of the beef, 50 percent of the fresh fruits and vegetables, and 20 percent of the shell eggs. During the same period the following foods were certified for quality and/or wholesomeness: 87 percent of the dried eggs, 80 percent of the frozen fruits and vegetables, 77 percent of the processed liquid eggs, 46 percent of the nonfat dry milk, and 40 percent of the canned fruits and vegetables.

Standards for meat and poultry products are pertinent guidelines to assist in the task of quality interpretation and cost evaluation. To qualify for this classification, a food must contain a minimum amount of meat or poultry as prescribed by the USDA. For example, ready-to-serve chicken soup must contain at least 2 percent chicken. Condensed chicken soup must contain 4 percent or more, since it would then contain at least 2 percent when diluted with water. But chicken-flavored soup, which is not considered a poultry product, may contain less chicken.

The standards for meat ingredients are usually based on the fresh weight of the product, whereas those for poultry are measured on the weight of the cooked, deboned product. Since meat and poultry shrink during cooking, standards take this fact into account. For instance, turkey pot pie must contain 14 percent or more cooked turkey; chicken burgers must be 100 percent chicken (a product containing fillers must be called chicken patties).

At present there are about 150 standards for prepared convenience entrees. Some examples are: Beef Stroganoff—at least 45 percent fresh uncooked beef or 30 percent cooked beef, and at least 10 percent sour cream, or a ''gourmet'' combination of at least 7.5 percent sour cream and 5 percent wine; Chop Suey—at least 25 percent meat; Fritters—at least 50 percent cooked meat; Chicken or turkey a la king—at least 20 percent poultry meat.

We can look forward to such standards being developed for all convenience entree products.

STORAGE

Improper and careless storage techniques will downgrade quality. Poor stock rotation and prolonged storing in any of the storage areas (dry, cooler, or freezer) may lead to flavor and texture changes. Positive storage control procedures will tend to eliminate these problems.

Haphazard food assembly methods (such as piling or stacking of food products), spillage, and mixing of liquids (such as sauces and gravies), so that they become contaminated with each other, will help to destroy the inherent character of the food. Spices, condiments, and herbs should be assembled in a neat, orderly fashion until needed for preparation. Sandwich spreads should be kept refrigerated and stored in tight containers during slack periods. Sandwich meats, fish, and other products that have a tendency to form a crust or hard surface when exposed to air should be mixed in small lots or covered. Improper thawing procedures for certain foods will affect quality. Items intended for microwave oven heating may require special thawing techniques to prevent uneven doneness. Foods that are to be cooked in the frozen state, like french fries, should not be allowed to thaw, but should be held in a freezer until used.

COOKING

Although cooking refers to all modes of food heating (fully or partially), factors affecting quality, such as temperature, timing, formulations, and equipment maintenance, are all involved in the final outcome. For example, a faulty timer on a microwave oven will yield inconsistent quality; unfiltered fat for deep frying will produce low quality fried products; a loose door or a worn gasket on a steam pressure cooker may give unsatisfactory results.

Employment of proper utensils is essential for consistent quality. The use of a 10-gallon container to heat 1 gallon of a product will cause excessive shrinkage, texture changes, and flavor losses.

Salad dressings should be added just prior to serving tossed or mixed salads containing soft-textured components (tomato slices) since they should not be allowed to stand for long periods of time. Lettuce and other salad vegetables should be kept dry to prevent browning and loss of crispness. Tossed or mixed salad ingredients should be stored in coolers until used. Before storage they should be wrapped in plastic film or placed in a covered vessel.

Forcing or inducing heating by the use of high temperatures or exposed flames will reduce flavor, decrease tenderness, increase shrinkage, and may produce a burnt taste. Cooking should always be performed at the right temperature and within the prescribed time cycle.

Formulations or recipes should be written clearly and precisely. All quantity measurements should be listed, together with the size of the measuring device to be used, such as ladle or scoop size, and number. Heating cycle and equipment should also be posted.

Holding food in a steam table, cabinet, or under infrared lamps for excessive periods of time will reduce quality, since it may affect food texture and flavor or increase shrinkage and loss of nutrients. Foods will become mealy, mushy, soggy, or dried out. Overproduction should be held to a minimum. Coffee should not be held over 1 hour and only at temperatures of 185° to 190°F. Desserts like cream or custard pies require refrigerated storage to prevent spoilage.

Leftover foods should be properly refrigerated, packed loosely in shallow, covered pans, labeled, and dated. Foods that will not be used should be thrown away. Fresh produce should always be washed before serving or use in salads or soup. Washing will remove excess soil, dust, insecticides, and surface bacteria.

PRODUCE*

General

Fruits and vegetables may be purchased in many stages of processing.[1] *Fresh* fruits and vegetables are those that have been picked and packed for delivery in the fresh state. Generally, these have been freed of soil and insects and cooled before packing. *Processed* fruits and vegetables are those that have undergone some form of treatment to preserve them. These treatments are known as:

1. *Canning.* The process of putting food into a container to which enough heat is applied to kill all bacteria. In addition to using high heat to kill bacteria, there are processes used which apply a combination of pressure and lower heat to reduce the boiling point needed to sterilize the product.
2. *Freezing.* A process whereby fruits and vegetables are kept at a low enough temperature to prevent spoilage.
3. *Dehydrating.* A process by which fruits and vegetables have most of their water extracted.
4. *Drying.* A process by which fruits and vegetables, mostly peas, beans, and cereal, are allowed to dry naturally or are machine-dried of most of their water content.
5. *Freeze-Drying.* A process in which fruits and vegetables are frozen and then dried in a vacuum so that the water content changes from ice to vapor, bypassing the liquid state. There is less damage to products that are freeze-dried than those that are dried or dehydrated.
6. *Dehydro-Freezing.* A process by which foods are dehydrated, then frozen.
7. *Irradiation.* A process by which the bacteria in foods is killed through exposure to radiation.

*See also Chapters 4 and 5.
[1]The author is grateful to the United Fresh Fruit and Vegetable Association for permission to use in this book the data on Uses, Marketing Season, Varieties, Containers, Servings and Weights and Quality from the association's Fruit and Vegetable Facts and Pointers, Fresh Facts, Supply Guide, Serving Costs, Buying, Handling and Using Fresh Fruits and Buying, Handling and Using Fresh Vegetables.

All of these processes compromise the quality of fresh fruits and vegetables. However, it is usually not economically possible to use all fresh produce, and the various types of processing make it possible to serve almost any kind of fruit or vegetable out of its growing season.

There are USDA Standards for fresh, canned, frozen, dehydrated, and dried fruits and vegetables. This book deals with those standards only, as the supply of freeze-dried, dehydro-frozen, and irradiated foods is not a market factor of significance at this time.

Applications of Refrigeration

Important applications of refrigeration to fresh fruits and vegetables include pre-cooling before shipment, cooling in short or long storage, air-conditioning of wholesale produce warehouses and retail produce departments, refrigeration of retail displays, storing produce in retail stores, and refrigeration in the home.

Pre-Cooling.   As the term implies, pre-cooling is the rapid, initial removal of field heat prior to shipment or storage. This is done as soon after harvest as possible. Tests show that pre-cooling slows the ripening process in fruit and the breakdown process in vegetables, checks development of molds and bacteria, and prolongs the market life of the produce. Various studies have shown that a reduction of 15° to 18°F in the temperature of deciduous fruits slows the ripening and the respiration rate by approximately one-half. While the ratio of reduction of temperature to slowing of respiration is not the same for all commodities, it is sufficient to justify pre-cooling of perishables before shipment.

Methods.   Methods of pre-cooling include: (1) placing packages in an ordinary refrigerated storage room (a slow process and, therefore, not as effective in increasing market life as some other methods); (2) hydro-cooling by means of an ice-cold water spray or water bath (a rapid process); (3) forced-air cooling in a tunnel or specially built room (a fairly rapid means); (4) cooling in refrigerated rail cars or trucks (fast or slow, depending on the process used); and (5) vacuum cooling (a rapid process).

Hydro-Cooling.   The most common form of hydro-cooler is a tunnel, constructed of metal sheets, through which the produce to be cooled is passed on a conveyor. Icy water is showered over the unlidded containers of produce. Often a chemical is put into the water as a sterilizing agent. A typical hydro-cooler, 31′ × 7′, operating efficiently, can reduce the pulp temperature of peaches from 85°F to 50°F in 12 to 14 minutes. It cools from 350 to 450 bushels an hour. A well-refrigerated storage room would take about 48 hours to reduce the temperature to the same extent.

Vacuum Cooling.   Vacuum cooling can reduce the temperature of lettuce from 73°F to 33°–35°F in 30 minutes. This period of time will cover the entire cycle of operations, from placing the lettuce cartons in the vacuum tank to removing them. One plant at Watsonville, Calif., has a cooling capacity of 75 carloads per day. In some plants, the tank will admit a railroad car. The lettuce is loaded, ready to ship, and the entire load is cooled in one operation.

The vacuum cooling system is based on two facts: (1) water evaporating from a surface cools the surface; and (2) as pressure is decreased, the boiling point of water is reduced. At the boiling point, evaporation is rapid. A vacuum cooler consists of a gas-tight chamber into which the produce is loaded. Pressure in the chamber is then reduced by exhausting air, resulting in rapid evaporation and cooling. A carton of lettuce (40 to 45 lb. net) loses about 2 to 2.5 percent of its weight.

Vacuum cooling can be applied to any of the leafy vegetables, as well as any other commodities to which a little water can be applied for evaporation.

Icing.   One of the common methods of refrigeration of fresh produce is with ice water, which provides both moisture and heat absorption. The ice may be placed in bunkers and air circulated through the load; or ice may be placed in the produce container or blown over the top of the load; or a combination of these methods may be used.

Continuous Refrigeration.   For best results, fruits and vegetables that have been refrigerated at shipping point and en route should continue under refrigeration at the receiving point. Wholesalers generally have cold rooms that are insulated and mechanically refrigerated. These are known as "holding rooms." They also have special ripening rooms for such commodities as bananas and tomatoes, which need to be kept relatively warm and humid until the correct stage of ripeness is reached.

Long Storage.   Items such as apples, pears, or potatoes may be held for several months in specially built storages. Temperature and other conditions are controlled. The operators have the special knowledge and equipment needed. These storages usually are at shipping point.

Standard Grades and Inspection

Buyers can purchase a carload or many carloads of fresh fruits and vegetables in a few minutes from someone thousands of miles away and know what they are getting after a phone call or a brief message on the teletype. This can be done because there are federal standard grades and packs, as well as state standards, and federally approved trade terms and definitions that apply to these perishable products.

In addition, a system of federal and state inspection is provided both to protect the public and to avoid the innumerable disputes that might otherwise arise between buyer and seller as to grade, quality, and condition of fresh produce.

Contract.   Each time a buyer and a seller of fresh produce close a deal, they have made a binding and enforceable contract, even though no detailed contract has been written and signed. An exchange of short, confirmatory messages by telegram or teletype accomplishes the same purpose as a lengthy document.

This is possible because such a brief statement, for example, as "U.S. Extra Number 1 topped Carrots" has a definite and detailed meaning known to buyer and seller and stated in the standards published by the U.S. Dept. of Agriculture. A federal or state inspector, examining a shipment of carrots, can determine whether they actually are of the stated grade.

About 40 percent of all shipments of fresh fruits and vegetables are officially inspected, mostly at shipping point. In many cases, inspection is a regular routine procedure. The fee for inspection is paid by the party ordering inspection. The fee is based on the quantity and number of kinds of commodities to be inspected.

Arrangements are also made, if desired, for continuous inspection of fresh fruits and vegetables at the packing plant. Such packages may then be labeled with the U.S. shield with the wording "Packed under continuous inspection of the U.S. Department of Agriculture." The inspection fees cover the government's costs for giving this service.

Voluntary Grading.   Use of the U.S. Standards and use of the inspection service is generally voluntary, but may be compulsory under certain circumstances. Under provisions of the Marketing Agreement Act of 1937, authority is granted for restriction of shipments of produce by grade, size, or maturity where marketing agreements are in effect. These agreements are adopted by vote of those concerned. Grading and inspection of certain products has been made compulsory in areas which have adopted marketing agreements and orders.

Compulsory Grading.   Laws of some states require grading of various fresh fruits and vegetables in accordance with official U.S. Standards or state grades. A few states also require inspection of some products.

The Export Apple and Pear Act makes it unlawful to ship fresh apples or pears to foreign countries in carlot quantities, unless they meet certain minimum grades prescribed by the Secretary of Agriculture.

What Grades Provide.   The grades prescribe and define quality terms such as "U.S. Fancy," "U.S. Extra No. 1," "U.S. No. 1," "U.S. Combination," and "U.S. No. 2." Grades may specify size, maturity, color, cleanliness, shape, freedom from specified injuries or damage, interior structure of the fruit or vegetable, absence of seedstems, or any other factor of quality. The grades also set up tolerances, that is, percentages of permissible variations from any specification. Tolerances are necessary because in commercial practice it is impossible to pack fruits or vegetables to meet specifications 100 percent.

As a rule, U.S. No. 1 grade represents good, average quality that is practicable to pack under commercial conditions. Usually, under normal growing conditions, more than half of a crop will be of U.S. No. 1 grade. The designation "U.S. No. 2" ordinarily represents the quality of the lowest grade that is deemed practicable to pack under normal conditions. Superior products are packed "U.S. Fancy" or "U.S. Extra No. 1."

Grades are worked out by USDA in response to requests of those interested. The policy of the department is not to issue standards for official use until they are considered practicable and workable.

Congressional action in 1913 paved the way for the promulgation in 1917 of the first standards for fruits and vegetables. Potatoes were the first product for which standards were adopted. The inspection service started in 1918 when Congress provided for inspection at receiving markets. In 1922 Congress extended the service to shipping points. Inspection offices now are maintained in 78 of the larger cities throughout the continental United States, 1 in Puerto Rico, and 1 in Hawaii.

Inspection Procedure.   Inspectors are trained people thoroughly conversant with grades and with all fruits and vegetables. Some specialize in certain products, but all are licensed to inspect any fresh fruit or vegetable.

Inspectors use a random sampling procedure. They select a number of boxes at random from the sorting line, car, or lot, and from each box examine a representative number of items, also selected at random. The sampling is large enough to make it reasonably certain that it reflects the quality of the entire lot.

The inspectors note findings as to each item inspected. If they find the samples lack uniformity, they will inspect more of the merchandise than they would otherwise. Upon completion of examination, the inspectors total their scores of various defects and calculate percentages of defects. They make up a worksheet and report, and from the report make up an inspection certificate. They note the condition of the car, how it is loaded, how it is iced, what the pack is, and the quality and condition of the merchandise.

Federal inspection certificates are prima facie evidence in any court of law.

Grade, Condition, and Quality.   A distinction should be noted with regard to the terms *grade, condition,* and *quality.* Grade, as used by the USDA, is the sum of the characteristics of a commodity at the time it is graded, and includes both quality and condition. Quality denotes those characteristics that are relatively permanent, such as shape, solidity, color, maturity, and freedom from insect damage. Condition relates to factors that may change, such as decay and firmness. If a commodity grades, for example, "U.S. Extra Fancy" when packed, it means that it not only has the quality characteristics of the grade, but is in good condition within the meaning of the grade (having no factor of poor condition outside the tolerances permitted).

A product that grades "U.S. Extra Fancy" when packed may, after a long journey or careless handling, be found out of grade due to its condition.

FRESH FRUITS

Here are important factors to specify for fresh fruits.

Grade.   When you specify a U.S. grade, such as "U.S. No. 1," it has definite, detailed meaning which makes it unnecessary to write out the details. A full set of U.S.

grade standards for fresh fruit and vegetables can be obtained free by writing the Fresh Products Standardization Section, Agricultural Marketing Service, Washington, D.C. 20250. In using grades, however, it should be noted that there can be quite a range of quality within the grade, due to tolerances provided in the grade. Also, though U.S. No. 1 is the highest grade for some commodities, it is a lower grade for others. Higher grades include U.S. Extra Fancy, U.S. Fancy, and U.S. Extra No. 1. Buyers should at all times specify that fruit must be up to the desirable grade at delivery, and not merely at the time it was shipped.

Quality.   Grade alone does not necessarily define all the quality factors the restaurateur is interested in when buying a fruit for a certain purpose. The buyer should specify any additional factors as necessary.

Variety.   In almost every instance it is necessary to specify variety because there are considerable differences which make one variety suitable for one purpose and another for a different purpose. Thus, Delicious apples might be wanted for table service or salads but would not be suitable for baking.

Size.   In almost all instances it is important to indicate size. The end use will determine what size is needed. The medium sizes generally cost more per package than either the very small or very large because mediums are more in demand. However, if a whole fruit is to be served, obviously a large fruit will cost more than a much smaller one. Size is usually indicated by the count in a standard container, the lowest counts meaning the largest sizes.

Quantity.   Quantity should be stated in precise terms appropriate to the commodity. In the case of strawberries, it could be 30 12-pt. trays. In the case of watermelons, it

USDA GRADE MARKS

could be 12 melons, average 30 lb. each. In the case of bananas, it could be 10 40-lb. cartons, also specifying the size of the bananas as small, medium, or large.

Brand.   It is advisable to specify brands, when possible, because fruits packed under some labels are consistently good. Judging labels requires experience, but the suppliers can help on this.

Growing Area.   Fruit from one area may be much different than fruit from another, so it is often desirable to specify the source from which the fruit is wanted. For example, because of climatic conditions, pears of the Far West are superior to those of the East.

What About Price?

Price is important, but buyers who shop on the basis of price only are likely to be poor buyers. If they get consistently low prices, they are also going to get consistently low quality and service. Fruit and vegetable dealers are as smart as the buyers, and they are not going to give something for nothing. Also, the price-only buyers tend to buy a little from one dealer and a little from another, splitting up their purchases so much that they may not be profitable customers for anyone. Thus they do not merit the attention and cooperation that others may deserve and get. It is axiomatic in the trade that produce offered as a bargain is likely to be anything but.

A GLOSSARY OF FRUIT TERMS*

Blossom End—The opposite end from the stem end. The stem end will have a scar or remains of the stem to identify it. The blossom end is often more rounded than the stem end.

Breakdown of Tissue—Decomposition or breaking down of cells due to pressure (bruise) or age (internal breakdown).

Decay—Decomposition of the fruit due to bacteria or fungus infection.

Ground Color—The basic background color of a fruit before the sun's rays cause the skin to redden. The ground color may be seen beneath and between the red blush of the fruit.

Hard—The terms ''hard,'' ''firm,'' and ''soft'' are subjective terms used to describe the degrees of maturity or ripeness of a fruit. A ''hard'' texture will not give when pressed; a ''firm'' texture will give slightly to pressure. A ''soft'' texture is, of course, soft to the touch. The term ''mature green'' is sometimes used instead of hard.

Mature—Describes a fruit that is ready to be picked, whether or not it is ripe at this time. If a fruit is picked when mature, it is capable of ripening properly, but if picked when immature, it will not ripen properly.

Netting—The vein-like network of lines running randomly across the rind of some melons.

Ripe—Describes a fruit that is ready to be eaten.

Russeting—A lacy, brownish, blemish-type coating on top of the skin.

Scald—A blemish or brownish discoloration, which develops occasionally in the skin of apples or other fruits in cold storage.

*Courtesy of USDA.

Inspection

When fruit is delivered, it should be inspected at once to ensure that it is of the kind, quantity, variety, grade, size, pack, and of any special quality that has been ordered. It is not necessary to remove and check every piece to make an adequate inspection. Professional inspectors of the U.S. Dept. of Agriculture do not do that. A random spot check of a reasonable number of samples from a reasonable number of packages is all that is necessary. Overinspection means overhandling, which increases damage. If fruit has been ordered by brand, check the trademarks to see if they conform. Check for ripeness. What is found may make it necessary to change plans as to when certain items will be served. If some fruits are too firm, such as pears, bananas, cantaloupe, and avocados, they will be much improved by holding at room temperature until they are at the best stage for eating.

Adequate Care

When good money has been spent to buy high quality fruits to serve discriminating customers, it is only good sense to spend some time and effort to give the fruits the right care. Here are the general rules:

1. Insist on gentle handling. It is not unusual for those who deliver fruits, as well as those who handle the packages in the foodservice operation, to be rough. It takes supervision, explanation, and a rather firm policy and follow-up to induce all concerned to place rather than to drop fruit packages. They should never be thrown or pushed roughly across the floor. They should be handled the same as a crate of eggs. It will be easier to persuade workers to handle the fruit carefully if backbreaking labor is eliminated by provision of suitable materials-handling equipment, such as 2-wheel hand trucks, a 4-wheel, bar-handle truck, semi-live skids and jack, a conveyor, or whatever the particular situation and volume handled calls for.

2. Handle as little as possible. Attention should be given to receiving and routing fruit efficiently so that it need not be removed repeatedly. This takes planning. No rule can be given, but certainly new fruit should not be stacked on top of older fruit or in such a way as to block efforts to reach and use the older fruit first. The rule should be first in, first out. Dating each package on receipt is a help.

3. Avoid letting fruit stand in danger areas. When fruit is received, it is sometimes allowed to stand almost any place before it is put in storage, and damage can result. A bad place, for example, is near a hot radiator, on a wet floor, or on a receiving platform in extreme cold, heat, or wind. If fruit is to be refrigerated, it should be moved into the cold room without delay.

4. Stack packages according to their shape and weight. Stack so that the pressure comes on the structure of the package, not on the fruit. Some packages are properly stacked on their bottoms, some on their sides, and some on end. Bulge packs should not be stacked on the bulge because that brings crushing pressure on the fruit. In general, keep stacks low for ease of handling and to avoid excessive pressure on the lower layers.

5. Temperature, humidity, and ventilation. Fresh fruits are alive. In a sense they "breathe," taking up oxygen and giving off carbon dioxide and other products such as ethylene. They generate heat which must be removed to maintain low temperatures. Fruits should be stacked so that air can circulate around the packages. No one rule as to temperature can be given.

It is recognized that most foodservice operations do not have facilities for keeping different kinds of produce at different temperatures and humidities. In most cases, the choice is simply between keeping a commodity refrigerated or at room temperature, and the refrigeration may be around 45°F. For brief periods, such as one or two days, neither exact temperature nor humidity is important, but for long periods proper control of both is essential. However, it should be noted that it is unwise to expose some fruits, such as bananas or avocados, to low temperatures (anywhere around 32°F) for even a short time. Quality is adversely affected.

FRESH VEGETABLES

Freshness

Specify and insist on freshness. If vegetables are wilted or stale, they should be rejected regardless of "bargain" prices. Check how well the original characteristics of the vegetable, such as bright, lovely color; crispness; good weight for size; good shape; lack of mechanical damage; and absence of decay have been preserved. Fresh vegetables are living, breathing organisms. Their life processes go on after harvest until death and decay. They use oxygen and give off heat. They gradually lose water. Retention of freshness requires lowering their temperature to retard the life processes and, in most cases—but not all—keeping humidity high to conserve moisture.

Vegetables that are warm on arrival should be considered suspect even if visible wilting has not yet occurred. The useful life of most vegetables is much shortened by allowing them to stay warm even for a few hours. (Exceptions include sweet potatoes, white potatoes, tomatoes, and others.)

Seasonality

Vegetables bought very early or very late in their season—except sweet corn which is often at its best in early and late periods—need to be bought with extra care. They will most certainly be high in price but will not necessarily be of high quality. Generally, vegetables are lower in price and are likely to be of better quality and flavor when they are in season. Check the availability chart.

A precise, detailed guide to availability and sources of each commodity by months is the annual USDA report on Fresh Fruit and Vegetable Unload Totals for 41 cities. All large scale buyers should have this at their fingertips. It is free from the USDA, Washington, D.C. 20250.

Price

The best buyers are not necessarily the ones who get everything for the least money. Instead, they are the ones who buy vegetables best suited to the particular use to which they are to be put and which please customers. Experience shows the cheapest vegetables often may not be the best value. Price needs to be balanced against such factors as freshness, tenderness, shape and appearance, size, trim loss, and total waste.

Grade

The U.S. and state standard grades are a handy tool for buyers. Instead of detailing lengthy specifications, they can ask for U.S. No. 1 celery or U.S. 1 cauliflower. They should specify that it must meet the grade at time of delivery to their receiving room. A vegetable that met the grade at shipping point might be below grade later. The purchasers can add any special requirements; for example, they may want pascal celery of a particular size from a preferred area, or they may want to specify film-wrapped cauliflower minus the jacket leaves and ribs. A set of the U.S. vegetable standards is available free from the Fruit and Vegetable Division, USDA, Washington, D.C. 20250, or may be found in *SPECS: The Comprehensive Foodservice Purchasing and Specification Manual* (1977).

Variety

For most vegetables, varietal distinctions are unimportant and are little used in institutional buying. Type but not variety is of considerable importance. Thus "pascal" is not a varietal name for celery but a type designation. "Danish" cabbage designates a type and so does "domestic round." Variety is more important for potatoes, but even so, type and origin is of more consequence. Even experts have trouble picking varieties out of a jumbled pile of many varieties of potatoes. In instances where variety is important, it is discussed under the vegetable subject heading.

Size

If size is important for a particular use, as it often is, it should be definitely specified: Such terms as *small* or *large* should only be used if these are defined in a standard grade specified in the order. Otherwise, size should be stated in terms such as length or diameter, or in terms of the number of units in a standard pack, such as 24s in lettuce, or in terms of weight, such as 20- to 25-lb. watermelons.

Packaging

Vegetables are available in many kinds of containers and packs, with different net weights, as well as different degrees of protection. Buyers should specify a container suitable for their purpose. For example, an institution probably would want brussels sprouts in a 25-lb. drum or carton rather than in a crate or tray containing pint cups.

Information on containers and net weights and other data on weights and measures for many products is available in Chapter 12.

Partially Prepared Vegetables

In many cases, local produce suppliers offer foodservice buyers a number of fresh vegetables in partially prepared form. Most universally available are pre-peeled potatoes, often marketed as peeled, whole; peeled and cut to various french fry sizes and styles; peeled and sliced for cottage fries; peeled, cut, and blanched for french fries. Other items offered by some suppliers include washed, cut, and mixed salad greens; coleslaw mixes; peeled, diced, sliced, or shredded carrots; washed and cut spinach; peeled, sliced, and chopped onions; and peeled and sliced or diced turnips and parsnips.

These partially prepared vegetables are not available everywhere at present, but *they can be* if the produce dealers are made aware of the need.

Inspection

When vegetables are delivered, they should be inspected at once to make sure they are the kind, quantity, grade, size, pack, brand, or of any special quality that has been ordered. Inspection should be by random sampling. It is wasteful of time and harmful to the products to unpack and repack everything in order to check each item. Professional inspection services use the sampling method.

Handling Care

While most vegetables need low temperature and high humidity during any holding period, there are exceptions, so each needs to be considered carefully and separately. All have in common the need for careful and knowledgeable handling. None should be banged around, thrown, or dropped. The term *hardware* is sometimes applied to such vegetables as potatoes and cabbage, but it is a false term. Much damage and loss results from the mistaken idea that some items can be handled roughly without harm. Handlers should be instructed about the need for gentleness, and this requirement should be enforced.

Vegetables should not be allowed to stand in frigid winter or hot summer temperatures or in high wind on the loading dock. Nor should they be placed temporarily next to a hot radiator or be allowed to stand in a puddle of water. Upon receipt and inspection, all should be placed promptly in storage with suitable temperature and humidity. All should have some ventilation space because fresh vegetables generate heat and need air movement to carry it away. Green leafy vegetables, in particular, generate a lot of heat.

Stacking

Crates, cartons, and other vegetable containers should be stacked properly to avoid pressure on the produce itself and to avoid toppling. Packages that have a bulge should be stacked to keep weight off the bulge. Height of stacks should be low enough to prevent crushing weight on the bottom packages. If vegetables are to be high stacked, then palletizing with suitable support for upper stacks is required.

Odors

Some vegetables, such as onions, give off odors that can penetrate and incorporate with other products such as butter, eggs, and cheese. Products that readily pick up odors should not be stored with vegetables even if their temperature requirements happen to be compatible.

Life and Storage

A booklet on storage temperatures (such as USDA Agriculture Handbook 66) gives data on the length of storage under certain conditions of temperature and humidity. However, these figures cannot be applied to vegetables as received at the foodservice operation. Their life has been shortened by their trip through the marketing process. Unless it is known that vegetables have been rapidly cooled immediately after harvest and have been kept at satisfactory temperatures, long storage is not desirable. Exceptions are vegetables that do not have critical temperature requirements, such as potatoes, and vegetables that naturally have a long keeping period, such as topped carrots.

It is recognized that foodservice operations, in most cases, cannot provide finely adjusted temperatures or humidity ranges required for different vegetables, and this is not necessary for brief periods. However, optimum temperature and humidity for commercial storage are quoted in this report to give the reader a yardstick for measuring the storage conditions that can be provided.

CANNED FRUITS AND VEGETABLES

Grades and standards of identity have been developed for a wide variety of canned fruits and vegetables and a number of related products such as peanut butter, jellies, etc. These grades are market classifications of quality. They classify products into groups according to established and generally accepted standards. The use of federal grades on the product is voluntary, but standards of identity, quality (wholesomeness), and fill are not.

Standards are measurements of quality, weight, or quantity. Minimum quality standards have been established for canned goods by the Federal Food, Drug, and Cosmetic Act. Provisions of this act prohibit the movement of adulterated and misbranded foods in interstate commerce. All canned foods covered by its provisions must conform to its general requirements under the threat of heavy penalty. Its provisions prescribe:

- A definition and standard of identity
- A standard of quality
- A standard of fill

A definition and standard of identity defines what a food is. For canned goods, it establishes the composition of the product in the can. This includes the name of, or synonym for, the product, specific mixture, and the ingredients used in canning. The ingredients need not be listed, unless the canner has added other ingredients, such as spices, herbs, artificial flavoring, or chemical preservatives. Definitions and standards of identity have been established for canned apricots, cherries, peaches, fruit cocktail, peas, corn, beans, tomatoes, and other fruits and vegetables.

A standard of quality defines a minimum level of quality for canned products. In the case of canned tomatoes, the minimum level of quality is based on drained weight, color, peel per pound, and blemishes per pound. For fruit cocktail, the product is defined by established mixtures of fruit and style of cut. If products do not meet these requirements, they must be labeled ''below'' standard in quality or ''good food not high grade.'' The reason may also be listed, such as: ''not well peeled,'' ''poor color,'' ''excessively trimmed.''

A standard of fill defines the fill of the can. Standards of fill vary for products. The standard of fill for some products is based on maximum head space. Peas must be filled within $\frac{3}{16}$ of an inch below the top of the double seam. For other products, such as tomatoes, corn, and potatoes, the standard of fill is based on the minimum percent of water capacity. They must be filled not less than 90 percent of total capacity. Other products such as apricots, cherries, peaches, and pears must be filled ''the maximum quantity of . . . ingredients which can be sealed in the container and processed by heat to prevent spoilage, without crushing or breaking such ingredients.'' In other words, they must be filled as ''full as commercially practical without impairment of the quality of the food product.'' If the products do not meet these requirements, they must be labeled ''Below Standard in Fill'' or ''Slack Fill.''

Label

As the old cliche goes, ''the label is the window of the can.'' Provisions under the Food, Drug, and Cosmetic Act prescribe certain minimum requirements which must be adhered to by all packers and distributors. The provisions for labeling are mandatory for all canned food products shipped in interstate commerce. The law requires that the label contain the following information:

1. The legal name of the product.
2. The name and address of canner or distributor.
3. The net contents in weight, measure, or numerical count.
4. The variety, style, and packing medium when relevant.
5. The dietary properties, if important.
6. Any artificial color, flavor, or preservative.
7. If the product falls below the quantity or standard of fill established by the Act, it must be so stated.
8. All information must be in English, unless an imported product with foreign language is distributed solely in an area with a predominant language other than English.

9. A statement of ingredients, unless a standard of identity has been established by the government.

Syrup Density

Federal law requires that the label state the type of packing medium. Fruits are packed in syrups consisting of water or juice, from plain syrup to extra-heavy syrup. Syrup density is not a factor in grading. However, as a general rule, the syrup with the greatest amount of sugar is used for the best grades. Syrup density for the same grades will differ according to the fruit canned because of the individual characteristics of fruit. This is illustrated in the following table.

DIFFERENCE IN SYRUP DENSITIES FOR FRUITS, BRIX MEASUREMENTS

Syrup	Apricots	Cherries	Grapes
Extra Heavy Syrup	25–40 degrees	24–35 degrees	22–35 degrees
Heavy	21–25 degrees	19–24 degrees	18–22 degrees
Light	16–21 degrees	14–19 degrees	14–18 degrees
Slightly Sweetened	Less than 16°	Less than 14°	Less than 14°

The reason for the difference in the Brix or syrup density for the three products is that sweet cherries and grapes would break down, if packed in a heavier syrup than 35°F, because of their delicate nature.

The Brix is a measurement of the sugar content obtained by means of a reading in degrees taken on a Brix hydrometer or refractometer, fifteen days or more after packing. Each degree of Brix may be estimated to have 1 percent sugar content.

Grades

Grades are essentially market classifications of quality. Grading is simply a process of classifying units of commodity in groups according to established and generally accepted standards.

Grades have been developed for a wide variety of canned fruits and vegetables by the U.S. Dept. of Agriculture. The U.S. grades for canned fruits and vegetables are as follows:

- U.S. Fancy, or U.S. Grade A
- U.S. Choice for Fruits, or U.S. Grade B
- U.S. Extra Standard for Vegetables, or U.S. Grade B
- U.S. Standard, or U.S. Grade C

All canned foods not meeting the minimum quality standards for Grade C are graded substandard and must be prominently labeled as such.

For some products, there are grades A and C, but no grade B; for other products, grade C is omitted. For example, tomato puree is graded A and C; fruit cocktail is graded A, B, and Substandard; canned clingstone peaches are graded A, B, C, D, or Substandard, Grade C, Solid Pack, and Substandard Solid Pack.

Top Grade Not Always Best

Each grade has its best use, but no one grade, even the top grade or most expensive product, is always the best for all purposes in a quantity foodservice program. It is important to remember that canned foods sold under the lower grades are perfectly wholesome and have essentially the same nutritional value. They differ mainly in appearance and, to a lesser degree, in taste and flavor.

In general, Grade A, or Fancy, consists of fruits and vegetables of the highest quality. They have been carefully selected for uniformity in size, color, maturity, and tenderness, and are practically free from defects or blemishes. When appearance and flavor are most important, Grade A, or Fancy, should be used.

Grade B (Choice for Fruits, Extra Standard Vegetables) is a fine quality but scores somewhat lower in one or more of the factors in grade than Grade A, or Fancy. Grade B products are not so uniform in color, size, or maturity, and they generally have larger tolerances to defects.

Grade C, or Standard, is a good quality product but fails to meet the more exacting standards of Grade B. It is just as nutritious and wholesome as the higher grades. The products are less uniform in size and color, slightly less tender, or have more blemishes. Where appearance or tenderness is not important, Grade C is of value. This grade is good for cooked fruit desserts or in dishes where the product has to be cooked further, or when the product is one of several ingredients in a recipe.

Substandard does not mean that the food is unwholesome. All canned goods must be wholesome under the provisions of the Food, Drug, and Cosmetic Act. Substandard merely means that the food has some quality defect greater than allowed in the standard grade. It may be considerably broken up, off color, or it may contain more than the allowed amount of defects. When form and appearance are not important, substandard foods may be used. Substandard canned goods are usually sold as "seconds."

Grades give buyers information on which to base their choice of quality as related to the planned use of the food in the menu. This is an advantage in the terms of cost, as the lower grades can be used in many forms of food preparation where appearance is of minor importance.

Scoring Factors

Grades are based on scoring factors. The total score determines the grade. The factors include color, uniformity of size, absence of defects, character, flavor, consistency, finish, size, symmetry, liquor or clearness of liquor, maturity, texture, wholeness, and cut. There can be variations in any one of these items. In many cases, a variation will cause a product to be downgraded. This does not necessarily indicate low nutritional quality or edibility. It means that the product may contain more than the allowed amounts of defects, be off color, or be broken.

There is no substitute for experience when it comes to determining the essential variations within each factor. Nevertheless, an effective job can be done if the buyer will keep in mind this general scoring and tolerance outline:

USDA Grade A must be practically perfect in every respect allowing a tolerance of from 15 percent to 18 percent within the grade which is scored between 85 to 100 points inclusive.

USDA Grade B must be reasonably perfect in every respect allowing a tolerance of from 16⅔ percent to 20 percent within the grade which is scored between 75 to 89 points inclusive.

USDA Grade C must be fairly perfect in every respect allowing a tolerance of from 20 percent to 25 percent within the grade which is scored between 60 to 74 points inclusive.

The exceptions are those products where only 2 grades are commercially packed. In such instances the general scoring and tolerance outline is:

USDA Grade A must be practically perfect in every respect allowing a tolerance of from 15 percent to 18 percent within the grade which is scored between 85 to 100 points inclusive.

USDA Grade B must be fairly perfect in every respect allowing a tolerance of from 18 percent to 22 percent within the grade which is scored between 70 to 84 points inclusive.

Flavor—Because there is such a great variation in the individual's likes and dislikes, it is exceedingly difficult to score so elusive a factor as "Flavor." In most of the U.S. Standards for Grades of Foods, the term *Normal Flavor* is used. In commercial grading, however, *Flavor* is the prime factor. If what we eat tastes good, we somehow overlook minor deficiencies.

General Appearance—My own judgment places the factor of "eat with their eyes" even before they taste what they see. If a food does not look good, the prejudice may very well affect one's opinion of Flavor. For this reason, some food experts rate "General Appearance" every bit as important as "Flavor."

The relative importance of all other factors depends entirely upon the product being judged. While no attempt will be made here to score "Quality" or "Standard" factors for the available grades, the important factors by which to judge the quality of some of the more popular, everyday products are emphasized here to help food buyers make certain that deliveries conform to purchase specifications.

Color—This factor is the chief subdivision of "General Appearance," and to receive proper rating, "Color" should be typical of the product. Many food experts score "Color" on a par with flavor for some items.

Type—This means distinctive classifications of a specific product. For example, Culturally Bleached Asparagus is one distinct type, and All-Green Asparagus is a separate distinct type.

Style—When we refer to "Style" we think of prevalent approved ideas of form adaptable to popular food items which canners and processors make available to buyers. A good example is: Peaches—Sliced or Halves.

Count—Actual number of pieces found upon opening and examination of container contents.

Uniformity of Size—The degree of consistency relative to freedom from variation or difference. Sameness or alikeness.

Symmetry—The degree of consistently harmonious proportions of units in container.

Absence of Defects—The degree of freedom from grit, harmless foreign or other extraneous material, and damage from poor or careless handling, or from mechanical, pathological, insect, or other similar injury.

General Character—Under this factor, consideration is given to degree of ripeness or maturity, the texture and condition of flesh, the firmness and tenderness of the product, its tendency to retain its apparent original conformation and size without material disintegration, the wholeness or cut, consistency or finish, and clearness of liquor or syrup.

Maturity—This factor refers to the degree of development or ripeness of the product.

Texture—The structural composition or character of the product tissues.

Firmness—The degree of soundness of product structure.

Tenderness—The degree of freedom from tough or hard fibers.

In addition to these factors, there are general requirements that must be met. Examples of these are the fill in the container, drained weight, and syrup density. The grading factors vary with individual canned fruits and vegetables, but the scoring range is the same. For some canned items there is no Grade B. Where canned foods are graded only A and C, the scoring range is greater. Following is a summary of the total scores all grades.

SCORING RANGES FOR THE GRADES OF CANNED FOODS

Grades	Where There is a Grade B	When There is No Grade B
A (Fancy)	90–100	85–100
B (Choice, Extra Standard)	75–89	
C (Standard)	60–74	70–84
Substandard	0–59	0–69

Canned tomatoes must score 90 points or higher to be graded A, since there is a Grade B in the standards for canned tomatoes. Tomato juice needs to score only 85 or higher to be graded A, since there is no Grade B for tomato juice.

Occasionally, a product may not qualify for a high grade, even though its total score is above the minimum established for that grade. This is the result of a "limiting rule." Each grading factor is assigned a score range. Under the limiting rule, if the product fails to score above a certain scoring range on an important factor, it cannot be graded higher, regardless of the total score.

Knowing the score of canned fruits and vegetables is of value to the buyer. For example, let us take tomatoes. Tomatoes are graded on the basis of drained weight, wholeness, color, and absence of defects.

Grade A whole tomatoes must have a net drained weight of 54.7 to 67.9 oz.; Grade A tomatoes must have a net drained weight of 72.2 oz. to 76.6 oz.; Grade B tomatoes must have a net drained weight of 63.5 oz. to 67.9 oz., and Grade C tomatoes must have a net drained weight of 54.7 oz. to 59.1 oz.

The difference between 72.2 oz. and 76.6 oz. is 4.4 oz. This could mean the difference of one or two extra tomatoes. If you are quoted the same price for tomatoes at 72.2 oz. and 76.6 oz., you would be getting approximately 6 percent more tomatoes for the money by purchasing 76.6 oz.

So if you ask three purveyors, "What's your price on tomatoes today?" how are you going to receive comparable quotes if you do not specify grade and weight?

Buyers should be aware of the point spread that determines the various grades. For example, a lot of canned peas may score 88 or 89 points and be classified as Grade B. This lot may be closely related in quality to the lot of canned peas that just scored 99 points and is graded Grade A. The only major difference between the two major lots will be the prices because of grade classification. If the color factor were graded low and the other factors were graded high, and color was not an important factor to you, then the lot scoring 88 or 89 points would be a better buy.

It is difficult, if not impossible, for most buyers to determine the point spread because of the lack of time and equipment. However, buyers can obtain the scores by requesting a copy of the grader's certificate.

U.S. Grade A

Fancy—Excellent high quality foods. Practically uniform in size and very symmetrical. Practically perfect in every respect, color, texture. Succulent, tender, represents the best of the crop.
Fruits are usually packed in extra heavy syrup.

U.S. Grade B

Choice—Fruits
Extra Standard—Vegetables
High quality foods, reasonably uniform in size. Reasonably good color and texture. Reasonably free from defects.
Fruits are usually packed in heavy syrup.

U.S. Grade C

Standard—Fairly good to quality foods. Fairly uniform in size, color, texture. Fairly free from defects. Fruits are usually packed in light syrup.

CONTAINER SIZE CONVERSION—TIN AND GLASS

Name of Container 1	Diameter x Height 2	Min. Vol. Fil (Cu.In.) 3	Total Capac. Avoir ozs. Water at 68°F 4	No. 303 Can Equiv. 5	No. 2 Can Equiv. 6	No. 2½ Can Equiv. 7	No. 3 CyL Can Equiv. 8	No. 10 Can Equiv. 9
2z Mushroom	202x204	5.45	3.60	0.207	0.170	0.117	0.068	0.032
5 z Baby Food	202x214	7.63	4.80	.290	.238	.164	.095	.045
6z Jitney	202x308	9.42	6.00	.358	.294	.203	.117	.055
6½z	202x314	10.62	......	.404	.332	.229	.132	.062
Baby	208x211	9.32	6.00	.354	.291	.201	.116	.055
4z Pimiento	211x200	7.18	4.90	.273	.224	.155	.089	.042
211 Baby Food	211x200	10.38	4.90	.395	.324	.223	.129	.061
4z Mushroom	211x212	11.19	7.15	.423	.348	.239	.138	.065
8z Short	211x300	12.34	7.90	.469	.386	.266	.153	.072
8z Tall	211x304	13.48	8.65	.512	.421	.291	.167	.079
No. 1 Picnic	211x400	17.06	10.90	.648	.533	.367	.212	.100
211 Cylinder (12r)	211x414	21.28	13.55	.809	.665	.455	.264	.125
Pint Olive	211x600	26.47	16.95	1.006	.827	.570	.329	.155
4z Flat Pimento	300x108	5.59	4.20	.212	.175	.120	.069	.033
7z Pimento	300x206	11.37	7.50	.432	.355	.245	.141	.067
	300x308	18.03	11.70	.685	.563	.383	.224	.106
No. 1 Square	300x308x308	26.96	......	1.025	.843	.580	.335	.158
No. 2½ Square	300x308x604	50.68	......	1.926	1.584	1.091	.629	.297
8z Mushroom	300x400	21.11	13.55	.802	.660	.545	.262	.124
No. 300	300x407	23.71	15.20	.901	.741	.511	.294	.139
No. 300 Cylinder	300x509	30.17	19.40	1.147	.943	.651	.375	.177
No. 1 Tall	301x411	25.99	16.60	.988	.812	.561	.323	.152
No. 303	303x406	26.31	16.85	1.000	.822	.566	.327	.154
No. 303 Cylinder	303x509	34.11	21.85	1.296	1.066	.734	.424	.200
No. 1 Flat	307x203	13.21	8.90	.502	.413	.298	.164	.077
No. 2 Flat	307x204	14.40	9.20	.547	.450	.310	.179	.084
Kitchenette	307x214	19.17	12.25	.729	.599	.413	.238	.112
No. 2 Squat	307x302	21.06	13.45	.800	.658	.453	.261	.123
No. 2 Vac. (12z Vac.) ...	307x306	22.90	14.70	.870	.716	.493	.284	.134
No. 95	307x400	27.63	17.75	1.050	.863	.595	.343	.162
No. 2	307x409	32.00	20.50	1.216	1.000	.689	.397	.187
No. 2 XT	307x506	38.30	......	1.456	1.197	.825	.476	.224
Jumbo	307x510	40.28	25.70	1.531	1.259	.867	.500	.286
No. 2 Cylinder	307x512	40.95	26.35	1.556	1.280	.886	.508	.240
No. 2 Tall	307x604	44.99	28.80	1.710	1.406	.969	.559	.264
29Z	307x700	50.65	32.48	1.925	1.583	1.090	.629	.297
Quart Olive	307x704	52.62	33.70	2.000	1.644	1.133	.653	.308
32Z (Quart)	307x710	55.43	35.54	2.107	1.732	1.193	.688	.325
	312x508	47.52	30.45	1.806	1.485	1.023	.590	.278
No. 1¼ (Veg.)	401x206	21.51	13.80	.818	.672	.463	.267	.126
No. 1¼ (Pineapple)	401x207.5	22.07	......	.839	.690	.475	.274	.129
No. 2½	401x411	46.45	29.75	1.765	1.452	1.000	.577	.272
	401x602	61.85	39.63	2.351	1.933	1.332	.768	.362
No. 3 Vac	404x307	37.19	23.85	1.414	1.162	.801	.462	.218
No. 3	404x414	54.09	35.05	2.056	1.690	1.165	.672	.317
	404x506	60.80	38.95	2.311	1.900	1.309	.755	.356
No. 3 Cyl. (46z)	404x700	80.54	51.70	3.061	2.517	1.735	1.000	.472
No. 5	502x510	92.20	59.10	3.504	2.881	1.985	1.145	.540
No. 5 Squat	603x408	106.30	68.15	4.040	3.322	2.288	1.320	.623
No. 10	603x700	170.71	109.45	6.488	5.335	3.673	2.120	1.000
No. 12 (Gal.)	603x812	215.82	138.35	8.203	6.744	4.646	2.680	1.264
GLASS CONTAINERS								
8z		12.12	......	.461	0.379	0.261	.150	.071
12z		18.18	......	.691	.568	.391	.226	.106
14z		21.21	......	.906	.663	.457	.263	.124
16z (No. 303 or 1 lb. jar)		27.97	......	1.063	.874	.602	.347	.164
30z No. 2½		48.06	......	1.827	1.502	1.035	.597	.282
32z		53.02	......	2.015	1.657	1.143	.658	.312
64z		115.20	......	4.390	3.069	2.487	1.434	.677
128z (1 gal. jug)		231.00	......	8.780	7.219	4.973	2.868	1.353

Instructions: To convert a given quantity of cans, glass jars or bottles of the size listed in column 1 to No. 303's, 2's 2½'s or 10's *multiply* by corresponding factor in columns 5, 6, 7 and 8. To convert *from* 303's, 2's 2½'s or 10's to a particular size in column 1, *divide* by corresponding factor. The equivalents are based on a comparison of minimum volume fill in cubic inches.

Source: *The Almanac of the Canning, Freezing, and Preserving Industries,* National Canners Association and Agricultural Marketing Service.

U.S. Grade D

Substandard—Products that fail to meet the requirements of Grade C or the standard of quality outlined under the Pure Food and Drug Law.

Noticeable departure from these characteristics for any product is a good indication the product is of a lower quality. Among the key checks on quality include: color; texture; odor; absence of defects, such as cuts and bruises; uniformity of size and shape; and degree of firmness.

Careful review of quality checks covered in this manual will provide buyers added insurance that products delivered meet the standards specified in their purchasing order.

Scoring. Qualified experts employ a point scoring range to determine a product's quality bracket. The point factors vary somewhat from product to product.

The usual scoring point range is: 90–100 points, Grade A (Fancy); 80–89 points, Grade B (Choice) for fruits or (Extra Standard) for vegetables; 70–79 points, Grade C (Standard); below 70 points is substandard. There are a few notable exceptions:

Applesauce
   Grade A (Fancy):   85–100 points
   Grade C (Standard):   70–84 points
Fruit Cocktail
   Grade A (Fancy):   85–100
   Grade B (Choice):   70–84
Tomato Puree and Tomato Paste
   Grade A (Fancy):   90–100
   Grade C (Standard):   80–89
   Substandard: 79 and under

All scoring factors are based upon the U.S. Dept. of Agriculture Consumer and Marketing Service standards. Experienced inspectors, either resident USDA personnel in canneries or trained inspectors employed by the companies, examine sample lots. The grade assigned to the lot represents an average score of the sampled products.

Inspectors do not always agree on grades of identical products. For example, the best of a crop of peaches might be scored Fancy by a local inspector. Yet an inspector from a preferred growing area might score them Choice in comparison to peaches from his or her region.

Because of the qualitative and geographical scoring differences, alert volume foodservice buyers prefer to use basic quality checks in determining grade and to select suppliers noted for purchasing the best products within each grade.

Drained Weights

Minimum drained weights designate the minimum amount of food per single can. The average drained weight of all the cans in one case should be greater than the minimum.

Ordinary kitchen equipment seldom will enable buyers to determine exact weight as defined by Food and Drug regulations. As a result, measuring headspace is a method often used for checking the percent of fill.

The usual method of checking contents or percent of fill is to measure the distance from the top of the opened can to the top of the contents. This is called headspace. Maximum gross headspace allowable in No. 10 or No. 3 cylinder cans is $^{27}/_{32}$ of an inch, which is greater than will be found in properly filled cans of most products.

In addition, solid contents of the can should usually be nearly level with the liquid surface level. If they seem unreasonably lower than the surface level, it would be best to request an official USDA certificate to fill weight from the packer.

Drained weights are not a factor on many foods, such as peas, Elberta peaches, cream-style corn, tomato puree, etc. On these products, the USDA uses a standard of fill of the container and a fill weight. For example, canned peas meet the fill standard when all contents (including liquid) are removed from the can and, when returned, completely fill the container—with or without the juice—after 15 seconds of settling.

Proper fill for fruits is determined by the maximum quantity that can be processed and sealed in the container without crushing or breaking the contents.

The Federal Food, Drug, and Cosmetic Act permits variations from the stated weights, measure, or numerical count on individual cans due to avoidable weighing, measuring, or counting deviations that occasionally occur in even the best packaging circumstances.

Variation that results in the average of packs in a shipment falling below the stated individual quantity is not permitted.

Unreasonable shortages are never allowed, such as twenty peach halves in a can when it was specified that it should contain 30 to 35 count halves.

Packing Fruits and Vegetables

Fruits and vegetables are grown and packed in nearly all sections of the United States, but certain areas consistently produce superior products. Time of harvest is also an important factor in product quality. These geographic and seasonal factors play important roles in food processors' guidelines for selecting raw products for canning. These guidelines are strictly followed except when nature fails to conform to normal moisture and warmth patterns.

Good Timing Leads to Good Buys

Prime harvest period for most fruits and vegetables used in volume feeding usually runs from July until late September or October.

Packers evaluate the products in October and November. As the season's canning activities progress, lot numbers are assigned to daily production runs and samples are rechecked against standards. When the harvest is in the cans, the "opening price" is computed using cost of materials, labor, and other price factors.

Prior to firming up "opening prices," suppliers can only quote interim prices, based on the apparent harvest projected from the acreage planted and weather conditions. Interim prices are an educated guess at best because of the effect of heavy rain-fall, hail, extreme dryness, and a host of other factors.

Preparing Accurate Bids: The Do's and Don'ts

Do:

List products clearly.

A good bid sheet is an accurate bid sheet. Any products listed on a bid sheet should be fully described by including the following factors:

Bid Description	Example
Product	Apples
Style of Product	Sliced
Count Range (or Sieve Size)	
Can Size and Pack	6/10
Source	Eastern
Variety	York Imperial
U.S. Grade	Grade A (Fancy)
Point Score	85 or better
Packing Medium	Solid-Pack—No Sugar Added
Minimum Drained Weight (or fill of container)	96 oz.

All of the information above is in accordance with canning industry and U.S. Government standards. Conformity with these standards makes it possible for bidders to quote on essentially the same product and, at the same time, permits the buyers to better evaluate the quotations and make the best possible purchase.

Do:

Make heading sheets as clear as the specifications.

Heading sheets on bid forms can be as simple or detailed as the buyer desires. However, certain information should be included on every covering sheet.

- Buyer's name and address
- Closing date and hour for return of bids
- Delivery address
- Date or dates when deliveries are desired
- Payment terms and dates

State and local regulations often require considerably more information than this minimum bid heading to avoid confusion among suppliers and to eliminate any questions about bidding procedures. The more extensive bid sheets generally include the following information:

- Number of invoices required
- How to submit samples, if required
- Final adjustment of quantities shown on bid
- Prices quoted should or should not include prepaid transtation charges
- Products requiring grade certificates
- Method of price quoting, i.e., by the case; total quantity of each lot; any other method
- Identification of products by brand or trade name
- Method of quoting on a different size container and/or case
- Method and time of delivery
- Right to accept or reject any or all bids
- Penalties for nonperformance
- Any other pertinent regulations or instructions

Do:

Single out statements of intent.

Many misunderstandings may be avoided by clearly worded statements clarifying the buyer's intent or any special conditions of sale. For example, ''the interpretation of descriptive terms of grade shall be in accordance with the U.S. Standards for grade in effect on the date of the invitation for bid.''

One of the most common areas covered by amplifying statements concerns disposition of delivered products that are apparently not the grade specified. This problem can be avoided by including a clarifying statement in the bid heading to the effect: ''When delivered products appear to be below the grade of the products specified, the buyer reserves the right to submit items in doubt to the nearest local or regional USDA office for official inspection and grading. In such cases, it is agreed the party in error will pay the cost of the inspection.''

Official inspection of processed fruits, vegetables, and other products is readily available nationally through regional offices of the U.S. Dept. of Agriculture. Inspection applications should be addressed to:

Processed Products Inspection
Fruit and Vegetable Division
Consumer and Marketing Service
U.S. Dept. of Agriculture

Simply consult the U.S. Government listing in your local telephone book for the inspection office nearest you, or write to the division's main office in Washington, D.C. 20250.

Don't:

Use incorrect terminology in an effort to obtain special grades or items.

For example, don't use the term Extra Fancy Grade; the correct name is Fancy Grade. To indicate that you want the top range of the fancy grade, you can adjust your point score specifications to read ''score 95 or better.'' You can similarly adjust your point score specification in any grade as long as you stay within the boundaries of the prescribed scoring range for the grade product.

Likewise, do not state Grade C (Standard) (fruit item) packed in extra heavy syrup; Grade C fruits are packed in light syrup only. Each grade of fruit is usually packed in its proper degree of syrup. Any grade of fruit may be packed in a lighter syrup, in water, or as ''solid pack.'' You will not find any grade of fruit packed in a syrup heavier than that which is customarily used for the grade.

Don't:

Be vague or general in your specifications.

For example, the items listed below were abstracted from an actual bid request, exactly as they were written by the customer.

Item	Size Can	Amount
Peaches, halves	No. 10	200 cases
Pears, Bartlett, halves	No. 10	175 cases
Peas, Early June	No. 10	300 cases
Green Beans, Blue Lake, cut	No. 10	300 cases

This particular bid request contained a list of twenty-five items totaling 4,500 cases, and each item was written like these examples.

You can readily see how impossible it would be for suppliers to submit quotations on identical items, and for the buyer to make an intelligent evaluation of the quotations submitted.

FROZEN

Frozen fruits and vegetables are graded identically, for the most part, with their canned equivalents. The grade standards for these items are shown in the text of their section only to the extent to which they differ from the canned product.

Frozen vegetables offer the advantage of having been frozen quite close to picking time, and thus offer the operator the advantage of not having been cooked in the canning process.

Frozen vegetables are purchased in a variety of packs and cases, with the most common commercial sizes being 2-lb., 2½-lb., and 3-lb. packages, 12 packages to the case. There are also 10-oz., 12-oz., 1-lb., and 5-lb. packages available. Some items such as peas and corn are available, usually in the ''B'' grade, in 20-lb. bulk packages.

Frozen fruits are generally packed in either a sugar or syrup to preserve flavor, texture, and color. The fruit-sugar ratio of 4:1 or 5:1 should be part of the purchase specifications. Frozen fruits usually come in 6-lb., 6½-lb., 20-lb., 25-lb., and 30-lb. containers although there are some 10-oz., 12 oz., and 1-lb. packs available.

DEHYDRATED AND DRIED

These items are limited in their uses in foodservice. Some, such as potato flakes, potato buds, etc., are quite common, while others, like dehydrated pears or peaches, are not frequently seen. The buyer should require grading certificates on low moisture and dried fruits, as the defects in these items become less evident than with their canned and frozen cousins.

Pack sizes range from 1 lb. to 50 lb. It is recommended that no more than a few weeks' supply be purchased at a time because insects prey upon dehydrated and dried foods.

JUICES*

Canned juices may be sweetened or unsweetened. The product should taste and look very much like the fresh product, allowing for some difference due to processing. The federal grades are U.S. Grade A (85 points); U.S. Grade C (70 points), and U.S. Grade D (less than 70 points). Purchase of U.S. Grade A is recommended.

Concentrate juices may or may not be purchased frozen. Both have grading levels of 85 and 70 points; U.S. Grade A and U.S. Grade C for canned, and U.S. Grade A and U.S. Grade B for frozen. The water/juice ratios for reconstitution vary from 2:1 to 18:1, an important factor in specifying for bids.

Only orange and grapefruit juice have federal grades in the dehydrated state, although some other dehydrated juices are marketed. The federal grades are U.S. Grade A (85) and U.S. Grade B (70); buy the former.

FROZEN FOODS

Code of Recommended Practices for Handling Frozen Foods

To safeguard frozen food quality for the consumer, eleven related trade groups some years ago established a code of recommended handling practices. The subjects covered by these practices relate to merchandising aspects of frozen foods. The groups that joined in subscribing to these practices did so in an organized effort to insure that new technological developments will continually be made available, and concurrently to update good practices for the care and handling of frozen foods.

These recommended practices are based upon extensive research in frozen food time-temperature-tolerance by the Western Utilization Research and Development Laboratory of the USDA which were concurred in by the Refrigeration Research Foundation. These practices do not replace more demanding company or industry practices which may be in effect. The industry's goal is to maintain reasonably uniform frozen food product temperatures of 0°F or lower, and to insure their proper care, from packer to consumer.

*See also Chapter 4.

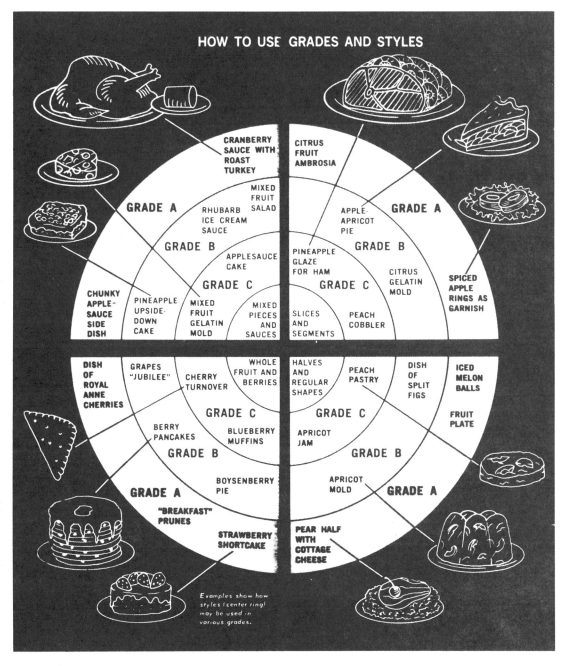

HOW TO USE GRADES AND STYLES

CRANBERRY SAUCE WITH ROAST TURKEY

CITRUS FRUIT AMBROSIA

GRADE A

MIXED FRUIT SALAD

RHUBARB ICE CREAM SAUCE

APPLE-APRICOT PIE

GRADE A

GRADE B

APPLESAUCE CAKE

PINEAPPLE GLAZE FOR HAM

GRADE B

CITRUS GELATIN MOLD

GRADE C

GRADE C

CHUNKY APPLE-SAUCE SIDE DISH

PINEAPPLE UPSIDE-DOWN CAKE

MIXED FRUIT GELATIN MOLD

MIXED PIECES AND SAUCES

SLICES AND SEGMENTS

PEACH COBBLER

SPICED APPLE RINGS AS GARNISH

DISH OF ROYAL ANNE CHERRIES

GRAPES "JUBILEE"

CHERRY TURNOVER

WHOLE FRUIT AND BERRIES

HALVES AND REGULAR SHAPES

PEACH PASTRY

DISH OF SPLIT FIGS

ICED MELON BALLS

GRADE C

GRADE C

FRUIT PLATE

BERRY PANCAKES

BLUEBERRY MUFFINS

APRICOT JAM

GRADE B

GRADE B

GRADE A

BOYSENBERRY PIE

APRICOT MOLD

GRADE A

"BREAKFAST" PRUNES

STRAWBERRY SHORTCAKE

PEAR HALF WITH COTTAGE CHEESE

Examples show how styles (center ring) may be used in various grades.

Source: USDA

The development of these recommendations was based upon the principle that voluntary action by industry members would result in more rapid advancement and attention to good care and handling practice than would be produced by compulsion of laws and regulations.

Foods for Freezing

1. Raw products should be harvested at optimum maturity, then delivered promptly to the plant where they should be prepared for freezing, frozen, and packaged (or placed in proper bulk storage) with all reasonable speed. Similarly, frozen products to be used as ingredients in prepared frozen foods should be of best quality for the intended purpose, handled at temperatures of 0°F or lower, and only permitted to thaw for the time and to the extent necessary for their incorporation into the end product.

2. Similar care should be used by processors without freezing facilities in moving prepared-for-packaging products to refrigerated warehouses for freezing.

3. Where processors have their own freezers and warehouses, products leaving the warehouse should be at 0°F or lower.

4. In movement from processors who freeze but do not have sufficient warehouse space to complete freezing, the product should leave the plant without delay, at 10°F or lower, in an insulated and refrigerated vehicle. Such movement to the primary warehouse for reduction of temperature to 0°F or lower, should not exceed 8 hours.

5. Product temperatures should be reduced to 0°F or lower, promptly upon reaching the primary warehouse.

Warehouse Equipment

1. Each warehouse should be of adequate capacity and should be equipped with suitable mechanical refrigeration to provide, under extreme conditions of outside temperature and peak load conditions, for maintaining an air temperature of 0°F or lower, in all rooms in which frozen foods are stored.

2. Each storage room should be equipped with an accurate temperature measuring device so installed as to correctly reflect the average air temperature of the room. Each day the warehouse is open, temperatures of each room should be recorded, dated, and a file of such temperatures maintained for a period of at least 2 years.

Warehouse Handling Practices

1. Warehouse operators should record product temperature of each lot of frozen foods received and should accept custody in accordance with good commercial practice. They should retain lot arrival temperature records for a period of at least 1 year.

2. Whenever frozen foods are received with product temperatures of 15°F or higher, warehouse personnel should immediately notify the owner or consignee and request instructions for special handling. These procedures may consist of any available method for effectively lowering temperatures, such as blast freezing, low temperature rooms with air circulation, and proper use of dunnage or separators in stacking.

3. Before a lot of frozen food is placed in storage, it should be code marked for effective identification.

4. Frozen foods should be moved over dock areas promptly to minimize exposure to elevated temperatures, rainfall, or other adverse weather conditions.

5. If frozen foods are purchased for resale directly to consumers, such products should be stored in the purchaser's own premises (regardless of whether such premises

are owned or leased from a public warehouse or others) so that the purchaser would have complete control of all of the conditions for which he or she is responsible in adhering to the code. The "first-in, first-out" method of inventory control is desirable.

6. During defrosting of overhead coils in storage rooms, stacks of frozen foods should be effectively protected by tarpaulins, or other protective covering, or by removal from beneath the coils.

7. Frozen foods going into a separate break-up room for order assembly must be moved out promptly unless break-up room is maintained uniformly at 0°F or lower.

Transportation Equipment

1. All vehicles—railway cars, motor trucks, trailers, and ships—should be: (a) so constructed and properly insulated that, when equipped with appropriate refrigeration units, they will be capable of maintaining product temperature of 0°F or lower throughout the load in all movements; (b) equipped with an appropriate temperature measurement device to accurately indicate air temperature inside the vehicle. The dial or reading element of the device should be mounted in a readily accessible position outside the vehicle; (c) equipped with air leak-proof cargo spaces, including tight fitting doors and suitable closures for drain holes to prevent air leakage; (d) racked, stripped, baffled, or otherwise so constructed as to provide clearance for air circulation around the load, unless of coldwall or envelope type construction (Note: Floor racks will not be necessary when product is palletized or is loaded on extruded floors; however, such floors must be free from any dirt and debris. It is recommended that ceiling air circulation ducts extend from the air circulating fans to at least ¾ the length of the load.); and (e) entirely free from any dirt, debris, or offensive odors when placed for loading.

2. Route delivery trucks should comply with all the provisions of Section 1 above and, in addition, should be equipped with curtains or flaps in the doorway area or with port doors, to minimize loss of refrigeration during delivery stops.

3. Self-refrigerated containers and other self-contained units utilized in making small shipments of frozen food, such as those which might move in LCL or LTL lots via aircraft, pickup trucks, and other nonrefrigerated vehicles, should be so constructed as to give the product adequate protection against physical damage in transit, and be equipped with a refrigerant or refrigerating system capable of maintaining a product temperature of 0°F or lower during the anticipated movement. All such containers should be free from dirt, debris, and offensive odors when offered for loading.

Handling Practices for Line-haul or Over-the-Road Transportation

1. All vehicles should be pre-cooled to an inside air temperature of 20°F or lower prior to loading, and after completing pre-tripping procedures.

2. Frozen foods should be securely packaged before they are offered for transportation.

3. Product temperature should be 0°F or lower when tendered to carrier for loading. Carrier should not accept products tendered at temperature higher than 0°F. Shippers, consignors, or warehouse personnel should not tender to a carrier any container which has been damaged or defaced to the extent that it is in an unsalable condition.

4. Carriers should provide their personnel with appropriate testing thermometers and instruction in proper procedure to determine that the product they receive is at 0°F or lower. Arrival product temperatures should be taken inside the vehicle within a reasonable time after arrival and prior to any unloading. However, the carrier must continue to protect the product until such time as the consignee is ready to accept that which the carrier is ready to tender.

5. No product should be loaded in such manner in any vehicle that it will interfere with the free flow of air into or out of the refrigeration unit, or with the free flow of air around the load in vehicles of other than envelope or coldwall type construction, or those using Freon or liquid nitrogen as a refrigerant.

6. Vehicles should be loaded and unloaded within allowable free time as provided for in governing tariffs to prevent accrual of detention charges.

7. The vehicle's refrigeration unit should be turned on and the doors kept closed during any period when loading and unloading operations cease.

8. The thermostat on the vehicle's refrigeration unit should be set at 0°F or lower.

9. All frozen foods shall be held, tendered, and transported at an air temperature of 0°F or lower, except for defrost cycles, loading and unloading, or other temporary conditions beyond the immediate control of the person under whose care and supervision the frozen food is held. The internal product temperature of frozen food shall be maintained at 0°F as quickly as possible.

10. After loading has been completed and the vehicle doors closed, the carrier's equipment should be checked prior to departure to insure that the refrigeration system is in proper working order.

Handling Practices for Route Delivery

1. All applicable sections under the part on over-the-road haul transportation above should be followed in the case of route delivery.

2. In addition, each lot for individual consignment should be refrigerated by means of mechanical refrigeration, or by any other method of maintaining product temperature.

3. Vehicles or containers should be pre-cooled to a temperature of 20°F or lower before being loaded with frozen foods.

4. Doors of route delivery trucks should be kept closed during any period when loading or unloading operations cease. In addition, door curtains or flaps should be used during actual unloading, if the vehicle is not equipped with port doors, to minimize loss of refrigeration.

Storage Facilities for Foodservice Installations

1. Frozen food storage facilities should be maintained at an air temperature of 0°F or lower.

2. Total storage facilities should be of sufficient cubic capacity to easily accommodate frozen foods in quantities anticipated for operation of the installation, taking into account frequency of deliveries, probable peak requirements, ordering practices, and related factors.

3. Cabinet-type frozen food storage facilities should be equipped with an accurate thermometer indicating a representative air temperature, and should be defrosted as frequently as necessary to maintain refrigeration efficiency.

4. Walk-in type storage facilities should have provision for circulation of refrigerated air and should be defrosted as frequently as necessary to maintain refrigeration efficiency. Such facilities should be equipped with an accurate thermometer, the sensing element of which should be located in the upper ⅓ of the distance between the floor and ceiling, and away from any entrance door or direct air blast from cooling unit or evaporator coil.

Foodservice Installation Handling Practices

1. Frozen foods should not be accepted by a foodservice installation when product delivery temperature exceeds 0°F. Installation managers or their designees should approve rejection.

2. All frozen foods received at a foodservice installation should be placed promptly in storage facilities having the characteristics described above. Products should be removed from storage in quantities only sufficient for immediate use.

3. Foodservice installations should rotate frozen food inventories on a "first-in, first-out" basis.

Product Temperature

1. Product temperature is that steady temperature that may be determined two ways. The first is by opening the top of the case, removing 2 corner packages, punching a hole through the case wall proceeding from the inside at a point coincident with the center of the first stack of packages and the first and second layer of packages, inserting the sensing element of an accurate dial thermometer (or other appropriate means of temperature measurement) about 3 inches from the outside so that it will fit snugly between the packages, replacing the 2 corner packages, closing the case, and placing a couple of cases on top to insure good contact with the sensing element of the thermometer.

The second way calls for using a sharp blade and partially cutting out a small section of the case wall in the approximate area of the first stack of packages and the first and second layer of packages, slitting the cut section to allow for insertion of the sensing element, and then proceeding as in the first method above.

2. Only when an accurate determination of temperature is impossible without sacrifice of packages of frozen foods should representative packages or units be opened to allow for insertion of the temperature sensing element to the approximate center of the packages in question.

3. All temperature measuring equipment should be of high quality and subject to periodic checking for accuracy, employing methods recommended by the manufacturer.

It is recommended that frozen food handlers concerned with taking temperatures of frozen foods refer to Technical Service Bulletin No. 7, "Frozen Food Temperatures—Their Meaning and Measurement," by the American Frozen Food Institute.

This outlines in detail correct methods for taking product temperatures, describes appropriate equipment for the purpose, discusses certain consideration for proper care and handling of frozen food, and cites certain pertinent provisions of the AFDOUS Model Frozen Food Code.

This code is endorsed and subscribed to by: American Frozen Food Institute, Frozen Potato Products Institute, International Foodservice Manufacturers Association, National Association of Food Chains, National Fisheries Institute, National Association of Refrigerated Warehouses, National Food Brokers Association, National Frozen Food Association, National Institute of Locker & Freezer Provisioners, National Prepared Frozen Food Processors Association, and the National Restaurant Association.

MEAT BUYING KNOW-HOW*

Meat buying is a complicated matter. It takes much experience in all phases of meat production, from slaughter to stew, to know all that is desirable for the wise purchasing and usage of meats. The purpose of this section is to present the *basic* facts about meat so that buyers will know what is behind the terminology. It must be emphasized here that the rules set forth later in this section for the writing and the use of specifications must be *strictly* adhered to or else substantial money and/or quality loss will be suffered. The specifications that appear later in this section should be used *with* the pictures of the various meat cuts and with a ruler or meat-measuring device. Only after long experience can one be certain that a visual check, without the above mentioned aids, will be accurate. Few people have that ability. There is a large variety of ways in which meat can be cut; *caveat emptor* applies more to meat than to any other product used in the foodservice industry.

Inspections

There are many labels, stamps, and codes used in the meat industry. The ones most to be trusted are those of the United States Department of Agriculture. These federal certifications are standardized throughout the country. Some state and local governments maintain their own inspection programs. These programs vary widely from state to state and area to area and, consequently, generally cannot be relied upon to be of the quality of the USDA programs.

The military inspection programs are of the same quality as the USDA programs and are interchangeable so far as military meat purchasing is concerned. Religious inspections such as Kosher or Kasruth are certification that the meat has met certain religious codes regarding method of slaughter and butchering. These religious certifications carry no guarantee of quality.

Federal Inspection. Label (a) certifies that the meat has met certain criteria of wholesomeness. The stamp must appear on all meat and meat products that are offered

---

*See also Chapter 11.

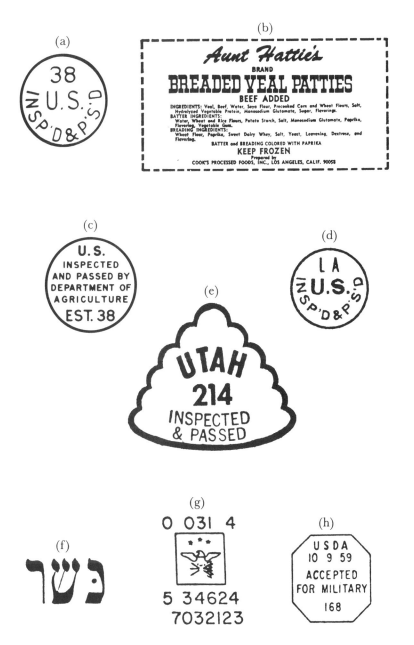

(a)

38
U.S.
INSP'D & P'S'D

(b)

Aunt Hattie's
BRAND
BREADED VEAL PATTIES
BEEF ADDED

INGREDIENTS: Veal, Beef, Water, Soya Flour, Precooked Corn and Wheat Flours, Salt, Hydrolyzed Vegetable Protein, Monosodium Glutamate, Sugar, Flavorings.
BATTER INGREDIENTS:
Water, Wheat and Rice Flours, Potato Starch, Salt, Monosodium Glutamate, Paprika, Flavoring, Vegetable Gum.
BREADING INGREDIENTS:
Wheat Flour, Paprika, Sweet Dairy Whey, Salt, Yeast, Leavening, Dextrose, and Flavoring.
BATTER and BREADING COLORED WITH PAPRIKA
KEEP FROZEN
Prepared by
COOK'S PROCESSED FOODS, INC., LOS ANGELES, CALIF. 90058

(c)

U.S.
INSPECTED
AND PASSED BY
DEPARTMENT OF
AGRICULTURE
EST. 38

(d)

LA
U.S.
INSP'D & P'S'D

(e)

UTAH
214
INSPECTED
& PASSED

(f)

כשר

(g)

O 031 4

5 34624
7032123

(h)

USDA
10 9 59
ACCEPTED
FOR MILITARY
168

in interstate commerce. This label on the carcass of the meat or on the label attached to a further processed meat or meat product has met the following standards:

- The carcass has been thoroughly examined for disease and any unwholesome part has been removed and destroyed.
- The meat has been handled and prepared in a sanitary fashion in a meat plant which meets rigid federal standards of sanitation.

- No known harmful substances have been added to the meat.
- The federal stamp has been affixed. The number in the circle identifies the plant where the meat was prepared.

A label (b) attached to further processed meats must meet certain federal criteria and must be approved before they can be used. The information on the label must include: the circular inspection stamp, the name and address of the plant, the net weight, and a list of ingredients in the order of their dominance.

If meat is packed in a container for shipping, then the container must be labeled. The Domestic Meat Label (c) must be affixed to the outside of the container.

Imported Meat.   Imported meats that meet USDA standards are stamped (d) at the port of entry.

Exemption from Inspection.   Although the cost of maintaining an on-premises USDA inspector is less than 75 cents per animal, there are some companies engaged in interstate commerce that are allowed an exemption from the requirement. These are the hotels or restaurants who raise their own meat. However, their plants must undergo periodic inspection, and their exemption is revocable.

Other Inspection Programs.   The state and local programs for inspection are varied in their standards. Some areas have no inspection. Before a buyer decides to purchase meat which has been inspected only by the state or local inspectors, it would be wise to make a personal comparison between those standards *and their enforcement* and the federal standards. The Utah State Inspection stamp and label are shown (e).

The Kosher stamp (f) is not a substitute for federal or state wholesomeness inspection. This is an additional label which indicates *religious* wholesomeness only.

The Military Inspection Program closely relates to the USDA Inspection Program. Meat is so inspected for the military service only. The military inspection stamps are shown (g) (h).

Grading

The U.S. Dept. of Agriculture maintains a voluntary meat grading service. These federal grades are applied to meat as a means of giving consumers a clear-cut guide as to the quality of the meat he buys. The grading standards are the same throughout the country. Since the grading standards are complicated, it is important that the meat buyer understand the meaning of the various grades and how they are determined. With this understanding, the buyer will be able to choose the grade of meat which is appropriate for the use intended.

Although a lot of the meat in the United States is graded by the Federal Grading Service, there are some meat packers who choose to apply their own grades instead of subscribing to federal grading.

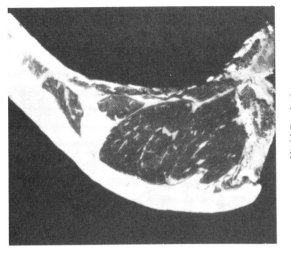

Yield Grade 3

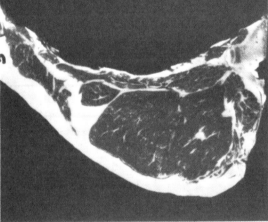

Yield Grade 2

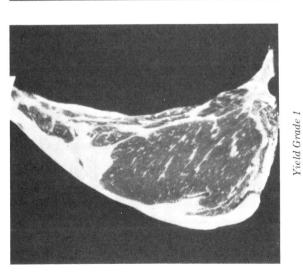

Yield Grade 1

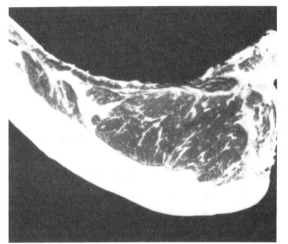

Yield Grade 5

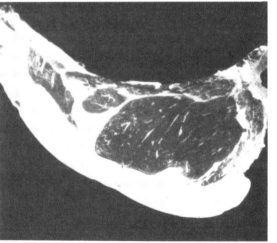

Yield Grade 4

Photos: NLS & MB.

The buyer should beware of such grading. The USDA grades are carefully worked out and consistent throughout the land. Private packer grading is capricious at best, and virtually fraudulent at worst. The professional meat buyer buys the measured, standardized, reliable federal grades and nothing else.

There are two types of federal grading. The first type, with which most people are familiar, is quality grading. Quality grading classifies meat according to a number of factors which contribute to how well the meat "eats" and "tastes."

The second type of grading is cutability grading or yield grading. The yield grade tells the buyer how much lean to expect from the cut carcass.

The quality grade is determined by an examination of the kind (class) of animal, the sex, the shape (conformation), the amount of exterior fat (finish), the amount of interior fat (marbling), and the firmness of the lean and the fat. The specifics vary depending upon the class of animal. These specifics of grading quality are explained later on in the section where specifications are given for each separate class.

Class

The classes (kinds) of meat and the grades for which they are eligible are listed next. The stamps shown appear in red on all the major cuts of meat. Since the stamp is rolled down the uncut carcass, there are some interior cuts of meat which cannot bear the stamp.

Beef
Steer, Heifer, Bullock
USDA GRADES—Prime, Choice, Good, Standard, Commercial, Utility, Cutter, Canner.
Cow
USDA GRADES—Choice, Good, Standard, Commercial, Utility, Cutter, Canner.
Bull, Stag
USDA GRADES—Choice, Good, Commercial, Utility, Cutter, Canner.
Veal and Calf
USDA GRADES—Prime, Choice, Good, Standard, Utility, Cull.

Ovine
Lamb, Yearling, Mutton
USDA GRADES—Prime, Choice, Good, Utility, Cull.
Mutton
USDA GRADES—Choice, Good, Utility, Cull.

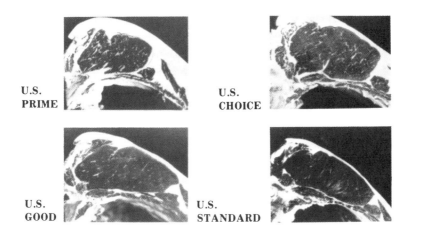

U.S.
PRIME

U.S.
CHOICE

U.S.
GOOD

U.S.
STANDARD

Pork (Hogs)

Barrows, Gilts
USDA GRADES—U.S. No. 1, U.S. No. 2, U.S. No. 3, U.S. No. 4, U.S. Utility.
Sows
USDA GRADES—U.S. No. 1, U.S. No. 2, U.S. No. 3, Medium, Cull.

The cuts of meat that have the greatest monetary value in the marketplace are from the back or hindquarter of the animal. The female animal usually has a heavier and, therefore, more valuable hindquarter than the male animal. When a male animal has its male hormones removed at an early age, the muscular development is then much like the female with the hindquarters being heavy.

Beef

Steer—a male animal that has had the male hormones removed at a very young age.

Heifer—a female animal that has never borne a calf.

Cow—a female animal that has borne one or more calves.

Bull—a male animal that has matured with male hormones intact.

Bullock—a young bull.

Stag—a male animal that is heavier and fatter than a bull. Male hormones removed after a certain stage of maturity is reached.

When buying beef, buyers will not know if they are buying steer, heifer, or cow except by examination of the pelvic area. The steer has rough fat in the cod area, a very small pelvic cavity, and a small "pizzle eye." The heifer has smooth cod fat and a larger pelvic cavity than the steer. A cow has a very large pelvic cavity and, usually being an old animal, the bones are hard and white as opposed to the softer, pink bones of a young animal.

Bulls and Stags are graded on a different set of standards than the Steer, Heifer, and Cow. A bull will have very heavy muscle development at the rounds, neck, shoulder, a large "pizzle eye," and coarse, dark meat.

The Stag will be less heavy and coarse than the bull, but not as light nor as finely fleshed as a steer.

Veal and Calf—a bovine of an age up to three months is classified as veal. Veal has a very light pink, actually almost gray colored, lean meat. The lean and fat are very soft, smooth, and flexible. The bones are very red, and the rib bones are very narrow.

A calf is a bovine that is older than three months. The calf has a pink to reddish-pink lean meat, which is soft and pliable to a degree not as great as veal, but is not nearly as firm as beef. The bones are pink and starting to harden. The rib bones are wider than on veal.

Ovine

Lamb is classified according to age. The very young, under weaning age, lamb is often called *Hothouse Lamb* or *Genuine Spring Lamb*. A lamb between two and five months of age may be called spring lamb or, sometimes, milk lamb or milk-fed lamb. Lamb has soft, porous bones, very light pink lean meat, and creamy white to pink fat which is soft and pliable. Perhaps the foremost indicator is the *break joint* of the foreleg. These joints break into four well-defined ridges which are smooth, soft, and blood-red.

Yearling Mutton has flesh which is light red to red; fat which is white and fairly firm; and graining in the flesh, which is fine, but it does not have as little grain as lamb. The break joint in yearling mutton has four ridges, as with lamb, but the edges are not smooth, and the bone is hard and white.

Mutton has medium red to dark red flesh, with a grain similar to calf or young steer. The fat is quite white and has a brittle consistency. The foreleg of mutton will not break as with lamb and yearling mutton. Instead, a hard, shiny, smooth knuckle with two prominent ridges forms. Whereas sex has a bearing upon the classification of lamb and yearling mutton, mutton is classified according to sex.

Mutton

Ewe—a female animal.
Wether—a male animal that has had its male hormones removed at a young age.
Buck—a mature male that has not been sexually altered.

Pork (Hogs)

Barrow—a male animal that has had the male hormones removed when very young.
Gilt—a female animal that has never borne pigs.
Sow—a female animal that has borne pigs.
Boar—a male animal that has matured with male hormones intact.
Stag—a male animal that has had its male hormones removed after reaching maturity.

ILLUSTRATIONS OF THE LOWER LIMITS OF CERTAIN DEGREES OF TYPICAL MARBLING REFERRED TO IN THE OFFICIAL UNITED STATES STANDARDS FOR GRADES OF CARCASS BEEF

Illustrations adapted from negatives furnished by New York State College of Agriculture, Cornell University

1—Very abundant	4—Slightly abundant	7—Small
2—Abundant	5—Moderate	8—Slight
3—Moderately abundant	6—Modest	9—Traces

(Practically devoid not shown)

UNITED STATES DEPARTMENT OF AGRICULTURE
CONSUMER AND MARKETING SERVICE
LIVESTOCK DIVISION

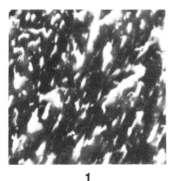

1

2

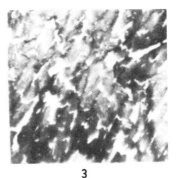

3

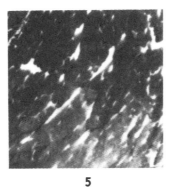

4

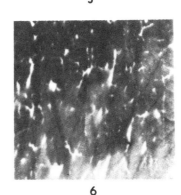

5

6

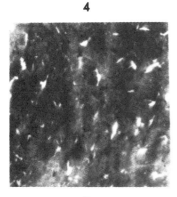

7

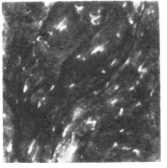

8

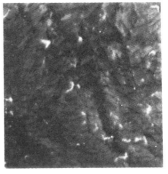

9

USDA.

It is very easy to remember hog classifications by equating the animals with their rough equivalent in bovines:

Barrow—Steer

Gilt—Heifer

Sow—Cow

Boar—Bull

Stag—Stag

Hogs are essentially graded in three categories. The grades U.S. No. 1, U.S. No. 2, and U.S. No. 3 are the Choice grades. The differences between these grades have to do with the ratio of lean to fat and the yield of the loin, the ham, the picnic, and the Boston Butt. The U.S. No. 4 (barrows, gilts) and U.S. Medium (sow) are the next level down in the grading and the bottom of the consumer grades. U.S. Utility (barrow, gilt) and U.S. Cull are not marketed for retail consumption.

FISH AND SHELLFISH*

Vertebrate, or fin fish. These are characterized by backbone and fins, and are of two types: lean and fat. Fat fish, such as mackerel, salmon, and swordfish, are broiled or baked. Lean types, such as cod, flounder, and haddock, are best for frying.

Shellfish. These fish items have bodies partially or completely covered with a shell. Shellfish are further divided into two classes:

1. Crustaceans: These shellfish have hard shells over the back portions of the body and over the claws, and softer shells for protection of the underparts of the body and legs. Shrimp and lobster are examples.
2. Mollusks: Shellfish in this class have two shells of the same size and shape, usually hard, which are ordinarily held tightly closed. Clams, oysters, and scallops are examples.

Market Forms

Round (Whole)—As it comes from the water.

Drawn—Eviscerated.

Dressed—Eviscerated, head, tail, and fins off.

Fillets—One-half the fish (backbone to belly) removed from the head, tail, fins, and skin.

Sticks—Blocks of fish meat of uniform size.

Steaks—A cross-section of one fish cut from a dressed fish with the skin off.

---

*See also Chapter 9.

Fresh Fish

Evidence of quality: Bright, shiny skin; no loose scales; bright, bulging, clean eyes; red inside the gills; firm flesh that bounces back when pressed; no strong odors; no slime.

Because fish deteriorates so very quickly, it is advisable to buy fresh fish, but only if it is to be used within 48 hours. There are approximately 200 varieties of fish marketed in the United States. All of the most popular varieties of fish are available frozen.

Frozen Fish

Evidence of quality: Shiny skin with no discoloration, red inside the gills; no strong odors; a surface glaze of ice (6 percent minimum) is permitted. Chapter 9 details the grading standards on the 14 frozen fish which are graded by the U.S. Fish and Wildlife of the Department of the Interior.

Shellfish, Fresh

Evidence of quality: Clear color and clean odor of flesh, clear liquids; no slime or slipperyness of surface; shells of crustaceans turn red when cooked; strong muscle tension.

FISH AND SHELLFISH: FACTORS RELATING TO SPECIFIED WEIGHTS OF FISH AND SHELLFISH[1]

Specification	Factors for converting to			
	Round weight[2]	Reported weight[3]	Dressed weight[4]	Edible weight[5]
Fish, fresh and frozen:				
Not packaged, domestically produced:				
Round weight	1.000	1.000	0.700	0.450
Dressed weight	1.429	—	1.000	0.643
Edible weight	2.222	—	1.556	1.000
Packaged, domestically produced:				
Round weight	1.000	0.338	—	0.338
Packaged weight	2.959	1.000	—	1.000
Imports, reported weight	1.948	1.000	1.364	0.877
Shellfish, fresh and frozen:				
Not packaged:				
(shrimp, oysters, crab, lobster, etc.)				
Reported weight	—	1.000	—	0.450
Edible weight	—	2.222	—	1.000
Packaged: (including fresh shucked oysters, clams, shrimp, etc.)	—	1.000	—	1.000
Fish, cured, all types:				
(includes smoked, pickled, salted and dried fish):				
Reported weight (i.e., cured weight)	1.500	1.000	—	0.750
Edible weight	2.000	1.333	—	1.000

1. Factors are for specified groups and are not applicable to individual species.
2. Weight of the fish as removed from the water.
3. Production as reported to the Fish and Wildlife Service; imports as reported by the Bureau of the Census.
4. Weight of fin fish after removal of entrails, head, tail, and fins.
5. Weight of the edible portion of the fish or shellfish.

SHELLFISH: NET WEIGHT PER GALLON OF SPECIFIED SHELLFISH

Product	Pounds per gallon
Clams	8.75
Oysters	8.75
Scallops	8.75

When purchasing shellfish, the buyer should be sure that the product is alive. The only exception to this is in the purchase of shrimp, which should be iced. Live shellfish will react to being touched or prodded.

Canned Fish

Evidence of quality: Evenly colored flesh with no blood or blood spots, bruises, scales; clear liquid with no off odors; firm flesh.

CANNED FISH: NET WEIGHT PER STANDARD CASE OF SPECIFIED CANNED FISH AND SHELLFISH

Product	Pounds per case
Alewives	45
Anchovies	31.25
Mackerel	45
Salmon	48
Sardines:	
Maine	23.4
Pacific	45
Shad	45
Tuna and tuna-like fish:	
Solid	21
Chunks	19.5
Flakes and grated	18
Crab meat, natural	19.5
Shrimp, wet pack[1]	15
Clam products:	
Whole and minced[1]	15
Juices, chowders, broth, etc.	30
Oysters, natural[1]	14
All other	48

1. "Cut out" or "drained" weights of can contents are given for shrimp, whole or minced clams, and oysters. Net can contents are given for other products.

EGGS*

All eggs and egg products processed for human consumption must be inspected for wholesomeness; all eggs which are inedible (leakers, checks, or dirties) cannot be used for human consumption, even as processed eggs.

The Egg Products Inspection Act (1970) provides not only for wholesomeness inspection, but also for standards, grades, and weight classes.

Egg grading considers the following factors:

1. *Shell.* Cleanliness, shape, texture, and total lack of cracks. An uncracked shell egg will give a tuning fork or bell tone when tapped against another shell egg; the shell exterior must be clean and have a normal egg shape with a smooth, fine texture. Brown-shelled eggs are no different than white-shelled eggs. Eggs with an irregular shape are lowered in grade.

2. *Air Cell.* When held to a light (or "candled"), a pocket of air called an air cell will be seen in an egg. The depth of the air cell, as well as the consistency of that air cell, is a determinant of quality. A small air cell of less that ⅛ in. will be found in the highest quality eggs; an air cell of more than ⅜ in., with a bubbly consistency, will be found in the eggs which fail to meet the lowest grade.

3. *White.* A fresh, high quality egg has a thick, white area which is milky in color. Eggs which are not properly refrigerated lose quality rapidly. As the egg gets older, the white becomes thinner in consistency and clearer in color.

4. *Yolk.* The yolk of a high quality egg is located in the middle of the egg, and is surrounded by a thin, barely visible membrane. As quality decreases, the yolk becomes flat due to the weakened membrane. No blood or meat spots are allowable.

There are two types of egg grades. Consumer Grades and Procurement Grades, fully explained in Chapter 8.

Processed Eggs

Frozen eggs must be pasteurized, just like milk, to prevent bacterial growth. The market forms are as follows:

Whole Eggs. This is the entire egg, without the shell, cracked, pasteurized, and packaged in 4-lb., 5-lb., 10-lb., or 30-lb. containers. Those with the best "eating" quality will have no additives or stabilizers. When comparing the price of shell eggs to whole frozen eggs, remember that 11 percent to 12 percent of the weight of shell eggs is in the shell. Pricing reciprocal: 1.12.

Egg Whites. This is the entire egg without shell and yolk. The white represents 58 percent of the whole egg. Pricing reciprocal: 1.72.

---

*See also Chapter 10.

Interior Quality of Eggs
'Recommended standards for scoring the quality of broken-out eggs)

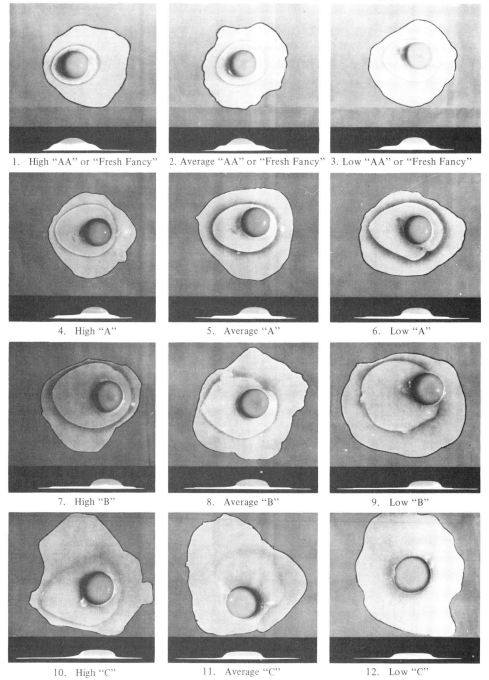

1. High "AA" or "Fresh Fancy"   2. Average "AA" or "Fresh Fancy"   3. Low "AA" or "Fresh Fancy"

4. High "A"   5. Average "A"   6. Low "A"

7. High "B"   8. Average "B"   9. Low "B"

10. High "C"   11. Average "C"   12. Low "C"

The pictures on this chart show the interior quality of eggs that meet the specifications of the U.S. Standards for Quality of Individual Shell Eggs with respect to albumen and yolk quality. Quality factors dealing with the shell, air cell, and defects are not included. Scores 1, 2, and 3 represent the appearance of broken-out eggs of high, average, and low AA Quality or Fresh Fancy Quality; 4, 5, and 6 represent high, average, and low A Quality; 7, 8, and 9, high, average, and low B Quality, and 10, 11 and 12 high, average, and low C Quality. (*Source:* USDA.)

Egg Yolk.   The whole egg without shell and white. The yolk represents 31 percent of the whole egg. Pricing reciprocal: 3.23.

Egg Yolk, Sugared.   Egg yolk, as above, with about 11 percent sugar added, and as much as 5 percent glycerine added to prevent hardening of the yolks.

The frozen eggs are excellent for use in baking and in making souffles, scrambled eggs, and omelets because no labor need be expended in shelling eggs or in separating yolks and whites.

Frozen Egg Roll

The Ralston-Purina Company markets a frozen, processed roll of egg which gives the same number of center-cut slices as seventeen hard-cooked eggs. Many operators have found this most practical for such uses as sliced egg salads and Eggs a la Russe. The "Gourm Egg" has food starch and stabilizers added, but this does not markedly affect the taste.

Hard-Cooked Refrigerated Eggs

In some areas of the country, hard-cooked eggs can be purchased already shelled, with a refrigerated shelf-life of up to three weeks.

The buyer should make sure that all frozen eggs have been federally inspected, and should try to buy frozen eggs that are guaranteed to be salmonella-free.

Dried Eggs

Eggs are dried either by a roller process or a spray process. They are also treated with enzymes to remove glucose. There is a high bacteria count in dried eggs, thus the buyer should attempt to buy dried eggs that are guaranteed salmonella-free, and the operator should refrigerate such products.

There are many dried egg-based egg-nog and custard bases on the market which are of high quality. There are no federal quality standards in this area so the buyer must test them for preference.

MILK

The responsibility for quality milk in a community is shared by the dairy industry, the medical profession, public health officials, and the consumers in that community, together with the public health officials of the federal government.

Protecting the Quality of Milk through Cooperative Action

Grade A Pasteurized Milk Ordinance.   Every state, and most municipalities, operate a rigid milk regulation program. The Grade A Pasteurized Milk Ordinance recommended by the U.S. Public Health Service, first published in 1924 and revised periodically, sets forth in detail a type of regulation that is desirable. This Ordinance is formulated as a guide for state and local communities, and represents recommendations of federal and state Departments of Agriculture; national, state, and local health authorities; and officials of the dairy industry. The milk supplies of much of the United States are covered by the Ordinance.

Industry and Government Cooperate.   Legal responsibility for health protection of milk supplies for the market is exercised, for the most part, by state and local governments. The dairy industry works cooperatively with both state and municipalities to maintain the standards for the milk supply. The industry is continuously interested in technological advances in procedures, equipment, and research to make sure any technological change produces quality milk.

Pasteurization and Sanitation.   Proper pasteurization is the only practical commercial measure today that destroys all disease organisms in fluid milk. Examination of cows and milk handlers can be done only at intervals. Disease organisms may enter milk accidentally from sources such as flies, contaminated water, and utensils. Pasteurization is by no means a substitute for sanitary dairy practices, but rather it is an additional safeguard for the consumer's health.

Unintentional Additives.   The dairy industry and public health officials have met a succession of technological problems, and today they are faced with the problem of unintentional additives to fluid milk. The chance that radioactive materials, insecticides, antibiotics, or carcinogens may appear in milk is occasion for much study and research. The Food and Drug Administration has set zero tolerance levels for a number of these substances. Both industry and government are dedicated to protecting the consumer from possible adulterants in the nation's milk supply.

Radioactive Fallout.   Radioactivity from natural sources constitutes a part of man's normal environment. Nuclear explosions increase these radiation levels. Radioactive elements reach humans directly through water and atmosphere, and indirectly through soil, plants, and animals. The radioisotopes of three elements in particular, strontium, cesium, and iodine, have been the subject of study. Study has been made through surveys and experimental procedures for the purpose of measuring current levels and of predicting equilibrium results.

Milk has probably been the most important single item for analysis because milk is convenient to handle and is produced on a year-round basis. The important parameter, however, is the level of contamination of the total human diet rather than concentration in any one food of any one kind.

Federal, state, and local health officials monitor the American food supply for possible contamination from radioactivity. Responsible experts in the fields of medicine, nutrition, and radiation health concur that countermeasures against fallout are not presently needed. In the meantime, the successful completion of the research now in progress should provide suitable countermeasures should these become necessary.

Pesticides. Pesticides are needed to achieve maximum production of acceptable foodstuffs. Even the best farming practices cannot control pests without some of the pesticide remaining on the plant at harvest. For this reason, the USDA and the Food and Drug Administration have established toxicity tests that are as rigorous and thorough as current knowledge allows. The dairy farmer, who must have pest control, complies with the official policy of no pesticides in milk. As long as present regulations prevail, pesticides do not appear to present a public health problem. However, the problem is under constant study and review. Industry and government continue to cooperate to protect the public health.

Supervision of Milk Supply

Principles that govern a quality milk supply can be briefed as follows:

1. Inspection and sanitary control of farms and milk plants.
2. Examination and testing of herds for the elimination of bovine diseases related to public health.
3. Regular instruction on desirable sanitary practices for persons engaged in production, processing, and distribution of milk.
4. Proper pasteurization of milk.
5. Laboratory examination of milk.
6. Monitoring of milk supplies by federal, state, and local health officials to protect against unintentional additives.

Grades of Milk

Grade A designates quality fluid milk and is the grade purchased in retail stores and delivered to consumers. Milk used for manufacturing milk products—butter, cheese, and ice cream—is designated by the term Manufacturing Grade.

These grades are based on the conditions under which the milk is produced and handled, and on the bacterial count of the final product. The grades and their meanings vary only slightly, according to local regulations. Where the U.S. Public Health Service Grade A Pasteurized Milk Ordinance has been adopted, uniform standards are prescribed.

In different parts of the world, the milk of various species of animals is used for food. In the United States, however, the cow furnishes virtually all of the available market milk. Therefore, unless otherwise specified, the term ''milk'' as used in the book refers to cows' milk.

The Attributes of Quality Milk

This centuries-old food is among the most perishable of all foods. Milk, as it comes from the cow, provides an excellent medium for bacterial growth and is subject to many possible flavor changes unless it is protected constantly from contamination each step of the way from the cow to the consumer. Milk is relied upon as an important source of many of the nutrients known to be necessary for proper development and maintenance of the human body. Maximum retention of these nutrients must be assured as milk is stored, processed, transported, and distributed in its many different forms.

Milk should be stored promptly in the refrigerator or consumed quickly. After a milk container is opened, it should be covered before storage. Milk removed from the original container should not be returned to it.

Quality milk has been described as milk that has low bacterial count, good flavor and appearance, satisfactory keeping quality, and high nutritive value. It is free from disease-producing bacteria, toxic substances, and foreign material.

Progress in dairy technology and public health results in milk that can be depended upon as a safe, nutritious, pleasing food, even though it may be produced hundreds or thousands of miles away. Vigilance is exercised continuously in maintaining this quality as new challenges arise in the environment. Pasteurization is a basic safeguard in the processing of all milk.

CHEESE

There are two kinds of cheese. One is commonly called natural cheese. This is cheese that is made from the milk of one of several kinds of animals. The other kind of cheese is process cheese; it is made by combining or blending two or more natural cheeses.

Cheese is made by the modification of milk in the following steps:

1. Curdling. This is usually done by heating the milk to anywhere from 80°F to 135°F (depending on the type of cheese to be made); adding rennet, and waiting for the cheese to curdle into curds and whey. Farm cheese is sometimes made by waiting for the lactic acid in the milk to curdle the milk, instead of adding rennet.
2. Removal of Whey. The curdled mass is broken into small pieces, and drained off.
3. Curing. Hard cheeses are kept in a cool environment for as long as three years. Salt, certain bacteria, and molds may be added to the cheese to help it develop its characteristic flavor.

There are federal standards for many cheeses produced in America. Where these standards exist, the specification is listed in Chapter 8. The cheeses of other countries differ according to the producer, as many different types of milks and curing processes are used. The listings of cheeses presented in Chapter 8 attempt to cover only the most common varieties. There are at least 600 different varieties on the market in the United States; obviously, space does not allow the classification of all of them.

BUTTER

''Butter'' means the food product usually known as butter, which is made exclusively from milk or cream, or both, with or without common salt, and with or without additional coloring matter, and containing not less than 80 percent by weight of milkfat, all tolerances having been allowed for.

The U.S. grade of butter is determined on the basis of classifying first the flavor characteristics, and then the characteristics in body, color, and salt. Flavor is the basic quality factor in grading butter, and is determined organoleptically by taste and smell. The flavor characteristic is identified and, together with its relative intensity, is rated according to the applicable classification. When more than one flavor characteristic is discernible in a sample of butter, the flavor classification of the sample shall be established on the basis of the flavor that carries the lowest rating. Body, color, and salt characteristics are then noted, and any defects are disrated in accordance with the established classification, subject to disratings for body, color, and salt; when the disratings for body, color, and salt exceed the permitted amount for any flavor classification, the final U.S. grade shall be lowered accordingly.

The specifications for the U.S. grades of butter are as listed in Chapter 8.

Cream

The term "cream" means cream separated from milk produced by healthy cows. The cream shall be pasteurized at a temperature not less than 165°F, and held continuously in a vat at such temperature for not less than 30 minutes; or pasteurized at a temperature of not less than 185°F, for not less than 15 seconds; or it shall be pasteurized by other approved methods giving equivalent results.

POULTRY

Standards and Grades

The difference between standards of quality and the grades assigned to poultry is sometimes misunderstood. The standards of quality cover the various factors that determine the grade. These factors, such as fat covering, fleshing, exposed flesh, discolorations, etc., when evaluated collectively, determine the grade of the bird.

The U.S. Consumer Grades for Poultry are used at the retail level. The U.S. Consumer Grades are: U.S. Grade A, U.S. Grade B, and U.S. Grade C.

The U.S. Procurement Grades are designed primarily for institutional use. These grades are: U.S. Procurement Grade 1 and U.S. Procurement Grade 2. The Procurement Grades place more emphasis on meat yield than on appearance.

Official Identification by Graders Licensed by the U.S. Dept. of Agriculture

Anyone having a financial interest in a lot of processed poultry may make application to the U.S. Dept. of Agriculture to have an official grade designation placed on the lot. This service, which is available throughout the country, is operated on a self-supporting basis. A nominal fee is charged which covers the time and travel expense of the grader, plus the cost of administering the program. The U.S. Dept of Agriculture enters into cooperative agreements with state departments of agriculture, making it possible to license qualified state employees to grade and certify the quality of poultry.

Many processors utilize full-time resident graders in their plants. This enables the plant to apply the U.S. grade mark to each individual package or each individual bird.

The military, federal, state, county, and city institutions, as well as other large-scale buyers such as steamship lines, independent and chain stores, and private hospitals, make use of the grading service by specifying U.S. grades in their contracts for poultry products.

Commercial firms often use the U.S. Standards and Grades as a basis for establishing specifications for their own product.

Classes

Some states provide a voluntary grading and inspection program. Such programs generally follow the U.S. Standards and Grades in whole or in part. Producers, as well as processors, may use the standards of quality as a basis for sorting or selecting birds for market.

"Kind" refers to the different species of poultry, such as chickens, turkeys, ducks, geese, guineas, and pigeons. The kinds of poultry are divided into "classes" by groups that are essentially of the same physical characteristics such as fryers or hens. These physical characteristics are associated with age and sex.

The kinds and classes of live, dressed, and ready-to-cook poultry listed in the U.S. Classes, Standards, and Grades are in general use in all segments of the poultry industry.

Included is a summary chart of specifications for standards of quality, applicable to live poultry, dressed poultry, and individual carcasses of ready-to-cook poultry, in determining the kind of poultry and its class.

QUESTIONS

1. Define the following terms:

quotations	condition
MBG specs	commodity
IMPS	scald
processed fruits	netting
Hydro-cooling	ground color
specifications	drained weight
grades	

2. How is quality measured?
3. What are the best temperatures to taste a particular flavor? How does the time of day affect taste acuity?

SUMMARY OF SPECIFICATIONS FOR STANDARDS OF QUALITY FOR INDIVIDUAL CARCASSES OF READY-TO-COOK POULTRY AND PARTS THEREFROM (MINIMUM REQUIREMENTS AND MAXIMUM DEFECTS PERMITTED), SEPTEMBER 1, 1965

FACTOR	A QUALITY			B QUALITY			C QUALITY
CONFORMATION: Breastbone Back Legs and Wings	Normal Slight curve or dent Normal (except slight curve) Normal			Moderate deformities Moderately dented, curved Moderately crooked Moderately misshapen			Abnormal Seriously curved or crooked Seriously crooked Misshapen
FLESHING:	Well-fleshed, moderately long, deep and rounded breast			Moderately fleshed, considering kind, class and part			Poorly fleshed
FAT COVERING:	Well-covered — especially between heavy feather tracts on breast, and considering kind, class, and part.			Sufficient fat on breast and legs to prevent distinct appearance of flesh through the skin.			Lacking in fat covering over all parts of carcass
PINFEATHERS: Nonprotruding pins and hair Protruding pins	Free Free			Few scattered Free			Scattering Free

EXPOSED FLESH:[1]								
Carcass Weight:		Breast and legs	Elsewhere	Part	Breast and legs	Else-where[2]	Part	
Minimum	Maximum							
None	1-1/2 lb.	None	3/4 in.	(slight	3/4 in.	1-1/2 in.	(moderate amount of the flesh normally covered)	No Limit
Over 1-1/2 lb.	6 lb.	None	1-1/2 in.	trim on	1-1/2 in.	3 in.		
Over 6 lb.	16 lb.	None	2 in.	edge)	2 in.	4 in.		
Over 16 lb.	None	None	3 in.		3 in.	5 in.		

1. Total aggregate area of flesh exposed by all cuts and tears and missing skin.
2. A carcass meeting the requirements of A Quality for fleshing may be trimmed to remove skin and flesh defects, provided that no more than one-third of the flesh is exposed on any part, and the meat yield is not appreciably affected.

4. Describe the use of the Abbe Refractometer. What products would be measured? Describe the use of the Brix Hydrometer. For what products would it be used? What does a high Brix point indicate?

5. For which food products must the buyer require federal grading?

6. Describe how poor handling, cooling techniques, or faulty equipment affect food quality.

7. What is the effect of pre-cooling of fruits and vegetables on quality?

8. Considering the perishability of products, packing, the long distance from field to market, how can the buyer be assured of high quality products?

9. Give example of how a specification may be given for the following items. Indicate best use.

beef	celery
apples	lemons
grapefruits	canned peaches
potatoes	canned tomatoes

10. What is the difference between U.S. Fancy Apples and U.S. No. 2.?
11. Size is indicated in a specification by its _____.
12. What factors will a buyer inspect when inspecting fresh fruit he or she has ordered?
13. The rule "first in, first out" applies to what product groups? Why?
14. How important is price when purchasing?
15. Proper storage of vegetables requires what temperature and what humidity?
16. List the minimum quality levels for canned tomatoes.
17. What are the FDCA requirements for labels?
18. What is the importance of yield grading of beef?
19. What are acceptable quality standards when purchasing a split carcass?
20. How will Grades A, B, C, of peas differ?
21. Can you distinguish between the following size cans? Rank order the largest to smallest.
    #303
    #2
    #2½
    #3
    #10
22. How is headspace determined? What does it indicate?
23. Prepare a bid sheet for commonly used beef items.
24. How does the air cell in an egg determine degree of quality?

EXHIBITS

Purpose of a Specification
1. To help insure the product desired is the product delivered. Make sure the product in the specification is the product the company bids on. Check the product specified against the one that is delivered to be sure they are the same.

Specification
The specification is a description of the product desired. This is developed from information on the style and variety of each kind of item. It is important that the specification be thoroughly understood by the person receiving the delivery of the item.

Fresh Commodity	Unit	Approx. Net Wt. #s	Common Count/Unit
Apples	Box	48	88–138
	Bushel	45–50	100
Apricots	Lug	18 & 22	6–10
	Crate	24	6–10
Asparagus	Crate	12 & 30	—
	Bunch	2.5–3	12–20 med.
Avocado	Box	—	3/lb.
Bananas	Box	40	—
Beans, Snap	Hamper	28–30	—
	Bushel		
Cabbage	Sack	50 & 75	15 med.
	Crate		
Cantaloupe	Crate	70	23–45
Carrots, Cello	Crate	48	1 lb. pkg.
Cauliflower, Cello	Crate	20	12–14 heads
Celery	Crate	45	24, 30, 36 stalks
Cherries, Bing	Lug	12 & 15	—
Corn, Whole	Crate	35–40	5 dz.
	Sack		
Cranberries	Bag	24	24–1 lb. cello/cs.
Cucumbers	Bushel	48–50	10–12
Grapefruit	Carton	36	18–48
Grapes	Lug	28	—
Lemons	Carton	40	95–235
Limes	Carton	10	80–84
Lettuce, Head	Carton	40–50	24–30
Melon, Honeydew	Crate	6–12	—
Melon, Watermelon	Crate	25–50	—
Onions, Dry	Sack	50	5/1# med.
Oranges, Calif.	Carton	40	48–180
Parsley	Bushel	15–20	5 dz. Bunches
Peaches	Bushel	50	80–88
	Lug	18–24	55 med.
Pears	Box	50	80–180
	Bushel	30–35	—
Peas	Bushel	25–28	110 med.
Peppers, Green	Bushel	18–20	9–15
Pineapple	Crate	50	—
Potatoes, Irish	Sack	100	—
Potatoes, Sweet	Hamper	50	—
Squash, Summer	Hamper	25	—
Squash, Winter	Crate	70–80	—
Strawberries	Flat	10	12 pt. boxes
	Crate	—	16 qt. or 24 pt.
Tangerines	Crate	45	150, 176
Tomatoes	Lug	28	5 × 6, 6 × 6
Turnips	Sack or Bushel	50	—

Definition of Terms

Flavor—Because there is such a great variation in the individual's likes and dislikes, it is exceedingly difficult to score so elusive a factor as *flavor.* In most of the U.S. Standards for Grades of Foods, the term *normal flavor* is used. In commercial grading, however, *flavor* is the prime factor. If what we eat tastes good, we somehow overlook minor deficiencies.

General Appearance—Our judgment places the factor of "eating with our eyes" even before we taste of what we see. If a food does not look good, the prejudice may very well affect one's opinion of *flavor.* For this reason, some food experts rate *general appearance* every bit as important as *flavor..*

The relative importance of all other factors depends entirely upon the product being judged. While no attempt will be made here to score *quality* or *standard* factors for the available grades, the important factors by which to judge the quality of some of the more popular, everyday products are emphasized here to help food buyers make certain that deliveries conform to purchase specifications.

Color—The factor of *color* is the chief subdivision of *general appearance*, and to receive proper rating *color* should be typical of the product. Many food experts score *color* on a par with *flavor* for some items.

Type—By *type* is meant distinctive classifications of a specific product. For example, Culturally Bleached Asparagus is one distinct type, and all Green Asparagus is a separate distinct type.

Style—When we refer to *style* we think of prevalent approved ideas of form adaptable to popular food items that canners and processors make available to buyers. A good example is: Peaches—sliced or halves.

Count—Actual number of pieces found upon opening and examination of container contents.

Uniformity of Size—The degree of consistency relative to freedom from variation or difference. Sameness or alikeness.

Symmetry—The degree of consistently harmonious proportions of units in container.

Absence of Defects—By *absence of defects* we refer to the degree of freedom from grit, from harmless foreign or other extraneous material, and damage from poor or careless handling, or from mechanical, pathological, insect, or other similar injury.

General Character—Under the factor *general character,* consideration is given to degree of ripeness or maturity, the texture and condition of flesh, the firmness and tenderness of the product, its tendency to retain its apparent original conformation and size without material disintegration, the wholeness or cut, consistency or finish, and clearness of liquor or syrup.

Maturity—This factor refers to the degree of development or ripeness of the product.

Texture—By *texture* we refer to structural composition or character of the product tissues.

(cont.)

Firmness—The degree of soundness of product structure.

Tenderness—The degree of freedom from tough or hard fibers.

Wholeness—The state of completeness or entirety.

Cut—This refers to the character of cut; that is, the effect of the cut on the appearance of the product.

Consistency—In some products, such as fruit butters, this factor refers to viscosity, that is, stickiness or gumminess. In other products, such as tomato catsup and tomato puree, the term is applied to density or specific gravity.

Finish—This factor especially refers to the size and texture of particles; the smoothness, evenness and uniformity of grain.

Clearness of Liquor—This factor requires no elaboration. The degree of sediment and cloudiness materially affects score for quality.

Clearness of Syrup—Any degree of sediment or cloudiness materially affects grading score.

Syrup Density—The degree or percentage, by weight, of sugar going into the solution as measured by either the Brix or Balling scale on hydrometers or saccharometers.

Drained Weight—The weight of the product after draining of liquor or syrup according to method prescribed by the National Canners Association or the USDA.

3

STORAGE AND HANDLING

INTRODUCTION

Changes in the quality of a food in storage is a result of the cumulation of environmental conditions during processing, warehousing, distribution, and retail outlet stages. There are a number of ways operators can maximize their food dollar through effective purchasing, storage, and handling.

Food processors pay great attention to optimizing the shelf life of their products since deterioration results in losses of color, flavor, texture, nutrients, and general appearances. Special ingredients such as antioxidants, stabilizers, and preservatives are added to retard the chemical and physical changes in food during storage.

It has been found that the single most important factor in maintaining quality of perishable food items during distribution and storage is consistent low temperatures. Temperatures of foods upon delivery, in cold or dry storage, are all discussed in this chapter.

Properly trained receiving personnel can perform a valuable function in identifying acceptable quality and quality determinants for the operation. Careful controls can ensure that invoice prices match quotations, counts, grades, proper weights, and other specifications.

Examples are given on cold storage units as well as dry storage. Operators need to carefully plan the equipment which best suits their needs. In addition, systematic storage procedures will maximize quality and economical practice.

The flow of materials through a foodservice operation begins in the receiving and storage areas. Careful consideration should be given to receiving and storage procedures as well as to the construction and physical needs of both areas. In planning, there should be a straight line from receiving dock to the storeroom and/or refrigerators and preferably on the same level as the kitchen. A short distance between receiving and storage will reduce handling labor, lessen pilferage hazards, and cause the least amount of deterioration in food products.

SHELF LIFE[1]

The quality of food products is a fragile thing because of their very nature. They are susceptible to spoilage, loss of nutrients, insect infestation, changes in color, flavor, or odor, and even package corrosion and leakage. Food technologists use the term *shelf life* when they speak of the period between the manufacture and the retail purchase of a food product. During this finite shelf life, the product is in a state of satisfactory quality in terms of nutritional value, taste, texture, and appearance.

The shelf lives of food products vary, but they are generally determined routinely for each particular product by its manufacturer or processor. This information is an essential factor in determining the kinds of conditions and methods used in distribution of the product.

Storage studies are part of each product development program, whether it includes a new product, a product improvement, or simply a change in type or specification of an ingredient. The manufacturer attempts to provide the longest shelf life practical, consistent with costs and the pattern of handling and use by distributors, retailers, and consumers.

For example, a manufacturer may package cake mixes, dessert mixes, and sauce mixes in heat-sealed plastic pouches to protect them against oxygen and moisture absorption. Prescribed procedures will be followed for pasteurization of perishable foods and avoidance of bacterial contamination. The manufacturer will also use special ingredients—such as preservatives, antioxidants, emulsifiers, stabilizers, and chelating agents—to retard chemical and physical changes in foods during storage.

Obviously, inadequate shelf life will lead to consumer dissatisfaction or complaints. At best, such dissatisfaction will eventually affect the acceptance and sales of brand name products. At worst, it can lead to malnutrition or even illness. For these reasons, food processors pay great attention to adequate storage stability or shelf life.

Major areas involved in a food's shelf life include:

- Loss of nutrient value, such as vitamin loss and protein breakdown
- Spoilage by microorganisms, enzymatic action, or insect infestation
- Loss of aesthetic qualities, such as color, flavor, aroma, texture, or general appearance
- Loss of functional properties, such as leavening activity in baking powder, thickening power in sauce mixes, or the ''set'' in instant puddings

Foods can be divided into two main categories: shelf-stable and perishable (including semi-perishable). Shelf-stable foods are considered ''nonperishable'' at room temperatures. Many unprocessed foods fall into this category, and are unaffected by microorganisms because of their low water content; included are such foods as cereal

---

[1]The author thanks *Food Technology* magazine for permission to use material from ''Shelf Life of Food,'' August 1974.

grains or nuts. Processed food products can be shelf-stable if they are preserved by heat sterilization (e.g., canning), formulated as dry mixes (e.g., cake mixes), or processed to reduce their water content (e.g., raisins or crackers).

Perishable foods are those that must be held under refrigerated or freezing conditions if they are to be kept for more than short periods. Cold temperatures inhibit the growth of spoilage bacteria, yeasts, and molds, and slow the action of enzymes. "Semi-perishable" is a term applied to foods that contain natural inhibitors (as in some cheeses, root vegetables, and eggs), or those that have received some type of mild preservation treatment which produces greater tolerance to environmental conditions and abuse during distribution and handling, such as pasteurization in milk, smoking in hams, or pickling.

Bacteria, molds, yeasts, and enzymatic breakdown are the main causes of deterioration of perishable foods. Usually, bacterial deterioration occurs well before chemical or physical changes can be noticed. Bacteria grow under a wide range of environmental conditions and are responsible for a variety of changes in food products. Some bacteria, for example, produce acid, while others produce off-flavors or cause a product to separate into two phases, as in sour milk. All these actions adversely affect the acceptability of the food. Everyone has seen mold growth on bread or preserves, an obvious visible sign of deterioration. Yeast growth also is noticeable in the fermentation of grape juice or home-made root beer. Enzymatic activity can be derived from natural systems, such as bruising or darkening in apples, or derived from microbial growth.

The most important factor in maintaining quality during the time a perishable food is in the distribution and supply system is a consistent low temperature. The maintenance of chilling or freezing temperatures is an absolute requirement for perishable foods such as fresh meat, milk, and fruit juices. For semi-perishable foods such as cured meats, cheese, and eggs, the temperatures need not be as low, but they should still be consistently maintained. Semi-perishable foods can have a shelf life of 30 to 90 days under refrigeration temperatures (depending on the food), while perishable foods usually can be held only 5 to 7 days under the same conditions. For longer storage of perishable foods, freezing is required, followed by storage at $-10°F$ (unless more drastic processing—such as canning—is done).

Some changes do occur during storage, even in a food which is classified as "shelf-stable," either because of its natural form or because it has been processed to destroy or inhibit bacteria and enzymes. Each component of a food is susceptible to a different type of deterioration, and the changes are subtle and complex. For example, fats are subject to what the chemist calls oxidation, hydrolysis, and reversion. The structure of protein molecules breaks down, which can lead to textural changes in foods as well as loss of functional properties such as whipping, gelling, and thickening. Then there are the "browning" reactions which involve sugars and the amino groups found in proteins. Pigments change color as they oxidize, and chemical deterioration of certain micronutrients such as vitamins can occur. If storage is prolonged or products are stored at excessively high temperatures, reactions can even take place between the food and the container, as in can corrosion.

These reactions and breakdowns become quite obvious to the naked eye, as products fade in color or turn brown, cake, harden or soften, or grow cloudy. Off-odors are another sign of staleness, as are off-flavors—although tasting can be dangerous.

It is difficult to make general statements as to losses of nutrient value that occur in processed foods during storage. Certainly, fresh fruit and vegetables suffer varying amounts of deterioration in food value during the period between harvest and consumption, as do commodities such as meat, milk, and eggs. With canned foods, however, most of whatever changes do occur take place prior to and during the processing itself, and losses during prolonged storage are limited to the more vulnerable vitamins.

For example, only 5 to 15 percent of vitamin C is lost when canned foods are stored for one year at 65°F, a representative storage temperature in food warehouses in temperate climates. At 80°F, losses rise to 15 to 30 percent over the course of storage. Depending on the pH (acidity) of the food, thiamine losses are similar or somewhat larger. Carotene, riboflavin, and niacin values decrease only slightly on storage.

Various chemical and biological reactions take place in all stored food, and their type and rate are influenced greatly by the storage environment. Many of these reactions involve oxygen, which is one of the main enemies of stored food. Protection against oxygen can be achieved in a variety of ways. For example, the packaging system can be tailored specifically to avoid oxygen, as in canning or hermetic sealing in plastic pouches. Or chemical additives (antioxidants) can be used to increase the food's resistance to oxygen uptake.

Moisture is another enemy of stored foods, since chemical and biological reactions take place more readily in moist media than in dry. Packaging materials play an important part here, too—moisture gain or loss can be prevented by using packaging materials with low moisture permeability. High humidity in storage areas frequently will need to be controlled.

As indicated earlier, storage temperatures are very important factors affecting shelf life, regardless of the type of processing involved. The rate of simple chemical reactions, for example, increases as the temperature is raised. As a rough guide, the rate of reaction doubles for every 10°C (18°F) rise in temperature. The effect of increasing temperature on a reaction in a food system, however, is often far greater, since biochemical systems and enzymes are involved. The rates of reaction in foods commonly *quadruple* with each 10°C rise. Obviously, such increases in reaction rate cannot go on indefinitely—enzyme action generally ceases above 60°C (140°F), and other "cooking" reactions begin at about the same temperature.

Bacterial growth is another major aspect determining shelf life. Again, temperature plays a major role. Most bacteria multiply rapidly in the temperature range of 70 to 100°F (a warm room temperature). At temperatures on either side of this range, their growth rate is reduced. Under ideal growth conditions, bacteria can double in number as frequently as every 20 minutes. At this rate, a single bacterium could produce a colony of over 2,000,000 within 7 hours!

The temperature *history* of stored frozen food has a definite impact on its shelf life, as well. Frozen food may be subject to more widespread abuses in temperature maintenance during storage and distribution than canned or packaged goods because of greater difficulty in control. Such abuse will have a major effect on its quality.

Considerable progress is being made in the development of temperature monitoring devices for frozen foods that can be attached to shipping containers, cases, or even individual packages. Devices are available which show whether the temperature of frozen food has ever reached some specified level (e.g., has ever thawed), and several time-temperature devices are also available which "add up" the total time intervals spent in various temperature ranges. Another device utilizes an enzyme system to produce a color change as the temperature increases.

As yet, these time-temperature monitoring devices are too expensive for use in anything other than bulk shipments.

It should be obvious that the total change in the quality of a food in storage is the sum of a series of successive exposures at various environmental conditions during the steps of processing, warehousing, and distribution, and the time spent in retail outlets as well as in the home before the food is consumed. This fact must always be kept in mind when considering the whole concept of "shelf life." A food with a shelf life of a few weeks at 100°F could be good for 3 years at 45°F.

Fortunately, most perishable foods will clearly show disagreeable evidence of spoilage before they become a danger to health. Nevertheless, there is always the potential danger that spoilage will not be detected for one reason or another, and that overage or abused perishable foods will cause food poisoning if the food is eaten without heating.

Given the complexities of food storage, what should you do?

1. Expect and insist on freshness for those products where freshness is important for function and sensory appeal. Where open dating is used, check to see if the dates are valid (be sure products that have not reached the date on the label are truly fresh). If not, complain to the store manager and expect corrective action.
2. Buy only what you need for a reasonable time.
3. Check products for staleness, off-quality, and spoilage, regardless of the date or time since purchase.
4. Check the label for special instructions on holding and storing the product.
5. Learn the basic facts about proper storage of food, including dried products.
6. Use perishable products within one or two days—longer only where experience has shown that the product keeps well.
7. Rotate frozen and canned products so that older packages or cans are used before more recent purchases.

By following these guidelines, operators can be assured of obtaining the maximum shelf life of their food purchases.

RECEIVING CONTROL

In both small and large foodservice operations, it is vitally important that meats, vegetables, and all other foods be carefully checked, weighed, and compared to the invoice accompanying the merchandise. Receiving personnel should be trained to weigh meats, fresh produce, eggs, etc., to verify quantity as well as quality. Scales capable of weighing large meat items should be available to assure that the operator is paying only for the merchandise received.

Products that are spoiled or damaged should be reported to the operator so that the defective merchandise may be returned, and credit may be received from the vendor. When vendors are aware that all merchandise is being carefully inspected, there will be less chance of receiving inferior products. The operator should send a printed copy of quality specifications used in the operation to all vendors in order to inform them of the operation's quality standards.

If a receiving sheet is kept, the receiving clerk should also make certain that the unit price listed on the receiving sheet is the same as that on the invoice. Occasionally, vendors will quote one price and charge another, a discrepancy which can easily be overlooked within the foodservice operation.

The manager should provide the receiver with:[2]

1. Purchase order information, including
   a Name of supplier.
   b. Name of delivery agent if special entrance permission is required by client.
   c. Approximate time of delivery.
   d. Exact quantities of items ordered.
   e. Product descriptions and specifications for each item ordered.
   f. Unit price of each item ordered.
2. Alphabetical, expansion, file portfolio for purchase order information and daily delivery tickets.
3. Purveyor invoices or delivery tickets, clearly stating
   a. Exact product quantities shipped for each item.
   b. Exact product description as specified by the order.
   c. Unit prices and price extensions.
4. Adequate receiving scale.
   a. Minimum requirements depend upon:
      (1) Size of unit
      (2) Weight of products received
   b. Requirements to consider:
      (1) Accuracy—checked periodically by a reputable scale representative
      (2) Maximum weight—determined by individual unit needs
      (3) Minimum weight gradations—usually ¼ pound
      (4) Readability of scale
      (5) Height of platform
      (6) Platform pan or cradle
      (7) Invoice imprinter
   c. Location—scale should be located in normal flow of received merchandise, near delivery entrance.

[2]The author is grateful to ARA Services, Inc., for help in compiling these checklists.

Receivers should:

1. Have proper invoices or delivery tickets.
   a. Any shortage should be noted and reported.
   b. Any overages should be refused or reported to the person who placed the order.
2. Verify each container against delivery invoice whenever possible, checking for:
   a. Short or excessive counts—*count* each item bought by count.
   b. Short or excessive weights—*weigh* each item bought by weight. (Do not include weights of packing medium or the container.)
   c. Short fills or short packs—*examine* the fill of containers or packages, particularly items that are usually repacked (such as fruits and vegetables). Occasionally weigh loaves of bread, checking weight of each loaf and number of usable slices.
   d. Shrinkage, leakage, or breakage.
3. Inspect delivered product condition for:
   a. Specified quality.
      (1) Ingredients as listed on label
      (2) Order of listed ingredients (ingredients are listed in descending order or predominance)
      (3) Label brands or quality declarations
      (4) Meat trim or fat cover
      (5) USDA Inspection Stamps
      (6) USDA Grade Shields
   b. Product Wholesomeness.
      (1) Discoloration
      (2) Odors
      (3) Mold
      (4) Spores
      (5) Bruises
      (6) Softness due to decay or deterioration
      (7) Immaturity—green or hard
      (8) Viscosity
   c. Packaging date codes—dates of packing and expiration.
   d. Spot-check temperatures of:
      (1) Dairy products, 38°F-45°F
      (2) Meat and fowl, 33°F-38°F
      (3) Fish and shellfish, 23°F-30°F
      (4) Frozen foods, such as meats, fruits, and vegetables, 0°-minus 20°F
4. Verify receiving documents with rubber receiving stamp and receiving signature.
   a. Purveyor's delivery copy stamped and signed.
   b. Your receiving copy stamped, signed, and attached to purchase order for your accounting.
5. See that product is delivered to proper storage area.

DRY STORAGE CONTROL

Food is normally stored in dry or refrigerated areas. Both need to be carefully planned so that buying can be controlled and food can be stored efficiently, which ultimately will save the operation many dollars. The storeroom should be well ventilated in order to remove odors; it should also be well lighted, dry, and clean.

Good lighting is achieved by the use of 2 or 3 watts for each square foot of floor area. Control of temperature in storage areas is vitally important when planning storage spaces. Too often, dry storage space is given little attention, and whatever space remains after all other functions have been assigned is given over to it; frequently the dry storage space is fitted with water heaters, hot water pipes, and other heat-producing devices. Ideally, no equipment requiring on-going maintenance should be located in the dry storage area. Temperatures should be controlled in a range of 40°F to 70°F. In no case should the temperature exceed 80°F, as this may damage food products and later cause spoilage.

The floors of the storeroom should be of heavy concrete. Walls should be constructed of a material that is easily washed. The room should be secured with a lock and opened only when receiving and storing or issuing items for use.

The storeroom should be kept neat and orderly at all times to ensure that items are not "lost," and that control is maintained. The area should look very much like a small supermarket. Stored items represent an investment and, in addition to the initial outlay of cash for these products, there are other cost factors which add to the original cost. These include: interest on the money invested, insurance, color, cost of storage, and possible losses due to shrinkage and deterioration. These factors influence the purchase quantities.

Some operators purchase according to a "par" stock level whereby each item in the storeroom has a set minimum and maximum level based on the usage of that item. As the quantity of an item reaches its minimum level, it is reordered up to its maximum level. In this way the operator seldom runs out of necessary items. This system of purchasing to par stock on every item used may, however, have its limitations by resulting in excessive inventories and overbuying. Some operators employ a combination of two methods of purchasing: (1) acquiring "par" stock levels for those items used daily which are not greatly affected by the menu, and (2) purchasing meats, vegetables, and other more expensive and perishable items on an "as needed" basis. This system tends to control inventory costs more satisfactorily while providing the security of not running out of needed items.

In determining the amount of space required for dry storage, the operator needs to give thorough consideration to the menu, the type of operation, the volume of business, the purchasing policies, and the frequency of deliveries. There are varying procedures for calculating storage space requirements. A simple and effective method is to take the total meal load for the heaviest day expected and divide this number by 2, which results in the number of square feet needed for a storeroom in an average operation for a 30-day supply of dry goods and supplies. For bi-monthly deliveries of supplies, the operator divides again by 2 or for weekly deliveries, by 4.

The 3 most common materials used for storeroom shelving are wood, formed steel, and wire. Metal is the ideal material for shelving because of its strength and durability, ease of maintenance, and versatility in adjusting shelf levels. Metal shelving is available in standard, prefabricated sizes and is easily assembled. The standard size is 7 shelves high and 36 inches wide.

Another type of shelving that many operators use, although more expensive, is made of heavy chrome-plated wire. Standard units come in sections 12 inches or 18 inches wide and 36 inches or 48 inches long. Sections are bolted together to achieve desired depth. Spacing is adjustable to a 7-foot height.

Some typical sizes listed below may help the operator plan shelving requirements and arrangements:

- No. 10 cans; 4 deep, 21-inch wide shelf;
                2 deep, 14-inch wide shelf
- Dish and glass racks; 20 by 24 inches, 21-inch wide shelf
- Gallon jugs; 2 deep, 14-inch wide shelf
- Cafeteria pans; 18 by 26-inch size, 21-inch wide shelf;
                12 by 20-inch size, 21-inch wide shelf
- No. 2 cans; 6 deep, 21-inch wide shelf

Storage shelves should be labeled with the name of the item routinely found there, as well as its container size. Items should be placed in the same order as they appear on the inventory form in order to facilitate taking inventory. Some operators choose to arrange storeroom items alphabetically, while others arrange them according to product groups, such as fruits, vegetables, fats and oils, etc. Whatever the arrangement, storage on shelving should always be neat and orderly.

Within the storeroom, items should be rotated and issued so that items received first are used before new items. Commonly referred to as "first in, first out," this procedure generally insures that products will be of highest quality when served to the consumer.

FROZEN FOOD STORAGE CONTROL

The use of frozen foods within a foodservice operation has increased steadily in recent years. Frozen foods offer definite advantages to the operator: (1) limited waste, (2) year-round availability, (3) less preparation time, (4) long storage life, (5) many sources of supply, and (6) more menu variety.

This increasing use of frozen foods requires the operator to have additional storage space. Frozen food storage requires lower temperature conditions than do other types of storage. Freezers provide storage space at 0°F, or lower, at all times. Freezers should also be capable of freezing foods quickly, since the faster the process, the smaller the ice crystals that form within the food, thereby maintaining it at a higher quality. Food should be frozen in a three-step process: (1) refrigeration to cool, (2) sharp freezing, and (3) holding at low temperature.

Frozen foods are highly perishable and deteriorate quickly if not handled correctly. For this reason, the operator should check frozen items as they are received and store them as quickly as possible in a 0°F freezer. Frozen foods never return to original quality once they begin to break down. Quality in frozen foods is judged by color, flavor, texture, appearance, and nutritive value of the product. Quantities ordered also affect the quality of the product as smaller inventories with more turnover generally result in higher quality products, as compared with large inventories maintained over a long period of time.

It is advisable to store food items in the original shipping cartons. Foods should be packed in vapor-proof containers to prevent dehydration, oxidation, discoloration, odor absorption, and loss of volatile flavors. Operators should check the condition of the containers to verify that there are no breaks which will cause freezer burn on food items.

The following points should help the operator to improve the overall efficiency in the use of freezers:

1. When unloading food items in the freezer, move loaded cart directly into the freezer, if possible. If the cart is too large for the freezer, move it as close to the freezer as possible. This will reduce handling time and protect the frozen food against exposure to temperatures above 0°F.

2. Rotate stock by marking new frozen foods to show the date received so that the oldest dated food will be used first.

3. Arrange frozen foods in the freezer by product groups. Labels should be available so that foods can easily be identified. This reduces handling time and helps to keep the freezer arranged in an orderly manner.

4. Maintain optimum air circulation in the walk-in type freezer by keeping foods off the floors, away from ceilings and walls. To ensure proper air circulation, platform racks are often used for stacking boxes on floors.

5. Train employees to open freezers only when necessary. Remove as many items at one time as possible, in order to minimize door opening.

6. Install a thermometer to measure the average temperature of the freezer so that it will not be affected by the opening of the door, by the cooling coils, or by direct air from the cooling unit. The thermometer should be placed where it is easy to see. In walk-in freezers, the thermometer should be attached to the outside. An alarm system should also be installed to indicate mechanical failure. Occasionally, the temperature of the products should be checked with a calibrated, dial-type, hand thermometer.

7. Defrost freezers regularly to prevent excessive formation of ice. This will increase efficiency and also reduce operating costs, labor, and damage to the product.

8. Maintain a clean, orderly, and well-organized freezer. This requires daily clean-up, but is well worth the time and effort since it will result in better utilization of products and reduction in damage to frozen foods.

9. Establish a regular service schedule to be followed regardless of the type of freezer being used.

Cold Storage

There is a great deal of information operators should know when planning the freezer equipment needed for their operation. First, operators should be familiar with the correct terminology used when referring to various pieces of equipment.

Frozen food storage, also called "low temperature reach-in" or "walk-in space," is equipment designed to store frozen food usually at 10°F to −10°F.

Processing freezer, the equipment designed to actually freeze food, operates at −20°F and is sometimes referred to as a "blast freezer," "plate freezer," or "tunnel freezer." After the freezing of food is completed, the food is transferred to frozen food storage. Based on current menu needs and projections of future changes, operators can determine their frozen food processing and storage requirements. The following facts should, however, also be determined:

1. Quality of off-premise prepared foods or ingredients specified during peak periods.
2. Frequency of frozen food deliveries.
3. Possibility of buying larger frozen quantities to reduce per pound or per serving costs.
4. Maximum length of time on-premise that prepared frozen items are held.
5. Amount of on-premise frozen foods to be stored.
6. Unusual consumption peaks.
7. Short-term space needed for pre-dished foods.
8. Anticipated use of government commodities.
9. Time and equipment factors, if any, involved in proper defrosting.

The two major types of storage facilities for frozen foods are reach-in and walk-in freezers. Reach-in units usually have less storage space. They may use either forced air or freezer plates to maintain temperatures. Those with plates cannot be defrosted automatically. Consider the following check points when purchasing reach-in equipment:

- Construction—properly sealed, easily cleaned
- Exterior—rust resistant; in keeping with decor if location makes this important
- Adequate insulation
- Doors—well constructed, easily opened, hinges easy to operate
- Lights—adequate; consider automatic light switch on door
- Shelves—easy to clean and adjust; maximum load provisions
- Condensing unit—sufficient horsepower; type; location; necessary ventilation
- Temperature control—visible thermometer or temperature record; automatic alarm system
- Defrosting system
- Amount of floor space required

Reach-ins can be adapted to a wide variety of institutional requirements because of the optional accessories available, including tray and pan slides, roll-out shelves, and drawers. One disadvantage of this type of storage is that it is more difficult to control the merchandise within the reach-in unit.

Walk-in freezer units provide more efficient use of storage space and make handling easier. Unlike reach-in units, walk-ins can function either as holding units or as processing units. They come in a wide range of standard ready-to-install models. Some of the popular walk-in models provide the following cubic content: 4' × 6'—117 cu. ft.; 6' × 8'—184 cu. ft.; 8' × 10'—435 cu. ft.; 10' × 18'—1022 cu. ft. Walk-ins provide a bulk storage capacity that enables operators to buy ahead. In many operations, frozen food walk-ins are located inside refrigeration walk-ins. These are called dual temperature walk-ins (part cooler, +35°F, and part freezer, 0°F to –10°F). As operators continue to use more frozen food products, pre-fabricated walk-ins are expected to best serve their space needs, as they may be added either inside or outside the building.

Insulation is important in food holding and processing equipment. The thickness of the insulation varies with different manufacturers. One manufacturer specifies 6 inches of insulation for –5°F temperatures, and 8 inches insulation for –20°F. A more recent development by manufacturers is 4 inches of polyurethane for either cooler (+35°F) or freezer (0° to –20°F) units. This material can be used for temperatures between –20°F and 40°F and gives the operator the flexibility of easily converting coolers to freezers by merely changing the refrigeration system.

Consider the following factors when planning walk-in space:

- Exterior—material offering long life, easy cleaning
- Interior—tight, easily maintained
- Insulation—adequate for temperatures required
- Assembly—easy, tight, minimum cost
- Refrigeration system—sufficient capacity to maintain required temperature; conditions surrounding location where it is to be installed
- Amount of cubic space needed for storage
- Defrost system—how is it controlled; automatic
- Door construction
- Floor level—should provide easy movement of food
- Transportation cost
- Alarm system
- Accessories—shelving, racks, display doors, etc.

The importance of the above factors cannot be over-emphasized nor can the choice of the manufacturer from whom you purchase the equipment. In the long run, it will pay the operator to purchase from a reputable manufacturer.

When installing reach-in or walk-in frozen holding or processing equipment, locate the cabinets away from any heat-producing equipment. If the unit is self-contained, there should be necessary circulation of air around the equipment. Careful attention should be given to the amperage and voltage supply at the compressor locations to ensure proper electrical service. Floors should be checked for stability to ensure that they will be able to support the weight of freezers and their contents. Furthermore, floors should also be level to enable the cabinets to rest evenly on all four corners. Before the door is installed, the operator must determine satisfactory height and width dimensions based on the institution's food-handling procedures. Some questions worth pondering when planning the efficient use of a walk-in unit are whether the door should swing right or left, whether it should open and close automatically, and whether glass panels should be installed in the door in order to check contents.

Because of the increasing quest for space, many operators are solving their frozen storage problem by installing a prefabricated walk-in unit outside. The units are designed for blast freezing or for holding frozen food, thereby permitting the purchase of larger quantities for maximum discounts while releasing expensive inside space for a more profitable use. An added advantage is that the equipment may be placed on a base, is delivered completely equipped and ready to use, and is designed to be easily expanded in size as the needs for frozen foods change.

In general, fresh and prepared foods are refrigerated between 30° to 45°F to keep them safe from harmful bacteria. If separate refrigerators are used for each food, they should be kept at the following temperatures:

45° to 50°F	Fruits
40° to 45°F	Vegetables, eggs, processed foods, pastry
38° to 40°F	Dairy products
34° to 38°F	Fresh meats
32° to 36°F	Fresh poultry, fish, and seafood
−10° to 0°F	Frozen foods

For accurately checking these temperatures, a thermometer should be located in the warmest place in each refrigerator.

Foodservice operators must carefully determine the best equipment and products to use in their establishment. In the case of refrigerated storage, the models to choose from are many:

- Walk-in
- Reach-in
- Roll-in
- Compartmentalized
- Pass-through
- Counter refrigeration
- Display refrigeration
- Portable refrigeration
- Refrigerated dispensers.

All of the types listed above can be used to help ''extend'' the amount of refrigerated space in an operation. Operators are purchasing more and more foods which are partially or completely prepared and which, therefore, require immediate refrigeration. How do operators decide which units can meet their needs most economically? Experts in this specialized area of refrigerated storage have suggested that operators estimate what percentage of a typical meal will consist of fresh food. In addition, they should determine how many days' supply of each kind of food must be refrigerated according to delivery schedules. From these calculations, it is recommended that: 20 to 25 percent of the space be allocated for meat (if portion cuts are used, the space needed would be 10 to 15 percent); 30 to 35 percent for fruits and vegetables; 20 to 25 percent for dairy products; and 5 to 10 percent for salads, sandwich material, bakery products, and leftovers.

The type of menu used and the type of establishment influence the amount of refrigeration space required. For example, a school lunch kitchen with a limited menu will require less refrigerated space than an expensive gourmet restaurant which serves many more fresh, refrigerated items.

The walk-in refrigerator is used extensively in the foodservice industry. One authority suggests that walk-ins are feasible in operations serving 300 to 400 meals per day. Some of the advantages of this type of storage include:

- The operator's ability to carry a greater variety of food to purchase in greater quantities with discount savings
- Decreases in the number of expensive deliveries
- The availability of more space for leftovers which reduces food loss.

Walk-ins today usually are assembled from pre-fabricated sections. For this reason, they can be enlarged easily and/or relocated, if required. The metal walls are easily cleaned, protect against rodents, etc., and require little maintenance. As with frozen walk-in space discussed earlier, the operator should check the following points, as summarized by Kotschevar and Terrell in *Food Service Planning,*[3] in choosing a particular unit.

- Proper insulation—at least 3 inches thick
- Floor on level plane for walk-in
- Vapor-proof walls, ceilings, and floors
- Sturdy, well-insulated door with heavy-duty lock
- Opening device on the inside
- Sturdy, durable, and adjustable shelving
- Outside thermometer
- Adequate storage space—1½ to 2 feet on either side of aisle, 42–inch aisles preferable, wide enough to accommodate whatever mobile equipment is used in the walk-in
- Audiovisual alarm system to alert personnel when a change in holding temperature occurs.

Operators have the option of leasing these pre-fab units from the manufacturer, thereby releasing available funds for other equipment, building projects, and related needs.

---

[3]L. Kotschevar and M. Terrell, *Food Service Planning,* (New York: John Wiley and Sons, Inc., 1961).

To be sure, there are many alternatives when choosing refrigerated storage. New innovations such as refrigerated drawers, refrigerated sandwich units, under-counter units, dispensers, display cases, and many more items give operators a certain flexibility in planning. Manufacturers of modern refrigeration equipment can provide operators with whatever units are needed to solve an organization's refrigerated storage problems.

The following guidelines, from *The Complete Book of Cooking Equipment* may help operators to attain optimum utilization from whatever type of refrigeration is used.

What You Do	**Why You Do It**
1. Pack food loosely	1. To get circulation
2. Hang van meats away from walls	2. Cold air needs to circulate to keep food from spoiling
3. Cover food (below) with wax or other covering paper	3. Prevent dripping
4. Discard things not needed	4. To prevent crowding and increase circulation
5. Place new purchases at back	5. Use older things first
6. Wash refrigerator frequently	6. It must be kept clean
7. Defrost before ¼-inch frost gathers	7. Frost slows cooling process
8. Open door only when necessary	8. Open door raises temperature

INVENTORY CONTROL

How to Determine Your Needs

The important adjective to remember about inventory is *adequate*. If you buy and store too much you are risking the "using a little bit more because it's there" method of increasing food costs.

Plan ahead. Your determination of what you will require should be based on:

1. A Customer Participation Forecast. Working from a basic plant employment count, or student board contracts figure, or patient count, or student enrollment, determine from prior experience what effect weather conditions, special function preregistration, seasonal or holiday trends, or other changeable factors, will have on the number of customers you can expect at each meal during the week.

2. A Menu Plan. In choosing items, consider customer preferences. In estimating quantities of raw materials needed, consult your recipe file for a listing of ingredients for each item.

3. A Review of Previous Food Production Records. Past food production records can guide you in forecasting customer participation and required product quantities.

Acceptable Inventory Levels

The table below shows typical amounts of products that should be carried in inventory. Naturally, these levels must be adjusted to suit such local conditions as source of supply, contract terms, weather severity at certain seasons, etc.

Type of Product	Acceptable Average Weeks for Inventory on Hand
Meats, seafood, etc.	0.8 to 1.0
Fresh and frozen	0.4 to 0.6
Groceries	1.5 to 2.0
Cafeteria supplies*	2.0 to 3.5

*This ratio varies considerably as a function of the amount of paper service used in the operation, and with the extent of cleaning responsibilities.

Each operation may find it worthwhile to establish current actual inventory levels for these product categories and then attempt to reduce them gradually until a "reasonable, comfortable" level is reached.

QUESTIONS

1. Define the following terms: shelf life, shelf-stable, processing freezer.
2. How does a food processor influence the shelf life of a product? For what specific losses is the food process or concerned?
3. What is the difference between items termed *perishable* and *semi-perishable?*
4. List the principle enemies of storage food and ways the operator may combat them.
5. The operator can use various safeguards to diminish the incidence of spoiled food. List these.
6. How can the operator be protected from being quoted one price and being charged another?
7. List the specifications required of a scale to be used in the receiving area.
8. The delivery invoice can be used by the receiver to check many areas. List them and explain.
9. In checking temperatures of products upon arrival, the receiver can expect that meat and fowl will be delivered between what temperatures? Dairy products?
10. Describe one acceptable method for purchasing employed to control inventory costs.
11. How will frozen food containers affect quality?
12. Describe a storage system that an operator can use to optimize frozen food items.
13. A plan used to control costs in an operation will include what systems? Discuss importance of each.
14. Why is it acceptable to have an average of 2 to 3.5 weeks of cafeteria inventory supplies on hand and only .8 to 1.0 weeks of meat and seafood?

EXHIBITS

Recommended Frozen Storage Practices
Promptly store frozen foods at a temperature of 0°F. (−18° C.) or below.
Check freezer thermometer frequently.
Cover all food containers.
Wrap all food well to prevent freezer burn.
Defrost as necessary to eliminate excessive frost build-up. If practical, defrost when the least amount of food is in storage.
Plan your opening of the freezer. Get what you need at one time to reduce the loss of cold air.
Remove contents to another freezer when defrosting to permit thorough cleaning and to keep contents dry.
Date all merchandise upon receipt and rotate inventory on a "first-in, first-out" basis.
Keep shelving and floor clean at all times.
Establish preventive maintenance program for equipment.

Source: National Restaurant Association

Recommended Refrigerated Storage Practices
All cooked food or other products removed from original container must be enclosed in clean, sanitized, covered container and identified.
Do not store packaged food in contact with water or undrained ice.
Check refrigerator thermometer regularly.

Recommended temperatures

produce	45°F. (7°C.) or below
dairy and meat	40°F. (4° C.) or below
seafood	30° F. (−1° C.) or below

Store large pieces of meat and all foods to permit free circulation of cool air on all surfaces.
Do not store food directly on floor or base.
Schedule cleaning of equipment and refrigerated storage rooms at regular intervals.
Date all merchandise upon receipt and rotate inventory on a "first-in, first-out" basis.
Check fruits and vegetables daily for spoilage.
Store dairy products separately from strong-odored foods. Store fish apart from other food products.
Establish preventive maintenance program for equipment.

Source: National Restaurant Association

4
FRUITS

INTRODUCTION

This chapter begins with a preface giving general facts about fruits and factors affecting them such as availability, transportation, distribution, and waste and loss. The different stages of fruits available for purchase are discussed, which includes both fresh and processed forms. It also includes a brief discussion of defining and grading canned products, along with recommendations for the foodservice operator to use when buying specific products.

A brief listing of commodities, the main containers used in shipping, and approximate net weights is available. Common counts of fruits, purchase specifications for canned vegetables, tomato products, and canned juices can be found in this chapter. Another quick reference the author has included is case equivalents for different can sizes, a guide to common can sizes, cost per serving table for #10 fruits and vegetables, and approximate packing dates.

Detailed specifications for fruits follow. A table listing many of the fruits alphabetically includes fresh, canned, frozen, dehydrated, dried, and sulfured U.S. grade orders. It also gives the can size, net weight, and drained weight in ounces. Specific tables and drawings will also be found throughout this chapter.

FRUITS*

General

Fruits and vegetables may be purchased in many stages of processing.[1] *Fresh* fruits and vegetables are those that have been picked and packed for delivery in the fresh state. Generally, these have been freed of soil and insects and cooled before packing. *Processed* fruits and vegetables are those that have undergone some form of treatment to preserve them. These treatments are known as:

1. Canning. The process of putting food into a container to which enough heat is applied to kill all bacteria. In addition to using high heat to kill bacteria, there are processes used which apply a combination of pressure and lower heat to reduce the boiling point needed to sterilize the product.
2. Freezing. A process whereby fruits and vegetables are kept at a low enough temperature to prevent spoilage.
3. Dehydrating. A process by which fruits and vegetables have most of their water extracted.
4. Drying. A process by which fruits and vegetables, mostly peas, beans and cereal, are allowed to dry naturally or are machine-dried of most of their water content.
5. Freeze-Drying. A process in which fruits and vegetables are frozen and then dried in a vacuum so that the water content changes from ice to vapor, by-passing the liquid state. There is less damage to products that are freeze-dried than those that are dried or dehydrated.
6. Dehydro-Freezing. A process by which foods are dehydrated, then frozen.
7. Irradiation. A process by which the bacteria in foods is killed through exposure to radiation.

All of these processes compromise the quality of fresh fruits and vegetables. However, it is usually not economically possible to use all fresh produce, and the various types of processing make it possible to serve almost any kind of fruit or vegetable out of its growing season.

There are USDA Standards for fresh, canned, frozen, dehydrated, and dried fruits and vegetables. This book deals with those standards only, as the supply of freeze-dried, dehydro-frozen, and irradiated foods is not a market factor of significance at this time.

---

*See also Chapter 5.

[1]The author is grateful to the United Fresh Fruit and Vegetable Association for permission to use in this book the data on Uses, Marketing Season, Varieties, Containers, Servings and Weights and Quality from the association's Fruit and Vegetable Facts and Pointers, Fresh Facts, Supply Guide, Serving Costs, Buying, Handling and Using Fresh Fruits and Buying, Handling and Using Fresh Vegetables. The author also thanks Blue Goose, Inc. for allowing substantial use from *The Buying Guide for Fresh Fruit, Vegetables, Herbs, and Nuts,* sixth revised edition.

A large variety of fresh fruits and vegetables is available at all seasons. It is not unusual for 70 or more distinctly different kinds of fresh produce (not counting the several varieties of each) to be on the market at the same time. During the year, more than 100 kinds of fresh produce are on sale, and if only the main varieties are counted, the number rises to 285.

Availability at All Seasons

Even in mid-winter, a shopper in one of the big supermarkets can probably buy about fifty different fresh fruits and vegetables, plus various varieties, and even more in some markets that have extensive produce departments.

The extension of the period of availability is due to such factors as increased production of truck crops in southern areas during the winter and early spring; planting of varieties that have been developed to produce earlier or later than previously; increased imports; improvement in storage methods; and improvements in transportation and terminal distribution which permit the transfer of tender produce for long distances during which they are maintained in good condition. The big change in all these factors has occurred in the last ten years; further improvements are expected to occur in the future.

Specialized Production

Because of the growing complexity of producing and marketing fresh produce, the trend is away from the very small market garden, or small home orchard, toward concentration in large tracts in areas where soil, climate, and water are most favorable. Big, specialized farms and orchards, run by well-trained operators, are able to take advantage of the most modern equipment, chemicals, and methods. Since costs of labor, material, and capital are rising, increased efficiency in production, packing, and marketing is essential.

While very small acreages far from market are no longer economical, there are still many truck farms of 40 to 60 acres, more or less, that are operated with much success. Orchards somewhat smaller than this are also successful. Many are located close to city markets.

The trend in fruit and vegetable growing is in line with the general trend in agriculture, i.e., toward fewer and larger farms in selected areas.

Packing

In the last 15 years, a revolution in packing has taken place, and it is continuing. One trend is the elimination of waste parts, such as carrot tops, radish tops, cauliflower jacket leaves, celery tops, and inedible parts of greens. Transportation, material, and labor are so costly that it has become essential not to ship inedible parts when they can be removed at shipping point.

Another trend is toward automatic assembling, filling, and closing of shipping containers. This is coupled with mechanized washing, sorting, and conveying. Automatic checking of color by electronic means is used in some cases.

Almost all bagging of produce at the shipping point, and at repackaging houses at terminals, is done more or less automatically. Commodities are weighed by various mechanical means and are poured into the bag, which is then closed mechanically.

There is a trend toward packing fruits and vegetables in consumer units at the shipping point, then placing the consumer units in a master container for shipment. Not all commodities are suitable (with technology at its present stage) for packaging in small units at places distant from market, but there are many.

Another trend apparent in the last few years is a shift from large, heavy shipping packages to smaller ones that are more easily handled. The size and weight of a package is an important consideration in restaurants and other institutions, and in retail stores where they may be lifted by hand.

A great deal of research and experimentation with various kinds of containers, liners, and trays is continuing.

The type of package used is important. It is intended to protect the packed commodity from crushing or bruising; permit easy stacking and securing in a rail car or truck; permit refrigeration as required; and perform other functions, such as, in some cases, providing an atmosphere low in oxygen or providing chemical inhibition of development of molds. The container needs to be designed for easy assembling, filling, and closing. Its weight should be as small as possible, and costs need to be as low as attainable, and still permit requirements to be met.

Transportation

Rapid transportation is of major importance in the commodity industry. Fresh produce is perishable to highly perishable; it cannot stand long delays, wide variations in temperature, or rough handling. Smooth, rapid movement at well-controlled, suitable temperatures is necessary. Transportation has improved considerably since the turn of the century both as to speed and protection of products from damage. Equipment is much better than it used to be.

On the average, it takes about eight days to haul a carload of fresh produce by rail freight from the West Coast to the East Coast. Express is faster, but it costs more. Trucks are used widely for hauls up to 1,500 miles or even farther.

Transportation is one of the major costs of marketing fresh produce, and may range from a few percent of the consumer's dollar spent for these products to 20 percent or more. Transportation rates have gone up in line with prices of other services. Rail rates for fresh produce are, in general, about two-thirds higher now than they were in 1945. Truck rates are correspondingly higher.

One of the newer developments is "piggy-backing." A truck is loaded on a special flat car and unloaded at destination ready to roll to its delivery point. Or a truck body or other container, minus wheels, may be loaded in the same way, then placed on a wheeled chassis at the receiving terminal. The Interstate Commerce Commission says trailer-on-flat-car operations are continuing to grow.

Progress is also being made with air transport of produce. Since air transport, in most cases, is more expensive than other types of carriage, it is applicable especially to commodities of relatively high value for their bulk and weight. Development of new jet transports designed for cargoes is expected to stimulate air shipment of highly perishable commodities.

Temperature Control

The use of refrigeration or other methods of temperature control is on the increase at all stages of fresh fruit and vegetable marketing, from shortly after harvest right through to the consumer. While large quantities of produce are marketed near where they are grown and, as a rule, are not refrigerated en route, vast amounts are moved long distances and must be kept at a suitable temperature to keep them in good condition. This involves cooling or warming of the load, depending on outside temperatures. At the same time, high relative humidity, about 90 percent, is desirable for most commodities to prevent wilting or moisture loss. Humidity in both iced and mechanically refrigerated cars usually is high. Ice, on top of the load or in the package, is used for some commodities, especially the leafy vegetables, to provide added moisture and refrigeration. Evaporation also is reduced by use of film box liners and film bags for both fruits and vegetables.

Distribution

No matter how plentiful and fine fresh fruits and vegetables are in the field or orchard, they would have little value if effective marketing channels did not exist. The function of placing foods where people who want them can buy them is carried out by distributors, the so-called "middlemen." The functions of the distributor are not as well understood by the public as the functions of the producer, leading to misunderstanding as to the value marketing adds to a product.

Distributive Links.   The distributive chain in a simple form is grower-to-shipper-to-transportation company-to-wholesaler-to-retailer-to-consumer. The variations, however, are many and important.

The produce may be packed, shipped, and sold by a cooperative agency owned by the growers. A broker may buy at shipping point for a distant receiver; the commodities may be serviced by a packing and cooling agency; the produce may be stored for later sale either in a general storage warehouse or a specialized house; it may be packaged in consumer units at shipping point or shipped for repacking at the terminal.

It may be shipped directly to a buyer in a terminal market, or it may occasionally be shipped as a "roller," to be sold while en route and diverted to the buyer. It may be shipped on consignment to a receiver who sells it and then deducts a service charge or commission. It may be shipped to an auction house which sells it to the highest bidder. It may be handled through a broker at its destination.

Produce also may be shipped to a service wholesaler who buys for his or her own account and who warehouses, stores, ripens, repacks as necessary, and delivers to retail stores. The ultimate distributor, for example a retail chain, may buy commodities in the field or orchard, or at the packing house, and handle them all the way through the stores, even transporting them long distances in its own trucks.

Repackers may buy commodities by the carload for delivery to their warehouses, or buy at auction or at the terminal market, and then repack items in consumer-size packages for retailers.

According to a study, about 26 percent of fresh fruits and vegetables in 23 principal markets were shipped directly to central warehouses of retailers. Most of the remainder apparently were shipped to produce terminals, where many wholesalers are grouped in one area, or to individual wholesale warehouses outside the terminals.

These are only a few of the complex distribution channels which have developed.

Licensed Dealers.   Wholesale distribution of fresh produce is largely carried on by about 25,000 licensed dealers. Under the Perishable Agricultural Commodities Act, all commission merchants, brokers, and dealers, buying or selling fresh fruits and vegetables in wholesale or jobbing quantities in interstate commerce, must have a license from the U.S. Dept. of Agriculture. All licensed dealers must carry on their business under the requirements of the Act.

Those who violate this law, for example by failure to pay promptly for produce they have purchased and which has been delivered in accordance with the contract, can be called to account under the PAC Act. If necessary, the license of a dealer can be suspended or revoked by the Secretary of Agriculture. In the absence of a license, the dealer cannot continue in business.

Trading Rules.   Under the PAC Act, trading rules are laid down. Since dealers are operating under known rules enforceable by law, they can deal quickly at a distance. Marketing terms are defined under the Act so that a specific and binding agreement for sale of large quantities of fresh produce can be made with a few words. The rules and the enforcement machinery have helped to speed up buying and selling of fresh produce. This is important because delays can cause great loss of perishable products.

Dealers Approve.   Reliable firms in the trade express their approval of the PAC Act and the way it is administered by the USDA. The Act has helped raise business standards in the commodity industry to a relatively high level.

Brokers.   Brokers are middlemen who do not take title to merchandise. Rather, their principal function is to bring buyer and seller together. They transact business in the name of this principal function. Brokers deal in large units, which in the case of fruits and vegetables is the carload or truckload. Brokers are generally classified as buying brokers and selling brokers. They take a commission, for instance $25 or $35 per car, or so much per package, depending on value.

Auctions.   Fresh produce is sold at auction at some shipping points and at some terminal markets. The auction operates at high speed and in a spectacular way. The auctioneers call for bids, each in their own special sing-song, almost hypnotic fashion. They know each buyer in the room and instantly recognize his or her bid signal, which may be a word or gesture. The hammer bangs down to sell the lot to the highest bidder. If bids are slow in coming on any lot, the auctioneer may pass it and go on to another, returning later to the slow lot. Everything possible is done to sell fast.

Onlookers unfamiliar with auctions usually cannot make head or tail of the proceedings. No merchandise is in sight. The buyers work from lists of the merchandise which they have previously inspected. The seasoned buyers have no difficulty in following the rapid-fire offers.

New York City, Chicago, Philadelphia, Boston, Cleveland, St. Louis, and Detroit have auctions that operate all year.

Wholesaling. Wholesale trade in fresh produce is carried on by 9,554 establishments, including 6,291 merchant wholesalers, 986 merchandise agents and brokers, and 2,227 assemblers of farm products. These establishments had total sales of $6.4 billion in a recent year.

The 6,291 classified as ''merchant wholesalers'' buy and sell largely for their own account; that is, they own the merchandise.

About 23 percent of the wholesale operators are packing houses, assemblers, and buyers who buy from, or pack for, farmers, and ship to the wholesale markets or the warehouses of retailers.

Wholesaling (aside from packing and shipping) accounts for about 10 percent of the consumer's dollar spent for fresh fruits and vegetables.

The wholesaler's general function is to assemble merchandise in large lots, mostly carlots or trucklots, and then store, reassemble, and sell to retailers, in accordance with their requirements. There is wide variation in service given by wholesalers. Some sell only to those who come to their stores and truck away the fruits and vegetables they buy. Others give a wide range of services.

Service Wholesaler. A merchant wholesaler whose functions are not too well understood is the service wholesaler. The word *service* indicates that he or she does more than just buy and sell. Service wholesalers also warehouse, deliver, extend credit, provide market information, may send out salesmen, and may, when necessary, aid retail customers with their merchandising.

The customers of service wholesalers are varied. They include independent retailers, voluntary and cooperative associations of retailers, chain stores, and institutions such as restaurants and hospitals.

Ordinarily a service wholesaler has both rail and truck docks; receives merchandise in carload or truckload lots; has common and refrigerated storage areas; banana ripening rooms; tomato ripening rooms; and often has facilities for packaging produce in consumer units. The service wholesaler maintains large and small trucks and may serve an area within a radius of one hundred or more miles. A firm may serve several hundred stores and institutions.

Restaurants and Mass Feeding Institutions.   According to the Bureau of Labor Statistics, about 17 percent of all food is consumed away from home; that is, in restaurants or other eating places, large scale feeding establishments such as in-plant cafeterias, and in public and private institutions such as hospitals.

Large restaurants and institutional eating places buy their produce from service wholesalers specializing in these commodities or from restaurant and hotel supply houses that handle an extensive line of both fresh and processed commodities of all kinds. Smaller restaurants often buy from these retailers.

Waste and Loss

Despite all the advances made in growing, harvesting, storing, and distributing fresh fruits and vegetables, a large amount of waste still occurs. Some waste is inevitable, as in eliminating culls and in trimming vegetables for marketing, but much waste can be prevented or reduced. Great strides have been made in combatting losses in growing due to pests such as insects, weeds, rodents, nematodes, fungi, and bacterial and viral organisms. Losses in marketing also have been greatly reduced by improved temperature control, better packages, faster transportation, and use of chemicals to inhibit development of molds and bacteria. Waxing some items has cut down loss of moisture and preserved them longer.

Loss in the marketing process, aside from normal trimming of vegetables for display, is still heavy. USDA has estimated that of the fruit sent to market, 11 percent is lost during the marketing process. The loss figure given for vegetables is 8 percent. Such a loss would amount to $424 million worth of vegetables and $308 million worth of fruit, a total of $732 million a year.

While all general loss figures are necessarily estimates, various detailed studies of losses of particular items indicate these estimates are conservative.

Grading

A relatively new system of grading is being studied and currently being used only on canned Yellow Cling Peaches. It is called the *Attribute System* of grading and is discussed generally later in this book in the Cling Peach section. Suffice it to say here, it appears that sometime in the future the Attribute System will be applied to most canned products, and this book, as well as industry terminology will be changed accordingly.

We have briefly discussed the basic systems used to define and grade canned products. These systems serve as excellent tools for developing a common understanding of products. We recommend, however, that it is necessary for the foodservice operators not to rely strictly on these systems for specifying their products, but rather to determine the styles, characteristics, and levels of quality of the characteristics which they require for their operation. In so doing, the operator should remember two things:

1. Specify products in a realistic manner. Determine what is realistically possible within the capabilities of the supplier and distributor, develop quality criteria accord-

ingly, and communicate your needs in accurate terms which are meaningful to the rest of the industry.

2. Remember that a top-grade product is not necessarily the best product. No one grade is always the best for all purposes in a foodservice program. Canned foods sold under the lower grades are perfectly wholesome and have excellent application in many operations. For example, in most steam-table operations, items such as *Extra-Standard* green beans and peas usually hold up much better and give a better appearance than Fancy Grade beans and peas. In school feeding, special-cut or mixed sieve green beans are often preferred to the more expensive regular cut beans. Distributor personnel and foodservice operators should be aware of product styles and grades available, and determine which is best for specific operations.[2]

FRUIT OR VEGETABLE?

California heads the list of leading vegetable-growing states in the United States, with 13.8 million tons produced each year. Rounding out the top five vegetable-growing states are Illinois, Iowa, Idaho, and Indiana. On the fruit-growing scale, California again takes top honors with Florida, Washington, New York, Michigan, Pennsylvania, Virginia, South Carolina, Georgia, Oregon, New Jersey, and Arizona placing high.

From a scientific point, fruit refers to the seeds of a plant, together with the parts in which it is enclosed. Vegetable generally refers to the foods we obtain from the leaves, stems, flower clusters, roots, or tubers of plants.

The botanist will tell you that all plants, including vegetables, produce fruits. However, it has been accepted to refer to fruits as those crops grown on trees, shrubs, vines, and fleshy stemmed plants, with the trees and plants living and producing fruit for a number of years. Cucumbers, eggplants, peppers, squashes, tomatoes, and string beans, all of which are commonly called vegetables, are technically fruits.

So sum it up this way: fruits are juicy, fleshy, pulpy tissue that are not usually eaten as part of the meal's main course, while vegetables refer to those plants that are served with the main course.

With our recent expanded understanding of the importance of nutrition, we know that it is vital to include both fruit and vegetables in our everyday diet.

Some vegetables are important because of their leaves or stems. Included here are cabbage, lettuce, spinach, parsley, asparagus, and rhubarb. Vegetables having roots or underground stems and leaves include onions, parsnips, turnips, potatoes, sweet potatoes, beets, and carrots. The seeds of other vegetables are important in our diet: sweet corn, peas, soybeans and beans.

---

[2]Information courtesy of Linda Raynes, Stewart—Tucker, Inc., Menlo Park, CA.

Three Classes

In general, fruit falls into three classes: tropical, which includes bananas and pine-apples; subtropical, which includes avocados and citrus fruits; and temperate-zone, which includes a tremendous number ranging from apples to grapes. Listed with the temperate-zone fruits are all of the berries, including strawberries, raspberries, black-berries, cranberries, currants, gooseberries, and blueberries, and also the important tree crops of apricots, cherries, peaches, pears, and plums.

In the specifications part of this chapter the classification system used for fruits and vegetables follows the model of the U.S. Department of Agriculture and the United Fresh Fruit and Vegetable Association, which are not in complete accord with the botanical classifications. That which is a fruit and that which is a vegetable is, from time to time, a point of debate among hospitality professionals. I am reminded of a dietitian friend who recently lost her paycheck (to her husband) in a bet over the definition of a "Smithfield" ham. Yes, they *are* fed a diet mostly consisting of peanuts!

Specifications

The buyer needs technical information in quantity in order to write specifications that leave no doubt as to any detail. This information is quite voluminous, so much so that to provide all the details would have added 700 pages to this text. That volume of information is available in the companion reference work which preceded this text, *SPECS: The Comprehensive Foodservice Purchasing and Specifications Manual* (Cahners, 1977). For the purpose of acquainting you with the detail and methods that lie behind the abbreviated specifications that follow, certain figures reproduce the detail given in the aforementioned book:

CONTAINER NET WEIGHTS

COMMODITY	CONTAINERS	NET WEIGHT (lbs. approx.)	COMMODITY	CONTAINERS	NET WEIGHT (lbs. approx.)
Alfalfa sprouts	Ctns, holding 12 4-oz plastic cups	3½	Avocados	2-lyr Bliss ctns & lugs, tray pack	25-28
				1-lyr Bliss ctns, tray pack (from CA)	12½
Anise	15½'' wbd crates	40-50		1-lyr flat ctns & boxes (from FL)	13-13½
	Ctns & crates, packed 1½-2½ dz	25	Bananas	Ctns	40
Apples	Ctns & boxes, loose pack	38-42			
	Ctns & boxes, tray pack	40-45	Bean sprouts	Ctns, holding 12 8-oz cello bags	6
	Ctns, cell pack	37-43		Lugs	10
Apricots	Sanger lugs	24-26	Beans, snap	Bu wbd crates & bu hampers	26-31
	L.A. lugs	26		Ctns, incl semi-telescope type	25-30
	Brentwood lugs, double faced, row pack	25-26		Ctns	20-22
			Beets, bunched	½ crates	35
Artichokes	Ctns & boxes, 7'' deep, by count and loose pack	20-25		4/5-bu crates	32
Asparagus	Pyramid crates, loose pack	32	Berries, misc. raspberries, black-berries & boysenberries	12 ½-pts in fiberboard tray	5½-7½
	½ pyramid crates	15-17			
	Ctns, holding 16 1½-lb pkgs	24-25			
	Pyramid wbd crates, holding 12 bchs (from NJ)	30	Blueberries	12-pt trays	11-12

COMMODITY	CONTAINERS	NET WEIGHT (lbs. approx.)
Broccoli	½ ctns, packed 14 bchs	20-23
Brussels sprouts	Ctns, loose pack	25
	Flats & ctns, 12 10-oz cups	7½-8
Cabbage, green	Flat crates (1¾ bu)	53-60
	Sacks, mesh	50
	Ctns	53
Carrots, bunched	Ctns, packed 2-dz bchs	23-27
Carrots, with tops removed	48 1-lb film bags in master ctns, wbd crates and mesh sacks	50
	Burlap sacks	74-80
Cauliflower	2-lyr ctns, holding 12-16 trimmed heads, film wrpd	18-24
	Long Island type crates	45-50
Celery	15½ '' crates & wbd crates, flat pack (from CA)	60-65
	14½ '' wbd crates (from FL)	55-60
Celery hearts	Ctns, holding 12 or 18 film bags (2-3 stalks per bag)	24-28
	Ctns, same as above (from FL)	32-38
Cherries, sweet	Calex lugs	18-20
Chinese cabbage	WGA crates	80-85
	14½ '' wbd crates	45-54
	15½ '' wbd crates	50
	1-1/9-bu wbd crates	50-53
Chives	Flats, holding 12 pots	10
Coconuts, bald	Burlap sacks, 40-50 nuts	75-80
Coconuts, husk	½-cantaloupe crates, 12s (from Mexico)	30-34
Corn, sweet	Wbd crates	42-50
	Wbd crates, early season, Coachella Valley (CA)	40-45
	Wbd crates, mid & late season districts (CA)	45-60
Cranberries	Ctns	50
	Ctns, holding 24 1-lb pkgs	24
Cucumbers, field grown	1-1/9-bu ctns & wbd crates	55
	Bu ctns & wbd crates	47-55
	Ctns	26-32
	L.A. lugs	28-32
Cucumbers, greenhouse	Ctns, 12-18 count	16
Dates	Ctns of many sizes	*
Eggplant	Bu ctns, 1-1/9-bu ctns, & wbd crates	33
	Ctns, packed 18s & 24s	20-23

COMMODITY	CONTAINERS	NET WEIGHT (lbs. approx.)
Escarole & endive	1-1/9-bu wbd crates	25
	Ctns & wbd crates, holding 24 heads	30-36
Endive, Belgian	European cartons	10
Figs	1-lyr flats, tray packed	5-6
	2-lyr flats, tray packed	10-15
Garlic	Ctns, holding 12 1-dz display ctns	*
	Ctns, holding 12 tube or film bag pkgs (2 cloves per pkg)	10
	Telescope ctns, bulk	30
Ginger	Ctns (from Fiji and Hawaii)	30
Grapefruit, FL	4/5-bu ctns & wbd crates	42½
Grapefruit, TX	7/10-bu ctns	40
	Crates	80
Grapefruit, Western	Ctns, packed in desert areas	34
	Ctns, packed in summer areas	36
	6 8-lb film bags in master ctns	48
	10 5-lb film bags in master ctns	50
Grapes, table (Coachella Valley)	Lugs, plain pack Coachella Valley	22
Grapes, table (other CA districts)	Lugs & ctns, plain pack	23-24
	Chests, sawdust pack	32-34
Greens**	Bu baskets, crates & ctns, 24 pack	20-25
	1-2/5-bu- & 1-3/5-bu wbd crates	30-35
	Crates & ctns, 12-24 bchs (from NJ)	*
Horseradish	Sacks	60
	Sacks	50
	Cello	5
Kiwifruit	1-lyr ctns (from New Zealand)	5-6
	1-lyr flats (from CA)	11-12
Kumquats	Ctns, loose	10
	Ctns, holding 16 8-oz Vexar bags	8
Leeks	Wbd crates, holding 10 1-lb cello bags	10
Lemons	Ctns	38
Lettuce, Big Boston	1-1/9-bu eastern wbd crates	20
Lettuce, Iceberg	Western iceberg ctns	43-48
Lettuce, Romaine	1-1/9-bu wbd crates	23
Lettuce, other loose leaf	Ctns & wbd crates, packed 24	20-25
	Bibb	10
	Leaf	13
Lettuce, leaf, greenhouse	Wood baskets	10
Limes	Pony ctns	10
	4/5-bu ctns	38-40

COMMODITY	CONTAINERS	NET WEIGHT (lbs. approx.)
Mangos	Lugs (from Mexico)	10-11
	Flats (from FL)	14
Melons: Cantaloupe	½ ctns, packed 9, 12, 18, 23	38-41
	⅔ ctns & crates, packed 12, 14	
	18, 24, 30	53-55
	Jumbo crates, packed 18-45	80-85
	Std crates	70
	½ wbd crates	45-50
Melons: Casaba	Bliss ctns, packed 4, 5, 6	32-34
	Flat crates, packed 5, 6	48-51
Melons: Crenshaw	Bliss ctns, packed 4, 5, 6, 8	32-34
	Flat crates	35-50
Melons: Honeydew	Bliss ctns, 7¾" depth	29-32
	⅔ ctns, packed 5 - 10	30-34
Melons: Persian	Jumbo ctns	29-30
	Std ctns	26-27
Watermelons	See alphabetical listing for *Watermelons*	
Mushrooms	Ctns, holding 8 1-lb pkgs	8
	Ctns, holding 9 8-oz pkgs	4½
	Ctns, loose pack	10
Nectarines	Sanger lugs, 2 lyr, tray pack	19-22
	L.A. lugs, 2 lyr, tray pack	22-29
	Ctns & lugs	26-27
Okra	Bu hampers & crates	30
	5/9-bu crates	18
	Ctns	18
	Bu crates & ctns (from Mexico)	18-20
	12-quart baskets	15-18
Onions, dry	Sacks	50
Onions, green	Ctns & wbd crates, holding 4-dz bchs	18
	Ctns	25-29
	Cabbage crates	47-54
Onions, pearl (red, gold, white)	Ctns, holding 12 10-oz pkgs	8
Oranges, FL	4/5-bu ctns & wbd crates	45
	8 5-lb mesh and film bags in master container	40
Oranges, TX	7/10-bu ctns	40-45
	Crates	90
Oranges, Western	Ctns	37-38
	8 5-lb film bags in master container	40
Oriental vegetables, misc.	L.A. lugs	25-28
	WGA crates	75-80
	Ctns	20-22
	Wbd crates	45

COMMODITY	CONTAINERS	NET WEIGHT (lbs. approx.)
Papayas	Ctns	10
Parsley	Cantaloupe jumbo crates, 5-dz bchs	20-25
	Ctns, 5-dz bchs	21
	Bu baskets, 5-dz bchs	21
Parsnips	Film bags	25
	Ctns, holding 12 1-lb cello bags	12
Peaches	¾-bu crates & ctns	38
	Sanger lugs, 2 lyr, tray pack (5-1/8" head)	19-22
	L.A. lugs, 2 lyr, tray pack (5¾" head without cleat)	22-29
	Ctns, 2 lyr, tray pack	20-24
	5/8-bu crates & ctns	25
Pears	Std boxes, wrap pack	45-48
	Ctns, tight-fill pack	36-37
	Lugs, wrpd (from CA)	23
Peas, blackeyed	Ctns, holding 12 11-oz cello pkgs	9¼
	Bu crates (from FL)	24
Peas, green (English type)	Bu wbd crates	30-32
	Bu baskets	28-30
Peppers, "California Wonder" type	Bu ctns	25
	1-1/9-bu wbd crates	28
	Ctns (from CA)	30
Peppers, chili	L.A. lugs & ctns, loose pack (short green & short yellow types, from CA)	16-25
	Ctns (from TX & Mexico)	20
	Ctns, retail pack	10
Persimmons	2-lyr lugs & ctns, tray pack	20-25
	1-lyr flats & ctns, tray pack	9-12
Pineapples	Ctns	40
	½ ctns	20
Plantains	Ctns	50
Plums (& prunes)	Ctns, loose pack	28
	Lugs & ctns, tight-fill pack	28
Prunes, fresh	Ctns	30
Pomegranates	Lugs, 2 lyr, place pack	25
	Ctns, 2 lyr, tray pack	25
Potatoes	100-lb sacks	100
	50-lb ctns and sacks	50
	20-lb film bags	20
	10-lb film bags	10

COMMODITY	CONTAINERS	NET WEIGHT (lbs. approx.)
Prickly pears	Boxes, wrap pack	18
Pumpkins	Various types of crates	*
Quince	Lugs & ctns, 2 lyr, tray pack	22
Radishes, with tops removed	Ctns, packed 30 6-oz film bags (from FL)	15
	Ctns, packed 30 6-oz film bags (from CA)	11½
	25-lb film bags	25
Rhubarb	Ctns, place pack	20
	10 1-lb film bags in master ctns	10
Rutabagas	Bags and ctns (from CA)	25
	Sacks and ctns (from Canada)	50
Salad mix	Ctns, holding 8 5-lb film bags	40
Shallots	Bags	5
Spinach	Ctns & wbd crates, packed 2 doz	20-22
	12 10-oz film bags in master container	7½-8
	Bu baskets & bu crates	20-25
Squash, hard types	1-1/9-bu crates	42
	Bulk bin ctns, collapsible and reuseable	800-900
	Various bulk bins	900-2000
	Flats, for chayotes	15
Squash, soft types	5/9-bu crates & ctns	21
	Ctns and L.A. lugs	24-28
	¾ lugs	18-22
	1-1/9-bu crates	42
	½-bu baskets & ctns	21
Strawberries	12 1-pt trays (from CA and Mexico)	11-12
	12 1-pt trays (from FL)	10¼
	16-qt crates	32

COMMODITY	CONTAINERS	NET WEIGHT (lbs. approx.)
Sunchokes (Jerusalem artichokes)	Ctns, holding 12 1-lb film bags	12
Sweetpotatoes	Ctns, crates & bu baskets	50
	Ctns	40
Tangelos	4/5-bu ctns & wbd crates	45
	½-bu ctns	25-30
	Ctns, holding 10 3-lb film bags	30
	Ctns, holding 16 3-lb film bags	48
Tangerines	4/5-bu ctns & wbd crates	47½
	½-bu ctns, volume-fill pack	25
	Ctns, holding 16 3-lb film bags	48
Tomatoes, cherry type	Baskets	8
Tomatoes, mature green	Ctns and wbd crates, volume-fill pack	30
Tomatoes, pinks and ripes	2-lyr flats & ctns, tray pack	20
	3-lyr lugs & ctns, tray pack	28
	Ctns, loose pack	30
Tomatoes, greenhouse	Baskets	8
Turnips, with tops removed	Film bags	25
	Film and mesh bags	50
	Ctns, holding 24 1-lb film bags	24
Watercress	Ctns, holding 12 bchs, iced (from CA)	7
	Ctns, holding 24 bchs, iced (from CA)	14
	Ctns (from FL)	5-6
	Ctns (from FL)	10-11
Watermelons	Various containers	*
	Bulk (from the West & Mexico)	34,000
	Bulk (from FL, TX & other states)	45,000
	Bulk bins, small size	800-1000
	Bulk bins, medium size	1400-1800
	WGA crates	80
	Ctns, holding 3 - 5 melons	55-80

* weight not available
** includes kale, kohlrabi, collards, cabbage sprouts, dandelion, Swiss chard, mustard and turnip tops

Abbreviations: bch(d)(s) *bunch(ed)(es)*; bu *bushel*; CA *California*; ctns *cartons*; dz *dozen*; FL *Florida*; incl *including*; L.A. *Los Angeles*; lb *pound*; lyr *layer*; NJ *New Jersey*; pkgs *packages*; pt *pint*; std *standard*; TX *Texas*; wbd *wirebound*; WGA *Western Growers Association*; wrpd *wrapped*. These abbreviations correspond with Market News Service terminology, which was standardized in 1975.

COMMON COUNTS OF FRUITS

Cherries, Sweet—Canned

8 oz.—20/25; 25/30; 30/35; 35/40
No. 2½—50/60; 60/65; 65/70; 70/80; 80/90; 90/105; 105/130; and 130/145
No. 10—210/235; 225/240; 240/260; 260/290; 290/335; 335/390; 390/480; and 480/540

Figs, Kadota—Canned

No. 2½—12/17; 17/22; 22/28; and 28/35
No. 10—50/70; 70/90; 90/110; and 110/140

Peaches, Canned

8 oz.—3/4; 5/6; and 6/7
No. 2½—5/6; 6/8; 8/10; 10/12; 13/15; 16/18; and 19/21
No. 10—18/22; 20/25; 25/30; 28/32; 30/35; 35/40; 40/45; and 45/55

Pears, Canned

8 oz.—3/4; 4/5; 5/6; and 6/7
No. 2½—5/6; 6/8; 7/9; 9/12; 10/14; and 12/17
No. 10—18/22; 20/25; 25/30; 28/32; 30/35; 35/40; 40/45; 40/50; and 45/55

Pineapple, Canned

No. 2½—8 whole slices or 16 half slices
No. 10—50 whole slices (⅜ in. thick); 28 whole slices (½ in. thick); 44 whole slices; or 60 whole slices

Plums, Canned

No. 2½—Purple Plums: 12/18; 18/24; and 24/30
Gage and Egg Plums: 10/15 and 15/20
No. 10—Purple Plums: 45/65; 65/90, and 90/110
Gage and Egg Plums: 35/55 and 55/75

Prunes, Dried—Canned

20/30 Size
No. 2½—33/37 (Regular Pack)
No. 10—120/140 (Regular Pack)
            190/210 (Nectarized Pack)

30/40 Size
No. 2½—44/50 (Regular Pack)
No. 10—160/180 (Regular Pack)
　　　240/260 (Nectarized Pack)
40/50 Size
No. 2½—52/57 (Regular Pack)
No. 10—190/210 (Regular Pack)
　　　290/310 (Nectarized Pack)
50/60 Size
No. 2½—60/68 (Regular Pack)
No. 10—220/250 (Regular Pack)
　　　340/360 (Nectarized Pack)

SPECIFICATIONS

PURCHASE SPECIFICATIONS FOR CANNED FRUITS

PRODUCT	UNIT PER CASE	U.S.D.A.	MINIMUM U.S.D.A. SCORE	APPROX. SIZE OR COUNT	REQUIREMENTS
APPLES	6/#10	FANCY	—	1/8 OR 1/4's AS SPECIFIED	YORK IMP. HEAVYPACK
APPLESAUCE, SWEETENED	6/#10	FANCY	90	—	MIN. 16° BRIX. COARSE FINISH
APRICOT HALVES	6/#10	CHOICE	82	85/115	UNPEELED, HEAVY SYRUP
BLUEBERRIES	6/#10	FANCY	—	—	WATER PACK
CHERRIES, LIGHT, SWEET	6/#10	CHOICE	84	270/330	UNPITTED, HEAVY SYRUP
CHERRIES, MARASCH. WHOLE OR BROKEN, AS SPECIFIED.	48/8 OZ. 24/8 OZ. OR 4/1 GAL.	*	—	—	PITTED, WITHOUT STEMS
CHERRIES, RSP	6/#10	FANCY OR STAND.	—	—	WATER PACK MONTMORENCY TYPE
CRANBERRY SCE.	6/#10	FANCY	—	—	STRAINED
FIGS, KADOTA	6/#10	CHOICE	84	70/90	HEAVY SYRUP STYLE: WHOLE
FRUIT COCKTAIL	6/#10	FANCY	90	—	HEAVY SYRUP
GRAPEFRUIT, WHOLE SECTIONS.	12/#5	FANCY	—	—	LIGHT SYRUP
PEACHES, HALVES, YELLOW CLING	6/#10	CHOICE	84	30/35	HEAVY SYRUP
PEACHES, SLICED YELLOW CLING	6/#10	CHOICE	84	—	THICK SLICES, HEAVY SYRUP
PEAR HALVES, BARTLETT	6/#10	CHOICE	84	25/30	HEAVY SYRUP
PINEAPPLE, HAWAIIAN,	6/#10	FANCY			HEAVY SYRUP
PINEAPPLE, HAWAIIAN CRUSHED	6/#10	FANCY	90	52	EXTRA HEAVY SYRUP
PLUMS, PURPLE	6/#10	CHOICE	84	70/80	HEAVY SYRUP

Jacques W. Bloch, Director of Food Service of Montefiore Hospital & Medical Center

CASE EQUIVALENTS

The following table gives the equivalent in cases of 24/303's, 24/2's, 24/2½'s and 6/10's, of the more commonly used cans.

Case of		No. 303 equiv. cases	No. 2 equiv. cases	No. 2½ equiv. cases	No. 10 equiv. cases	Case of:		No. 303 equiv. cases	No. 2 equiv. cases	No. 2½ equiv. cases	No. 10 equiv. cases
48 6Z	=	.72	.59	.41	.441	24 #303	=	. . . . . .	.82	.57	.616
48 8Z Tall	=	1.03	.84	.58	.632	36 #303	=	1.50	1.23	.85	.924
24 8Z Tall	=	.515	.421	.290	.316	24 12Z Vac.	=	.87	.72	.49	.536
24 8Z short	=	.469	.386	.266	.289	24 #2 Vac.	=	.87	.72	.49	.536
48 8Z Short	=	.94	.77	.53	.576	24 #2	=	1.22	. . . . . .	.69	.748
48 #1 Flat	=	1.05	.87	.60	.619	24 #2 Cyl.	=	1.56	1.284	.89	.960
48 #1 Pic.	=	1.30	1.06	.73	.800	24 #2½	=	1.77	1.45	. . . . . .	1.088
24 #1 Tall	=	.99	.81	.56	.609	24 #3	=	2.08	1.71	1.16	1.268
48 #1 Tall	=	1.97	1.63	1.12	1.216	24 #3 Vac.	=	1.42	1.16	.80	.871
24 #1 Sqr.	=	1.02	.84	.58	.732	12 #29Z	=	.96	.79	.55	.593
24 #211 Cyl.	=	.80	.66	.46	.499	12 #32Z	=	1.05	.86	.60	.649
48 #211 Cyl.	=	1.61	1.32	.91	1.000	12 #3 Cyl.	=	1.53	1.26	.87	.944
24 #300	=	.90	.74	.51	.556	6 #10	=	1.62	1.33	.92	. . . . . .
24 #300 Cyl.	=	1.15	.94	.65	.707	6 #5 Squat	=	1.01	.83	.57	.623

The capacity of a 16 oz. and No. 2½ glass jar is approximately the same as the No. 303 and No. 2½ can respectively.

Case equivalents may be computed from Minimum Volume Fill by following the example below.

Problem: Develop an equivalent to convert 24/303 to 6/10
Volume of #303 = 26.31   Volume of #10 = 170.71

Formula: Case Equivalent = (Cont. per case x Vol. of #303) ÷ (Cont. per case x Vol. of #10)
= (24 x 26.31) ÷ (6 x 170.71)
= 631.44 ÷ 1,024.26
= .616

Multiply No. of 24/303's by .616 to obtain equivalent No. of 6/10's

COST PER SERVING TABLE
FOR #10 FRUITS AND VEGETABLES

Cost		Cost Per Serving			
Per Case (6/10)	Per Can	22 Servings	19* Servings	16 Servings	13 Servings
$3.00	$.50	$.023	$.026	$.031	$.038
3.50	.58	.026	.031	.036	.045
4.00	.67	.030	.035	.042	.052
4.50	.75	.034	.039	.047	.058
5.00	.83	.038	.044	.052	.064
5.50	.92	.042	.048	.058	.071
6.00	1.00	.045	.053	.063	.077
6.50	1.08	.049	.057	.068	.083
7.00	1.17	.053	.062	.073	.090
7.50	1.25	.057	.066	.078	.096
8.00	1.33	.060	.070	.083	.102
8.50	1.42	.065	.075	.089	.109
9.00	1.50	.068	.079	.094	.115
9.50	1.58	.072	.083	.099	.122
10.00	1.66	.075	.087	.104	.128

*19 servings based on 3.5 oz. portions

Reprinted with permission of Stewart-Tucker, Inc., Menlo Park, CA.

A GUIDE TO COMMON CAN SIZES

6-oz.	Used principally for frozen concentrated juices, as well as regular single strength fruit and vegetable juices.	Approximately ¾ cup 6 fl. oz.
8-oz.	Distributed principally in metropolitan areas and used for most fruit and vegetables, as well as for ripe olives.	Approximately 1 cup 8 oz. (7¾ fl. oz.)
No. 1 (picnic)	Used principally for condensed soups and some fruits, vegetables, meat, and fish products.	Approximately 1¼ cups 10½ oz. (9½ fl. oz.)
No. 300	For specialty items, such as beans with pork, spaghetti, macaroni, chili con carne, date and nut bread, and clams, also a variety of fruits, including cranberry sauce and blueberries.	Approximately 1¾ cups 15½ oz. (13½ fl. oz.)
No. 303	Used more extensively than any other can for a complete range of vegetables, plus fruits such as sweet and sour cherries, fruit cocktail, and apple sauce.	Approximately 2 cups 1 lb. (15 fl. oz.)
No. 2	Used for all vegetable items, plus a wide range of fruits and fruit and tomato juices.	Approximately 2½ cups 1 lb. 4 oz. (1 pt. 2 fl. oz.)
No. 2½	Used principally for fruits, such as peaches, pears, plums and fruit cocktail, plus vegetables such as tomatoes, sauerkraut, and pumpkin.	Approximately 3½ cups 1 lb. 13 oz. (1 pt. 10 fl. oz.)
46-oz. (No. 3 cylinder)	Used almost exclusively for vegetable and fruit juices. Whole chicken is also packed in this can.	Approximately 5½ cups 46 oz. (1 qt. 14 fl. oz.)
No. 10	So-called "institutional" or "restaurant" size container, most fruits and vegetables are packed in it. It is not ordinarily available in retail stores.	Approximately 12 cups 6 lbs. 9 oz. (3 qts.)

Substituting One Can for Another Size				**Food Weight of Various Scoops**
1 No. 10 can = 7 No. 303	(1 lb.)	cans		# 8 Scoop = 4 to 5 oz.
1 No. 10 can = 5 No. 2	(1 lb. 4 oz.)	cans		#10 Scoop = 3 to 4 oz.
1 No. 10 can = 4 No. 2½	(1 lb. 13 oz.)	cans		#12 Scoop = 2½ to 3 oz.
1 No. 10 can = 2 No. 3 Cyl.	(46 to 50 oz.)	cans		#20 Scoop = 1¾ to 2 oz.

Product	Fresh U.S. Grade Order	Canned U.S. Grade Order	Size of Can	Net Wt. Oz.	Drained Wt. Oz.	Frozen U.S. Grade Order	Dehyd. U.S. Grade Order	Dried U.S. Grade Order	Sulfured U.S. Grade Order
Apples	x-fcy, fcy, No. 1 util, comb	85, 70, <70	303	15.2	14.0	85, 70, <70	85, 70, <70	fcy, choice, s-stand	
			2½	26.8	26.0				
			10	98.5	96.0				
Apricots	No. 1, No. 2	90, 80, 70, <70 (solid pack) 70, <70	10	89.5			85, 70, <70	fcy, choice, stand, s-stand	
Mixed Pieces									
x-hvy, hvy syrup			8Z T	—	4.2				
			303	—	8.7				
			2½	18.7	15.5				
			10	70.5	59.7				
other liquids			8Z T	—	4.3				
			303	—	8.9				
			2½	18.7	16.0				
			10	70.5	61.7				
Halves									
x-hvy, hvy syrup			8Z T	5.3	4.2				
			303	10.4	8.7				
			2½	18.4	15.5				
			10	69.5	59.7				
other liquids			8Z T	5.3	4.3				
			303	10.4	8.9				
			2½	18.4	16.0				
			10	69.5	61.7				
Slices									
x-hvy, hvy syrup			8Z T	5.6	4.2				
			303	11.0	8.7				
			2½	19.4	15.5				
			10	72.4	59.7				
other liquids			8Z T	5.6	4.3				
			303	11.0	8.9				
			2½	19.4	16.0				
			10	72.5	61.7				
Whole Unpeeled									
x-hvy, hvy syrup			8Z T	4.6	3.7				
			303	9.2	7.6				
			2½	16.5	13.8				
			10	65.0	57.5				

Product	Grades	Color	Can size			Color
other liquids			8Z T	4.6	3.8	
			303	9.2	7.8	
			2½	16.5	14.2	
			10	65.0	59.0	
Whole Peeled x-hvy, hvy syrup			8Z T	5.0	3.8	
			303	9.9	8.0	
			2½	17.5	14.4	
			10	66.5	57.9	
other liquids			8Z T	5.0	3.9	
			303	9.9	8.2	
			2½	17.5	14.8	
			10	66.5	59.5	
Avocados	No. 1, comb, No. 2, No. 3	90, 80, 70, <70				
	No. 1, No. 2					
Blackberries x-hvy, hvy syrup		90, 80, 70, <70	8Z T	7.8	4.25	85, 70, <70
			303	15.2	8.50	
			10	98.5	62.00	
lt. syr. and water			8Z T	7.8	4.75	
			303	15.2	9.25	
			10	98.5	66.00	
Blueberries	No. 1	90, 80, 70, <70	10	98.5	55.0	90, 80, 70, <70
Dewberries and Similar Berries x-hvy, hvy syrup	No. 1, No. 2	90, 80, 70, <70	303	15.2	7.75	85, 70, <70
			10	98.5	55.00	
lt. syr. and water			303	15.2	8.25	
			10	98.5	60.00	
Raspberries Syr. A and B Black	No. 1, No. 2	90, 80, 70, <70	8Z T	7.8	5.0	85, 70, <70
			303	15.2	8.0	
			2½	26.8	14.5	
			10	98.5	55.0	
Syr. A and B Red and Purple			8Z T	7.8	4.0	
			303	15.2	8.0	
			2½	26.8	14.5	
			10	98.5	53.0	

Product	Fresh U.S. Grade Order	Canned U.S. Grade Order	Size of Can	Net Wt. Oz.	Drained Wt. Oz.	Frozen U.S. Grade Order	Dehyd. U.S. Grade Order	Dried U.S. Grade Order	Sulfured U.S. Grade Order
Water C and S-									
Stand. Red and Purple			8Z T	7.8	4.50				
			303	15.2	8.25				
			2½	26.8	14.50				
			10	98.5	60.00				
Water C and S-									
Stand. Black			8Z T	7.8	5.25				
			303	15.2	8.25				
			2½	26.8	14.50				
			10	98.5	65.00				
Strawberries	No. 1, comb	90, 80, 70, <70							
Sweet Cherries						90, 80, 70, <70 fcy, stand, s-stand			85, 70, <70
Lt. Syrup									
unpitted			8Z T	5.4	4.8				
			303	10.7	9.5				
			2½	19.0	17.6				
			10	71.5	68.2				
pitted			8Z T	5.5	4.8				
			303	10.9	9.5				
			2½	19.4	17.6				
			10	73.0	68.2				
X-Hvy and Diet.									
unpitted			8Z T	5.4	4.3				
			303	10.7	9.0				
			2½	19.0	16.6				
			10	71.5	61.7				
pitted			8Z T	5.5	4.3				
			303	10.9	9.0				
			2½	19.4	16.6				
			10	73.0	61.7				
Hvy Syrup									
unpitted			8Z T	5.4	4.6				
			303	107.	9.3				
			2½	19.0	17.1				
			10	71.5	63.7				

	Grade	Grade	Can Size			Grade	Grade
pitted							85, 70, <70
Red Tart Pitted Cherries	90, 80, 70, <70		8Z T	5.5	4.6		
			303	10.9	9.3		
			2½	19.4	17.1		
			10	73.0	63.7		
Pkd in Water or Cherry Juice			303	72.9	10.7	90, 80, 70, <70	fcy, choice, s-stand
			10	86.7	71.2		
Pkd in Syrup or Sweet. Water			303	72.9	9.9	90, 80, 70, <70	fcy, choice, s-stand
			10	86.7	69.4		
Cranberries							
Currents	No. 1						
Dates	fcy, choice, choice (dry), stand (dry), s-stand						
Figs	90, 80, 70, <70						
Whole			8Z T	5.3	4.2		fcy, choice, stand, s-stand
			303	10.5	9.0		
			2½	19.0	16.6		
			10	69.0	60.5		
Other Styles			303	10.8	9.0		
			2½	19.2	16.6		
			10	71.0	63.5		
Fruit Cocktail	85, 70, <70		8Z T	6.1	5.1		
			303	11.7	10.3		
			2½	20.7	18.3		
			10	77.0	69.4		
Canned Fruits for Salad	85, 70, <70		8Z T	5.4	4.7		
			303	10.6	9.3		
			2½	18.7	16.9		
			10	70.5	62.4		

Product	Fresh U.S. Grade Order	Canned U.S. Grade Order	Size of Can	Net Wt. Oz.	Drained Wt. Oz.	Frozen U.S. Grade Order	Dehyd. U.S. Grade Order	Dried U.S. Grade Order	Sulfured U.S. Grade Order
Grapefruit and Oranges Grade A		90, 80, 70, <70	8Z T	90% vol.	4.85				
			303	90% vol.	9.50				
Grade B or Brkn.			8Z T	90% vol.	4.60				
			303	90% vol.	8.95				
S-Standard			8Z T	90% vol.	4.35				
			303	90% vol.	8.45				
Grapefruit		90, 80, 70, <70	8Z T	full as practicable	4.25	90, 80, 70,			
			303		8.50	<70			
Cal. and Ariz.	fcy, No. 1, No. 2, comb, No. 3								
Florida	fcy, No. 1, No. 1 bright, No. 1 gold, No. 1 bronze, No. 1 russet, No. 2, No. 2 bright, No. 2 russet, No. 3								
Tex. and Others	fcy, No. 1, No. 1 bright, No. 1 bronze comb, No. 2, No. 2 russet								
Grapes		85, 70, <70	8Z T	6.0	4.7				
			303	11.4	9.4				
			2½	20.3	16.1				
			10	74.5	60.3				
Am. Bunch	fcy table, No. 1 table, No. 1 juice								
European or Vinifera Table	x-fcy table, x-fcy export, fcy table, fcy export, No. 1 table								

Commodity	Grades	
Lemons	No. 1, export / No. 1, comb, / No. 2	
Persian (Tahiti) Limes	No. 1, comb, / No. 2	
Tangelos	fcy, No. 1 / bright, No. 1, / No. 1 gold, No. / 1 bronze, No. 1 / russet, No. 2 / bright, No. 2, / No. 2 russet, / No. 3	
Tangerines	fcy, No. 1, No. / 1 bronze, No. / 2, No. 2 russet, / No. 3	
Florida	fcy, No. 1, No. / 1 bronze, No. 1 / russet, No. 2, / No. 2 russet, / No. 3	
Cantaloupes	fcy, No. 1, / comm, No. 2	90, 80, <80
Honeydew and Honeyball Melons	No. 1, comm, / No. 2	90, 80, <80
Nectarines	fcy, ex-No. 1, / No. 1, No. 2	
Oranges	fcy, No. 1 / bright, No. 1, / No. 1 gold, No. / 1 bronze, No. 1 / russet, No. 2 / bright, No. 2, / No. 2 russet, / No. 3	
Cal. and Ariz.	fcy, No. 1, / comb, No. 2	

Product	Fresh U.S. Grade Order	Canned U.S. Grade Order	Size of Can	Net Wt. Oz.	Drained Wt. Oz.	Frozen U.S. Grade Order	Dehyd. U.S. Grade Order	Dried U.S. Grade Order	Sulfured U.S. Grade Order
Tex. and Others	fcy, No. 1, No. 1 bright, No. 1 bronze, comb, No. 2, No. 2 russet, No. 3								
Peaches	fcy, ex-No. 1 No. 1, No. 2						85, 70, <70	fcy, choice, stand, s-stand	
Clingstone		90, 80, 70, 60, <60							
sliced, x-hvy syrup			8Z T	5.4	4.3				
			303	10.7	9.1				
			2½	19.0	16.3				
			10	72.0	62.5				
sliced, hvy syrup			8Z T	5.4	4.5				
			303	10.7	9.3				
			2½	19.0	16.7				
			10	72.0	64.5				
sliced, other liquids			8Z T	5.4	4.6				
			303	10.7	9.5				
			2½	19.0	17.1				
			10	72.0	66.5				
diced, any liq.			8Z T	6.1	4.7				
			303	11.7	9.8				
			2½	20.7	17.5				
			10	77.0	68.2				
diced, hvy pack			2½	—	18.6				
			10	86.0	73.5				
diced, solid pk unsweet.			2½	—	24.1				
			10	—	89.5				
halves, x-hvy syrup			8Z T	5.4	4.3				
			303	10.6	9.1				

Product	Can	Count		
halves, hvy syrup	2½	7ct +	18.7	16.2
	2½	6ct –	18.0	15.6
	10	24ct +	70.5	62.0
	10	32ct –	69.0	60.5
	8Z T	—	5.4	4.5
	303		10.6	9.3
halves, other liquid	2½	7ct +	18.7	16.6
	2½	6ct –	18.0	16.0
	10	24ct +	70.5	64.0
	10	23ct –	69.0	62.5
	8Z T	—	5.4	4.6
	303		10.6	9.5
quarters, x-hvy syrup	2½	7ct +	18.7	17.0
	2½	6ct –	18.0	16.4
	10	24ct +	70.5	66.0
	10	23ct –	69.0	64.5
	8Z T	—	5.5	4.3
	303		11.0	9.1
	2½		19.3	16.2
	10		74.0	62.0

Product	Fresh U.S. Grade Order	Canned U.S. Grade Order	Size of Can	Net Wt. Oz.	Drained Wt. Oz.	Frozen U.S. Grade Order	Dehyd. U.S. Grade Order	Dried U.S. Grade Order	Sulfured U.S. Grade Order
quarters, hvy syrup			8Z T	5.5	4.5				
			303	11.0	9.3				
			2½	19.3	16.6				
			10	74.0	64.0				
quarters, other liquid			8Z T	5.5	4.6				
			303	11.0	9.5				
			2½	19.3	17.0				
			10	74.0	66.0				
mixed pieces, x-hvy syrup			8Z T	—	4.3				
			303	—	9.1				
			2½	19.3	16.2				
			10	74.0	62.0				
mixed pieces hvy syrup			8Z T	—	4.5				
			303	—	9.3				
			2½	19.3	16.6				
			10	74.0	64.0				
mixed pieces, other liquid			8Z T	—	4.6				
			303	—	9.5				
			2½	19.3	17.0				
			10	74.0	66.0				
Freestone		90, 80, 70, 60, <60							
halves, x-hvy syrup			8Z T	5.6	4.1				
			303	11.0	8.6				
			2½ 7ct +	19.4	15.2				
			6ct −	19.0	14.8				
			10 24 ct +	73.0	68.5				
			23 ct −	72.0	57.5				

Style	Grade	Can size			Brix
halves, other liquid		8Z T	5.6	4.3	
		303	11.0	8.9	
		2½	19.4	15.7	
		7ct +	19.0	15.3	
		6ct −			
		10	73.0	60.0	
		24			
		ct +	72.0	59.0	
		23			
		ct −			
quarter, mixed, x-hvy syrup		8Z T	5.7	4.2	
		303	11.3	8.8	
		2½	19.9	15.5	
		10	76.0	60.5	
quarters, mixed, other liquid		8Z T	5.7	4.4	
		303	11.3	9.1	
		2½	19.9	16.0	
		10	76.0	62.0	
sliced, x-hvy syrup		8Z T	5.6	4.1	
		303	11.1	8.6	
		2½	19.6	15.2	
		10	74.0	58.0	
sliced, other liquid		8Z T	5.6	4.3	
		303	11.1	8.9	
		2½	19.6	15.2	
		10	74.0	59.0	
solid pack, unsweetened		2½	—	22.6	
		10	—	87.5	
		10	—	67.5	
Pineapples hvy pack	fcy, No. 1				90, 80, 70, <70
	No. 2				
Chunks		8Z T	7.8	5.00	90, 80, 70, <70
		2½	26.8	18.25	
		10	98.5	65.75	
Cubes		8Z T	7.8	5.00	
		2½	26.8	18.25	
		10	98.5	71.24	

Product	Fresh U.S. Grade Order	Canned U.S. Grade Order	Size of Can	Net Wt. Oz.	Drained Wt. Oz.	Frozen U.S. Grade Order	Dehyd. U.S. Grade Order	Dried U.S. Grade Order	Sulfured U.S. Grade Order
Tidbits			8Z T	7.8	5.00				
			2½	26.8	18.25				
			10	98.5	65.75				
Spears Slices			2½	26.8	18.25				
			2½	26.8	18.25				
			10	98.5	61.50				
Half Slices			2½	26.8	18.00				
Broken Slices			2½	26.8	18.00				
			10	98.5	62.50				
"Solid Pack" Crushed					not <78% of contents				
"Hvy Pack" Crushed					73–78% of contents				
Others					not <63% of contents				
Plums	fcy, No. 1, comb, No. 2	90, 80, 70, <70				85, 70, <70			
Purple halves Unpeeled			8Z T	5.2	4.2				
			303	10.7	8.9				
			2½	18.7	15.0				
			10	70.0	57.7				
Purple whole Unpeeled			8Z T	4.6	3.7				
			303	9.8	7.5				
			2½ >17 17–22	17.0					
			23+ 10	17.5	13.5				
				18.0					
			>70	66.0	52.3				
			70+	68.0					

Product	Grade	Scores	Can size		
Green, Yellow Whole Unpeeled			8Z T	5.1	3.7
			303	10.0	7.5
			2½	18.2	71.5
			10	67.0	52.3
Green, Yellow Whole Peeled			8Z T	5.3	3.7
			303	10.5	7.5
			2½	18.7	13.5
			10	68.8	52.3
Prunes	fcy, No. 1 comb, No. 2	90, 75, 60, <60			
	fcy, choice, stand, s-stand	85, 70, <70			
Metal Cont. Reg. Pack			2½	26.8	19.0
			10	98.5	70.0
Metal Cont. Hvy Pack			2½	26.8	29.0
			10	98.5	110.0
Glass Cont. Reg. Pack			2½	26.8	18.0
			10	98.5	—
Tomatoes	No. 1, No. 2, No. 3, comb	90, 80, 70, <70			
Whole			8Z T	7.8	4.3
			303	15.2	8.5
			2½	26.8	14.9
			10	98.5	54.7
Grade A			8Z T	7.8	5.7
			303	15.2	11.1
			2½	26.8	19.6
			10	98.5	72.2
Grade B			8Z T	7.8	5.0
			303	15.2	9.8
			2½	26.8	17.3
			10	98.5	63.5
Grade C			8Z T	7.8	4.3
			303	15.2	8.5
			2½	26.8	14.9
			10	98.5	54.7

FRUITS—DRIED

Fruits, dried, regular and low-moisture, as purchased	Unit of purchase	Weight per unit	Yield, as served	Portion as served	Portions per purchase unit	Approximate purchase units for— 25 portions	Approximate purchase units for— 100 portions
REGULAR		*Pounds*	*Percent*		*Number*	*Number*	*Number*
Apple slices	Pound	1.00	412	4 ounces	16.48	1¾	6¼
				⅙ 9-inch pie (⅓ pound per pie)	18.00	1½	5¾
Apricots	Carton	5.00	412	4 ounces	82.40	(1)	1¼
	11-ounce package	.69	344	do	9.46	2¾	10¾
	Pound	1.00	344	do	13.76	2	7½
	Carton	30.00	344	do	412.80	(1)	(1)
Dates	12-ounce package	.75	100	3 ounces	4.00	6¼	25
	Pound	1.00	100	do	5.33	4¾	19
	Carton	15.00	100	do	80.00	(1)	1¼
Peaches	11-ounce package	.69	422	4 ounces	11.60	2¼	8¾
	Pound	1.00	422	4 ounces	16.88	1½	6
				⅙ 9-inch pie (⅓ pound per pie)	18.00	1½	5¾
	Carton	30.00	422	4 ounces	506.40	(1)	(1)
Prunes	Pound	1.00	253	do	10.12	2½	10
	2-pound package	2.00	253	do	20.24	1¼	5
	Carton	30.00	253	do	303.60	(1)	(1)
Raisins	Pound	1.00	100	½ cup	6.00	4¼	16¾
LOW-MOISTURE							
Apples	Pound	1.00	584	4 ounces	23.36	1¼	4½
				⅙ 9-inch pie (¼ pound per pie).	24.00	1¼	4¼
Applesauce	No. 10 can	1.50	584	4 ounces	35.04	(1)	3
	Pound	1.00	911	do	36.44	(1)	2¾
	No. 10 can	2.50	911	do	91.10	(1)	1¼
Apricots	Pound	1.00	505	do	20.20	1¼	5
	No. 10 can	3.50	505	do	70.70	(1)	1½
Fruit cocktail	Pound	1.00	558	do	22.32	1¼	4½
	No. 10 can	2.75	558	do	61.38	(1)	1¾
Peaches	Pound	1.00	534	4 ounces	21.36	1¼	4¾
				⅙ 9-inch pie (¼ pound per pie).	24.00	1¼	4¼
	No. 10 can	3.00	534	4 ounces	64.08	(1)	1¾
Prunes, whole, pitted	Pound	1.00	462	do	18.48	1½	5½
	No. 10 can	3.00	462	do	55.44	(1)	2

[1] Number of purchase units needed is less than one.

Apples

There is no such thing as the typical apple flavor, as each variety has its own distinctive taste—sweet, mellow, or tart. Some apples are better suited for baking, some for eating out of hand, while others make better sauce because of their firmness of flesh as well as their flavor characteristics. There are 7,000 varieties of apples grown in the United States and listed by the Department of Agriculture's division of plant industry. Of these varieties, 13 provide about 90 percent of the total production.

Commercial apple production is dominated by nine leading varieties. Red Delicious is the leader with approximately 30 percent of the total; the second spot in varietal ranking goes to Golden Delicious, followed by McIntosh, Rome, Jonathan, York, Stayman, Winesap, and Newtown Pippin. The nine leaders account for about 85 percent of total commercial production!

The size of apples is described in terms of the number of apples contained in a box: 48s, for example, are extremely large apples, while 216s are the smallest that are commercially packed.

The most widely used standard of maturity used by orchardists is the pressure test. Similar to the oldtime hand scale, the plunger of the tester is pressed against the surface of the apple after a thin layer of peeling has been removed. The amount of pressure, as recorded by the instrument, required to cause an indenture of approximately ¼ inch, determines whether the apple is hard, firm, firm-ripe, or ripe.

Another method employed to determine maturity is a refractometer. A wedge of flesh is cut from the apple, squeezed to secure a drop of juice, and placed on a glass slide enclosed in the telescope-like refractometer. By holding it up to the light, the tester can automatically determine, from a self-enclosed gauge, the amount of sugar in that drop of juice.

In a general way, the grade of an apple is not so much determined upon the general defects of its skin, as it is of its color. The Extra Fancy or U.S. Fancy grade apples are more colorful (for variety) than others. Although there is more taste appeal to a fully-colored red apple, the same variety of apples with some bright, red color—and no greenish or sallow coloring—could also provide the same taste pleasure, and will probably cost you considerably less.

In selecting apples, secure those that have good color for their variety and are firm to the touch. This latter point is particularly important when buying the large sizes. Big apples tend to mature more rapidly than the smaller ones and, when soft, usually have a mealy or mushy texture with an overripe flavor too mellow for real taste enjoyment.

Here are a few points to bear in mind when buying apples. Those that measure 2½ inches or more in diameter are ideal for general all-around use. The larger sizes (3 inches and up) of the baking varieties are best for that purpose. This does not mean that those smaller should be neglected entirely, for they are often priced so as to be more economical for cooking than the larger ones. Check the skins. They should be smooth and reasonably bruise free. Too many bruises end up as decay spots, indicating too ripe or too poorly handled. Don't pinch them—you may add another bruise.

Light russet doesn't hurt the quality or the flavor. Are the apples bright and sparkly? On red varieties, the background color should be a slightly yellowish-green—the darker and greener the green, the more immature the apple. Too green a ground color will indicate poor flavor, too starchy, and hard.

Warm temperatures hasten the ripening process and cause apples to lose their crispness and tangy flavor very rapidly. If you keep reserve supplies in the refrigerator or some equally cool spot, they will be at their best when you are ready to use them.

The availability of fresh, crisp, juicy apples throughout the winter and into the spring depends largely upon scientific cold storage. After November 1, virtually all apples come from storage. Two principal methods of storage are employed—regular cold storage with temperatures maintained around the 30°F mark, and CA (controlled atmosphere) storage.

U.S. Department of Agriculture research has proved that apples lose crispness ten times as fast at 70°F as at 32°F. And, they soften nearly five times as quickly at 40°F as at 32°F—and this applies any time in the marketing season!

Overripe apples: Indicated by a yielding to slight pressure on the skin and soft, mealy flesh. Apples with bruised areas and decay. Scald on apples (irregular shaped tan or brown areas) may not seriously affect the eating quality of the apple.

APPLE PURCHASE DATA

Purchase Unit	Servings per Pur-chase Unit	Serving Size or Portion	Purchase Units for 100 Servings	Additional Yield Information
lb.	4.00	1 small raw apple (about 1/2 cup)	25	
lb.	5.60	1/2 cup raw, chopped, diced, or sliced	18	1 lb. as purchased - 0.76 lb. ready to cook or serve raw
	11.20	1/4 cup raw, chopped, diced, or sliced	9	
lb.	3.00	1 medium baked apple (about 1/2 cup cooked)	33-1/2	1 lb. as purchased - 0.63 lb. cooked
lb.	2.64	1/2 cup cooked, sliced	38	
	5.28	1/4 cup cooked, sliced	19	

Buy: Grade A Canned: Uniform, bright color, maximum ¼ inch thickness variation; maximum 5 percent damaged units; maximum 5 percent mushy.

Deterioration: Hardness or softness. Excessive brown, gray, or pink color. Inedible tissue, excessive skin, bruises, or other defects.

Deterioration in Frozen: Hardness or softness. Excessive brown, gray, or pink color. Inedible tissue, excessive skin, bruises, or other defects. Same as canned except 3 percent mushy.

Grade A Dehydrated: Bright light yellow to yellow white; uniform size (Pie pieces: ¾ inch to 1 inch long, ³⁄₁₆ inch or less thick; Flakes: less than ¾ inch long and ³⁄₁₆ inch thick; Wedges: less than 1 inch long and 5/8 inch thick; Sauce pieces: maximum 10 percent pass through No. 8 sieve), brittle and, upon cooking, uniformly tender.

Deterioration: Variable or dark color. Presence of small pieces, loose core material, stems, or calyxes, hard or dry units, and sulfur dioxide in excess of 500 PPM.

Apples, Lady

This is one of the most exotic and unusual looking apples in the world of fruits. It is delightfully flavored. Hardly one in a thousand Lady Apples qualify as Pomme d'Apie Glacee.

The latter is almost transparent in appearance, which lends itself to a different type of decorative effect if placed so that light shines through it. The apple has an unusual grape-like flavor, with a size similar to an apricot.

The fruit is grown by a few orchardists in the United States, one of the largest being in Missouri; yet this Lady Apple orchard is not considered large in the commercial sense. There are a few hundred trees in Washington and perhaps this many scattered throughout Ohio and the Appalachian states.

Applesauce

The Fancy Grade products should flow not more than 6.5 centimeters in Regular style, nor more than 7.5 centimeters in Chunky style on the USDA Flow Sheet #1. There should not be more than 0.7 centimeter free liquid present in Regular, nor more than a slight amount of free liquid present in Chunky. The Choice Grade products should not flow more than 8.5 centimeters in Regular style, nor more than 9.5 centimeters in Chunky, with no more than 1.0 centimeter free liquor present in Regular, nor more than a moderate amount of free liquid in Chunky.

Fancy Grade Regular style sauce should possess a granular texture with particles evenly divided. It should have a crisp texture upon eating (not lumpy) and should be free from a "pasty" or "salvy" texture. The Fancy Grade Chunky style has a high proportion of apple chunks and any fine apple particles present should not more than moderately affect appearance and/or eating quality. The product should have a distinct flavor free from off-flavor due to overripe apples, oxidation, or carmelization. In sweetened applesauce the product should have a good sugar-acid balance and may range from slightly tart to sweet. It should be free from astringent flavors and test not less than 16.5 degrees Brix for Fancy Grade or 14.5 degrees Brix for Choice Grade.

Deterioration: Thin consistency. Dull or poor color or pink color. Off-flavor, particles of seeds, flecks from bruised portions, and peel or inedible tissue.

Dehydrated: Variable or dark color. Presence of small pieces, loose core material, stems or calyxes, hard or dry units, and sulfur dioxide in excess of 500 PPM.

Canned Apple Juice. This unfermented liquid is prepared from the first-pressing juice of properly-prepared, sound, fresh apples, excluding the liquid obtained from any residual apple material. Such apple juice is prepared without any concentration, without dilution, and without the addition of sweetening ingredients. The two basic styles are clear (clarified) apple juice, or cloudy (nonclarified) apple juice which does not indicate a crushed or disintegrated apple product.

The product should possess a good color which is bright and typical of freshly pressed juice and may vary from characteristic light non-amber shades to medium-amber shades. Clarified juice should be sparkling clear and transparent. Nonclarified juice may range from a slight translucent appearance to a definitely hazy appearance. Apple juice of this quality may possess a slight amount of sediment or residue of an amorphous nature. It should be free from particles of seed, coarse particles of pulp, or other defects.

The flavor should be a distinct fruity flavor, free from astringent flavors, and free from flavors due to overripe apples, oxidation, or carmelization. The apple juice must have a Brix reading of not less than 11.5 degrees.

Deterioration: Oxidized or astringent flavor. Presence of apple pulp, seeds or other sediments.

Years ago, apple cider was packed early in the year when the apples had less sugar, giving it a tart flavor. Apple juice was prepared later in the season from apples having more natural sugar, thus producing a sweeter product.

Now the only reason both are offered is to satisfy customer preference—some request apple juice, others request apple cider. Both products are prepared from similar varieties of apples and are processed and packaged in the same manner.

Apple-Pear

For such a minor item in the produce world, this fruit is known by a variety of names: Japanese Pears, Asian Pears, Pear-Apples, Chalea (if you're from British Columbia), Oriental Pears, and Shalea.

In recent years, several varieties have come into the United States from China and Japan, imported through a long process of post-entry quarantine. Two prominent Japanese varieties are the Yashi and the twentieth century. The apple-pear is a distinctive varietal type and is not a cross between an apple and a pear. When it is ready-to-eat, it is still quite firm; eating it reveals a crispness somewhat similar to an apple. The fruit is shaped like a pear, generally quite small in size, has a slight russeting, and appears somewhat like a small Anjou or even Comice.

Apple, Star

In Cuba, Jamaica, and several other tropical American countries, the star apple is a common dooryard tree and its fruit is held in much the same estimation as the sapote. The fruit is commonly round, 2 to 4 inches, and the surface is smooth, somewhat dull purple in some varieties, light green in others. The fruit is usually eaten fresh, but in Jamaica it is sometimes made into preserves. A star apple must be left on tree until fully ripe or it is astringent. It is cultivated to some extent in Mexico, Florida, and South America, and a very little in Hawaii. The flesh is melting, sweet, and pleasantly flavored.

Apricots

The apricot is a stone fruit (drupe) of the Rose family and of the genus *Prunus,* which also includes plums, peaches, nectarines, cherries, and almonds. All these named are drupes; that is, a fleshy, one-seeded fruit that does not split open of itself, and with the seed enclosed in a stony endocarp called a pit.

Golden-yellow color, plumpness, and firmness are indications of quality in apricots. Since they are an extremely delicate fruit, you should avoid buying those that are soft to the touch or have a wilted or shriveled look about them. Such fruit decays quickly and lacks good flavor.

The three principal varieties of this delicacy are the Moorpark, Royal, and Tilton, with other popular varieties being the Blenheim, King Derby, and Perfection.

Servings and Weights. A pound of fresh apricots serves six, with two medium raw apricots apiece, about half a cup. On this basis it takes 16¾ lb. for 100 servings. A pound of apricots provides 5.41 portions of ½ cup of raw halves and it takes 18½ lb. to serve 100. A pound provides 10.82 servings of ¼ cup of raw halves and it takes 9¼ lb. to serve 100. One pound as purchased equals 0.94 lb. ready to serve raw.

Buy: Grade B Canned: May possess pale yellow or light greenish yellow areas; weigh minimum 2.5 ounces each half; no pit material; not mushy.

Deterioration: Pale yellow color exceeding more than half of each apricot and light greenish yellow color exceeding more than one fourth each apricot. Noticeable brown coloring. Excessive broken or crushed halves, lack of uniformity in size and thickness. Presence of ''loose'' pits, dirt, grit, excessive damage, and oxidation.

Grade A Dehydrated: Bright reddish orange; Nuggets: ⅝ inch square; Diced: ¼ to ½ inch cubes; Sliced: ¼ to ½ inch wide and ¾ inch long; maximum 5 percent damaged; coarse, grainy texture.

Deterioration: Dark or oxidation discoloration. Dull orange to amber color.

Grade A Dried: May possess yellow areas at stem; maximum 10 percent in slabs, with pits, physical, or insect injury, maximum .1 percent decayed.

Avocados

Avocados vary widely in weight, texture, shape, and thickness of skin. The color may range from green to black, depending on the type of fruit and the section of the country in which it was produced. In any case, you should avoid those that have dark, soft, sunken spots on their surface or appear badly bruised.

Avocados are best for eating when they yield to light pressure on the outer rind. Like pears and bananas, they may be purchased slightly underripe and ripened at ordinary room temperatures. Ripening time can be shortened by placing the fruit in a paper or plastic bag slightly closed and held at room temperature. After cutting the avocado, the exposed surfaces should be coated with lemon or lime juice to retain the green-gold color of the interior.

Do not cut an avocado until it is ripe! Besides the above method of testing for ripeness, a very simple way is to stick a toothpick in the fruit at the stem end. If it flows freely in and out of the fruit, it is ripe, ready to eat.

Some authorities estimate there are more than 700 varieties, but California provides more than 75 percent of the avocados consumed in the U.S.

Hass. The production leader. Almost ideally adapted to market requirements of size, stability, resistance to bruising during shipping or consumer handling. Long marketing season, April to November. Ovoid shaped with thick skin protecting it from hot summer sun. Color ranges from emerald green at maturity, through black, as it becomes ready to eat.

Fuerte. Second largest tonnage variety. Principally marketed October to March. Fruit is green, pear-shaped, 8–16 ounces, thin, pliable and leathery, somewhat-pebbled skin. Flavor good.

Bacon and Zutano. The two principal varieties, which, with Fuerte, make up the "fall and winter" crop. Both are pear-shaped, green, thin-skinned.

Rincon and MacArthur. Combined with Hass, make up the "spring and summer" supply of "greens." Pear-shaped, with a medium-thick green skin.

Nabal. Almost round, smooth, and green.

Anaheim. Pear-shaped, green fruit.

Reed. A round, green fruit.

All the above are California varieties of importance. Florida varieties, in order of commercial importance, are vastly different and listed as follows:

Booth 8 and Booth 7. Booth 8 is oblong-ovate, small to medium large, medium green, rather dull skin that is slightly roughened. Booth 7 fruit is rounded obovate, medium size, bright green, and slightly pebbled, glossy skin.

Lula. Fruit is pyriform, or occasionally necked, medium large, light green with a nearly smooth skin.

Waldin. Oblong to oval with a characteristic flattening on one side of blossom end, medium to large, pale green, smooth skin.

Bananas

There are two principal varieties of bananas imported from the tropics. The Gros Michel variety was prominent in retail stores many years ago; today it is almost a rarity. Generally a long type with a tapered point, it has a pleasant flavor, ripens uniformly, and generally is highly resistant to bruising and discoloration. In the tropics, the plant is very susceptible to Panama disease, and thus, the present and future production will probably be reduced.

The leading variety today is the Cavendish. The variety has been under cultivation for many years but it requires a greater degree of care to prevent bruising in handling and shipping, as well as advanced techniques in obtaining uniform ripening results. In the tropics, the plant is immune to the Panama disease. The distinguishing feature of the variety is that the fruit tips are blunt and generally curved.

A small quantity of small-fingered red bananas is also imported into the United States and Canada.

The apple banana is a form of the Lacatan variety—a small, blunt-fingered fruit similar to the Cavendish but not more than 3 to 5 inches long. Like red bananas, they are limited in production, bruise quite easily, and are heavier in sugar content.

Once they have reached the stage of ripeness best suited to the individual taste, bananas can be placed in the refrigerator and held for several days if desired. (The skin will turn dark in several hours, when refrigerated, but the edible portion will remain unchanged for 3 to 6 days, then begin to discolor.)

Deterioration: Bruised fruit; discolored skins; decay; a dull, grayish, aged appearance (showing that the bananas have been exposed to cold and will not ripen properly).

Grades or Specifications.   There are no standard U.S. grades for bananas. The major banana companies have their own grading systems.

There are no official international quality standards for bananas. The Study Group on Bananas of F.A.O., United Nations, while favoring international standards in theory, noted:

The difficulties of developing meaningful standards were very great, due to varietal differences, and even different characteristics of the same varieties grown under different environmental conditions, the highly perishable nature of the fruit, and the long distances over which it had to be shipped. It was also pointed out that there were different grade standards which had been developed in accordance with the difference in taste, preferences, and requirements of different consumers.

Scope: This specification covers the requirements for form, size, stage of ripeness, grade, and method of packing fresh bananas. Classification: Fresh bananas shall be of the following form, size, stage of ripeness, and grade, as specified. Form: Bananas shall be in individual "fingers," "clusters," "hands," full "stems," or in combinations of two or more of these forms, as specified. Size: (If other than required in the grade) shall be as specified. Stage of Ripeness: Bananas shall be of the stage or stages of ripeness specified. Grade: Bananas shall be No. 1 grade.

Description of Grades: No. 1 consists of bananas of a yellow variety which have reached a stage of maturity which will insure satisfactory completion of the ripening process, and which are clean, bright, firm, well developed, and free from damage materially affecting appearance, shipping quality, or edible quality caused by scars or other discoloration, decay, disease, chilling, heat, sunburn, sprayburn, chemicals, mechanical, or other means. . . . When bananas are in "hands" or "clusters," the "hands" or "clusters" show a smooth cut where detached from the stalk and are free from portions of stalk. Each "hand" has eight or more "fingers," each "cluster" has three or more "fingers." Unless otherwise specified, the maximum diameter of each banana shall be not less than 1⅛ in.; and the length of each banana shall not be less than 6 in., measured along the line of the outer curve from the blossom end of pulp.

Tolerances: For defects: Not more than 10 percent, by count, of individual bananas (fingers) in any lot may fail to meet grade requirements, including therein not more than 1 percent with defects which seriously affect edible quality. For undersize fingers: Not more than 15 percent by count may be smaller than required by the grade, or otherwise specified; but not more than 10 percent may be undersize for either diameter or length. For "clusters," "hands," or "stems": Not more than 5 percent of either "clusters," "hands," or "stems" may fail to meet the requirements of the grade for trimming, or the specified size of "cluster," "hand," or "stem." Application of Tolerances: The contents of individual packages or individual "stems" in the lot, based on sample inspection, are subject to the following limitations (provided that the averages for the entire lot are within tolerances specified): For a tolerance of 10 percent or more, not more than 1½ times the tolerance specified; and for a tolerance of less than 10 percent, not more than double the tolerance specified; except that in the case of "clusters," "hands," or "stems" this variation applies to "fingers" only, not to the tolerance of 5 percent for "clusters," "hands," or "stems" as a whole.

Stages of Ripeness. Color No. 1, peel color green; No. 2, light green, breaking slightly toward yellow; No. 3, yellowish green; No. 4, greenish yellow, more yellow than green; No. 5, yellow with green tips; No. 6, yellow; No. 7, yellow, flecked with brown.[3]

Servings and Weights.   The following table prepared by the U.S. Dept. of Agriculture gives information about purchasing and serving units. "A.P." means "As purchased."

Food as Purchased	Purchase Unit	Servings per Purchase Unit	Serving Size or Portion	Purchase Units for 100 Servings	Additional Yield Information
BANANAS					
Fresh	lb.	3.00	1 medium banana (about 2/3 cup)	33-1/2	1 lb. AP= 0.68 lb. ready-to-serve raw
	lb.	4.39	1/2 cup sliced	23	
		8.78	1/4 cup sliced	11-1/2	

Berries

A berry is defined as any fleshy, simple fruit with one or more seeds and a skin. True berries include the banana, cranberry, grape, and tomato.

Here are two good tips to remember about berries: (1) Keep in mind that only the popular strawberry is privileged to wear a cap as a sign of maturity. All other berries that are mature should be free of their hull. (2) For best quality and taste, select those berries that are firm, plump, and full-colored for the variety.

Learn to distinguish the different types: red and black raspberries: the core separates from the fruit; blackberries and dewberries: much alike and used the same way; loganberries: big, dark red berries from the Far West; and boysenberries: greatly resemble loganberries.

---

[3]USDA Code.

Large-size blueberries are preferred to smaller ones as they have a better flavor. The cultivated blueberry in today's retail store is distinctly different from the wild huckleberry, the latter having ten large seeds that crackle as the berry is eaten.

For practically every member of the berry family, optimum storage conditions are 32°F and 90 percent relative humidity. Plan to use them quickly, as they have a short life!

Practically all "berries" mentioned in this section are covered by a USDA grade specification, generally U.S. No. 1 or better. There are so many variables in color, size, and general appearance, they are seldom sold by grade. For instance, few people know blueberry size is based on count in a half-pint basket; 90 or less, 90 to 130, 130 to 190, and 190 or more are acceptable specifications.

Buy: Grade B Canned: May lack luster and vary in color; maximum 15 percent less than $^{18}/_{32}$ inch diameter; maximum 8 percent damaged; maximum 15 percent crushed.

Grade A Frozen: Intense luster; maximum 5 percent damaged; fleshy, tender; maximum 10 percent crushed.

Blackberries—Dewberries

Dewberries are trailing, ground-running kinds of blackberries, while the blackberry is one of the bramble fruits, and grows on an erect plant. As marketed, they look so much alike, they cannot be distinguished.

Boysenberries are a dewberry variety grown mainly in California, but also to some extent in Oregon and Texas. Berries are large and long, 1¼ inch long by 1 inch thick, dark reddish-black when fully ripe, and slightly acid.

Loganberries, the oldest trailing blackberry variety of the Pacific Coast, are of California origin. Berries are large, long, dark red, acid and high-flavored.

The *Olallie* berry is grown extensively in California, but is of Oregon origin. It is a cross between Black Logan and Young; berries are bright black, medium-sized, firm. They are principally for local shipments.

Deterioration: Dull appearance, softness, and mold are signs of age and waste. Excessive irregularity of size. Off-color, noticeably hard or seedy berries, and mashed or soft berries. Marked presence of leaves and stems.

Deterioration of Frozen: Presence of leaves, large stems, cap stems, or undeveloped berries. Crushed, mushy, or soft berries. Grit or sand.

Blueberries

Blueberries are the third most popular noncitrus fruit in the United States. While they are found on almost every continent of the world, the United States and Canada grow more blueberries commercially than the rest of the world combined. Both nations are large consumers.

In the United States, fresh blueberries begin coming to market in May and continue through September, with July the peak month. In May and June, supplies orinate from North Carolina, July from New Jersey, and late July and August into September from Michigan.

Deterioration: Dull appearance, softness, and mold are signs of age and waste.

Presence of leaves, large stems, cap stems, and undeveloped berries. Crushed, mushy or soft berries, and grit or sand.

Servings and Weights.   One cup of blueberries weighs about 140 grams or 5 oz. One pt. of blueberries makes 4 to 5 half-cup servings; 22 pt. serve 100.

Elderberries

These small black berries of the elder bush, are principally used in jelly and wine-making, pies, and breads.

Gooseberries

Approximately 50 species are distributed over the northern hemisphere, with the greatest number in North America.

Because this plant acts as a host to a fungus that attacks the white pine, one of the most valuable trees in the country, federal and state laws regulate interstate shipments of gooseberries and the areas in which they may be grown. When available through local supplies or on farmers markets, fresh gooseberries are in season May through August, with June and July as peak months. Ripe gooseberries are easy to recognize: they are soft, have a light amber color, with the large ones being generally of preferred quality.

Raspberries

The wild red raspberry is native of the northern states, while the black raspberry is native farther South. There are yellow or golden and apricot or amber-colored berries, as well as black, red, purple, and various shades in between.

Raspberries are on the market from mid-April through November, with peak months of June and July.

Deterioration: Dull appearance, softness, and mold are signs of age and waste.

Buy: Grade B Canned: Minimum 85 percent bright, typical color; 9/16 inch diameter; maximum 5 percent undeveloped or damaged berries; thick fleshed, well ripened; maximum 10 percent broken or mashed.

Grade A Frozen: 95 percent bright, typical color; ¼ square inch extraneous material, 2 stems per 16 ounces; maximum 5 percent damaged or undeveloped; mature, well ripened; maximum 10 percent red raspberries crushed or 5 percent black raspberries crushed.

Deterioration: Presence of leaves, large stems, cap stems, or underdeveloped berries. Crushed, mushy, or soft berries. Grit or sand.

Strawberries

Large strawberries are the choicest for eating, although size is not a true sign of sweetness. Today, strawberry season is all year-round. Peak production and low prices generally prevail between mid-April and mid-July.

Deterioration: Soft or moldy berries are either overripe or decayed.

Servings.   There is no agreement as to what constitutes a "portion" or serving of any fresh fruit or vegetable. However, there are some guidelines, including USDA's *Food Buying Guide for Type A School Lunches.* This suggests three possible servings: 1 cup, ½ cup, and ¼ cup. If the serving is 1 cup, and the purchase unit is the pint, then 1 pt. provides 2.125 servings, and it would take 47.2 pt. for 100.

If the serving is ½ cup, there are 4.25 servings per pint, and it would take 23.6 pt. to serve 100. A ¼ cup serving, which would be more a garnish than a serving, would run 8.5 servings per pint and would require 11.8 pt. for 100 servings.

One pint of strawberries, as purchased, is estimated to weigh 0.78 lb. and would provide 0.7 lb. ready-to-serve raw. It is also estimated that 1 lb. as purchased would provide 0.89 lb. ready-to-serve. One pound provides 5.41 servings of ½ cup raw whole berries; or 10.82 servings of ¼ cup, or 2.7 servings of 1 cup.

Grades.   United States standards for grades of strawberries, effective July 1, 1965, are U.S. 1, U.S. Combination, and U.S. 2. The principal grade is U.S. 1.

U.S. 1 consists of strawberries of one variety or similar varietal characteristics with the cap (calyx) attached, which are firm, not overripe or undeveloped, and which are free from mold or decay, and free from damage caused by dirt, moisture, foreign matter, disease, insects, or mechanical orother means. Each strawberry has not less than ¾ of its surface showing a pink or red color.

Size: Unless otherwise specified, the minimum diameter of each strawberry is not less than ¾ in.

Tolerances: In order to allow for variations incident to proper grading and handling the following tolerances, by volume, are provided as specified: For defects: Not more than 10 percent for strawberries in any lot which fail to meet the requirements of this grade, but not more than one-half of this tolerance, or 5 percent, shall be allowed for defects causing serious damage, including therein not more than ⅖ of this latter amount or 2 percent for strawberries affected by decay. For off-size: Not more than 5 percent for strawberries in any lot which are below the specified minimum size.[4]

Buy: Grade B Frozen: Pink to red color with minimal dull, gray, or reddish-brown; no grit or sand, ½ square inch leaves, cups, etc., per 16 ounces or 4 stems or 32 short stems; reasonably firm, whole: maximum of 20 percent partial or mushy; sliced: maximum of 30 percent mushy.

---

[4]USDA Code.

Deterioration: Dull gray, reddish-brown, or white color. Presence of grit, sand, weeds, grass, seedy units, insect damage, stems, caps, sepal bracts, or mushy berries. Off-flavors or odors.

Breadfruit

A member of the mulberry family and widely dispersed in the torrid zones, breadfruit is a staple fruit of Polynesia. Oval or round in shape, it may grow up to watermelon size: 5 to 9 inches long, 4 to 8 inches in diameter, and 2 to 15 pounds or more. The rind is yellowish-green, and the pulp is fibrous and white to yellowish when mature. The cultivated breadfruit is seedless; the wild breadfruit has seeds. The seed-bearing form is usually called breadnut and may be raised from seeds. This is grown primarily for the seeds, which are roasted or boiled.

Cakee

Cakee (also known as Seso Vegetal) is a favorite Jamaican food grown on a tropical evergreen tree. The tri-valved fruits turn yellow and red as they ripen. The mature fruit splits open along three sutures, exposing three large, shiny-black seeds which are attached to a white or milky-white aril. The firm and oily aril is the edible portion and is consumed fresh or is cooked and used as a vegetable. The firm, yellow fingers should be curried, baked, or cooked with saltwater fish. Only the naturally-opened fruits can be eaten.

Carambola

The carambola varies in size from a hen's egg to a large orange. It may be ovate, or an acutely five-angled fruit. The Golden Star fruit is ovoid or ellipsoid in shape, from 4 to 5 inches in length, with 4 to 6 prominent, longitudinal ribs. The skin is bright golden-yellow in color and has a thick, waxy cuticle. The flesh is juicy and crisp in texture and contains no fiber. It is grown sparingly in southern California and Florida, as well as the West Indies and Hawaii. Many consider different varieties resulting in "sweet" types and "sour" types; however, fruits from seedlings produce the unpleasantly sour product and those from vegetatively propagated plants produce the superior fruit desired. It is used in beverages, jellies, and jams. It continues to grow in popularity in southern Florida as a dooryard tree, but its super-sensitivity to cold weather and water have deterred large commercial growings. Fully ripe fruits have an agreeable flavor, mildly sub-acid to sweet.

Cherimoya

The cherimoya (chair-i-moy-a) is almost heart-shaped, green-colored when ripe, with the skin marked faintly in medalions. It is grown in southern Florida, Indies, Australia, California. It is sometimes called "custard apple" or "sherbet fruit" because of its natural sherbet texture when chilled. Flavor resembles a combination of fresh pineapple, strawberry, and banana.

Choose ones with fairly uniform green color. The larger fruit is usually the best. Surface brown scars do not indicate poor quality, but avoid cherimoya with mold or cracks at the stem end, or those with dark brown skins, as they are probably overripe. Ripen at room temperature until they yield to gentle pressure from the palms of the hands.

It is cut in halves or quarters to eat with a spoon. The many seeds are removed as it is eaten.

Cherries

The two principal varieties of sweet cherries grown for fresh market are Bing and Lambert. The Bing matures before the Lambert in all districts and is characterized by its large size and round, plump shape, plus the dark mahogany color. It is the most popular of the fresh market varieties and is primarily grown in the Western areas that have just the right climatic conditions for this variety. It is an excellent "shipper."

The Lambert is similar to the Bing in many ways. It matures a week to ten days after the Bing and is grown in the same producing areas. It has the same rich flavor as the Bing, but is more elongated or heart-shaped. The Lambert variety is also hardy.

A third, and newer, variety of sweet cherries, the Van, has gained favor among the fresh buying trade. It is used as a pollenizer for Bings and has many of the same characteristics. Except for a somewhat shorter stem, it is difficult to distinguish it from the Bing, maturing about one week later.

The Chinnok variety is an early black, sweet cherry of good size that is used as a pollenizer for Bings. It matures just ahead of the Bing, is very flavorful, slightly softer than the Bing, but is not considered an ideal shipping variety.

Black Tartarian, Burbank, Chapman, and Burlat are varieties that are grown in California, primarily because of their early-maturing characteristics. Although there are quality variances between these varieties, they generally are all dark red, soft, mostly small size, and are considered to be of fair quality.

The Black Republican variety is considered an excellent pollenizer in the Northwest, but is seldom shipped for fresh market. They are quite small and very firm, but the quality is just fair. Black Republicans mature during the Lambert season.

Royal Ann and Rainier (Golden Bing) are both light or white sweet cherries. They gain excellent size, have outstanding flavor, but are very poor shippers. The light skin emphasizes even the slightest bruising, which detracts from the appearance of these varieties.

Schmidt and Windsor are Eastern sweet cherry varieties and both are grown mainly as processing varieties. They are dark, sweet cherries, characterized by good size and a quite firm, meaty texture. They are considered good for canning and brining.

Cherries are so delicate that they must be handled carefully to avoid bruising or other damage. Prime quality fruit should appear fresh, firm, well matured, and well colored for the variety; be juicy and of fine flavor. Use the taste test.

Buy: Grade A Canned: Pinkish yellow to pale amber with varying depth of blush; minimum 2.84 gram weight; minimum ³⁄₁₆ inch diameter; practically free of defects; pitted may have 1 pit per 20 ounces and 10 percent slightly damaged; thick fleshed, tender but not soft; maximum 5 percent with cracks.

Grade A Frozen: color typical of well-ripened cherries; minimum ¼ inch diameter; maximum 1 piece extraneous material per 20 ounces, 1 pit per 20 ounces in pitted; maximum 7 percent damaged; tender, fleshy texture.

Deterioration: Dull-appearing, soft, or shriveled fruits with brown stems are usually overripe and of poor flavor or inedible.

Cherry sizes are described in "rows," dating back to when the industry place-packed the top layer in the box. A tight fit of ten cherries across the narrow face of the lug became "10 row" cherries. Depending on variety, 9-row is generally the very largest packed, 13-row the smallest. But a 10-row California cherry is smaller than a 10-row shipped from Washington—just to keep you thoroughly confused. Reason: California ships an eighteen-pound net lug, Washington a larger, twenty-pound lug.

Tart Cherry Varieties.   Early Richmond is mainly grown in the midwestern and eastern U.S. It matures in early June, is dark red, round, medium to large, juicy, and considered good for canning only.

English Morello, again, is mainly a midwestern and eastern variety. It is harvested around July 15, is dark red, medium to large, juicy, and considered good for canning only.

Montmorency is grown in all sections. It is harvested in July, is light to dark red, medium to large, and juicy. It is the most popular of the sour cherry varieties and may be eaten fresh.

Buy: Grade A Canned: Bright, typical color.

Grade A Frozen: As with canned except maximum 15 percent vary from "good red color."

Deterioration: Excessive number of pits, loose, soft, tough, or leathery cherries, and defects that extend into fruit tissue.

Deterioration of Frozen: Poor, pale color, or the presence of pits or pit fragments, scab blemishes, hail injury, discolored areas, or scar tissue. Thin flesh, leathery, tough, or soft texture or off-flavor.

Varieties: Royal Anne, Yellow Spanish, Napoleon.   Canned maraschino cherries are prepared from the sound, ripe fruit of the Royal Anne, Yellow Spanish, Napoleon, and like varieties of sweet cherries. The Royal Anne Light Sweet is by far the most predominant variety used. These sweet cherries have pale meat and yellow skin, with a red blush which makes them easy to bleach and dye. The finished product exhibits a bright, clear, red color, with a slight "almond" flavor.

The product possesses a sugar content of 37 to 40 degrees Brix and firm, crisp texture. The cherries are available in various sizes, pitted or unpitted, with or without stem, and of various quality categories.

At the brining plant the cherries are inspected and placed in large brining tanks which hold from 200 to 300 barrels of cherries. They remain there approximately two months while they are bleached. The brining solution contains 0.75 percent to 1.50

percent sulphur dioxide, in addition to calcium ions. Bleaching removes all flavor and color, leaving the cellulose structure intact. The brine acts as a preservative, enabling the cherries to keep as long as three years. This brining solution also gives the cherries firmer texture and stronger stem attachment, and it loosens the meat from the pit. When the brined cherries, now a pale golden color, are ready for finishing, they are moved by conveyor to machines which remove the pit and sort them according to size. Next, the cherries are sorted and graded—either by hand or machine—for color, absence of defects, size, and presence of stem. Brined cherries are available in various quality categories. Shipments of brined cherries to finishers usually are made in poly-lined drums containing 250 pounds net cherries.

For finishing, cherries are put into processing tanks and leached of brining solution. Then FDA-approved Red Number 4 food coloring and a sugar solution are added under controlled temperatures. Five interchanges of sugar over a five- to seven-day period are necessary before the cherries reach the 37 to 40 degree Brix or sugar content, which makes them maraschino cherries.

An almond flavor is added to red maraschinos to complete the manufacturing process. Maraschino cherries produced in the United States have no alcoholic content.

Coconuts

There are three soft spots at the top of the shell of the coconut. To get to the meat and milk, pierce these spots with an ice pick, or similar sharp instrument, and drain the milk. Then tap all over with a hammer until the hard shell cracks and falls off. Another way to break the shell is to heat the coconut in the oven for thirty minutes at 350°F.

Coconuts are on the market all year with peak availability in October, November, and December. Good quality coconuts are those which are heavy for their size and in which the milk sloshes around. Coconuts without milk are spoiled. Nuts with moldy or wet "eyes" are unsound.

They are best stored at 32 to 35°F, relative humidity of 90 percent. Under these conditions, they can be held for one or two months. The dry kernel, or meat, is the copra of commerce from which coconut oil is expressed.

Crabapples

Crabapples are mostly used in making jellies, jams, and preserves. They're small in size (about 1½ inches in diameter), with a sour taste that makes them unsuitable for eating out of hand. Choose them in the same manner as you would regular varieties of apples.

Cranberries

Mechanical pickers harvest an annual crop of 200,000,000 pounds of cranberries. Massachusetts and Wisconsin produce the largest supply with New Jersey, Washington, and Oregon contributing a substantial share. Unlike the wild berries of long ago, today's fruit is cultivated to grow larger, brighter in color, and more flavorful.

Fresh cranberry size, shape, and color will depend on the variety. As a general rule they all are glossy, firm, plump, and red. Poor quality is indicated by shriveling, dull appearance, softness, or stickiness. While cranberries keep longer than most berries, they do need to be stored in the refrigerator. They may be left in their store container, then, just before cooking time, rinse in cold water and remove any stems or bruised fruit.

Deterioration: Soft, spongy, or leaky berries may produce an off-flavor when cooked.

Buy: Grade B Frozen: Reasonably good color, slightly soft to moderately firm; minor blemishes.

Cranberry Sauce

Buy: Grade B Canned: Bright, dark red color; slightly firm gel in jellied and strained; free from foreign matter; tender; maximum 3 defective berries per 12 ounces; slightly tart flavor with no trace of carmelized flavor.

Deterioration: Excessive number of stems or pieces of leaf. Poor color.

Currants

Select firm, ripe currants for jelly-making. Overripe fruit does not "jell" so well. The three main varieties are red, white, and black, and are in season from June to August.

Buy: Dried Grade A: Possesses a good typical color; good characteristic flavor shows development characteristic of dried currants prepared from well-matured grapes, containing not more than 20 percent moisture. Not more than 1 piece of stem per 24 oz. of dried currants may be present; not more than 12 seeds per 16 oz. may be present in seeded dried currants; not more than 1½ percent of dried currants may possess capstems; not more than 1 percent, by weight, may be undeveloped, and not more than 2 percent be damaged; not more than 5 percent may be sugared; not more than 5 percent may be moldy. The appearance or edibility may not be affected by dried currants damaged by fermentation; and no grit, sand, or silt may be present that affects the appearance and edibility.

Dates

There are more than one hundred varieties of dates grown in the Coachella Valley of southern California. It is the only area in the western hemisphere where dates are grown on a commercial basis.

Dates are classified as soft, semi-dry, and dry, depending upon the softness of the ripe fruit. Another classification is according to the kind of sugar contained in the ripe fruit, with most soft varieties being invert-sugar dates and most dry varieties cane-sugar dates.

The principal commercial variety in the United States is the Deglet Noor, meaning "Date of the Light." It is a semi-dry variety, an excellent eating date, has high cane-sugar content, and ripens late in the season. Commercially, it accounts for about

85 percent of the total date acreage. It is the only semi-dry variety that is a cane-sugar date; the others are invert-sugar varieties.

The Halaway, Khadrawy, and Azhidi varieties are invert-sugar dates. The Khadrawy is a soft variety, while Halaway and Zahidi are semi-dry. These varieties are in great demand by the people who must guard their sugar intake. This is a natural sugar (like honey), and is composed of dextrose and levulose.

When fully ripe, fresh dates are plump and lustrous with a golden brown color and smooth skin. They are sold pitted and unpitted, and are available throughout the year. The season of top abundance is from September to May, with the peak in November.

Dates will keep indefinitely if properly cared for and stored. Like any delicately-flavored fruit, certain precautions must be taken to insure keeping the dates in prime condition. Ideal storage conditions are between 30 and 40°F, relative humidity of 75 to 80 percent. The lower the temperature, the longer the fruit will retain its original quality. Dates should not be stored near flour, cereal, or any other items that might be infested. Do not store near onions, fish, or other odorous items, for dates tend to absorb such odors.

Dry varieties usually contain only a small amount of moisture when ripe, and they are nonperishable. The soft and semi-dry varieties contain a considerable amount of moisture and are usually highly perishable.

Buy: Grade A: Light amber color; 90 percent of dates in the container must be the same size; maximum 1 pit per 25 ounces; minimum 75 percent well developed, well fleshed and soft; no dry ends.

Deterioration: Variable size and color, and presence of dirt, deformed units, puffiness, and sunburn.

Feijoa

The feijoa (fee-jo-a) is a great new taste treat from primarily New Zealand. Scattered trees have been planted in Florida, California, and Hawaii, but there are no commercial acreages in production at this time. Feijoa trees are rather small, to 15 feet, with evergreen leaves 2 to 3 inches long. They will endure winter temperatures down to 15°F. The fruit is generally oval in shape, 1½ to 3 inches long. A prominent calyx is persistent. The skin is waxy, generally dark green but occasionally greenish-yellow. It looks like a slightly elongated guava, and the true, botanical variation can best be described as a pineapple guava.

Only the interior pulp is scooped or spooned out and eaten immediately as a dessert or in salads—or combined with all other fruit you can think of. It may be stewed or used in jams or other similar recipes. Plan to store for only short periods, at 33 to 35°F.

Figs

The commercial fig is not a fruit in the strict botanical sense, but a hollow, fleshy receptacle with the many true fruits or ''seeds'' on the inside of it, and an opening at the top through which passes the insect that pollinates the minute fruit.

California produces the largest volume of figs, both Mission (or Adriatic) and the Smyrna types. The latter requires special provision for pollination by a gall wasp. In Texas and in the eastern states, only the Adriatic type is grown, which requires no pollination to set fruit.

There are many varieties of figs, but they are classified by shape, color of skin, and color of flesh. The shape is round or turbinate in some, pyriform or obovate in others.

Smyrna is the common imported dried fig of commerce which is produced in considerable quantities in California. This variety does not develop its fruit to maturity, as a rule, except when it is pollinated by a certain fig wasp, known as a Blastophaga, which lives over the winter in a caprifig. (Caprifigs produce pollen, but their fruit is of little or no value for edible purposes.)

The Celest is the variety very largely grown throughout all but the Texas portion of the Fig Belt. In the Gulf Coast region of Texas, the Magnolia is of similar, or perhaps even greater, relative importance than the Celest is elsewhere.

Figs grown in the humid regions of the South Atlantic Coastal Plain and the Gulf Regions are extremely perishable. They will ferment and sour under ordinary conditions within a comparatively short time after they are picked. Prompt utilization of the fruit, as it ripens, is imperative. (All figs will spoil more quickly in damp, muggy, rainy weather than in bright, clear weather.)

The Black Mission variety has a skin that is almost black when fully ripe. They are good for eating out of hand, stewing, or for pies and cakes.

Brown Turkey (or Brown Naples of Blue Burgundy) figs are medium to large, short, and pear-shaped. They have a thick stalk, a red flesh, and are brownish-purple with bluish bloom. They are juicy and richly flavored.

The Brunswick variety is very large, broad, and pear-shaped, with short, rather slender stalk. Ribs are well marked, with a dark brown tough skin. The pulp is thick, pink, and soft. The Brunswick is of fair quality and produced mid- to late-season.

The Calimyrna is a generally large, greenish-yellow, very sweet fig. Its somewhat nut-like flavor makes it ideal for hand-eating.

Celeste figs are small to medium in size, pear-shaped, ribbed, violet in color, but sometimes shaded purplish-brown. They have short, stout stems; white flesh (shading to rose-color at center); and are firm, juicy, sweet, and of excellent quality. Celeste is one of the hardiest varieties of figs and can be grown far outside the usual limits of culture. Its season is early. They are very desirable for canning and preserving.

Known as the Dottato in some countries, the Kadota figs are large, green or yellowish-green, pear-shaped with a thick neck. They have violet-tinted flesh, and are juicy and excellent quality.

Optimum storage is at 32°F and 90 percent relative humidity—but it is best to plan on eating immediately! Ripeness can be ascertained by the degree of softness to the touch, while overripeness is detected by a sour odor, due to fermentation of the juice.

Most fruits are picked mature-green for shipping, but the fig must be tree-ripened to reach its full sugar content and provide proper eating quality.

Buy: Grade B Canned: Bright light green color; 75 percent difference in weight range allowed; maximum 3 severed figs, maximum 2 tough woody stems per 30 ounces and 1 piece extraneous material per 10 ounces; maximum 20 percent defects; tender texture.

Grade B Dried: Reasonably well matured and uniform size; typical color, good flavor, no foreign material.

Fruit Cocktail

Buy: Grade A Canned: Reasonably clear, bright syrup; fruit typically colored with no pink stain; peaches, pears, and pineapple: ⅜ to ¾ inch arc, ½ to ⁵⁄₁₆ inch thick, ¾ to 1¼ inches long; grapes, 300 percent maximum weight variation; 33⅓ percent maximum cherry half-length variation; practically free from defects and extraneous material; 5 percent blemishes, tender fruit.

Deterioration: Excessive sediment, poor color, presence of hard or mushy pieces of fruit, and excessive number of cap stems on the grapes. Fruit variability in size or excessively small.

Fruits for Salad

Buy: Grade A Canned: Reasonably uniform, bright, typical well matured fruit with only slight pink staining; apricots: maximum 75 percent weight difference; peaches or pears: maximum 60 percent weight difference; pineapple: ⁵⁄₁₆ to ½ inch thick, ¹¹⁄₁₆ to 1¼ inches long; must have some characteristics as Grade A or B apricots, pears, peaches and Grade A pineapple.

Deterioration: Excessive sediment in packing medium. Poor color with oxidation. Peel, hard, crushed, or frayed fruit.

Canned fruits for salad consist of apricots, yellow cling peaches, pears, pineapple, cherries, and/or grapes in the styles and proportions stated in the following table.

PROPORTION OF FRUITS

Fruits	Forms (or styles)	Proportion Not Less Than	Not More Than
Apricots	Unpeeled or peeled quarters or halves	15%	30%
Yellow cling peaches	Peeled quarters or slices	23%	45%
Pears	Peeled quarters or slices	19%	38%
Pineapple	Wedge-shaped segments from slices	8%	16%
Cherries	Whole, artificially-colored red, and/or artificially-flavored	3%	8%
Grapes	Whole, natural, seedless	6%	12%

**FRUITS FOR SALAD: GRADE A MINIMUM
COUNTS OF FRUIT UNITS**

Style	#2½ Cans	#10 Cans
Halves apricots	5 each of	20 each of
Quartered peaches	5 fruits	3 or more
Quartered pears		fruits

Tropical Fruits for Salad

This product is packed in the Philippines only, by one major processor. The approximate ingredient percentages are:

Pineapple tidbits:45%
Papaya, diced:37%
Banana slices:15%
Cherry halves (artificially-colored): 3%

The packing medium, consisting of Guava puree, Pineapple juice, and passion fruit juice, can and should be used as part of the serving portion in weight. This generally offers more servings per container than fruits for salad, diced fruit mix, or fruit cocktail.

As yet there are no U.S. Standards for Grade on this item, but the color should be bright, the sizing of each unit practically uniform, and the texture tender. The bananas used are of a specific variety which resists darkening, even when exposed to the air for long periods of time.

Granadilla

Passion Fruit: This fruit, sometimes called the purple granadilla (gran-a-dill-a), grows extensively in South America and Australia and is now being cultivated in California in increasing quantities. Passion fruit, which is the size and shape of an egg, has a tough, purple skin. The meat is yellow, with many black seeds, and is generally eaten in the fresh stage with a spoon. It is also used in cakes, jellies, or made into a beverage.

Sweet Granadilla: Not as well-known as the purple granadilla, its flavor is considered even finer. It is oval shaped, 3 to 6 inches long, with an orange-brown, tough, leathery skin. The pulp is translucent and whitish. Its uses are the same as passion fruit.

Giant Granadilla: The largest of the granadillas, its fruit is oblong, measuring up to 10 inches in length. Resembling a short, thick vegetable marrow, the giant granadilla is yellow-green in color and contains a mass of purple sweet-acid pulp mixed with flat seeds. Its flavor is inferior to purple and sweet granadillas. In the West Indies, it is called "watermelon."

Grapefruit

Two grapefruit of the same size will often vary in taste and juiciness. One will be heavy, firm, and smoothly textured, with a well-rounded shape, or flattened—a good indication of fine, juicy grapefruit. The other will be coarse, puffy, and rough—indicative of lack of juice, as well as taste. Since grapefruit is, on the average, over three-quarters liquid, heaviness is a good indication of juice content.

Do not rely solely on color as an index to flavor, as good grapefruit can range from pale yellow to russet or bronze. Brightly colored fruit is naturally more appealing, yet a russeted fruit may often be tastier and juicier. Minor surface blemishes do not affect the eating quality, although the presence of a bad bruise may indicate some internal breakdown, which is not apparent on the outside.

Skin color does not indicate ripeness. As in all citrus, a grapefruit tree may have blossoms, immature fruit, and ripe fruit on it all at the same time. In the spring, extra chlorophyll produced for new bloom tinges the already ripened fruit with green color. This natural process is called *regreening* and in no way affects the quality. Grapefruit is never artificially colored.

Florida and Texas are the principal producing states between the months of September and June, supplemented between January and June by grapefruit growing in the deserts of Arizona and California. Summer grapefruit originates principally in California. The two main types are the Duncan, containing numerous seeds, and the Marsh seedless, which has very few seeds. The pink-meated grapefruit, relatively a newcomer in the citrus realm, is a cross-bred creation, and many people consider the ''pink-meats'' somewhat sweeter than others. These popular varieties are known as Foster Pinks, Thompson Pinks or Marsh Pinks, and Ruby Reds—the latter two varieties being relatively seedless.

For purely psychological reasons, the favorite of most consumers is the Ruby Red grapefruit, because of its ''eye'' appeal. The variety is one of nature's million dollar mistakes! It was discovered as a bud mutation on a Thompson pink tree. Horticulturists grafted bud wood to several orange rootstocks, thus propagating what we know now as the ''Ruby Red'' grapefruit. It is the primary grapefruit grown in Texas, and is also grown in large quantities in Florida.

Today, the Star Ruby is a new strain developed in Texas and is reputed to have a much deeper red than the Ruby Red, and to be sweeter and have a higher acid content. Also, it is supposed to hold its color later in the season and have a reddish-gold peel color that could be extraordinary.

The Indian River area of Florida, a narrow strip of land along the east coast of the state, stretching from Daytona on the north to West Palm Beach on the south, has long been noted for its production of top quality citrus. About 50 percent of the state's fresh-marketed grapefruit crop is grown in the area and has been the backbone of the area's citrus production; orange and various mandarin tree plantings have increased dramatically in recent years.

Little known even in the industry is the basic size-of-fruit difference between Florida and ''other'' grapefruit. Since this fruit, like many others, is sized and sold by count per half-box carton, the larger-sized carton used in Florida makes their fruit, size for size, about one size larger than the same count-size fruit from Texas, California, or Arizona!

Grapefruit should be held at 50°F and 85 percent relative humidity.

Deterioration: Rough, ridged, or wrinkled skin, or pointed shape may indicate thick skin, pulpiness, and lack of juice.

U.S. No. 1 grade for Florida grapefruit consists of grapefruit which meet the following requirements: [a] Basic requirements: (1) discoloration: (i) Not more than one-third of the surface, in the aggregate, may be affected by discoloration; (2) Fairly smooth texture; (3) Fairly well colored; (4) Firm; (5) Mature; (6) Similar varietal characteristics; and (7) Well formed. [b] Free from: (1) Bruises; (2) Cuts not healed; (3) Decay; (4) Growth cracks; (5) Wormy fruit. [c] Free from damage caused by: (1) Ammoniation; (2) Buckskin; (3) Caked melanose; (4) Dirt or other foreign material; (5) Disease; (6) Dryness or mushy condition; (7) Green spots; (8) Hail; (9) Insects; (10) Oil spots; (11) Scab; (12) Scale; (13) Scars; (14) Skin breakdown; (15) Sprayburn; (16) Sprouting; (17) Sunburn; (18) Thorn scratches; and (19) Other means.[5]

Size and Count	Pack	Rows	Layers	Diameter Range
18	2 × 2	3	3	9/16 in.
23	3 × 2	3	3	9/16 in.
32	4 × 3	3	3	7/16 in.
40	4 × 5	3	3	7/16 in.
48	3 × 3	4	4	5/16 in.
56	4 × 3	4	4	5/16 in.

Buy: Grade B Canned: Fairly bright but not off color; 50 percent whole segments; no serious dry, ricey or fibrous cells.

Deterioration of Canned Sections: Color lacking brightness, noticeable tinge of amber color, and excessive number of broken segments. Floating free cells and mushy, fibrous segments. Prominent presence of seeds and portions of membranes. Noticeable scorched, bitter, or flat taste.

Canned Grapefruit Juice: Should be of the unfermented liquid obtained from nature-fresh grapefruit, properly-prepared, and with the juice extracted and processed in a manner to assure a clean, wholesome product. Top grade juice must possess a good color of either a pale yellow to very slightly amber, typical of the juice of properly ripened white-fleshed grapefruit; or slightly red, typical of the juice of red or deep pink-fleshed grapefruit. It should be practically free from defects such as seeds or seed portions, discolored specks, and particles of membrane, core, and peel material from the fruit. The juice must possess a fine, distinct flavor, typical of freshly-extracted grapefruit juice, free from excessive bitterness or container flavors.

Deterioration: Carmelized or oxodized flavor. Dull, murky, or off color. Excessive seed particles, suspended pulp, or residue.

---

[5]USDA Code.

Grade B Frozen: Same as canned; maximum 10 percent damaged; fleshy, firm.

Deterioration of Frozen, Concentrated: Tan or gray off-color. Excessive amounts of pulp and small seed particles.

Blended grapefruit/orange juice is the wholesome product prepared from a combination of undiluted, unconcentrated, unfermented juices obtained from mature fresh grapefruit and sweet oranges. The blend in the juices used is usually 50 percent grapefruit and 50 percent orange juice. When oranges yielding light-colored juice are used, as much as 75 percent orange juice may be used.

Top grade product should possess a light yellow-orange color which is bright and typical of freshly extracted juice, and be free from browning due to scorching, oxidation, carmelization, or other causes. The juice should be practically free from particles of membrane, core, skin material and seeds, or portions of seeds. The blended juices should possess a flavor that is fine, distinct, and substantially typical of freshly-extracted grapefruit and orange juice, free from off-flavors, from the container, or processing and storage.

GRAPEFRUIT COST TABLE Cost per Grapefruit—in cents

COST PER CARTON IN DOLLARS	SIZE OF GRAPEFRUIT						
	(LARGE)		(MEDIUM)			(SMALL)	
	27	32	36	40	48	56	64
4.00	14¾¢	12½¢	11 ¢	10 ¢	8¼¢	7¼¢	6¼¢
4.50	16¼	14	12½	11¼	9½	8	7
5.00	18½	15½	13¾	12½	10¼	8¾	7¾
5.50	20¼	17¼	15¼	13¾	11½	9¾	8½
6.00	22¼	18¾	16½	15	12½	10¾	9¼
6.50	24	20¼	18	16¼	13½	11½	10
7.00	26	22	19¼	17½	14½	12½	11
7.50	27¾	23¼	20¾	18¾	15½	13¼	11¾
8.00	29½	25	22¼	20	16½	14¼	12½
8.50	31½	26½	23½	21¼	17½	15¼	13¼
9.00	33¼	28	25	22½	18¾	16	14
9.50	35	29½	26¼	23¾	19¾	17	14¾
10.00	37	31¼	27¾	25	20¾	17¾	15½

Reprinted with permission Sunkist Growers, Inc. SUNKIST is a trademark of Sunkist Growers, Inc.

EQUIVALENTS OF FOOD MEASURES

Grapefruit, medium . . . . 1 . . . . 10 to 12 sections

Grapefruit, medium . . . . 1 . . . . ⅔ cup juice

CHECK THIS SIZE CHART TO FIND THE SIZE GRAPEFRUIT BEST SUITED TO YOUR SERVICE.

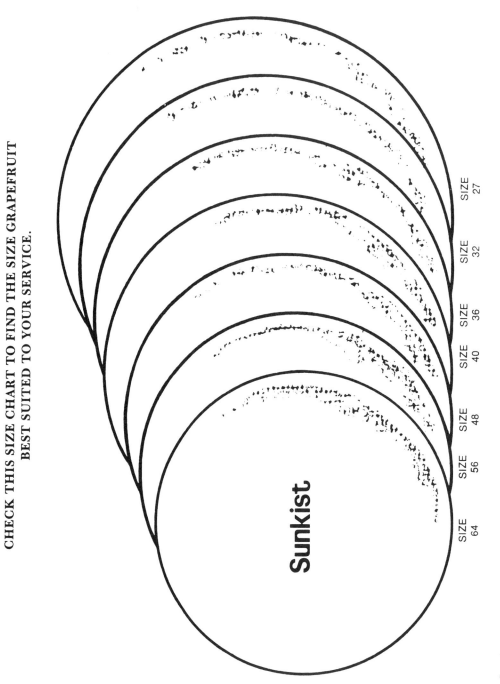

SIZE 27

SIZE 32

SIZE 36

SIZE 40

SIZE 48

SIZE 56

SIZE 64

Sunkist

Reprinted with permission Sunkist Growers, Inc. SUNKIST is a trademark of Sunkist Growers, Inc.

Grapefruit and Orange for Salad

Buy: Grade B Canned: Fairly bright typical color; 50 percent to 75 percent whole segments; maximum 15 percent damaged; no serious dry, ricey, or fibrous cells; orange 32½ percent, grapefruit 60 percent.

Deterioration: Color lacking brightness, noticeable tinge of amber color, and excessive number of broken segments. Floating free cells and mushy, fibrous segments. Prominent presence of seeds and portions of membranes. Noticeable scorched, bitter, or flat taste.

Grapes

Grapes for commercial use are divided into four major groups: table, raisin, wine, and juice. Canning is a minor group. The same grape may be in more than one, or even in all, groups, such as the Thompson Seedless, which is suitable for all five types of uses. A limited number of varieties produce wines of good quality—and raisins, for example, are produced mainly from three varieties.

Table grapes are those intended for use as fresh fruit, either for food or decorative purposes. Fewer than a dozen varieties are grown extensively for table grapes.

When selecting grapes, choose those bunches that are well formed and good looking. Color is a good guide to ripeness. The darker varieties should be free of a green tinge, while white grapes should have a decided amber coloring when completely matured. Fully ripened grapes are fairly soft to the touch and tender to the taste.

Unlike some other fruit, grapes will not improve in color, sugar, nor quality after they have been harvested. Therefore, they should not be expected to ripen after leaving the vine.

California produces about 90 percent of the table and juice grapes, all of the European (Vitis vinifera) species. Table grapes are available from early June through April or May. The eastern states produce the Vitis labrusca (American type) species and these grapes are available in fall months only.

You will find that the skin of a California grape adheres tightly to the pulp, but its seeds are easily removed. This, however, is just the opposite of the eastern grape, for the skin of the latter separates from the pulp easily while its seeds are difficult to pry away from the meat.

Generally speaking, the western varieties are the sweeter of the two, although eastern varieties are eaten out of hand, and made into jellies, wines, or grape juices.

In California and Arizona, several varieties are sprayed at bloom time with a gibberellin material as a thinning spray; and for Thompson's and most varieties, it is frequently used as a post-bloom application to increase the berry size. The method of application is in a water spray with a wetting agent. The material lengthens stems and delays maturity in proportion to the increase in berry size. Used on Perlettes, Thompson Seedless, Beauty Seedless, and Emperors, the gibberellin-treated grapes produce large, oval-shaped berries with firm flesh, mild taste, and a sweet, fine flavor. Berry size for Thompson's will increase 40 to 60 percent over untreated grapes.

Listed below (alphabetically, not in order of importance) are the most important varieties:

Almeria. A yellow-green, fairly sweet white grape, slight Muscat flavor.

Calmeria. Large, elongated berry with firm pulp. Green-white color with fairly thick skin. Mild in flavor.

Cardinal. Handsome dark-red berries that may attain an inch or more in diameter. Clusters are long and conical. Mild tasting, delicious.

Catawba. Large, purplish-red, distinctive flavor. Sometimes a table grape, but mostly used for wine and juice. Best storing of the American type.

Concord. Blue; the standard eastern variety, unexcelled for grape juice, jelly, or table use. Now the principal American type grape.

Delaware. Small, pink, tender skin. Used as table grape and for wine.

Emperor. Red; the latest maturing California variety; large, red festive berries with a cherry flavor. Clusters are large and very full.

Exotic. Large, black berry; clusters are long, full, and handsome. Flesh is crisp; taste is subtle.

Flame Tokay. Red, large, round berries; medium to large bunches.

Lady Finger. A pale green, large, very elongated white grape.

Malaga. White Malaga, medium-size bunches, round-white, medium-size berries; Red Malaga, larger, round-red berries.

Muscat. A greenish-yellow, oval-white grape, used for wine.

Niagara. Large, amber, with heavy gray bloom; medium sugar content; coarse and rather sour flavor.

Perlettes. A white, rather small, round to olive-shaped berry; fairly small to medium-sized bunches, rather compact, tight bunches. The earliest maturing California variety, seedless.

Ribier. Black, large, round berries; small to large bunches.

Thompson Seedless. White, small, olive-shaped berries; sweet and seedless.

Grapes are highly perishable, so handle them carefully. They should be refrigerated near 32°F, 90 percent relative humidity. Use them quickly, while they are at their very best!

Deterioration: Soft or wrinkled berries, grapes with bleached areas around the stem end, leaking and decayed berries.

U.S. No. 1 grade consists of bunches of well developed grapes of one variety (except when designated as assorted varieties) which are mature and fairly well colored. The berries shall be:

firm, firmly attached to capstems, and shall not be weak, materially shriveled at capstems, shattered, split, crushed, or wet, and shall be free from decay, waterberry, and sunburn, and free from damage caused by scarring, discoloration, heat, Almeria Spot, mildew, other diseases, freezing, insects, or mechanical, or other means.

Bunches shall not be straggly. They shall be free from damage caused by shot berries, dried berries, or other defective berries, or by the trimming away of defective berries, and each bunch shall weigh not less than one-fourth pound.

Stems shall not be weak, or dry and brittle, and shall be free from mold, and free from damage caused by mildew or freezing.[6]

Buy: Grade A Canned: Reasonably uniform color typical of variety; reasonably uniform size and consistency.

Canned grape juice is unfermented, unconcentrated, undiluted liquid obtained from properly-matured fresh grapes. If the product is made from concentrate it must so state on the label.

Two types of grape juice are available on the market:

1. Pure Concord Grape Juice: Prepared solely from the juice of Concord grapes. This is generally accepted as the most desirable juice in color, flavor, and overall appeal.
2. Blended Grape Juice: Prepared from a blend of Brazilian and California white and red grapes which may or may not be blended with Concord grape juice. It is a general rule that the smaller the percentage of Concord grape juice used in the blend, the lower the quality and price of the end-product.

Top grade juice should possess a good bright purple or bright reddish-purple translucent color. Blended juices should have a color typical of the varietal types from which the product has been prepared. The juice must be practically free from sediment and other residue; particles of skin, pulp, and seed; and other defects which detract from the overall quality of the product. The flavor should be distinct and normal, typical of well-matured grapes. The canned juice should be free from traces of scorched, astringent, carmelized, or other objectionable off-flavors of any kind.

Deterioration: Tartrate crystals, skins and pulp, scorched or carmelized flavor.

Deterioration in Frozen, Concentrated: Tartrate crystals, skins and pulp, scorched or carmelized flavor.

Guava

Grown extensively in Hawaii, Florida, and southern California, but native to Mexico and South America, guava (gwá-va) is a member of the custard apple family, grown on small trees or bushes.

Fruit varies in size, shape, color, and flavor. Most common varieties are pineapple and strawberry, so-called because of their similarity in flavor to these fruits. Shape is round, 1 to 4 inches in length, usually with flesh ranging from white to deep pink or salmon red. Numerous small seeds are embedded in flesh toward the center of the fruit. Skin color is from green to yellow, depending on variety.

For cooking, choose guavas that are firm to the touch; for eating out-of-hand, ripen at room temperature until they give slightly to gentle pressure. They may be refrigerated after reaching the ripe stage and will keep for some time.

[6]USDA Code.

Kiwi Fruit

Native of China, the Kiwi (kee-wee) was first introduced into New Zealand in 1906 and has been commercially cultivated only in that country. The fruit is really a Chinese gooseberry.

The fruit is light brown, ''furry'' appearing, measuring 2½ to 3½ inches in length. It is elongated with a very tender, soft skin. The interior texture is very similar to the American gooseberry and quite delectable.

It should be soft as a ripe pear for best eating. Ripen at room temperature and then refrigerate. It can be eaten out-of-hand after peeling, incorporated into salads or fruit compotes. Kiwi is in the market from June to March.

Kumquats

Native of China, the kumquat (come-kwat) resembles an orange, but the size is generally 2 to 2½ inches, football-shaped. This fruit is unusual in that the skin is sweet and the flesh is tart. It is used for Christmas table decorations, preserves, jellies, and candied fruit. It may be eaten raw, skin and all. Choose firm kumquats; they will keep for some time without refrigeration.

Lemons

Most lemons are sorted and re-sorted throughout the season to secure proper color and maturity. An expensive ''electric eye'' machine has been developed to separate yellow, silver, light green, or dark green at the rate of 40 fruits per second, with high accuracy, but most color separating is still done by the experienced ''naked eye.'' Similar to a terminal market tomato ripening-packing operation, as lemons are graded, the too-green are separated back into field boxes or bins, and sent to ''curing rooms.'' They are eventually withdrawn at a later date and again color-graded.

The best lemons have a fine-textured skin and are heavy for their size. Those that are coarse skinned, or light in weight, have less juice. The fruit that has a slightly greenish cast is likely to have more acid than those that are deep yellow. Deep yellow lemons are usually more mature than light yellow, and not quite as acid.

Under ideal storage conditions, 58 to 60°F and 89 to 91 percent relative humidity, a USDA test revealed that: (1) lemons lost weight at the rate of only 2 to 3 percent a month; (2) juice content of the individual lemons increased after 1 to 2 months in storage; (3) acid yield increased the first month; and (4) ascorbic acid concentration remained nearly constant throughout seven months' storage.

Deterioration: Fruit that is shriveled, hard-skinned, or soft or spongy, or with brown discolored sunken areas are indications of aging and deterioration.

CHECK THIS SIZE CHART TO FIND THE SIZE OF LEMON BEST SUITED TO YOUR SERVICE

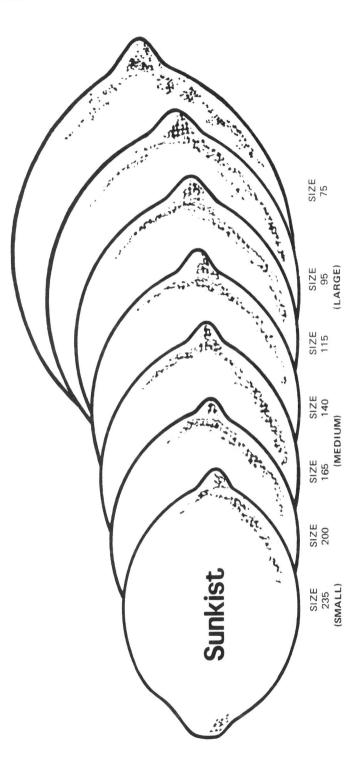

SIZE
75

SIZE
95
(LARGE)

SIZE
115

SIZE
140
(MEDIUM)

SIZE
165

SIZE
200

SIZE
235
(SMALL)

Sunkist

Reprinted with permission Sunkist Growers, Inc. SUNKIST is a trademark of Sunkist Growers, Inc.

LEMON COST TABLE (COST PER LEMON—IN CENTS)

Cost per Carton in Dollars	Size of Lemons						
	(Large)		(Medium)		(Small)		
	75	95	115	140	165	200	235
6.00	8	6 ¼	5	4 ¼	3 ½	3	2 ½
7.00	9 ¼	7 ¼	6	5	4 ¼	3 ½	3
8.00	10 ½	8 ¼	6 ¾	5 ¾	4 ¾	4	3 ¼
9.00	12	9 ½	7 ¾	6 ½	5 ½	4 ½	3 ¾
10.00	13 ¼	10 ½	8 ¾	7 ¼	6	5	4 ¼
11.00	14 ½	11 ½	9 ½	7 ¾	6 ½	5 ½	4 ¾
12.00	16	12 ½	10 ½	8 ½	7 ¼	6	5
13.00	17 ¼	13 ½	11 ¼	9 ¼	7 ¾	6 ½	5 ½
14.00	18 ½	14 ¾	12	10	8 ½	7	6
15.00	20	15 ½	13	10 ½	9	7 ¼	6 ¼
16.00	21 ¼	16 ¾	13 ¾	11 ¼	9 ½	8	6 ¾

Reprinted with permission Sunkist Growers, Inc. SUNKIST is a trademark of Sunkist Growers, Inc.

Limes

Only acid type limes are grown in the United States, while sweet limes are popular in many other citrus growing areas. Acid limes are further divided into Tahiti (large fruits) and Mexican (small fruits with thin rinds) types.

Varieties of the Tahiti type include *Persian* (called Tahiti in California), *Bearss, Idemore,* and *Pond.* The Persian variety is the most extensively grown commercially. Its outstanding characteristics include large size, fine grained pulp, light greenish-yellow color, very acid, and highly flavored. Fruit color, when fully ripe, is light orange-yellow (marketed at green mature state). Fruit matures the year-round.

The Bearss is the principal lime variety in California. It is distinguished from the Persian by its smaller fruit and very juicy pulp. It is very acid, of excellent quality, with no seeds. Fruit color, when fully ripe, is light lemon-yellow. Its season is winter to late spring, with fruit maturing more or less throughout the year.

Under the Mexican group is the Key lime of Florida, known as *Mexican* in southwestern United States; as *Dominican* when imported from the Dominican Republic; or *West Indian* when imported from any of the West Indies. Mexican limes are distinguished by light lemon-yellow color of fruit, round to oval shape, and small size. The rind is smooth, leathery, and very thin. The juice is abundant, and the flavor is strong and very acid. Its season is late fall to spring, maturing more or less in some volume throughout the year. Mexican limes are marketed when fully ripe.

With reference to Persian type limes, those that are green in color and heavy for their size are the most desirable.

Deterioration: Dull, dry skin is an indication of aging and loss of acid flavor.

Litchi or Lychee

Methods of spelling this fruit are as numerous as Chinese dialects! The litchi or lychee (lee-chee or lye-chee) is a schizophrenic fruit which can become a nut if it is dried after maturing. Vastly popular in Asia for 2,000 years, it is now grown in Jamaica, Hawaii, Brazil, Florida, and California. The matured fruit looks like overgrown strawberries prior to being picked. After picking, the attractive red color disappears. Fruit can be stored for two or three weeks without losing its flavor, which is similar to a Muscat grape (although some say it tastes more like raisins or Royal Ann cherries).

The outer covering is hard and bitter, rough on the surface, and divided into small scale-like areas from which short conical protuberances usually arise.

As a dried fruit, it is well-known and is shipped to the United States and other countries, while considerable quantity is preserved in syrup and exported. Like most other fruits, however, it is considered most delicious when fresh.

Loquat

The loquat (lo-kwatt) is produced in Northern India and Japan. It is popular in Mediterranean countries, but rare in the United States. The fruit is round or oval, 1 to 3 inches in length, pale yellow or orange, with a somewhat downy surface and up to 10 large seeds. Thin skin, flesh firm and mealy, color from white to deep orange, juicy, of sub-acid flavor, the loquat is somewhat reminiscent of a cherry. They may be eaten fresh, stewed, or made into pies and jelly or sauce. They are available during April and May. Reportedly, a loquat is a cross between the banana and pineapple.

Mandarins

Mandarins botanically refer to three classifications of oranges: (1) Satsumas, (2) Tangerines, and (3) Miscellaneous hybrids, which include the Tangelo (Orlando, Minneola, etc.), the Tangors (King, Murcott, Temple), and complex hybrids (Robinson, Lee, Page, etc.).

There are a multitude of tangerine varieties, and an even greater number of "complex hybrids." Throughout the United States, retailers generally identify the varieties that are rather small, deep-orange colored, with a rather soft, short-necked, pebbly skin as "tangerines." "Tangelos" are generally identified in this way—and some retailers add the "Orlando" or "Minneola" to their description.

Despite the urging of receivers, California and Arizona continue to designate their mandarin sizes with alleged word descriptions, having no reference to pieces of fruit per container.

For storage, temperatures of 38 to 40°F, with a relative humidity of 90 to 95 percent is considered ideal. During transport, the humidity may be the same, but temperature should be 32 to 38°F.

Select fruit that is heavy for its size, which indicates ample juice content, and that is a deep orange, or almost red, color. A "puffy" appearance and "feel" is normal for

Size Designation	Diameter Inches
Super Colossal	3.25–3.75
Colossal	3.00–3.25
Mammoth	2.75–3.00
Jumbo	2.50–2.75
Large	2.25–2.50
Medium	2.00–2.25
Small	1.75–2.00

many varieties, but it should still have the weight, and there should be no soft, water-soaked areas or mold.

Following is a brief description of some of the major mandarins:

Clementine (Algerial) Mandarin. One of the earliest varieties to reach our markets. Generally called an Algerian tangerine. Fruit size is medium to large, and shape varies from slightly elongated to slightly flattened. The fruit has a red-orange pebbled rind which peels easily. Seed number varies from none to many.

Dancy Tangerine. Has a lively, sweet-tart flavor with many seeds in a loose, easy-to-peel rind. When the fruit becomes overripe, the rind looks dry and puffy.

Fairchild Tangerine. Principally grown in desert areas. Generally medium to large size, slightly flat, smooth skin, and deep orange color. Peels easily, many seeds, has a rich and sweet taste.

Fortune Tangerine. Principally grown in desert areas. Fruit slightly flat, red-orange color, slightly ''lumpy'' appearing with a tight rind sometimes difficult to peel. Many seeds, flavor brisk and sub-acid.

Fremont Tangerine. Grown in desert areas, slightly flat, red-orange color, and smooth skin easy to peel. Many seeds, a slightly acid, but sweet, flavor.

Kara Mandarin. A hybrid, it is a rather large mandarin with a pebbled to slightly rough, orange-colored rind. Fruit is deep oblate, usually with a small neck. Peels fairly well, has an attractive deep orange pulp, a medium number of seeds, and an excellent, rich flavor.

Kinnow. This is another hybrid Tangor whose trees are alternate bearers with consequent small fruit size in the heavy crop years. The fruit is slightly flattened with no neck, and it has a smooth, orange rind. The number of seeds is high and the segments do not separate easily. Fruit grown in the desert areas peel better than when grown elsewhere. It has a rich and sweet flavor with thin, tender membranes around the segments. Very heavy fruit for its size.

Minneola Tangelo. This is actually a grapefruit-tangerine cross, but in all characteristics, it resembles the tangerine. Well-suited for growing in the desert areas, produces fruit of good size and appearance; red-orange; and slightly elongated, often with some neck. Pulp is tender and fine-textured. Flavor is fair to good with a grapefruit-like tartness.

Murcott (recently renamed *Honey Tangerine*). A Tangor fruit grown principally in Florida. Exceedingly sweet, rich, thin-skinned; fairly easily peeled. Like the Kinnow, very heavy for its size, very firm, extraordinarily good keeping qualities.

Orlando. This Tangelo has the same parentage as the Minneola. Fruit is of medium size, slightly flattened, and has an attractive, deep orange rind. Does not peel easily.

Satsuma. This is the principal variety of Japan. Fruit size is medium to small. Fruit may be smooth and rather flattened but sometimes quite rough and necked. The rind is orange, pebbled, and peels readily. Essentially seedless.

Temple. No one knows the exact parentage, but it is believed to be a cross between a tangerine and an orange. It is one of the finest quality citrus fruits grown in the United States, but it has not done well in California. Generally of large size with a slightly rough red-orange rind. Shape varies from spherical to slightly flattened. Generally firm and juicy with quite a few seeds. The flavor is distinct, rich, spicy, and sweet-tart.

Wilking Mandarin. This is a hybrid that has excellent flavor, but the trees are extreme alternate bearing and in most areas have small fruit in heavy crop years. The fruit is firm, slightly flattened, and without a neck. The rind is orange, fine-pebbled, and peels fairly well. Flesh is deep orange, with a considerable number of seeds.

Mangos

Mangos may be varied in size and shape, depending on variety and the area in which they are grown. They are generally eaten raw, but green mangos are often used in many forms of sauces or preserves, as well as for pickling. Buy mangos that are firm, and then let ripen at room temperature until the fruit gives easily to slight pressure. Refrigerate until ready for use. Mangos should not be cut until just before serving, in order to conserve the aroma.

Once fully ripened, mangos should be stored at 50°F and 85 percent relative humidity. Mangos are on the market from January through late August from various shipping areas.

Mangosteen

Native to the Far East, this unusual fruit is similar in taste to the lychee and mango. It may be eaten out-of-hand or made into preserves. The exterior is reddish-brown in color with a thick and very hard rind enclosing a number of segments (like those of an orange). The juicy flesh has a flavor suggesting those of the peach and pineapple. The pericarp of this fruit is used as an astringent. The mangosteen is the size of a mandarin orange, round, and slightly flattened at each end. It has a white juicy pulp with a cool and refreshing sweet-tart flavor. It may contain 5 to 7 segments, and probably 1 to 3 of the segments will contain seeds, which are very flavorful.

Melons

There is no absolutely sure guide for determining quality in melons from the outside, but some indicators are fairly dependable.

For cantaloupes, there should be no trace of a stem; there should be a very definite, pronounced cavity where the melon was pulled from the vine. If a cantaloupe is reasonably mature, the stem that attached it to the vine will slip easily and completely away. Experienced produce buyers look for this "full slip" condition when making their purchases.

Also observe the netting and shape, for if the netting covers the cantaloupe thickly and stands out like a whipcord, the melon has another merit point. The background color under the netting should ideally be a slight golden, or, at worst, a light greenish-gray. (Avoid completely a dull, dark green background color.)

Ideally, a cantaloupe should be football-shaped, or almost round, at worst. (Avoid lopsided or heavily indented melons.) It should have a delicate melon aroma. A slight rattling of the seeds, when shaken, is another sign of maturity; however, loose, watery seeds are, more than likely, the first sign of the last stages of maturity, and it could be slightly sour.

Plan to give cantaloupes two or three days at room temperature before serving. Time and warmth will not make it sweeter, but will soften the meat and make it juicier—two factors essential to melon appreciation.

Serve them in halves or wedges, or cut up the "meat" to use in fruit cups or salads. Another serving suggestion is to make an attractive dessert or main dish with melon balls.

Grades.   Federal cantaloupe grades as amended June 30, 1968 are U.S. Fancy, U.S. 1, U.S. Commercial, and U.S. 2. The grade used most is U.S. 1. This grade

> consists of cantaloupes of one type which are mature and have good internal quality, but are not overripe or soft or wilted, which are well formed, well netted and free from decay, wet slip and sunscald, and free from damage caused by liquid in the seed cavity, sunburn, hail, dirt, surface mold or other disease, aphids or other insects, scars, cracks, sunken areas, ground spot, bruises or mechanical or other means.[7]

A fully mature honeydew should be creamy white or pale yellow, even on the underside. Fruit should be large, at least 6½ to 7 inches in diameter, weighing about 5 to 7 pounds. Test the aroma, since a ripe honeydew has a distinct and pleasing fragrance. A very slight, oily film generally is noticeable on the outer rind, also.

Because large honeydew melons are "crown fruit" (those growing closest to the root of the plant), these are generally the best eating quality and more "meaty." Seldom is a small honeydew really fine eating, nor does it have a thick meat. Avoid completely honeydews with a noticeable greenish-white exterior.

Most honeydews must be shipped in a hard condition, and will then be pre-ripened in banana-ripening rooms before offered to the public. If the melon you purchase is hard, but meets the size, weight, and color requirements, let it stand in a warm room for several hours (or days), away from sunlight, preferably in high humidity, until the aroma and softness at the stem and blossom end appear. This is the only time you should then cut the melon for eating.

---

[7]USDA Code.

The honeyball is smaller than the honeydew and, instead of being smooth-surfaced, is covered with a thin but plainly visible netting. Honeyballs, when ripe, are slightly soft and fragrant. Generally their flesh is a light white-green color, although some varieties are pink-meated. Their season is from June to November.

Grades. U.S. standards for honeydews and honeyballs include:

> U.S. 1 consists of honeydew or honeyball type melons which are mature, firm, well formed, which are free from decay, and free from damage caused by dirt, aphis stain, rust spots, bruises, cracks, broken skin, sunscald, sunburn, hail, moisture, insects, disease or other means. . . . In order to allow for variations incident to proper grading and handling. . . , the following tolerances, by count, are provided as specified: (a) 10 percent for melons in any lot which fail to meet the requirements of the grade; provided that not more than one-half of this amount, or 5 percent, shall be allowed for defects causing serious damage, including in this latter amount not more than 1 percent for melons affected by decay . . .[8]

Among other melon varieties, you'll find the Casaba, large and round in shape, with a rigid and furrowed rind. It is golden yellow when ripe, with a white meat. The Santa Claus or Christmas melon looks like a small watermelon, but has the flesh of a honeydew. The Persian melon looks like a large flattened cantaloupe, but has a yellow skin and netting and pink meat.

One of the finest eating melons is the Crenshaw; this is a hybrid variety of muskmelon. It generally weighs 7 to 9 pounds, round at the base, and comes to a point at the stem end. It has a gold and green rind, which is smooth, with no netting and a little ribbing. The meat is a bright salmon color, thick, juicy, and very good when ripe.

As a general guide to selection of all of the above melons, the outer skin should be a good color, give off a rich aroma, and be slightly soft at the blossom end. Never cut any of these melons unless they are ripe—they do not ripen satisfactorily after cutting.

The essential factors of watermelon quality are maturity and size. The larger melons have more edible flesh, proportionately, than the smaller ones.

Color is the best key to ripeness in watermelons. A yellowish underside, regardless of the rich green color of the rest of the melon, is a good sign of ripeness. A watermelon is somewhat like a book, in that you can't always tell its contents by its cover. When you go to buy a whole melon, look for one that is symmetrically shaped and has a velvety bloom—a dull, rather than a shiney surface. The underside should be turning from white or pale green to a light yellowish color.

Avoid ''white heart'' in watermelons—a hard, white streak running lengthwise through the melon. Seeds, too, give a clue to ripeness. If the melon is fully matured, the seeds are usually dark brown or black. (Only one variety, the Improved Garrisonian, has white seeds.)

Deterioration: Melons with cuts or punctures through the rind, large bruised areas, and decay.

---

[8]USDA Code.

**MONTHLY AVAILABILITY OF WATERMELONS AS
PERCENTAGE OF TOTAL ANNUAL SUPPLY**

Jan. %	Feb. %	Mar. %	Apr. %	May %	June %
*	*	1	2	10	29

July %	Aug. %	Sept. %	Oct. %	Nov. %	Dec. %
31	20	6	1	*	*

*less than .5 percent

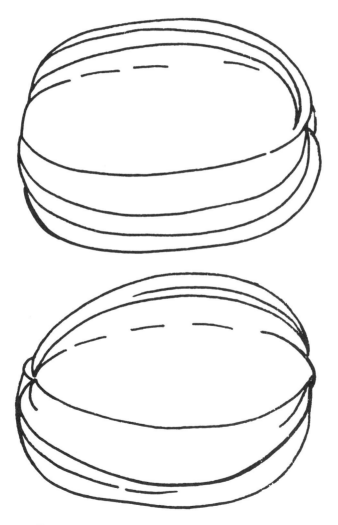

Two melons of round type illustrated
above are permitted in U. S. No. 1 grade

SHAPES OF LONG TYPE MELONS

Permissible in U. S. No. 1 Grade

Permissible in U. S. No. 2 Grade

Cull. Not Permissible in U. S. No. 2 Grade

Grades. U.S. standards for watermelons, effective March 22, 1954, provide for three grades: U.S. 1, U.S. Commercial and U.S. 2.

> U.S. 1 consists of watermelons of similar varietal characteristics which are mature but not overripe, fairly well formed, and which are free from anthracnose, decay, sunscald, and free from damage caused by other diseases, sunburn, hail, scars, insects, hollow heart, whiteheart, or mechanical or other means.
>
> Tolerances: In order to allow for variations incident to proper grading and handling, not more than a total of 10 percent, by count, of the watermelons in any lot may fail to meet the requirements of this grade; provided that not more than one-half of this amount, or 5 percent, may be badly misshapen, or seriously damaged by any means, including therein not more than 1 percent for decay.[9]

Melon Balls

Buy: Grade A Frozen: Bright overall appearance; reasonably uniform color; free from pale cantaloupe, dark green honeydew; maximum 20 percent rind spots; tender, well ripened melons that are not soft, mushy, fibrous, tough, or rubbery.

Nectarines

Historically, early nectarine varieties were small, fast-softening, and white-fleshed —primarily adapted to the home and local markets. But the new and better varieties have peach "blood" in the crosses, in order to get large size and firmness. When peaches are brought into the breeding, however, all the first generation progeny come in as peaches, making it necessary to back-cross the breeding to get the one out of four nectarines in recessive segregation.

Thus, a nectarine is a nectarine—it is not a fuzzless peach, and it is not (as popularly believed) a cross between a peach and a plum. Like other stone fruits, including cherries and apricots, it is a member of the rose family and closely related to peaches and almonds.

Like the peach, the nectarine does not gain sugar after harvest and, if not well matured when picked, it will be unsatisfactory tasting. In addition to maturity, ideal storage conditions of 32°F and 90 percent relative humidity will keep the product in ideal condition for short periods of time.

Newer nectarine varieties are large sized, bright red in color, and usually yellow fleshed freestones. Since most new varieties of nectarines have full, red color before they are mature, color is not a good maturity index. The development of flesh color and rounding out of the fruit are much better criteria of maturity. Bright-looking, plump fruit with an orange-yellow color between the red areas, firm to moderately hard, will probably ripen normally within 2 to 3 days at room temperature. Avoid fruit that is hard, dull, or slightly shriveled, for it was probably immature when picked. Avoid those with cracked or punctured skin or bruising. Russeting or staining of the skin may detract from appearance, but should have no effect on eating quality.

---

[9]USDA Code.

Deterioration: Hard, dull, or shriveled fruit may be immature. Fruit that has cracked or punctured skin or which is soft, overripe, or decayed.

U.S. No. 1 consists of nectarines of one variety which are mature but not soft or overripe, which are well formed, clean and free from decay, broken skins which are not healed, worms, worm holes, and free from injury caused by split pit, and free from damage caused by bruises, growth cracks, hail, sunburn, sprayburn, scab, bacterial spot, scale, scars, russeting, other disease, insects or mechanical, or other means. At least 75 percent of the nectarines in any lot shall show some blushed or red color, except that there are no color requirements for nectarines of the John Rivers variety in this grade.[10]

Fruit Nectars

Fruit nectars should be prepared from sound, ripe, raw produce with nutritive sweeteners, water, and citric acid added. Ascorbic acid may be added to preserve the color and improve the flavor. The product should be free of large specks and practically free of small specks. The product should be smooth and there should be no tendency for separation of insoluble solids from the liquid phase. The product should possess a distinct flavor typical of ripe fruit and be free from off-flavors.

Oranges

The weight of an orange is indicative of its juice content. Also, the fruit should be firm and have a skin that is not too rough.

Color is not a sure guide to quality because much of the Florida and Texas crop has coloring added to the outer skin. Such fruit is dipped in, or sprayed with, a harmless vegetable die solution at packing time. This process has absolutely no effect on the eating quality of the fruit; it simply gives the outer skin the deep orange color expected by consumers. The law requires that all oranges treated this way must be stamped "Color Added" and must have passed very strict maturity tests.

Varieties of oranges are generally divided into two general classifications: sour and sweet. The former is valuable only as a rootstock, but it is grown in some countries, particularly Spain, for its bitter or sour fruits. Mandarins or tangerines are considered distinct from the sweet orange grown in the United States, but the tangor hybrid Temple orange represents a sizeable volume.

The sweet orange can be divided into four principal kinds: the common (such as the Florida or California valencia); the book, or pigmented orange (such as the ruby); the acidless (grown in some Mediterranean areas); and the navel (grown principally in California but to smaller extent in Florida and Texas). These are not botanical classifications.

Valencia oranges, regardless of where produced, have a tendency late in the season to turn from a bright orange hue to a greenish tinge, particularly around the stem

---

[10]USDA Code.

end. Do not be misled by this change in color, as it affects only the outer skin. Actually these oranges are amply matured, and the inside is fully ripe, sweet, and juicy.

Optimum storage conditions are 32°F and 90 percent relative humidity. A common phrase, "Best for Juice and Every Use" applies to this fruit. For hand-eating, salads, or added as a topping to ice cream or day-old cake, oranges will add zest.

Since all oranges are still identified for size by count (72s and 88s being much larger than 113s or 100s), few people recognize that a Florida orange is approximately one size larger than the same count size from California, Arizona, or Texas!

Deterioration: Dull, dry skin and spongy texture, and discolored, weakened areas around the stem end indicate aging and deteriorated eating quality.

Servings and Weights. USDA reports that a California winter navel, 2⅘ in. in diameter, weighs 180 grams (6.3 oz.) and a Florida orange 3 in. in diameter weighs 210 grams or 7.35 oz. One cup of California Valencia (summer) orange juice weighs 249 grams; a cup of early and mid-season Florida juice, 247 grams; and a cup of Florida late season Valencia juice, 248 grams.

Small oranges, 3 to a lb., provide about ½ cup of fruit and juice per orange; or 3 servings per lb.; and require 33½ lb., as purchased, to serve 100 persons. A *medium orange,* 2 to the lb., provides about ⅔ cup of fruit and juice per orange, 2 servings per lb., and requires 50 lb. to serve 100.

ORANGE COST TABLE (COST PER ORANGE, IN CENTS)

Cost per Carton in Dollars	Size of Oranges						
	48	**56**	**72**	**88**	**113**	**138**	**163**
$3.00	6¼¢	5¼¢	4¼¢	3½¢	2¾¢	2¼¢	1¾¢
3.25	6¾	5¾	4½	3¾	3	2¼	2
3.50	7¼	6¼	4¾	4	3	2½	2¼
3.75	7¾	6¾	5¼	4¼	3¼	2¾	2¼
4.00	8¼	7¼	5½	4½	3½	3	2½
4.25	8¾	7½	6	4¾	3¾	3	2½
4.50	9½	8	6¼	5	4	3¼	2¾
4.75	10	8½	6½	5½	4¼	3½	3
5.00	10½	9	7	5¾	4½	3½	3
5.25	11	9½	7¼	6	4¾	3¾	3¼
5.50	11½	9¾	7½	6¼	4¾	4	3¼
5.75	12	10¼	8	6½	5	4¼	3½
6.00	12½	10¾	8¼	6¾	5¼	4¼	3¾
6.25	13	11¼	8¾	7	5½	4½	3¾
6.50	13½	11½	9	7¼	5¾	4¾	4
6.75	14	12	9¼	7¾	6	5	4¼
7.00	14½	12½	9¾	8	6¼	5	4¼

Reprinted with permission Sunkist Growers, Inc., SUNKIST is a trademark of Sunkist Growers, Inc.

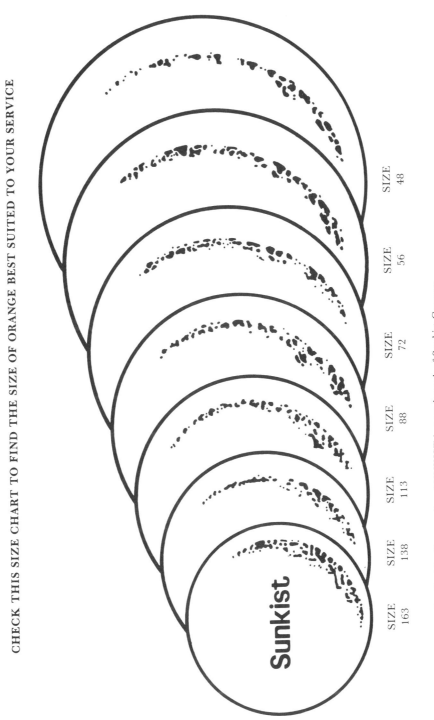

CHECK THIS SIZE CHART TO FIND THE SIZE OF ORANGE BEST SUITED TO YOUR SERVICE

SIZE 48

SIZE 56

SIZE 72

SIZE 88

SIZE 113

SIZE 138

SIZE 163

Sunkist

Reprinted with permission Sunkist Growers Inc. SUNKIST is a trademark of Sunkist Growers.

A *pound of oranges,* any size, is considered to provide 2.82 servings of ½ cup sections *with membrane,* requiring 35½ lb., as purchased, for 100 servings; or 5.64 ¼ cup sections with membrane, requiring 17¼ lb., as purchased, for 100 servings. One pound, as purchased, equals 0.7 lb. ready to serve.

A *pound of oranges* provides 2.26 servings of ½-cup sections *without membrane,* and requires 44¼ lb., as purchased, to serve 100; and 1 lb. provides 4.52 servings of ¼ cup sections without membrane and requires 22¼ lb. to serve 100. With such servings, 1 lb., as purchased, provides 0.56 lb. ready to serve.

A *pound of oranges* provides 1.83 servings of ½ cup of juice, requiring 54¾ lb., as purchased, for 100 servings; and 1 lb. of oranges provides 3.66 servings of ¼ cup of juice, requiring 27½ lb., as purchased, for 100 servings. One pound, as purchased, yields 0.5 lb. (1 cup) of juice.

Canned orange juice is prepared from the unfermented, undiluted, unconcentrated liquid from mature, fresh oranges. The juice extracted and processed in a manner to assure a clean, wholesome product.

There are two types of canned, fresh orange juice: Mid-Season juice, packed year-round from various varieties and blends of oranges, and Valencia juice, packed only during the summer months, from oranges of the Valencia variety. The Valencia product yields a more desirable juice in both color and flavor and demands a premium price in the market.

Top grade juice should possess a good, bright yellow to yellow-orange color, with no evidence of browning or carmelization due to scorching during processing. The product should be practically free from defects such as particles of membrane, core, skin, or seed. Canned orange juice must possess a fine, distinct flavor, definitely free from traces of scorched, oxidized or other off-flavors.

Deterioration: Carmelized or oxidized flavor. Dull, murky, or off-color. Excessive seed particles, suspended pulp, or residue.

Deterioration of Frozen, Concentrated: Low Brix. Off color and flavor. Seeds, peel, or excessive pulp.

Papayas

The papaya (pa-pie-ya) is native to tropical America but the original home is unknown. The plant grows almost like weeds throughout the tropics. They are extensively cultivated for export in Hawaii, while considerable amounts are grown in Puerto Rico and Florida. California grows some in the far south; however, the main source of supply for consumption is Hawaii.

Select fruit that is well colored, not green, but at least half yellow. The fruit should be smooth, unbruised, unbroken, showing no signs of deterioration or shriveling and be well shaped.

Papayas are available year-round, with peak production in the late winter and early spring.

The fruit is picked in the firm-ripe state and will ripen in 3 to 5 days at room temperature. After ripening, papayas can be stored as low as 32°F without damage. Fruit that is all yellow is generally ready to eat, and will keep for a week or two. The seeds are also edible. The milk-like juice of the papaya is prized as a remedy for dyspepsia because of its papain content, and in some eastern cities, it is being bottled and marketed as a healthful soft drink.

Grades. Hawaii has 3 grades in its Wholesale-Standards for Hawaii-Grown Papayas, Hawaii Fancy, Hawaii No. 1, and Hawaii No. 2.

> Hawaii No. 1 consists of Solo-type (a variety) papayas, which are mature but not overripe, clean, well trimmed, meet soluble solids requirements, fairly well formed, fairly smooth; and which are free from decay, breakdown, internal hard lumps, catfaces, brown spot, scars, disease, insects, mechanical, or other means. Unless otherwise specified or unless destined for export, the weight of each papaya shall be not less than 14 oz. nor more than 32 oz. in weight. Unless destined for export, papayas shall be pyriform in shape. (Note: Shipments to the U.S. are not exports but domestic, so that the detailed weight requirements of the grade apply.)[11]

Papaws

Native to North America, the papaw (paw-paw) is the oblong, yellowish fruit of an annonaceous tree of central and southern United States. The fruit has a sweet, many-seeded banana-like pulp. Papaws are often confused with papayas, but actually these two fruits are different. Papaws are about 6 inches in length, with a width of about 3 inches, and an average weight of ¾ pound. Its flesh is yellow, creamy in texture, and has a pungent odor. They are often not enjoyed at first—a taste for them has to be acquired.

Passion Fruit

See ''Granadilla'' elsewhere in this section.

Peaches

When purchasing peaches, the best thing to remember is that they must look good to be good. Buy peaches that are fairly firm, or becoming a trifle soft. A red color, or ''blush'' on the peach, in varying degrees, is not, alone, a true sign of edible quality. The skin color between the red areas (ground color) should be yellow, or at least creamy. Avoid very firm or hard peaches with a distinctly green ground color, for they are probably immature and will not ripen properly. Don't buy peaches with large, flattened bruises, for they will not ripen properly. Overripeness is generally indicated by the deeper reddish-brown color and a softness of the fruit—even a shriveling of the skin at the stem end. Peaches in this stage are suitable for immediate use, but cannot be held for any length of time.

New varieties, with more exterior glamour and taste appeal, are fast replacing some old favorites, such as the Elberta. In a general way, all early-maturing varieties

---

[11]USDA Code.

TALLY SHEET FOR CANNED CLINGSTONE PEACHES
(SAMPLE UNIT SIZE - 25 HALVES)

PLANT (Name)

| INSPECTOR (Name) | DATE | RING MARK | CAN SIZE | | CODE |
| GRADER (Name) | SHIFT | | SAMPLING FREQUENCY | | |

PERIOD CODE / LINE NUMBER						
TIME						
NET WEIGHT						
VACUUM						
HEAD SPACE						
COUNT						
SIRUP						
FILL WEIGHT / DRAINED WEIGHT						

LOT GRADE

CASE COUNT

☐ CASED ☐ LABELED ☐ PLAIN ☐ FULLY INSIDE ENAMELED

☐ UNCASED ☐ UNLABELED ☐ BEADED ☐ INSIDE ENAMELED ENDS

CONDITION OF CONTAINER

☐ MEETS ☐ FAILS

			S	T	L						
P* R E R E Q U I S I T E S	**C O O K E D**	Sim. Varietal Char. **									
		Brightness	F - - FIRM								
		Character C **	S - - SOFT								
		SStd **	FR - - FRAYED M - - MUSHY								
		GRADE									
		Flavor and Odor									
	U N C O O K E D	Crushed or Broken									
		CUSUM	1	2	3						
		Peel (Area) CM2									
		** M A T E R I A L / P I T	Large Pieces								
		CUSUM	1	.5	2						
		Small Pieces									
		CUSUM	1	3	3						
C L A S S I F I E D D E F E C T S	**C R I T**	EVM-Small Pieces									
		TOTAL CRITICAL									
		CUSUM Grade A	.3	.1	.9						
		Grade B	0	.5	.5						
		Grade C	0	1.0	1.0						
	S E V E R E	Color-Poor									
		Blemished									
		Off-Suture									
		Other Mech. Damage									
		Gouges									
		TOTAL SEVERE									
		CUSUM Grade A	0	1	1						
		Grade B	1.5	1.5	3						
		Grade C	1	5	3						
	M A J O R	Color-Fairly Good									
		Blemished									
		Off-Suture									
		Detached Pieces									
		Other Mech. Damage									
		Shelly									
		Gouges									
		TOTAL MAJOR									
		CUSUM Grade A	0	3	2						
		Grade B	1	4	3						
		Grade C	1	6	4						
	M I N O R	Blemished									
		Units Vary 1 cm									
		Off-Suture									
		Partially Detached Pc.									
		Other Mech. Damage									
		Gouges									
		Short Stems									
		TOTAL MINOR									
	T O T A L	**TOTAL ALL CLASSES**									
		CUSUM Grade A	1	4	3						
		Grade B	1	6	4						
		Grace C	1	10	4						

SAMPLE UNIT GRADE

| PACKERS GRADE | FINAL GRADE |

CASE COUNT PER CODE

FVQ FORM 364-46-2
MAR. 1979   *See Grading Manual for Clingstone Peaches · Lot Inspection Section   USDA - FSQS

Reprinted with permission USDA.

are either clingstone or semi-cling, all others are freestone. The hundreds of known peach varieties are classified in this manner, clingstone or freestone. In freestone varieties, the fruit can be easily separated from the stone or pit; in clingstones, as implied by the name, the flesh adheres tightly to the pit. Both types may have either yellow or white flesh.

To some extent, varieties grown in western states are somewhat different from the varieties grown in midwestern and eastern states. Elsewhere in this section we have listed the major California varieties, together with their appearance on the marketing scene. All fourteen varieties listed are yellow-meated.

In midwestern and eastern states, the following are a few of the major varieties in order of marketing appearance: Springgold, Early Amber, Springcrest (yellow flesh, semi-freestone); Sentinal, Keystone, Candor, Cardinal (yellow flesh, semi-freestone); Surecrop, Redcap, Early Red (yellow, cling); Harvester, Harbelle, Redhaven, Jerseyland, Loring, Washington, Redglobe, Madison, Redskin, Dixiland, Jefferson, Blake, Monroe, Richhaven, Cresthaven, Jersey Queen, Marqueen, and Marsun (all yellow, freestone).

Hydrocooling peaches is a common practice in eastern and southern states. It is a process whereby peaches pass over a continuous chain conveyor and are subjected to a shower of ice water, which may contain a fungicide solution. The pit temperature of the fruit usually is reduced by 20 to 30° in 15 to 20 minutes.

Peaches are hydrocooled after packing, although a few shippers hydrocool fruit prior to packing. The process reduces the temperature of the fruit rapidly, delays ripening, and deters or eliminates decay during transit. It also permits marketing ripe fruit, reduces shipping and marketing losses, and results in better quality peaches for the consumer.

Peaches ripen rapidly at room temperature, but if they are to be held, 32°F and 90 percent relative humidity is ideal.

Peaches can be peeled easily by dipping them in boiling water for 20 to 30 seconds and then plunging them immediately into ice water. The skins will slip off readily.

From the standpoint of pure economics—and recognizing that the grower is probably the biggest gambler in the world—peaches cost about $20.00 a ton less to produce than nectarines, and about $50.00 a ton less than plums. These favorable margins for peaches will probably be maintained for the next several years. Peach breeders in recent years have done a great job in making new peach varieties more attractive.

Deterioration: Small, round, tan spots of decay usually enlarge and cause waste.

Servings and Weights.   One cup of sliced peaches weighs 168 gr. or 6 oz. . . . One peach 2½ × 2 in. in diameter weighs 114 gr. (4.1 oz.). The skin and pit is 12 percent of the weight of such a peach.''[12]

One lb. of medium-sized peaches serves 4; and 25 lb. serve 100. A pound when sliced raw provides 3½ servings or ½ cup and 29 lb. sliced serves 100. For 1 lb., ready-to-serve raw, use 1.32 lb. (about 1 lb. 5 oz.) as purchased. One quart of raw sliced peaches weighs 1.68 lb. (about 1 lb. 11 oz.). A bushel of peaches weighs 47 to 52 lb.

[12]Agriculture Handbook No. 8, USDA.

Buy: Grade B Canned: Yellowish orange to greenish yellow color; maximum 60 percent weight variation in whole, halves, or quarters; maximum 20 percent suture cuts, maximum 10 percent partial slices, diced are maximum ¾ inch; reasonably fleshy, tender, intact; clingstone may have more ragged edges than freestone.

Deterioration: Off-color or wide color variation. Excessive variation in size, symmetry, and thickness. Discoloration, excessive softness, or hard units. Crushed or broken pieces, presence of excessive loose pits, stems, and leaves.

Grade B Frozen: Maximum 20 percent have green or brown color; maximum 100 percent weight variation, 20 percent off suture cuts; slices: maximum 20 percent partial or broken; some allowances made for pit material and extraneous matter; firm ripe fruit, maximum 20 percent mushy, 5 percent hard.

Deterioration: Variable color, off-color, dull color, or excessive brown oxidation. Presence of misshapen units, pits, stem, peel, scab, or insect injury. Hard, rubbery, or soft, mushy texture. Excessively frayed units or off-flavor or odor.

Grade A Dehydrated: Deep rich yellow to orange amber color; approximately ⅛ inch size for nuggets, coarse grainy texture with no hard pieces; diced: ¼ to ½ inch cube; maximum 5 percent damaged units.

Deterioration: Dark or oxidation discoloration. Dull orange to amber color.

Persimmons

Known as the "apple of the orient," this rich, sweet fruit is an excellent addition to your menu. Persimmons come in two major varieties: *Hachiya,* which is slightly pointed in shape and a bright orange color; and the *Fuyu* (Fuji), with the same bright color but flatter in shape.

Hachiya is the leading variety in this country (accounts for 90 percent of the total). They must be soft-ripe before they are eaten. The Fuyu variety is eaten out of hand like an apple, as well as being sliced. Buy soft ones for immediate use and firm ones to ripen at home and use as desired. They should be refrigerated as soon as possible because they become soft.

Persimmons are available from October to January, and they ripen best in a cool, dark place. They are relished for their luscious taste.

There has been a widespread notion that persimmons are "astringent" in flavor, but this is largely a myth, generated by some persons attempting to eat the fruit before it has properly ripened. Unlike many fruits, persimmons attain full skin color *before they are ripe!* Persimmons are picked when mature, but must be shipped while hard, in order to ripen at the market.

Grade.   There are no U.S. standards for persimmons. However, California, which grows almost all the commercial persimmons, has standard requirements in Section 805 of the Agricultural Code.

Persimmons shall be mature but not over-ripe. Hachiya variety shall have 90 percent of surface at time of picking orange or reddish color. Other Oriental varieties shall have 75 percent of surface at time of picking orange or reddish, balance at least yellowish green color. Free from: mold, decay, serious damage wasting 10 percent by weight by:

cuts, bruises, broken skin, hail, growth cracks, other causes. Total tolerance of defects 10 percent by count, only 5 percent of any one defect allowed. Packing requirements: variation in size of not over $\frac{1}{2}$ in. allowed when packed or partially packed. Shall not be deceptively packed. No markings required but when any markings used shall not be false or misleading.[13]

Pears

Canning pears are harvested in full size, but in a green, immature state. The grower tests the fruit's firmness before harvest with a pressure gauge. When the sample pears register 14 to 18 pounds per square inch resistance on the gauge, harvest begins. After arriving at the cannery in 1,000-pound bins, they are first size-graded and then ripened for five to seven days under controlled conditions in large ripening rooms where the temperature is maintained at approximately 80°F, and the humidity at about 90 percent. Very small quantities of Ethylene gas are sometimes introduced to speed and ensure uniform ripening and color development. Throughout the ripening period, plant personnel monitor the pressure reading of random pear samples. When the sample units offer 3 to 6 pounds per square inch resistance, they are ready for the canning process.

One particular aspect of pear processing that is important to the final quality has to do with the way in which the product is peeled. Two methods are commonly used to peel pears:

1. Lye Peeling: Substantial quantities of pears are peeled by passing them through a very dilute lye and steam bath which loosens and removes the peel. This is a common method used to peel many products for canning.
2. Mechanical Peeling: Large quantities of pears are processed through a machine which not only cores and halves, slices, or quarters the pear, but also peels each unit with a small "mechanical knife."

Though both systems yield a clean, attractive product, it is generally felt that the mechanical system of peel removal yields an even better product for "grade pack" (halves, quarters, slices). The mechanically-peeled pear exhibits a clean, white translucent appearance, as opposed to a duller, sloughy appearance which is oftentimes the result of lye peeling. One can determine if a pear has been mechanically peeled by noting the faint parallel ridges or lines on the "back" of the pear which are left by the mechanical knife.

The majority of lye-peeled pears are oriented for use in Fruit Cocktail and Fruit Mix, while every effort is made to utilize the mechanically-peeled pears for grade pack.

Deterioration: Noticeable "dead white" or "chalky" pears or pears with a decided pink or brown cast. Mushiness or partly crushed or broken pears. Presence of toughness hardness, or graininess and misshapen units that are poorly peeled and trimmed. Presence of interior stems.

---

[13]USDA Code.

Pineapples

Most pineapples shipped for fresh sales are picked at the peak of ripeness and flavor. Unlike bananas and pears, pineapples do not have a starch reserve, and thus have no material to convert to sugar. *They cannot ripen after harvest.*

Our best advice is to use pineapple soon after purchase. Storing a pineapple after harvest may result in a change in shell color and softening due to respiration and acid loss—but *it does not actually "ripen."*

In choosing a pineapple, select one that is plump, fresh looking, and as large as possible; the larger the fruit, the greater the proportion of edible flesh. Fresh, deep-green crown leaves are a good sign, but contrary to popular belief, the ease with which these leaves can be pulled out is not necessarily a sure sign of quality. Thumping is of no value. Avoid fruit that is old looking, dry, with brown leaves. Fragrance is a good sign. Avoid bruised fruit, or those with soft spots. A very slight separation of the eyes (pips) generally indicates maturity. Overmaturity is most frequently shown by slight decay at the base or on the sides with dark, soft, watery spots.

To lose some of the natural acid present in pineapples, keep at room temperature, away from heat or sun, then refrigerate at 45°F, relative humidity of 85 to 90 percent. Pineapples are very sensitive to chilling when not fully ripe.

Fresh pineapples are sliced, grated, or cubed and eaten plain, dipped in sugar, or mixed with other fruits. They are used as an appetizer, salad, or dessert. Add to lemon pies, cook with meats, or combine with cheese chunks for hor d'oeurves.

Deterioration: A dull yellowish-green color, sunken or slightly pointed pips, and a dried appearance.

Servings and Weights. The following table, from USDA, gives the yield in percent and number of portions per purchase unit for pineapple; also the approximate number of purchase units necessary to yield 25 or 100 portions.

Pineapple, first cultivated by the Chinese as early as 1640, was introduced to Europe in the seventeenth century, where it was cultivated in hothouses. Prized as a

Unit of Purchase	Weight per unit [lb.]	Yield as served [percent]	Portion as served	Portions per purchase units [Number]	Approximate purchase units for	
					25 portions	100 portions
Pound	1.00	52	3 oz. cubed	2.77	9-1/4	36-1/4
1/2 crate	35.00	52	3 oz. cubed	97.07	less than 1	1-1/4
1/2 gal. jar (chunks)	4.36	100	4 oz.	17.44	1-1/2	5-3/4

"rare fruit," it was used by the wealthy to adorn banquet tables, and soon became a subtle symbol of elite social standing, symbolizing high living and opulence.

Production has increased substantially since then, especially in the last 70 years, as total pack has gone from 1,893 cases in 1903, to a world production of 37.6 million cases in 1977, with Hawaiian pineapple accounting for slightly more than one-third of this amount, followed by Taiwan, Malaysia, Philippines, South Africa, Australia, Okinawa, and Mexico as important foreign producers.

Botanically-related to the same plant family as Spanish Moss, which grows on trees, pineapple is the only plant in this family that bears an edible fruit.

Pineapple is not grown from seed but from slips and suckers off the plant, or crown atop the fruit. Nearly two years of cultivation and caring go into each pineapple before it is canned. The pineapple plant bears its first fruit 18 to 22 months after planting. By this time the plant has grown to approximately 3 feet in height, and 4 inches in width. The first harvest of each plant produces a single 4- to 5-pound pineapple. If it is part of a ratoon (second or third) crop, it will have one or two smaller, but equally good pineapples. Normally sweetest from January through September, the peak season for processing pineapple is between May and August.

Harvesting is done with the aid of a boom harvester-conveyor. A crew of 6 to 12 people follows the machine, walking between the rows. Each person selects a ripe fruit and snaps off the crown as it is placed on a conveyor belt running along the boom. The fruit travels up the boom and is eased into a bin on a truck and rushed to the cannery for processing.

Arriving at the cannery, the pineapples are dropped in water-filled troughs, washed, and cushioned as they are elevated to the Genaca machine for processing.

Invented in 1913 by Henry Genaca, an engineer, the Genaca machine makes possible the mass production of canned pineapple. This machine drives a smooth steel cylinder straight through each pineapple, simultaneously removing the shell, core, and both ends of the fruit, to form a golden cylinder. (It even scrapes the shell, leaving the husk nearly dry, ready to be made into bran.) The pineapple cylinders are sent to the trimming tables at the rate of up to 106 per minute. On high-speed stainless steel conveyors, the cylinders are sliced, sorted, and matched by hand labor, according to color. Cans move to be filled with the various styles of pineapple, topped with natural juice or a syrup-packing medium. Vacuum seamers attach and seal lids, and the canned fruit is then sterilized and cooked in retorts at 212°F for 7 to 15 minutes, depending on the size of can and style of product.

Deterioration: Off-color, excess of light-colored units, or white markings. Units excessively blemished with deep eyes, brown spots, bruises, or peel.

Canned pineapple and canned prune juice items should possess good, bright color and be free from specks and other objectionable particles which affect the appearance or palatability of the juice. The flavor should be distinct and characteristic of juice from a properly-matured and properly-ripened raw product. The juice should be free from any carmelized flavor or odor.

Deterioration of Pineapple Juice: Off-flavor, seed particles and excessive free and suspended pulp. Dull or dark color, and coagulated pulp.

Plantain

Plantain is an important food in all tropical countries. While resembling a green banana, they are longer and thicker than bananas, with quite rough skins and a number of blemishes. Frequently used as a vegetable, rather than a fruit, plantains are usually found on the vegetable stand rather than in the fruit department. Even when fully ripe, the fruit remains starchy and is thus used primarily for baking, mashing, and frying. It is never eaten raw. Plantain may be used as a substitute for baked potatoes, or they are excellent fried as a meat accompaniment. Do not refrigerate the fruit unless it becomes quite soft.

Plumcots

A cross between the plum and apricot, plumcots have a red flesh and a purple skin. Select them as you would apricots. Plumcots have very little acceptance in the market, as they are not very widely known or grown.

Plums

Plums come in a bewildering variety. There are more than 2,000 varieties but it is fairly easy to become an expert if you remember there are two main types: the *Japanese* varieties and the *European* varieties.

The Japanese varieties are medium to large—they are famous for their juiciness. They may be a variety of shapes, but *never* blue or purple.

European varieties are *always* blue or purple. They are generally smaller, and oval or roundish. Compared to Japanese varieties, most European plums are milder in flavor and have a firmer texture.

Following are some of the more popular plum varieties, in approximate order of appearance on the market:

Red Beaut. Firm, yellow-colored flesh, bright red exterior. One of the earliest varieties.

Beauty. Medium-sized, heart-shaped, bright crimson in color when ripe. Flesh is amber, streaked with scarlet.

Burmosa. Semi-heart-shaped, attractive in appearance with a red blush. Flesh is light amber, soft, and fine-textured, with a mild and pleasant flavor.

Santa Rosa. Perhaps the "queen" of plums, there is the regular Santa Rosa and the late Santa Rosa, referring particularly to maturity. Conical in shape, purplish-crimson in color, the flesh is yellow to dark red near the skin. A rich, pleasing-tart flavor and very juicy.

Wickson. Large, heart-shaped, yellow skin with whitish bloom; ripens to a yellow-red color. Flesh is bright yellow, juicy; excellent flavor.

Tragedy. Medium in size, oval in shape, skin is dark blue-purple in color with a yellow-green, firm flesh. Sweet and well-flavored.

Mariposa. A red-fleshed plum, almost perfectly round in shape, skin color is red with a very heavy cover of cray bloom, and, as the fruit ripens, it becomes dark, red-purple in color.

El Dorado. Black-red skin with light amber flesh that turns to pink when cooked. Firm, easy to slice, and holds shape well when canned or cooked.

Laroda. A generally large plum with medium red over-color, yellow under-color. Yellow flesh, good "shipper."

Duarte. Dark red or dull-red skin, flesh is dark red when ripe; juicy and good flavor. Heart-shaped.

Nubiana. Large, flat type with oval shape; purple-black at maturity; yellow flesh; hard; good flavor.

Queen Ann. Large plum with deep, mahogany color. Flesh is light amber in color throughout, and when fully mature, has a rich, honey-like flavor.

President. Fruit is large, oval-shaped, very dark purple in color; good texture and flavor; outer skin generally has a "frosty" look.

Sim-Ka (also called *New Yorker*). Fruit is large; purple-colored skin and yellow flesh with good keeping quality.

Red Rosa. Purplish-red colored skin, yellow flesh; good keeping quality.

Casselman. A bud mutation of Late Santa Rosa, similar in size and shape, but has a lighter red over-color and ripens a few days later.

Elephant Heart. A large fruit with bright red flesh; excellent dessert quality.

Sharkey. Round, mottled red on yellow background; yellow-flesh; good flavor.

Sugar. Oval shape, purple skin; yellow, dry, sweet meat.

Standard. Dark blue in color with yellow flesh.

All plums should have good color for the variety, and be in a fairly firm-to-slightly-soft stage of ripeness (soft enough to yield to slight pressure). Optimum storage conditions are 32°F and 90 percent relative humidity.

The industry has started to switch to a "tight-fill" pack of plums and a volume-fill pack of prune plums, both in 28 pound net weight fibreboard. Minimizing hand labor, fruit will be directly conveyed from the grading-sizing belt to the container, with the tight-fill being given a three-second machine vibration to allow the fruit to "nest" properly. A tight-fitting lid on both types of packs prevents vertical motion of the fruit during shipping.

Deterioration: Fruit that has skin breaks or punctures, brown discoloration, or that is excessively soft, leaking, or decayed.

Weights and Servings The following table from USDA provides measures and equivalents useful in determining food quantities.

Buy: Grade B Canned: Reasonably uniform color, maximum 75 percent weight variation; minor stems, extraneous matter; good character, soft to slightly firm, 20 to 25 percent may be thinly fleshed.

Grade A Frozen: Uniform bright typical color with no evidence of oxidation; 50 percent maximum weight variation; 5 percent maximum crushed or broken; 10 percent maximum blemished; tender, fleshy, well ripened.

Deterioration: Off-color or brown color. Fruit excessively crushed or broken. Soft or tough, shriveled plums. Noticeable number of loose skins, gum pockets identified by surface scab or blemishes.

Food as Purchased	Purchase Unit	Servings per Purchase Unit	Serving Size or Portion	Purchase Units for 100 Servings	Additional Yield Information
PLUMS					
Fresh	lb.	4.00	2 medium raw plums (about 1/2 cup)	25	1 lb. AP= 0.94 lb. ready-to-oook or serve raw.
	lb.	4.67	1/2 cup raw halves	21-1/2	
		9.34	1/4 cup raw halves	10-3/4	
	lb.	4.20	1/2 cup raw sliced	24	
		8.40	1/4 cup raw sliced	12	
	lb.	3.27	1/2 cup cooked	30-3/4	
		6.54	1/4 cup cooked	15-1/2	

Pomegranates

The pomegranate is grown in many subtropical areas. In the United States, it can be grown in the southern areas, but all commercial production is in California.

"Pomegranate" literally means "apple with many seeds." This is a colorful autumn fruit about the size of a large apple, hard-rinded, and varying in color from yellow to deep red.

The Wonderful or Red Wonderful is the principal commercial variety. The fruit is large, glossy, and of deep red or purple color. They are in season from September until the early part of December, with 60 percent of the supplies in October.

Large sizes are better as the kernels are juicier and better developed inside; but, regardless of the size of pomegranate, all pomegranates have approximately the same number of seeds. Each seed and its edible pulp is surrounded by a spongy-soft membrane, which is quite bitter. Only the seed is edible for fresh use.

Sprinkle a few pomegranate seeds into a salad—they make a bright jewel-like garnish and have an unusual flavor and texture. The seeds in their pulp capsules are easily removed when the fruit is cut in half and they can be held in the freezer indefinitely. When keeping the whole fruit for short periods of time, room temperature, out of sunlight, is ideal. Refrigeration will not hurt; it could aid storage by adding moisture. Pomegranate juice is the base for grenadine syrup, so the fresh juice is very compatible to tropical drinks. It too can be frozen and used as desired.

Quality. Fruit should have unbroken rind with no sign of decay; be heavy for its size; and have a fresh, not dried-out, appearance. There are no U.S. standards.

Quality of pomegranates for shipment fresh or for processing is regulated by the California Agricultural Code. The acid content of juice extracted from a sample of the pomegranates is limited to not more than 1.85 percent. The code also provides requirements for the color of juice. Methods of selecting the sample and for testing are prescribed. Color must be a shade of red equal to or darker than Munsell color chart 5R-512, Lot 8730.

Prickly Pears

Prickly pears (Indian fig, barberry fig, and tuna) are the delicious fruit of a species of cactus and are most abundant during fall and early winter. They range in color from yellow to crimson and have spines that can be easily removed by singeing before the fruit is peeled. Heaviest supplies originate in Washington and Oregon.

Choose those that are firm but not hard, with a bright, fresh appearance. Prickly pears are red when ripe. Most of the prickly pears in the markets have been de-spined. They are cut into pieces, or sliced, for eating.

Prunes

Prunes are actually a variety of plum particularly suitable for drying purposes, as a fresh, ripe prune can be separated from the pit like a freestone peach. They are blue-black, oval, firm-fleshed and represent the late plum crop. The Italian variety is most commonly shipped in the fresh stage, with most supplies coming from Oregon, Idaho, and Washington.

Quality characteristics for both plums and prunes are similar. They should be good color for the variety, and in a fairly firm-to-slightly-soft stage of ripeness (soft enough to yield to slight pressure).

Buy: Grade A Dried Canned: Black, blue, or reddish-brown color; maximum 75 percent weight variation; thick fleshed, maximum 10 percent hard or soft, maximum 5 percent fibrous or tough.

Grade A Dehydrated: Light chocolate to dark brown; nuggets: 5/8 inch; whole pitted: maximum 133 per pound; 5 percent maximum damage, pit, fragments; coarse or grainy uniform texture.

Grade A Dried: As with Grade A Dried Canned.

Deterioration: Excessive number of prunes with thick scab, leathery areas on the skin, or tough skin. Noticeable size variation and dull chocolate-brown color, as well as shriveled prunes that fail to rehydrate.

Deterioration of Dried: Mixed varieties (unless requested), mixed sizes, variable texture and color, and defects such as scars, scabs, cracked or split units. Excessively moist units.

Quince

The quince is an autumn fruit that is generally grown for use in jelly-making and preserving. Good quality quinces are firm, free from blemishes, and show a pale yellow color when fully ripe. They bruise very easily and must be handled carefully, although they may be kept for a very long period of time in a dry, cool place. Quinces may be round or pear-shaped, resembling an apple with a rather misshapen stem end. There is usually a rather woolly surface on the yellow skin. The flavor is more acid-bitter than an apple, and it has numerous hard seeds throughout.

Choose quinces that are large and smooth, as the small knotty ones are wasteful. They may be used for sauce, dessert, or in puddings, pies, and tarts. They are excellent baked. Some of the oldtimers in the business tell us that if you place a quince in a closet or cupboard, it will keep the air fresh.

Sapote

Also called the Mexican custard apple, the sapote (sa-po-tee or sa-po-tay) is one of the principal foods of that country. It is grown in many citrus areas in a small way. Clusters of the fruit are large and greenish-yellow. The White sapote is the most readily available on a commercial basis in the United States. It resembles a green apple, but without an indentation on the blossom end.

Choose firm sapotes, free of bruises, with green to yellow-green color. Allow to ripen and soften at room temperature and then refrigerate. Sapotes, also referred to as marmalade plums, may be eaten fresh out-of-hand or made into a preserve or jam.

There are four principal varieties: sapote, black sapote, white sapote, and yellow sapote. Store as you would plums.

Tamarind

The fruit is a pod, cinnamon brown in color, 3 to 8 inches long, and flattened. Within its brittle covering are several obovate compressed seeds surrounded by brown pulp of acid taste. These seeds are used in cooking and in preparing refreshing drinks. It is widely used in Oriental chutneys and curries; is also used, with the addition of sugar and water, to yield a cooling drink or "refresco," especially well-known in Latin America.

Tangelos

Servings and Weights.   The following servings and weights apply to oranges, but the figures are comparable for tangelos. One pound of tangelos provide 2.82 servings each of ½ cup sections with membranes. To serve 100, use 35½ lb. of tangelos. One pound of tangelos, as purchased, equals 0.70 lb. ready-to-serve.

Tangerines

Grades.   U.S. Standards for Grades of Florida Tangerines provide for the following grades: U.S. Fancy; U.S. 1; U.S. 1 Bronze; U.S. 1 Russet; U.S. 2, U.S. 2 Russet, and U.S. 3. Tangerines produced in other states are covered by the U.S. Standards for Tangerines, an entirely separate set of standards.

U.S. 1 is the basic trading grade. Florida standards require that U.S. 1 tangerines be:

> fairly well colored; firm; mature; well formed; free from bruises, decay, unhealed skin breaks, and wormy fruit; and free from damage caused by ammoniation, buckskin, caked melanose, creasing, dirt or other foreign material, disease, dryness or mushy condition, green spots, hail, insects, oil spots, scab, scale, scars, skin breakdown, sprayburn, sunburn, unsightly discoloration, and other means. Not more than one-third of the surface, in the aggregate, may be affected by discoloration.[14]

Tomatoes

It may surprise you to learn that tomatoes, once known as "love apples," are actually a fruit, not a vegetable. Among fruits, it is a berry, being pulpy and containing one or more seeds that are not stones. It is also one of the few fruits and vegetables that gains weight as it matures.

There are probably four basic factors on which you should evaluate the quality of tomatoes: (1) color or general appearance, (2) firmness and weight of the fruit (in relation to size), (3) internal appearance of the sliced fruit, and (4) flavor. A tomato can be of good quality whether large or small; size is a matter of preference. The ideal tomato, from the consumer's viewpoint, is one that is full size, vine ripened, unblemished, and characteristically tomato-red.

Many tomatoes shipped to distant markets are harvested at the "mature-green" stage. At this stage, the fruits are about full grown, have heightened gloss because of the waxy skin that cannot be torn by scraping, internally have well-formed jelly-like substance, and show no red color (but may show cream-colored streaks at the blossom end). Tomatoes, with stems attached, lose moisture more slowly and will keep fresh for a longer time than those with stems removed.

The best ripening temperatures for mature-green tomatoes are 65 to 70°F, with relative humidity of 85 to 88 percent. Tomatoes that are not fully ripened will ripen satisfactorily at home if placed in an area with good air circulation and normal temperature and humidity. They should not be refrigerated until such time as they are fully ripened. After ripening, they can be held at 50°F or lower.

Deterioration: Soft, bruised tomatoes with deep, long cracks. This requires much trimming and excessive waste.

Servings and Weights.   The following table prepared by USDA gives information about purchasing and serving units. "AP" means "As Purchased."

Another guide states that for a 2-slice portion, a 1-lb. tomato results in 7½ portions; and for 25 portions, 3.5 lb. would be needed; and for 100 portions, 13.5 pounds

---

[14]USDA Code.

Food as Purchased	Purchase Unit	Servings per Purchase Unit	Serving Size or Portion	Purchase Units for 100 Servings	Additional Yield Information
TOMATOES					
Fresh	Pound	4.00	1 small tomato (about 1/2 cup)	25	1 lb. AP = 0.91 lb. ready-to-serve raw
	Pound	5.06	1/2 cup raw, diced or sliced	20	
		10.12	1/4 cup raw, diced or sliced	10	

are needed. A pound cut into wedges provides 12 portions; and 2¼ lb. are needed for 25 portions, and 8½ lb. are needed for 100 portions. Yield from tomatoes as purchased is 91 percent.

Grades. U.S. Standards for fresh tomatoes were first issued in 1922, and have been revised many times.

BASIC TRADING GRADES—At present, the four grades for fresh tomatoes are U.S. No. 1, U.S. Combination, U.S. No. 2, and U.S. No. 3.

U.S. No. 1 consists of tomatoes of similar varietal characteristics which are mature but not overripe or soft, which are clean, well developed, fairly well formed, fairly smooth, and which are free from decay, freezing injury, and sunscald, and free from damage caused by bruises, from cuts and broken skins, internal discoloration, sunburn, puffiness, catfaces, other scars, growth cracks, hail, insects, disease, or mechanical or other means.

U.S. Combination consists of a combination of U.S. No. 1 and U.S. No. 2 tomatoes where at least 60 percent, by count, meet the requirements of the U.S. No. 1 grade. The reader should refer to the Standards for tolerances on U.S. Combination and for descriptions and tolerances on U.S. No. 2 and U.S. No. 3 grades. The term ''unclassified'' is not a grade, but means only that no grade has been applied to the lot.[15]

Raw product tomatoes average about 5.4 percent Natural Tomato Soluble Solids, hereafter referred to as NTSS.

---

[15]USDA Code.

Four main processing steps make the difference in tomato products:

1. Hot or cold break. In cold break, immediately after pulping the raw product, the temperature is raised into the range of 160 to 180°F. In hot break, immediately after pulping the raw product, the temperature is raised into the range of 195 to 210°F. The difference is that the higher temperatures in the hot break effectively inactivate enzymes which break down pectins. This yields a more viscous finished product in the hot break, as it is pectin retention which produces thickness or consistency in tomato products.

2. The screen size the finished product goes through. In a continual process, pulped product is pumped in and out of the hot break tanks with a predetermined dwell time to assure complete heat penetration. From these tanks it generally goes through three finishers. The first usually has a large screen with ³⁄₁₆-inch holes. All of the stems and most of the peel and seeds are removed. The next two finishers will have the screen size as desired for the finished product. A fine screen, used for fine-finish tomato products and tomato juice, will remove all seeds and practically all peel. Screens with .033- or .045-inch openings will leave small pieces of peel, but no seeds. A .060-inch screen will leave larger pieces of peel, and occasional small pieces of seeds. The pieces of peel are rolled and up to ¼-inch long, giving the product more body for use in products such as Chili Sauces, Special Heavy Catsup, coarse-finish Purees, etc.

3. The degree of concentration or water removal. As previously stated, raw product tomatoes are about 5.4 percent NTSS. A product is considered tomato juice until it is concentrated to 8.0 percent NTSS, the point where it is legally puree. Water can be removed from the product by boiling in the atmosphere. However, when placed in a high vacuum the product will boil at a lower temperature and, therefore, it will retain a bright-red color without darkening.

4. The absence or amount of salt and/or seasoning. Tomato Juice is not deliberately concentrated, but in the normal process, some water is removed. Diet Tomato Juice (without salt) is approximately 5.7 percent NTSS. After salt is added to make regular Tomato Juice, the product will have about 6.6 percent *total* solids. This, of course, means that the amount of added salt is about 0.9 percent by weight. The small finisher screen sizes virtually eliminate pieces of peel and gives a fine finish.

Tomato Puree, at some degree of concentration with a specific type of finish, is used as the basic ingredient in making Catsup, Concentrated Tomato Juice, and sauces of all types.

Tomato Sauce uses approximately 11.0 percent NTSS Puree, to which is added salt and spices.

Tomato Catsup uses three levels of Puree to Make Fancy, Extra Standard, or Standard Catsup. To these respective concentrations of Puree is added syrup, salt, vinegar, and seasoning in different quantities, according to one of the three finished Tomato Catsup grades.

Vegetable Juice Cocktail uses tomato juice, some water, and seasonings.

Tomato paste must have a minimum of 24 percent NTSS. Most of the Tomato Paste packs range from 24.0 percent to 35.1 percent NTSS. Tomato Paste does not have any salt or spices added. It is just tomato pulp, usually hot break, with finisher screen sizes from .023 to .060 inches.

Buy: Grade A.

Deterioration: Pale red color or yellow and green portions. Excessive skin, core material, or blemished units. Noticeably watery or soft pieces. Presence of mold or insects and poor flavor.

Cherry Tomatoes. Cherry Tomatoes are a relatively minor crop in California, but are a comparatively high value crop. Red Cherry, Large, is probably the most popular variety. Plants are usually trained for erect growth by the use of stakes and horizontal strings. These tomatoes may grow as large as 2 inches in diameter, but generally 1 to 1½ inches. They may or may not have some of the green calyx attached.

Whole Peeled. Canned Tomatoes should be prepared from firm, clean, fully-ripened tomatoes. Color should be typically tomato-red with no heavy green or yellow shoulders, and practically free from any yellow coloration.

The units should be fairly large and uniform within the can, with no broken, split, or severely cracked units. The product should be practically free of peel, stems, large stem scars, or other blemishes.

Standard Grade Whole Peeled Tomatoes should be typically tomato-red to orange-yellow shade, free from green. They should consist of well-sized units of reasonable uniformity, retain a somewhat similar shape after processing, and be fairly free of broken, split, or cracked units.

Tomato Catsup. Tomato Catsup should have a good, distinctive, spicy tomato flavor free from scorching or any objectionable flavor of any kind. It should possess a uniform deep-red color and be free from seeds and skin.

Fancy Catsup has a total solids content of at least 33 percent, and I recommend that it should flow not more than 6.0 cm on the Bostwick Consistometer under standard conditions.

Special Heavy Catsup will have a solids content of approximately 27 percent, and should not flow more than 6.0 cm on the Bostwick Consistometer under standard conditions. The product is of coarse texture and, therefore, contains slightly more particles of seeds and skin in the finished product.

Extra Standard Catsup has a solids content of at least 29 percent, and should flow not more than 8.0 cm on the Bostwick Consistometer under standard conditions.

Standard Catsup will be of fancy color, but may be of standard quality for defects (dark specks, scale-like particles, etc.)

Deterioration: Dark brown discoloration around neck of bottles. Black specks, lack of spicing, or overspicing. Sour, scorched, or bitter flavor, and noticeable pale yellow color.

Tomato Sauce. Tomato Sauce is the concentrated product prepared from the liquid extracted from mature, sound, whole tomatoes, to which salt and spices are added and to which may be added one or more nutritive sweetening ingredients, a vinegar or vinegars, and onion, garlic, or other vegetable flavoring ingredients. The product is generally of medium texture and should be practically free from defects. Specks, seed particles, peel, and core material should not more than slightly affect appearance. The product may exhibit very slight separation, but no excessive "weeping." It is recommended that Tomato Sauce should flow not more than 10 cm on the Bostwick Consistometer under standard conditions, and possess a good flavor and odor.

Deterioration: Off-color, predominantly yellowish red solids. Scorched, bitter, salty, or green tomato flavor. Excessive dark specks and scale-like particles from seeds, tomato peel, or core. Poor consistency tending to thinness.

Tomato Paste.   Tomato Paste is prepared from the pulp of mature, whole, sound, red tomatoes, which have been rapidly concentrated to a total solids content of at least 24 percent NTSS ("light" concentration). The product may vary in texture from "fine" to "coarse," and should possess a good, red, ripe tomato color. It should possess a mild, sweet flavor and odor without any off-flavors or off-odors such as from scorched, bitter, or green fruit pulp. Solids level, thickness and finish (texture) should be considered when specifying this item.

Deterioration: Off-color, scorched, bitter, or green tomato flavor. Excessive black specks. Ready separation of watery liquid.

Tomato Puree.   Tomato Puree is the product prepared from the pulp of mature, whole, sound red tomatoes which have been rapidly concentrated to contain not less than 8.0 percent NTSS, nor more than 23.9 percent NTSS. The product is packed with "fine," "medium," and "coarse" texture. However, the "coarse" texture (.060-inch screen) is generally preferred in the Foodservice industry. Tomato Puree should possess a mild, sweet flavor and odor without any off-flavors or off-odors such as from scorched, bitter, or green fruit pulp. Solids level, thickness, and finish (texture) should be considered when specifying this item.

Deterioration: Off-color, predominately yellowish red solids. Scorched, bitter, salty, or green tomato flavor. Excessive dark specks, and scale-like particles from seeds, tomato peel, or core. Poor consistency tending to thinness.

In January 1970, a revision of the Standards of Identity for Tomato Puree and Paste went into effect specifying a new method for reporting solids content. The old standard specified that solids be reported as "salt-free" solids based upon determination of total solids by the official vacuum-drying method and subtracting from this the total salt content of the sample including natural as well as added salt. In place of a vacuum oven, solids were usually determined by means of a refractometer and conversion tables used to convert the refractometer readings to salt-free solids by vacuum oven-drying.

In the new standards, solids content is reported as "Natural Tomato Soluble Solids" (NTSS) based upon the readings obtained on the saugar scale of a refractometer at 20°C. Solids readings are no longer based upon the vacuum oven determination and hence no conversion tables are needed. Another difference between the two standards is that in the new standard only added salt is subtracted from the reading. No correction is made for the natural salt content of the product if no salt has been added.

Since the old standard was based upon total solids, whereas the new standard is based upon soluble solids, the values obtained for solids according to the new standards are always numerically lower than those specified in the old standards. This necessitated a change in the solids limits specified in the standards and may require a change in the solids specifications for the purchase of Puree and Paste products.

Ground Tomatoes in Puree.   The style of this product can vary from packer to packer. Basically it is a mixture of 50 percent ground peeled or unpeeled tomatoes and 50 percent puree. Different packers utilize different concentrations of puree. Whatever the specific gravity necessary to achieve the proper consistency and appearance is the type of puree which is used. Various tomatoes varieties and sizes of tomato pieces are also used, which can result in differences in appearance.

Though this product from different canners *generally* bears the same characteristics, there are many terms used to identify the product (i.e., Tomato Magic, All for One, Ground Tomatoes, All-Purpose, 7-11, and so forth).

The demand for this type of tomato product has accelerated dramatically over the past few years due to its excellent "fresh" tomato flavor and color which carry through to the numerous end-products in which it can be used.

Chili Sauce.   This product is a heavy-bodied, very coarse-texture sauce made from sound, ripe, red tomatoes, sugar, vinegar, onions, salt, and spices. It will consist of 30 to 32 percent solids, and possess a good, bright tomato color, with a spicy, tangy aroma without any off-flavors.

Flow, as measured with a Bostwick Consistometer shall not exceed 5.5 cm in 30 seconds.

Deterioration: Dark brown discoloration around neck of bottles. Black specks, lack of spicing, or overspicing. Sour, scorched, or bitter flavor and noticeable pale yellow color.

Tomato Juice.   Canned Tomato Juice is unconcentrated fancy-quality juice with salt added. It should be prepared from clean, sound, well-colored tomatoes.

The finished product should possess a bright, rich, red color and be of medium-heavy to heavy consistency (45 to 70 seconds on the Lamb-Lewis Viscometer.) The product should be free of large specks and practically free of small specks.

Ugli Fruit

A native to Jamaica, ugli (ugly) fruit has become popular because it is such a miserable looking piece of fruit. About the size of a grapefruit, it has an extremely rough peel, is badly disfigured, and has light-green blemishes which turn orange when the fruit is mature. It is very juicy, with large quantities of pulp and a rather delightful orange-like flavor. Ugli fruit has a spherical to oblate appearance, with rather loose skin. Besides Jamaica, it is also grown in small quantities in Florida. It should be used and stored as other citrus.

ARTIFICIALLY SWEETENED CANNED FRUITS

Apricots, Canned, Artificially Sweetened
[27.14 6/23/59]

Cherries, Canned, Artificially Sweetened
[27.34 6/23/59]

Figs, Canned, Artificially Sweetened
[27.73 6/23/59]

Peaches, Canned, Artificially Sweetened
[27.6 6/23/59]

Pears, Canned, Artificially Sweetened
[27.24 6/23/59]

Pineapple, Canned, Artificially Sweetened
[27.57 2/26/62]

Artificially sweetened canned fruits are the foods which conform to the definition and standards of identity prescribed for the above-mentioned canned fruits, except that the packing medium used is water artificially sweetened with saccharin, sodium saccharin, or a combination of both. Such packing medium may be thickened with pectin and may contain any mixture of any edible organic acid or acids as a flavor-enhancing agent, in a quantity not more than is reasonably required for this purpose.

The specified name of the food is ''artificially sweetened ____,'' the blank being filled in with the name prescribed for the above-mentioned canned fruit having the same optional ingredient.

The artificially sweetened food is subject to the requirements for label statement of optional ingredients used, as prescribed for the above-mentioned canned fruits. If the packing medium is thickened with pectin, the label shall bear the statement ''thickened with pectin.'' When any organic salt or acid or any mixture of two or more of these is added, the label shall bear the common or usual name of each such ingredient.

Canned Apricots with Rum [1/21/78]

Canned Cherries with Rum [1/21/78]

Canned Peaches with Rum [1/21/78]

Canned Pears with Rum [1/21/78]

The above-mentioned canned fruits with rum conform to the definitions and standards of identity and each is subject to the requirements for label statement of optional ingredients, prescribed for the above-mentioned canned fruits, except that it contains added rum in such amount that its alcoholic content is more than 3 percent but less than 5 percent by weight.

QUESTIONS

1. List the seven methods of processing fruits.
2. Describe and give reasons for the evolution of the present packing system.
3. Describe and give examples of three different links in the distribution process.

4. What is the PAC Act?
5. Describe the difference between fruits and vegetables and give examples.
6. Give an example of each of the three classes of fruit.
7. Why would apricots be most expensive in May?
8. How is apple maturity determined?
9. Why are apricots and plums considered to be in the same family?
10. When ordering apricots to be served as a breakfast fruit the can size you order is unavailable. What can size would be ordered as a replacement?
11. What two factors should a buyer be aware of when purchasing apricots and apples?
12. List two varieties of avocados from both California and Florida.
13. Explain the different forms of bananas available on the market.
14. What does #1 Grade mean in reference to bananas and who gives it?
15. Which berry is allowed to have a stem?
16. Why are cherries described in rows? What is inconsistent about rows?
17. What defects are legally allowed for sweet cherries?
18. What are the two methods used to remove the shell from a coconut?
19. What precautions are needed for storing fresh dates?
20. What are the specifications for buying Grade A dates?
21. Name fruits which must ripen before being picked.
22. Explain the size-of-fruit difference between Florida and ''other'' grapefruit.
23. List the four major and one minor groups for grapes.
24. Describe a 7¢ lemon and the specifications used for ordering.
25. Give a brief description of a mandarin orange acceptable on delivery.
26. List the most reliable indicators for purchasing melons of good quality.
27. List fruits which will ripen after being picked.
28. What is the difference between a clingstone and freestone peach? List the reasons for specification of each.
29. List factors considered when purchasing pineapple.
30. What is the difference between a plantain and a banana?
31. What are the reasons for different specifications among plums?
32. Are tomatoes a fruit or a vegetable? Why?
33. Compare and contrast freestone and clingstone peaches. On what processing state would you buy each type for use as a dessert? as a recipe ingredient (for a cake?) Why?
34. Explain the following terms:

Standard of Identity
Standard of Quality
Standard of Fill

35. You have peaches on the menu for a dessert. What grade will you buy in fresh? Canned? Calculate the labor cost and food cost for 200 portions of each type to be served to high school sophomores.
36. What information must be provided on a label?

37. Define:

   leaker
   swell
   puffer
   hydrogen swell

   flipper
   springer
   flat sour

38. You have pears on the menu for a dessert. What grade will you buy in fresh? Canned? Disregarding labor cost, at what price is fresh cheaper if canned is $16.00 per 6/10, 30/35 count can, case?

39. Twenty-nine pounds of raw peaches serve 100, and one case of canned peaches serves 210. Which is the best buy? How does this relate to your group experience?

40. What are some ways that raw fruit maturity is determined and how does this impact the canning process?

41. List ten items that might be included in a bid description. Which one(s) might be eliminated? Why?

42. What is a typical fruit to sugar ratio in frozen strawberries? What percentage sugar does light syrup have? What is that in terms of Brix?

43. What is the difference between U.S. Choice and U.S. Fancy pears? Please be specific.

44. Make a list of ten canned goods grading tools that a large operation should consider owning and using.

45. What is the impact of count specification in canned fruits? Give an example using 200 teenagers on 25/30 fruit vs. 35/40 fruit.

EXHIBITS

Canned Specification	
Peaches	Product
Clingstone	Variety
Halves	Style
35/40	Count
6/10	Pack
67.1 oz.	Dry Weight Minimum
Light Syrup	Pack Medium
Min. 16°	Brix
U.S. Choice	Grade
Min. 84 pts.	Point Score

Can Equivalents

Can Number (No.)

	300	303	2	2½	3 cyl	10	12 (gal)
300	1.000	.901	.751	.511	.294	.139	.110
303	1.111	1.000	.822	.566	.347	.154	.122
2	1.350	1.216	1.000	.689	.397	.187	.148
2½	1.957	1.765	1.452	1.000	.577	.272	.215
3 cyl	3.401	3.061	2.517	1.735	1.000	.472	.373
10	7.194	6.488	5.355	3.673	2.120	1.000	.791
12 (gal)	9.102	8.203	6.744	4.646	2.680	1.264	1.000

Computed from National Canners Association Data

Case Equivalents

Can Number (No.)

	303	2	2½	10
24/300	.90	.74	.51	.556
24/303	1.00	.82	.57	.616
24/2	1.22	1.00	.69	.748
24/2½	1.77	1.45	1.00	1.088
12/3 cyl	1.53	1.26	.87	.944
6/10	1.62	1.33	.92	

Source: National Canners Association

To convert: multiply figure in the first row (horizontal) by the figure in the desired vertical column *or* divide the figure in desired vertical column by the desired size in the horizontal row.

| Canned Fruits | (½ cup servings) | | |
	6 cans/cs. Suggested Size #10 Can	24 cans/cs. Suggested Size #2½ Can	#303
Apples (sliced)	24	6.5	4
Applesauce	27	7	4
Apricots (halves)	15–16	3.5–4	4
Bananas (mashed)	29	7	4
Cranberry Sauce	29	7	4
Cherries (red tart)	24–26	—	3–4
Cherries (sweet)	27	7	3–4
Grapefruit Sections	—	—	4
Fruit Cocktail	27	7.5	4–4.5
Peaches (halves or slices)	25	7	3
Pears (halves)	25	7	3
Pineapple (chunks)	27	7.5	—
Raspberries	27	—	4
Strawberries	27	—	4

5

VEGETABLES

INTRODUCTION

To introduce this chapter is a table which alphabetically lists each of the different vegetables. This includes the product name and the fresh, canned, frozen, dehydrated, and dried and sulfured U.S. grade order where applicable. It also states the can size, net weight in ounces, and drained weight in ounces.

Following this, detailed specifications for each of the vegetables are cited. The chapter reveals the etiology of certain vegetables, descriptions of prevalent varieties, information regarding storage, and servings and weights relating to certain varieties, grades, and standards. The specifications tell you what grades to buy in regard to fresh, canned, and frozen vegetables. Vegetables such as beans and sweet potatoes have drawings that indicate shapes that are considered acceptable. Defects to be aware of when selecting these products are also included.

Included also is information on little known vegetables such as burdock, malanga, and cardoon. Drawings are also available for some of the varying vegetable sizes.

[1]The author thanks Blue Goose, Inc. for allowing the use of substantial material from *The Buying Guide for Fresh Fruits, Vegetables, Herbs, and Nuts*, sixth revised edition (Fullerton, CA: Blue Goose, Inc., 1976).

Product	Fresh U.S. Grade Order	Canned U.S. Grade Order	Size of Can	Net Wt. Oz.	Drained Wt. Oz.	Frozen U.S. Grade Order	Dehyd. U.S. Grade Order	Dried U.S. Grade Order	Sulfured U.S. Grade Order
Artichokes Globe	No. 1, No. 2 No. 1, No. 2								
Green and Wax Beans	fcy, No. 1, comb, No. 2	90, 80, 70, <70				fcy, x-stand, stand, s-stand			
Whole			8Z T	7.8	4.0				
			303	15.2	8.5				
			2½	26.8	16.0				
			10	98.5	57.5				
Whole Vert. Pk and Asparagus Style			8Z T	7.8	4.6				
			303	15.2	9.5				
			2½	26.8	17.0				
Short Cuts and <1½"			8Z T	7.8	4.5				
			303	15.2	9.2				
			2½	26.8	16.4				
			10	98.5	63.0				
Cuts 1½" +			8Z T	7.8	4.1				
			303	15.2	8.7				
			2½	26.8	16.2				
			10	98.5	60.0				
Mixed and Short Cuts			8Z T	7.8	4.5				
			303	15.2	9.2				
			2½	26.8	16.4				
			10	98.5	63.0				
Sliced, Length or French Style			8Z T	7.8	4.1				
			303	15.2	8.7				
			2½	26.8	16.2				
			10	98.5	59.0				

Product	US Grades	Min Scores	Can Size	Fill	Min Drained Weight	Min Scores	Min Scores
Lima Beans	No. 1, comb, No. 2 / No. 2	90, 80, 70, <70	8Z T	full as practicable	5.5	90, 80, 70, <70	85, 70, <70
			303	full as practicable	11.0		
			10	full as practicable	72.0		
Speckled Butter Beets — Whole, No. 1–3 Incl.	No. 1, No. 2	85, 70, <70	8Z T	7.8	5.5	90, 80, <80	
			303	15.2	10.0		
			2½	26.8	19.5		
			10	98.5	69.0		
Whole, No. 4–6 Incl.			8Z T	7.8	5.0		
			303	15.2	9.5		
			2½	26.8	19.0		
			10	98.5	68.0		
Sliced Small			8Z T	7.8	5.50		
			303	15.2	10.25		
			2½	26.8	19.00		
			10	98.5	69.00		
Sliced, Med. and Large			8Z T	7.8	5.00		
			303	15.2	9.75		
			2½	26.8	18.50		
			10	98.5	68.00		
Diced			8Z T	7.8	5.5		
			303	15.2	10.5		
			2½	26.8	19.0		
			10	98.5	72.0		
Quartered			8Z T	7.8	5.5		
			303	15.2	10.5		
			2½	26.8	18.5		
			10	98.5	70.0		

Product	Fresh U.S. Grade Order	Canned U.S. Grade Order	Size of Can	Net Wt. Oz.	Drained Wt. Oz.	Frozen U.S. Grade Order	Dehyd. U.S. Grade Order	Dried U.S. Grade Order	Sulfured U.S. Grade Order
Julienne			8Z T	7.8	5.25				
			303	15.2	9.00				
			2½	26.8	18.25				
			10	98.5	68.00				
Bunched Ital. Sprout. Broccoli	fcy, No. 1 No. 2								
Broccoli						fcy, stand, s-stand			
Brussels Sprouts	No. 1, No. 2					90, 80, 70, <70			
Carrots	No. 1, comm	85, 70, <70				90, 80, <80			
Topped Carrots	x-No. 1, No. 1 No. 1 jumbo, No. 2								
short-trimmed	No. 1, comm								
Whole, <1½" Diameter			8Z T	7.8	5.50				
			303	15.2	9.75				
			2½	26.8	19.50				
			10	98.5	69.00				
Whole, 1½" + Diameter			8Z T	7.8	5.00				
			303	15.2	9.25				
			2½	26.8	19.00				
			10	98.5	68.00				
Sliced, <1½" Diameter			8Z T	7.8	5.5				
			303	15.2	10.0				
			2½	26.8	19.0				
			10	98.5	69.0				
Sliced, 1½" + Diameter			8Z T	7.8	5.0				
			303	15.2	9.5				
			2½	26.8	18.5				
			10	98.5	68.0				

Style	Grade	Factor A	Can size	Min. fill (oz)	Min. drained wt (oz)	Factor B
Diced			8Z T	7.8	5.5	
			303	15.2	10.5	
			2½	26.8	19.0	
			10	98.5	72.0	
Quartered			8Z T	7.8	5.5	
			303	15.2	10.5	
			2½	26.8	18.5	
			10	98.5	70.0	
Julienne			8Z T	7.8	5.25	
			303	15.2	9.00	
			2½	26.8	18.25	
			10	98.5	68.00	
Cauliflower	No. 1, comm					
Celery	No. 1, No. 2					
Corn						
Green	fcy, No. 1, No. 2	85, 70, <70				90, 80, 70, <70
Whole Kernel		90, 80, 70, <70				90, 80, 70, <70
Grade A			8Z T	full as practicable	5.25	
			303	full as practicable	10.50	
			10	full as practicable	70.00	
Grades B, C and s-stand			8Z T	full as practicable	5.50	
			303	full as practicable	10.75	
			10	full as practicable	72.00	
Cream Style						90, 80, 70, <70
Corn-On-The-Cob		90, 80, <80				

Product	Fresh U.S. Grade Order	Canned U.S. Grade Order	Size of Can	Net Wt. Oz.	Drained Wt. Oz.	Frozen U.S. Grade Order	Dehyd. U.S. Grade Order	Dried U.S. Grade Order	Sulfured U.S. Grade Order
Cucumbers	fcy, x-No. 1, No. 1, No. 1 small, No. 1 large, No. 2								
Pickling Cu.	No. 1, No. 2, No. 3								
Greenhouse Cu.	fcy, No. 1, No. 2								
Eggplant	fcy, No. 1, No. 2								
Endive, Escarole, Chicory									
Garlic	No. 1								
Hominy	No. 1	85, 70, <70							
Style 1			303	full as practicable	10.0				
			2½	full as practicable	18.0				
			10	full as practicable	72.0				
Style 2			303	full as practicable	12.00				
			2½	full as practicable	21.25				
			10	full as practicable	76.00				
Horseradish Roots	fcy, No. 1, No. 2								
Kale	No. 1, comm								

Commodity	Grade	Color/Quality	Can size			
Leafy Greens Other Than Spinach						
Mustard, Turnip Greens	No. 1					
Kale	No. 1, comm					
Dandelion Gr.	No. 1					
Collard, Broccoli Greens	No. 1					
Beet Greens	No. 1	fcy, x-stand, s-stand	8Z T	7.8	4.8	85, 70, <70
			303	15.2	10.2	
			2½	26.8	17.6	
			10	98.5	54.7	
Lettuce	fcy, No. 1, comm, No. 2					
Greenhouse Leaf	fcy, No. 1					
Mixed Vegetables	No. 1, No. 2	90, 80, <80, 85, 70, <70				90, 80, 70, <70
Mushrooms	No. 1	90, 80, <70				90, 80, <80
Okra						
Whole or Salad			8Z T	7.8	4.5	
			303	15.2	10.0	
			2½	26.8	17.8	
			10	98.5	60.0	
Cut			8Z T	7.8	5.0	
			303	15.2	10.5	
			2½	26.8	18.8	
			10	98.5	60.0	
Okra and Tomatoes		85, 70, <70				
Onions						
Creole	No. 1, No. 2 comb					
Bermuda-Granex-Grano	No. 1, comb, No. 2					

Product	Fresh U.S. Grade Order	Canned U.S. Grade Order	Size of Can	Net Wt. Oz.	Drained Wt. Oz.	Frozen U.S. Grade Order	Dehyd. U.S. Grade Order	Dried U.S. Grade Order	Sulfured U.S. Grade Order
Green	No. 1, No. 2								
Bunched Shallots	No. 1, No. 2								
All Others	No. 1, Export No. 1, comm, No. 1 boilers, No. 1 picklers, No. 2	85, 70, <70							
tiny			8Z T	7.8	4.5				
			303	15.2	9.5				
			10	98.5	64.0				
small			8Z T	7.8	4.5				
			303	15.2	9.0				
			10	98.5	63.0				
medium			8Z T	7.8	4.5				
			303	15.2	9.0				
			10	98.5	60.0				
Breaded Onion Rings									
Parsley	No. 1					85, 70, <70			
Parsnips	No. 1, No. 2								
Peas	No. 1, fcy	90, 80, 70, <70					90, 80, 70, <70		
So. Peas (Field, Black-eye)	No. 1, comm	85, 70, <70	303	15.2	11.0	90, 80, <80			
			10	98.5	72.0				
Peas and Carrots		90, 80, <80				90, 80, 70, <70			
Peas	No. 1, fcy								
Carrots	A and B		8Z T	7.8	5.5				
			303	15.2	10.6				
			10	98.5	70.0				
Carrots Sliced or Strips									

Product	Grades	Container	Fill	Drained weight	Grade %
Carrots Diced or Dble. Diced	fcy, No. 1, No. 2				90, 80, <80
Sweet Peppers		8Z T, 303, 10	7.8, 15.2, 98.5	5.5, 10.8, 71.0	85, 70, <70
Pimentos Whole, Halves		303, 2½, 10	full as practicable	11.0, 20.2, 70.7	
Whole and Pieces		303, 2½, 10	full as practicable	11.2, 20.5, 72.2	
Pieces, Diced or Chopped		303, 2½, 10	full as practicable	11.2, 20.5, 74.0	
Sliced		303, 2½, 10	full as practicable	11.0, 20.2, 71.7	
Potatoes	x-No. 1, No. 1, comm, No. 2				

Product	Fresh U.S. Grade Order	Canned U.S. Grade Order	Size of Can	Net Wt. Oz.	Drained Wt. Oz.	Frozen U.S. Grade Order	Dehyd. U.S. Grade Order	Dried U.S. Grade Order	Sulfured U.S. Grade Order
Seed Potatoes	No. 1 seed potatoes								
White Potatoes		85, 70, <70	2½ 10	26.8 98.5	19.0 74.0				
Peeled Potatoes		85, 70, <70							
French Fried Potatoes						90, 90, 80, <80			
Pumpkin	No. 1, comm								
Radishes	fcy, No. 1, No. 2								
Rhubarb		85, 70, <70				85, 70, <70			
Turnips or Rutabagas	No. 1, No. 2					85, 70, <70			
Spinach		fcy, x-stand, s-stand	8Z T 303 2½ 10	7.8 15.2 26.8 98.5	4.8 9.6 17.6 54.7	90, 80, <80			
Leaves	x-No. 1, No. 1, comm								
Plants	No. 1, comm								
Fall and Winter Squash	No. 1, No. 2	85, 70, <70	8Z T 303 2½ 10	7.8 15.2 26.8 98.5	— — —	85, 70, <70			
Summer Squash Whole	No. 1, No. 2	85, 70, <70	8Z T 303 10	7.8 15.2 98.5	4.5 10.8 70.0	85, 70, <70			
Sliced or Cut			8Z T 303 10	7.8 15.2 98.5	5.5 11.0 70.0				
Sweet Potatoes	x-No. 1, No. 1, comm. No. 2	fcy, stand, s-stand				90, 80, <80			
Succotash		fcy, x-stand, stand, s-stand	8Z T 303 2½ 10	7.8 15.2 26.8 98.5	— — — —	90, 80, 70, <70			

APPROXIMATE PACKING DATES WEST COAST VEGETABLES

Item	Jan.	Feb.	March	April	May	June	July	Aug.	Sept.	Oct.	Nov.	Dec.
Asparagus			■	■	■	■						
Beans - Green (Cal.)						■	■	■				
Beans - Green (NW)								■	■			
Beans - Italian							■	■				
Beans - Wax							■	■				
Beets							■	■	■			
Carrots								■	■	■	■	
Corn								■	■			
Lima Beans									■			
Olives	■									■		■
Peas (Calif.)					■							
Peas (NW)							■					
Spinach			■	■								
Tomatoes							■	■	■	■		

Reprinted with permission Stewart-Tucker, Inc.; Menlo Park, CA.

**PURCHASE SPECIFICATIONS FOR
CANNED VEGETABLES**

PRODUCT	UNIT PER CASE	U.S.D.A. GRADE	MIN. U.S.D.A. SCORE	SIZE OR COUNT	REQUIREMENTS
ASPARAGUS, CUT	6/#10	STAND.	—	—	ALL GREEN
ASPARAGUS, WHOLE SPEARS	6/#5 SQUAT OR 24/#2 OR 24/#300 (14 OZ)	FANCY	92	4/80 17/24	ALL GREEN MAMMOTH, CALIFORNIA
BEANS, BAKED VEGETARIAN	6/#10	FANCY	—	—	WHITE BEANS IN TOMATO SAUCE
BEANS, GREEN, CUT	6/#10	EX. STAND.	82	4 OR 5 SIEVE	"BLUELAKE", ROUND, 1-1/2" CUT.
BEANS, LIMA	6/#10	EX. STAND.	—	#3 SIZE	GREEN & WHITE MIXED
BEANS, RED KIDNEY	6/#10	FANCY	—	—	DARK RED IN SAUCE
BEANS, WAX, CUT	6/#10	FANCY	—	SIZE #3 OR 4 OR 3 & 4 MIXED	ROUND OR FLAT
BEETS, SLICED	6/#10	FANCY	90	2-1/2" DIA. OR UNDER	MEDIUM
BEETS, DICED	6/#10	FANCY	90	—	—
CARROTS, SLICED	6/#10	FANCY	90	—	SMALL
CARROTS, DICED	6/#10	FANCY	90	—	—
CORN, CRM, STYLE	6/#10	FANCY	—	—	GOLDEN, EXTRA HEAVY CONSISTENCY
CORN, WHOLE KERNEL	6/#10	FANCY	90	—	GOLDEN, SMALL KERNEL
MUSHROOMS	48/#1 OR 24/#1 (8 OZ) OR 24/#2-1/2 (16 OZ)	STAND.	—	—	STEMS & PIECES, DOMESTIC OR IMPORTED. CREAM COLOR.

Jaques Bloch, FHCFA, Montefiore Hospital, New York, NY.

SPECIFICATIONS

Anise

Anise, also called sweet fennel or finocchi, is similar in appearance to celery, but it has a spicy, licorice flavor. This edible type of anise should not be confused with the variety that is grown only for the oil that is secreted by its leaves.

The stocks should be fresh, clean, crisp, solid, and of characteristic color. It should be tender and have a well-developed bulb. Bulbs showing extensive brown areas, and tops that are yellow and brown are signs of old age or damage from rough handling.

Anise has many applications as a spice, accenting a variety of foods. The bulbs are quartered and eaten raw with salt, or they make an interesting addition to a salad. They may be braised or steamed in any of the ways appropriate for celery, or boiled and served with a cream sauce. It should be kept refrigerated at 32°F, 95 percent relative humidity.

MONTHLY AVAILABILITY OF ANISE AS
PERCENTAGE OF TOTAL ANNUAL SUPPLY

Jan. %	Feb. %	Mar. %	Apr. %	May %	June %
7	1	4		*	

July %	Aug. %	Sept. %	Oct. %	Nov. %	Dec. %
		*	14	30	37

Grades. The U.S. standards for so-called "sweet anise" (finocchio) adopted in 1930, provide one grade, U.S. 1. This

> shall consist of stalks of sweet anise which are firm, tender, well trimmed, and fairly well blanched; which are free from decay and from damage caused by growth cracks, pithy branches, wilting, freezing, seed stems, dirt, discoloration, disease, insects, or mechanical or other means. Unless otherwise specified the minimum diameter of each bulb shall be not less than 2 in.[2]

Artichokes

The artichoke plant, *Cynara scolymus,* is a herbaceous perennial with strong, prickly, deeply-cut leaves, and large terminal heads, which are harvested before they bloom. It is a member of the *Compositae* family, so named because the members have small flowers (florets) born in dense composite heads resembling single flowers. It derives its common name from the northern Italian words *articocal* and *articoclos.*

The Globe artichoke is the large, unopened flower bud of the thistle-like plant which is available all year-round, with heavy supplies in April and May. Most of the production is from California.

Size has little to do with quality or flavor, but those with compact, heavy, plump globes that yield slightly to pressure and that have large, tightly clinging, fleshy leaf scales of a good, green color are the best. Browning may mean old age, bruise injury, or frost.

Winter is the most critical period for artichoke growers. At freezing temperatures, the outer skin of the scales is broken, causing the bud to appear blistered and whitish. After several days, this blistered skin becomes dark and the industry calls them "Winter Kist." Under these conditions, quality is not impaired, but the black appearance has a detrimental effect on sales.

Artichokes should not be stored for any long period of time, but for brief holding, 32°F and a high humidity of 95 percent is desirable to prevent wilting or drying.

Jerusalem artichokes are actually a tuber, the root of a variety of sunflower plant. They are sometimes marketed under the name "sunchokes." One of the true natives of North America, Jerusalem artichokes really aren't artichokes at all, and they have nothing to do with Jerusalem.

---

[2]USDA Code.

Grades.   U.S. Grade Standards for artichokes provide two grades, U.S. No. 1 and U.S. No. 2.

> U.S. No. 1 shall consist of artichokes which are properly trimmed, fairly well formed, fairly compact, not overdeveloped; and which are free from damage caused by worms, snails, bruising, freezing, disease, insects, or other means. In order to allow for variations incident to proper grading and handling, not more than 10 percent, by count, of any lot may be below the requirements of this grade but no part of this tolerance shall be allowed for decay.[3]

Artichokes, Chinese

Also known as Chorogi or Knotroot, the plant is mint-like, grows up to 18 inches in height with ovate to lanceolate leaves. It produces numerous small slender tubers with the edible portion just under the soil surface. Tubers are white with crisp flesh which can be eaten raw or cooked. Chinese artichokes are somewhat comparable in appearance to potatoes, but the tubers do not store well. They are not grown commercially in the United States.

Asparagus

Buy: U.S. No. 1 Fresh, Grade A Canned, Grade B Frozen.

Deterioration: Wilted, flabby spears or mushy condition of tips indicate age and objectionable flavor.

Deterioration of Canned: Soft, mushy, or tough fibrous cuts. Shattered open or flowered heads. Off-color (very light yellow-green) or uneven colored cuts. Stringy or frayed edges. Presence of considerable grit. Too few heads. Noticeable bitter or undesirable taste.

Deterioration of Frozen: Tough fibrous units, shattered, open, or flowered heads. Off-color, stringy, or frayed cut edges. Presence of considerable grit, silt, or sand. Too few heads (in cuts and tips style). Off-flavor or odor.

Bamboo Shoots

Grown mostly in the southern states, edible bamboo shoots are the tender young stalks of a species of bamboo plant. They resemble asparagus spears in appearance. Freshness, crispness, and a good, green color are general indications of quality.

Bean Sprouts

These crisp tendrils have been around for centuries, spending most of their culinary lives in Oriental dishes. Cooked or raw, bean sprouts have a fresh, delicate flavor and an unusual shape and texture that adds a new dimension to vegetable combinations, salads, and main dishes. Bean sprouts should be fresh looking, crisp, with tips that are not dry. The shorter the bean sprout, the younger and more tender it is.

---

[3]USDA Code.

Store the sprouts in a refrigerator. If you plan to serve them raw, wash them well, float off the loose particles, and chill in ice water for half an hour before serving.

People generally mean "pea sprouts" when they say "bean sprouts." Pea sprouts are tiny shoots issuing from a little pea. When bought, the pea sprouts still carry an olive-green hood, which should be plucked off during the washing. If the roots at the tail of the snow-white stem are too long, they should also be plucked off. Bean sprouts are usually golden yellow in color and possess a stronger flavor and a rather crunchy texture. The hood color varies according to the type of bean used. This hood must be removed.

Bean threads are long, clear, dried "threads" made from mung beans, most commonly used in Chinese soups. The Japanese use them in sukiyaki. They have a bland flavor and add a desirable chewy quality to a dish. Before using, you must soak the threads in water for several hours or overnight.

The nutritional values in sprouts from soybeans are more than in the same amount of mung bean sprouts; however, all varieties mentioned have a high content of water, generally represent some volume of protein, vitamins, and minerals—but not importantly so.

Deterioration: Dark, dull gray, or yellow-colored sprouts. Bitter, musty, sour, or excessive acid flavor. Excessive loose hulls and strings. Sprouts that are tough and stringy.

Beans

String or stringless beans (practically all produced today are stringless) with long straight pods, crisp enough to snap easily between your fingers, are your best buy. When the beans start to ridge and bulge the pods, they usually are old, tough, and leathery. Some string beans are green, others are waxy yellow (wax beans). Some are flat and some are round, but all are equally good. String beans, found on the market all year, are in reality the immature pods of kidney beans, picked while the seeds are tiny.

Beans are of two general types: *bush* (such as described above) or *vining,* such as "pole" beans, the latter growing on trellis or vines, the principal variety of which is the Kentucky Wonder.

Lima beans are flat and kidney-shaped, the smaller sizes being known as butter limas and the larger beans as potato limas. When making your purchase, look for clean, well-filled pods of a dark green color, as flabby pods generally indicate poor quality. The bean itself should be plump, with a tender skin of good green or greenish-white color.

Fava beans are a comparative newcomer to America. They are a long, round, velvety-podded variety held in high esteem by epicures. They resemble the lima bean except they are rounder, with thick, somewhat larger pods.

Garbanzo beans are the "slick chick" of the pea family. Sometimes called chick peas, they are widely used in the Mediterranean and Spanish-American cuisines.

A high Vitamin A content . . . one-third the daily requirement in one-half cup, pressure cooked . . . is the major nutritional value of regular green beans.

Beans can be held successfully for a short period of time at 45 to 50°F with relative humidity of 85 percent. An effective method of storage is to place them in a plastic film

SIZES OF GREEN BEANS

| Sieve Designation | Word Designation | | Measurement of Thickness in 64ths of One Inch |
	Whole Beans	Cut or Short Cut Beans	
Size 1	Tiny	Small	Less than 14 ½
Size 2	Small	Small	14 ½ , but not including 18 ½
Size 3	Medium	Small	18 ½ , but not including 21
Size 4	Medium Large	Medium	21, but not including 24
Size 5	Large	Large	24, but not including 27
Size 6	Extra Large	Extra Large	27 or more

Reprinted with permission Stewart–Tucker, Inc., Menlo Park, CA.

bag, which helps greatly to retain moisture, and store them in the hydrator. Washing them before they are placed in the refrigerator will aid in preventing dehydration. Green beans are high in Vitamin A content. One-half cup, pressure cooked, provides one-third the daily requirement.

Deterioration: Wilted and dry beans are signs of aging after picking, resulting in poor flavor. Older beans with enlarged seeds are likely to be tough and fibrous.

GREEN AND WAX BEAN SIZES

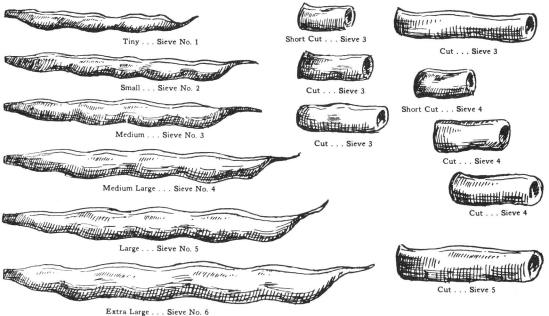

Tiny . . . Sieve No. 1

Small . . . Sieve No. 2

Medium . . . Sieve No. 3

Medium Large . . . Sieve No. 4

Large . . . Sieve No. 5

Extra Large . . . Sieve No. 6

Short Cut . . . Sieve 3

Cut . . . Sieve 3

Cut . . . Sieve 3

Cut . . . Sieve 3

Short Cut . . . Sieve 4

Cut . . . Sieve 4

Cut . . . Sieve 4

Cut . . . Sieve 5

Frosty Acres Buyers Guide—The Frozen Food Forum, Inc.; Atlanta, Ga.

GREEN BEANS—APPROXIMATE SIZES OF DIFFERENT CUT AND WHOLE STYLES

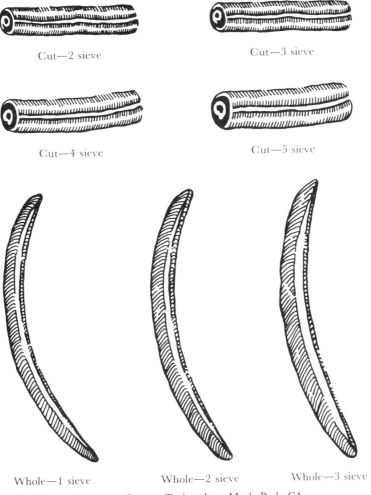

Cut—2 sieve

Cut—3 sieve

Cut—4 sieve

Cut—5 sieve

Whole—1 sieve

Whole—2 sieve

Whole—3 sieve

Reprinted with permission Stewart–Tucker, Inc., Menlo Park, CA.

Servings and Weights. The usual serving is ½ cup of cooked snap beans. A pound of fresh beans, as purchased, provides 4½ servings. It takes 22 lb. to serve 100. For 1 lb. ready-to-cook, use 1.14 lb. (about 1 lb., 2 oz.) as purchased. One quart of beans ready to cook equals 0.94 lb. (about 15 oz.). One bushel is 28 to 30 lb., as purchased.

Buy: Grade B Canned: 90 percent uniform color; maximum of 15 percent of d.w. in defects; young and tender with some loss of fleshy structure, practically free of fiber; maximum of 10 percent tough strings; liquor may be cloudy.

PRODUCT FLOW CHART: GREEN AND WAX BEANS

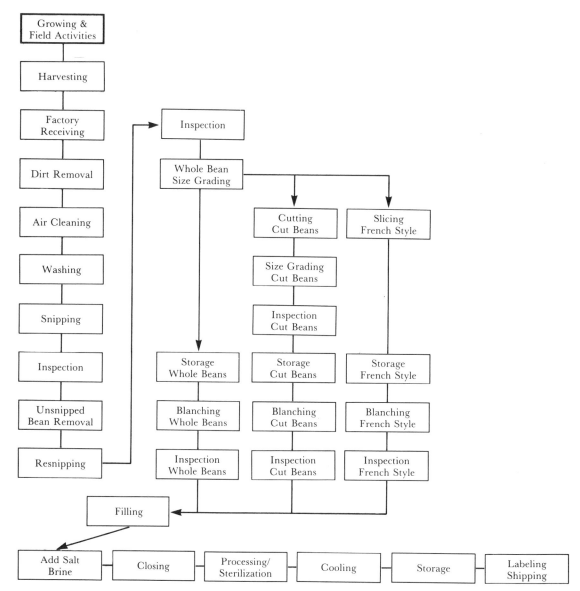

Reprinted with permission Stewart—Tucker, Inc.; Menlo Park, CA.

Deterioration: Excessively cloudy or off-color liquid. Spotted beans. Beans with large seeds or worm holes. Noticeably soft or mushy beans, lacking a fleshy texture. Presence of excessive unsnipped ends, loose stem ends, tough inedible strings, uneven and ragged units, split units, and small pieces of pod.

Grade B Frozen: As with canned; maximum 6 tough string units per 10 ounces in sliced lengthwise or 4 percent in other varieties.

Deterioration: Off-color or mixed varieties. Presence of loose stems, unstemmed units, or small pieces. Presence of damaged, or blemished units, tough stringy units, and excess sloughing. Off-odor or flavor.

Beans, Lima

Buy: Grade B Canned: 50 percent green, 50 percent lighter, maximum of 25 percent white; 1 square inch defects per 30 ounces; reasonably young and tender; cloudy liquor with considerable sediment.

Grade B Frozen: 60 to 65 percent green; light discolorations; minor amounts of vegetable matter; maximum 10 percent shriveled, 4 percent sprouted, 3 percent blemished units.

Deterioration of Canned: Off-color. Excessive number of white beans and extraneous material, broken beans, loose skins, blemished beans, and off flavor or odor.

Deterioration of Frozen: Off-color or excessive number of white beans. Extraneous material, broken beans, loose skins, or blemished beans. Off-flavor or odor.

LIMA BEAN SIZES

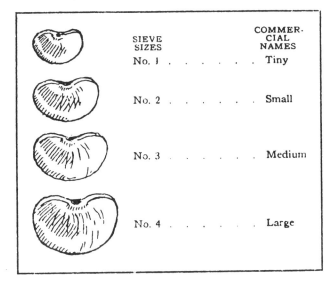

	SIEVE SIZES	COMMERCIAL NAMES
	No. 1	Tiny
	No. 2	Small
	No. 3	Medium
	No. 4	Large

Beans, Speckled Butter (Lima)

Buy: Grade A Frozen: Color mix: maximum 15 percent light green, 20 percent light tan to tan; 4 beans per 10 ounces brown; practically free from defects such as shriveled or sprouted beans or extraneous material; reasonably tender, uniform texture.

Beans, Dried Canned

Buy: Grade A; Color: Typical good color. Consistency: Beans in Tomato sauce and in sweetened sauce—Sauce is smooth and is neither grainy nor lumpy, and product forms a slightly mounded mass with not more than a slight separation of liquid. Beans in brine—Packing medium is neither grainy nor lumpy, and the product may possess a thick consistency or there may be a separation of liquid. Defects: Practically free from defects. Maximum Tolerance: Not more than 5 percent by count of loose skins and broken and mashed units; and not more than 4 percent may be damaged units. Character: Possesses typical texture that may be slightly granular or slightly firm with skins that are tender.

Beans, Baked, Canned

"Canned baked beans" is the product prepared from dry mature beans used for canning, but not including soybeans. Any safe and suitable ingredients permissible under the provisions of the Federal Food, Drug, and Cosmetic Act may be used. The product is prepared by washing, soaking, and baking by the application of dry heat in open or loosely covered containers in a closed oven at atmospheric pressure for sufficient prolonged time to produce a typical texture and flavor. It is packed in hermetically sealed containers and sufficiently processed by heat to assure preservation.

"Reasonably good character" means that the baked beans have a reasonably good, typical texture, that may be firm or soft but not hard or mushy; and that the skins may be slightly tough.

Types of canned baked beans include: White beans, Red Kidney beans, Yellow-eye beans, and beans of other colors or types except soybeans. Styles include: "In Brown Sugar, Molasses, New England Sauce, or Tomato Sauce."

U.S. Grade A = 90 points, U.S. Grade B = 80 points, Substandard = less than 80 points.

Buy Grade A: uniform color, holds well-rounded mound without beans separating; characteristic flavor; tender skins, beans may be slightly soft or firm.

Pork and Beans, Canned

Types include: Pea (Navy) Beans, Small white beans, flat white beans, Great northern beans, other white beans, excluding white lima beans.

"Canned pork and beans" (Canned dried white beans with pork) is the product prepared from dry mature white beans with pork or pork fat; and with a packing medium or sauce consisting of water, tomato products, and any other safe and suitable ingredients permissible under the provisions of the Federal Food, Drug, and Cosmetic Act. The product is prepared by washing, soaking, blanching, or other processing. It is packed in hermetically sealed containers and sufficiently processed by heat to assure preservation.

U.S. Grade A = 90 points, U.S. Grade B = 80 points, Substandard = less than 80 points.

Buy Grade A: Beans alike in shape, size, and color with maximum 1 percent contrasting varieties; bright typical color of beans; rich, distinct flavor; smooth sauce, makes slightly mounded mass; good texture, tender skins.

Beans, Chinese Long (Dow Kwok)

Chinese long beans are available the year-round from California and Mexico. They are pencil-thin, light green and tender, usually about 12 inches long, but may attain a length of 20 to 25 inches! Usually cooked with beef, the tiny bean within the pod resembles immature black-eyed peas.

Beets

Beets are marketed with or without tops—the fall crop, which is sometimes stored, being the one usually sold with only the root remaining. They are available the year-round.

Fresh, prime quality beets should have a good globular shape, with a smooth, firm flesh and a rich, deep-red color. Those of medium size are less likely to be tough. In the early crop, a poor appearance of the leaves is no certain indication of inferiority, for beet tops deteriorate rapidly without affecting the root quality.

Beet tops are frequently taken from young plants, bunched, and sold as salad greens. Here the color and appearance of the tops are important, as their edibility depends upon their being young and tender. Select those that are thin-ribbed, fresh green, and not wilted or slimy.

Best storage temperature is 32°F, at 95 percent relative humidity. Bunched beets should be stored only briefly, for the beet tops are extremely perishable.

Servings and Weights.   A pound of fresh, untrimmed beet greens provides 2.37 portions of ½ cup cooked; or 4.74 portions of ¼ cup cooked. It takes 42¼ lb. as purchased for 100 servings of ½ cup; and 21¼ lb. for 100 servings of ¼ cup. A pound, as purchased, provides 0.56 lb. ready to cook.

A pound of fresh beets without tops provides 3.76 servings of ½ cup cooked, diced or sliced; and 7.52 portions of ¼ cup cooked, diced or sliced. It takes 26¾ lb. as purchased to provide 100 portions of ½ cup; and 13½ lb. to provide 100 portions of ¼ cup. One pound as purchased provides 0.76 lb. cooked.

A bushel of beets weighs 50 to 56 lb. A bunch weighs from 1 to 1½ lb.

Grades.   The federal grades are U.S. 1 and U.S. 2, and in each the styles are designated as bunched beets, beets with short-trimmed tops, and topped beets. Beets called bunched mean beets tied in bunches with tops full length or removed to not less than 6 in. Beets with short-trimmed tops are those showing leaf-stems ranging to not more than 4 in. long. Topped beets are those with tops removed to not more than ½ in. in length. Standard bunches shall be fairly uniform in size, and each bunch *shall weigh not less than 1 lb.* and contain at least 3 beets. Not more than 10 percent of the bunches in any lot may fail to meet the requirements.

Buy Grade A Canned: All styles: good color, maximum 15 percent blemished. Whole: maximum 2¼ inch diameter; Sliced: maximum ⅝ inch thick, 3½ inch diameter; Quartered: cut from maximum 2½ inch diameter beets; Cut: ¼ ounce to 2 ounce pieces; Julienne, French Style, or Shoestring: maximum 3/16 inch square, maximum 10 percent unblemished.

Deterioration: Excessive number of end cuts, woodiness, coarse texture, and excessive softness. Black spots, pieces of peel, frayed edges and off-color, brown, or light pink beets. Deep cuts indicating mechanical or insect injury.

Bitter Melon

Balsam pear, commonly known as Bitter Melon, a clear vegetable, is about the size of a cucumber and possesses a wrinkled surface. Inside is a layer of white or pink spongy pulp and seeds. They are 6 to 8 inches long, used for sour flavoring or fried with beef. Bitter melons are available from June to October.

Bok Choy (Chinese Chard)

Bok choy resembles both chard and celery. It is also called white mustard cabbage. It is a very leafy green vegetable with a white stem and shiny dark leaves, often topped with a pale yellow flower. You can usually buy either the whole cluster, including tougher stalks, or just the heart of tender stem cluster, with the tough exterior stalks removed. Either is sold by the pound. Flavor is slightly stronger than that of Chinese cabbage, but it is good cooked as a vegetable or in soups, and generally used in the preparation of Chinese chop suey and chow mein. Leaves should be prepared as you would spinach.

Broccoli

The term "broccoli," as generally used, refers to sprouting broccoli rather than the heading type. The word comes from the Italian "brocco," meaning arm or branch.

When you buy broccoli, look for plenty of green color in the heads as well as the leaves and stems. Size of heads may vary, but this bears no relation to the eating quality. Stalks should be tender and firm with compact dark green or purplish-green buds in the head. Old, frequently tough broccoli can be detected by yellow "flowers" visible inside the buds. The more yellow flowers you see, the less desirable it is.

Use broccoli as soon as possible; store it only briefly at 32°F and 95 percent relative humidity.

Deterioration: Soft, slippery, watersoaked spots or irregular brown spots are signs of decay. Heads that are spreading, wilted, turning yellow, or have many enlarged flower buds are old and probably will have an off-flavor.

Grades. U.S. grade standards effective July 12, 1943 for bunched Italian sprouting broccoli are U.S. Fancy, U.S. 1 and U.S. 2.

U.S. 1 shall consist of bunched stalks of Italian sprouting broccoli. Each bunch shall be free from decay, and from damage caused by over-maturity, discoloration of bud clusters or leaves, freezing, wilting, dirt or other foreign material, disease, insects, mechanical or other means. The bud clusters in each bunch shall be generally fairly compact. Each bunch shall be neatly and fairly evenly cut off at the base, and well trimmed, unless otherwise specified as "closely trimmed," "fairly well trimmed," or "leafy." There are no requirements for diameter but diameter may be specified for any lot as shown under "Size Specification." Unless otherwise specified, the length of each stalk shall be not less than 5 in. or more than 9 in.[4]

Broccoli, Frozen

Buy: Grade A: Bright green, 1 piece extraneous matter per 30 ounces, tender, no tough fibers, minimum 80 percent well developed. Spears: 2 inches maximum, usually 90 percent 1 inch; Short Spears: 95 percent largest; largest maximum 3 times smallest; Cut, Chopped: maximum 6 percent, 4 percent damaged or extraneous material; maximum ½ inch cuts, maximum ¾ inch chopped; Pieces: no grade A, 10 percent damage in Grade B.

Deterioration of Grade A and Grade B: Dull, off-color units. Presence of grit, silt, or extraneous material. Defective units, excessively trimmed units, or blemished units. Presence of flowering units or units with excessive fiber. Off-flavor or color.

Brussels Sprouts

Brussels sprouts look like miniature cabbages and are at their best between October and March. They receive their name from the Belgian city of Brussels, where they were first grown in the thirteenth century.

Good sprouts are firm, compact, fresh, and of bright appearance and good green color. Puffy or soft sprouts are usually poor in quality and flavor. Wilted or yellowing leaves indicate aging.

They are commonly not sold by varietal name. Size and color are more likely to be the best buying criteria.

Deterioration: Sprouts with yellow or otherwise discolored leaves or sprouts which are soft, open or wilted. Small holes or ragged leaves may indicate worm damage.

Servings and Weights. One pound of fresh brussels sprouts provides 4.42 portions of ½ cup cooked, or 8.84 portions of ¼ cup cooked. It takes 22¾ lb. as purchased for 100 servings of ½ cup, and 11½ lb. for 100 servings of ¼ cup. A pound, as purchased, provides 0.74 lb. ready to cook.

---

[4]USDA Code.

Grades. The U.S. Standards for fresh brussels sprouts provide for two grades, U.S. No. 1 and U.S. No. 2. U.S. No. 1 consists of:

> Brussels sprouts which are well colored, firm, not withered or burst, which are free from soft decay and seed stems, and free from damage caused by discoloration, dirt or other foreign material, freezing, disease, insects, or mechanical or other means. Unless otherwise specified, the diameter of each brussels sprout shall be not less than 1 in., and the length shall be not more than 2¾ in. In order to allow for variations incident to proper grading and handling other than for size, not more than a total of 10 percent, by weight, of the brussels sprouts in any lot may fail to meet the requirements of the grade: provided, that not more than ⅕ of this amount, or 2 percent, shall be allowed for soft decay. In addition, not more than a total of 5 percent, by weight, of the brussels sprouts in any lot may be smaller than the specified minimum diameter, and not more than 10 percent may be longer than the specified maximum length. "Well colored" means that the brussels sprout has a light green or a darker shade of green color characteristic of well-grown brussels sprouts. "Firm" means that the brussels sprout is of reasonable solidity and is fairly compact but may yield slightly to moderate pressure.[5]

Brussels Sprouts, Frozen

Buy: Grade B: Green with 5 to 25 percent yellow units; no grit or silt; 1 piece extraneous material per 20 ounces; maximum 20 percent damaged; minimum 50 percent well developed; maximum 10 percent loose heads.

Deterioration: Off-color units. Presence of excessive grit or silt, loose leaves, small pieces, poorly trimmed or damaged units. Units that are soft or very loose structured. Off-flavor or odor.

Burdock (Gobo)

Species of Arctium, from the Green word for "bear," probably alluded to the shaggy "bur." Gobo is heavily cultivated in Japan for its root, which has been greatly thickened and ameliorated, affording a popular vegetable. The Burdock is a common and despised weed in this country.

Cabbage

Despite its plentifulness, cabbage can be expensive if you do not pay attention to its careful selection. There are numerous common varieties but the quality characteristics are generally the same for all types.

Well-trimmed, reasonably solid heads that are heavy for their size and show no discolored veins are your best buy. Early or new cabbage is not so firm as some of the Fall and Winter strains, which are suitable for storing.

One of the most unusual-appearing varieties is called Savoy cabbage. Its yellowish, crimped leaves form a head usually not much harder than that of Iceberg let-

---

[5]USDA Code.

tuce. Another novel type is Celery cabbage, also called Chinese cabbage, which has some of the characteristics of both Romaine and cabbage. This variety is used principally for salads and its long, oval-shaped head should be firm, fresh and well blanched.

Except for color, red cabbage is identical to other "headed" types.

Cabbage stores well at 32°F and 90 percent relative humidity, if well ventilated. It wilts quickly in dry storage.

To retain all the nutrients of cabbage, the method of cooking is important, especially to conserve Vitamin C. It should not be shredded and left exposed to air, especially not to warm air. It should be cooked quickly, then used soon, and not kept warm for a long period.

Deterioration: Faded green and yellowing or wilted outer leaves are objectionable. Worm and insect injury may penetrate the head and require excessive trimming. Heads with decay should be avoided.

Servings and Weights.   One pound of cabbage will yield 6.32 portions of coleslaw, 2 oz. each, for a yield of 79 percent as served. To obtain 25 portions, a buyer would need to order 4 lb.; 100 portions, 16 lb. One pound will yield about 4 portions of cooked slices or wedges, 3 oz. each, for a yield of 75 to 80 percent as served. To obtain 25 portions, a buyer would need to order 6 lb.; 100 portions, about 25 lb.

A 50-lb. crate or sack of cabbage will provide about 213 3-oz. portions of cooked slices or wedges, a yield of 80 percent.

Grades.   U.S. standards for cabbage, effective Sept. 1, 1945, provide for 2 grades: U.S. 1 and U.S. Commercial.

U.S. 1 shall consist of heads of cabbage of one variety, or similar varietal characteristics, which are of reasonable solidity, and are not withered, puffy, or burst, and which are free from soft rot, seedstems, and from damage caused by discoloration, freezing, disease, insects, or mechanical or other means. Stems shall be cut so that they do not extend more than ½ in. beyond the point of attachment of the outermost leaves. Unless otherwise specified, each head shall be well trimmed. However, cabbage which has fairly good green color and is specified as "U.S. 1 Green," and red cabbage which is specified as "U.S. 1 New Red" need be only fairly well trimmed.[6]

Cactus Leaves (Nopales)

In April and May, cactus plants make new growth. The little leaves, or pencos, are light green and as crisp and tender as lettuce. Nopales are a favorite Mexican vegetable, with flavor and texture similar to green beans, but firmer. The smaller leaves are more tender.

To prepare for cooking, the cactus thorns must be carefully removed with a potato peeler or sharp-pointed knife. Cut the de-spined nopales into half-inch squares and boil in salted water with ¼ tsp. of soda and one chopped onion for 20 small, tender nopales. It should require from 5 to 10 minutes to cook them tender. Drain, season to taste, and serve.

---

[6]USDA Code.

Cardoon

A long celery-like vegetable, measuring nearly two feet, with a narrow, coarse top leaf, the cardoon is thought to be of the same species as the Globe artichoke and to have been developed from it by long cultivation and selection.

The plant has been introduced in South America and has grown wild extensively in the Pampas.

Leaves should be very dark green. Select cardoon with a small shank as this indicates a young, tender plant. Remove the outer stems as they only become tougher when cooked. The inner leaves and stalks have a pleasant flavor and can be substituted for celery. Store like celery. Vinegar added to the water (about 1 tsp. to a cup) will keep the cardoon white. The roots and leaf stalks are usually cooked and eaten in soups.

Carrots

Look for firm, well-formed, smooth, orange to orange-red carrots with well trimmed tops. Wilted, flabby, soft, shriveled carrots—or carrots with large green areas (sunburn) at the top—should be avoided. Also avoid topped carrots that have green shoots and bunched carrots that have yellow tops—they are too old and have not been stored properly. Excessive forking, and rough or cracked carrots will cause considerable waste in preparation.

Deterioration: Sunken or mushy spots, mold, or flabbiness are indications of age and poor condition.

Servings and Weights. One cup of grated fresh carrots weighs 110 grams (1 lb. is 454 grams); and 1 carrot (5½ by 1 in., or 25 thin carrot strips) weighs 50 grams.

A pound of carrots, ready to cook, provides 1¼ servings of ½ cup each of cooked, diced or sliced vegetables. To serve 100, the requirement is 24 lb. of carrots ready to cook. For 1 lb. ready to cook or to serve raw, use 1.22 lb. (about 1 lb, 4 oz. as purchased). One qt. cooked, diced, or sliced equals 1.23 lb., about 1 lb., 4 oz.

A pound of carrots grated or shredded gives 6¼ servings of ½ cup each; and it takes 16 lb. for 100 such servings. One quart raw, grated, or shredded equals 1.04 lb., about 1 lb., 1 oz.

A pound of carrots raw, diced, sliced, or in strips, provides 5 servings of 1/2 cup each; and it takes 20 lb. for 100 such servings. One quart raw, diced, sliced, or strips, equals 1.28 lb., about 1 lb., 5 oz.

A bushel of carrots (2150 cu. in.) weighs about 50 lb.

Grades. There are U.S. wholesale standard grades for bunched, topped, and short-trimmed carrots. There are also consumer grades for fresh carrots as a whole, but they are little used and are, therefore, only mentioned here. The grades that are of most interest are for topped carrots. These are U.S. Extra No. 1, U.S. No. 1, and U.S. No. 2. Texts of all grades can be obtained by writing Agricultural Marketing Service, Washington, D.C. Space here permits giving a sample of only one of the grades.

Topped carrots: U.S. Extra No. 1 consists of carrots of similar varietal characteristics which are well trimmed, firm, clean, fairly well colored, fairly smooth, well formed, and which are free from damage caused by freezing, growth cracks, sunburn, pithiness, woodiness, internal discoloration, oil spray, dry rot, other disease, insects, or mechanical or other means.

Size: Unless otherwise specified, the diameter of each carrot shall be not less than ¾ in. nor more than 1½ in., and the length shall be not less than 5 in.

For bunched carrots and for carrots with short trimmed tops, there are two grades: U.S. No. 1 and U.S. Commercial.

Carrots, Canned

Buy: Grade A: Orange-yellow color; maximum 15 percent defective except 10 percent in diced and shoestring, tender, firm, not fibrous.

Diced: 88 percent larger than ½ volume of smallest cube.

Shoestring: ³⁄₁₆ inch cross-section, maximum 12 percent ½ inch or less.

Cut: from maximum 2½ inch diameter carrot, minimum ¼ ounce; 50 percent weight variation second smallest to largest.

Deterioration: Off-color, showing a grayish or brownish cast; excessive number of pale and white carrots. Presence of tough or woody carrots showing softness. Poor trimming and peeling. Deep cuts resulting from insect or mechanical injury.

Carrots, Frozen

Buy: Grade B: Reasonably bright; one ⅜ inch square defect per 40 ounces; 14 damaged units per 10 ounces, maximum 17 percent smaller than ½ of volume, tender, not fibrous, uniform texture.

Deterioration: Excessive green or off-color. Excessive number of broken, crushed, cracked, unpeeled, tough, fibrous, or mushy units. Off-flavor or odor.

Cauliflower

The word "cauliflower" comes from two Latin terms and literally means cabbage flower or stalk flower. Cauliflower is a cultivated descendant of common cabbage.

For years, the primary instructions for buying good cauliflower included the phrase, "Should wear a jacket of bright green, denoting freshness." Today, most cauliflower is shipped with the head only packaged in a clear-film wrap, thus eliminating the very perishable and heavy, ribbed leaves. The film helps to preserve freshness and nutrients, elimination of the heavily-ribbed leaves saves better than one-third the cost of shipping the product.

Regardless, there are still some sure signs in selecting good quality cauliflower. Size of the head does not affect quality, nor do the tiny leaves you occasionally find growing through the curds; however, the small "flowers" in the head must not have started to grow, or the cauliflower will be inferior eating quality. It should not have a rice-like appearance. The curd should be white, or only slightly creamy-white, very firm, and compact. (Loose, open flower clusters indicate over-maturity.) Spotted, speckled, or bruised curds should be avoided, unless this portion can be trimmed with little waste—and the curd meets all other requirements.

Ideal storage temperature is 32°F, relative humidity 90 percent.

Avoid overcooking. When the stem end yields to the touch of a fork, boiled cauliflower is done. It may be served buttered, creamed, au gratin, or polonaise. Small bits of flowerettes are also used raw in salads, and the vegetable may also be used in making soup.

Cauliflower is one of those white vegetables that can pick up an unattractive yellowish appearance if cooked in "hard" or alkaline water. Add a teaspoonful of fresh lemon juice to the water and the cauliflower will stay white.

A new, green cauliflower variety is now commercially grown. A cross between conventional cauliflower and broccoli, it requires no hand tying in the field and will stay green through cooking. The curd (head) resembles cauliflower and is chartreuse green rather than dark green, such as broccoli. The new variety is higher in dry matter, cooks faster with less tendency to discolor, more tasty, and less odoriferous while cooking.

Deterioration: Spotted or spreading heads are a sign of aging, overmaturity, or disease.

Grades. There is only one U.S. grade for cauliflower, U.S. 1.

> This consists of compact heads of cauliflower which are not discolored or overmature; and which are free from soft or wet decay and are free from damage caused by wilting, fuzziness, riciness, enlarged bracts, bruises, hollow stems, dirt, or other foreign matter, disease, insects, or mechanical or other means. Unless otherwise specified, the heads shall be not less than 4 in. in diameter. Jacket leaves shall be fresh, green, and free from damage caused by disease and free from serious damage by any other cause. Unless otherwise specified, jacket leaves shall be well trimmed. In order to allow for variations other than for size, incident to proper grading and handling, not more than a total of 10 percent, by count, of the cauliflower in any lot may fail to meet the requirements of this grade, but not more than ¹⁄₁₀ of this amount, or 1 percent may be affected by soft rot or wet decay affecting the curd. In addition, not more than 5 percent, by count, of the heads in any lot may be smaller than the specified minimum size.[7]

Cauliflower, Frozen

Buy: Grade A: White to cream color with green or bluish tint on branches; free from pieces and fragments; maximum 15 percent poor trim or damage; minimum 80 percent firm, compact clusters; 20 percent may be slightly soft, rice-like, or fuzzy.

Deterioration: Off-color or more than a slight tint of green, blue, or purple on stalks. Excessive amounts of small pieces and detached fragments, excessive number of damaged units or loose, soft, rice-like, or fuzzy units. Off-flavors or odors.

Celeriac

Also known as *celery root,* this vegetable is cultivated for its root instead of its stalk. It is grown the same as celery, for the thickened edible corm, except that no branching is required. The leaves are not eaten.

---

[7]USDA Code.

Choose celeriac that is small, since the smaller celeriac will be more tender and less woody. Trim roots and tops and store in refrigerator, 32°F, with high humidity.

Celeriac is a light brown bulb-type root. It is best to peel it before cooking. Primarily used in stews and soups, celeriac can be braised or used as a substitute for cooked potatoes.

Grade and Quality.   No standards for celeriac have been established by the USDA. When grown properly, the roots should be solid and tender. Celeriac may come to market washed or unwashed.

Celery

There are two distinct types of celery: Golden Heart, which is bleached white, and Pascal, which is a dark or light green. The latter has practically replaced the former variety because of its distinctive flavor and almost complete lack of stringiness.

Quality characteristics for both varieties are the same. Leaf stems or stalks should be brittle enough to snap easily, and be of medium length and thickness. The inside of the stem should be smooth. If it feels rough or puffy to your finger, the celery is likely to be pithy. A good heart formation usually indicates good celery, and examining stalks for this feature will reveal whether there is any black heart, a rot commonly found in stalks of celery. Leaflets should be fresh or only slightly wilted. Stalks of light green, glossy surface, will taste best.

Favorable storage temperature is 32°F, relative humidity 90 to 95 percent.

Deterioration: Stalks with wilted, flabby branches, predominantly yellow leaves, dark streaks inside the branches or coarse central stems. Avoid celery with brown to black discoloration of the small center branches or insect injury.

Servings and weights.   One quart of raw chopped celery is about a pound, according to USDA which also states that for 1 lb. ready-to-cook or serve raw, use 1.33 lb. (about 1 lb., 5 oz.) as purchased. In the school lunch program, 1 lb. is figured as providing 5 servings; and 20 lb. provides 100 servings, these two figures relating to pounds ready to serve. According to USDA, 3 small inner stalks (5 in. long, ¾ in. wide) weigh 50 grams. One large outer stalk (8 in. long, 1 in. wide, 1½ in. at root end), 40 grams. One cup raw diced celery, 100 grams. One cup of diced cooked celery, however, weighs 130 grams.

Grades.   U.S. standards for celery for use at shipping point and wholesale are U.S. Extra No. 1, U.S. No. 1, and U.S. No. 2. There are also U.S. Consumer Standards for celery stalks, for use at retail, but these grades are little used. They are U.S. Grade AA, U.S. Grade A, and U.S. Grade B.

U.S. Extra No. 1 consists of stalks of celery of similar varietal characteristics which are well developed, well formed, clean, well trimmed, compact, and which are free from black-heart, brown stem, soft rot, doubles, and free from damage caused by freezing, growth cracks, horizontal cracks, pithy branches, seedstems, suckers, wilting, blight, other disease, insects, or mechanical or other means. Stalks shall be green unless speci-

**CELERY: WELL-FORMED
LOWER LIMIT
"BOWING"   U.S.   EXTRA
NO. 1**

USDA

fied as fairly well blanched or mixed blanch. (a) The average midrib length of the outer whorl of branches shall be not less than 7 in. (b) Unless otherwise specified in connection with the grade, stalks shall be of such length as to extend from one side, end, or bottom of the container to within 1½ in. of the corresponding opposite side, end, or top of the container. Such measurement shall not include the bulge. In any container when stalk length is specified, it shall be the minimum length in terms of whole inches of even number, as 12 in., 14 in. etc., in accordance with the facts.[8]

Celtuce

A comparatively new vegetable in the United States, celtuce has been grown in China for many years. This type has an enlarged stem and no head. The leaves are not palat-

[8]USDA Code.

able, as those of other types, except possibly while they are young and tender. It is grown principally for its large, fleshy stems which are peeled and eaten raw or cooked. Its flavor is a combination of celery and lettuce, from which it derives its name. Choose and store the same as you would lettuce.

Chard

Swiss chard is a type of beet that develops no enlarged fleshy root. It has large leaves with thickened mid-ribs; both ribs and leaves are palatable. The roots are hard and woody. Like all salad greens, it is important the leaves be fresh, crisp, and of a good, green color. Ideal storage is at 34°F, at 90 percent humidity.

In effect, it is two vegetables in one, since the leaves may be cooked as greens and the white stems may be cooked like celery. The fiber is very delicate, similar to asparagus. It should always be steamed, never boiled. The leaves should be cooked like spinach, using only the water that clings to them after washing.

Quality. There are no U.S. standard grades for Swiss chard. Like all leafy greens, this vegetable should be fresh, crisp, not showing yellow or browned portions, and should be free of aphis or other insect infestation. It should be clean and *cold*. Unless it is under refrigeration, the quality is doubtful. Stalks that are wilted and rubbery will be tough and unsatisfactory. Coarse stalks indicate pithiness. This may be discovered by pressing or twisting the stalk.

Chayote (Vegetable pears)

Grown successfully in California, Louisiana, and Florida, chayote is round to pear-shaped, smooth or corrugated, and the surface sometimes is covered with small soft spines. Quality vegetable pears are quite fiberless, with little or no seed coat around the single flat seed. The deeply wrinkled, fibrous seed coat makes it unfit to eat. The darker green and the harder they are, the better. Chayote is more delicately flavored than the squash. A single vine may yield 50 to 100 fruits a season. Chayote is easily shipped, and it may be stored at room temperature for 2 to 4 months. It is a cousin to the cucumber and squash.

Creole cooks call it Mirliton, South Americans call it mango squash. Floridians call it the vegetable pear. Whatever name you use, it is one of the most versatile of all fresh vegetables. It may be used in soups, salads, main dishes, and in desserts.

Choose chayotes like a vegetable, not as a fruit.

Chervil

Member of the parsley family, salad chervil is a leafy vegetable used like parsley. Turnip-rooted chervil, sometimes called parsnip chervil, is served with its roots cooked like parsnips. It is grown as a spring or autumn crop, not thriving in the heat of summer. Chervil is a native of Caucasus, Southern Russia and Western Asia.

Collards

Good quality collards are fresh, crisp, clean, and free from insect injury. Wilting and yellowing of the leaves indicate age or other form of damage. They should have a healthy, green color, free of blemishes. Store at 32°F, 90 percent humidity. Crushed ice in the package of greens will help keep them fresh.

Closely related to kale, collards is one of the most primitive and oldest members of the cabbage family. Georgia and Virginia have the largest acreages, but a good many other states also grow a large supply.

Deterioration: Extremely tough, fibrous leaf stems, or decayed, yellowed, or badly wilted leaves indicate overage and poor eating quality.

Deterioration of Canned: Poor flavor or odor. Off-color and tough, coarse leaves or stems. Root stubs, weeds, and seed heads in greens.

Deterioration of Frozen: Off-color. Presence of silt, sand, grit, weeds, grass, discoloration, tough or coarse stems, or leaves. Off-flavor or odor.

Grades.   US. standards for collard greens or broccoli, effective April 1953, provide for one grade, U.S. 1. This

consists of collard greens . . . of similar varietal characteristics which are fresh, fairly tender, fairly clean, well trimmed, and of characteristic color for the variety or type; which are free from decay, and free from damage caused by coarse stalks and seed-stems, discoloration, freezing, foreign material, disease, insects, or mechanical or other means.[9]

Coriander/Cilantro

Coriander, native to southern Europe and the Orient, has a very ancient history. The ripe seeds of coriander have served as a spice and a seasoning from very ancient times. Coriander seeds have been found in excavated Egyptian tombs.

The plant is, or has been, widely cultivated in most of Europe and Asia. In the United States, Kentucky produces more coriander plants than any other state.

Cilantro, the Spanish name for coriander, is sometimes called Chinese parsley or Mexican parsley. It is the parsley-like leaf of the coriander plant. The leaves are much more tender than parsley, but may be used in any manner parsley is used. The flavor is zesty and lingers on the tongue. When substituting cilantro for parsley, use it with care, for you'll need less cilantro than your usual parsley.

While many people use the two words as though they were one and the same, coriander is actually the dried, ripe fruits of the plant; cilantro is the leaf.

When selecting the latter, good, green color and fresh, unwilted leaves mean good quality. Wash well and store in refrigerator drawer in plastic bag after drying.

---

[9]USDA Code.

Corn

Our present-day sweet corns are generally hybrids which are grouped by kernel color: yellow, bi-color, and white. There are over 200 varieties of sweet corn being grown in the United States. The most important commercial varieties are yellow hybrids, with new varieties constantly being developed, having characteristics especially suited for an area of production. Whether it is white or yellow corn, generally the best, most properly-developed corn will be an even-numbered row of kernels—generally 12 to 14 rows. (White sweet corn is generally favored in southern states.)

In best quality corn, the husk is a fresh green color while the kernels are tender, milky, and sufficiently large to leave no space between the rows. They should be just firm enough to puncture rather easily when slight pressure is applied. Ears generally should be filled to the tip, with no rows of missing kernels. If you see cobs with kernels that are very soft and very small, you can be quite sure that the corn is immature.

Deterioration: Undeveloped ears, and kernels that are depressed and deep yellow. Also avoid ears with yellowed, wilted, or dried husks.

Servings and Weights.   In order to obtain 25 portions of sweet corn, a buyer for group feeding would need to purchase 1¾ doz. ears for 3 oz. portions of cooked kernels; for 25 portions of sweet corn cooked on the cob, he would need to purchase 25 ears; the usual 5-doz. crate or bag of sweet corn would provide 60 portions (1 ear each) of corn-on-the-cob.

The following table from USDA's *Food Buying Guide for Type A School Lunches,* January 1964, gives yields of sweet corn, with and without husks, by various size portions, and purchase units (in pounds) for 100 servings of each:

Food as Purchased	Purchase Unit	Servings per Purchase Unit	Serving Size or Portion	Purchase Units for 100 Servings	Additional Yield Information
With husks	lb.	2.00	1 medium ear (about 1/2 cup cooked)	50	1 lb. AP = 0.37 lb. edible portion cooked
	lb.	2.14	1/2 cup cooked	46-3/4	
		4.28	1/4 cup cooked	23-1/2	
Without husks	lb.	3.00	1 medium ear (about 1/2 cup cooked)	33-1/2	
	lb.	3.30	1/2 cup cooked	30-1/2	1 lb. AP = 0.55 lb.
		6.60	1/4 cup cooked	15-1/4	raw cut corn.

Grades. U.S. grade standards for green corn provide three grades, U.S. Fancy, U.S. 1, and U.S. 2.

> U.S. Fancy consists of ears of green corn of similar varietal characteristics, which are well trimmed, well developed, and which are free from smut, decay, worms, or insect injury, and free from injury caused by rust, discoloration, birds, other disease, or mechanical or other means. Cobs shall be fairly well filled, with plump and milky kernels, and well covered with fresh husks. The length of each cob shall be not less than 6 in. and the ears shall not be clipped.

> U.S. 1 consists of ears of green corn of similar varietal characteristics which are well trimmed, well developed, and which are free from smut and decay, and free from injury caused by rust, and free from damage caused by discoloration, birds, worms, other insects, other disease, or mechanical or other means. Cobs shall be fairly well filled, with plump and milky kernels, and fairly well covered with fresh husks. Each ear may be clipped, but each clipped ear shall be properly clipped. Unless otherwise specified, the length of each cob, clipped or unclipped, shall be not less than 5 in.[10]

It should be noted that the standards specify green corn, not sweet corn. It would be advisable, therefore, for a buyer to specify ''sweet corn'' of a certain grade to avoid the chance of receiving field corn which otherwise meets the grade standards.

Corn, Whole Kernel, Canned

Buy: Grade B: Reasonably uniform color, may lack brightness; minimal ragged, torn, or irregular cut kernels; cream stage of maturity, tender texture; good flavor and odor.
Grade B Frozen: As with canned.
Deterioration: Dull color in golden varieties; and a brownish cast in white varieties. Irregular or ragged cut kernels with cob tissue attached, tough or leathery kernels, clusters of grain, and worm-eaten kernels. Excessively sweetened or salted corn and ''can black.''

Corn, Cream Style, Canned

Buy: Grade B: May lack brightness, moderate appearance of curdling, stiff mound at two minutes, minimal defects; tender; good odor and flavor.
Deterioration: Dull color in golden varieties and a brownish color in white varieties. Cob tissue and tough or leathery kernels, clusters of kernels, worm-eaten kernels. Excessively sweetened or salted corn and ''can black.''

Corn-on-the-Cob, Frozen

Buy: Grade B: No objectionable flavors and odors; fairly uniform color, maximum 15 kernels per ear off-variety; pericarp is tender, no blister stage ears.
Deterioration: Dull color, off-color. Excessive crushed, broken, or ragged kernels; pieces of cob, silk, or husk. Damaged or seriously damaged kernels, tough kernels, and off-flavor or odors.

---

[10]USDA Code.

This special testing device was developed by FDA to check cream style corn. Corn is too ''soupy'' to meet the quality standard if a given quantity spreads too far on graduated plated.

Cucumbers

A good guide in buying cucumbers is to remember that those that are firm, fresh, and with good green color are best. The shade of color is important, as the older ones tend to be of rather dull green or sometimes yellow. Poor quality is also indicated by an outer rind that has a decided "give" to it when slight pressure is applied.

Washing or brushing, grading for size and defects, waxing the outer surface in central packing plants, have become common practices. Waxing (a harmless vegetable wax) is done to enhance appearance and to retard evaporation.

Cucumbers are divided into three classes, based on their use. The field-grown (generally) slicing or table cukes, are characterized by the presence of small, white spines, and generally grow thick and long. Second, the pickling varieties, also field-grown, may be either black or white-spined. They are much smaller than the slicing varieties, and less tapered at the tip. Third, the forcing or greenhouse varieties are adapted to culture under artificial heat.

There are about twenty species of cucumbers, divided into numerous subspecies. These are then subdivided even further. There are green, white, and yellow cukes; long, short, thin, as well as stubby; smooth-skinned and rough-skinned; early and late maturing. Fairly new on the scene are the European (some call it English) cucumbers—a lighter green color than field-grown, a 2 to 2¼ inch diameter, and 12 to 20 inches in length. These are exclusively of the parthenocarpic (seedless) type bred for greenhouse culture with no pollinating insects.

Cucumbers should be kept moderately cold, 45 to 50°F, at 85 percent relative humidity. They are an ideal accompaniment to summer meals.

Deterioration: Cucumbers having a thick cross section and with faded or yellowing color. These are probably overmature. Avoid wilted, spongy, shriveled, or decayed cucumbers.

Grades.   U.S. grade standards effective March 1, 1958, for field grown cucumbers provide for six grades, U.S. Fancy, U.S. Extra 1, U.S. 1, U.S. 1 Small, U.S. 1 Large, and U.S. 2. It is practical to give only samples of these grades here.

U.S. 1 consists of cucumbers which are fairly well colored, fairly well formed, not overgrown, and which are fresh, firm, and free from decay, sunscald, and from damage caused by scars, yellowing sunburn, dirt or other foreign material, freezing, mosaic or other disease, insects, cuts, bruises, mechanical or other means. (a) Unless otherwise specified, the maximum diameter of each cucumber shall be not more than 2⅜ in. and the length of each cucumber shall be not less than 6 in.

U.S. 1 Small consists of cucumbers which meet all requirements for the U.S. 1 grade except for size. (a) The diameter of each cucumber shall be not less than 1½ in. or more than 2 in. There are no requirements for length.

U.S. 1 Large consists of cucumbers which meet all requirements for U.S. 1 grade except for size. (a) The minimum diameter of each cucumber shall be not less than 2¼ in. and, unless otherwise specified, the length of each cucumber shall be not less than 6 in. There are no maximum diameter and length requirements."[11]

---

[11]USDA Code.

**MINIMUM SHAPES PERMISSIBLE IN U.S. NO. 1 GRADE
CUCUMBERS (ABOUT ⅓ ACTUAL SIZE)**

Daikon

The daikon is a Japanese radish, about 8 to 10 inches long, and about 1¼ to 1½ inches in diameter at the top. It has a flavor similar to ordinary radishes but a bit hotter. Pickled whole in large tubs with rice hulls added to the brine, it is served shredded as a relish, thinly sliced in soups, or cut in thin strips on vegetable trays. It is an excellent keeper and should be stored like radishes in refrigerator.

As an indication of its importance, nearly one-third of the tonnage of vegetables grown in Japan is daikon.

Dandelions

Dandelions, when used as a food, are usually served as a salad green. However, cooked dandelion greens are an excellent source of Vitamin A, a half-cup supplies more than enough of this element to meet the normal daily requirement.

Good quality is characterized by a fresh green appearance and comparatively large, tender leaves. If a portion of the root is still attached, they will probably be more succulent. Avoid dandelions which show excessive dirt and insect damage, and those that are wilted, flabby, and have yellow or tough leaves.

Store at 32°F, 90 percent relative humidity—preferably placing crushed ice in the container with the greens.

They top all other vegetables and fruits in iron and Vitamin A. One pound (raw) contains no refuse and provides 200 calories.

Uses. The leaves of the dandelion plant are used as a green vegetable. They are gathered when young and tender and thoroughly cleaned. They can be eaten raw in a green salad or cooked, like spinach. To cook, put greens in a pan with a small amount of water, cover, and steam 10 to 20 minutes. Serve with butter or vinegar. Bacon, fat salt pork, or sauteed onions can be added before cooking for complementary flavoring. For more elaborate dishes, dandelion greens can be substituted for spinach in recipes such as quiche, eggs florentine, and creamed spinach.

Dandelion wine is made from the flowers of the plant. The basic ingredients are the flower heads and water in equal amounts, sugar, yeast, and chopped oranges and lemons. Dandelion "coffee" is made from the tap root of a mature plant, which may be as long as 3 ft. The root is dug up, cleaned, roasted in an oven until brown, and then ground in a coffee mill.

A substance called Taraxacum can be extracted from dandelion roots. It has long been used in medicine and home remedies, although there is no convincing reason for believing it possesses any therapeutic virtues.

Quality. Very young, fresh, green plants with tender leaves are the most desirable. Leaves still attached to roots are likely to be succulent; when leaves are separated from the base, they wilt rapidly. Avoid plants which are wilted, flabby, tough, or yellow as these are signs of age.

Grades. U.S. standards for dandelion greens, effective Feb. 4, 1955, provide for one grade, U.S. 1.

U.S. 1 consists of dandelion greens of similar varietal characteristics which are fresh, fairly tender, fairly clean, well trimmed, and which are free from decay, and free from damage caused by seedstems, discoloration, freezing, foreign material, disease, insects, or mechanical or other means.[12]

---

[12]USDA Code.

Eggplant

Depending upon variety, eggplant has a white, purple, purple-black, yellowish-white, red, or striped color. Most world production is the dark purple, egg-shaped to nearly globular, variety.

Purple eggplants should be a clear, dark, glossy color that covers the entire surface. Heaviness and firmness of flesh are also important. Watch the size of eggplants you buy. A good rule to follow is to choose pear-shaped eggplants from 3 to 6 inches in diameter. Store only briefly at 45 to 50°F, 85 percent relative humidity.

Grades.   U.S. standards for eggplant are U.S. Fancy, U.S. No. 1, and U.S. No. 2.

> U.S. No. 1 consists of eggplant of similar varietal characteristics, which are fairly well colored, firm, clean, fairly well shaped, and which are free from decay and worm holes, and free from damage caused by scars, freezing, disease, insects, or mechanical or other means. If count is specified, the eggplant shall be reasonably uniform in size in the containers. Not more than 10 percent by count of the eggplant in any container may be below the requirements, including not more than 1 percent for decay. "Well colored" means that the eggplant has a uniform good color characteristic for that variety over practically the entire surface. "Firm" means that the eggplant is not soft, flabby, or shriveled.[13]

Endive

Considerable confusion in using three terms has resulted throughout the country because of local misinterpretations of the exact vegetable to which they apply. For instance, endive is called escarole or chicory in some localities; chickory is misnamed endive, and so on. However, the descriptions and illustrations given here should facilitate your identification of each of these leafy greens.

Curly endive grows in a bunchy head with narrow, ragged-edge leaves that curl at the ends. The center of the head is a yellowish white and has a milder taste than the darker green outer leaves, which tend to be slightly bitter. If this center is not as white as desired when the endive is purchased, it can be further bleached by covering overnight with a damp cloth.

There is another variety of endive with broad leaves (Batavian endive) that do not curl at the tips. It is this type which is almost universally marketed as *escarole.*

Witlof chicory is a rather tightly folded plant that grows upright in a thin, elongated stalk, rather than flat or bushy like endive or escarole. This vegetable is usually bleached a decided white while growing, and it is known far more commonly as French endive than by its true botanical name.

Another form of chicory is grown for its large roots, which are dried and used as a supplement for coffee.

In buying, look for freshness, crispness, tenderness, and a good green color of outer leaves, avoiding those heads with brownish or yellowish discolorations.

---

[13]USDA Code.

Hold briefly at 32°F, relative humidity 90 percent. It keeps better with crushed ice in or around the package.

Deterioration: Materially wilted or yellowed plants are unsatisfactory.

Servings and Weights. One pound as purchased equals 0.74 lb. ready to serve raw. A pound as purchased 8.4 ½ cup servings for salad or 16.8 ¼ cup servings. To serve ½ cup portions to 100 takes 12 lb. as purchased; and to serve ¼ cup portions to 100 takes 6 lb.

Grades. The U.S. standard grade for endive, escarole, or chicory (but not including so-called ''French endive'' or ''Witloof'' or chicory which is marketed for its roots) is U.S. No. 1. This

> shall consist of plants of similar varietal characteristics, which are fresh, well trimmed, fairly well blanched, free from decay, and from damage caused by seedstems, broken, bruised, spotted or discolored leaves, wilting, dirt, disease, insects, or mechanical or other means. In order to allow for variations incident to proper grading and handling, not more than 10 percent by count of the plants in any container may be below the requirements of this grade, but not to exceed a total of 5 percent shall be allowed for defects causing serious damage, and not more than ⅖ of this amount, or 2 percent shall be allowed for decay.[14]

Fiddleheads

These are the young shoots of the ostrich fern, and they get their name from their coiled shape resembling the scrolled head of a violin. Fiddleheads can be served as a vegetable, salad green, or in soup. Basically, it is a snob-appeal vegetable growing wild in eastern Canada and presumed to replace old favorites such as asparagus, truffles, and wild rice. They are commercially exploited, primarily in the province of Quebec.

Freeze-Dried Vegetables

Varieties	Chives, Green Bell Peppers, Red Bell Peppers, Dill, Leeks, Shallots, Parsley (Italian and Curly)
Growing Areas California (Santa Clara Valley):	Chives, Dill, Leeks, Shallots, Parsley (Italian and Curly)
California (Central Valleys):	Green Bell Peppers, Red Bell Peppers

---

[14]USDA Code.

Packing Season

Chives:	Mid-March to Mid-October
Green Bell Peppers:	Mid-August to Mid-September
Red Bell Peppers:	Mid-September to First Frost
Dill:	Mid-July to Mid-September
Shallots:	September to October
Leeks, Parsley	
(Italian and Curly):	Year-Round

The Freeze-Drying Process

The important steps in freeze-drying include raw material selection, grading, size separation, washing, peeling or removal of undesirable parts, sorting, preparation to final shape (slice, dice, chop, etc.), blanching, freezing, freeze-drying, inspection screening, and finally, packaging for sale.

The freeze-drying process removes all but 3 to 4 percent of the moisture in a product and may require 9 hours or longer.

The basic steps in the actual freeze-drying process are: (1) the raw product is frozen to −25°F, and (2) air pressure in the drying chamber is lowered so that a very high vacuum is created.

Garlic

Closely allied to the onion, garlic has been described as the "atomic bomb of the vegetable world." It is a member of the lily family and can point to a very distinguished background.

It is a bulbous-rooted perennial plant. The root is a compound bulb consisting of several smaller sections, or cloves, which are enveloped by a common skin or membrane. It differs from the onion by being more powerful in its effects and more distinctive in its taste.

Garlic should be stored dry, away from onions and potatoes, preferably in a cool, dark area.

Three general types of garlic are grown throughout the world: Creole, Italian, and Tahiti. The Creole generally has larger cloves, while the Italian has the smallest cloves with the strongest flavor—and the cloves are pinkish in color. The Tahiti has large, individual cloves, and they are generally darker in color. Most experts claim this latter type is not a true garlic and dub it "elephant garlic."

Unless garlic is kept in a closed jar, its strong, pungent odor penetrates all food close to it. For ideal, long storage, and yet somewhat inhibiting the odor, place cloves in a jar, lid loose, and store in a dark, dry area at 30 to 40°F.

Grades. U.S. standards for garlic, adopted in 1944, provide for one grade, U.S. No. 1.

U.S. No. 1 consists of garlic of similar varietal characteristics which is mature and well cured, compact, with cloves well filled and fairly plump, free from mold, decay, shattered cloves, and from damage caused by dirt or staining, sunburn, sunscald, cuts, sprouts, tops, roots, disease, insects, or mechanical or other means. Each bulb shall be fairly well enclosed in its outer sheath. Unless otherwise specified, the minimum diameter of each bulb shall be not less than 1½ in.[15]

Garlic, Dehydrated

Dehydrated garlic is produced from bulbs of properly-matured, clean, sound garlic. As garlic is a delicate and expensive crop to grow, most acreage for dehydration is grown on a contract basis. This is due in part to the cost of purchasing state-inspected and certified garlic stock that is free from disease and pests. Vegetative propagation accomplished through planting of individual garlic cloves and hand-harvesting also add to the cost of the raw product. Great care must be taken during harvesting to ensure gentle handling as the bulbs are extremely delicate and bruise easily, losing quality.

The finished product quality must meet the standards set forth by the American Dehydrated Onion and Garlic Association (ADOGA). The color shall be white to bright-white, with a maximum dark speck tolerance of 25/0.1 gm in granulated, and 25/0.5 gm in powdered. All garlic products shall be dehydrated to a final maximum moisture content of 6.75 percent. This ensures proper product storage and flavor stability. The maximum defect tolerance limit is 1 percent by weight. Defects include black or dark brown pieces, roots, stems, and foreign materials such as other vegetables.

Ginger Root

This is possibly one of the least glamorous appearing items in the market, but it can elevate an ordinary fruit salad into something quite outstanding. This plant is native to India and China. Medicinal ginger is prepared from the dried "root," condimental ginger from the green. Candied ginger is made from carefully selected, succulent young rhizomes which are washed and peeled and then preserved in jars of syrup.

Choose tubers that are fresh looking and firm. The new little sprouts that appear on the sides of the ginger root have a more delicate flavor than the main part of the root, and they may be grated and used.

To substitute ginger root for powdered ginger, use 1 tablespoon of grated or shredded fresh ginger root in place of ⅛ teaspoon of powdered ginger.

Gourds, ornamental

These are a result of cross-pollination and have become quite popular in recent years as a colorful table decoration for Thanksgiving and Christmas, and to herald the coming of fall and winter. Otherwise, gourds have no value.

---

[15]USDA Code.

Hominy

Canned hominy is the product prepared from clean, sound, field corn, either White or Golden, by removing the pericarp (hull), and pre-cooking or processing, soaking, and sorting. The product may be packed in a liquid or jelled packing medium, depending on the style.

There are two basic styles of canned hominy:

1. Whole Kernel: White or golden hominy packed in brine or vacuum pack condition.
2. Grits: Prepared from coarse ground hominy kernel particles of White or Golden field corn. The pericarp and germ have been removed. May be packed in a brine or a jelled packing medium, in a regular brine, or a vacuum pack can. This is not a major product and will not be covered in the following parts of this section.

The first step in canning hominy is to treat the dry kernels of field corn in a boiling 2 percent lye solution, stirring until the skins slip off easily. This requires about 25 to 35 minutes. After the lye treatment, the corn kernels are washed with fresh water, then run through a hominy huller with a coarse wire screen. The hulled corn is transferred to a tank where it is washed and then boiled in several changes of water to rinse out the lye and cook the kernels. During this first part of the boiling process, the hominy may be bleached to produce white hominy by addition of sodium bisulfite (.1 percent solution) to the water for approximately 15 minutes. The bisulfite must then be thoroughly leached from the hominy before canning. The boiling process, along with the retorting in the cans, is what increases the size of the kernel.

Buy: Grade A: Light, slightly cloudy, viscous liquid with few globules or sediment; bright white or gold color; maximum 2 percent off variety kernels; maximum 2 percent damaged or with pericarps; reasonably firm, but tender; free from excessively soft kernels.

Horseradish

Horseradish (German mustard) is grown mainly for its root, which is ground up and mixed with vinegar for a condiment. It has a hot taste given to it by its pungent, highly volatile oil.

Horseradish belongs to the cabbage, turnip, mustard family. It comes to us from Great Britain, where it is thought to have been naturalized from some eastern Europe country. It is often found growing wild in moist locations, such as margins of streams, in cool woods, and damp meadows.

Jicama

A root tuber grown in tropical America, the jicama is used by Mexican families as the potato is used in the United States. It is said to be a great favorite with travellers because it quenches thirst and is nutritious. Resembling a turnip in appearance, the jicama has a bland flavor similar to the water chestnut. It is an excellent substitute for the more expensive water chestnut. Choose just as you would a potato; however, the smaller ones are better (the larger ones may be woody). Store in a cool, dry place.

Kale

Kale is a large, hardy, curly-leafed green, inexpensive and usually abundant throughout the winter. Dark green kale is best but a few leaves with slightly browned edges are not objectionable, as they can readily be trimmed. Leaves should be crisp, clean, and free from bruising or crushing. Kale should be kept cold and moist. Do not plan to store it for any length of time but, if necessary, hold at 40°F, with very high humidity.

Deterioration: Extremely tough, fibrous leaf stems or decayed, yellowed, or badly wilted leaves indicate overripeness and poor eating quality.

Deterioration of Canned: Poor flavor or odor. Off-color and tough, coarse, leaves or stems. Root stubs, weeds, and seed heads in greens.

Deterioration of Frozen: Off-color. Presence of silt, sand, grit, weeds, grass, discoloration, tough or coarse stems, or leaves. Off-flavor or odor.

Grades.   The U.S. standards for kale provide two grades U.S. 1 and U.S. Commercial. The grade customarily used, U.S.1

shall consist of plants of kale of one type which are well trimmed, not stunted, free from decay, and from damage caused by yellow or discolored leaves, seedstems, wilting, but burn, freezing, dirt, disease, insects, or mechanical or other means. In order to allow for variations incident to proper grading and handling, not more than 10 percent, by weight, of the plants in any container may be below the requirements of the grade, but not more than $\frac{1}{10}$ of this tolerance, or 1 percent, shall be allowed for kale which is affected by wet decay.[16]

Kohlrabi

This is a member of the cabbage family and a native of northern Europe. The name is taken directly from the German language, meaning, ''cabbage turnip.''

It has an unusual appearance which distinguishes it from other members of the cabbage family. Instead of a head of closely packed leaves, there is a globular swelling of the stem, some 3 or 4 inches in diameter, just above the ground. The leaves are similar to those of a turnip.

Store Kohlrabi at 32°F, and 95 to 98 percent relative humidity. The young, small globes, not over 3 inches in diameter, are the best and have the most delicate flavor. The young leaves of kohlrabi may be cooked like spinach.

Leafy Greens, Canned

Buy: Grade B: Good flavor and odor; no major color defects; not mushy, ragged cut, or shredded; no root stub; only minor grit, sand, or silt; 3 inch or less weeds or extraneous material.

---

[16]USDA Code.

Leafy Greens (other than spinach), Frozen

Buy: Grade B: Reasonably uniform color; only a trace of grit, sand, silt, seedstems, and roots; 8 square inch damage per 12 ounces; 12 inch maximum grass or weeds; tender leaves.

Lettuce

There are five general types of lettuce: crisphead (iceberg), butterhead (Boston, Bibb), Cos (Romaine), leaf (bunching), and stem. These "greens" comprise the major types of lettuce used in salads today.

Iceberg lettuce, the common name for crisphead varieties, is by far the most popular of all salad greens with most of the U.S. supply (over 85 percent) originating in California and Arizona.

Lettuce does not "ripen" en route like some commodities. It is harvested when mature and through various means, respiration is retarded so that, hopefully, it will arrive at the retail store in exactly the same quality and condition it was in the field.

Refrigeration, per se, tends to pull moisture from the head, severely hampering freshness. So, along with refrigeration, it's wise to make sure the lettuce moisture content is replenished and maintained. A living plant, respiration can be slowed by refrigeration, and deterioration increases rapidly as the temperature rises—5 times as great at 75° as at 32°F.

When selecting iceberg lettuce, look for heads that are firm but not hard, free from burned or rusty-looking tips, and have a general fresh appearance. Lighter, springier heads will have a sweeter taste and be easier to separate for use in salads or sandwiches.

The butterhead varieties are distinguished by their soft, pliable leaves and delicate buttery flavor. The veins are finer and the ribs less prominent than those of the crisphead varieties. Principal varieties of butterhead lettuce are Big Boston, White Boston, Bibb, and May King.

Big Boston, sometimes called "Butterhead" is another rather well-known variety of lettuce, particularly in the east and southeast. This type forms heads somewhat softer and lighter than Iceberg and not so crisp in texture. Boston lettuce is not as sweet and tender as other butterhead varieties. It is medium in size, with light green outer leaves and light yellow leaves inside.

Bibb lettuce leaves are a deep, rich, green and blend into a whitish green toward the core. Quality is excellent—it has a delicate, buttery flavor, sweet and tender. Grown principally in greenhouses, it is erroneously referred to as "limestone." The flavor is best described as "distinctly lettuce with a touch of cultivated Dandelion or Italian Chicoria flavor."

Cos, or romaine, grown mainly in the east and south, has a long, loaf-shaped head and long, narrow leaves. The varieties of Cos are divided into self-closing and loose-closing types. The leaves appear coarse, but they are tender, sweet, tasty, and less bitter than other varieties. It has dark green outer leaves and golden-yellow inner ones, and a stronger flavor than Iceberg.

Leaf lettuce, as the name implies, grows with leaves loosely branching from its stalk—these varieties do not form heads. The leaves are clustered or pressed together but only the young ones at the center of the plant overlap to any extent. Leaf lettuce has a crisp texture preferred by many people.

The edible part of the stem lettuce is the enlarged stem or seedstalk. It may be peeled and eaten raw or it may be boiled, stewed, or creamed. Stem lettuce is an ingredient of many Chinese dishes. Celtuce is the only variety offered for sale in the United States.

Corn salad, a lettuce-like vegetable, is also known as lamb's lettuce or fetticus. Its leaves are generally used in the fresh state but are also sometimes cooked as greens.

Vacuum-cooling of crisphead lettuce at shipping point has created a revolutionary change in the handling of lettuce. The process permits the use of any type of container for packaging lettuce, providing the container admits ventilation. The principle of vacuum-cooling has long been known. Evaporative cooling was utilized early in the history of man to cool water. Today, the pulp temperature of lettuce is quickly cooled to 32 to 34°F by placing individual cartons (or even whole carloads of cartons) of lettuce in large, metal "tubes." Mechanically, a vacuum is immediately created, and within 28 to 30 minutes the pulp temperature of the lettuce is drawn down to the above temperatures. Weight losses during the cooling process are small.

Deterioration of Iceberg Head: Very firm heads showing tan or brownish discoloration of leaf stems at the base of the head are likely to be of poor quality. Tip burn, a tan or brown discoloration along the outer margin of the head leaves, often extends to many leaves inside the head and is objectionable.

Deterioration of Romaine: Heads that lack green color. Heads with irregular shapes, which indicates the presence of overgrown central stems. Tip burn, a tan or brown area around the margins of the leaves. Serious discoloration or soft decay should be avoided.

Deterioration of Leaf: Lots that are noticeably wilted or showing numerous discolored leaves or spots of soft decay will cause too much waste.

Servings and Weights.   Yield of head lettuce is about 74 percent per pound purchased. One pound as purchased provides 5.92 portions of 2 oz. raw. The amount as purchased for such portions for 25 persons is 4.25 lb.; and for 100 is 17 lb.

A carton of Iceberg lettuce, 2 dozen heads, provides 144 portions of ⅙ head each. For 25 persons, such portions require 4¼ heads as purchased; and for 100, the total is 17 heads.

The yield of romaine is about 64 percent of the amount purchased. One pound yields 10.24 portions of 1 oz. each. For portions of this size for 25, about 2½ lb. are required; and for 100, 10 lb.

Grades.   U.S. grade standards for lettuce, effective June 16, 1970, provide four grades, U.S. Fancy, U.S. 1, U.S. Commercial, and U.S. 2. For full details, see the standard available from Consumer and Marketing Service, Washington, D.C. 20250.

Since U.S. 1 is the main trading grade, the information given here is for that grade, but is not complete.

U.S. No. 1 consists of heads of lettuce of similar varietal characteristics which are fresh and green, which are not soft or burst, and which are free from decay and doubles, and from damage caused by tipburn, downy mildew, opening, seedstems, broken midribs, freezing, discoloration, dirt disease, insects, or mechanical or other means. Each head shall be fairly well trimmed, unless specified as closely trimmed. In any lot of Iceberg type lettuce, the percentages of hard and firm heads or the combined percentage of hard and firm heads shall be specified in connection with the grade.

Standard pack: Heads of lettuce shall be fairly uniform in size and tightly but not excessively tightly packed in uniform layers in the containers, according to the approved and recognized methods, except that in standard fiberboard containers a "bridge" of 6 heads may be used in a 2½ doz. pack; and in standard wooden crates a "bridge" may be used with sizes smaller than 5-doz. count.

Solidity classification: (a) The following terms shall be used in describing the solidity of lettuce: (1) "Hard" means that the head is compact and solid. This term represents the highest degree of solidity. (2) "Firm" means that the head is compact, but may yield slightly to moderate pressure. (3) "Fairly firm" means that although the head is not firm, it is not soft and spongy, and has good head formation, and edible content. (4) "Soft" means that the head is easily compressed or spongy.[17]

Malanga

Large herbs of tropical America, malangas have thick, tuberous rhizomes. They are grown in the tropics for the edible roots and sometimes as greenhouse foliage plants.

Mushrooms

Freshness, color, and shape are the three points generally considered in buying mushrooms. Variety is not a factor, since all of the cultivated mushrooms on the U.S. market are of the same variety.

Avoid withered mushrooms, since this is a sign of age. Mushrooms that look bright and attractive in the store can be kept in the home refrigerator for 4 to 5 days with little effect. All mushrooms, however, will eventually oxidize and turn dark. This will occur very quickly when exposed to room temperature, but more slowly when refrigerated. An open "veil" around the base of the cap is also a sign of old age.

Normal color is white to pallid brown; however, a darkened or spotted mushroom is not necessarily spoiled, but instead, may be bruised. The cap is more tender than the stem. The size of mushrooms is not a reliable indication of whether they are tender.

A 1977 arrival is a new mushroom from Japan called the *yuki no shita,* which, translated, means "under the snow." And that's just where it grows in its natural state. More popularly known as enoki-dake—or "snow puff"—it only faintly resembles our regular mushroom, the stem being the thickness of a matchstick about 3 to 5 inches long, with a "cap" at the top about ¼ inch across. It looks almost like a beansprout with a cap! It is very delicate, with a pale ivory-white color.

---

[17]USDA Code.

Grades. U.S. standards for Grades of Mushrooms, effective July 15, 1966, provide for two grades: U.S. 1 and U.S. 2.

> U.S. No. 1 consists of fresh mushrooms of similar varietal characteristics which are mature, at least fairly well shaped, well trimmed, free from open veils, disease, spots, insect injury, and decay, and from damage by any cause. Size is specified in terms of diameter and, unless otherwise specified, meets the requirements of one of the following size classifications: (1) small to medium—up to $1\frac{5}{8}$ in. in diameter; (2) large—over $1\frac{5}{8}$ in. in diameter.
>
> The following specific defects shall be considered as damage: Discoloration when the color of the cap or stem materially affects the appearance or marketing quality of the mushrooms. Dirt when any amount (of soil or compost material) is embedded in the cap or stem. "Length of stem" means the greatest distance as measured from the point of attachment of the veils on the stem to the butt. "Diameter" means the greatest dimension of the cap measured at right angles to the stem."[18]

Mushrooms, Canned

Buy: Grade B: Cap may be dark cream, gills may be brownish gray; 10 percent minor damage, 2 percent serious.

"Whole" and "Buttons": Cap size variation maximum of ¼ inch.

"Sliced Whole" and "Sliced Buttons": Maximum 10 percent small side-slices; maximum diameter variation of ⅝ inch.

"Random Sliced": Maximum 10 percent small side slices.

All: Tender to slightly soft, not fibrous nor rubbery; 90 percent possess closed veil.

Deterioration: Excessive white or dark color. Tough or rubbery units, and fibrous or woody caps.

Mustard Greens

The species most often grown for commercial production is known as *leaf mustard*. A species grown in home gardens is called *mustard spinach* or *tendergreen mustard*. Seeds of various species can be used to make the mustard that goes on the hot dog or hamburger. The large-leaved, fancy, pungent garden mustards grown in this country as pot herbs are generally the brown or Indian mustard. They are grown mainly in California and the Pacific Northwest for their seeds.

Mustard greens should be fresh, tender, crisp, and of a good, green color. Wilted, dirty, discolored, or spotted leaves are indications of poor condition and quality. The presence of seed stems is a sure indication of age and toughness. The smaller leaves, 6 to 12 inches long, are preferred.

They should be cooled as near 32°F as possible and kept at or near that temperature until used. Humidity should be high, 90 to 95 percent. If temperature is kept low and humidity high, leafy greens have a shelf life of 10 to 14 days.

Deterioration: Coarse, tough leaf stems, yellowish color, excessively bruised leaves, or soft decay, are all signs of poor eating quality.

---

[18]USDA Code.

Uses.   The young, tender leaves of mustard greens can be used as salad, either alone or mixed with other salad greens and ingredients. The older, but tender, leaves are used for cooking and should be handled like other pot herbs. After washing, cook in a covered pan in a little water for 15 to 20 minutes. Season to taste. Salt, pepper, and butter, or salt, pepper, and lemon juice or vinegar enhance the pungency of the greens. In the South, mustard is cooked in water in which salt pork or ham has been simmered, but keep the water to a minimum and use it in sauce or gravy. Any water in which greens have been cooked will have its share of vitamins and minerals, as well as flavor. In addition to their uses as salad or side dish, the leaves can provide flavor in soups and stews.

Quality.   All kinds of greens should be fresh, young, tender, free from blemishes, and have a good green color. Some mustard greens show a slight bronze tint (this is normal), and some are naturally light green. However, avoid mustard greens that are distinctly yellowed. Any that are wilted are not worth buying. Avoid greens that are coarse and fibrous, or that are soft, or decayed. Any with evidence of insects, especially aphids, should be rejected.

Grades.   U.S. grade standards for mustard greens and turnip greens, effective in 1953, provide for one grade, U. S. 1. This consists of greens of

> similar varietal characteristics which are fresh, fairly tender, fairly clean, and which are free from decay, and free from damage caused by seedstems, discoloration, freezing, foreign material, disease, insects, or mechanical or other means. In order to allow for variations incident to proper grading and handling, other than for size of roots and mixtures of plants and leaves, not more than a total of 10 percent, by weight, of the units in any lot, may fail to meet the requirements of the grade: provided, that not more than ½ of this amount, or 5 percent, shall be allowed for serious damage by any cause, and including therein not more than 2 percent for decay. Not more than 5 percent, by weight, of the mustard . . . greens may consist of cut leaves in a lot consisting of plants or of plants in a lot consisting of cut leaves.[19]

Deterioration of Canned: Poor flavor or odor. Off color and tough, coarse, leaves or stems. Root stubs, weeds, and seed heads in greens.

Deterioration of Frozen: Off-color. Presence of silt, sand, grit, weeds, grass, discoloration, tough or coarse stems, or leaves. Off-flavor or odor.

Nappa

Chinese cabbage, or Sui Choy, Chow Choy, Won Bok. Select and care as though regular cabbage.

Nopales

See ''Cactus Leaves.''

---

[19]USDA Code.

Okra

Okra is commonly called quingumbo or gumbo in the United States. In other parts of the world, it is called "Lady's Fingers" or simply "Gumbo." The plant is an annual of the edible hibiscus family (Mallow). Many plants of this species are used as food but cotton is the most important economic plant belonging to the Mallow family.

Good quality okra may be green or white in color, with pods that are either long and thin or short and chunky. In all cases, freshness can be determined by the tenderness of the pods—those that snap easily or puncture on slight pressure being best. Young, tender, fresh, clean pods of small-to-medium size, ranging from 2 to 4 inches in length, usually are of good quality. Pods that have passed their prime will present a somewhat dull, dry appearance. Okra can be stored a maximum of 2 weeks at 50°F, and 85 to 95 percent relative humidity.

Deterioration: Pods that are long, very pale in color, very firm or dry in appearance are likely to be tough and fibrous.

Grades. The U.S. standards for okra were established in 1928 and codified in 1967.

U.S. No. 1 shall consist of pods of okra of similar varietal characteristics which are fresh, tender, not badly misshapen, free from decay, and from damage caused by dirt or other foreign matter, disease, insects, mechanical or other means.[20]

Okra, Canned

Buy: Grade A: Uniform color; some damaged units and extraneous material allowed; tender and practically free of fibrous material; 90 percent uniform pods; 3½ inch maximum length; 100 percent length variation.

Deterioration: Poor or unpleasant flavor. Ragged cut or trim, and discolored or diseased spots on pods.

Deterioration of Frozen: Dull, off-color pods. Excessive defects such as blemishes, inedible stems, or collapsed pods.

Okra and Tomatoes, Canned

Buy: Grade A: Tomatoes have good red color, okra is color of young tender okra; maximum 10 percent yellow tomato; typical okra and tomato flavors; minor sand, silt, grit or extraneous material; whole or almost whole tomato flesh and intact okra pods; maximum 2 percent fibrous material.

Deterioration: Okra with poor or unpleasant flavor, ragged cut or trim pods, and discolored or diseased pods. Tomatoes with pale red color or yellow and green portions, and with excessive skin, core material, or blemish units. Tomatoes with noticeable watery or soft pieces and presence of mold or insects. Tomatoes with poor flavor.

---

[20]USDA Code.

Olives

Canned Ripe Olives are produced only in California, nowhere else in the United States (except in a very small section of Arizona). California also produces a product sometimes known as the "Green Ripe" or "Ripe Green" olive. This style has the true nut-like flavor of the ripe olive, but is green in color.

Harvesting of the fruit for pickling is done in the fall, after the fruit has changed from a deep green to a straw or cherry red color, but before it turns black. Harvesting usually continues for about 2 months, or until the fruit becomes damaged by frost. Temperatures of 27 to 28°F for several hours are likely to injure the tissues so the fruit cannot be used for pickling; such frozen fruits can be allowed to remain on the trees, however, to be harvested later for oil extraction. The table-oil harvest is done by hand-picking into baskets or buckets; ladders are used to climb into the trees.

Fresh, unprocessed olives are inedible, being extremely bitter. The bitterness is caused by a glucoside which must be neutralized, usually by treatments with a dilute sodium hydroxide solution.

In the Mediterranean countries much of the table olive crop is processed by the green Spanish-style method, in which the fruits are picked when they are a light-green to straw color. They are immediately placed in a diluted hydroxide solution, with the treatment continuing until the lye has penetrated about ¾ of the distance to the pit. The lye solution is then removed and replaced with several changes of water to wash the lye from the fruit. During treatment and washing, undue exposure to air is avoided, as this results in an undesirable darkening of the fruit.

The fruit is then placed in large wood barrels and kept there for 1 to 6 months, or longer, to undergo lactic acid fermentation. During this treatment, the fruits are kept in a 6 to 8 percent salt solution, and sugar is added after several weeks to maintain the fermentation process. Following this, the olives are packed in barrels or glass containers.

Deterioration: Off-color fruit, off-flavor, and odor. Units with internal or external discoloration, pits or pit fragments.

Onions

Onions are used as a main vegetable dish or as a flavorful ingredient of main meat dishes. They are good boiled, broiled, baked, creamed, steamed, fried, french fried, roasted, pickled, in soups, and stews, for onion rings, sliced raw, and diced raw in salads. A glance through any good cookbook reveals few recipes, other than desserts, which do not include at least a suspicion of onion, says *Wise Encyclopedia of Cookery*.

There are enough variations to keep the onion a popular repeater on the menu circuit. It develops different and interesting nuances without ever losing the distinctive individuality of its flavor. It contributes zip and nip even to such mild dishes as the souffle.

Look for hard or firm onions which are dry and have small necks. They should be covered with papery outer scales and reasonably free from green sunburn spots and other blemishes. Avoid onions with wet or very soft necks, which usually are immature

CALIFORNIA CANNED RIPE OLIVES
INSTITUTIONAL SIZE—GRADES

Equivalent Size - Grades Spanish Green Olives Kilo = 2.2046 lbs.		Comparable Size - Grades California Ripe Olives	Whole - Unpitted			Pitted		
			Drained Net Wt. #10 Can	Approx. No. Per Can	Av. No. Per Lb.	Drained Net Wt. #10 Can	Approx. No. Per Can	Av. No. Per Lb.
280-300		Small Select Standard	66 oz.	557	135	51 oz.	578	135
240-260		Medium	66 oz.	466	113	51 oz.	486	113
200-220		Large	66 oz.	404	98	51 oz.	402	98
160-180		Extra Large Picnic	66 oz.	338	82	51 oz. 51 oz.	334 343	82 82
140-150 150-160		Mammoth Gem	66 oz.	288	70	51 oz. 50 oz.	278 298	70 70
120-130 130-140		Giant	64 oz.	228	53-60	49 oz.	245	53-60
90-100 100-110 110-120		Jumbo	64 oz.	192	46-50	49 oz.	199	46-50

Stewart–Tucker, Inc., Menlo Park, CA. Reprinted with permission.

or affected by decay. Also avoid onions with thick, hollow, woody centers in the neck, or with fresh sprouts. Size has nothing to do with onion quality. Selection for size depends on the use to which the onions are to be put, that is, specify large onions for slicing, medium or small onions for roasting or boiling, and small onions for boiling or pickling.

On the American market, there are three basic types of "dry" onions: the early Bermuda-Granex-Grano; the late crop onions; and the Creole type.

The Bermuda-Granex-Grano type are flat to top-shaped, with varying amounts of intermediate shapes. These onions belong to the group considered "early maturing" or "short day." The granex is probably the most widely grown short-day onion, due to its attractiveness and productiveness. The bulbs have thin, yellow scales and medium-firm flesh. They are crisp and exceptionally mild in flavor. The Yellow Bermuda is another of the short-day variety. The bulbs are flat and the flesh is soft and mild. Storage life is short. Both of these may be yellow or white skinned.

The late or main crop onions are mostly of the globe type and have distinctly yellow, white, or red skins. Yellow globe is a commercial term applied to several varieties and strains.

The Yellow Sweet Spanish is strictly a "long-day" onion adapted to the more northern districts of the semi-arid irrigated regions of the western United States. The large bulbs are globe-shaped, the dry scales are dark-yellow and adhere fairly well. The necks are fairly heavy with the flesh medium firm and mild. Sweet Spanish onions, originally introduced from Spain, are produced in large quantities.

Red varieties are from the Creole family and are usually a strong-flavored onion; however, pungency is not entirely related to variety, since it has been found that the same variety can have considerably different flavor when grown in different locations and on different soils.

Onions of any of these varieties are often called "boilers" when they range from 1 to 1½ inches in diameter. Any that are smaller than that are termed "picklers."

When selecting onions, look for those that are well shaped and dry enough to crackle. Thin necks and bright, hard bulbs are two other indications of quality.

Grades.   U.S. grade standards effective Dec. 15, 1966 for dry onions other than Bermuda-Granex-Grano and Creole types provide 6 grades, U.S. 1, U.S. Export 1, U.S. Commercial, U.S. 1 Boilers, U.S. 1 Picklers, and U.S. 2. U.S. grade standards for Bermuda-Granex-Grano type onions effective Jan. 1, 1960, and amended March 18, 1962, provide for 3 grades, U.S. 1, U.S. Combination, and U.S. 2.

U.S. 1 onions (other than Bermuda-Granex-Grano-Creole) consist of onions of similar varietal characteristics which are mature, fairly firm, fairly well shaped, and which are free from decay, wet sunscald, doubles, bottlenecks, scallions, and free from damage caused by seedstems, splits, tops, roots, dry sunscald, sunburn, sprouts, freezing, peeling, cracked fleshy scales, watery scales, dirt or staining, foreign matter, disease, insects, or other means.

Size Classifications: (a) The size of onions may be specified in accordance with one of the following classifications: (1) "Small" shall be from 1 to 2¼ in. in diameter; (2)

"Medium" shall be from 2 to 3¼ in. in diameter, except that for onions grown in Minnesota, Iowa, and states east of the Mississippi River, "Medium" shall be 1½ to 3¼ in. in diameter, with percentage of onions 2 in. and larger in diameter as specified in Sec. 51.2830(a); or, (3) "Large" or "Jumbo" shall be 3 in. or larger in diameter.[21]

Green onions are merely onions that are harvested green. Many like to munch the tops, as well as the small bulb. Sometimes the greens are chopped and mixed with cottage cheese. Often green onions are cut up and put in salad. They may also be boiled and served like asparagus. In selecting, they should have good, green-colored tops and white, bleached stems up to about 3 inches from the roots.

Uses. Green onions are a savory morsel eaten raw with meat, cheese, or fish. The tops are more nutritious than the white parts. Hot green onions served on toast with a rich cheese are tasty. Green onions combine well into Chinese dishes. Serve them with meat loaf, with hash, hamburgers, even scrambled eggs. One good way of cooking green onions, according to the Western Growers Assn., is to boil in 1 in. of salted water until barely tender, 8 to 10 min.

Quality. Aside from grade at time of federal or state inspection, the consumer should expect green onions to have green, fresh tops, medium-sized necks, and be well blanched for 2 or 3 in. from the root, and that the onions are young, crisp, and tender. Wilted or discolored tops indicate poor quality.

Grades. The U.S. standard grades for common green onions are U.S. 1 and U.S. 2. These standards do not apply to leeks, Welch or Japanese multiplier onions, or to shallots.

U.S. 1 shall consist of green onions which are fairly well formed, firm, young and tender, fairly clean, free from decay, and from damage caused by seedstems, roots, foreign material, disease, insects, mechanical or other means. The bulbs shall be well trimmed. The tops shall be fresh, of good green color, free from damage caused by broken or bruised leaves, or by clipping. When all the tops of the onions have been evenly clipped back in accordance with good commercial practice, they shall be specified as "Clipped Tops" in connection with the grade.[22]

The *shallot,* sometimes called "scallion," belongs to the same group as onions, leeks, chives, and garlic. This group is one of the oldest, having been known for many thousands of years. Many persons confuse shallots with green onions, scallions, or leeks. Green onions have a definite bulb formation; scallions are any shoots from the white onion varieties that are pulled before the bulb has formed; while leeks are similar in appearance to scallions, but have flat leaves, a white stalk with a diameter of about 1½ inches, and a length of 6 to 8 inches. The shallot can be distinguished from these others by its distinctive bulbs, which are made up of cloves, like garlic. Chives are tiny onions whose roots and tops are both used for flavoring, generally sold in pots, all green, and are pencil-lead thin.

[21]USDA Code.
[22]USDA Code.

Uses.   Shallots are a gourmet's delight. Nearly every French or European recipe calls for their use in flavoring. Every part of the plant, from the fresh crisp green leaves to the white elongated bulb, is edible. They are chopped and added to salads, soups, stews, and other meat dishes. They have a characteristic alliaceous odor due to the presence of allyl sulphide, but they are milder and more aromatic than the onion. They also make excellent pickles. The bulbs of shallots are sometimes cured in the same manner as onions and marketed in dry form. These cloves are used in the same way as the green shallots.

Quality.   Green shallots of good quality have green fresh tops, and medium-sized necks which are well blanched for at least 2 or 3 in. from the root and which are young, crisp, and tender. Bruised, yellowed, wilted, or otherwise damaged tops are not attractive and may indicate poor quality or damaged necks. The wilting and yellowing of the top may indicate age and flabby, tough, fibrous necks. This condition can be ascertained by puncturing with the thumbnail and twisting. Bruised tops are unimportant, if they can be trimmed without waste or without spoiling the appearance for table use.

Grades.   U.S. standards specify two grades for green shallots, U.S. No. 1 and U.S. No. 2.

> U.S. No. 1 shall consist of shallots of similar varietal characteristics, which are fairly well formed, firm, young and tender, well trimmed, fairly clean, free from decay, and from damage caused by seedstems, foreign material, disease, insects, mechanical or other means. The tops shall be fresh, of good green color, and free from damage caused by broken or bruised leaves. *Unless otherwise specified,* the overall length (roots excepted) of the shallots shall not exceed 22 in., and the shallots shall be not less than ¼ in. or more than ¾ in. in diameter. In order to allow for variations, other than size, incident to proper grading and handling, not more than a total of 10 percent, by count, of the shallots in any lot may fail to meet the requirements of this grade, but *not more than 5 percent shall be allowed for defects* causing serious damage, including not more than 2 percent for shallots affected by decay. Not more than a total of 10 percent, by count, of the shallots in any lot may fail to meet the requirements as to the specified length, minimum diameter, or maximum diameter, *but not more than 5 percent shall be allowed for any one of the requirements for size.* Bunches shall be fairly uniform in size, and the shallots in the individual bunches shall also be of fairly uniform size. The weight of the bunches shall be not less than 4 lb. per dozen bunches. The weight of the bunched shallots shall be determined after they have been wet and shaken or drained to remove excess water.[23]

For "dry" onions, cold storage is not essential but dry storage is desirable, with a 70 to 75 percent relative humidity. At higher humidities, onions are subject to root growth and decay in time. They should never be stored with potatoes, for example, because they will take on moisture from the potatoes and decay quickly.

Medium "dry" onions are good for chopping, boiling, and stuffing. Large Yellow are all-purpose, but excellent for stuffing and slicing for hamburgers. Jumbo onions

---

[23]USDA Code.

are excellent for hamburgers and french fried onion rings. Red onions are good mainly for salads and other garnishes where rings are used, since the outside is the only part that is red.

"Cocktail onions" are fairly new on the scene. They are produced in much the same way as onion sets with very heavy, close seeding of pickling-type onions. Being crowded together, they tend to bulb early in their growth. Special varieties are selected. The "Pearl Onion" name came from the Pearl variety, plus the fact that the small, white onion simulated a pearl (with a stretch of the imagination).

Onions, Canned

Buy: Grade A: Bright typical color with maximum 10 percent greenish color on bulbs. 300 percent weight variation allowed; maximum 10 percent poorly shaped; 95 percent well trimmed; firm, tender, maximum 10 percent soft or spongy.

Onion, Dehydrated

Dehydrated onions are produced from firm, white fruit at the peak of maturity. They possess a high solids content ranging from 15 to 20 percent. They should be free from mold, sunburn, and other diseases. Large bulbs are preferred for economy in field harvesting and plant preparation. The development of suitable varieties of onion and the quality control from planting to harvest is achieved through a joint effort involving grower and packer.

The finished product must meet the Quality Standards set forth by the American Dehydrated Onion and Garlic Association (ADOGA). The color shall be white or yellowish-white, with very few dark specks. Chopped, sliced, and diced onion shall have a maximum total defect tolerance of 0.5 percent by weight. These defects consist of root crown, outer skin, neck, hair roots, rocks and other foreign materials. The size shall be uniform with little variation within each style.

Powdered onion products shall have a moisture content of 4.5 percent with all other onion products maintaining a level of 5.0 percent.

Onion Rings, Breaded, Frozen:

Buy: Grade A: Cream to golden uniform color; maximum 25 percent imperfect rings; minor carbon specks, extraneous material; after heating: moderately crisp, not soggy, oily or dry; onion is succulent and tender.

Parsley

Like other greens, parsley keeps best at low temperatures (32°F) and high humidity. Use of crushed ice is desirable in keeping parsley.

The most frequent use is as a garnish. It should be bright green and fresh-looking to be completely effective. Chopped parsley should be folded into a towel and wrung out thoroughly so that it dries out quickly. Besides using as a garnish, it may be a dominant seasoning for soups, bisques, bread spread, and a sauce. Use it chopped or shredded in butter—for bread or sweet corn.

In selecting parsley, look for a healthy green, preferably dark, with no yellowing, for the latter is an indication of age. It should be crisp and firm. Especially the more popular curly parsley should spring back with a slight pressure between your fingers or fist. Black, watery areas indicate bruising.

Deterioration: Watersoaked, discolored, or slimy leaves affected by decay indicate poor quality.

Grade. U.S. standards were established in 1930 for *curly and plain parsley* (do not apply to parsley tops marketed with a part of the entire root attached.) There is one grade, U.S. No. 1, which

> shall consist of parsley of similar varietal characteristics, and of good green color; which is free from decay, and from damage caused by seedstems, yellow or discolored leaves, wilting, freezing, dirt, or other foreign material, disease, insects, or mechanical or other means. In order to allow for variations incident to proper grading and handling, not more than 5 percent, by weight, of any lot may be below the requirements of this grade, but not more than ½ of 1 percent shall be allowed for parsley which is affected by decay.[24]

Parsnips

Parsnips are a member of a Umbelliferae family, which also includes carrots, fennel, parsley, celery, celeriac, and chervil. The word is from the Latin *Pastinaca sativa*—"Pastus" meaning food, and "sativa" meaning cultivated.

Parsnips are one of the hardiest vegetables on the market and hold up well under either warm or quite cold temperatures. However, many authorities state that the parsnip's flavor is not really brought out until it has been stored for some time at a temperature close to 32°F. Small-to-medium size parsnips are usually the best quality, provided they are firm and well shaped. The jumbo sizes are likely to have a "woody" core. They should be free of straggly rootlets and fairly smooth.

Best temperature for storage is 32°F, relative humidity 90 percent. They wilt readily under dry conditions. Stews, soups, and mashed probably offer the best potentials for service. They are delicious when creamed, sauteed, or deep fat fried in thin slices in batter. When properly cooked (steamed, not boiled), parsnips have a sweet, nutty flavor.

Grades. U.S. standard grades are U.S. No. 1 and U.S. No. 2.

> U.S. No. 1 shall consist of parsnips of similar varietal characteristics which are well trimmed, fairly well formed, fairly smooth, fairly clean, fairly firm, free from woodiness, soft rot, or wet breakdown, and from damage caused by discoloration, bruises,

---

[24]USDA Code.

cuts, rodents, growth cracks, pithiness, disease, insects, mechanical or other means. Unless otherwise specified, the diameter of each parsnip shall be not less than 1½ in. The maximum diameter of the parsnips in any lot may be specified in terms of inches and quarter inches, in accordance with the facts.[25]

Peas

Peas have been used as far back as prehistoric time. In all forms—fresh, canned, and frozen—it is still a very major item. National consumption far exceeds the fresh consumption of ten years ago! Peas are recognized as a good source of protein, calcium, phosphorus, iron, potassium, thiamine, riboflavin, and a good amount of Vitamins A and C. The greatest nutrient value is found in "fresh" peas.

When buying fresh peas, get them at their sweetest, most flavorful stage. Select fairly large, bright green, angular pods that are well filled and snap readily. A yellowish pod generally indicates overmaturity and, consequently, toughness. Mildew, swollen, or highly specked pods should also be avoided.

Green peas, like sweet corn, tend to lose part of their sugar content unless they are promptly cooled to near 32°F shortly after being picked. They will store better in the pod, rather than shelled, but keep them cold and moist if you must store them!

Sugar Peas. Other names are Sit Dow, Soot Dow, and French peas, plus the most popular name, "Snow Peas." This is a flat Chinese pea, 3 to 4 inches long, about 1 inch wide, most plentiful from May through September, but available in some supply throughout the year. The pea within the pod is extremely small. Many Oriental dishes include the whole pod in the recipe. The tiny, tender pea within the pod adds a special taste to the crisp pod when eaten.

China Peas. Also known as How Lon Dow, these are slightly smaller in size than sugar peas, and more tender. They are frequently eaten raw.

Pigeon Peas. Also known as Grandules, these are grown mainly in Puerto Rico and the Dominican Republic, then shipped chiefly to the New York area.

Early Dwarf. Many people use this designation for small English Peas, but fresh distribution is practically nonexistent. It is actually a variety of English peas.

Deterioration: Pods that are whitish-green, turning yellow, badly wilted, or warm are likely to have peas that are hard, starchy, and of poor flavor.

Peas, Canned

Buy: Grade B: Liquid may be cloudy; typical pea color; ¼ square inch extraneous material per 50 ounce net; maximum 5 percent ruptured skins; percent to sink in percent salt solution: 15 percent in 13 percent salt, 4 percent in 13 percent salt; early peas: 30 percent in 13½ percent salt, 8 percent in 15 percent salt.

The determination of maturity and tenderness is based on the brine flotation test which utilizes salt solutions of various specific gravities to separate the peas according to "maturity." The more tender, less starchy peas tend to float and are syphoned off

---

[25]USDA Code.

PEA SIZES

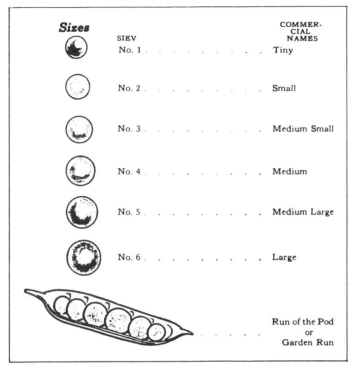

Frosty Acres Buyers Guide—The Frozen Food Forum, Inc.; Atlanta, Ga.

accordingly. The starchier, more mature peas which sink to the bottom of the testing receptacle within 10 seconds after immersion are counted as defects. For Fancy Grade A not more than 12 percent, by count, of Sweet peas will sink in 11 percent salt solution; not more than 2 percent in a 13 percent salt solution; for Early peas, not more than 20 percent, by count, in an 11 percent solution, and not more than 2 percent, by count, in a 13½ percent solution.

Deterioration: Noticeable cloudy liquid and accumulation of sediment. Variations of color, off-color peas, presence of spotted, discolored, or broken peas. Excessive hardness or mushiness. Variability of color, tough or mealy peas, presence of foreign material such as pea pods and thistle buds.

Peas, Frozen

Buy: Grade B: Bright uniform green color; about ½ inch extraneous material per 30 ounces net; maximum 10 percent pea pieces; tender, 12 percent sink in 15 percent salt solution.

Deterioration: Dull, off-color peas. Extraneous material, broken peas, loose skins, or blemished peas. Off-flavor or odor.

Field and Black-eye Peas, Canned and Frozen

Buy: Grade A: Uniform color typical of young peas; minor extraneous material, tender and in early maturity.

Grade B Frozen: As above with greater amount of minor extraneous material.

Deterioration: Poorly colored peas and mashed or broken peas. Cloudy packing medium and mealy or hard peas as well as mixed varieties.

Peas and Carrots, Canned

Buy: Grade B: Good overall color, may be dull but not off-color; sizes conform with B standard of carrots; 1 piece extraneous material per 30 ounces; carrots not tough, hard or mushy; peas tender and comply with B pea standards.

Deterioration: Noticeable cloudy liquid and accumulation of sediment. Variations of color and off-color peas. Presence of spotted, discolored, or broken peas. Excessive hardness or mushiness. Variability of color, and tough or mealy peas. Presence of foreign material such as pea pods and thistle buds. Off-color carrots showing a grayish or brownish cast. Excessive number of pale and white carrots. Presence of tough or woody carrots showing softness, poor trimming, and peeling. Deep cuts resulting from insect or mechanical injury.

Peas and Carrots, Frozen

Buy: Grade B: As with canned; maximum 14 damaged units per 10 ounces; maximum 100 percent size variation in maximum 17 percent of carrot dice; tender peas and carrots of uniform texture.

Deterioration: Dull, off-color peas. Extraneous material, broken peas, loose skins, or blemished peas. Off-flavor or odor in peas. Excessive green or off-color carrots. Excessive number of broken, crushed, cracked, unpeeled or tough fibrous, by units. Off-flavor or odor in carrots.

Peppers

In the United States, the sweet, mild pepper is usually preferred and may be bought either green or red, according to the stage of maturity desired.

Best quality peppers are well-shaped, thick walled, and firm, with a uniform glossy color. Pale color and soft seeds are signs of immaturity, while sunken blister-like spots on the surface indicate that decay may set in rather quickly.

The varieties of garden peppers may be classified in two categories: those with mild or sweet fleshed fruit, and those with hot or pungent-fleshed fruits. Within each of these groups is a remarkable range of sizes, shapes, and colors of fruits. The California Wonder, or Bell, are the most popular because of highly desirable size, shape, and attractiveness.

Chili, Pimiento, and Cayenne are varieties of hot peppers that are often dried and sold in strings. Pimiento peppers are canned extensively for use in preparing such foods

SWEET PEPPERS—LOWER LIMIT
"NOT SERIOUSLY MISSHAPEN"
U.S. No. 2

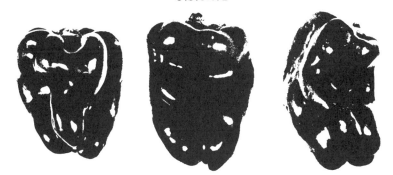

as pimiento cheese and the red stuffing for olives. Paprika is the finely ground fruit walls of paprika peppers, a mild type.

Mature-green peppers should not be stored at temperatures below 45°F, and the ideal temperature is about 46 to 48°F, with relative humidity of 85 percent. Under the most favorable conditions, peppers can be stored successfully for only 12 to 14 days.

Red Sweet peppers are sometimes diced and mixed with sweet corn or other vegetables. The Red Sweet pepper is a rich green before changing colors.

Green Sweet peppers are delicious stuffed and baked. They are delicious, too, fried Italian style—in olive oil flavored with a noticeable bit of crushed garlic. Additionally, sweet peppers are canned or pickled in brine for use in salads or other foods. They are also french fried, and used in soups and stews. They are good boiled, plain, or with other vegetables.

Garden peppers—hot and mild types—are not related to the pepper that gives us black pepper.

Deterioration: Pale green, dull color, or lack of firmness indicate poor quality. Soft, mushy spots of decay progress rapidly and cause excessive waste. Green to black slimy decay around stems may often be overlooked, but this decay will also progress rapidly.

Grades. U.S. grade standards for sweet peppers provide three grades, U.S. Fancy, U.S. 1 and U.S. 2.

> U.S. Fancy consists of mature, green sweet peppers of similar varietal characteristics which are firm, well shaped, and free from sunscald, freezing injury, decay, and from injury caused by scars, hail, sunburn, disease, insects, mechanical or other means. Size: The diameter of each pepper shall not be less than 3 in. and the length of each pepper shall be not less than 3½ in. Color: Any lot of peppers which meets all the requirements of this grade, except those relating to color, may be designated as "U.S. Fancy Red" if at least 90 percent of the peppers show any amount of a shade of red color; or as "U.S. Fancy Mixed Color" if the peppers fail to meet the color requirements of either "U.S. Fancy" or "U.S. Fancy Red."[26]

[26]USDA Code.

Peppers, Sweet, Frozen

Buy: Grade A: Characteristic light color; pods well trimmed with little grit, sand, silt, seeds, core, stem or serious damage; firm, full fleshed, tender.

Whole stemmed: 90 percent minimum 2½ inches long.

Sliced: Maximum 30 percent less than 1¼ inch long.

Diced: Maximum 10 percent markedly large or small, practically uniform size and weight.

Deterioration: Off-color, bronzing, poorly cut units, seeds, cores, and stems.

Potatoes

The word "potato" apparently came from the Spanish "patata" or "batata," which was applied to sweet potatoes, and, by mistake, to the white potato. Botanically, it is a succulent, nonwoody annual plant of the night-shade family. Few of the latter are of economic importance, except the cultivated eggplant.

A great many people are misinformed about white or Irish potatoes on two counts. First, they are not native to Ireland, and were not introduced to the Irish until 1585. Second, white potatoes, contrary to popular belief, are not an exceptionally fattening food. As a matter of fact, one medium-size potato contains no more calories than a large apple or a single baking powder biscuit of average size.

Furthermore, the potato is a fair source of Vitamins B_1, C, and G, and it has an abundant content of iron, phosphorus, and other minerals.

A large part of the U.S. potato crop must be stored, since most of it is harvested in September to November. Storage is generally done on the farm or at a controlled air storage of an association or corporation. Potatoes are generally held in common storage rather than cold storage. In storing potatoes, temperature maintained in the storage is dependent a great deal on ultimate use intended. For general fresh use, outside winter air permits fan injection into the storage area to maintain optimum storage temperatures with moderate air circulation.

Early or "new" potatoes are shipped directly from the field after harvesting. On occasions, they are excessively "skinned" or "feathered" because of immaturity, coupled with rough handling. The feathered area is likely to turn brown or black, causing the potato to wilt or shrivel at normal room temperatures. While there is much consumer preference for new potatoes, don't plan to home-store them for more than a few days.

Much experimentation has been made by use of gamma rays to inhibit sprouting of potatoes. Government tests have shown that by such radiation they can completely inhibit the sprouting of potatoes to preserve for future use; however, at this writing, there are no commercial installations for this method because of cost.

Use of chemical sprout inhibitors on the fall crop is increasing. This may be applied to the potatoes as a gas or dust at the time of placement in storage, or in the wash water as they are withdrawn from storage. These inhibitors are harmless and do not change the color, taste, or texture of the food.

Throughout the world, potato tubers are of a great many sizes, shapes, and colors. The flesh color may be white, yellow, pink, red, or blue—but only the white fleshed types are acceptable in the United States.

In the industry, potatoes are generally classified in five basic types: the Round White, Russet Burbank (long Russet group), Russet Rural or Round Russet, Round Red group, and the Long White.

Each variety listed here was developed for specific, or perhaps general, home or commerical use. Unfortunately, the seed used, the climate under which the tubers were grown, the amount of water and fertilizer, and the temperature and humidity of the storage prior to shipment—all have an effect on cooking qualities. Using the following guide, in combination with the variety marked on the consumer size unit purchased, should serve your purpose:

Cherokee. Short, elliptical, frequently flattened area on one side toward stem end, medium shallow eyes, and white flesh. Good for boiling, baking.

Chippewa. Elliptical to oblong, shallow eyes with white skin; ideal for boiling with no darkening after cooking.

Cobbler (Irish). Roundish with white, smooth skin and shallow to rather deep eyes; best for boiling, may be baked; darkens after cooking.

Green Mountain. Oblong, broad, flattened with smooth, sometimes netted, white skin and medium deep eyes. Good for boiling, baking; flesh generally darkens after cooking.

Hunter. Elliptical, medium thick, skin smooth, dark cream buff; eyes shallow, moderately well distributed; white flesh. Good for boiling or baking with no darkening after cooking.

Katahdin. Tubers are short elliptical to round, medium thick with shallow eyes and smooth, white skin. Ideal for boiling, slight darkening after cooking; also used for french fries.

Kennebec. Elliptical to oblong with shallow eyes, white skin and flesh; good for boiling, baking, french fries; generally no darkening after cooking.

Keswick. Elliptical to oblong tubers with eyes medium in depth; dark cream skin color with white flesh; good for boiling, baking, with no discoloration after cooking.

McClure, Red. Entire supply from San Luis Valley of Colorado; tubers generally medium size, round, flattened, skin sometimes somewhat netted, red. Eyes few, mostly at seed end, very shallow except bud-eye cluster, which is frequently depressed.

Norgold Russet. Oblong to long, heavy netting to skin, uniform russeting; shallow eyes, very well distributed. Good for boiling or french fries; no darkening after cooking.

Norland. Oblong, smooth red skin and shallow eyes with white flesh. Ideal for boiling with no darkening of skin.

Pungo. Elliptical, somewhat rounded tubers with white, flaked skin, medium deep eyes, and white flesh. Good for boiling and baking with no skin discoloration.

Red LaSoda. Semi-round to slightly oblong with bright, red skin, very smooth. Eyes are medium in depth to shallow. Ideal for boiling; no darkening after cooking.

Red Pontiac. Round to oblong with smooth or sometimes netted, intense red skin, medium deep eyes and white flesh. Ideal for boiling; slight darkening after cooking.

Russet Burbank (Netted Gem). Long, cylindrical, or slightly flattened with russeted, heavy-netted skin and numerous, well distributed shallow eyes and white flesh. Good for every purpose but ideal for baking and french fries. Slight discoloration after cooking.

Sebago. Elliptical to round, with smooth, white skin and shallow eyes; good for boiling, baking, with no darkening after cooking.

White Rose (Long White). Large, long, elliptical, flattened tubers with smooth, white skin and numerous medium-deep eyes with white flesh. Ideal for boiling; generally no darkening after cooking.

Potatoes of any kind or size should be firm, relatively smooth, clean, and reasonably well shaped. They should not be badly cut, bruised, wilted, sprouted, sunburned or light-burned. Size does not affect quality and is a matter of choice for the particular use.

Some red potato varieties, in some areas of production, are artificially colored with a red dye and wax. The wax and color used are nontoxic and used to enhance the appearance and preserve the freshness. Federal Food and Drug regulations require the potatoes so treated to be plainly marked on the package or at the display area. A number of years ago, as a result of imperfect color in some of the new varieties of red potatoes, color-waxing was employed by many areas of production to provide a uniformity of color and ready identification of the red potatoes. Because boiling of this type of potato, with the skin on, caused an objectionable residue in the pan, many states have established laws prohibiting sale of color-waxed potatoes.

Today, some areas also clear-wax their Russet and White varieties to enhance the appearance and preserve freshness. The objectionable pan residue has virtually been eliminated.

In the future, potatoes will probably be sold not only by grade and size, but also specific gravity. The latter test is your very best guide to cooking characteristics. The higher the specific gravity of the potato, the more mealy it usually is; thus, ideal for baking. The potato of slightly lower specific gravity is better for boiling, and one of still lower specific gravity is preferred for frying.

If a potato placed in a 1.08 salt solution sinks, its specific gravity is greater than 1.08. If it floats, it may be placed in a 1.07 solution and the test repeated. Rather ideal specific gravity for baking and mashing potatoes is considered 1.08. For boilers, between 1.07 and 1.08; for fryers, below 1.07.

To know the cooking characteristics of your potatoes, make a solution of 22 oz. of common salt in 11 pints of water. Potatoes of specific gravity of 1.08 or higher will sink in such a solution.

The "greening" on the surface of the skin of a potato is a result of development of chlorophyl in potatoes that have been exposed to either sunlight or artificial light. This greening is an indication of the possible presence of an alkaloid called solanine. If the greening has developed far enough, it will cause the potatoes to have a bitter taste. Large amounts could cause illness in the consumer. It is best to completely peel-away this green area of the potato. If you find several potatoes green, return them to the seller. When storing potatoes in the home, it is best to store in a cool, dry, dark area, as greening takes place more rapidly at room temperature than in a cool area. But for best eating quality, do not store your raw potatoes in the refrigerator.

Deterioration: Badly sprouted or soft, flabby potatoes are unsatisfactory. Potatoes that are soft due to freezing are unsatisfactory.

Servings and Weights. For potatoes to be pared by hand: 1 lb. provides 3 boiled potatoes of medium size; 8½ lb. provides 25 portions; and 3½ lb. provides 100.

For french fries: 1 lb. provides 4.32 portions of 1 oz. each; 6 lb. provides 25 portions; and 23½ lb. provides 100.

For cubed and diced, cooked: 1 lb. provides 4.27 portions of 3 oz. each; 6 lb. provides 25 portions; and 23½ lb. provides 100.

For mashed potatoes: 1 lb. provides 3.80 portions of 4 oz. each; 6¾ lb. provides 25 portions; and 26½ lb. provides 100.

To be pared by machine: 1 lb. provides 3 portions of 1 medium boiled; 8½ lb. provides 25 portions; and 33½ lb. provides 100.

For french fries: 1 lb. provides 4.16 portions of 2 oz. each, 6¼ lb. provides 25 portions; and 24¼ lb. provides 100.

For cubed, diced, and cooked: 1 lb. provides 4.05 portions of 3 oz. each; 6¼ lb. provides 25 portions; and 24¾ lb. provides 100.

For mashed: 1 lb. provides 3.60 portions of 4 oz. each; 8½ lb. provides 25 portions; and 33½ lb. provides 100.

With ready-to-cook potatoes: 1 lb. provides 3 portions of medium boiled; 8½ lb. provides 25 portions; and 33½ lb. provides 100.

For french fries: 1 lb. provides 5.44 portions of 2 oz. each; 4¾ lb. provides 25 portions; and 18½ lb. provides 100.

For mashed: 1 lb. provides 4.76 portions of 4 oz. each; 5¼ lb. provides 25 portions; and 21¼ lb. provides 100.

Grades. Potato grade standards, as promulgated by the USDA, with approval of the trade, were revised as of Sept. 1, 1971. The new grades are "tighter" than those in effect since 1958, that is, potatoes must be cleaner and have fewer defects to make the grade than before. Even though the new grades are tighter than the old ones, there is still a great deal of room between potatoes at the top of U.S. 1 grade and at the bottom. It cannot be considered that two shipments are of similar quality merely because both grade U.S. 1. This is still a pretty loose grade, apparently because the trade has not been able to agree on stricter requirements.

Yet, the new grades provide total tolerance for defects in U.S. 1 of 8 percent, compared with 11 percent in the old grades; moderately shriveled, spongy, or flabby potatoes, formerly permitted in U.S. 1, are ruled out; artificial color, formerly not mentioned and, therefore, permitted, is scored as an external defect if it is unsightly, conceals other defects, or causes more than 5 percent waste when discolored flesh is removed; and scoring of sprouts or clusters of sprouts as defects is tightened.

The U.S. potato standards provide for U.S. extra 1, U.S. Commercial and U.S. 2 grades. Since U.S. 1 is the principal trading grade, only this grade will be outlined here, but space does not permit giving full details.

U.S. 1 consists of potatoes which meet the following requirements: (a) similar varietal characteristics; (b) firm; (c) fairly clean; (d) fairly well shaped; (e) free from (1) freezing, (2) blackheart, (3) late blight, southern bacterial wilt, and ring rot; and (4) soft rot and wet breakdown; (f) free from damage by any other cause; (g) size. Not less than 1⅞ inches in diameter, unless otherwise specified in connection with the grade; (h) tolerances (as specified.)

Size: The minimum size or minimum and maximum sizes may be specified in connection with the grade in terms of diameter or weight of the individual potato, or in accordance with one of the size designations . . . : size A minimum diameter of 1-⅞ inc., with at least 40 percent 2½ in. in diameter, or 6 oz. in weight or larger; size B, 1½ in. minimum, 2¼ in. maximum; Small, 1¾ to 2½ in. in diameter; Medium, 2¼ in. or 5 oz. to 3¼ in. or 10 oz; and Large, 3 in. or 10 oz. to 4¼ in. or 16 oz. . . . Count and weight of the individual potato [is] from 50 count, which is 15 oz. minimum, to over 140 count, which is 4 oz. minimum, to 8 oz. maximum, the size designations to apply to potatoes packed in any size container.[27]

WHITE POTATOES

Approximate potato size found in various counts. Certain counts require blending of potato sizes. Illustrations therefore must be considered only as average diameter of potatoes in various counts.

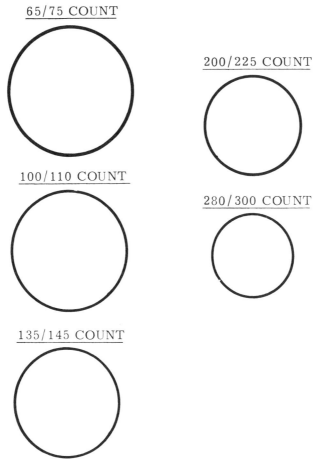

65/75 COUNT

200/225 COUNT

100/110 COUNT

280/300 COUNT

135/145 COUNT

Frosty Acres Buyers Guide—The Frozen Food Forum, Inc.; Atlanta, Ga.

---

[27]USDA Code.

White Potatoes, Canned

Buy: Grade A: Uniform light color; free from oxidation, some blemish; typical firm, even grain texture; may have slight degree of sloughing.

Whole: Maximum 2 inch diameter, 300 percent weight variation, ½ square inch peel per 20 ounces.

Sliced: 150 percent diameter variation allowed to 2 inch maximum; maximum ¾ inch thick; ½ square inch extraneous material per 20 ounce net; maximum 10 percent blemished.

Diced: 10 percent maximum + or −½ inch cube; uniform size and shape.

Shoestring: Maximum 10 percent less than ½ inch long; uniform thickness; 4 percent maximum blemished; ½ ounce peel per 20 ounces.

Pieces: ½ to 2 ounce pieces with maximum 100 percent weight variation.

Deterioration: Oxidized units. Poor peeling, grit, and gouges.

Dehydrated Potato Products

Regular Potato Granules

These are the result of drying clean, trimmed, sound potato tubers to a final moisture content of 6 to 7 percent. Each granule consists of a single potato cell or an aggregate of 5 to 7 cells. These small granules compact together to form a very dense mixture—close to the density of water. This is why they must be prepared in a high-speed mechanical mixer to whip the granules and allow the water to be totally interspersed around each granule, thus allowing full rehydration of each granule to yield the desired fluffy mashed potato product.

If the *granules are not prepared* in a high-speed mechanical mixer, up to 10 percent of the stated *yield is lost*.

With seasoned potato granules, the milk,[28] spices, etc., are blended dry with the potato granules.

Following peeling and trimming, the potatoes are usually sliced (thickness ⅜ to ¾ inches) to promote uniformity of cooking. Cooking is done in steam at atmospheric pressure, with the potatoes on a moving belt at a depth of about 6 to 8 inches. Cooking time depends on the raw material and on the altitude, but it is usually in the range of 30 to 40 minutes. Mashing and mixing with the dry "add-back" granules is then performed.

The "add-back" process takes place when cooked potatoes are partially dried by "adding back" enough previously dried granules to give a "moist mix" which, after holding, can be satisfactorily granulated to a fine powder. This process was developed

---

[28]Actually the practice of adding nonfat dry milk to all seasoned *granule* products has been discontinued, and whey protein solids have been introduced. (This does not apply to agglomerated potatoes, i.e., Kwik Tatoes, Potato Pearls, etc., where nonfat milk is still used.) Whey is the highly-nutritive byproduct of cheese and cottage cheese production and, therefore, is a readily available, low-cost source of milk protein. Tests indicate there are no detectable differences in product flavor or nutritional values since the introduction of whey protein solids in potato granules.

to assure gentle shearing and pressing of the cooked potato cells with a minimum of ruptured cells. Rupture of cells releases free starch; the product becomes unduly sticky or pasty if this is excessive.

The resultant moist-mix is cooled to approximately 60 to 80°F. It is then conditioned by holding for about 1 hour at this temperature, mixed, dried, in one or two stages to about 12 to 13 percent moisture content, and screened. Material coarser than about 60 to 80 mesh is returned to the process as add-back for succeeding cycles. A part of the fine material passing through the screen is also returned as add-back, but the major part to be used as product of the cycle, is further dried to a final moisture content of about 6 percent.

The rule of thumb is that one #10 can of potato granules will replace 40 pounds of raw potatoes.

Agglomerated Complex Mix Potato Granules

These items (i.e., Kwik Tatoes, Potato Pearls) are top-of-the-line dehydrated potato products. Agglomerated potato granules are prepared from regular potato granules in the following manner:

The granules are mixed and coated with a wet mixture of nonfat milk, butter, and spices. These ingredients help "glue" or attach 10 to 20 separate potato granules together. This is where the term "agglomerated" arises. The agglomerated granules are then screened and broken down into uniform particles and dried again in a modified fluidized bed dryer.

At this point in the process, the agglomerated granules are less uniform in shape and do not compact together as densely as regular granules. This characteristic allows the water to more easily intersperse around each agglomerated granule to fully rehydrate the product. Due to this ease of rehydration, the product can be prepared by simply hand-mixing right in the serving tray. Also, it is excellent for use in dispenser machines and may be mixed in a high-speed mechanical mixer for up to a 10 percent greater yield.

Although the case cost of this item is ½ to ¾ times more than regular potato granules, it is a tremendous convenience item. Add the cost of labor for preparation, equipment clean-up, and milk and butter seasoning to regular potato granules, and the final per-serving cost difference between the two items is almost negligible.

Potato Flakes

These are produced by applying cooked mashed potatoes to the surface of a steam-heated rotating drum-drying apparatus fitted with applicator rolls. The deposited layers of potato solids are dried almost instantly and, as the drum rotates, are removed in large sheets which are then broken into flakes for packaging.

Because potato flakes are dried quickly in a single step, the potato cells are easily rehydrated, as the potato starch retains its absorbing power. Of all forms of dried potatoes, potato flakes alone are most easily *rehydrated with cold water*. In fact, if boiling water is used, it will damage the potato cell structure, resulting in a very "pasty," glue-like mashed potato product. Best results are obtained when flakes are added *to* the liquid which first has been cooled down by adding cold milk. Mixing may then be done by hand right in the serving tray. *Do not whip* potato flakes with a mechanical mixer, as they have already been whipped during processing. Additional whipping is unnecessary and actually harms the potatoes.

Potatoes, White, French Fried

Deterioration: Excessive light or dark colored units. Excessive number of chips, slivers, or irregular sized pieces. Carbon specks, dark discolorations, excessive oiliness or sogginess after heating. Off-flavor or odor.

Pumpkin

All pumpkins and squashes are of the cucurbit family, which includes watermelons, cucumbers, muskmelons, and gourds. Basically, there is no distinction between squashes and pumpkins; thus, the word has merely become a culinary term traced back traditionally to the early settlers.

Size and shape have little to do with a pumpkin's flavor, although the smaller ones have less waste and usually a more tender flesh.

Quality.   There are no grades specifically for pumpkins, but the same general criteria apply as to other winter squashes. They should be well matured, not broken or cracked, free from soft rot or wet breakdown, excessive scarring, and indications of disease or freezing, and they should be clean. Generally, pumpkins are expected to have a rich, orange color.

Pumpkin, Canned

Buy: Grade A: Uniform, light color; holds mound of height 50 percent of length of container; maximum 10 cc liquid separation per 30 ounce net; no grit, sand, silt.

Deterioration: Gray, tan, or dull color. Excessive free liquid. Coarse, pasty finish. Excessive pieces of seed, dark particles, and fiber.

Radishes

Good quality in fresh radishes is not indicated by the condition or color of the leaves, but by the root, which should be smooth, crisp, and firm, never soft or spongy. The long, white, mild-flavored ones are called "icicles" but the red "button" variety is more popular. Round radishes vary in size from about 1 inch in diameter up to 4 inches; the long ones from 3 to 10 inches in length. They are plentiful every month of the year.

In addition to the most popular varieties just mentioned, there are also round white and round black radishes.

Best storage temperature is 32°F, with very high humidity. If storing bunched radishes, addition of ice helps keep tops fresh.

Deterioration: Radishes with cuts or gouges often discolor and decay rapidly.

Grades. Grades for topped or bunched radishes are U.S. No. 1 and U.S. Commercial.

> U.S. No. 1 consists of radishes of similar varietal characteristics, the roots of which are clean, well-formed, smooth, firm, tender, and free from decay, and which are free from damage caused by freezing, growth cracks or air cracks, cuts, pithiness, disease, insects, or mechanical or other means. Bunched radishes shall have tops which are fresh, and free from decay, and free from damage caused by freezing, seedstems, yellowing or other discoloration, disease, insects, or mechanical or other means.
>
> Styles: "Bunched radishes" means radishes with full length tops which are tied in bunches. "Topped radishes" means radishes with the tops clipped back to not more than ⅜ in. in length.
>
> Standard bunches of radishes shall be fairly uniform in size, and radishes in the individual bunches shall not vary more than ½ in. in diameter. Not more than 10 percent of the bunches in any lot may fail to meet the requirements for "standard bunching."
>
> Size terms: (1) "Small" means less than ¾ in. in diameter; (2) "Medium" means ¾ to 1 in. in diameter; (3) "Large" means over 1 to 1¼ in. in diameter; and (4) "Very large" means over 1¼ in. in diameter.[29]

Rappini

Rappini is a very small turnip plant with no bulb development. It is pulled by hand and marketed with the roots attached. The name is derived from the Latin name for turnip (*rapa*) and the suffix (*ini*), meaning small.

Rhubarb

Fresh rhubarb is frequently referred to as "pieplant." Botanically, rhubarb is a vegetable, but in use, it is considered a fruit because of its high acidity and flavor.

Field-grown rhubarb is rich, dark red in color, with coarse, green foliage and a very tart flavor. It is sold with leaves attached or removed. Hothouse rhubarb is a light pink with small leaves and is almost stringless. It has a milder flavor and tops are usually trimmed before selling.

Rhubarb of good quality is fresh, firm, crisp, tender, and either cherry red or pink in color. The stalks should be fairly thick, with the younger stems (on which the leaves are not fully grown) usually the most tender and delicate in flavor. Stale rhubarb usu-

---

[29]USDA Code.

ally has a wilted, flabby appearance. Condition of the leaves is a reliable guide in judging freshness of this vegetable.

Fresh rhubarb stalks in good condition can be stored 2 to 4 weeks at 32°F, high relative humidity. Rhubarb wilts rapidly at room temperature.

Only the stalk of the rhubarb is suitable for consumption. The leaf is very bitter, containing oxalic acid—if any quantity of leaves is eaten, it could be fatal.

Grades.   Three U.S. grades are provided for rhubarb (field grown). U.S. Fancy, U.S. No. 1, and U.S. No. 2.

> U.S. Fancy consists of stalks of rhubarb of similar varietal characteristics which are very well colored, fresh, tender, straight, clean, well trimmed, and not pithy; which are free from decay and free from damage caused by scars, freezing, disease, insects, or mechanical, or other means. (a) The diameter of each stalk is not less than 1 in., and the length is not less than 10 in.[30]

U.S. No. 1 and 2 are basically the same as U.S. Fancy, except for color, sizing, and shape.

Rutabagas

While there are white-fleshed and yellow-fleshed varieties, commercial rutabagas are virtually all yellow-fleshed.

Storage rutabagas are generally dipped in an edible vegetable wax to make them keep better, since the hot coating is effective in preventing wilting and loss of weight. It also improves the appearance (luster) slightly. Such a coated root is usually preferable. This comes off when the root is peeled, of course.

Rutabagas are round and slightly longish and have a more solid flesh than the turnip. They should be stored at 32°F, relative humidity of 95 percent. This is one of the few vegetables that has to be peeled before cooking.

Grades.   U.S. grade standards for turnips or rutabagas, effective Aug. 1, 1955, provide for two grades, U.S. 1 and U.S. 2. Information given here applies to topped turnips or rutabagas, with tops removed to not more than ¾ in. in length. The following are excerpts:

> U.S. 1 consists of turnips or rutabagas of similar varietal characteristics, the roots of which are well trimmed, firm, fairly smooth, farily well shaped, fairly clean, and free from soft rot, and free from damage caused by cuts, discoloration, freezing, growth cracks, pithiness, woodiness, watercore, dry rot, other disease, insects, or rodents, or mechanical or other means. (a) Unless otherwise specified, the diameter of each turnip or rutabaga shall be not less than 1¾ in.[31]

---

[30]USDA Code.
[31]USDA Code.

Salsify

A member of the sunflower family, salsify is sometimes called oyster plant, vegetable oyster, and, incorrectly, vegetable marrow. It is a garden esculent, grown for the fleshy root, which has the flavor of oysters. Salsify is very hardy. The seeds (which are really fruits) are sown in early spring.

Salsify is similar in appearance and quality characteristics to parsnips, except that the tops look like heavy grass. It also resembles the parsnip in that its flavor is improved after exposure to cold temperatures.

Sorrel

A member of the buckwheat family, and identifiable by its arrow-shaped leaves, sorrel is cooked as a green. The name ''sorrel'' is applied to two distinct types of plants which are used as a food. Both have a relatively high content of oxalic acid, which gives them a sour flavor, but in other respects, are quite different.

The type known as *garden sorrel* is of some commercial importance and closely resembles the common sheep sorrel. The leaves are of a light-dull green color and are narrow and pointed in shape like an arrowhead. It should be bought and handled the same as you would spinach, with which it is usually cooked to add flavor.

The other type is known as *oxalis, wood sorrel, sour grass,* or *sour clover,* and is of practically no commercial importance. The leaves are small, light-green, and composed of three rounded leaflets resembling those of clover. The stems are upright, tender, and vary from light green to red.

Soybeans

Fresh, edible soybeans are seen more and more in the markets and can be distinguished by their fuzzy pods, which are about the same length as those of peas, but much flatter.

Spinach

Well-developed plants with fresh, crisp, clean leaves of good green color are the best quality. Small, straggly, or overgrown stalky plants are often tough. Those that are wilted or have started to turn yellow usually show sliminess and rot. Both the curly and flat-leaf types are good for cooking. Ideal storage temperature is 32°F, relatively humidity 95 to 98 percent.

Deterioration: Coarse, tough leaf stems, yellowish color, excessively bruised leaves, or soft decay, are all signs of poor eating quality.

Grades.   There are U.S. standards for spinach plants, fresh spinach leaves, and fresh spinach for canning. The standards for *spinach plants* are U.S. No. 1 and U.S. Commercial; for *fresh spinach leaves,* U.S. Extra No. 1, U.S. No. 1, and U.S. Commercial; for *canning,* U.S. No. 1, U.S. No. 2, and U.S. 3. There are also U.S. *consumer standards* for fresh spinach leaves, that is, standards that can be applied to spinach placed in consumer size packages and sold to the consumer under a federal grade. The consumer standards are U.S. Grade A and U.S. Grade B.

As an example of the grades, U.S. Extra No. 1 for fresh spinach leaves

shall consist of spinach leaves of similar varietal characteristics which are fairly clean, well trimmed, free from coarse stalks, seedstems, seedbuds, crowns and roots, sandburs or other kinds of burs, decay, and from damage caused by clusters of leaves, wilting, discoloration, freezing, foreign material, disease, insects, mechanical or other means. . . . Not more than 5 percent, by count, of any lot may fail to meet the requirements of this grade, including not more than 1 percent for spinach leaves which are affected by decay.[32]

Spinach, Canned

Buy: Grade B: Good flavor and odor, has only minor off-color, mushy texture, disintegration, ragged cutting or shredded leaves or extraneous material.

Deterioration: Pale color or a decided brown cast. Presence of grit, grass blades, or small weeds. Soft, mushy leaves or presence of tough fibrous stems and leaves and leaves damaged by insects, mildew, etc.

Spinach, Frozen

Buy: Grade B: As with canned but of brighter color.

Deterioration: Off-color. Presence of silt, sand, grit, weeds, grass, discoloration, tough or coarse stems, or leaves. Off-flavor or odor.

Squash

The terms "summer" and "winter" for squash are only based on current usage, not on actuality. Summer types are on the market all winter; and winter types are on the market in the late summer and fall as well as winter, and some are on the market all year.

The soft-shell, immature squashes, such as *Yellow Crookneck,* and *Zucchini,* should be obviously fresh, fairly heavy for size, and of characteristic color. Rind should be so tender it is easily punctured with the fingernail. Seeds should be soft and fully edible.

There are two general types: Long and Short, differing mainly in size. Hard-shelled mature squashes are not expected to be fresh in the same sense as immature squash. The shell should be intact and show no decay. In this type of squash, the seeds are expected to be hard and inedible and are scooped out before or after cooking. Avoid squash that shows any soft or watery areas. These varieties are adapted for long storage. *Hubbards* can be successfully stored for 6 months or longer; *Table Queen* (Acorn) can be kept 3 to 6 months.

The popular varieties of squash in the soft-shelled, immature category include:

[32]USDA Code.

Yellow-Crookneck is one of the most widely grown. It is available all year, though not storage. Curved at the neck and larger at the apex than at the base; moderately warted, light yellow skin at early edible stage, turning to deeper color in mature state; creamy yellow flesh. *Yellow Straightneck* is similar to Crookneck, but relatively straight. *Zucchini* is also widely grown and on the market all year. They are cylindrical, straight in shape; skin color is moderately dark green over a ground color of pale yellow. Sometimes sold as "Italian" squash. *Cocozelle* is a bush squash with fruit almost cylindrical when young, with very slightly enlarged apex. Skin is smooth but ribbed widely and shallowly, alternately striped in rather definite lines with very dark green or dull greenish black or pale greenish-yellow coloring. *Scallops* (pattypans) are widely grown and on the market all year. They are disk or flared—bowl shape with prominent ribbing on edge, giving escalloped appearance. Size is generally 3 to 4 inches across. In the white type, they are pale green when young, becoming whiter later. Skin is smooth or slightly warted, flesh is green tinged.

The hard-shelled, mature varieties include *Acorn* (Table Queen), which is widely grown and available all year. This squash is acorn-shaped, hence the name. *Buttercup* falls into this category and is so named because of the turban-like cap at the blossom end; the shape is somewhat drumlike, with sides slightly tapering near the apex. *Butternut* is also of this category, available all year; nearly cylindrical but with a slightly bulbous base; light creamy brown or dark yellow skin; smooth and hard shell; yellow or orange flesh and fine grained. *Large Banana* is on the market August through March. Fruit is nearly cylindrical and moderately tapering at base and apex; skin is moderately smooth to obscurely wrinkled and pock-marked; color is pale olive gray changing to creamy pink in storage.

For hard shell squash, ideal temperature for storage is 50°F, relative humidity 70 to 75 percent. For soft-shelled, immature squash, best temperature is 32 to 40°F, relative humidity 85 to 90 percent.

Deterioration of Summer: Those with dull surface and tough rind are overgrown or overaged, and are likely to have poor texture and flavor.

Deterioration of Winter: Watersoaked or moldy spots indicate freezing injury or early stages of decay.

Grades. U.S. standard grades were established in 1944 on fall and winter type squash and in 1945 on summer squash. In each case, the grades are U.S. No. 1 and U.S. No. 2. *The fall and winter grades* apply to such varieties as Hubbard, Turban, Table Queen (Acorn), Marrow, Delicious, Butternut, and others, that have hard rinds and are eaten when seeds are mature. The *summer squash standards* apply to squash picked in the immature stage and eaten without the removal of seeds or seed cavity tissue. Such squashes include Yellow Crookneck, Yellow Straightneck, White Scallop (Pattypan), Zucchini, Cocozelle.

In the case of winter squash,

U.S. No. 1 shall consist of squash of one variety which are well matured, not broken or cracked, and which are free from soft rot or wet breakdown, and from damage caused by scars, dry rot, freezing, dirt, disease, insects, mechanical or other means. . . . In order to allow for variations other than size, incident to proper grading and handling, not more than a total of 10 percent, by weight, of the squash in any lot may fail to meet the requirements of the foregoing grades, including not more than 2 percent for squash which are affected by soft rot or wet breakdown, or are seriously damaged by dry rot. In addition, not more than 5 percent, by weight, of any lot may consist of squash smaller than any minimum weight specified, and not more than 15 percent, by weight, of any lot may consist of squash larger than any maximum weight specified. . . . In view of the size variations in different varieties, and because of market demands for squash of various sizes, it is not considered advisable to require a minimum size in the grade. It is therefore suggested that a minimum size or a range of sizes be specified in connection with the grade as, "U.S. No. 1, 6 lb. min.," "U.S. No. 2, 4 lb. min.," "U.S. No. 1, 6 to 12 lb.," in accordance with the facts.[33]

In the case of fall and winter squash,

"Well Matured" means that the squash has completed its ripening process to a stage of development which is indicative of good handling and keeping quality for the variety. . . . [Damage that throws winter squash out of grade includes] scars (except stem scars) caused by rodents or other means which are not well healed and corked over, or which cover more than 10 percent of the surface, or which form depressions or pits that materially affect the appearance of the squash.[34]

Damage also means stem scars which are unhealed on Hubbard, Delicious, Marros, and other varieties which normally retain their stems after harvesting.

In the case of summer squash,

U.S. No. 1 shall consist of squash of one variety or similar varietal characteristics, with stems or portions of stems attached, *which are fairly young and fairly tender,* fairly well formed, firm, free from decay and breakdown, and from damage caused by discoloration, cuts, bruises and scars, freezing, dirt or other foreign material, disease, mechanical or other means. . . . In order to allow for variations incident to proper grading and handling, not more than 10 percent, by weight, of the squash in any lot may fail to meet the requirements of this grade, but not more than ½ of this tolerance, or 5 percent, shall be allowed for defects causing serious damage, and not more than ⅕ of this amount, or 1 percent, shall be allowed for squash affected by decay or breakdown. . . .

Because of the size differences between varieties and the difference in size preference in various markets, there are no size requirements in the grades. However, if so desired, size may be specified in connection with the grade, in terms of minimum or maximum diameter or both, or minimum length or both. When size is specified, it shall be stated in terms of inches and quarter inches. In order to allow for variations incident to proper sizing, not more than 5 percent, by weight, of any lot may consist of squash smaller than any minimum size specified; and not more than 10 percent, by weight, of any lot may consist of squash larger than any maximum size specified.[35]

---

[33]USDA Code.
[34]USDA Code.
[35]USDA Code.

Squash, Summer Type, Canned and Frozen

Buy: Grade A: Light, typical color of variety; no grit, sand, or silt; 1 piece extraneous material per 12 ounces; 12 percent of units may be damaged; units intact, fleshy, tender, with seeds in immature stage. In frozen, buy Grade A, maximum 6 percent poorly cut or mechanically damaged.

Deterioration: Mixed varieties. Off color and broken or mashed units.

Squash, Cooked, Frozen

Buy: Grade A: Warmed, mixed squash has only minor separation at 2 minutes; light typical color, no oxidation; even texture, little or no grit, sand, silt.

Deterioration: Oxidized or off-color squash, hard particles, lumps, and pieces of rind.

Spaghetti Squash

Also known as Cucuzzi, Calabash, and Suzza melon. It is an edible gourd, often classed as a summer squash, but not a true squash. The plant is a vining annual with large, pubescent leaves on long petioles which form a canopy over the stems and fruits. The fruit grows up to 2 to 3 feet long and 3 inches in diameter. It is light green, with a smooth skin.

To bake, cut desired sections, place in 325°F oven, and cook about 2 hours. Or, place whole or cut sections in boiling water for 20 to 30 minutes.

Sweet Potatoes

Sweet potatoes are of two types: dry-meated and moist-meated. The "moist" type is often called "yam;" however, the true yam is of a different genus.

The skin of the dry type is usually light yellowish-tan or fawn-colored, while the skin of the moist-fleshed varieties vary in color from whitish-tan to brownish-red.

Disregard color in sweet potato buying, but remember that thick, chunky, medium-size sweets, which taper toward the ends, are preferable. Avoid those with any sign of decay, as such deterioration spreads rapidly, affecting the taste of the entire potato. Buy bright, clean sweets that are free from blemishes. You can enjoy them the year-round.

The top seven ranking varieties of production are:

Centennial. Soft-flesh type; roots tapered to cylindrical; medium to large; orange skin and deep-orange flesh.

Nemagold. Flesh fairly soft when baked. Roots medium size, short to long spindle, with russet-golden-orange skin and deep-orange flesh. Skin usually smooth, but sometimes veined.

Goldrush. Excellent quality for market and canning. Soft-flesh type. Roots tapered, spindle uniform, attractive bright orange skin and deep-orange flesh. Smooth skin.

Georgia Red. Soft-fleshed type. Roots slightly variable. Purplish-red to copper-red skin and orange flesh. Excellent for baking.

SWEET POTATOES—SHAPE—FAIRLY WELL SHAPED
(One Usable Piece Available.)

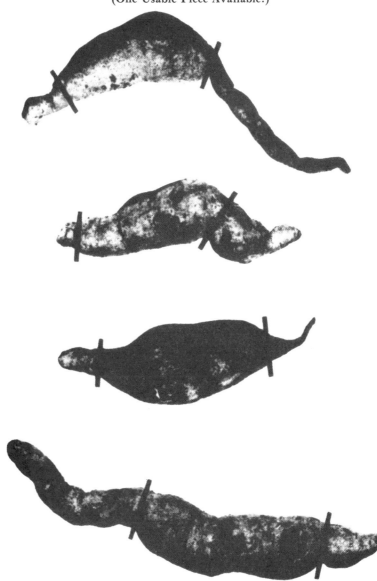

Porto Rico. Light rose to rose skin color with orange-yellow flesh. Shape of root is fusiform to globular and irregular, but smooth.

For short periods of storage, approximately 55°F with low humidity, is best.

Deterioration: Worm holes and other penetrating defects cause excessive waste.

Grades. U.S. grades for sweet potatoes are U.S. Extra No. 1, U.S. No. 1, U.S. Commercial, and U.S. No. 2. U.S. No 1 is the chief trading grade.

U.S. No 1 shall consist of sweet potatoes of one type which are firm, fairly smooth, fairly clean, not more than slightly misshapen, which are free from freezing injury, internal breakdown, black rot, other decay, or wet breakdown, except soil rot, and from damage caused by secondary rootlets, sprouts, cuts, bruises, scars, growth cracks, scurf, soil rot, or other diseases, wireworms, weevils or other insects, mechanical or other means. Unless otherwise specified, each sweet potatoe shall be not less than 3 in. in length and 1¾ in. in diameter, and shall not exceed 10 in. in length. In no case shall the sweet potato be more than 3¾ in. in diameter or weigh more than 20 oz.

Tolerance for defects: In order to allow for variations other than size, incident to proper grading and handling, not more than a total of 10 percent, by weight, of the sweet potatoes in any lot may fail to meet the requirements of this grade, but not to exceed a total of 5 percent shall be allowed for defects causing serious damage, including not more than 2 percent for sweet potatoes affected by soft rot or wet breakdown, except soil rot.[36]

Sweet Potatoes, Canned

Buy: Grade A: Yellow or golden color with reasonable variations.

Whole and Pieces: Largest piece maximum 8 times weight of 2 smallest; soft to firm without disintegration, smooth texture, no coarse fibers.

Whole Process and Mashed: Stiff consistency, may show slight separation of liquid; only minor peel rootlets, discoloration; smooth texture.

Deterioration: Presence of coarse fibers, fibrous ends, irregular shapes, broken pieces, and very light color. Tendency to mushiness.

In the United States today, the word "yam" is used as an industry trademark to identify the nutritionally superior "moist-fleshed" type of sweet potatoes, improved in Louisiana and now grown in many of the other southern states. It is also the type grown in the central valleys of California. North Carolina has become the number one tonnage producer. The flesh of this type of sweet potato is an orangish-color. It turns soft and moist during cooking, and is sweet to the taste. The other type of sweet potato produced for food in the United States—the "dry-fleshed" type—has a pale-yellow to light-orange color and remains dry and firm when cooked. It is less sweet to the taste than the sweet potatoes called "yams." These varieties grow best further north in New Jersey, and other mid-Atlantic seaboard states.

In light of this information one could build up reference to yams as compared to just sweet potatoes. "Sweet Potatoes" must be shown on the label, as this is their legal definition under the Standards of Identity in the FDA grades. "Yams" may be shown on the label also, because in the marketplace, a yam is considered to be a specific type of sweet potato of the moist-fleshed variety.

Sweet Potatoes, Frozen

Buy: Grade B: Yellow, golden, or mixed.

---

[36]USDA Code.

Succotash, Canned

Buy: Grade A.

Succotash, Frozen

Buy: Grade B.

Sugar Cane

Sugar cane is from the cane of the same name. It is generally packaged in cellophane, 8 to 10 inch sticks. Strip hard cover, chew or shred inner fibrous sugar.

Sunchokes

See "Artichokes."

Sunflower Seeds

These seeds are from the sunflower plant. In recent years, the seeds have become a snack food, the eaters cracking the hull with their fingers, or between their teeth, to secure the tiny, edible kernel. In the organic food movement, the kernels are favored for their heavy protein content. Growing sunflowers has become a very large, commercial venture.

Tamarillo (Tree tomato)

This is known in some areas as Cyphomandra. All our research indicates these two items are actually the same; therefore, we are treating them as Tamarillos, since this is the name commonly known in the United States.

Tamarillo is commercially grown in New Zealand. It is oval to egg-shaped, about 2 inches long with a stem attached. Its greenish-purple color changes to reddish-purple when ripe. It can be used both as a fruit or vegetable as they combine well with either sweet or savory foods.

Taro Root

Also known as Dasheen, taro root is thought to have come originally from China. It is raised and used mostly in the southern states, cultivated in many warm regions of the temperate zones. In Hawaii, taro is eaten mostly in the form of poi.

The starch grains in taro are the smallest in any plant, making them readily digestible. The flesh of cooked dasheens ranges from purple or violet to a cream shade. The deep violet-colored "corms," as the tubers are called, are regarded as having a better flavor than the light or cream-colored ones. It can be baked, steamed, boiled, or used in soups like potatoes. When buying, the entire tuber should be very firm. Store in refrigerator.

Tarragon

Tarragon plants may grow to 2 feet. The leaves are used for seasoning.

Tomatillos

Commonly known as ground tomatoes, these little husk-covered green vegetables grow on vines along the ground. They resemble a small green tomato, but taste like a slightly green plum in their raw state. The skin is tough, though thin, like a chili. Quality is good if they are clean and firm, with color from bright green to yellowish green. Husks are always dry. Do not wash until ready to serve. Store in refrigerator.

Topepo

This vegetable derives its name from the fact that it is a cross between the tomato and Chinese sweet pepper. Topepoes are generally used in salads and should be selected the same way as you would tomatoes.

Truffles, White

Related to the mushroom, the truffle is bulbous and unimpressive looking; it has an odor some find offensive. It grows underground on the roots of trees and is found only in parts of northern Italy. Truffle lovers call it the "diamond of the vegetable world."

Since Roman times, true gourmets have paid up to $200.00 a pound for white truffles, slicing or dicing it and sprinkling it on salads and other dishes. Its tangy, delicate flavor is quite distinctive.

Truffles grow wild, up to 2 or more feet below the surface of the ground; efforts to seed them have been unsuccessful. Their hiding places are sniffed out by specially-trained dogs, the owner gently unearthing the truffles.

Turnips

Turnips are generally sold with the tops removed, although those from early crops are sometimes sold in bunches with tops on. The eating quality of turnip greens depends largely on their freshness when purchased. Turnip greens are not suitable for storage for more than a week or two after being cut. They vary considerably in appearance, depending upon the variety and the stage of development at which they are harvested.

Best storage temperature is 32°F, relative humidity 95 to 98 percent. White turnips are especially good in soups and stews. Yellow turnips are most often mashed.

Deterioration: Coarse, tough leaf stems, yellowish color, excessively bruised leaves, or soft decay, are all signs of poor eating quality. Large turnips with too many leaf scars around crown and with obvious fibrous roots, deep cuts, or decay.

Deterioration of Canned: Poor flavor or odor. Off color and tough, coarse, leaves or stems. Root stubs, weeds, and seed heads in greens.

Grades. U.S. grade standards for turnips or rutabagas, effective August 1, 1955, provide for two grades, U.S. No. 1 and U.S. No. 2, including bunched, topped, and short-trimmed turnips. U.S. Standards for mustard greens and turnip greens, effective March 8, 1953, provide for one grade, U.S. No. 1. It is not possible to reprint the entire standards here, but excerpts are given, and the complete text may be obtained free from Fruit and Vegetable Division, Agricultural Marketing Service, USDA, Washington, D.C. 20250.

"Bunched turnips" means turnips which are tied in bunches. The tops shall be full length or removed to not less than 6 in. Turnips with short-trimmed tops means, unless otherwise specified, turnips showing leafstems ranging to not more than 4 in. in length. "Topped turnips". . . means turnips with tops removed to not more than ¾ in. in length.

U.S. 1 consists of turnips or rutabagas of similar varietal characteristics, the roots of which are well trimmed, firm, fairly smooth, fairly well shaped, fairly clean, and free from soft rot, and free from damage caused by cuts, discoloration, freezing, growth cracks, pithiness, woodiness, watercore, dry rot, other disease, insects or rodents, or mechanical or other means. Bunched turnips, or turnips with short-trimmed tops, shall have tops which are fresh and free from decay, and free from damage caused by discoloration, freezing, disease, insects, or mechanical or other means. Unless otherwise specified, the diameter of each turnip or rutabaga shall be not less than 1¾ in.[37]

Turnip Greens with Turnips, Frozen

Buy: Grade A.

Deterioration: Off-color. Presence of silt, sand, grit, weeds, grass, discoloration, tough or coarse stems, or leaves. Off-flavor or odor.

Vegetable Marrow

Vegetable marrow, a member of the squash family, should be eaten young, about ¼ or ⅙ the full-grown size. It is a green, cucumber-looking vegetable with thin yellow stripes. In Europe it is much prized, but in this country, the Crookneck and Scallop types of squash are more popular. Choose and store it like squash. It is also called Chinese squash (Faahn Gwaah) and "marrow squash."

Verdolagas

Verdolagas are also known as Purslanem or Fatweed. They are common, trailing weeds with fleshy, succulent stems, widely distributed. Improved strains are cultivated as pot herbs. The leaves are small, spatulate, or narrow-obovate, thick and green. Cultivated forms are for upright growing, and are larger and of better flavor. Plants may be grown from seeds or from cuttings. Verdolagas are rarely cultivated in the United States; they are grown primarily in Mexico and Central America.

[37]USDA Code.

Water Chestnut

"Chinese water chestnut" and "waternut" are common English names for a tropical sedge, which is widespread in the tropics of the Old World. This species has long been cultivated for its corms, or so-called tubers. These are esteemed as a nutritious delicacy in Chinese cookery and are extensively eaten raw. The skin is a chestnut-brown color, with white flesh. It has a chestnutty flavor and texture. A plant with the same name is a floating aquatic plant and is considered a pest in some streams in the eastern United States. Although the corms of this plant can also be eaten, the fruits are quite distinct from the highly edible corms of the Chinese water chestnut.

Corms vary considerably in size; however, in general, only corms of 1 to $\frac{3}{16}$ inch or more in diameter are acceptable to the trade.

Water chestnuts can be successfully stored in a jar, with the lid applied *but not airtight* in the refrigerator. If storage temperatures are too high, sprouting of the water chestnuts may occur. They may also be stored in plastic bags for short periods, providing the bags are not sealed tight.

Chinese water chestnuts are in greatest demand in the fresh form; however, they are also found canned and frozen. Canned water chestnuts lose much of their flavor but retain their crispness, whereas frozen water chestnuts retain the flavor but are less crisp than the canned product.

Their crisp, white, applelike flesh is both sweet and starchy. Its flavor is similar to fresh coconut.

Watercress

Watercress is a perennial aquatic plant, generally cultivated in large ponds. It has long stems and small, thick leaves having a pungent flavor. It is most easily produced in water from springs in limestone regions. The best product comes from clear, running water, or near springs where it can be watered frequently.

There is only one variety of the plant we call watercress; however, there are other cresses that grow wild and under similar conditions. Two field or land cresses that are seen on the market are peppergrass (sometimes called Fine Curled or Curled), which is a hardy, quick-growing annual having finely curled, deep-green foliage with pleasing flavor; and Upland cress, a dwarf plant with slender stalks and oval-notched leaves rather like watercress in shape and flavor. There are many other cresses, generally growing wild, mainly gathered in the spring and used as greens or as a substitute for watercress. The only true watercresses belong to the egenus Nasturtium of the mustard family.

Watercress should be selected with an eye to its fresh, bright-green color and crispness of its rather long stems. Presence of wilted, bruised, or yellowing leaves is a sign of age or poor handling.

As in other leafy greens, favorable storage temperature is 32°F, very high humidity. It can be kept in the refrigerator for a week or more when proper care is taken in storage. It should be washed gently, but thoroughly, in cold water, drained well, and dried on a towel or absorbent paper.

Winter Melon

A pumpkin-like melon with a frosty greenish skin, winter melon is most frequently cooked in a pork meat stock to make soup. The Chinese sometimes peel off the rind and quick-cook thin squares for a vegetable dish.

In spite of its name, you will see the winter melon throughout the year. They are very large and may weigh 20 to 30 pounds.

Yucca (or Yuca) Root

Also known as Cassava (or Casava) and ''manoic,'' yucca root applies to any of various tropical American plants of the genus Manihot; especially, M. esculenta, having a large, starchy root. The starch derived from the root of this plant is used to make tapioca and as a staple food in the tropics.

QUESTIONS

1. Define the following:

    "Winter Kist"   Celtuce
    Butter lima   Collards
    Chick peas   Daikon
    "Brocco"   ADOGA
    Gobo   Pericarp
    Pencose

2. Jerusalem artichokes are actually a true native of North America. (True or False)
3. List the sieve sizes of lima beans in relation to their commercial name.
4. A poor appearance of the leaves of beet roots is an indication of poor quality beets. (True or False)
5. Briefly explain the proper cooking method for cabbage to retain its nutritional value.
6. At what stage of growth is cauliflower of inferior eating quality?
7. Describe a U.S. No. 1 grade of cauliflower.
8. How many pounds of sweet corn on the cob without husks would you need to purchase to serve 100 people?
9. One-half cup serving of cooked dandelions will supply your daily Vitamin A requirements. (True or False)
10. Briefly differentiate between the following: curly endive, escarole, witlof chicory.
11. What are the steps used in the freeze-drying process?
12. List the five types of lettuce and briefly describe them.
13. Of what importance is the specific gravity of potatoes?
14. You have ample kitchen staff. You need sauce for pizza for 200 teenagers. How much of each of the following do you need: (a) fresh tomatoes, (b) canned whole tomatoes, (c) tomato puree, (d) tomato sauce. What impact does grade have on this decision?

15. What is the principal difference between U.S. Fancy and U.S. Extra Standard Canned Whole Kernel Corn? If you used the latter, how would you overcome this disadvantage?

16. Construct a table showing what a No. 10 can equals in No. 303's, No. 2's, No. 2½'s, and No. 3 cyl.

17. List five pitfalls of vague specifications.

18. How can the specific gravity of a potato be determined in the school lunch kitchen? Why might it be useful to use this method?

19. There are two factors that can make catsup "slow." What are they? How can you use this knowledge in your facilities?

20. Compare and contrast Canned and Frozen Carrots. What makes U.S. Standard Carrots unacceptable for school lunch?

21. Does it make any difference whether you use frozen or canned vegetables? If so, what?

22. What is the color grading system for french fried potatoes? Is length a factor? How do you know if you got what you ordered?

23. If canned green beans are $12.00 per case, at what price are frozen green beans cheaper? Given tight staffing, which would you use? Which state is the "better" product?

24. Should Mexicali Corn be bought or should you mix your own?

25. What information, other than required on the label, does a case and can of product give you? How can that information be used?

26. Does quality in canned fruits and vegetables really matter? Shouldn't we buy the cheapest product regardless of quality?

EXHIBITS

Frozen Specification	
Peas	Product
Sweet	Style/Type
4 Sieve	Count/Sieve
2016 Bulk	Pack
Agricpack	Source
Telephone	Variety
AAB	U.S. Grade
85 Min	Point Score

Canned Vegetables	(½ cup servings) 6 cans/cs. Suggested Size #10 Can	24 cans/cs. Suggested Size #2½ Can	#303
Asparagus (cuts and tips)	20	—	—
Beans (lima)	24	—	4
Beans (snap, green, or wax)	21	5.5	3
Beets (sliced)	23	—	3.25
Carrots (sliced)	23	—	3.25
Corn (whole kernel)	23	—	3.5
Okra	20	—	3.5
Onions (small, whole)	20	—	3
Peas (green)	23	—	3
Potatoes (small, whole)	25	—	—
Pumpkin (mashed)	26.5	7	—
Spinach	15	4.5–5	3
Squash (summer)	17.5	—	3
Tomatoes	25.5	7	4
Catsup	111	—	—

Fruit Juices:	18 fluid-ounce can yields 4.5 sugs.
	46 fluid-ounce can yields 11.50 sugs.
	96 fluid-ounce can yields 24 sugs.
Vegetable Juices:	23 fluid-ounce can yields 5.75 sugs.
	46 fluid-ounce can yields 11.50 sugs.
	96 fluid-ounce can yields 24 sugs.

Portion as served = 3 ounces cooked

Frozen Vegetable	Yield/#
Asparagus (cuts and tips)	4.27
Beans (lima)	5.33
Beans (snap, green, or wax)	4.85
Broccoli (cut or chopped)	4.53
Carrots (sliced)	5.12
Corn (whole kernel)	5.17
Okra	4.37
Peas (green)	5.12
Potatoes (French fries)	8 (10 pieces)
Spinach	4.27
Squash (summer)	4.64

Green Peas			
	(bushel) Fresh	(#10) Canned	(2½#) Frozen
3 oz. Serving	51	24	13
1000 Serving	19.6 bushels	41⅔ cans	62.5 boxes
Preparation Time	100 min/bushels	—	—
Wage Rate	$ 4.00/hr	—	—
Added Cost	$130.67	—	—
Space Requirement			
Price	$ 3.00/bu	$ 2.00/cn	$ 0.54/#
$/1000	$ 58.80	$83.34	$84.37
Added Cost	$130.67	—	—
Total	$189.47	$83.34	$84.37

6

WINES, SPIRITS, AND BEER

INTRODUCTION

A successful restaurateur's wine cellar will be determined by the customers rather than by the restaurateur's choice of an imposing wine selection. Wine cellar selection can be done through observation of other area restaurants, asking knowledgeable persons, or sampling the wine.

The vigneron, soil, and sun all affect the future of a wine. Too little sun or sun at the wrong time decreases wine quality. Soil type indicates the type of grapes that will produce a desired wine. The vigneron is the master, who constantly checks for grapes at perfection for harvesting, crushing, fermenting, and storing. The wine will go through a series of "transfers" and fermentations before it is bottled in two to three years. The length of time to bottle and cork quality indicate the better wines.

Tasting a wine should be taken seriously. Foods affecting the taste buds and smoking should be avoided. Time allowed for breathing is determined by the age of the wine. Appearance is checked first. Is it cloudy? What color is it? Bouquet is the smell of the grape and is most evident in a young wine, but not necessarily absent in an older wine. Taste is highly subjective and based on personal experience. Wine should be tasted one against another for a frame of reference. One is frequently able to detect subtleties of the wine in the aftertaste.

The Act of 1911 was instituted to protect the description Bordeaux. Previously many wines were termed Bordeaux when they were not from the region. The Description of Origin Act (1919), Capus Act (1927), and Decree Act (1935) helped limit wine fraud. Wines by description are strictly controlled now.

Bordeaux is the largest wine-growing area in France. Burgundy is another wine-growing area in France. Champagne strictly controls the wines that originate from this area. Beaujolais is becoming the "quick study" wine, although it is a young wine and doesn't travel particularly well. There are four main categories of Chablis, and they have existed since 1938.

German wines are classified according to grape sugar content rather than by vineyards as the French do. Italian wines have three standards of controls which began in

1963. Spanish wines are not controlled and tend to be young except for one area close to the French border, which ages the wines for a longer period of time.

California produces a great deal of wine and has regions similar to those in Europe. New York also produces a large amount of wine.

Stocking and inventory of a wine cellar can be elaborate or simple. Standard practice is to set minimum and maximum levels for the cellar and floor stock. Wines should be stored at 55°F, away from direct sunlight, in a dry, well ventilated area.

Distilling wine with a still produces brandy. The simplest form of a still is a fire, pan, and tubing called a "worm." A craftsman is required for the proper blending of flavors.

[1]With wines, as with any other food or beverage, a restaurant that serves its patrons something they like well enough to buy again is the restaurant that builds a permanent business. Each wine must be palatable to the taste of the patrons for whom it is intended and in harmony with the food items with which it is to be served. Tart, strong-flavored, heavy-bodied Burgundy may be a "natural" for a restaurant specializing in Italian dishes, but the dining room of a cosmopolitan hotel will sell more semi-sweet Sauterne than Burgundy, at least until its patrons' wine tastes have been further developed. It is more important to have wines that satisfy customers than it is to have an elaborate and imposing selection.

Successful buying is always done with the selling price in mind. Wine buying must enable the restaurant to offer its patrons the essential combination of a satisfactory quantity at a reasonable price.

Restaurateurs who do not yet know wines can do the same things any merchant does when entering a new field. They can observe what wines other comparable restaurants are selling successfully. They can seek impartial advice from people who know wine. More important, they can sample the wines personally and get their staff and friends to sample them. Even if they are novices, it is a safe assumption that if they like a wine, the patrons will like it too, and if the restaurateur and the staff do not like it, the patrons will not like it either. A common mistake is to offer an unsuitable wine on the assumption that people who like wine will like this one even though the restaurateur and the staff do not. (Sampling should continue after the original purchase to insure that the wines remain in good condition and that successive shipments retain the original quality.) Those buying wine for the first time should buy cautiously and watch the reactions of their patrons. By such careful buying, the wine assortment can be refined gradually until it is adequate to sustain a continuing successful wine-selling program.

WINE MAKING

Three things go into the making of wine, whether it be good, bad, or indifferent: (1) the soil from which the vine grows, (2) the sun or the amount of sun that shines upon the vine in any given year, and (3) the hand of the *vigneron* who makes the wine. The first is immovable and permanent, the second is variable, and the third and last is human. When these three come into alignment, the result can be a near miracle.

---

[1]Reprinted from *The Sale of Wine in Restaurants* by permission of the Wine Institute.

The first element, the soil upon which the vines are grown, does not alter from year to year, but like any other soil it can become exhausted if it is not constantly fed with the right kind of humus, although its mineral-bearing qualities will be unimpaired whatever happens. It is just these mineral-bearing qualities that provide those mysterious saccharomycetes and yeasts which form in the bloom of the grape and which, in conjunction with the fermenting elements and the sugar of the grape itself, form the special flavor and character of the grape.

It is unquestionably true that the grapes from which the finest wines are made grow on the thinnest of soils, consequently they produce the smallest of yields. The quality of the soil can change from field to field. One-half of the field may be quite white and then suddenly the whole color value changes and the other end is brown. It is quite possible that only a narrow path will separate the vineyard making the wine of the very first order from another producing grapes which are of the third or fourth growth. This is the first element in wine-making—the soil upon which the grapes are grown. It is vulnerable to sun and storm, and it must be kept in first-class condition by the person who makes the wine.

The second factor—the sun—is responsible for most of the worries of the vineyard. By sun, we mean the lack of it, for generally speaking, it can be assumed that if the grapes ripen, you will get good wine, and if they do not ripen properly, you won't. There are varying degrees of ripeness, and it is this factor that makes all the difference to a good, bad, or indifferent year. The function of the sun is to promote the sugar in the grape which becomes alcohol in fermentation.

If the sun shines when the buds are burgeoning on the vine, it is a very good thing; and if the sun shines when the flowers are blooming, that is also a good thing, but most of all the sun is wanted when the grapes have formed and are beginning to swell. Then a little rain won't hurt, and if a fine month is experienced before the vintage, you are likely to get some extraordinarily good wine. If, on the other hand, the weather is wet and damp, all the very horrible diseases that the vine grower has to contend with will start to raise their extremely ugly heads—nasty things connected with mildew and bugs which thrive in damp and wet. They take their toll by reducing the crop and spoiling the wine.

Too much sun will also do damage, although not by any means on the same scale. The grapes become *brule,* or burnt, and the wine is hot and rather harsh. It is for this reason that some of the Greek and Mediterranean wine is pretty harsh.

The basic process of making wine is simple and universal. The grapes are gathered; they are stripped of their stalks and they are dumped together in a large press and pressed; the juice is run off into large vats, and in a few hours fermentation commences. (If red wine is being made, the black grape skins are left in, for it is the pigment in the grape skins dissolved in fermentation which gives red wine its color. White wine is often made from black grapes, cf. Champagne, but the skins are removed before fermentation starts.) This fermentation is, as it is called, boisterous; that is, it bubbles away rather like a mud volcano. At just the right time, the *vigneron* will stop the first fermentation by drawing off the wine into barrels and a period of secondary fermentation is commenced. This varies from place to place and according to the method of storage, but let us assume that we are discussing very good wine in, say, the Bordeaux district. In the first year, the wine is stored in *barriques,* large barrels containing about a hogshead (or 48 gallons), in what is called the *chais*. (The *chais* is the large hall or shed adjoining the *pressoir* where the wine is made and where the fermenting vats stand, usually above ground, and where the new wine is racked by transferring it from barrel to barrel, about three times during the first year, while undergoing its slow secondary fermentation.) From the *chais*, the wine is removed to the cellar where it is racked yet again, once in its second year, and in the third year it is bottled. In the case of minor wines, and more common wines (perhaps ''little wines'' is a better expression), the second fermentation is accelerated by technical processes as it is intended for quick consumption. It is not expected to adorn your cellar or mine for ten or twenty years before it is drunk.

To return to our better wines, in the third year it is bottled. In all these conditions, there is a very human factor—that of timing. In the moment of time when a wine should be at its most perfect, the vintner must first stop fermentation in the vat by putting his wine into barrels. He must choose the exact (within a few days) time in which the wine in its first year should be racked, and again the second year, and above all, the moment in time when the wine in the barrel shall be bottled.

The vast majority of wine is exported in bulk after the secondary fermentations have stopped, and before bottling. It is much cheaper and easier to move wine in quantities of 50 gallons than in a case of a dozen bottles (2 gallons). If the wine is bottled at its chateau or domain or schloss, it is to be assumed that the *vigneron* will know the best moment at which to bottle his own wine. If he is a bad *vigneron*, he won't. That is why many wines have ceased to live up to their reputations. It is much the same with your wine merchant who imports wine in barrels. He or she must, by constant tasting and by good cellarage, choose the day on which that wine should be bottled in order to give it its very best chance. This is a matter of great experience and not a little inspiration.

The wine is now in the bottles and we must assume whether it is done in the chateau, or in the cellars of a local and trusted wine merchant, or in the wholesaler's warehouse, that the expert has done his or her job properly and the wine has been given its best chance on the day of bottling.

Now there is the matter of the cork, and it is upon the cork that the whole reputation of the wine will rest from the time of bottling forward, for wine is rendered bad only through the air which enters through the cork. If you buy your wine chateau-bottled or if you buy it through a first-class wine merchant, you will find they are using what is called the long cork (2¼ inches long) even on moderate quantities of wine. Wine merchants who wish to save money use a short and, therefore, cheaper cork. The better the cork, the better you can keep your wine because the air will not get through it quite so quickly. Cheap corks are short and porous and the air will get in and will turn your wine into vinegar.

TASTING*

Tasting has become ritualistic with wine lovers for it is through a formal observance of procedures that you become acquainted with each wine you encounter. To identify the

---

*Robards, T. *Wine Cellar Journal,* New York: Quadrangle/The New York Times Book Co., 1974. Reprinted with permission.

qualities of a wine, you must give them maximum opportunity to emerge. Unfortunately, the tasting ritual occasionally gives rise to wine snobbism. Those who follow the ceremony for purposes other than to taste the wine limit their enjoyment, but those who observe the proper wine-tasting procedure to maximize their experience are creating the conditions that will reveal the wine at its best.

The ritual begins long before you actually drink the wine. To assure that your taste buds are at their peak, you should avoid food or drink that would deaden your ability to taste. Raw onions, garlic, mustard, hot peppers, and vinegar will prevent your taste buds from recognizing the subtleties of a good wine. Most salads, therefore, should be served at the end of the meal, as they traditionally are in France. Most mixed drinks or cocktails will also numb your tasting senses. A good alternative during the cocktail hour is a light wine-based aperitif, a glass of white wine, or Champagne. Vodka and water on ice can be a viable compromise as well. Smoking also impairs the ability to enjoy wine.

With your taste buds in optimum condition, you must be certain that the wine is able to perform well. This means removing the cork from the bottle and permitting the wine to "breathe," or be exposed to the air, for a time before serving it. In general, the younger the wine, the more breathing is required. Old wines need not breathe more than a few minutes. A good red Bordeaux (Boar-duh), Chianti (Key-an-ti) Classico, or California Cabernet Sauvignon (Kub-err-nay) (So-veey-naw) from a good vintage may need 2 to 3 hours of breathing prior to drinking if it is less than a decade old. Red Burgundies need less time to mature; most reach their peak in 6 to 8 years and need less airing than Bordeaux. A good host or hostess will sample a bottle ahead of time to determine how much time it needs to be left uncorked. It is well to remember that almost all red table wines benefit from *some* breathing.

White table wines should be drunk young and need less breathing. Sparkling wines, such as Champagne (Shaum-pahn), should not be permitted to breath at all in advance of tasting as they will lose their bubbles with exposure to air.

Once the wine is ready for tasting and the tasters are equally prepared, the ritual can begin. Four major characteristics should be considered and noted: appearance, bouquet, taste, and aftertaste.

Appearance

Your first clue about the soundness of a wine will come with how it looks in your glass. First, determine its clarity. Pour no more than a half-ounce and tip your glass on its side, being careful to hold it by the stem and not by the bowl. Ideally, you will have a white tablecloth for background. Is the wine crystal-clear? Is it free of sediment or floating particles? Or is it slightly cloudy? A sound wine should be limpid, without a hint of cloudiness.

A mature red wine is likely to contain sediment, but the sediment should be settled on the side or at the bottom of the bottle. The first serving of wine, regardless of its age, should be clear. To be certain that old red wines are clear, they should be decanted.

Color is a very important aspect of a wine's appearance, and some information about the manner in which a bottle has been cellared can be obtained from its hue. A reliable rule of thumb is that all wines tend to turn brown with age. Sometimes the brownness can be perceived only by looking at the very edge of the wine in a tilted glass against a white background. Sometimes the brownness is all too evident. This goes for both red and white wines. Obviously, a wine that is brown at too young an age has something wrong with it. It may have been improperly made or improperly stored.

Older white wines also turn progressively brown. A Sauterne with 20 years in the bottle will have a deep caramel color, but it may still be sound because Sauterne is a sweet wine whose natural sugar and higher alcoholic content help preserve it. On the other hand, white Burgundy, Rhine, or Mosel (Mos-l) with an obvious brown tinge may have begun to deteriorate. As a rule, a properly made dry white wine should retain its light golden hue for at least 6 years. After that, its color will deepen. A white table wine less than 6 years old that begins to darken has not necessarily gone bad. Although some wine aficionados prefer the taste of a brownish-tinged white wine, the degree of color should be carefully noted as an indication of maturity.

Red table wines turn brown less easily than white wines. This is because red wines contain greater amounts of tannin, a substance imparted to the wine by the skins, stems, and seeds of grapes, which are permitted to ferment for a longer time in producing red wines than in whites. The red wine that is coarse and harsh with an abundance of tannin when it is young is the wine that may live for decades, slowly but invariably improving in the bottle. Even now, some of the great Bordeaux from the magnificent 1928 vintage show a deep crimson hue with only a hint of mahogany. Red Burgundies tend to reach maturity earlier in their lives, but, when properly stored, they too last decades.

You should search out wines that have maintained their scarlet hue despite decades in a bottle, or the properly mature reds that have turned only slightly brown around the edges. Beware, however, when the brownness extends beyond the edges and the wine appears to have lost the color of the grape. Wines from the 1800s sold at auctions in the United States and London often fetch enormous sums, but they may contain brown wine of questionable quality. It is prudent to avoid red wines that have turned heavily brown at less than a decade of bottle age. (Bottle age begins when the wine is transferred from aging vat to bottle.)

Bouquet

The grape develops on the vine only after the plant has flowered. By a quirk of nature, the aroma of the flower often remains in the fermented grape juice that becomes wine. At its peak, a fine table wine will exude an aroma that can only be described as a bouquet. The smell of the grape will be evident but not obvious. In a great wine, it will be complex and challenging, sometimes evoking such diverse scents as herbs, spices, violets, and lilacs. The bouquet of a great wine may grow ever more complex over the decades. While losing its intensity, it will always be balanced so the taste of the wine will not be overwhelmed by a single obvious characteristic.

Because the bouquet of a great wine tends to diminish with age, the lack of a pronounced aroma should not be used as a determinant of wine quality. It is wise to avoid wines whose aroma is odd or distasteful—experience helps identify these negative characteristics. You should remember that the aroma of a great wine is always either pleasant or nonexistent.

Taste

How is wine meant to taste? This question is perhaps the most frequently asked and the most difficult to answer. A great Red Bordeaux from a good vintage should taste a certain way. A great Bordeaux from a mediocre vintage will not taste as good, but it will taste better than most of the other wines produced that year. A great Red Burgundy should be big and robust, with all sorts of complexities in its bouquet and body. Yet some of the finest Burgundies are extraordinarily subtle wines. A 1934 Musigny (Mew-seen-yee) Comte de Vogué tasted in 1972 by a group of highly qualified oenophiles ranked far ahead of the 1929 Chateau Latour, the 1929 Chateau Lafite-Rothschild, and the 1929 Chateau Haut-Brion (Oh-bree-yahw), among others sampled the same evening. If any rule is worth following in evaluating taste, it certainly must be that taste is highly subjective and based on personal experience. The bouquet should be complex without being overwhelming, and it should be challenging. A good table wine is light without being thin, full-bodied without being heavy, and, above all, balanced.

To make judgments on taste, you must have a frame of reference. That means tasting on your own—always with one wine against another. It is not helpful to taste a single wine, all by itself, without any basis for comparison. You should progress from one good wine to another, gradually increasing your own sophistication until you have reached the point where you can return and identify what pleases you.

Only at that point will you know that the Meursault (Mair-so) for which you may have laid out a modest sum is actually a much more characteristically rounded White Burgundy than the Pouilly-Fuisse (Poo-ee-foo-ee-say) that costs twice as much. You will come to know that an Italian Chianti Classico from one of the outstanding vineyards in Tuscany may be able to challenge many good chateau-bottled Bordeaux, or that a Cabernet Sauvignon from California may display a whole range of traits alien to a fine Bordeaux made from the same kind of grapes, but nevertheless taste sound and special. You will learn that a Beaujolais should be fruity and zesty with youth, even though it is a red wine, and that you should not demand from a full-bodied Red Barolo from Italy the same subtlety and elegance that you expect from a Romanee-Conti (Ro-man-ee-Kawn-tee) from the Burgundian Cote d'Or (Cout-dohr) in France.

Naturally, the food that accompanies wine tends to have an important impact on how the wine tastes. Even assuming that you follow the rules about avoiding those strong-tasting salad dressings and garlic-based sauces, the same wine may display strikingly different characteristics when tasted with contrasting foods. The Chablis (Shab-lee) that seems dry and steely with oysters on the half-shell may be completely overwhelmed by a rich turbot, even though both are fish. The big and rich Burgundy that was so perfect with a Beef Wellington may seem inappropriate with a veal dish.

When you are tasting, always allow the wine to rest in your mouth for a moment and roll it around your tongue before swallowing. This allows you to savor the various tastes present in the wine.

Aftertaste

Commercial wine buyers will always spit out the wine they taste when they are trying to decide on their purchases. The main reason for this is to avoid the buildup of alcohol in their systems that will hamper their ability to make wise investment decisions. But in refusing to swallow, they must, by necessity, deprive themselves of a key element in the tasting experience. The aftertaste can be quite different from the impressions your tastebuds receive before you swallow. Often, a wine's acidity will be most apparent in the aftertaste. Other subtleties will become evident too, partly because your intake of air after swallowing tends to accentuate the characteristics of the small amount of wine that remains in your mouth. How *should* you react to aftertaste? As in the taste itself, there are no set rules. Some very fine wines may leave nothing whatever behind, while poor ones may yield an unpleasant aftertaste. The most important thing to remember is that your tasting experience does not end as soon as you have swallowed the wine.

APPELLATIONS CONTRÔLÉE

These "descriptions of origin" are so loaded with references, and they express the idea of collective heritage and ownership so well that, not so long ago, their delimitation gave rise to a hot dispute which was finally settled by a decree published in the *Official Gazette* of February 19th, 1911.

Before they came to their decision, the legislators were bombarded with more or less justified claims that the description Bordeaux should be extended to wines which were sometimes far removed from the city of that name.

The archivist Brutails helped them to decide on the limits by bringing his historical knowledge to bear and making a clear distinction between the wines of the seneschalcy and those of the Uplands (Haut-Pays) in accordance with traditions dating from the Middle Ages.

In that distant era, the only wines entitled to the description Bordeaux were those harvested in the immediate vicinity of the city by winegrowers who were freemen of the city and dwelt *intra muros*. To guard the privilege, King John had stated on April 15th, 1214: "We desire that all the wines of our citizens of Bordeaux, which come from the vines of their city, should travel freely on the river." In other words, all other wines were subject to a blockade and were discriminated against fiscally.

Like waves spreading out from a stone splashing in water, the description—or, more exactly, the privilege—was then extended to the 350 parishes of the seneschalcy of Guienne. Such was the legal position of the vineyards in 1789. It was not too critical.

The new administrative division of France into departments, on the threshold of the nineteenth century, once again extended the area of the description Bordeaux. Instead of the 350 parishes of the seneschalcy, it covered almost all the 554 communes of the Gironde. It was only a strike by the Council General that prevented the description being also extended to 63 communes of the Dordogne and Lot-et-Garonne.

After the decree of 1911, the winegrowers of the Lot-et-Garonne tried to call their wines "wines of the Bordeaux Uplands." This attempt was rejected by the courts since the description *Haut-Pays Bordelais* was not a traditional one—quite the contrary, in fact, since the term "Haut-Pays" was used to identify wines other than those known by the trademark Bordeaux. Cutting the city wines with wines made from the Haut-Pays had always been prohibited, as is evidenced by numerous fiats of the Bordeaux *parlement* down the centuries. The Act of 1911 was thus perfectly straightforward. Its purpose was to fit the place-of-origin concept into the framework of modern law and to protect the description Bordeaux from the concept of "provenance" with all the possibilities of generalized fraud it entailed.

At this stage of regulation, however, the name "Bordeaux" covered all the growths of the Bordeaux region without distinction, including the Great Growths which had been the beneficiaries of the 1855 classification and which had made use of all their prestige to obtain the decree.

In early 1919, the problem of descriptions of origin came up again with a new urgency owing to the Peace Conference being held at Versailles. If respect for descriptions of origin was to be imposed upon Germany, internal regulations had to be set up. The Descriptions of Origin Act was promulgated on May 6th, 1919. From then on, legislation proliferated. The most decisive laws were the Capus Act of 1927 and the Decree Act of 1935. The fact was that the winegrowers were unable to accept geographical origin as the sole criterion entitling to a "description." The 1919 Act was supplemented therefore by others which took account of new factors such as soil, vine species, degree of alcohol, and yield per acre. Thus were born the *appellations d'origine contrôlée* (AOC), the guaranteed descriptions of origin.

In the case of the Bordeaux region, the result of these provisions was a sort of hierarchy. It may, perhaps, have been a mistake to put the most limited description at the top and gradually descend to more and more general descriptions with an increasingly large production. Thus, in order of descent, a Pauillac growth was entitled to the descriptions Pauillac, Médoc, and Bordeaux.

To put it another way, a Pauillac wine which was considered to be unworthy of its name of origin and which lacked the characteristics required of a good Médoc could always be marketed as a Bordeaux. This use of the description Bordeaux as a catch-all was to produce great confusion in view of the worldwide renown of the greatest fine-wine producing region in France. However famous some celebrated châteaux or a few restricted descriptions might be, the foreign wine-lover had great difficulty in understanding that the word Bordeaux standing alone indicated the more modest products of the Bordeaux region. The most recent example of this regrettable confusion was given by the world press when commenting on a speech made by the then French Minister of Agriculture, Mr. Edgard Pisani, during a visit to Bordeaux. He said: "I have been and still am struck by the fact that the 'Bordeaux' flag is fast reaching the stage when it waves over the most mediocre goods and that so much disorder has been created in this wine-growing area that the first care of every winegrower is to put on a château label instead of the Bordeaux one."

Being badly informed about the AOC legislation, all that some journalists gleaned from his statement was the inference that Bordeaux wine was mediocre in general. Nonetheless, the Minister's criticism was perfectly justified and the reluctance of some Girondin producers to use the name Bordeaux was quite understandable. It does not mean, however, that they were entirely in the right. Although the descriptions Bordeaux and Bordeaux Supérieur were used to denote the more mediocre products, the great mass of Bordeaux wines in terms of the Capus Act were of excellent quality and widely used to improve growths better placed economically.

It was necessary to escape from that blind alley and take up the challenge to logic. The question was who would take the first step on the way back to a sound tradition.

One solution would have been for the Great Growths to meet their historic responsibilities and once more inscribe the name of Bordeaux on the pediment of their fame. In that way, they would have taken up anew their centuries old mission and, like true nobles, would have returned to the head of their troops and imposed discipline amongst them. The hesitation to sign such a blank cheque, however, was quite understandable. The other solution, more in keeping with the style of our era, was for those involved to take the revaluation of the description Bordeaux into their own hands; in fact, that was what they did.

Thanks to Mr. Pierre Perromat, President of the National Institute of Descriptions of Origin, but who never abandoned the presidency of the Bordeaux Superieur wine syndicate, these wines have, since 1967, enjoyed full descriptions of origin. They are subject to tasting and analytical tests like most of the other Gironde descriptions and have recovered their independence. There is no longer a catch-all description. Henceforth, the only refuge for disinherited Bordeaux descriptions in the category: ''wines for everyday consumption.''

The description Bordeaux Clairet, which derives from the description Bordeaux, has been highly fashionable in recent years. It is a rosé wine from any red grape already covered by the regional description and is obtained by ''bleeding'' the vat before the must has taken on its full colour. Bordeaux Clairet has nothing in common with the old claret, which was a briefly fermented red wine.

Bordeaux is France's largest wine-growing area and the most prolific. The Red Clarets and White Sauternes of Bordeaux are the standard by which other wine-producing areas of the world are judged.

The Bordeaux area has five major regions and several minor ones.

Bordeaux District Wines
Red, White, or Rosé

Appellation Contrôlée Bordeaux.   From anywhere in the Bordeaux district. May be a blend. Sometimes labeled with trade of monopoly names. (A Bordeaux Superieur must by law have a slightly higher alcoholic content.)

Regional Wines of the Five Classic Regions
Red Wines

Appellation Contrôlée Médoc (or Haut-Médoc).   Though all the finest come from Haut-Médoc, appellation is often shortened to MÉDOC. Inner subdivisions:

Moulis	Listrac
Pauillac	St.-Julien
Margaux	St.-Estéphe

Appellation Contrôlée Graves.

Appellation Contrôlée Pomerol.   Subdivision bordering Pomerol:

Lalande de Pomerol

Appellation Contrôlée St.-Émilion. Subdivisions bordering St.-Émilion, authorized to hyphenate their names with St.-Émilion:

Lussac	Montagne
Puisseguin	St.-Georges
Parsac	Sables

White Wines

Appellation Contrôlée Graves.

Appellation Contrôlée Sauternes.   Subdivision of Sauternes with option to use its own Appellation Contrôlée:

Barsac

Other regions of Bordeaux Entitled to
Their Own Appellations Contrôlées

Côtes de Bourg or Bourg (red)	Entre-Deux-Mers (white)
Blaye (red)	Côtes-de-Bordeaux-St.-Macaire (white)
Néac (red)	Graves de Vayres (white)
Côtes de Fronsac (red)	Loupiac (white)
Côtes Canon-Fronsac (red)	Ste.-Croix-du-Mont (white)
Cérons (white)	Premiéres Cotes de Bordeaux (red and white)
	St.-Foy-de-Bordeaux (red and white)

Château Wines (Crus Classés)
Médoc or Haut-Médoc
(Moulis, Pauillac, Margaux, Listrac, St.-Julien, St.-Éstephe)

Graves	St.-Émilion
Pomerol	Sauternes (Barsac)

White and rosé wines of Haut-Médoc are entitled only to *Appellation Contrôlée Bordeaux.*

A Graves *Supérieure,* like a Bordeaux *Supérieur,* requires a slightly higher alcoholic content.

Both the terms *Haut-Sauternes* and *Haut-Barsac* on a label are entirely meaningless; likewise *Grand (Grand Médoc, Grand St.-Julien,* etc.).

Note: Bottles of Bordeaux wines bearing a seal with the initials ADEB (Association pour le Développment de l'Exportation du Vin de Bordeaux) indicate that the wine has been voluntarily submitted to a panel of Bordeaux experts before export.

(Crus Exceptionnels et Bourgeois)

Château Villegeorge	Château Chasse-Spleen
Château Angludet	Château Poujeaux-Theil
Château La Couronne	Château Bel-Air-Marquis-d'Aligre
Château Moulin-Riche	Château Fourcas-Hostein
Château Capbern	Cru Gressier-Grand-Poujeaux
Château Dutruch-Lambert	Château Lanessan
Château Fourcas-Dupré	Château de Pez
Château Le Boscq	Château Phélan-Ségur
Château Meyney	Château La Tour-de-Mons
Château Les-Ormes-de-Pez	Château Sénéjac
Château Paveil-de-Luze	Château Gloria

Classified Wines of the Cote D'or
Grands Crus
(Entitled to a vineyard Appellation Contrôlée)

Côte de Nuits[2]

(Le) Chambertin	Clos de la Roche
Chambertin-Clos de Bèze	Clost St.-Denis
Latricières-Chambertin	(Le) Musigny
Mazys-Chambertin (Mazis)	Clos de Vougeot
Mazoyéres-Chambertin	Grands Echézeaux (and Echézeaux)
Ruchottes-Chambertin	Romanée-Conti
Chapelle-Chambertin	La Romanée
Charmes-Chambertin	La Tâche
Griotte-Chambertin	Richebourg
Clos de Tart	Romanée-St.-Vivant
Bonnes-Mares	

Côte de Beaune[3]

Corton	Bâtard-Montrachet
Corton-Charlemagne	Chevalier-Montrachet
Charlemagne	Bienvenues-Bâtard-Montrachet
(Le) Montrachet	Criots-Bâtard-Montrachet

[2]All listed wines are red, with the exception of Musigny, whose vineyard also produces a rare, expensive white (Musigny Blanc.)
[3]All listed wines are white, with the exception of Corton, which may be either red or white (Corton Blanc).

Premiers Crus
(Vineyards entitled to the Appellation Contrôlée
of their own particular commune.
Labels need not bear the words Premier Cru.)

Côte de Nuits—Red Wines

Commune	Vineyard
Fixin	Clos de la Perrière
	Clos du Chapitre
	Les Hervelets
Gevrey-Chambertin	Clos de Ruchottes
	Clos St.-Jacques
	Varoilles
	Fouchère
	Estournelles (or Etournelles)
	Cazatiers
	Combottes
Morey-St.-Denis	Clos des Lambrays
	Calouère
	Les Charnières
Chambolle-Musigny	Les Amoureuses
	Les Baudes
	Les Charmes
Vougeot	Les Petits-Vougeot
	Le Cras
	Clos de la Perrière
Flagey-Eschézeaux	Les Beaumonts (Beaux-Monts)
	Champs-Traversin
	Clos St.-Denix
	Les Cruots (or Vignes-Blanches)
	Les Rouges-du-Bas
	Les Poulaillières
	Les Loachausses
	Les Quartiers-de-Nuits
	Les Treux
	En Orveaux
	Les Echézeaux-de-Dessus
Vosne-Romanee	Les Beaumonts (Beaux-Monts)
	Les Gaudichots
	Les Malconsorts (Clos Frantin)
	La Grande Rue
	Les Suchots (Grands Suchots)
	Aux Brûlèes
	Les Reignots
	Clos des Réas

Commune	*Vineyard*
	Les Petits-Monts
	Les Chaumes
Nuits-St.-Georges	Les St.-Georges
	Les Boudots
	Les Cailles
	Les Porrets (Porets)
	Les Pruliers
	Les Vaucrains
	Les Cras
	Les (Aux) Murgers
	Les Thorey (Clos de Thorey)
Nuits-St.-Georges-Prémeaux	Clos de la Maréchale
	Les Didiers-St.-Georges
	Clos des Forêts-St.-Georges
	Les Corvées (Les Corvees-Paget)
	Le Clos St.-Marc
	Clos des Argillières
	Clos Arlot (d'Arlot)
	Les Perdrix (Champs Perdrix)

Côte de Nuits—White Wines

Commune	*Vineyard*
Fixin	Clos de la Perrière Blanc
Morey-St.-Denis	Mont-Luisants Blanc
Vougeot	Clos Blanc de Vougeot
Nuits-St.-Georges	La Perrière
Nuits-St.-Georges-Prémeaux	Clos Arlot (d'Arlot) Blanc
Pernand-Vergelesses	Ile-des-Vergelesses
	Les Basses-Vergelesses
Aloxe-Corton	Corton-Bressandes
	Corton-Clos du Roi
	Corton-(Les) Renardes
	Corton-Chaumes
	Corton-Maréchaudes
	Corton-Vigne-au-Saint
	Corton-(Les) Perrières
	Corton-(Les) Grèves
	Corton-Pauland
	Corton-(Les) Meix
	Corton-(Les) Pougets

Commune	Vineyard
	Corton-Vergennes
Savigny-lés-Beaune	Les Vergelesses
	Les Marconnets
	Les Jarrons
Beaune	Les Grèves (Grèves de l'Enfant Jèsus)
	Les Fèves
	Les Marconnets
	Les Bressandes
	Le Clos des Mouches
	Le Clos de la Mousse
	Le Cras
	Les Champs-Pimonts
	Les Cent-Vignes
Pommard	Les Épenots (Épenaux) (Grands Épenots)
	Les Rugiens-Bas
	Le Clos Blanc
Volnay	Les Angles
	Les Caillerets
	Les Champans
	Les Fremiets
	Santenots (Volnay-Santenots)
	Les Petures
	Clos des Chenes
	Clos des Ducs
Auxey-Duresses	Les Duresses
	Le Bas-des-Duresses
	Les Bretterins
	Les Ecusseaux
	Les Grands-Champs
	Les Reugnes
	Clos du Val
Puligny-Montrachet	Le Cailleret
	Clavoillons
Chassagne-Montrachet	Abbaye de Morgeot
	Le Clos St.-Jean Morgeot
	Morgeot
	Clos de la Boudriotte (La Boudriotte)
	La Romanee
Meursault	Les Cras
Santenay	(Les) Gravieres
	Clos-de-Tavanne
	La Comme

Côte de Beaune—White Wines

Commune	*Vineyard*
Beaune	Clos des Mouches Blanc
Meursault	Clos des Perrières
(Les)	(Les) Perrières
	(Les) Genevrières
	(La) Goutte d'Or
	(Les) Charmes
	(Les) Santenots
	(Les) Bouchères
	La Pièce-sous-le-Bois
	Sous-le-Dos-d'Ãne
Puligny-Montrachet	Le Cailleret
	Les Combettes
	Hameau de Blagny Blanc
	Le Champ-Canet
	Les Pucelles
	Les Chalumeaux
Chassagne-Montrachet	Les Ruchottes
	Morgeot
	La Maltroie (Chateau de)

Classified Growths of Graves
(Crus Classés)

Red Wines
(Classified in 1953)

Château Bouscaut
Château Carbonnieux
Château Smith-Haut-Lafitte
Château La Mission-Haut-Brion
Château La Tour-Haut-Brion
Château Haut-Brion

Château Fieuzal
Château Malartic-Lagravière
Château Haut-Bailly
Domaine de Chevalier
Château Olivier
Château La Tour-Martillac
Château Pape-Clément

White Wines
(Classified in 1959)

Château Haut-Brion
Château Bouscaut
Domaine de Chevalier
Château Malartic-Lagraviére
Château Coubins

Château Carbonnieux
Château Olivier
Château La Tour-Martillac
Château Laville-Haut-Brion

Classified Growths of Sauternes and Barsac
(1855)

1. (Grand Premier Cru)
Chateau d'Yquem
2. (Premiers Crus)

Château La Tour-Blanche
Château Lafaurie-Peyraguey
Château de Suduiraut
Château Climens
Château Rieussec
Château Rabaud-Sigalas

Clos Haut-Peyraguey
Château Rayne-Vigneau
Château Cotet
Château Guiraud
Château Rabaud-Promis

3. (Deuxièmes Crus)

Château Myrat
Château Doisy-Védrines
Château Filhot
Château Nairac
Château Suau
Château Romer

Château Doisy-Daëne
Château d'Arche
Château Broustet
Château Caillou
Château de Malle
Château Lamothe

Classified Growths of St.-Emilion
(1953)

1. (Premiers Grands Crus Classés)

Château Ausone
Château Beauséjour
Château Canon
Château Figeac
Château Magdelaine
Château Trottevieille

Château Cheval Blanc
Château Belair
Clos Fourtet
Château La Gaffelière
Château Pavie

2. (Grands Crux Classés)

Château l'Angélus
Château Bellevue
Château Cadet-Bon
Château Canon-La-Gaffelière
Château Chapelle Madeleine
Château Corbin
Château Coutet
Château Curé Bon
Château Fonroque
Château Grand-Barrail-Lamarzelle

Château Grand-Corbin-Despagne
Château Grand Pontet
Château Guadet-St.-Julien
Clos des Jacobins
Château La Clotte
Château La Couspaude
Château Larcis-Ducasse
Château Lamarzelle
Château Chauvin
Château Corbin-Michotte

Château Croque-Michotte
Château Fonplégade
Château Franc-Mayne
Château Grand-Corbin-Figeac
Château Grand-Mayne
Château Grandes Murailles
Château Jean Faure
Château La Carte
Château La Cluzière
Château La Dominique
Clos La Madeleine
Château Laroze
Château La Tour-du-Pin-Figeac
Château Le Châtelet
Château Le Prieuré
Château Moulin-du-Cadet
Château Pavie-Macquin
Château Petit-Faurie-de-Souchard
Château Ripeau
Château St.-Georges-Cote-Pavie
Clos St.-Martin

Château Trimoulet
Château Troplong-Mondot
Château Yon-Figeac
Château Balestard-la-Tonnelle
Château Bergat
Château Cadet-Piola
Château Cap-de-Mourlin
Château Larmande
Château Lasserre
Château La Tour-Figeac
Château Le Couvent
Château Mauvezin
Château Pavie-Decesse
Château Pavillon-Cadet
Château Petit-Faurie-de-Soutard
Château Sansonnet
Château Soutard
Château Tertre-Daugay
Château Trois-Moulins
Château Villemaurine

Principal Red Wines of Pomerol
(Unofficial classification by the Pomerol Wine Growers Syndicate)

1. (Grands Premiers Crus)

Château Pétrus

Château Certan
Vieux-Château-Certan

2. (Premiers Crus)

Cru l'Evangile
Château Beauregard
Château Clinet
Château Lafleur
Château La Commanderie
Château Gazin
Château Le-Gay-La-Fleur
Château Guillot

Château Nénin
Château Petit-Village
Le Clos Lacombe
Le Clos de l'Eglise
Clos du Clocher
(Château) Certain-Sauteloup
Château Trotanoy

WHITE BURGUNDY[4]

Everything that really matters in the way of white wine produced in Burgundy, from Chablis on the north to Beaujolais Blanc and St. Véran (near Macon) on the south, is now officially made from the Chardonnay grape alone. Twenty years ago this was more often called the ''Pinot-Chardonnay'' and considered a cousin of the Pinot Noir, the great red-wine grape of Burgundy and of Champagne. Another cousin, not quite as good but possibly more authentic, went by the name of Pinot Blanc Vrai both in France and in California. Except in a few old vineyards, this has almost disappeared, but occasional white albino ''sports'' or clones come along in red-wine vineyards—notably even in Nuits-St. Georges, *La Perriére,* giving fine white wine in the very heart and citadel of Red Burgundy.

It is safe to assume, therefore, that all White Burgundies, except those labeled ''Aligoté'' (an inferior white grape grown mostly for common, daily table wine) are Chardonnay, even if the grape name does not appear. It is implicit in the geographical name which the wine bears.

Most of these fragrant, elegant, and delicious wines, thanks to modern cellar technique, can now be bottled and drunk when they are not much over a year old. Generally the good ones are close to their peak at three or four years. Only the very best, and only in great years, will they keep past the age of ten.

The Two First Crus of Chablis

Grands Crus

Blanchots	La Mouronne
Bougros	Les Preuses
Les Clos	Valmur
Grenouilles	Vaudésir

Premiers Crus

Beauroy (Boroy)	Fourchaume
Beugnon(s)	Les Lys
Butteaux	Melinots
Chapelots	Mont de Milieu
Châtains	Montée de Tonnerre
Côte de Fontenay	Montmains
Côte de Lèchet	Pied d'Aloup
Les Forêts	Sechêt (sechè)

---

[4]Frank Schoonmaker, *Almanac of Wine,* Hastings House Publishers, 1975. Reprinted by permission of publisher.

Roncières	Vaucoupin
Troême (Troene)	Vaulorent
Vaillons	Vosgros
Vaupulent	Vogiros (Vaugiraud)

The *Grand Cru* vineyard of La Moutonne has for some years been under a cloud of disputes within its family management and contentions with the Institute des Appellations d'Origine. When bottles under its own name have appeared, or reappear again, it is to be recommended as one of the finest.

Principal Wines of Southern Burgundy

Côte Chalonnaise—Red Wines

Commune (or Appellation Contrôlée)	Recommended Vineyards
Rully	La Fosse
	Marisou
Mercurey	Clos du Roi
	Clos des Fourneaux
	Clos Marcilly
Givry	Clos St.-Pierre
	Clos St.-Paul
	Cellier aux Moines

Beaujolais—Red Wines

Crus de Beaujolais	Vineyards
St.-Amour	Champ Grillè
	Château de St.-Amour
Juliénas	Château des Capitans (Les Capitans)
	Les Mouilles
Fleurie	Clos de la Roilette
	La Madonne
	Le Vivier
Moulin-à-Vent	Les Carquelins
	Le Moulin-à-Vent
	Les Burdelines
Chénas	La Rochelle
	Les Caves
	Les Vérillats
Chiroubles	Le Moulin
	Bel Air
Morgon	Château de Bellevue
Brouilly	Les Bussières
Côte de Brouilly	Le Pavé

Côte Chalonnaise—White Wines

Commune	*Vineyard*
Rully	Raclot
Mercurey	Clos de Petit Clou
Givry	Champs Pourot
Montagny	Vieux Château

Mâconnais—White Wines

Commune	*Vineyard*
Pouilly-Fuissé	Les Chailloux
	Les Bouthières
	Les Prâs
	La Frérie (Frairie)
	Château Fuissé
	Château Pouilly
	Les Champs
	Les Perrières
	Les Brulets
	Les Crays
	Les Chanrue
	Les Chevrieres
	Les Vignes-Blanches

Other Appellations Contrôlées for white wines of the Mâconnais include Pouilly-Loché and Pouilly-Vinzelles; Chardonnay, Viré, Lugny, Clessé and St.-Véran.

Note: Other wines are simply *Mâcon* and *Mâcon Supérieur Grand* or *Premier Cru* or *Tête de Cuvée;* labels of any wines from Pouilly-Fuisse or other parts of the Mâconnais are entirely meaningless, and should be viewed with suspicion. *Premier Cru* vineyards are, however, authorized for the Côte Chalonnaise and are indicative of officially recognized quality. The term *Cru de Beaujolais* in Beaujolais refers to one of the nine superior subdivisions.

RANGE OF CHAMPAGNE WINES

Champagne is obtained by blending wines from three different grapes: the *Pinot Noir,* the *Pinot Meunier,* both black grapes, and the *Chardonnay,* a white grape. Many people are surprised to learn that this wine, so pure and clear, is made to a large extent from black grapes.

As in other vineyards, grapes from the same stocks do not necessarily have the same flavor or qualities, since these are influenced by the soil and place where they are grown. A connoisseur can easily tell the difference between the varieties. But with Champagne, it is more difficult to distinguish the range of wines and their varieties because of the grape marriages which initiated the fame of Champagne and contributed to much of its glory. The different firms possess their own particular characteristics, and long experience is needed to distinguish between them.

The soil and a favorable location are so important and make for such a difference in the final variety of the grapes that certain coefficients have been granted to the producing regions by commune and according to the quality of their produce. It is true that these basic coefficients are liable to change every year, depending on the results of the wine harvests.

The coefficients range from 77 to 100 percent; those of 100 percent are traditionally known as *"grands crus,"* while those of 90 to 99 percent are entitled *"premiers crus."* These titles are rarely carried on the label because the guarantee of quality is, in most cases, given by the great names of the firms who absorb 80 percent of the production. The opposite is true for most other wines, which normally are only too pleased to be able to announce *"grand cru."*

Before examining the various types of Champagne, it is useful to recall the legal protection of the *appellation d'origine contrôlée,* which benefits producers and consumers alike. Only the following is recognized as Champagne:

1. Wine produced from vines planted from authorized stocks, within the limits of the viticultural Champagne region, pruned to the required height, of a limited yield per acre;
2. Wine of an assured quality guaranteed by a limited yield in must and by a minimum alcohol content;
3. Wine prepared in accordance with the natural procedure known as *méthode champenoise,* in premises within the Champagne region where only wines from this region may be stored;
4. Wine stored in bottles prior to shipping for at least 1 year (but for 3 years after the harvesting, in the case of wines with a *millésime*).

These principles, which have been progressively sanctioned by French law, are applied and controlled, to avoid any fraud, by the CIVC in the name of the public authority, vinegrowers, and wine-merchants.

After the final stage, the dosing of the wine, the various types of Champagne can be classified as follows:

Brut (without mention of year). This wine, usually light and lively, is very suitable as an aperitif as it prepares both the mind and the palate.

Brut Millésimé. This is a very good wine which comes from a good vintage year, since only wines of the same year may be blended together in order to produce a first-grade bottle. In some years it might even be a collector's bottle. This type of wine is often more full-bodied and more generous; it deserves to be savored with particular care. A few of the old vintage wines very difficult to find today include: 1928, 1933, 1934, 1937, 1943, 1945, 1949, and 1953. Their merits vary, but one should be wary of those which have been aged too long. Here again, one might ask if Champagne be drunk young or old. Several things must be considered. First, although the carbonic acid gas in the Champagne gives it a certain resistance to bacteria and assures its conservation, it does not mean that the wine is impervious to everything and can remain in optimum condition forever. It is as much alive as any other wine and must receive the same attention and care. It ages and may change. After ten years or so, it may take on a slight color and begin to maderize; this will continue with the years. It is then said to have become a *renarde* (a vixen). It remains drinkable, of course, but its essential qualities fade, just as a beautiful flower fades. Moreover, the pressure of the gas decreases and little by little the wine loses its life. There is no point, therefore—except as an experiment or perhaps in the case of a particularly good vintage year—in keeping Champagne for a long time. It is put on the market at the time in its life when it is suitable for consumption. This is one of the rules that controls the quality of Champagne.

Dry and Semi-dry Champagne. The present trend is toward the brut or extra dry variety. The sweeter type of Champagne, possessing perhaps a little less character, is certainly much less in demand today. These are wines which are very pleasant with desserts; they must, however, be served at a cooler temperature than the others.

Rosé. A very fruity wine with an excellent color, it is coming more and more into favor, and the big firms have no hesitation in offering it. Its bouquet varies according to the way it has been made. Some are produced by adding a small amount of red wine from Champagne; others (more preferable) are produced as a rosé from the start. It cannot compete with great classical Champagnes.

It should be added that the shippers also prepare wines for specific foreign markets, to meet specific preferences of their clients. The fruitiness and sweetness of these vary according to their destination.

There remain two other effervescent wines of Champagne which should be mentioned, both of which are very pleasant to drink:

Crémant. The gas content of crémant is lower than that of Champagne. This is done by reducing the amount of liqueur added to the wine before the second fermentation. These lithe, light, fruity wines go down very well, but they can never match their superiors. They have, nevertheless, their own place in the Champagne family.

Blanc de Blancs. This variety is made solely from white grapes, using the *Chardonnay* variety. It is a very elegant, light wine, with a particularly fine bouquet.

Finally, the Champagne region also produces noneffervescent, so-called "still wines."

The Still Wines of Champagne

The still white wines of Champagne are an excellent introduction to a better knowledge of Champagne. There is a *Blanc de Blancs* which has not been *champagnisé* (given a Champagne sparkle), and also a *Blanc de Noirs,* a much more full-bodied wine. The big firms market it. It offers the dominant characteristics of the Champagne vineyards, with its own particular spirit, color, and charm. The still red wines are simple and excellent, but somewhat fragile. Their flavor and strength remind one of the wines of Burgundy, while their tannin content recalls those of Bordeaux. The best known among them is the incomparable Bouzy, but Cumières, Ambonnay, Verzenay, Sillery, Mailly, Saint-Thierry also have excellent wines. The appearances of a red wine from

Champagne on the table is always greeted with surprise and interest. These amazing red wines have a very special fruity flavor, while their mischievousness is more apparent than real. They are great wines produced with care and should not be drunk at room temperature; they are at their best when cooled. In great vintage years, they are very full-bodied and may be kept for a long time. There is a limit, however. Wine of the year 1959, for example, is of a very different order, far removed from the lightheartedness of other years. These red wines at a certain age would seem to become almost too robust and to lose much of their original appeal.

Bouzy is marketed independently of the large Champagne producers by the individual growers since it is not a wine requiring the skilled blending of the sparkling Champagnes.

The Marketing of Champagne

The grape has ripened, the Champagne is born. Now it must be marketed—and it has long been known that the people of Champagne are as prudent as they are smart. The whole structure of commercialization and marketing in the Champagne area is as special as the wines. The marketing structure includes:

1. *Négociants-manipulants* who themselves vinify the wines from their own vines, or from the must which they buy from individual vinegrowers. They blend, marry, bottle, and market the wine themselves.
2. *Négociants non manipulants* are companies or individuals who market Champagne but do not make it.
3. *Récoltants-manipulants* are vintners who produce and then market their own wine.
4. *Co-opératives de manipulation* who press, vinify, and blend wines brought to them by member growers. The cooperatives also market the wine themselves.

In the English-speaking countries these terms are rarely met since almost all Champagne is exported by the *grande marque* houses such as Moët et Chandon, Heidsick, G. H. Mumm and Veuve Clicquot, who belong to the first category, the *négociants-manipulants*.

BEAUJOLAIS[5]

Today, American wine drinkers are on the lookout for something less expensive than Classified Bordeaux and Vintage Burgundy. They are doing what an actor would call ''a quick sketch.'' We seem at least to have learned what we really need to know about Beaujolais.

Beaujolais has often been called, perhaps not inaccurately, the Frenchman's best-loved wine. In its freshness and youth, its arrival is an annual November delight.

---

[5]*Almanac of Wine.*

This new wine can be called, progressively, *bourru* (still cloudy), *nouveau* (new), *Primeur* (fresh), or *de l'année* (of the current year). It improves with keeping about as much as fresh lettuce. It is one of the exceedingly rare wines which truly cannot "travel." It is never quite as good in Lyon as in the vineyard village where it was born. It is even slightly less good in Paris; decidedly less attractive in New York; and when it reaches Chicago or San Francisco, it is not at all what it was originally intended to be.

In France a great deal of it never sees a bottle at all. It arrives at one's favorite bistro in cask and it is served *en carafe* at the table or by the glass across the "zinc" of one's favorite bar. Before it can be shipped successfully to some place a long way from home, it has to be *travaillé,* or disciplined a little, or "stabilized," or possibly pasturized, in any case clarified or filtered, passed through a bottling machine, given a cork and capsule, then, at a tender age, subjected to the indignity of an ocean voyage. By that time its spirit is at least subdued, and it tastes a lot less like Beaujolais and more like just any young red wine.

Geographically speaking, the Beaujolais country is part of Burgundy, but fine Red Burgundy is truly a quite different and more serious wine. The Beaujolais are made from a different grape—the Gamay or Gamay Beaujolais. True Red Burgundy comes only from the Pinot Noir. If you plant the Pinot Noir on the clay and granite soil of Beaujolais, it rarely gives a wine of the quality expected, and the Gamay grape on the calcareous hillside of the noble Côte d'Or yields a disappointing and common wine at best. When Beaujolais, as it matures, begins to taste like a Côte d'Or wine, the peasants say, rather contemptuously, "*il morgonne*"—it begins to taste a bit like a wine from Morgon, by which they mean that it is changing its character—"like putting on airs and a foreign accent."

In classifying the wines of the Beaujolais country, the French have proceeded in their usual systematic fashion, and so we have the following special terms, special names, and categories.

First in order is Beaujolais Supérieur, less clearly defined, although legally limited to a somewhat lower production per acre and wines of a slightly higher alcoholic content. Next, and already getting well into the fine wine category, is Beaujolais Villages. These are worth looking for, particularly when they carry as well the name of the grower and a specific vineyard, chateau, or property. Beaujolais Villages almost always brings a somewhat higher price, which its quality fully justifies.

Finally, we come to the truly superior wines of this region, rarely bottled as *primeur,* but always under the name of the village, and generally that of the producer as well. In good vintages these improve in bottle for at least 2 to 4 years, and in some instances much longer.

The people of the Beaujolais countryside tend to be a joyous tribe, hospitable, musical, literary, and famous for their good cuisine. They like to say that just as the Greeks had their nine Muses, so Beaujolais has its nine, and they list the following: Moulin-à-Vent (the best of the nine); Fleurie (second best); Morgon, Chénas, and Juliénas mature more slowly; Brouilly and Côte de Brouilly tend to be big wines, mouth-filling, rather soft; Chiroubles and St. Amour are considered the most delicate and charming.

BEAUJOLAIS BLANC[6]

Beaujolais Blanc is almost unknown in France, and you may conceivably be sneered at by a would-be connoisseur who thinks there is no such thing. It is nevertheless an extremely pleasant, rather small wine, made from the Chardonnay grape just south of Macon in the villages where Maconnais ends and Beaujolais begins. The best of this is now sold as St. Véran (see White Burgundy). It is not unlike a lesser Pouilly-Fuissé, which appears to be a more appealing name. It is pleasant, dry, refreshing, and to be drunk young.

CHABLIS[7]

The vineyards of Chablis have been legally defined and delimited since 1938, and their wines divided into four main categories:

1. *Chablis Grand Cru.* Only seven small vineyards are entitled to this, the highest ranking appellation. All seven are on the right bank of the Serein River, facing south and southwest, and six of the seven (all except Blanchots, which is in Fyé) are in the township of Chablis proper. All produce wines of the highest class, but an expert might perhaps be disposed to list them in this order: *Vaudésir, Les Clos, Grenouilles, Valmur, Preuses, Blanchots,* and *Bougros.* Their wines must be of at least 10½ percent alcohol by volume, and their production may not exceed an average of 312 gallons per acre. Only the Chardonnay grape may be grown.

2. *Chablis Premier Cru.* These wines come from certain other specific vineyards (750 acres in all), and usually carry the vineyard name, and, of course, the important words *Premier Cru.* Until quite recently there were 21 such legally delimited vineyards each with its own name. They have now been grouped into 9 larger units, although the old names may still be used by growers who wish to do so.

The principal Premier Cru Vineyards include: Montée de Tonnerre, Vaillons, Beauroy, Monts de Milieu, Vaucoupin, Vosgros, Fourchaume, Côte de Lechet, Les Fourneaux, Montmains (Les Fôrets, Butteaux) and Mélinots.

3. *Chablis* (Also called ''Chablis tout court''). These wines are produced on certain delimited areas of chalky soil, from the Chardonnay grape, in 20 specific communes: Chablis, Beines, Beru, Chemillysur-Serein, Chichée, Courgis, Fleys, Fontenay, Fyé, La Chapelle-Vaupeltiegne, Ligny-le-Chatel, Lignorelles, Maligny, Milly, Poilly, Poinchy, Prehy, Rameau, Villey and Viviers. These wines must have a minimum alcohol content of 10 percent and a maximum average yield of 354 gallons.

4. *Petit Chablis.* These are lesser wines from the same twenty communes, also made from the Chardonnay grape. The minimum alcohol content is 9½ percent.

---

[6]*Almanac of Wine.*
[7]*Almanac of Wine.*

CÔTES-DU-RHONE[8]

For the thirsty American with a good palate and a thin pocketbook, these days about the only Happy-Hunting-Ground left in France is the Rhone Valley. This is mostly for red wines, of course, but over 90 percent of the Côtes-du-Rhône production is red or rosé anyway, so no matter. With 3 or 4 exceptions (Chateaneuf-du-Pape, Hermitage, Côte Rôtie, and perhaps the spicy white Condrieu), they are wines that you do not really have to lay away, but if you forget a few bottles for a few years in your cellar you will be glad you did when you open them. Nor do you have to be so careful in selecting vintages. Really poor years are not too frequent and the differences that separate good from very good from great are far less obvious than in Bordeaux and Burgundy.

This happy situation has come to exist thanks largely to the intelligent cooperation, over the past thirty years, of a number of well-informed and disinterested growers, a few competently managed cooperative cellars, and the INAO (the Appellation Contrôlée people in Paris). Thus, when the small producers in a given district have demonstrated their ability to produce, over a period of years, a superior wine of consistent quality and special character, they end up by getting a special *Appellation Contrôlée* of their own. The most recently accorded of these is *Coteaux de Mont Ventoux,* literally "Slopes of the Windy Mountain." It is, in fact, a famous landmark north of Avignon.

Other wines worth looking for, in the less expensive category, are those called simply "Côtes-du-Rhone," especially when followed by the word "villages," or the name of a specific village.

Of course, even more reassuring, is an Appellation Contrôlée which the particular wine itself has earned. There is a small constellation of such vineyards round Hermitage (Crozes-Hermitage, Cornas, St. Joseph), another group near Châteauneuf-du-Pape, farther south (Gigondas, Mont-Ventoux, etc.), and lastly, Avignon, with its famous old "*sur-le-Pont*" bridge (which as the initiates have learned, should be "Sous-le-Pont."[9] And, beyond the Rhône, on the road to Spain, is the Rosé Country—Travel, with Lirac just next door and nearly as good, and many others, sold as Côtes-du-Rhône, often with a village name appended.

Quite a number of good, dry white wines are produced, full-bodied, rather long-lived, and golden: White Hermitage, Crozes-Hermitage, St. Péray (also sparkling); Condrieu and Chateau-Grillet (both made from the Viognier grape, and doubtless the best), Châteauneuf-du-Pape Blanc, etc. It has not been my experience that they improve greatly with keeping.

---

[8]*Almanac of Wine.*

[9]The ruined Pont-St. Bénézet, the "Pont d'Avignon" of the old song, originally traversed not only the two branches of the Rhône, but the green meadows of the Ile-de-la-Barthelasse which then separates them. This broad, shady, and inviting island is, even today, a favorite spot for carnivals, fairs, and picnics. It was obviously here, "*sous-le-pont,*" not on the narrow old bridge itself, that the dancing took place.

VAL-DE-LOIRE[10]

This is the ancient and rather poetic name which the French now often use to mean the whole wide basin of the River Loire, including all of its tributaries. The Loire is the longest river of France, and in terms of American geography, its equivalent would be the Val-de-Mississippi, and would include Pittsburgh and Cheyenne, as well as Little Rock and New Orleans.

In France, the whole Loire country does have a certain special character all its own. It is, traditionally, the part of France where the best French is spoken; Touraine and Anjou, two of its ancient provinces, were called "the Garden of France" long before Thomas Cook was born; it was here that the French kings built their splendid chateaux and where they preferred to live; its countryside is consistently beautiful; its towns, castles, and cathedrals were scarcely damaged by war; its hotels, and restaurants, and village *auberges* are charming and picturesque; its cuisine is almost everywhere *raffinée* and excellent. There are vineyards almost everywhere, and the local wines are almost all good, occasionally outstanding, and hardly ever expensive. The whole district, from Nevers round to Nantes, is truly a *pays vinicole,* a wine-country.

The leading grape varieties are these:

Muscadet—Widely grown east and south of the old city of Nantes, near the mouth of the Loire, on the Atlantic. It is extremely productive, giving a fresh, pale, dry white wine, comparable to a lesser Chablis.

Gros Plant—Probably the Folle Blanche, this is an excellent *vin ordinaire,* very like the Muscadet. It usually carries the words "Pays Nantais" on its label.

Chenin Blanc. Also called, confusingly, the *Pineau de la Loire* (it is not a Pinot), is widely planted on the Loire and also in California, frequently to produce a semi-sweet wine with considerable bouquet. It gives us such illustrious wines as Vouvray, Montlouis, and the great white wines of Anjou.

Grolleau or *Groslot.* This very productive, mediocre grape is widely planted to give the rather common, mediocre, slightly sweet Rosé d'Anjou which is so popular in the United States.

Cabernet Franc. This is a blood brother or at least a first cousin of the Cabernet Sauvignon which gives us the best red wines of California—by no means just a cross, like the Ruby Cabernet. It is widely grown in the St. Emilion district, near Bordeaux. Cabernet Franc is usually rated above the Merlot; Rabelais called it the "Breton" and praised it unreservedly and often. It gives us such splendid reds as Chinon, Bourgueil, St. Nicolas-de-Bourgueil, Champigny, as well as almost all of the finer *vins rosés* of the whole Loire Valley.

Sauvignon Blanc. Traditionally, this is the classic variety of white Graves, in the Bordeaux Country. It has long been my conviction that this noble variety does even better in these upper reaches of the Loire Valley. It is interesting to compare them, and include Sancerre, Pouilly-Fumé, Quincy, and perhaps Reuilly, if you can find it, in the same tasting. These are certainly among the best dry white wines of France, possibly surpassed only by the great Chardonnays of Burgundy.

---

[10]*Almanac of Wine.*

PRINCIPAL WINES OF THE LOIRE

Whites

Appellation Contrôlée	*Vineyards*
Pouilly-Fumé (or Blanc-Fumé-de-Pouilly)	Château du Nozet
	Château de Tracy
	Coteaux des Loges
	La Loge aux Moines
	Coteau des Girarmes
	Domaine de Riaux
Sancerre	Château de Sancerre
	Clos de la Poussie
	Les Monts Damnés
	Perrières
	Bué (locality)
	Chavignol (locality)
Quincy	Rimonet
Reuilly	Clos des Messieurs
Montlouis	Hameau de la Milletière
Vouvray	Clos le Mont
	Château Moncontour
	Clos de la Taiserie
Saumur	Château de Parnay (Clos Cristal)
Quarts-de-Chaume	Château de Bellerive
	Château de Surronde
Coteaux du Layon	Château de la Fresnaye
Coteaux de l'Aubance	Roche de Mûrs
Savennières	La Coulée de Serrant
	La Roche aux Moines
	Clos du Papillon
	Château de Savennières
	Château d'Epiré
Bonnézeaux	Château de Fesle
Muscadet	La Chapelle
	Châteauguy

Reds

Appellation Controlee	*Vineyard*
Vin de l'Orléanais[11]	Beaugency (locality)
	St.-Jean-de-Braye (locality)
Chinon	Rochette-St.-Jean
	Le Closeaux

---

[11]VDQS appellation.

Appellation Controlee	*Vineyard*
Bourgueil	Clos de la Salpêtrerie
	Clos des Perriéres
St.-Nicolas-de-Bourgueil	Clos du Fondis
Saumur (Saumur-Champigny)	Château de Parnay
	Clos des Hospices

ALSACE[12]

In geography, in climate, and of course in grape varieties as well, the Alsatian wine country has much more in common with Germany than with the rest of France. Its fragrant Rieslings, its spicy Gewürztraminers, its light, fresh, rather dry Sylvaners, and its Pinot Gris (called Rülander in Germany) are basically Rhine wines, however indubitably French. Vintage years in Alsace tend to follow the German rather than the French pattern.

Alsatian wines, too, are generally a good bit dryer than their German cousins. They are made above all to be drunk with food and they complement, to perfection, the bountiful and excellent cuisine of their home province.

German wine laws do not classify vineyards as the French do. Any vineyard in Germany can theoretically produce top-class wine. Instead they specify exactly what degree of sugar the must (crushed grapes) should contain to qualify for each classification.

New laws made in 1971 lay down three basic grades of quality, wherever in Germany the wine comes from. They are:

1. *Tafelwein.* The most ordinary, which need not attain any particular strength or come from any particular place or grape. It is not allowed to use a vineyard name.

2. *Qualitätswein.* Must come from a particular region (Gebiet), from certain grape varieties, attain a certain must-weight[13] (60, which would give 7½ percent natural alcohol before adding sugar), and carry a test number.

3. *Qualitätswein mit Prädikat.* The grade for the traditional type wines that do not use sugar, thus, in practice, can only be made in good years when the grapes are really ripe. Their must-weight has to be 73 (the equivalent of 9½ percent alcohol), and their grapes of certain varieties. They must come from a particular area (Bereich), carry a test number, and may not be sugared.

Within the last grade the traditional classifications by sweetness of the top wines are given exact meanings. (Weights vary by area and grape variety.) They are:

- *Kabinett:* mimimum must-weight of 73 (or 70 in certain cold areas like the Mosel)
- *Spätlese:* minimum must-weight 85 (Mosel 76)

---

[12]*Almanac of Wine.*
[13]The number of grams by which one liter of must is heavier than one liter of distilled water.

- *Auslese:* minimum must-weight about 90
- *Beerenauslese:* minimum about 120
- *Trockenbeerenauslese:* minimum about 150

At the same time, the new law reduced the number of individual vineyards in Germany from 30,000 in the old land register to a considerably more manageable number. The process of doing so caused a vast upheaval in the German wine world, for in addition to forgetting many favorite old names and learning (admittedly fewer) new ones, wine-lovers will have to become more or less familiar with the concepts of *Gebiet, Bereich,* and *Grosslage.*

A *Gebiet* is simply a wine-growing region, e.g., Nahe, Rheinplalz.

A *Bereich* is a smaller district within a Gebiet.

The third subdivision is a *Grosslage,* an area formed by a number of neighboring vineyards (whether in the same village or not) and called by the name of the best-known of them. It is important to distinguish this from a ''site'' (*Einzellage*)—one individual vineyard. Site names will continue to be carried by all the top-class wines from the best growers.

ITALIAN WINE LAW

The Italian wine law of 1963 lays down three standards of control.

Denominazione Semplice is equivalent, more or less, to the German Tafelwein. Only a simple statement of ' ' region of production is allowed; there are no set standards.

Denominazione di O,.ç,ne Controllata is the next rank. A body of wine growers may apply to have their wine registered as DOC. They must suggest limits to where it can be produced and standards of quality which it must reach. A committee in Rome decides whether or not the wine merits DOC standing and confirms the specifications. DOC wines are subject to testing and must wear a DOC label, in addition to their own.

Denominazione Controllata e Garantita, the top rank, is awarded only to certain wines from certain producers, rather than whole regions. To be controllata e garantita, a wine must be bottled and sealed with a government seal by the producer or someone who takes full responsibility for it. Eventually all the best wines of Italy will be controllata e garantita; at present the scheme is only in embryo.

SPAIN[14]

Although California today produces about three times as much ''Sherry'' as Spain, the Spaniards, with the enthusiastic help of some 25 million foreign tourists, drink nearly three times as much table wine as the United States. Almost all of this is just *vino corriente,* sound and inexpensive and far from bad, rarely as much as two years old.

Only in one small corner of Spain, close to the French border, are wines produced which are more or less properly vintaged and which deserve this treatment. This is the

[14]*Almanac of Wine.*

Rioja district, about a hundred miles southwest of Biarritz and San Sebastian. All too little known, the Rioja produces some more than passable white wines, and some of the most remarkable red wines of Europe. The best of these can stand comparison with all but the very best of France, and forty years ago, a few of them used to bring as high prices in New York as Chateau Margaux.

Unfortunately, there is no organized system of chateau or estate bottling in Spain. Almost every producer buys grapes from neighbors to supplement their own production, and often makes several quite different qualities of wine in any given vintage. The less noteworthy lots are aged, bottled, and marketed normally when four or five years old, whereas the most outstanding cuvées are given more time in wood plus a good many years in bottle, and emerge ten or fifteen years later, as "Reservas," often under a different label and at a higher price.

PORTUGAL[15]

With the unique and spendid exception of Vintage Port, Portuguese wines hardly ever carry a vintage; when they do, this is much more in the nature of a not entirely dependable statement of age than any sort of indication of superior quality. One of the charms of Portuguese table wines—Vinho Verde, Dão, Colares, as well as the ever more popular rosés—is that they do not take themselves too seriously.

Port, of course, is another matter. In the last three years it carries the name Port only when shipped (in bottle) from England, the Portuguese having decided to give it its Portuguese name "Porto." This will make it easy to distinguish the true Portuguese Port from other wines so labelled from California, New York State, etc.

CALIFORNIA GRAPE GUIDE

Seventeen of the best varieties are described here, with the climate regions for which they are recommended by the University of California, and the normal yield per acre. One ton of grapes gives about 160 U.S. gallons (606 liters) of wine. So, 5 tons/acre = 3030 liters/acre, or approximately 73 hectoliters/hectare. Lower yields usually give higher quality. The 1975 acreage figures for the leading counties for each grape are given last.

Barbera (regions 3–4; 5–8 tons): Dark red wine with good balance of acidity even when grown in very hot conditions. Italian style. Fresno 5,694; Kern 4,313; Madera 3,751

Cabernet Sauvignon (regions 1–2; 4–6 tons): The best red wine; perfumed, fruity, dry, long-lasting. Needs aging at least four years. Monterey 5,634; Napa 5,209; Sonoma 4,164; Santa Barbara 1,889

Chardonnay (regions 1–2; 4–6 tons): The best white wine; dry but full and sappy; perfumed, grape flavor; improved by short time in oak. Lasts well. Monterey 2,929; Napa 2,249; Sonoma 1,808

---

[15]*Almanac of Wine.*

WINE AND FOOD CHART

Wine Class	Best-Known Types	Wine and Food Combinations
Appetizer Wines	Sherry Vermouth Flavored Wines	Before or between meals. Serve chilled, without food, or with hors d'oeuvres, nuts, cheeses.
White Dinner (or Table) Wines	Sauterne Sauvignon Blanc Semillon Chablis Chenin Blanc French Colombard Pinot Blanc Pinot Chardonnay Rhine Wine Sylvaner Riesling Traminer Gewurztraminer	With lighter dishes. Served well chilled, with chicken, fish, shellfish, omelets, any white meat. Sometimes also served as an appetizer wine.
Red Dinner (or Table) Wines	Burgundy Gamay Petite Sirah Pinot Noir Chianti Claret Cabernet Sauvignon Grignolino Merlot Ruby Cabernet Zinfandel Rosé ''Vino'' Types	With hearty dishes. Serve at cool room temperature with steaks, chops, roasts, game, cheese dishes, spaghetti. (Rosé with all foods.)
Dessert Wines	Muscatel Angelica Cream (Sweet) Sherry Port Tokay	At dessert. Served chilled or at cool room temperature, with fruits, cookies, nuts, cheese, fruit cake, pound cake.
Sparkling Wines	Champagne Natural (very dry) Brut (very dry) Sec (semi-dry) Doux (sweet) Pink Champagne Sparkling Burgundy Cold Duck	With all foods. Serve well chilled with any food—appetizers, the main course, or dessert (especially good in festive party punches).

Prepared and published for Wine Advisory Board by Wine Institute, 165 Post Street, San Francisco, CA.
Copyright 1975 Wine Advisory Board.

Chenin Blanc (region 1; 6-10 tons) (sometimes wrongly called White Pinot; is not Pinot Blanc): In hills sometimes makes well-balanced, rich but tart wine. Often not very distinctive. Kern 4,844; Fresno 2,373; Merced 2,377; Monterey 2,092

French Colombard (regions 3-4; 6-10 tons): Rather neutral dry white used for blending; in cooler areas fresh and pleasant unblended. Fresno 5,835; Kern 4,995; Madera 3,365; Merced 2,509

Gamay (regions 1-2; 6-9 tons) (also known as Napa Gamay): The true French Gamay, but only good for pink wine. Monterey 1,218; Napa 1,006; Kern 425; Sonoma 328

Gamay Beaujolais (regions 1-2; 3-4 tons): A form of Pinot Noir; light red wine, not comparable with french Beaujolais. Monterey 1,223; Napa 603; Mendocino 589; San Benito 518

Gewürztraminer (region 1; 4-6 tons): Gentle, often slightly sweet, distinctively spicy white wine. Monterey 795; Sonoma 473; Napa 300

Grenache (region 2; 5-9 tons): Very good for rosé; light-colored full-bodied red used for blending. Madera 3,967; Kern 3,578; Fresno 3,041

Petite Sirah (region 2; 4-8 tons) (also called Shiraz): Dark red, strong, tannic and long-lasting. Monterey 2,234; Kern 1,887; Fresno 1,358; Sonoma 1,194

Pinot Blanc (region 1; 4-6 tons): Fruity, dry, medium to good quality white. Monterey 670; San Benito 180; Sonoma 74

Pinot Noir (region 1; 3-4 tons): Good lightish red with distinctive grape aroma, rarely absolutely first-rank in California. Monterey 2,590; Napa 2,526 Sonoma 2,523; Santa Barbara 826

Ruby Cabernet (regions 3-4; 6-8 tons): New variety makes good dry table wine in hot areas; useful not great. Kern 4,802; Fresno 4,014; Madera 2,525

Sauvignon Blanc (regions 2-3; 4-7 tons): Good to very good earthy/grapy dry white. Monterey 1,027; Napa 534; Merced 390

Semillon (regions 2-3; 4-6 tons): Medium to sweet golden-white; occasionally excellent. Kern 670; Stanislaus 504; Monterey 519

White Riesling (regions 1-2; 4-6 tons) (also called Johannisberg Riesling): Scented, fruity, ideally tart, but often soft, first-class white. Monterey 2,374; Napa 1,414; Santa Barbara 1,009; Sonoma 814

Zinfandel (region 1; 4-6 tons): "California's Beaujolais"; raspberryish, spicy and good; also used for blending. San Joaquin 10,927; Sonoma 3,721; San Bernadino 3,303; Monterey, 3,194; Napa 1,315

NEW YORK GRAPE GUIDE

Baco Noir: Red hybrid from Vitis riparia. Great acidity but good clean dark wine.

Catawba: One of the earliest developments from V. labrusca and still one of the best. A pale red grape from which white, red, or rosé wine can be made. Not too acid.

Chelois: A hybrid developed by Seibel. Dry red wine, slightly foxy.

Concord: The dark red small V. labrusca which is most widely planted. Needs sugaring and makes strongly foxy wine.

De Chaunac: A good red French American hybrid; dark color; rich, heavy wine.

Delaware: A pink grape, only slightly foxy; ripens well and hardly needs sugaring.

Duchess: White wine; rather neutral.

Elvira: White wine; now not much planted.

French American: Several varieties, including the popular Aurora.

Isabella: Sweetish dark red grape, very foxy.

Moore's Diamond: For dry white wine fairly neutral.

Niagara: For sweet white wine; very foxy.

Seyve-Villa: Several varieties of white grape. Good but rather neutral.

WINE STOCK CONTROL[16]

The systems by which wine stocks are inventoried, requisitioned, and replenished are simple or elaborate depending upon the size of the restaurant, hotel, or club. In most large establishments the wine steward or beverage manager is responsible for maintaining and replenishing the reserve stock. This person in turn holds the service bar responsible for keeping up the main floor stock.

Normal practice is to set "par stock" and "minimum stock" quantities for each wine in the cellar, and to establish proportionately smaller par and minimum stocks for the main floor supply. These quantities are adjusted from time to time in accordance with the sales turnover experienced with each brand, size, and type. Whenever a stock of any item declines to the minimum, an additional supply is requisitioned to bring it to par. In some restaurants this is done automatically for the main floor stock by keeping a record of every wine item sold, and then sending a requisition to the storeroom at the close of the day to replace all such items.

In any establishment where the wine assortment is large enough to require it, every wine item is given a number that appears on the wine list and on the bins in both the wine cellar and the main floor stock. Usually these numbers are affixed to the bottles when the wine is first received and unpacked. Numbering of bottles is done either with pencil, or small gummed labels, or metal-edged tags. An advantage of the metal-edged tag is that it can be removed when the bottle is sold and deposited in a box, from which the requisition for replacements is made at the end of the day.

It is common practice to attach to each bin a perpetual inventory card showing the name and number, as well as the par and minimum stocks of the wine item in the bin. It is also well to keep a copy of the restaurant's wine list posted on the wall at eye level near the bins to show the selling price of each wine and the names and numbers.

Storing the Reserve Stock[17]

Some restaurants order their wines from week to week, but others keep large reserve stocks in storage. Requirements for good wine storage are simply that it protect the establishment's wine investment from spoilage and loss and that it be located and arranged for economical operation.

---

[16]Reprinted from *The Sale of Wine in Restaurants* by permission of the Wine Institute.

[17]The Wine Institute.

Modern air conditioning and insulating methods make it no longer necessary to locate wine cellars underground. The only specifications are: (1) the temperature should be even, not subject to frequent or sudden changes; (2) it should be neither too warm nor too cold (ideal is about 55°F); and (3) it should be away from direct sunlight and clean. A dry, well ventilated room is preferable, and is easier to keep clean. It is well that the room be away from furnaces, steam pipes, and radiators. Excessive vibration and fruit and vegetable odors have also been known to affect wines.

The simplest kind of cellar equipment consists of wooden or steel shelving, divided into bins. Corked dinner and sparkling wines should be stored on their sides to keep the corks moist and airtight. Dessert wines and dinner wines with screw caps may stand upright. Sparkling wines and white dinner wines, which are the most delicate, should be stored on the lower shelves where it is cooler, red dinner wines above the whites, and dessert wines on upper shelves. In the reserve stock, as in the main floor stock, bottles that have been longest in storage should be sold first.

If bottle racks are used instead of bins, they should be constructed to hold half bottles as well as large bottles. If wine is stored in unopened cases, the cases should rest on wooden strips to prevent mold from forming underneath. Cases should be so placed so that corked bottles of dinner and sparkling wines will rest horizontally.

If the reserve wine stock is large and the cellar elaborate, endless refinements are possible, such as different rooms with lower temperatures for the white and sparkling wines. However, few restaurants in the United States have yet developed their wine storage to this point.

HOW SPIRITS ARE MADE

Put at its simplest, distilling is a way of concentrating the strength and flavor of any alcoholic drink by removing most of the water. It relies on the fact that alcohol is more volatile than water—which is to say that it boils at a lower temperature. If you boil wine in a saucepan it will lose all its alcohol and most of its aromatic elements into the air long before the pan is dry. So if you collect the steam and condense it you will have the alcohol and very little of the water; you will have, in fact, brandy.

This fact has been known in the East for thousands of years. It entered the western world in the fourteenth century, via the Arabs, whose words *al embic* (meaning a still) and *al cohol* we still use.

The original form of still, the pot-still, is simply a kettle on a fire, with a long spout, usually curled into a worm, in which the vapor condenses. Even now this is the best design, and used for all the highest-quality spirits. Its great advantage is that it gives total control. The distiller can choose precisely what part of the vapor he wants to keep, as containing the desirable proportion of alcohol and flavor. He can eliminate undesirable elements which vaporize sooner than alcohol and "pass over" first, or which are less volatile and "pass over" later.

The pot-still's disadvantage is that it is slow, it needs a craftsman to operate it, and it needs to be cleaned out and filled up after every operation.

Most modern distilling is done in the patent continuous still, which was invented by an Irish exciseman called Coffey. It uses steam to vaporize the alcohol, letting the waste run away continuously, which makes it faster in operation than the pot-still and much cheaper to run. The only drawback is that you must distill at very high strength in order to get a clean enough spirit to drink. You cannot choose precisely which ''fraction'' of the vapor you will keep. Continuous-still spirits therefore normally have less of the congenerics, as the flavoring elements which ''pass over'' with the alcohol are called. They have less of the original taste and smell of the raw material; they also need less time in wood to mature.

BEER[18]

The base of beer is grain. Through the centuries the preferred grain has been barley, although almost everything else has been tried and some, such as corn and rice, are still widely used. When the barley ran short, early Americans became adventurous, even trying pumpkins as a substitute. The absence of pumpkin beer on supermarket shelves today suggests that the experiment was not entirely successful.

The grain is ground, and heated water is added to activate its enzymes. The grain begins to germinate, creating what is called the wort. At this point hops are added. Although hops are not essential (early ale was made without hops), it is the hops that give beer its tangy taste; without them beer is slightly sweet. Yeast is mixed into the wort and in effect ''eats'' the wort, turning it into alcohol and carbonic acid. Within about eight days the mixture is green beer, which then has to be aged in oxygen-free containers for up to three months.

A batch of beer was a very chancy quaff in those days before the significance of such variables as temperature control and cleanliness were well understood. Sometimes it was marvelous, sometimes terrible.

Partly for that reason, perhaps, beer lost some of its following in the eighteenth century to such competing beverages as wine, rum, cider, coffee, and tea. Still, beer was a great favorite among the founders of the new republic. George Washington most often called for a new variety of beer called porter—so named because of its popularity among London porters. It consisted of equal parts of beer, ale, and small beer, a weak malt meant to be downed shortly after brewing. And Thomas Jefferson, that genius craftsman who could put together everything from new houses to new nations, found time to dabble in the beer business as well. He installed a brewer at Monticello to make beer for his tenants and neighbors, and Jefferson himself often attended to such details as ordering bottles and corks.

The big breweries did not emerge until the nineteenth century, the first of them founded by Matthew Vassar, an English immigrant who deserves nomination as the patron saint of college men. Settling in Poughkeepsie, New York, Vassar began brewing beer on a small scale in 1812. His enterprise thrived so well that by 1860 M. Vassar and Co.'s Brewery and Malt Works employed fifty men and turned out thirty thou-

[18]*Companion*, October, 1977.

sand barrels of ale a year. Having provided the beer, Vassar then endowed the college for young women that bears his name, thus giving the boys the girls with whom to drink the beer.

But even as the Englishman Vassar was enjoying his yeasty success, an enormous change was taking place that would alter the character of American beer and shape the American taste down to this day. And it would not be an English taste, but a German taste. In the middle of the nineteenth century waves of German immigrants landed on American shores, bringing their considerable brewing skills with them. The Germans favored lager beer, lager meaning ''storage.'' To make lager, green beer goes through a second fermentation in which it is stored at a temperature just above freezing for several months.

The middle of the nineteenth century was a sort of golden age for American breweries. In 1850 there were 431 breweries in the country producing around seven hundred fifty thousand barrels a year. A decade later there were three times as many breweries producing more than a million barrels. Beer gardens flourished in New York's Bowery, then a pleasant family gathering spot. But it was a great swath through the Midwest, from western Pennsylvania to the Dakotas, and from Missouri to Wisconsin, that filled with Germans and Scandinavians and became the country's beer belt. To this day, about half the beer consumed in this country is downed in the Midwest.

The great family names of brewing appeared; for example, Rupert, Schaeffer, and Heileman. Milwaukee became the capital of beer country and for an interesting reason. Cincinnati was closer to the population centers of the Midwest, but Milwaukee was closer to the frozen lakes of the North. To keep the beer cold during its fermentation, great blocks of ice had to be carved from the lakes and dragged into the storage caves.

By the 1870s the fundamental American taste had been shaped and remains pretty much unchanged to this day. Americans clearly preferred lager beer over British ale or porter. Moreover, of the lagers, Americans liked the Pilsen variety (pale, light-bodied, clear, and slightly effervescent) more than the heavier and darker Munich. The Pilsen (named for the Czech city of its origin) is also a little less alcoholic. That taste was modified somewhat by Prohibition, a period during which Americans started drinking seas of soft drinks and became addicted to carbonation. Much to the distress of purists, Americans are now inclined to choose fizzy beers, even when the carbonation is artificially, rather than naturally, induced.

Although the American taste has changed relatively little in the past one hundred years, the industry itself has changed enormously. Before Prohibition most of the beer came out of the breweries in oak barrels and was destined for saloons not too many miles away. The working man who wanted his mug of beer at home generally stopped off at his saloon and drew off a cardboard container full—''rushing the growler,'' as it was called.

Then came the revolution. On January 24, 1935, the Krueger Brewing Company of Newark, New Jersey, and the American Can Company brought forth canned beer, which went on sale for the first time in Richmond, Virginia. The industry hasn't been quite the same since. Today, about 60 percent of the beer sold in this country comes in cans, 23 percent in bottles, and the rest in kegs.

Cans make it relatively easy to ship beer over long distances, a capability that has hastened the consolidation of the industry. In 1910 there were about fifteen hundred breweries in the country, most of them selling not much beyond their own neighborhoods. By 1933 there were only seven hundred fifty, and today we are down to forty-nine. And even that number disguises the real concentration of the industry. Only ten years ago the five biggest brewers in the country accounted for only one-third of the entire market. Today the big five—Anheuser-Busch, Schlitz, Miller, Pabst, and Coors—have 69 percent of the market.

The small regional breweries have been decimated by rising costs, especially for grains, aluminum, and glass. The large national breweries, on the other hand, have been able to meet those costs without raising their prices substantially by bulk purchasing and through the labor-saving efficiencies of scale. Miller, for example, is building a brewery in Eden, North Carolina, that will be able to produce an oceanic twenty million barrels a year. And one regional brewery that does prosper, the G. Heileman Brewing Company of La Crosse, Wisconsin, does so only because it has purchased a string of other local breweries, such as Blatz in Wisconsin and Rainier in Washington, and has thereby been able to take advantage of some of the same economies of scale available to the big nationals.

A lively area of competition in the next few years is likely to be the calorie war. Typically, a can of beer contains about one hundred fifty calories. That can be brought down below one hundred by reducing the alcohol content a little and also filtering out some of the sugars that have not fermented from the original grain. The reasons for doing so are compelling. One of the traditional limitations of the beer business is that beer appeals principally to men between the ages of eighteen and thirty-four (they drink half the beer consumed in the country).

For years brewers tried to develop and package low-calorie beers in a way that would make beer appealing to women, but the efforts were never very successful. Dieting women, it seems, are unlikely to drink beer of any kind. Then, in January 1975, Miller introduced its Lite beer with a significantly different strategy, designed to make it appealing to men, especially middle-aged men. Men don't stop drinking at thirty-five; they simply drink less beer or turn to something else, partly, at least, because a man of fifty is more likely to feel a little bloated after a couple of beers than a man of twenty.

How does American beer stack up with beers around the world? The ingredient that makes the difference in beer is the hops, that vine of the nettle family that gives beer its tang. The experts argue over whether it is Bavaria or Czechoslovakia that produces the best hops, but they also acknowledge that those from the Yakim Valley in Washington and the Willamette Valley in Oregon are extremely close to the best European in quality.

Michael A. Weiner, an anthropologist with a prodigious capacity and unquenchable enthusiasm for beer, personally tested more than two hundred, including fifty-eight American brands. He reports the results in his attractive and handy book, *The Taster's Guide to Beer*. He awarded each beer from one to seven steins, "1" indicating poor, but drinkable, "7" denoting what he believes to be one of the world's best. Weiner gave "7s" to seven beers, none of them American. Three were German

(Dortmunder Union, Henninger, Lowenbrau); two English (Bass Pale Ale, Mackson Stout); one Czechoslovakian (Pilsner Urquell); and one Danish (Carlsberg Light).

But Weiner gave five American beers ''6s,'' which proclaims them almost perfect: Anchor Steam of California (''strong body, flavor, and bouquet'') and Anchor Steam Porter (''malty aroma, nut-like flavor, tart aftertaste''); McSorley's Ale of New York (''among the sharpest, most aromatic in the world''); Point Special of Wisconsin (''distinctive hops aroma with no aftertaste''); and Rolling Rock of Pennsylvania (''alive, tart, sharp, and very unusual''). And twenty-two of the remaining American beers received ''5s,'' which indicates they are above average.

QUESTIONS

1. Define and give an example:

vigneron	Extra Sec
brule	Dry Sec
germentation	Demi Sec
barriques	Magnum
chais	Methuselah
AOC	Nebuchadnezzar
ADEB	must
mise du Domaine	must-weight
mise par let proprietaire	noble rot
mise dans nos caves	distilling
Brut	continuous still

2. List some devices that a novice wine restaurateur may use to successfully stock a wine cellar.
3. What three factors affect wines?
4. What is the difference between red and white wine?
5. What do brown edges on a wine indicate? How soon do they appear?
6. If a wine is Chablis Grand Cru, what are the limiting factors which determine it?
7. What causes must weight to differ?
8. Explain why a high yield generally produces lower quality grapes.
9. List forms of inventory for wines in a restaurant with a large stock.
10. List California wine areas.
11. List how and where several types of wine should be stored.
12. What do Pinot Noir, Gamay, Gringnolino, Cabernet, Chardonney have in common?
13. How are the terms Frizzante, Moussex, Sext, Spirtzig related?

7

CEREALS, GRAINS, BAKERY PRODUCTS, AND SWEETENERS

INTRODUCTION

The variety of cereal grains we use each day appears in a multitude of different products. Attention is given in this chapter to the appropriate uses of these grains and their nutritive characteristics.

Most widely used of the grains is wheat. Grade requirements for wheat are given for each of the seven classes of wheat. Wheat flours used in breadmaking and other pastries are discussed. Special blending of the wheat flours make the flours more adaptable for special uses.

Federal standards are listed for pastas which include the ratio of various ingredients. Good pastas are hard and yellow and should break evenly. Different styles of macaroni products are shown in picture form.

In the refining, compounding, or processing of some foods, there is an unavoidable loss of vitamins and minerals. The explanation of the fortification and enrichment processes are given as means to curtail these losses.

Bakery products including breads and pastries are described from an ingredient standpoint as well as the various stages of frozen to ready-to-serve. The determinants of quality for pies and cakes are listed with particular emphasis on storage and handling.

Finally, the additives used in baking are presented, primarily sweeteners and soy products. Take note of the varieties available as well as the advantages to using particular products.

CEREALS AND GRAINS

The cereal[1] grains are the dried seeds of cultivated grasses which belong to the family Gramineae. They are rice, wheat, oats, barley, corn, rye, grain sorghum, and millet.

Barley is sold as pearled barley which is popular for use in soups. It is the whole grain which has had the hulls and bran removed. Barley flour is used in baby foods and in breakfast cereals.

Corn is made into cornmeal or grits which must be cooked. Ready-to-eat corn flakes are made by blending grits with malt, sugar, and other ingredients, followed by cooking, rolling, and toasting.

Wheat and rye for human food are milled into flour. Rye flour is used for making bread. A high proportion of the wheat crop is milled into flour.

One variety of wheat (Durum) is made into macaroni type products. Wheat is also converted into breakfast cereals to be cooked and served hot, like farina, cream of wheat, and rolled wheat, and ready-to-eat kinds such as puffed, shredded, and flaked wheat.

Among the foods made from oats, rolled oats have been available for the longest time. In the ready-to-eat oat cereals, there are flaked, puffed, and shredded forms, Rolled oats, whether old fashioned, quick, or instant, are made from the whole grain, including the bran and germ.

Rice is boiled or steamed to prepare it for the table. It may be white polished rice; brown rice, which retains part of the bran coat; or converted rice, which has been pre-cooked and dried before polishing.

Wheat is the grain of common wheat, club wheat, and durum wheat which, before the removal of the dockage, consists of 50 percent or more of one or more wheats and not more than 10 percent of other grains for which standards have been established under the U.S. Grain Standards Act and which, after the removal of the dockage, contains 50 percent or more of whole kernels of one or more of these wheats.

Dockage is weed seeds, weed stems, chaff, straw, grain other than wheat, sand, dirt, and any other material other than wheat, which can be removed readily from the wheat by the use of appropriate sieves and cleaning devices; also underdeveloped, shriveled, and small pieces of wheat kernels removed in properly separating the material other than wheat and which cannot be recovered by properly rescreening or re-cleaning.

Foreign material is all matter other than wheat which is not separated from the wheat in the proper determination of dockage.

Other grains are rye, oats, corn, grain sorghum, barley, hull-less barley, flaxseed, emmer, spelt, einkorn, Polish wheat, poulard wheat, cultivated buckwheat, and soybeans.

Damaged kernels are kernels and pieces of kernels of wheat and other grains which are heat damaged, sprouted, frosted, badly ground damaged, badly weather damaged, moldy, diseased, or otherwise materially damaged.

---

[1]USDA.

Wheat

Wheat is divided into the following seven classes: Hard Red Spring Wheat, Durum Wheat, Red Durum Wheat, Hard Red Winter Wheat, Soft Red Winter Wheat, White Wheat, and Mixed Wheat.

The class Hard Red Spring Wheat includes all varieties of hard red spring wheat. This class is divided into the following three subclasses:

1. Dark Northern Spring Wheat: Hard Red Spring Wheat with 75 percent or more of dark, hard, and vitreous kernels.
2. Northern Spring Wheat: Hard Red Spring Wheat with 25 percent or more but less than 75 percent of dark, hard, and vitreous kernels.
3. Red Spring Wheat: Hard Red Spring Wheat with less than 25 percent of dark, hard, and vitreous kernels.

The class Durum Wheat includes all varieties of white (amber) Durum Wheat. This class is divided into the following three subclasses:

1. Hard Amber Durum Wheat: Durum Wheat with 75 percent or more of hard and vitreous kernels of amber color.
2. Amber Durum Wheat: Durum Wheat with 60 percent or more but less than 75 percent of hard and vitreous kernels of amber color.
3. Durum Wheat: Durum Wheat with less than 60 percent of hard and vitreous kernels of amber color.

The class Red Durum Wheat includes all varieties of red durum wheat. There are no subclasses in this class.

The class Hard Red Winter Wheat includes all varieties of hard red winter wheat. This class is divided into the following three subclasses:

1. Dark Hard Winter Wheat: Hard Red Winter Wheat with 75 percent or more of dark, hard, and vitreous kernels.
2. Hard Winter Wheat: Hard Red Winter Wheat with 40 percent or more but less than 75 percent of dark, hard, and vitreous kernels.
3. Yellow Hard Winter Wheat: Hard Red Winter Wheat with less than 40 percent of dark, hard, and vitreous kernels.

The class Soft Red Winter Wheat includes all varieties of soft red winter wheat. There are no subclasses in this class.

The class White Wheat includes all varieties of white wheat. This class is divided into the following four subclasses:

1. Hard White Wheat: White Wheat with 75 percent or more of hard kernels which may contain not more than 10 percent of wheat of the white club varieties.
2. Soft White Wheat: White Wheat with less than 75 percent of hard kernels which may contain not more than 10 percent of wheat of the white club varieties.

3. White Club Wheat: White Wheat consisting of wheat of the white club varieties which may contain not more than 10 percent of other white wheat.
4. Western White Wheat: White Wheat containing more than 10 percent of wheat of the white club varieties and more than 10 percent of other white wheat.

The class Mixed Wheat is any mixture of wheat which consists of one of the following:

1. Two or more classes each of which constitutes more than 10 percent of the mixture; or
2. One class that constitutes more than 10 percent and 2 or more other classes in combination that exceed 10 percent of the mixture; or
3. Several classes none of which constitutes 10 percent or more of the mixture but which combined meet the definition for wheat.

Grades. Grades are the U.S. numerical grades, U.S. Sample grade, and special grades.

Mixed Wheat is graded according to the U.S. numerical and U.S. Sample grade requirements of the class of wheat which predominates in the mixture, except that the factor "wheat of other classes" is disregarded.

GRADE AND GRADE REQUIREMENTS FOR ALL CLASSES
OF WHEAT EXCEPT MIXED WHEAT

| Grade | Minimum Test Weight per Bushel | | Maximum Limits of— | | | | | | |
| | Hard Red Spring Wheat or White Club Wheat | All Other Classes and Sub-Classes | Defects | | | | | Wheat of other Classes* | |
			Heat-Damaged Kernels	Damaged Kernels [Total]	Foreign Material	Shrunken and Broken Kernels	Defects [Total]	Contrasting Classes	Wheat of Other Classes [Total]
	Pounds	*Pounds*	*Percent*	*Percent*	*Percent*	*Percent*	*Percent*	*Percent*	*Percent*
U.S. No. 1	58.0	60.0	0.1	2.0	0.5	3.0	3.0	1.0	3.0
U.S. No. 2	57.0	58.0	0.2	4.0	1.0	5.0	5.0	2.0	5.0
U.S. No. 3	55.0	56.0	0.5	7.0	2.0	8.0	8.0	3.0	10.0
U.S. No. 4	53.0	54.0	1.0	10.0	3.0	12.0	12.0	10.0	10.0
U.S. No. 5	50.0	51.0	3.0	15.0	5.0	20.0	20.0	10.0	10.0
U.S. Sample grade	U.S. Sample grade shall be wheat which does not meet the requirements for any of the grades from U.S. No. 1 to U.S. No. 5, inclusive; or which contains more than two crotalaria seeds (*Crotalaria spp.*) in 1,000 grams of grain, or contains castor beans (*Ricinus communis*), stones, broken glass, animal filth, an unknown foreign substance(s), or a commonly recognized harmful or toxic substance(s); or which is musty, sour, or heating; or which has any commercially objectionable foreign odor except of smut or garlic; or which contains a quantity of smut so great that any one or more of the grade requirements cannot be applied accurately; or which is otherwise of distinctly low quality.								

*Red Durum Wheat of any grade may contain not more than 10.0 percent of wheat of other classes.

Grade Designations for Wheat. The grade designations for wheat include the letters "U.S."; the number of the grade or the words "Sample grade," as the case may be; the name of the applicable subclass, or in the case of Red Durum Wheat, Soft Red Winter Wheat, and Mixed Wheat, the name of the class; the name of each applicable special grade; and when applicable the word "dockage" together with the percentage thereof. In the case of Western White Wheat, the grade designation also includes, following the name of the subclass, the name and percentage of white club wheat and other white wheat in the mixture. In the case of Mixed Wheat, the grade designation also includes, following the name of the class, the name and percentage of Hard Red Spring, Durum, Red Durum, Hard Red winter, Soft Red Winter, and White Wheat, if any, contained in the mixture.

Wheat Flours. The hard (spring) wheat flours are used for making breads and pastas. The flour that the operator buys depends upon the use to which it will be put. The rougher the handling the flour gets, the higher the protein value that the flour needs. Wheat is rolled and sifted many times, the flour being separated each time until the stage is reached that is called a *patent.* The earlier the patent is reached, the higher the protein value of the wheat. The patents, in order of quality, are Extra Short (or Fancy), Short (or First), Medium, Long, and Straight. Besides the "Bran" and "Shorts" that are left in the milling of wheat, after the patent is out, there is a material called "clear." The best patent flours make a fancy clear flour. The characteristics of some flours are:

- All-Purpose Flour—A mixture of hard and soft wheat flours.
- Cake Flour—Protein (gluten) of 8 percent.
- Durum Flour—Further refined to make pastas.
- Clear Flour—Wheat meal left over when patent flour is made.
- Graham Flour—Contains the wheat germ and lots of the bran.
- Gluten Flour—Has much of the starch removed. Ground gluten has virtually all the starch removed.
- Hard Flour—Used for bread; high in gluten.
- Self-Rising Flour—A soft wheat flour with leavening added.
- Wheat Germ—Germ of the wheat usually marketed with bran added.
- Whole Wheat Flour—Straight wheat which has been ground into flour instead of being separated. Bran is added. Whole Wheat Flour with only a little bran is called "light."

Pasta

Pastas are made from semolina, the inner part of durum wheat. Wheats other than durum make poor pastas and should be avoided.

Federal Standards. 13 percent maximum moisture; 5-1½ percent minimum egg solids if labeled "egg"; 3.8 percent minimum milk solids if labeled "milk"; 13 percent minimum protein; 2 percent minimum, 5 percent maximum spinach or tomatoes if so labeled; ½ percent to 2 percent egg white, bay leaf, celery, onions, and salt.

There are several classes of pastas:

1. Ropes or Strings—Spaghettini (1/16 in. d.); Spaghetti (0.06) to 0.11 in. d.); Vermicelli (0.06 in. d. max.); Fidellini.
2. Tubular—Foratini (3/32 in. d.); Forati (.125 in. d.); Mezzarrelli (5/32 in. d.); Macaroni (0.11 to 0.27 in. d.); Zitoni (½ in. d.); Zifi, Perciatelli, Mezzani.

3. Flat—Lasagne (1 to 2 in. w.); Broad Noodles (¼ in. w., 0.03 in. thick); Medium Noodles (⅛ in w. 0.033 in. thick); Fine Noodles (1/16 in. w., 0.035 in. thick); Linguine, Fettucini.
4. Tubular, called Elbows—Bonballati (⅜ in. d.); Ditali lisci (¼ in. to 7/10 in. d.); Rigatoni (9/16 in. d.); Tochetti (⅛ in. to 5/32 in. d.).
5. Envelopes—Ravioli, Manicotti, Canelloni.
6. Fancies—In all shapes but generally small sizes. Made to look like stars, letters, shells, etc.

Good pastas are hard and yellow in color, almost translucent, and should break evenly.

BREADS AND PASTRY

Flours[2] are made by grinding cereal grains to powders of varying fineness. A meal is coarsely ground flour.

Wheat is the preferred grain for flour. Present in wheat flour are the proteins gliadin and glutenin. Gliadin is of a sticky nature which imparts adhesiveness to the gluten, while glutenin imparts tenacity and strength. The combination of these two very different proteins with water is known as gluten. Gluten is the elastic part of dough which allows the batter or dough to expand as gas is released from the leavening agent. When heated, it coagulates and forms the structure, imparting form and lightness to the product.

There are several types of wheat—durum wheats, hard wheats, and soft wheats. These wheats vary in the amount of protein they contain. Special blending of the wheat flours makes the flours more adaptable for special uses, for example:

Pasta flours are milled from durum wheat which is high in protein, and their best use is to make noodles, macaroni, and spaghetti.

Bread flours are milled primarily for the baker. They are a blend of hard spring and hard winter wheats. They may be bleached or unbleached. These flours are somewhat granular to the touch.

Cake flours are bleached flours milled from soft wheats, and are the most finely ground of all the flours. Protein content of these flours is low.

Pastry flours are generally milled from soft wheat; however, they can be made from either hard or soft wheat. These flours are used largely by bakers, and are unbleached.

All-purpose flours can be blends of hard wheats or soft wheats or both, depending on what area of the country the wheat comes from. These flours are blended to obtain satisfactory results for general family cooking. Protein content is sufficient to make good yeast breads as well as quick breads.

Self-rising flour is an intimate mixture of flour, sodium bicarbonate (baking soda), and one or more of the acid-reacting substances—monocalcium phosphate, sodium acid pyrophosphate, and sodium aluminum phosphate (baking powder).

---

[2]USDA.

STYLES OF MACARONI

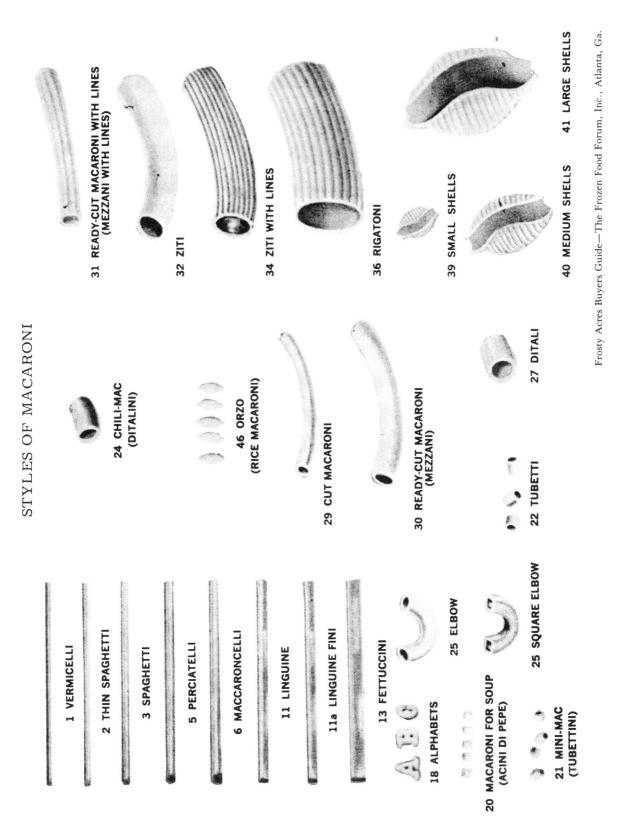

1 VERMICELLI

2 THIN SPAGHETTI

3 SPAGHETTI

5 PERCIATELLI

6 MACCARONCELLI

11 LINGUINE

11a LINGUINE FINI

13 FETTUCCINI

18 ALPHABETS

20 MACARONI FOR SOUP
(ACINI DI PEPE)

21 MINI-MAC
(TUBETTINI)

25 ELBOW

25 SQUARE ELBOW

24 CHILI-MAC
(DITALINI)

46 ORZO
(RICE MACARONI)

29 CUT MACARONI

30 READY-CUT MACARONI
(MEZZANI)

22 TUBETTI

27 DITALI

31 READY-CUT MACARONI WITH LINES
(MEZZANI WITH LINES)

32 ZITI

34 ZITI WITH LINES

36 RIGATONI

39 SMALL SHELLS

40 MEDIUM SHELLS

41 LARGE SHELLS

Frosty Acres Buyers Guide—The Frozen Food Forum, Inc., Atlanta, Ga.

Rye is second to wheat as a bread-making grain. This grain is used extensively with wheat in breads.

Rye flour is always darker than wheat flour. Bleaching has little effect on the color, but improves the baking properties. Rye gluten contains the same protein as wheat gluten, but in different proportions. Its proteins are very different in character and lack stability. Therefore, it is difficult to make a loaf of considerable volume.

Rye bread has a close texture and is difficult to bake. Pumpernickel is an example of an all-rye flour bread. Many varieties of bread are available currently with a rye and wheat grain combination.

Oats are rich in protein and are very nourishing although they are not suitable for breadmaking because they contain no gluten-forming protein.

Oats and oatmeal are important breakfast foods. They are also used with other flours to make tasty cookies.

Corn contains the protein gliadin but does not contain glutenin. This means that cornmeal cannot form gluten and must be used with a wheat flour for making breads. Cornmeal is used very extensively in the United States, particularly in the South, for making cornbread, spoonbread, muffins, and mush.

Barley is not normally used for breadmaking purposes. It is low in protein and fat, and high mineral content. This food is seldom used in our country except in soups.

Rice flour is milled from white rice. It is particularly useful in diets for persons who have allergies to other cereal grains. Rice flour can be used as a thickening agent or as flour in certain baked products such as cookies and pancakes.

Buckwheat is used only as pancake flour. It is not a true grain, but is used as a cereal.

In the refining, compounding, or processing of some foods, there is an unavoidable loss of vitamins and minerals. Enrichment is to replace or to restore the food by adding pure vitamins and minerals to the natural level of the original product.

Milling of low extraction fine white flour, cornmeal, and polished white rice results in unavoidable losses of some nutrients. The Food and Nutrition Board of the National Research Council, recognizing the deficiency of these products in vitamins and iron, recommended that all white flours be enriched. In the last several decades, the addition of thiamine, riboflavin, niacin, and iron to wheat flour, macaroni and noodle products, farina, rice, cornmeal, and corn grits has been gradually introduced as a legally required procedure in a large number of states. Besides these four required enrichment ingredients, calcium and Vitamin D.

A food may be considered fortified when one or more ingredients have been added to provide certain nutrients that may or may not be present naturally in foods. For example, since milk in its natural state does not contain Vitamin D, addition of the vitamin makes milk a fortified food. Today, both enrichment and fortification have become accepted routine steps in the manufacture of certain staple foods, and they contribute considerably to the nutritional welfare of our population.

What may start as mere enrichment may become modified to a combination of enrichment and fortification. Flour is a good example where enrichment was not limited to restoring previous natural values.

In setting legal requirements for enrichment of bread, human needs and the general dietary situation with respect to the nutrients involved were taken into consideration.

Standards for bread and flour shipped in interstate commerce and labeled as "enriched" became effective August 13, 1952. Bread or flour identified as enriched must contain amounts of the four required enrichment ingredients (thiamine, riboflavin, niacin, and iron) in each pound of bread or flour as are written in the FDA regulations. Calcium and Vitamin D are optional enrichment ingredients that may also be added to bread or to flour.

Food and drug inspectors maintain surveillance over the storage and transportation of grain in interstate commerce, as well as in the flour mill, to assure that adequate sanitation practices and other safeguards are followed. Flour labeled as "enriched" must contain the specified amounts of vitamins and minerals. FDA checks both by inspection and analysis to see that adequate amounts are present.

Flours and meals are attractive to insect pests. This contamination can sometimes result from unsatisfactory storage conditions. To sidestep this problem, flour and meal should be stored in tightly covered containers in a cool, dry area. Flour held at high temperatures may become unusable. The flour container should always be cleaned thoroughly before a new supply is added.

Barley

Used by the foodservice operator principally in soups and as an entree accompaniment. Barley is also used to make malt.

- Pearl—Has bran removed (brown)
- Dot—Husk removed (white)
- Scotch—Ground grains (brown)

Size.   24/1 lb., 10 lb., 25 lb., 100 lb. packs.

Bread

Follow these guidelines:

- Straight Breads—Only flour, shortening, water, milk (or buttermilk), sugar, salt, and yeast are allowed.
- Nut Breads, Raisin Breads—Should have 50 percent by weight of the added product.

Additives.   For softness, but tending to hold moisture, are used. White breads: Calcium propionate or Sodium propionate of 3.2 percent; other breads: 3.8 percent.

Quality.   Interior—Good color, not crumbly, soft to the touch. Exterior—even shape, even light brown, or typical color; no cuts or breaks.

Size.   Varies from 1 lb. to 3 lb. loaves with slice size up to 4 ½ in. square; slice thickness from ¼ in. to ½ in.

CEREAL ENRICHMENT STANDARDS

This table shows the final nutrient levels required for enriched cereal products as specified by the U.S. Food and Drug Administration and the USDA Agriculture Stabilization and Conservation Service (ASCS). All figures are in mg per pound of product except for Vitamin A which is in International Units (IU) per pound. When two figures are shown it indicates a minimum-maximum range. Where one number is shown it indicates the minimum level with overages left to good manufacturing practice. Standards in parentheses are optional.

Product	Thiamin	Ribo-flavin	Niacin	Iron	Calcium	Vitamin A
Enriched Flour	2.9	1.8	24	13.0–16.5	(960)[2]	
Enriched Self-Rising Flour	2.9	1.8	24	13.0–16.5	960	
Enriched Farina[1]	2.0–2.5	1.2–1.5	16–20	13.0	(500)[2]	
ASCS Domestic Wheat Flour	2.9	1.8	24	13.0–16.5		
ASCS Export Wheat Flour	2.9	1.8	24	13.0–16.5	500–625	4000–6000
ASCS 6% and 12% Soy Fortified Flour	2.0–2.5	1.2–1.5	16–20	13.0–16.5	6%: 500–1107 12%: 750–1364	4000–6000
Enriched Corn Meal and Grits	2.0–3.0	1.2–1.8	16–24	13–26	(500–750)[2]	
Enriched Self-Rising Corn Meal	2.0–3.0	1.2–1.8	16–24	13–26	(500–1750)[2]	
ASCS Domestic Corn Meal	2.0–3.0	1.2–1.8	16–24	13–26		
ASCS Domestic Corn Grits	2.0–3.0	1.2–1.8	16–24	21–26		
ASCS Export Corn Meal, Corn Flour, and Soy Fortified Corn Meal	2.0–3.0	1.2–1.8	16–24	13–26	500–750	4000–6000
Enriched Rice[3]	2.0–4.0	1.2–2.4	16–32	13–26	(500–1000)[2]	
Enriched Macaroni and Noodle Products[4]	4.0–5.0	1.7–2.2	27–34	13.0–16.5	(500–625)[2]	
Enriched Bread[5]	1.8	1.1	15	8.0–12.5	(600)[2]	
US RDA (mg or IU per day)	1.5	1.7	20	18	1000	5000

Cereal Foods World (November 1977).

Compliance with the appropriate standards is required: 1) For any ASCS commodity, 2) If any enrichment is used, 3) If the product is labeled or advertised as being "enriched" or containing enriched flour, 4) If the product is sold in States having mandatory enrichment laws. States requiring enrichment of FLOUR and BREAD are: AL, AK, AZ, AR, CA, CO, CT, FL, GA, HI, ID, IN, KS, KY, LA, ME, MA, MS, MT, NB, NH, NJ, NM, NY, ND, OH, OK, OR, PR, RI, SC, SD, TX, UT, WA, WV, WY; CORN MEAL: AL, AZ, CA, CT, GA, MS, NY, SC, UT; PASTA: CN, FL, NY, OR, WA; RICE: FL, NY, PR. States with the "25% RULE" are AZ, CA, UT. This rule requires that all fabricated foods containing 25% or more of a cereal product ingredient for which a standard of enrichment exists must be made with the enriched form of that product or have the equivalent nutrients added.

[1]FDA has proposed nutritional quality guidelines for fortified hot breakfast cereals including farina (39 FR 20896).

[2]No claim of calcium enrichment can be made when calcium is present for technological reasons at levels less than the minimum value shown except as required by nutritional labeling (21 CFR 1.17) and ingredient labeling (21 CFR 1.10).

[3]FDA has proposed revising the standards for enriched rice (42 FR 36487) which would make the maximum level shown a single minimum level. Riboflavin would be optional.

[4]Enriched pasta products are normally made from semolina, durum flour, or wheat flour enriched to these same levels. There are, however, no official standards for enriched cereals used in pasta production.

[5]Bread containing 62% or more of flour enriched to the standards for enriched flour will meet the standards for enriched bread.

The above is a condensation of regulations in effect as of August, 1977. It has been reviewed for correctness by the FDA and ASCS.

Buckwheat

The seed of the plant is ground into a flour which varies from brown to white in color with the amount of bran.

Corn Flour

Made from cornmeal.

Cornmeal

Ground white or yellow corn. Grind: Stone or machine; coarse or fine. Specify whether or not the bran and germ are included. Pack: 2 lb., 5 lb., 10 lb., 100 lb.

Cornstarch

A starch made from corn which is used to thicken food items. Gels at about 170°F.

Crackers

Crackers are baked from a dough that is made of flour, sugar, salt, and shortening. Specifications: 2 in. by 2 in.—¼ in. thick, 190 per lb.; 2 in. by 2 in.—³/₁₆ in. thick, 120 per lb.; 2 in. by 1⅓ in.—¼ in. thick, 180 per lb.; 2 in. by 1⅓ in.—³/₁₆ in. thick, 235 per lb.

Saltines.   1 percent salt topping by weight; 5 percent maximum water; 10 percent minimum fat.

Graham.   30 percent whole wheat flour; ¼ in. to ⅜ in. thick; 6 percent maximum water; 10 percent minimum fat.

Other varieties such as Rye Crisp, Ritz, Oyster, Zwieback are generally marketed by brand names and must be so specified according to the buyer's preference.

Cracker Crumbs and Cracker Meal

Broken or ground crackers of various types. Packed in 1 lb., 5 lb., and 10 lb. containers.

Oats

The endosperm of oats which is used to make oatmeal by cutting into small pieces and subjecting it to a steam treatment and dyeing.

- Steel-Cut—Very small pieces
- Stone-Ground—Buhr, old-fashioned or stone
- Quick-Cooking—Small pieces which have had extra steam treatment
- Quality Checks—No off-flavors or odors. Off-white color, even.

Rice

- Pearl—American and California
- Short Grain—Calora, Magnolia, Zenith
- Medium Grain—Blue Rose, Early Prolific
- Long Grain—Blue Bonnet, Edith, Fortuna, Lady Wright, Rexora
- White—All bran removed
- Undermilled—Most bran removed
- Brown—Unpolished, bran on
- Converted—Steamed, dried, enriched
- Instant—Cooked, dried
- Best Varieties—Long grain in Rexora or Calora. Buy Converted rice.

Grades. White Rice—U.S. No. 1, U.S. No. 2, U.S. No. 3, U.S. No. 4, U.S. No. 5, Sample Grade. Brown Rice—U.S. No. 1, U.S. No. 2, U.S. No. 3, U.S. No. 4. Buy U.S. No. 1 or U.S. No. 2 as the defects in the lower grades are too great. Rice flour is made from rice and is used as a modified starch in some recipes.

Rye

The grain is ground to make rye meal (rye graham) for pumpernickel bread. A coarse flour. Rye flour—for rye bread. A fine flour which is mixed with wheat flour for baking.

Grades. White, medium, dark.

Soy

Soybeans ground into a flour or a meal which is used with other products to enhance protein values.

Wild Rice

Not really rice but a grass seed (Zizania aquatica). Short, small, large.

BAKERY PRODUCTS[3]

Baked products include pastry, pie, cake, bread, rolls, buns, and quick breads. These products are obtainable in the following forms: ready-to-serve, partially baked, ready-to-serve frozen, prepared frozen, canned prepared, and prepared mixes.

1. *Ready-to-serve products* have been baked and are ready to be served. Breads, sweet rolls, doughnuts, pastries, and cookies are examples of these.

---

[3]Thorner and Manning, *Quality Control in Food Service* (Westport, Conn.: The AVI Publishing Co., Inc., 1976).

2. *Partially-baked products* are "half baked." Baking must be completed on premises before serving. Available forms are loaves of bread, rolls, and buns.
3. *Ready-to-serve frozen products* are fully prepared products ready to serve after thawing. If desired, these products can be heated before serving. Cakes, pastries, some pies, rolls, and buns are sold in this manner.
4. *Prepared frozen products* have not been baked prior to freezing. They require baking before serving. Breads, pies, and rolls are available in this fashion.
5. *Canned prepared products* must be completely baked before serving. Cookies, biscuits, and rolls are in this group.
6. *Prepared mixes* are convenient preparations containing basic ingredients like flour, shortening, sugar, and leavening. Ingredients such as water, milk, or eggs may have to be added. Pie crusts, cakes, and roll mixes are obtainable in this form.

Cakes

A number of factors are responsible for determining the quality of cakes.

1. The cake should have a uniform shape and be free of cracks and sags.
2. The color should be uniform. A light-colored cake should have a uniform golden brown hue on all sides.
3. The crust should be thin and tender.
4. The bottom should show no evidence of burning.
5. The crumb should be medium with a fine even grain. It should be moist and smooth but not tacky or soggy.
6. Unless the type of cake calls for a dominant flavor, the flavor should be balanced with no foreign or off-flavors (oily, starchy).
7. If icing is present, it should not be separated from the cake and not show any unevenness, nor should it run when thawed or pull apart when cut.
8. The top of the cake should show no discoloration, which may be caused by moisture as a result of intermittent thawing.

Handling Hints. Unfrosted cakes can be thawed in freezer wrapping. If a cake is frosted, it should be removed from the carton and the wrapping removed to prevent stickiness and injury to the frosting.

Unused cake should not be refrozen. It can be stored in a refrigerator for a short time.

Handling instructions provided by the processor should be read and followed.

Storage Life. Freezing is an ideal method of prolonging shelf life of most baked products. Bread, if quick frozen and held at 0°F (−18°C), will remain fresh for many months. When thawed, bread will have a freshness equivalent to a product held for two days at 70°F (22°C). Cakes and cookies will retain their palatability for at least 6 months at 0°F (−18°C) and longer at lower temperatures. Proper thawing conditions, such as a low-moisture atmosphere, are essential to prevent rapid staling. Although almost all kinds of cakes can be frozen and thawed without noticeable change, the following defects may occur as a result of prolonged storage: loss of volume, abnormal softness or compressibility, crumbliness, and tenderness.[4]

The following are examples of storage life of products held at 0°F (−18°C):

Angel cake, 4 mo	Pound cake, 9 mo
Cheese cake, 12 mo	Sponge cake (egg yolk), 2 mo
Chocolate cake, 6 mo	Sponge cake (whole egg), 6 mo
Cookies, 12 mo	Turnovers, 12 mo
Fruit cake, 12 mo	Yellow cake, 9 mo
Fruit pies, 12 mo	

Quick Breads

Quick breads are what the name implies. They are relatively easy to prepare and they are quick. Examples of quick breads are muffins, biscuits, waffles, pancakes and coffee cakes.

There are three types of quick bread mixes:

1. Drop batter, such as drop biscuits or muffins.
2. Pour batter, as a pancake or waffle batter.
3. Dough, such as rolled biscuits or dumplings.

Quick breads should not be overmixed. Overmixing develops the gluten too much, causing tunnels and coarseness in the finished product. Muffins are usually baked at 400°F (204°C) for 20 to 25 minutes until browned; biscuits are baked at 450°F (233°C) for 12 to 15 minutes or until golden brown.

Pre-prepared frozen waffles, pancakes, and French toast are all available and are widely distributed. Although these products are generally considered breakfast foods, they can be embellished in many novel ways and served as appealing desserts.

Pancakes that are prepared from mixes should be heated on a griddle at 385°F (197°C). Waffles are prepared in the conventional manner using a waffle baker.

Pre-prepared and frozen waffles and pancakes may be heated in an oven or toaster. They may be heated thawed or frozen. If thawing is preferred, allow them to thaw for 10 to 15 minutes. Place them in a pre-heated oven at 350°F (177°C) using standard-size sheet pans for 4 to 5 minutes. If heated from the frozen state, add another minute to the heating time. When a toaster is used, thaw for 10 to 15 minutes at medium setting or toast twice at light setting without thawing. These items may also be heated in a microwave oven. Prior testing is advised to determine the proper timing for the desired degrees of doneness.

---

[4]Tressler, VanArsdale, and Copley, *The Freezing Preservation of Food* (Westport, Ct: AVI, 1968).

Pies

A pie consists of two main sections and an optional section. The two main sections are the crust and filling. The optional section may be a compatible accompaniment in the form of garnishes, decorations, and toppings.

The ideal crust should be crisp, tender, and fragile, and should not shrink during baking. It should break short and should not be pasty or soggy. Its color should be golden with mottled brown running through it. It should exhibit a clean aroma with a fresh-baked character. The taste should be clean and free from foreign flavors such as oil or burned particles.

The filling must be clear and brilliant but not viscous. It may ooze without being watery. It should not be gelatinous, gummy, or stiff. The flavor of the main ingredient, if fruit, should be true and dominant, without being overpowering. The filling must also be free from foreign flavors and off-tastes.

The percentage of the main ingredient should be sufficient to fill the pie cavity when baked and to provide an adequate quantity for each portion.

Frozen Pies.   Frozen pies are available either fully baked or with unbaked crusts. Fully baked pies need no further preparation other than thawing to room temperature before serving.

Frozen pies with unbaked crusts are excellent when prepared according to instructions provided by the processor. The filling and fruit of frozen pies are already cooked. During the baking operation, both the crust and filling have identical time cycles, so that they are finished simultaneously. Dual completion is only possible if pies are baked from the frozen state. Conventional or convection ovens are suited for this type of baking.

The Lloyd J. Harriss Company of Saugatuck, Michigan, bakers of quality frozen pies, has provided the following information for the handling, baking, and serving of these products.

1. Cut a number of 1½ inch slits or prick the top crust with the tines of a fork. This allows steam to escape while baking. For custard and pumpkin pies, the protective wax sheet should be removed.
2. An aluminum cookie sheet should be placed on the lowest rack of an oven. Pies are then positioned on the metal sheet. Fruit pies are baked in a preheated oven at 425°F (219°C) from 45 to 55 minutes until a golden brown color appears on the outer surface of the crust. Custards and pumpkin require 55 to 65 minutes.
3. After baking, the pies should be air-cooled to room temperature before serving. For best acceptability, pies should never be served too hot or too cold.
4. Berry pies will tend to boil quicker than pies made from other fruits. To overcome this problem, such a pie may be baked for a shorter time and at a higher temperature (additional 25°F or 3.9°C).
5. Custard and pumpkin pies often require an additional 10 to 15 minutes of baking time. This facilitates moisture reduction and "sets" the pie filling. If these pies are

removed prior to completion of the "setting process," the filling may "run" and have poor flavor.

6. Ovens should not be overloaded. This may cause a heat loss which may prevent an oven from attaining proper temperature during the baking cycle. Experimentation with any oven is necessary to determine its optimum working capacity.

Pie Defects and Probable Causes.

1. *Raw pie:* May be caused by a pie that is too cold. Frozen pie temperature prior to baking should be 0 to 5°F (−18 to −12°C). Lower temperatures will result in slow heating, unless compensation is made by extending the baking cycle.
2. *Raw or soggy bottoms:* May be caused by an oven that is too cool, insufficient bottom heat, dirty oven floor, pie bottom dough too rich, or bottom rolled too thin.
3. *Burned pies:* May be caused by improper temperatures, usually the result of a faulty oven thermostat, or a pie that was partially thawed and cooked too rapidly.
4. *Burned bottoms:* May be caused by excessive bottom heat or an uneven distribution of heat.
5. *Blisters on crust:* Crust not stippled or docked and too much egg-wash.
6. *Filling runs out during baking:* Pies were filled too much, pies were not properly sealed, oven was too cool, too much sugar was used in the filling, or filling was too thin.
7. *Shrinkage of crust:* Oven too cool.

Pie and Tart Shells.   Pie and tart shells are available unbaked and frozen. They are versatile items and may be used for a base for many kinds of novel fillings. Depending on the processor's instructions, shells require baking for about 10 minutes in a preheated oven set at 400°F (204°C). Formation of a golden brown color is usually a good indication that a shell is completely baked. If a filling requires heating, shells should be partially baked to compensate for this condition.

Pie shells are ideal for cream, pecan, cheese custard, and pumpkin fillings. Graham cracker shells may also be used for cheese fillings.

Many fillings are adaptable for use in tart and pie shells. Tart shells make an excellent and attractive device to hold puddings, berries, and other fruit. Pre-prepared and canned puddings like vanilla, custard, chocolate, or lemon can be presented in a tart shell.

Baked Products from Frozen Dough

Baked products that are produced from frozen dough and finished on premises have taken a great step forward over the last ten years. A multitude of bakery items can be easily prepared from frozen dough.

Bread and rolls, over the years, have become highly abused menu items. Among the faults resulting from these improper handling practices are bread and rolls that are unappealing, soggy, doughy, underbaked, stale, and sour. Numerous feeding establishments have built fine reputations by serving interesting and appetizing assortments of baked items. Restaurants located in some American cities, such as San Francisco, Chicago, New York, Miami, New Orleans, and Boston, are expected to provide quality baked products, as one way to retain their clientele. Specialty items like brioche, pecan rolls, croissants, popovers, corn sticks, salt sticks, and many kinds of breads are served as part of the daily menu. With the advent of frozen dough on a commercial scale, foodservice establishments were provided with the means of upgrading their bread and roll service. Small bread loaves baked on premises and made in different sizes, shapes, and styles have met with national acceptance. Consumers seem captivated with the idea of slicing their own fragrant, fresh, hot bread at the table. This concept was introduced over a decade ago by Bridgeford Foods Corporation in Anaheim, California.

Standards of Identity for Bakery Products

Standards of Identity, promulgated by the FDA, are provided for the following bakery products:

1. Bread, white bread, rolls, white rolls, buns, and white buns.
2. Enriched bread and milk rolls or buns.
3. Milk bread and milk rolls or buns.
4. Raisin bread and raisin rolls or raisin buns.
5. Whole wheat bread, graham bread, entire wheat bread, whole wheat rolls, graham rolls, entire wheat rolls, whole wheat buns, graham buns, and entire wheat buns.

SWEETENERS[5]

Sweeteners are essential ingredients in most bakery foods. They make contributions not only to flavor, but also to leavening in yeast-raised products, to structure-building in cakes and cookies, to crust color development in most products, and to color and flavor development on tasting and browning. Powdered sweeteners are used for dusting and coating on various sweet foods and doughnuts, and in the preparation of icings and fillings.

Each type of sweetener has unique properties which make it suitable for specific uses. Replacement of one sweetener with another may be possible in some cases, particularly when the replacement level is well below 50 percent, but the sweeteners are sufficiently different so that expert guidance is usually required for best results.

The specifications and typical analyses listed throughout this survey were furnished by manufacturers of commercial products, as specifically identified. To simplify

---

[5]*Bakery,* May 1977; June 1977.

this complex area, the information is organized into three major categories and many suitable subcategories as listed below:

1. *Beet or Cane Sugar:* sucrose (dry, liquid); invert (liquid); molasses; brown sugar.
2. *Corn Sweetener:* dextrose (dry liquid); corn syrups, liquid (high fructose, 95 D.E., 60 to 70 D.E., 50 to 60 D.E., 40 to 50 D.E.); dry corn syrup solids (42, 36, 24 D.E. and low D.E. maltodextrins).
3. *Blends:* sucrose/dextrose; invert/dextrose; sucrose/corn syrup; invert/corn syrup.

Sucrose

Sucrose, the sweetener from cane or beets, is available dry or liquid. It is distinguished by its very pleasing sweet flavor, its ability to be fermented by yeast to raise yeast-leavened goods, its development of attractive foxy red crust color when breads and rolls are baked, its structure-building function in cakes, and the ability to form stable icings and coatings.

Invert is similar to sucrose in all yeast-leavened bakery foods because yeast converts sucrose to invert sugar in doughs almost instantaneously. Therefore, in yeast-leavened foods, sucrose and invert both function as invert. Invert is available only in the liquid form.

In nonyeast-leavened products invert differs from sucrose and is not suitable for all applications (where the basic structure of sucrose is what is needed, such as in icings, cakes, cookies, etc.). Molasses and brown sugar are used in dark breads, cakes, and cookies for appearance and flavor. These are sucrose products which have not been refined to the same degree as liquid or dry sucrose.

Corn Sweeteners

Corn sweeteners are available in many different consistencies and many different degrees of fermentability, both wet and dry. Dextrose Equivalent (D.E.) is a measure of the amount of reducing sugars present, expressed as dextrose. This ranges from a D.E. of 99+, representing highly purified dextrose (corn sugar available wet or dry), through the 95 D.E. corn syrup (available only wet), to the 60 to 70 D.E. corn syrups, and still lower conversions with 42 D.E. being considered. Also, 42 D.E. and lower conversion syrups are available wet or dry.

The 99+ D.E. product (wet or dry), and the 95+ D.E. syrup (available only liquid) are widely used in the manufacture of yeast-leavened bakery foods. The sweetness factor is 70 percent that of sucrose. Fermentability is excellent, matching that of sucrose. Crust color development is good, but the color is not as foxy red as produced when sucrose is used. These products are not able to replace sucrose in cakes and cookies, where structure-building is involved, although limited partial substitution is feasible. High fructose syrups are equivalent in all practical regards to invert sugar and can be used in yeast-leavened bakery foods with outstanding results. In nonyeast-leavened foods, the same cautions and limitations described for invert apply to high fructose corn syrups.

Corn Sugar

The acid-enzyme converted corn syrups, 60 to 70 D.E., are used in many yeast-leavened applications, particularly when blended with either sucrose or dextrose. The 60 to 70 D.E. syrups provide less sweetness and less fermentability, on a pound basis, than do the higher conversion sweeteners. When supplemented with sucrose or dextrose, or when used at higher levels, it is possible to achieve good results. Lower conversion syrups are often used in making bakers' jellies and fillings as well as in soft cookies and certain cakes, and in specialty glazes such as in sticky-buns. Dry corn syrup solids are usually below 42 D.E. They can be used conveniently in dry mixes and in certain kinds of pie fillings and similar products.

QUESTIONS

1. Define the following terms:

surum	enrichment
dockage	enzyme active sog
tough wheat	lipoxidose
weeirly wheat	lecithin
ergot	defatted flour
gultch	"short" pastry
semolina	TVP
gliodin	sucrose
glutenin	dextrose
fortified	

2. List the eight cereal grains.
3. Which wheat flours are used for making breads and pastas? Explain.
4. What are the characteristics of a high quality pasta? Which wheat makes the best pasta? Why?
5. How are flours made?
6. What is the characteristic by which we distinguish the several types of wheat?
7. Discuss the advantages and disadvantages of using rye flour in making bread?
8. What are the essential components in a bread flour?
9. What are the ingredients used in enriching flour and bread? Why is this process necessary?
10. What is the difference between ready-to-serve frozen pastry products and prepared frozen products?
11. Name four quality checks of a cake.
12. Discuss the preferred storage for cake, cookies, breads.
13. Give some examples of prolonged storage of pastry products.
14. Construct a scorecard for grading frozen fruit pies.
15. Discuss the advantages of using soy flours. In what products will you use them?
16. Give some examples of variety breads.

17. Discuss some of the applications of textured vegetable protein in bakery products.

18. You are making the following items. What sweetening agent will you use? Why?

Angel cake _____

Coffee cake _____

Glaze for Sticky Buns _____

Whole wheat rolls _____

Chocolate icing _____

Vanilla filling _____

8

DAIRY PRODUCTS

INTRODUCTION

Butter, cheese, milk, and frozen desserts are presented in this chapter on dairy products. The quality of these finished products is determined by the principal ingredient. Variations found in the composition of the milk fat used in these products is an important standard used in grading. Careful attention is given to the conditions which influence the stability of dairy products.

Quality shields and grades are given for all product groups. Flavor characteristics including factors for disrating body, color, and salt is included for butter. Also included, and of particular interest, is the definition of butter flavor characteristics.

Kinds of milk, cheese, and frozen desserts include tables listing processing and purchasing information. For example, the table on cheese provides information on aging period, color, texture, flavor, common purchase unit, milkfat, and moisture.

Production processes are described in detail explaining the factors which affect body, texture, flavor, and grade of each product.

BUTTER

Basically, the quality of the finished butter can be no higher than the quality of the raw milk and cream from which it is made. Careful grading and segregation at the receiving platform is very important. However, poor workmanship can result in disratings that would cause the butter to be down-graded, and could detract from the flavor and stability of the finished product. Therefore, it is extremely important that close attention be given to the workmanship factors, and especially to those conditions which influence spreadability and product stability. Every buttermaker should have a good butter trier, and should personally and carefully examine each churning of butter after the butter has been properly chilled for forty-eight hours.

Flavor

The flavor of butter is determined primarily by the senses of taste and smell. To register its full taste sensation, a substance must be soluble so that it can be carried quickly to the taste buds of the tongue.

The sense of smell supplements taste in determining flavor in butter. The warmth of the mouth melts the butter and frees its volatile aromas which then enter the olfactory chambers, coming forward into the nose. Moisture in the mouth and nasal passages enhances the transmission of flavor sensations.

There are only four primary taste sensations: sweet, sour, salt, and bitter. Sugar produces the sensation of sweetness; lactic acid or a tart apple produces a sour taste; common table salt produces a sensation of saltiness, and quinine produces a bitter sensation. When melted butter comes in direct contact with the taste buds, its sweet and salty characteristics are detected by the taste buds located at the tip of the tongue, its sour characteristics by those on the sides of the tongue, and its bitter characteristics by those at the back of the tongue.

The proper procedure in grading butter is first to use the sense of smell, and then the sense of taste to confirm and establish the character, probable origin, and degree of development of each flavor present. By discerning carefully the odor or aroma characteristics of the sample, the character, and degree of the flavor present, the grader is able to identify and classify the flavor properly.

Aroma in butter may be present to a greater or lesser degree. In the higher grades of butter, a pleasing aroma accentuates certain pleasing or desirable flavors. An objectionable aroma or odor is generally associated with flavors present in the lower grades of butter, and serves to accentuate the undesirable flavor characteristics. The aroma noted in butter before it is tasted reflects a general indication of its quality.

The temperature of the butter at the time of grading is important in determining the true characteristics of flavor and aroma. The temperature of the butter should preferably range from 40°F to 50°F. A temperature of about 70°F is preferable in the grading room; it should not be below 60°F.

Body

The factor of body in butter is considered from the standpoint of its characteristics or defects. Defects in body are disrated according to degree or intensity. Milkfat in butter is a mixture of various triglycerides of different melting points and appears in the form of fat globules and as free fat. In both of these forms, a part of the fat is crystalline and another part liquid. Some are solid at temperatures up to 100°F or even higher; others are still liquid at temperatures far below the freezing point. Because of this, butter at the temperatures at which it is usually handled is always a mixture of solid (crystallized) and liquid fat. The variations in the composition of milkfat thus have a great influence upon the texture and spreadability of butter.

In summer, when milkfat contains more liquid fat, butter tends to be weak and leaky, and, in winter, when its solid fat content is high, butter tends to be hard and brittle, resulting in unsatisfactory spreadability. The ratio between the crystalline and the liquid particles depends upon the composition of the butterfat (varying with the season of the year), manufacturing methods, and the temperature of the butter.

There may be a wide range of variation in the percentage of globular fat, also due presumably to differences in the composition of fat and manufacturing practices. Close attention should be given to the proper relationship between the temperatures of heating and cooling, the rate of cooling the cream, and the temperature of churning, washing, and working of the butter, at different seasons of the year when there are different fat conditions. This is important in maintaining a uniformly firm, waxy body possessing good spreadability.

The temperature of the cream after holding is a very important factor which determines the hardness of the butter. Butter with either a poor or excellent body may be made from cream containing either a hard or soft fat, depending upon the methods of processing. The state of the water droplets and air in butter also plays a vital role in the body of the butter.

Butter with a firm, waxy body has an attractive appearance, has granules that are close knit, and cuts clean when sliced, with good spreadability. The trier sample from such butter will show this clean-cut, smooth, waxy appearance.

The temperature of the butter at the time of grading is important in determining the true characteristics of body, and should be between 40°F and 50°F.

Color

The natural color of butter varies according to seasonal and sectional conditions. The color of butter is considered defective when it is uneven, or lacks uniformity within the same churning or package.

Salt

In grading butter, the factor of salt is considered from the standpoint of the degree of salt taste, and whether it is completely dissolved. A range in the salt content or salty taste of butter is permitted without considering it a defect. This range provides for the various market preferences for salt taste in butter. Uniformity of salt content between churnings from the same factory is desirable.

Grades

The specifications for the U.S. grades of butter are as follows:

1. U.S. Grade AA or U.S. 93 Score butter conforms to the following: Possesses a fine and highly pleasing butter flavor. May possess a slight feed and a definite cooked (fine) flavor. It is made from sweet cream of low natural acid to which a culture (starter) may or may not have been added. The permitted total disratings in body, color, and salt characteristics are limited to one-half ($\frac{1}{2}$). For detailed specifications and classification of flavor characteristics, as well as body, color, and salt characteristics, and disratings, see the accompanying tables.

2. U.S. Grade A or U.S. 92 Score butter conforms to the following: Possesses a pleasing and desirable butter flavor. May possess any of the following flavors to a slight degree: Aged, bitter, coarse-acid, flat, smothered, and storage. May possess feed and cooked (coarse) flavors to a definite degree. The permitted total disratings in body, color, and salt characteristics are limited to one-half (½), except when the flavor classification is AA, a disrating total of one (1) is permitted.

3. U.S. Grade B or U.S. 90 Score butter conforms to the following: Possesses a fairly pleasing butter flavor. May possess any of the following flavors to a slight degree: Lipase, malty, musty, neutralizer, scorched, utensil, weed, whey, and woody. May possess any of the following flavors to a definite degree: Aged, bitter, coarse-acid, smothered, storage, and old cream; feed flavor to a pronounced degree. The permitted total disratings in body, color, and salt characteristics are limited to one-half (½), except when the flavor classification is AA, a disrating total of one and one-half (1½) is permitted, and when the flavor classification is A, a disrating total of one (1) is permitted.

4. U.S. Grade C or U.S. 89 Score butter conforms to the following: May possess any of the following flavors to a slight degree: Barny, sour, wild onion or garlic, and yeasty. May possess any of the following flavors to a definite degree: Lipase, malty, musty, neutralizer, scorched, stale, utensil, weed, whey, and woody. The permitted total disratings in body, color, and salt characteristics are limited to one (1), except when the flavor classification is A, a disrating total of one and one-half (1½) is permitted.

5. General. Butter of all U.S. grades is free of foreign materials and visible mold. Butter possessing a flavor rating of AA or A and workmanship disratings in excess of one and one-half (1½) is given a flavor rating only; butter possessing a flavor rating of B or C and workmanship disrating in excess of one (1) is given a flavor rating only.

Butter which fails to meet the requirements for U.S. Grade C or U.S. 89 Score is not given a U.S. grade.

Butter, when tested, which does not comply with the provisions of the Federal Food, Drug and Cosmetic Act, including minimum milkfat requirements of 80.0 percent, is not assigned a U.S. grade.

GRADE AND QUALITY SHIELDS FOR CONSUMER PACKAGES OF DAIRY PRODUCTS MANUFACTURED UNDER THE GRADING AND QUALITY CONTROL SERVICE (AA SHIELD ON TOP LEVEL QUALITY FOR BUTTER)

Butter produced in a plant found on inspection to be using unsatisfactory manufacturing practices, equipment, or facilities, or to be operating under insanitary plant
conditions, is not assigned a U.S. grade.

Margarine

Margarines are fatty foods prepared by blending fats and oils with other ingredients
such as milk solids, salt, flavoring materials, and Vitamins A and D. By federal regulation, margarine must contain at least 80 percent fat. The fats used in margarines may be
of either animal or vegetable origin although vegetable oils are by far the most widely
used.

The fats may be prepared from single hydrogenated fats, from two or more
hydrogenated fats, or from a blend of hydrogenated fat and an unhydrogenated oil.

DEFINITION OF FLAVOR CHARACTERISTICS

Identified Flavors[1]	Flavor Classification			
	AA	**A**	**B**	**C**
Feed	S*	D*	P*	—
Cooked (fine)	D	—	—	—
Aged	—	S	D	—
Bitter	—	S	D	—
Coarse-acid	—	S	D	—
Flat	—	S	—	—
Smothered	—	S	D	—
Storage	—	S	D	—
Cooked (coarse)	—	D	—	—
Lipase	—	—	S	D
Malty	—	—	S	D
Musty	—	—	S	D
Neutralizer	—	—	S	D
Scorched	—	—	S	D
Utensil	—	—	S	D
Weed	—	—	S	D
Whey	—	—	S	D
Woody	—	—	S	D
Old cream	—	—	D	—
Barny	—	—	—	S
Metallic	—	—	—	S
Sour	—	—	—	S
Wild onion or garlic	—	—	—	S
Yeasty	—	—	—	S
Stale	—	—	—	D

*S—Slight; D—Definite; P—Pronounced.
1. When more than one flavor is discernible in a sample of butter, the flavor
classification of the sample shall be established on the basis of the flavor that
carries the lowest classification.

CHARACTERISTICS AND DISRATINGS
IN BODY, COLOR, AND SALT

BODY			
Characteristics	**Disratings**		
	S*	**D***	**P***
Crumbly	1/2	1	—
Gummy	1/2	1	—
Leaky	1/2	1	2
Mealy or grainy	1/2	1	—
Short	1/2	1	—
Weak	1/2	1	—
Sticky	1/2	1	—
Ragged boring	1	2	

COLOR			
Characteristics	**Disratings**		
	S	**D**	**P**
Wavy	1/2	1	—
Mottled	1	2	—
Streaked	1	2	—
Color specks	1	2	—

SALT			
Characteristics	**Disratings**		
	S	**D**	**P**
Sharp	1/2	1	—
Gritty	1	2	—

TABLE

Flavor Classification	Total Disratings	U.S. Grade or U.S. Score
AA	1/2	AA or 93
AA	1	A or 92
A	1/2	A or 92
AA	1 1/2	B or 90
A	1	B or 90
B	1/2	B or 90
A	1 1/2	C or 89
C	1	C or 89

*S—Slight; D—Definite; P—Pronounced.

Many manufacturers of margarines are now producing these products with substantially higher levels of polyunsaturated fatty acids, in response to medical research findings which suggest the advisability of higher levels of these fatty acids in the diet. These margarines contain fats having 22 to 60 percent polyunsaturated fatty acids and iodine values ranging from 92 to 130. In contrast, regular margarines contain 10 to 20 percent polyunsaturated fatty acids and have iodine values from 78 to 90. Some medical workers have referred to these products high in polyunsaturated fatty acids as ''special'' margarines because, in addition to their use in normal diets, they are also suitable for use in special diets where an increased level of linoleic acid is desired.

The range in fatty acid composition and iodine value for the various types of margarine products made from vegetable oils is included.

FATTY ACID COMPOSITION AND IODINE VALUE OF FAT AND OILS IN MARGARINE PRODUCTS

Type Margarine	% of Total Fatty Acids			Saturated Fatty Acids	Iodine Value
	Unsaturated Fatty Acids				
	Monoenoic	Dienoic	Trienoic		
Vegetable margarine —regular	42 to 63	10 to 20	0 to 0.5	16 to 25	78 to 90
Vegetable margarine —special	20 to 57	22 to 60	0 to 0.5	13 to 30	92 to 130

CHEESE[1]

Most of the cheese produced in the United States is made from cow's milk. However, the milk of other animals may be used. For example, goat's milk is used extensively in Norway; in France, sheep's milk is commonly used.

Milk is Main Ingredient

For certain types of cheese, both milk and cream are used. For others, a mixture of whole and partially defatted milk may be used. For example, cottage cheese is usually made from defatted milk, though cream may be added later. Cream cheese is made from milk enriched with cream. Virtually all American cheese is made from whole milk, the end result being a cheese with a minimum of 30.5 percent fat and a maximum of 39 percent water. Swiss and Edam, which are usually made from mixtures of whole and defatted milk, are generally of lower fat content than is American cheese.

---

[1] *Newer Knowledge of Cheese* (Rosemont, IL: National Diary Council, 1948), pp. 7—12.

Milk Quality Important

The quality of milk used in making cheese is of prime significance. The type of bacteria present in the milk used may play an important role in flavor development during the ripening of a given batch of cheese. Therefore, it is necessary to carefully control the quality of the milk going into cheese production. Obviously, the same measures customarily taken to insure a sanitary milk supply should be adhered to in cheese making.

Much of the hard and semi-hard cheese manufactured in the United States is made from unpasteurized milk, although there is an increasing tendency toward the use of pasteurized milk for the production of such types. Most of the cream cheese and cottage cheese is made from pasteurized milk. While it is believed that any pathogenic bacteria which originally may have been present in the milk lose vitality and die within a few months under proper curing conditions, health officials prefer that all milk going into cheese production be pasteurized.

Hard Cheese From Pasteurized Milk

From the public health standpoint, the importance of the use of pasteurized milk in making cheese is obvious. However, when its use for hard cheese first began, many cheese makers were of the opinion that American cheese made from pasteurized milk did not develop a satisfactory flavor. Exhaustive tests carried out over a period of years indicate, however, that cheese made from pasteurized milk develops, under suitably controlled conditions, an acceptable milk flavor. It is more uniform in quality and requires a shorter ripening period since higher curing temperatures are permissible.

Curd Formation

After the milk has been blended to assure a unifrom fat content, it is warmed, and a culture of lactic acid-producing bacteria is added as a "starter." These bacteria, which are of the same kind that normally cause the souring of milk, are allowed to act until the milk has reached the degree of acidity necessary to accelerate rennet action. At this point, rennet is added to coagulate the casein. This enzyme preparation is the coagulant used in the production of most cheese. The soft, unripened cheeses are the only ones in which acid coagulation alone is sometimes used.

The coagulum produced by rennet is elastic and has the ability to shrink, squeezing out the whey. Such a curd retains most of the calcium- and phosphorus-bearing salts of the milk. When rennet is not used, however, a larger proportion of these mineral salts is dissolved and thereby transferred to the whey. The extent to which the minerals are retained in a finished cheese of this type will be influenced by handling techniques.

The coagulation temperature employed is carefully controlled but varies according to the type of cheese being prepared. The range may extend from 68 to 104°F; ordinarily, it runs from 82 to 95°F. Soft, unripened cheeses usually require a lower temperature for proper flavor and curd development.

Cutting and Draining the Curd

After the casein has coagulated to the proper degree, the curd is cut with a suitable curd knife, heated (if called for) 30 to 40 minutes, and then drained of whey. This process, primarily as it influences the moisture content and, indirectly, texture and body, helps to determine the characteristics of the finished cheese. The cubes or flakes into which the curd is cut range from the size of a grain of wheat to that of a walnut, depending on the kind of cheese under production. It is necessary, however, to maintain uniformity of particle size in the manufacture of a given cheese if the proper texture (often a distinguishing characteristic) of the finished cheese is to be attained.

After heating and draining, the curd is placed in molds or hoops, pressed, and again drained. The curd may be salted either before or after this step, depending on the type of cheese involved. The method of salting also varies with the type of cheese. In some cases, the salt is mixed with the curd; in dry salting, it may be rubbed on the surface of the formed cheese; some cheeses may be salted by floating them in a brine bath.

Specific types of organisms not only help to produce a characteristic flavor, but also promote certain differences in texture. (For example, the holes in Swiss cheese are produced by the gas-forming *Propionibacterium shermanii*.) The temperature and humidity of the curing room influence the growth and development of these microorganisms.

MILK

Pasteurized Milk

How Milk is Pasteurized. Pasteurization is defined as the process of heating milk to at least 145°F, and holding it at, or above, this temperature continuously for at least 30 minutes, or heating it to at least 161°F, and holding it at, or above, this temperature continuously for at least 15 seconds, in approved and properly operated equipment. The latter method is predominant today. Following this treatment, the milk is cooled promptly to 45°F, or lower.

Effects of Pasteurization. Pasteurization destroys all pathogenic organisms, and most of the nonpathogenic bacteria, so that milk may be safely consumed. The keeping quality of milk also is improved. The food value is not changed significantly.

There is no apparent undesirable effect on the protein, fat, carbohydrate, or mineral content of milk, nor on Vitamins A, D, E, riboflavin, niacin, pyridoxine, or biotin. Both Vitamins A and E are subject to oxidative deterioration, but they appear to be quite stable in fluid dairy products. Only slight losses, if any, occur in Vitamins B_{12}, K, and pantothenic acid.

Greater losses of ascorbic acid and thiamine have been reported, but the level of ascorbic acid in milk is not of special importance. A varied American diet includes other sources rich in ascorbic acid. While pasteurization reduces thiamine somewhat, milk still supplies a significant amount in the daily diet. Carefully controlled, high-temperature-short-time pasteurization permits maximum retention of these two vitamins.

Homogenized Milk

Pasteurized Milk is Also Homogenized.   Today most whole milk is homogenized immediately after it is pasteurized. The milk is treated mechanically to break up the fat into smaller globules and then to disperse these permanently in a fine emulsion throughout the milk. The heated milk is channeled to the homogenizer where the milk, under high pressure, is forced through very tiny openings. Nothing is added or removed.

Effects of Homogenization.   Physically, homogenized milk differs from ordinary whole milk in that there is no separation of cream, and the product remains uniform throughout. Small differences in color and viscosity may be noted in the homogenized milk, and there is a slightly "richer" taste. Homogenization lowers the curd tension that results in the formation of a softer curd during human digestion.

Kinds of Milk

Today milk appears on the market in many forms to appeal to varied tastes of consumers and to satisfy their demands. A wide line of products has been developed to improve keeping quality, facilitate distribution and storage, make maximum use of by-products, and preserve surplus. The processing involved in producing each form of milk is designed and controlled to protect the health of the consumer. Some forms of milk are available in all communities; others may be found in only a few communities.

Standards of composition are generally established by state and local governments for all fluid milk products. Federal standards of identity have been established only on evaporated, condensed, and nonfat dry milk.

Whole Fresh Fluid Milk

Composition.   While the composition of milk is variable between cows and seasons of the year, minimum standards for the composition of whole milk have been set by individual states. Many states define whole milk as milk that contains not less than 3.25 percent milk fat and not less than 8.25 percent milk solids-not-fat. At the milk plant, the milk from different farms is pooled and "standardized" to meet or exceed the minimum legal requirements.

The standards of composition, however, vary with the different states. Even within the state, the milk composition may be well above the minimum standard. Milk of higher milk solids-not-fat and milk fat is available in most markets. This may be a premium product, or milk from certain breeds of cows that is sold by breed name in many communities.

Basic Processing.   Most of the whole fluid milk marketed in this country is pasteurized and homogenized. Milk that receives no heat treatment is called raw milk. Unless it is Certified Milk, raw milk should be pasteurized at home, or boiled, before it is consumed.

Certified Milk

What, Why, and Where.   Certified Milk originated in 1893 in response to a need for safe milk. Its certification on the container means that the conditions under which it was produced and distributed conform with the high standards for cleanliness set forth by the American Association of Medical Milk Commissions. These standards have been recognized in many state and local laws. The Grade A Pasteurized Milk Ordinance provides for the sale of certified pasteurized milk derived from certified raw milk.

Certified Milk continues to be available in only a few communities. Where it is available, it may be either raw or pasteurized, though most Certified Milk is now being pasteurized. It also may be homogenized, and may be fortified with Vitamin D.

Soft Curd Milk

For certain uses, it is considered desirable to modify cow's milk so that the curd tension is considerably less, and the curd formed in digestion is softer. In digestion, the curd formed from soft curd milk tends to leave the stomach more quickly than does the curd of ordinary milk.

Commercial Preparation.   Soft curd milk may be produced by homogenization, by enzymatic treatment, by sonic vibration, by ion-exchange, and by addition of various salts. Now that almost all fresh fluid milk sold is homogenized, and thus has a soft curd, the product labeled ''soft curd milk,'' prepared by the other processes, is seldom seen.

Home Preparation.   For infant formulas, softening the curd may be accomplished, depending on the doctor's recommendation, by dilution, by heating, or by acidification. Boiling for one minute usually brings the curd tension of ordinary milk into the soft curd class.

Low Sodium Milk

Ninety percent or more of the sodium that occurs naturally in milk can be removed by a process of ion-exchange. Fresh whole milk is passed through an ion-exchange resin to replace the sodium in milk with potassium. The milk is pasteurized and homogenized.

During the ion-exchange process, some B-vitamins and calcium are lost. Despite this loss, low-sodium milk has special use in certain sodium-restricted diets. It permits the inclusion of milk and other protein foods that may otherwise have to be severely limited because of their high sodium content. Low-sodium milk is available in various parts of the country as a dry, canned, or fresh product.

Fortified Milks

Fortified milks are those containing added amounts of one or more of the essential nutrients normally present in milk.

Vitamin D Milk. The Council on Foods and Nutrition of the American Medical Association recognized the fortification of milk with Vitamin D as being of public health significance.

Food in general does not contain appreciable quantities of Vitamin D. Its primary source is the action of sunlight on the skin. A small but not physiologically significant amount occurs normally in milk. However, milk is the only food the Council on Foods and Nutrition of the American Medical Association has approved for fortification with Vitamin D. Milk provides the proportion of calcium and phosphorus that must be present with Vitamin D for normal calcification of bones and teeth.

To meet the requirements for acceptance by that Council, Vitamin D milk must contain 400 International Units of Vitamin D per quart, usually added in the form of a concentrate. The fortification of a large proportion of the fresh milk, and almost all evaporated milk with Vitamin D has contributed to the decline in the incidence of rickets, once a common scourge of infancy.

Multiple Fortified Milk. Milk can be fortified with substances such as Vitamins A, D, multi-vitamin preparations, minerals, lactose, and nonfat dry milk. The substance added, and the amount of fortification, will vary depending on the dairy company. The dairy company, in turn, conforms to the state standards for multiple fortified milk, where these standards exist. Usually the products and amounts added must be declared on the label. Fortified milks will also vary in fat content. They can be made with whole, partially skimmed, or skim milk.

Concentrated Milks

Concentrated milks may be fresh, frozen, evaporated, condensed, or dried. Milks are concentrated by removal of varying amounts of water under carefully controlled conditions of heat and vacuum. All may be reconstituted by the addition of appropriate quantities of water.

Concentrated Fresh Milk. Fresh whole milk is concentrated by first pasteurizing and homogenizing, and then removing two-thirds of the water under vacuum. This 3:1 concentrate, standardized to about 10.5 percent milk fat, is rehomogenized, repasteurized, and packaged. Although perishable, concentrated fresh milk may retain its flavor and sweetness for as long as six weeks stored at near freezing temperature. This milk is available in only a few communities.

Concentrated Frozen Milk. To increase the keeping quality of fresh concentrated milk, it may be quickly frozen and held at $-10°$ to $-20°F$ for several months. Like other frozen foods, it must be used soon after defrosting. This milk, too, is available in only a few communities.

Concentrated Canned Milk. Considerable research is underway on the production of a concentrated, sterilized milk, aseptically packaged in cans. The product will keep three months on the shelf, or six months if refrigerated.

Evaporated Milk.   In the manufacture of evaporated milk, slightly more than half of the water is removed by heating pasteurized whole milk at 122° to 131°F in vacuum pans. After evaporation, the milk is homogenized, and usually Vitamin D is added to provide 400 I.U. per reconstituted quart. The evaporated milk is sealed in cans, and sterilized at about 239°F for 15 minutes, thus preventing bacterial spoilage. A can of evaporated milk requires no refrigeration until opened.

Condensed Milk.   In the preparation of condensed milk, sugar is added to the milk before the evaporation process is initiated. This milk contains not less than 28.0 percent milk solids and 8.3 percent milk fat. The sugar, which represents about 40 to 45 percent of the condensed milk, acts as a preservative. The milk, sealed in cans can be stored without further heat treatment and without refrigeration.

Dry Milk Nonfat.   Nonfat dry milk is made of fresh whole milk from which both water and fat have been removed. After the fat has been removed, the skim milk is pasteurized and about two-thirds of the water removed under vacuum. This concentrated skim milk is dried by spraying it into a chamber of hot, filtered air. The resulting product is a fine-textured powder of very low moisture content.

A further step, the instantizing process, produces a dry milk that dissolves in water instantly. By one method, the dry milk is moistened with steam, then redried. Except for small losses in ascorbic acid, Vitamin B_{12}, and biotin, the processing has no appreciable effect on the nutritive value. The presence of the milk fat does require special packaging to prevent oxidation during storage.

Skim Milk

Skim milk is milk from which fat has been removed by centrifugation to reduce its milk fat content to less than that of whole milk. In the skim milk ordinarily available, the fat content is 0.1 percent, although it may be lower or higher. Various states have established standards ranging from 8.0 to 9.25 percent as the minimum for the total solids in skim milk. The product is pasteurized.

With the exception of milk fat and the Vitamin A contained in the milk, fat, the other nutrients of milk—the protein, lactose, minerals, and water-soluble vitamins—remain for the most part in the skim milk.

Because the Vitamin A of whole milk is removed with the fat, a water-soluble Vitamin A and D concentrate is frequently added to skim milk. Such fortified skim milk often contains 2000 I.U. of Vitamin A and 400 I.U. of Vitamin D per quart. However, the amounts may vary as discussed under *Fortified Milks*. Fortified skim milk may also contain additional milk solids-not-fat.

Two Percent Milk

As its name implies, two percent milk contains 2 percent milk fat. Made from fresh whole and skim milk, two percent milk is pasteurized and homogenized. It may be enriched by adding milk solids-not-fat and various vitamin and mineral preparations.

Cultured Milks

Cultured milks are prepared from pasteurized (or sterilized) milk. Certain desirable bacterial cultures, whose growth under controlled conditions of sanitation, inoculation, and temperature yield a variety of milks, have been added. These fermented milks may exert a favorable influence on the flora of the intestinal tract.

Buttermilk.   Commercially produced buttermilk is a cultured product. Today it is not the by-product from churning cream into butter. Most of the cultured buttermilk marketed in the United States is made of fresh skim milk. However, cultured buttermilk may be made from fresh, fluid whole milk, concentrated fluid milk (whole or skim), or reconstituted, nonfat dry milk.

Pasteurized skim milk is cultured chiefly with *Streptococcus lactis* and incubated at 68° to 72°F until the acidity is 0.8 to 0.9 percent, expressed as lactic acid. The result is a milk with characteristic tangy flavor and smooth, rich body. Butter granules are sometimes added in an amount to produce a buttermilk testing one or less-than-one percent milk fat. The concentration of milk solids-not-fat is similar to that of whole milk.

Acidophilus Milk.   Pasteurized skim milk, cultured with *Lactobacillus acidophilus*, and incubated at 100°F, is called acidophilus milk. This tart milk, available in only a few communities, is sometimes used to combat excessive intestinal putrefaction by changing the bacterial flora of the intestine. As a therapeutic product, its use may be prescribed after antibiotic treatment to help reestablish a normal balance of bacterial flora in the intestine.

Yogurt.   Possessing a consistency resembling custard, yogurt is usually manufactured from fresh, partially skimmed milk, enriched with added milk solids-not-fat. Fermentation is accomplished by a mixed culture of one or more strains of organisms, as *Streptococcus thermophilus, Bacterium Bulgaricum,* and *Plocamo-bacterium yoghourtii.* The milk is pasteurized and homogenized, inoculated and incubated at 112° to 115°F. The final product has a tangy flavor, and contains between 11 and 12 percent milk solids. It is available in varied flavors.

Effects of Fermentation.   In fermented milks, changes due to bacterial growth include formation of lactic acid from lactose, and coagulation of the milk protein, casein. Bacterial enzyme action on protein and fat constituents, plus the effect of the increased concentration of acid, changes the physical properties and chemical structure of the milk.

A thicker body and a pleasing flavor and aroma are developed in the finished product that varies with the type of culture and kind of milk used, the concentration of milk fat and milk solids-not-fat, the fermentation process, and the temperature at which it is carried out. Some alteration in the vitamin concentration may occur, but there is no evidence of major changes in these nutrients. These products are said to promote biological synthesis of vitamins within the small intestine.

Flavored Milks and Milk Drinks

A flavored milk is whole milk with syrup or powder containing a wholesome flavoring agent, and sugar added. A flavored milk drink or dairy drink, is skim or partially skimmed milk similarly flavored and sweetened. These milks are pasteurized, and usually homogenized.

Chocolate Milk.   Whole milk flavored with a chocolate syrup or powder is called chocolate milk. Usually its milk fat content is the same as for whole milk, and it contains 1 percent cocoa or 1½ percent liquid chocolate, plus 5 percent sugar, and less than 1 percent stabilizers.

Chocolate Dairy Drink.   Skim or partially skimmed milk flavored with a chocolate syrup or powder is called chocolate dairy drink. Frequently its milk fat content is about 2.3 percent and its milk solids-not-fat about 90 percent of the amount in skim milk. Otherwise, it contains the same ingredients as chocolate milk and is processed in the same manner.

Food Value.   Research indicates that the addition of normal quantities of good grade chocolate has no appreciable effect upon the availability of either the calcium or protein of milk to human beings. Therefore, the nutritive value of milk is not significantly altered by the addition of this flavoring, except in regard to the increased caloric value, chiefly from the added sugar. The sugar and chocolate content bring the caloric value of chocolate dairy drink made of skim milk to a slightly higher level than that of plain whole milk, but to a lower level than the chocolate milk.

Canned Whole Milk

Whole milk that is homogenized, sterilized at 270° to 280°F for 8 to 10 seconds, and canned aseptically, is available chiefly for use on ships or for export. It can be stored at room temperature until opened, after which it requires refrigeration.

Frozen Whole Milk

Homogenized, pasteurized, whole milk can be quickly frozen and kept below −10°F for 6 weeks to 3 months. Like concentrated frozen milk, it must be used soon after defrosting. This milk, used on ships and at overseas military installations is not ordinarily available in retail markets.

Freezing does not measurably change the nutritive value of milk. Freezing causes a destabilization of the protein, however, and particles of precipitated protein may be visible on the glass when the milk thaws. On thawing, there is also a tendency for the fat to separate. Milk that has been accidentally frozen (on the doorstep in winter, for example) is quite safe to use. It is a wise precaution to boil the milk for all uses if, during freezing, the cap has been pushed out of the bottle.

**GRADE AND QUALITY SHIELDS FOR CONSUMER PACKAGES
OF DAIRY PRODUCTS MANUFACTURED UNDER THE
GRADING AND QUALITY CONTROL SERVICE. QUALITY
APPROVED SHIELD FOR CULTURED BUTTERMILK AND
CULTURED SOUR CREAM MEANS THESE PRODUCTS WERE
MANUFACTURED AND PACKAGED UNDER USDA'S GRADING
AND QUALITY CONTROL SERVICE.**

Dried Milk and Dried Buttermilk

Milk is dried (water removed) either by spraying through the air into a drying chamber (spray process) or by rolling inside a heated drum (roller method).

The Federal Grades for dried milks are U.S. Premium, U.S. Extra and U.S. Standard, with U.S. Premium applying only to dry whole milk. U.S. Premium may have "slight cooked flavors" and lumps that do not break up under "slight pressure"; U.S. Extra may have "definite cooked flavors" and lumps that do not break up under "moderate pressure"; U.S. Standard may have "definite scorched and storage flavors" and lumps that do not break up under "moderate pressure" as well as a moderate amount of brown and black scorched particles which are not allowed in the other grades.

Dry Whole Milk

"Dry whole milk" (made by the spray process or the atmospheric roller process) is the product resulting from the removal of water from milk. It contains the lactose, milk proteins, milk fat, and milk minerals in the same relative proportions as in the fresh milk from which made.

The term "milk" means milk produced by healthy cows and pasteurized at a temperature of 161°F for 15 seconds, or its equivalent in bacterial destruction, before or during the manufacture of the dry whole milk.

Nonfat Dry Milk

Basis for determination of U.S. grades of nonfat dry milk are determined on the basis of flavor and odor, physical appearance, bacterial estimate on the basis of standard

Kind	Maximum Bacterial Estimate per gram	Minimum Butterfat Content %	Maximum Coliform Count per gram	Maximum Moisture Content %
Dry Whole Milk—U.S. Premium	30,000	26	90	2.25
U.S. Extra	50,000	26	no req.	2.50
U.S. Standard	100,000	26	no req.	3.00
Nonfat Dry Milk—Roller Process				
U.S. Extra	50,000	1.25 max	no req.	4.00
U.S. Standard	100,000	1.50 max	no req.	5.00
Nonfat Dry Milk—Spray Process				
U.S. Extra	50,000	1.25 max	no req.	4.00
U.S. Standard	100,000	1.50 max	—	5.00
Instant Nonfat Dry Milk				
U.S. Extra	80,000	1.25 milk-fat max	10	—
Dry Buttermilk— U.S. Extra	50,000	4.50	—	4.0
U.S. Standard	200,000	4.50	—	5.0

plate count, butterfat content, moisture content, scorched particle content, solubility index, and titratable acidity.

The final U.S. grade is established on the basis of the lowest rating of any one of the quality characteristics.

Instant Nonfat Dry Milk

Instant nonfat dry milk is nonfat dry milk which has been produced in such a manner as to improve substantially its dispersing and reliquefication characteristics over those produced by the conventional processes.

"Nonfat dry milk" is the product resulting from the removal of fat and water from milk, and contains the lactose, milk proteins, and milk minerals in the same relative proportion as in the fresh milk from which it is made.

NONFAT DRY MILK

Dry Buttermilk

"Dry buttermilk" (made by the spray process or the atmospheric roller process) is the product resulting from drying liquid buttermilk, derived from the manufacture of sweet cream butter to which no alkali or other chemical has been added, and which has been pasteurized either before or during the process of manufacture, at a temperature of 161°F for 15 seconds, or its equivalent in bacterial destruction.

FROZEN DESSERTS

Manufacturers of ice cream may now use a USDA symbol to indicate that their product lives up to USDA standards for ingredients and composition. A regulation published in October, 1977, states that a manufacturer who wants (it is voluntary) to use the symbol may do so if: (1) the manufacturing plant is a USDA-approved plant; (2) the dairy ingredients used come from a USDA-approved plant; and (3) the ice cream is produced according to the USDA standard of composition under continuous inspection by USDA dairy inspectors. The symbol is a rectangular box, containing the words: "Meets USDA Ingredient Standard for Ice Cream."

The USDA standards of composition and symbol were mandated by Congress in the Food and Agriculture Act of 1977, so that consumers could distinguish between ice cream made with and without caseinates. Under the USDA standard, ice cream must contain: (1) at least 1.6 lb. total solids per gallon and weigh at least 4.5 lb. per gallon; and (2) at least 20 percent total milk solids, constituted of at least 10 percent milk fat and at least 6 percent milk-solids-not fat. Whey, by weight, can be no more than 25 percent of the milk-solids-not fat.

Ice Milk

- Milkfat: 2.0 percent minimum, 7.0 percent maximum
- Total milk solids: 11.0 percent minimum
- Stabilizer: 0.5 percent maximum
- Weight per gallon: 4.5 lb. minimum
- Food solids per gallon: 1.3 lb. minimum

Fruit, Nut, or Chocolate Ice Milk (and Bulky flavors)

- Milkfat: 2.0 percent minimum, 7.0 percent maximum
- Total milk solids: 11.0 percent minimum
- Stabilizer: 0.5 percent maximum
- Weight per gallon: 4.5 lb. minimum
- Food solids per gallon: 1.3 lb. minimum

Sherbet (Milk)

- Milkfat: 1.0 percent minimum, 2.0 percent maximum
- Total milk solids: 2.0 percent minimum, 5.0 percent maximum
- Acid: 0.35 percent minimum
- Stabilizer: 0.5 percent maximum
- Weight per gallon: 6.0 lb. minimum

Artifically Sweetened Ice Milk—Plain

- Milkfat: No standard. State standards may vary from 2.0 to 7.0 percent minimum and 4.99 to 8.0 percent maximum where they exist
- Total milk solids: No standard. State standards may vary from 10.0 to 30.0 percent minimum where they exist
- Stabilizer: No standard. State standards are 0.5 percent maximum where they exist.
- Artificial sweetener: No standard. Illegal in a few states
- Edible carbohydrates: No standard. Illegal in a few states
- Weight per gallon: No standard. State standards may vary from 4.2 to 4.5 lb minimum where they exist
- Food solids per gallon: No standard. State standards are 1.0 or 1.3 lb. minimum where they exist

Artificially Sweetened Ice Milk—Fruit, Nuts, Chocolate

- Milkfat: No standard. State standards may vary from 2.0 to 7.0 percent minimum and 4.99 to 8.0 percent maximum where they exist
- Total milk solids: No standard. State standards may vary from 10.8 to 30.0 percent minimum where they exist
- Stabilizer: No standard. State standards are .05 percent maximum where they exist
- Artificial sweetener: No standard. Illegal in a few states
- Edible carbohydrates: No standard. Illegal in a few states
- Weight per gallon: No standard. State standards may vary from 4.2 to 4.5 lb. minimum where they exist
- Food solids per gallon: No standard. State standards are 1.3 lb. minimum where they exist

Plain Ice Cream

- Milkfat: 10.0 percent minimum
- Total milk solids: 20.0 percent minimum
- Stabilizer: 0.5 percent maximum
- Weight per gallon: 4.5 lb. minimum
- Food solids per gallon: 1.6 lb. minimum

Fruit, Nut, or Chocolate Ice Cream (and Bulky Flavors)

- Milkfat: 8.0 percent minimum
- Total milk solids: 16.0 percent minimum
- Stabilizer: 0.5 percent maximum
- Weight per gallon: 4.5 lb. minimum
- Food solids per gallon: 1.6 lb. minimum

Artificially Sweetened Ice Cream—Plain

- Milkfat: No standard. State standards may vary from 6.0 to 12.0 percent minimum where they exist
- Total milk solids: No standard. State standards may vary from 18.0 to 20.0 percent minimum where standards exist
- Stabilizer: No standard. State standards are 0.5 or 0.6 percent minimum where they exist
- Artificial sweetener: No standard. Illegal in some states
- Edible Carbohydrates: No standard. Illegal in some states
- Weight per gallon: No standard. State standards may vary from 4.2 to 4.5 lb. minimum where standards exist
- Food solids per gallon: No standard. State standards may vary from 1.6 to 1.8 lb. minimum where standards exist

Artificially Sweetened Ice Cream—Fruit, Nuts or Chocolate

- Milkfat: No standard. State standards may vary from 7.0 to 10.0 percent minimum where they exist
- Total milk solids: No standard. State standards may vary from 14.0 to 20.0 percent minimum where they exist
- Stabilizer: No standard. State standards are 0.5 or 0.6 percent maximum where standards exist
- Artificial sweetener: No standard. Illegal in some states
- Edible carbohydrates: No standard. Illegal in some states
- Weight per gallon: No standard. State standards may vary from 4.2 to 4.5 lb. minimum where they exist
- Food solids per gallon: No standard. State standards are 1.6 lb. minimum where they exist

Frozen Custard

- Milkfat: 10.0 percent minimum
- Total milk solids: 20.0 percent minimum
- Stabilizer: 0.5 percent maximum
- Weight per gallon: 4.5 lb. minimum
- Food solids per gallon: 1.6 lb. minimum

- Egg yolks, per 90 lb.: No standard. State standards may vary from 1.5 to 5.0 dozen minimum where they exist
- Solids: 1.4 percent minimum

Frozen Dessert—Mellorine Type

- Fat, animal or vegetable: No standard. State standards may vary from 6.0 to 10.0 percent minimum where they exist
- Milk solids-not-fat: No standard. State standards may vary from 10.0 to 20.0 percent minimum where they exist
- Stabilizer: No standard. State standards may vary from 0.5 to 1.0 percent maximum where they exist
- Weight per gallon: No standard. State standards are 4.5 lb. minimum where they exist
- Food solids per gallon: No standard. State standards may vary from 1.3 to 1.6 lb. minimum where they exist

Milk Shake Mix

- Milkfat: No standard. State standards may vary from 2.0 to 4.0 percent minimum where they exist
- Total milk solids: No standard. State standards may vary from 10.0 to 25.0 percent minimum where they exist

QUESTIONS

1. Define the following terms.

ripen	acidophilus milk
curd	casein
starter	coagulation temperature
rennet	whey
raw milk	aging period
fortified milk	homogenized
concentrated	ultra-pasteurized
yogurt	

2. Describe the procedure used in grading butter.
3. Distinguish the importance of the aroma of butter prior to tasting. What effect does the temperature of the butter have on flavor and aroma?
4. Discuss the factors that influence the texture and spreadability of butter.
5. Name the four grades of butter discussed in this chapter and the general characteristics of each.
6. What is the primary difference between butter and margarine?
7. How is the fat content altered in the production of cheese?

8. What is the function of bacteria in cheese production?
9. List the advantages of using pasteurized milk in cheese.
10. What is the significance of propioni bacterium shermanii on Swiss cheese?
11. The length of the aging period effects the texture of cheese in what?
12. Describe the milk pasteurization process.
13. What are the standards for whole milk, i.e., milk fat and milk solids?
14. List the ingredients added to fortified milk.
15. Dried milk is graded according to three federal grades. Name them.
16. How is dry milk produced?
17. Under what conditions may manufacturers of ice cream use the USDA symbol?
18. Ice cream (USDA standard) contains what minimum percent of milk fat? Ice milk?

9

FISH AND SHELLFISH

INTRODUCTION

Grade standards for fishery products have been established by the Bureau of Commercial Fisheries, U.S. Department of the Interior. Quality grades for fishery products may be Grades A, B, C, and Substandard.

This chapter discusses grade and inspection standards for fish and shellfish. In addition, the various market forms of each product are listed with recommended preparation methods.

Quality acceptance standards are extremely important in fish and shellfish due to limited holding qualities and rapid deterioration when dead. The flesh and fish should appear pink, and the eyes should be bright and clear. It is recommended to purchase crabs, lobster, clams, and oysters fresh to insure the highest quality.

There are many fish products on the market with varying degrees of fish flesh. These products are usually made of cod, haddock, whiting, and pollock. Methods for sampling these ratios of fish flesh to breading are indicated. An encyclopedia of seafood information completes this chapter. This list includes various names for seafood, areas where it may be found, general characteristics, and the various market forms.

INSPECTION, STANDARDS, AND GRADES

The U.S. Department of the Interior, through the Bureau of Commercial Fisheries, makes available an official inspection service for all types of processed fishery products: fresh, frozen, canned, and cured. The service is voluntary, offered upon a fee-for-service basis.

Under continuous inspection, one or more inspectors are assigned to a processing plant whenever it is operating. They make continuous checks on quality of the raw product, as well as plant conditions under which the product is being prepared, processed, and packed. This service is made available only if the plant meets rigid sanitary requirements for facilities, equipment, and raw material.

Products packed in any plant operated under the continuous inspection program, and in compliance with USDI inspection regulations, may be labeled with the official USDI inspection shield which carries the statement ''Packed Under Continuous Inspection of the U.S. Department of the Interior.''

Grade standards have been established by the Bureau of Commercial Fisheries, U.S. Department of the Interior, for a total of 15 processed fishery products.

Quality grades for fishery products are Grade A, B, C, and substandard. The grade most widely sold in the stores is Grade A. It is produced in the greatest volume and retailers have found that this high quality product pleases their customers.

Grade A means top or best quality. Grade A products are uniform in size, practically free from blemishes and defects, and possess a good flavor.

Grade B means good quality. Grade B products may not be as uniform in size or as free from blemishes or defects as Grade A products. This grade may be termed a general commercial grade, and is quite suitable for most purposes.

Grade C means fairly good quality. Grade C products are just as wholesome and may be as nutritious as the higher grades. They have a definite value as a thrifty buy for use in dishes where appearance may not be quite so important.

If a product carries a grade label A, B, or C, it must meet quality requirements of the USDI Grade Standards. Any fishery products packed under continuous in-plant inspection of the U.S. Department of the Interior are permitted to use the prefix ''U.S.'' with the grade designation, such as U.S. Grade A.

Grade Standards:

1. Reflect different quality levels of products.
2. Form a basis for sales and purchases.
3. Provide guidelines for in-plant quality control.
4. Establish a basis for official inspection.

Many brand-name fishery products carry either one or both inspection marks on their labels. The following is a list of fish and shellfish products made from a variety of species of fish, which presently bear inspection marks.

- Frozen Raw Fish Fillets, Portions, and Sticks
- Frozen Fried Fish Fillets, Portions, and Sticks
- Fresh or Frozen Whole or Dressed Fish
- Frozen Raw Breaded Shrimp
- Frozen Whole Cooked Crabs and Crabmeat
- Fried Fish Seafood Cakes
- Raw and Fried Fish Dinners
- Fried Clams and Clam Cake Dinners
- Fried Scallops and Fried Scallop Dinners
- Raw and Raw Breaded Scallops
- Frozen Fish Steaks
- Raw Peeled and Deveined Shrimp
- Cooked Crabmeat, Legs, and Claws
- Fish and Shellfish in Sauce Dinners

SPECIFICATIONS

Fish and shellfish are sold in many different forms or cuts. Learning to recognize these forms, and how best to use them, is very important in buying and serving fish and shellfish. Unless otherwise stated, most market forms of fish and shellfish are available both fresh and frozen, are usually sold by weight, and are ready to cook, heat, or serve as purchased.

Market Forms of Fish

In this country "fish" means fin fish. There are many different market forms of fish.

Whole fish are sold just as they come from the water. Before cooking, the fish must be scaled, eviscerated, and usually the head, tail, and fins are removed. Some small fish, like smelt, are often cooked with only their entrails removed.

Dressed fish are scaled, eviscerated, and sometimes the head, tail, and fins removed. The smaller size fish are called *pan-dressed*.

Steaks are cross-section slices from a large dressed fish cut ⅝ to 1 inch thick. A cross section of the backbone is usually the only bone in a steak. *Chunks* are cross-sections of a large dressed fish. A cross section of the backbone is usually the only bone in a chunk.

Single fillets, the most common type, are the sides of the fish cut lengthwise away from the backbone. They are practically boneless and may or may not be skinned. *Butterfly fillets* are the two sides of the fish cut lengthwise away from the backbone and held together by the uncut flesh and skin of the belly. These fillets are practically boneless.

Frozen raw or fried breaded fish portions are cut from frozen fish blocks, coated with a batter, breaded, packaged, and frozen. Portions weigh more than 1½ ounces and are at least ⅜ inch thick. Raw portions must contain not less than 75 percent and fried por-

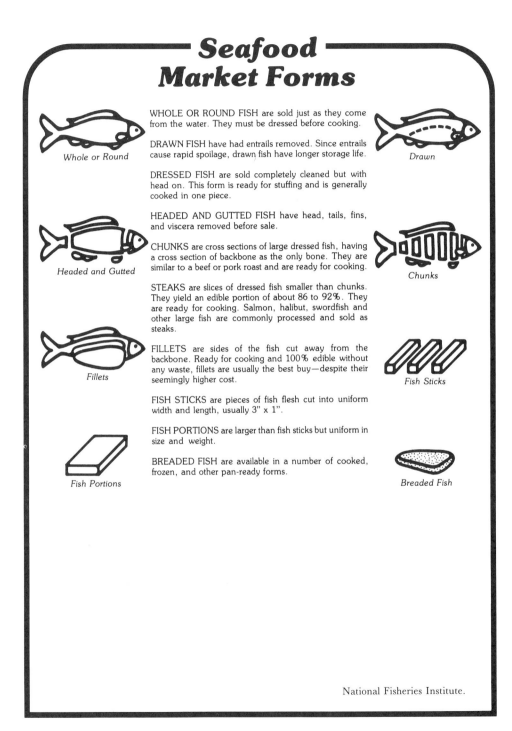

Seafood Market Forms

Whole or Round

Drawn

Headed and Gutted

Chunks

Fillets

Fish Sticks

Fish Portions

Breaded Fish

WHOLE OR ROUND FISH are sold just as they come from the water. They must be dressed before cooking.

DRAWN FISH have had entrails removed. Since entrails cause rapid spoilage, drawn fish have longer storage life.

DRESSED FISH are sold completely cleaned but with head on. This form is ready for stuffing and is generally cooked in one piece.

HEADED AND GUTTED FISH have head, tails, fins, and viscera removed before sale.

CHUNKS are cross sections of large dressed fish, having a cross section of backbone as the only bone. They are similar to a beef or pork roast and are ready for cooking.

STEAKS are slices of dressed fish smaller than chunks. They yield an edible portion of about 86 to 92%. They are ready for cooking. Salmon, halibut, swordfish and other large fish are commonly processed and sold as steaks.

FILLETS are sides of the fish cut away from the backbone. Ready for cooking and 100% edible without any waste, fillets are usually the best buy—despite their seemingly higher cost.

FISH STICKS are pieces of fish flesh cut into uniform width and length, usually 3" x 1".

FISH PORTIONS are larger than fish sticks but uniform in size and weight.

BREADED FISH are available in a number of cooked, frozen, and other pan-ready forms.

National Fisheries Institute.

CUTS AND SHAPES OF PREPARED FISH

Aberdeen Cut	Rhombus shape, cut from block, sides squared or tapered.
American Cut	Tapered or beveled edges of fish portions, or fillets.
Bits	Also known as bites, nuggets, cubes—small pieces of fish from blocks less than ½ to 1 oz., each in square, round, or irregular shapes.
Cakes	Rounded, flat cakes of minced or ground fish, usually breaded.
Chunks	Large pieces, cross-section slices, similar to steaks.
Custom Cut	Same as Aberdeen Cut.
Diamond Cut	Same as Aberdeen Cut.
Fillet	Boneless piece of fish cut lengthwise from backbone. With/without skin. Butterflied fillets are two sides of fish held together by skin and flesh of back. Natural cut is cut from block.
Fish 'n' Cheese	Portion topped with cheese, or may be combined with fish.
French Cut	Same as Aberdeen Cut.
Portion	Usually a square or rectangle, cut from block, 1½ to 6 oz., breaded or unbreaded, raw or precooked. *Grated fish portions* is term used for portions made from mechanically separated fish flesh.

tions not less than 65 percent fish flesh, according to USDI standards. They may be purchased raw or partially cooked.

Frozen fried sticks are cut from frozen fish blocks, coated with a batter, breaded, partially cooked, packaged, and frozen. Fried fish sticks weigh up to 1½ ounces, must be at least ⅜ inch thick, and contain not less than 60 percent fish flesh, according to USDI standards.

Canned fish include a great variety of convenience and specialty items as well as the ever popular tuna, salmon, and Maine sardines.

Tuna is packed from six species. The catch includes albacore, blackfin, bluefin, skipjack, yellowfin, and little tuna. Albacore has lighter meat than the others and is the only tuna permitted to be labeled ''white meat'' tuna. The other species are labeled ''light meat'' tuna. Canned tuna is packed in oil or water. In descending order of price, the packs of tuna are: solid, chunk, and flaked or grated.

Salmon is packed from five species. Canned salmon is usually sold by the name of the fish since there is a difference in the color, texture, and flavor of the salmon. Higher priced varieties are deeper red in color and have a higher oil content. In descending order of price, the packs of salmon are: red or sockeye; chinook or king; medium red, silver, or coho; pink; and chum or keta.

Cured fish are processed from many different species. Some of the more common cured fish on the market are pickled and spiced herring; salt cod and salmon; smoked chubs, salmon, and whitefish; as well as many convenience and specialty items.

Market Forms of Shellfish

In the United States, ''shellfish'' means crustaceans and mollusks. The crustaceans include crabs, lobsters, and shrimp. Clams, oysters, and scallops are mollusks.

Clams.   Several species of clams are widely used for food. On the Atlantic coast, they are the hard, soft, and surf clams. On the Pacific coast, the most common species are the butter, littleneck, razor, and pismo clams. The hard clams, or hard-shell clams, are commonly called ''quahog'' in New England, where ''clam'' generally means the soft-shell variety. Littlenecks and cherrystones are the trade names for the smaller-sized hard clams generally served raw on the half shell. The larger sizes of hard, soft, and surf clams are called ''chowders'' and are used mainly for chowders and soups. Clams are sold by the dozen or by weight.

Clams in the shell are just as they come from the water. Fresh clams should be alive when purchased and the shells should close tightly when tapped. Shucked clams are the meat removed from the shells. The meat is pale to deep orange in color and has a fresh, mild odor. Fresh shucked clams are packed in little or no liquid.

Frozen raw or fried breaded clams are shucked clams coated with a batter, breaded, packaged, and frozen. They may be purchased raw or partially cooked. Canned clams are available whole, minced, or in chowder, bouillon, broth, and nectar.

Crabs.   The three principal species of crabs are the blue, Dungeness, and king. Blue crabs come from the Atlantic and Gulf coasts and weigh from ¼ to 1 pound. Dungeness crabs are from the Pacific coast and weigh from 1¼ to 2½ pounds. King crabs come from the coast of Alaska and weigh from 6 to 20 pounds. A big king crab can easily measure 6 feet across from the tip of one leg to the tip of the opposite leg. Growing in popularity are the stone crabs from Florida and the tanner crabs from Alaska.

Crabs in the shell are sold fresh, frozen, or cooked. Fresh crabs should be alive and active when purchased. Cooked crabs are bright red and have a mild odor. Blue crabs are sold by the dozen, and Dungeness crabs are sold individually.

Soft-shell crabs are molting blue crabs just after they have shed their shells and before the new shells have hardened. They are sold just as they come from the water. They should be alive and active when purchased.

Frozen crab legs are the legs of cooked king and tanner crabs which have been frozen and split or cut into sections. The meat is white with an attractive red tint on the outside.

Crab meat is the meat removed from cooked crabs. The meat is packed and chilled, frozen, pasteurized, or canned. The body meat from Dungeness crab is white and the claw meat has a brownish-red tint on the outside. King crab meat is primarily leg meat. It is white with an attractive reddish tint on the outside.

In descending order of price, the packs of blue crab are: Lump meat, whole lumps of white meat from the two body muscles which operate the swimming legs; flake meat, small pieces of white meat from the body; flake and lump, a combination of the first two kinds; and claw meat, brownish tinted meat from the claws.

Lobsters.   Northern lobsters are caught in the cold waters off the coast of Maine and Massachusetts. Off the coasts of California and Florida another shellfish is caught which is known locally as ''lobster.'' More properly, it is a spiny or rock lobster. The large, heavy claws of the northern lobsters distinguish them from the spiny lobsters, which have no claws. Lobsters usually weigh from ¾ to 4 pounds.

The market sizes of lobsters are:

1. Chicken: ¾ to 1 pound
2. Quarters: 1¼ to 1½ pounds
3. Large: 1½ to 2½ pounds
4. Jumbo: Over 3 pounds

Lobsters in the shell are sold fresh, frozen, or cooked. The fresh lobster should be alive and active when purchased. The "tail" of a live lobster curls under the body and does not hang down when the lobster is picked up. Cooked lobsters should be bright red and have a fresh, mild odor.

Frozen spiny lobster tails are spiny lobsters with their heads removed, graded according to size, and frozen. Spiny lobster tails should have clean, white meat and no odor. The average market size of spiny lobster tails is 2 to 8 ounces.

Lobster meat is the meat removed from cooked lobsters. The meat is packed and chilled, frozen, or canned. It is white with an attractive reddish tint on the outside.

Oysters. The three principal species of oysters are the Eastern, Pacific, and Western. Eastern oysters are found or cultivated from Massachusetts to Texas. The large Pacific oysters and small Western oysters are found or cultivated from Washington to Mexico.

Oysters in the shell are sold just as they come from the water. They should be alive when purchased. The shells should close tightly when tapped. Live oysters are sold by the dozen.

Shucked oysters are oysters removed from the shells; they should be plump and have a natural creamy color and clear liquid. Shucked oysters have a fresh, mild odor and are packed in little or no liquid. Avoid oysters with an excessive amount of liquid because this indicates poor quality and careless handling. Shucked oysters are graded according to their size.

Frozen raw or fried breaded oysters are shucked oysters coated with a batter, breaded, packaged, and frozen. They are available raw or partially cooked. Canned oysters are available on the market whole and as stew.

Scallops. Many people are not aware that scallops are a shellfish—a mollusk with two shells, similar to the clams and oysters. In at least one respect, however, scallops differ from clams and oysters because they are active swimmers, moving freely through the water and over the ocean floor. Actively snapping its shells together provides locomotion for the scallop and results in development of an oversized muscle that's called the adductor muscle. This excellently flavored muscle is the only part eaten by Americans.

The two principal species of scallops on the market are bay and sea. Large sea scallops are taken from the deep waters of the North and Middle Atlantic. The sea scallop's shell is saucer shaped and sometimes grows as large as 8 inches across. The adductor muscle may be as large as 2 inches across. Small bay scallops are taken from inshore bays and estuaries from New England to the Gulf of Mexico.

The shell of the bay scallop is much smaller than the sea scallop. Its maximum width is about 4 inches. It resembles the sea scallop in shape except that the shell is grooved and has serrated or scalloped edges. The adductor muscle of the bay scallop is about a half inch across. Increasing in popularity are calico scallops from Florida and sea scallops from Alaska.

Shucked scallops are the adductor muscles removed from the shells. The meat is a creamy white, light tan, orange, or pinkish. Fresh scallops should have a sweetish odor and be packed in little or no liquid. Frozen raw or fried breaded scallops are shucked scallops coated with a batter, breaded, packaged, and frozen. Fried scallops must contain not less than 60 percent scallop meat, according to USDI standards. They are available raw or partially cooked.

Shrimp.   Kinds of shrimp common in the United States are white shrimp, which is greenish-gray; brown or Brazilian shrimp, which is brownish-red; pink or coral shrimp; and Alaska, California, and Maine varieties, which vary in color and are relatively small. Although raw shrimp range in color from greenish-gray to brownish-red, when cooked they all take on an attractive reddish tint. There is very little difference in the appearance and flavor of the cooked shrimp. Shrimp are caught in all our coastal waters from Maine to Alaska, with the bulk of the catch coming from the Gulf. Shrimp are sold according to size, the larger the size the higher the price.

Headless shrimp are, of course, shrimp with the heads removed. They are graded according to size. Fresh shrimp have a fresh, mild odor and firm meat. "Green shrimp" does not refer to the color of the shrimp but is the term used by the trade to describe raw shrimp.

Peeled and cleaned shrimp are headless shrimp with the shell and intestinal tract removed. They may be sold raw or cooked. The cooked shrimp should have an attractive reddish tint and a mild odor. They may be purchased fresh, frozen, and canned.

Frozen raw or fried breaded shrimp are peeled and cleaned shrimp coated with a batter, breaded, packaged, and frozen.

Fresh Fish—Quality Indicators[1]

First look at the eyes. They should be bright, clear, and protruding slightly from the head. If they have sunken into the head, the fish probably is not fresh.

Next look at the gills. They should be bright red or pink. As quality slips, the gills quickly begin to darken.

If the fish is drawn or gutted, turn it over and look at the intestinal cavity, which should be pink and have a fresh clean appearance.

Any fresh fillet or cut of fish should have firm flesh that will spring back when gently pressed with the finger. The skin should be shiny, with a mild, fresh, clean odor.

---

[1]*NOAA Magazine,* (January, 1975).

Crabs and Lobsters

If they are fresh, look for movement of the legs, to ensure that the animals are alive. If they are cooked, look for a bright orangey-red color, and make sure that they have no disagreeable odor.

Clams and Oysters

They should be alive when bought in the shell. If the shells are closed, the shellfish are alive. If the shell is open, tap it gently to see if it closes. If it doesn't, reject it.

Shucked Oysters

Check them for plumpness and to see that they have a natural creamy color and a clear liquid.

Frozen Fishery Products

Make sure that the fish is solidly frozen and has no objectionable odor. It may be glazed (fish processors will sometimes dip the frozen fish into water one or more times, quickly freezing the water, so that the entire fish is covered with an icy glaze that protects the flesh from dehydration). As long as the glaze remains intact and the fish remains frozen, it will keep quite well. If the glaze has melted or is chipped, the unprotected flesh may turn a cottony white. This is freezer burn, and even though the fillet is frozen, the exposed flesh has begun to suffer a cellular breakdown. Reject the fish.

The National Marine Fisheries Service has established criteria for the amount of flesh that must be in the breaded portions in order for the company to use the Grade A shield and inspection mark. Raw breaded portions must have 75 percent flesh; fish sticks, 72 percent; and precooked breaded portions must have 65 percent flesh.

There are two methods that inspectors can use to determine the amount of fish flesh in the stick or portion. They may use the on-line method or the scrape method. If the on-line method is used, inspectors go to the production line and get a completed box of 15 portions. They then go to the front of the line and get 15 portions which have been cut to the proper size but have not been otherwise processed. Inspectors then weigh the portions and use a mathematical formula to determine the percentage of flesh found in the completed portion.

If the scrape method is used, inspectors take samples of the finished breaded product and weigh them. They then scrape the batter and breading from the flesh and weigh the flesh again. By using another formula the inspectors are able to determine the ratio of flesh to breading. If the amount of flesh is below the minimum requirement then additional samples are taken from the line and tested to verify the original results. This retesting is done several times while production corrections are being made.

After the sample has been tested for proper weight and ratio of breading to flesh, it is cooked, split, and checked for odor and taste, and to see that there are no bones or other foreign matter in the portion.

Breaded Shrimp[2]

Frozen raw breaded shrimp are made from whole, clean headless shrimp that have been peeled and deveined. The shrimp are coated with a wholesome batter and/or breading. Shrimp are termed "whole" if they consist of five or more segments of shrimp flesh.

Breaded shrimp are prepared and frozen in accordance with good commercial practice. The frozen product is maintained at temperatures which preserve its quality. Frozen raw breaded shrimp must contain at least 50 percent by weight of shrimp material, according to U.S. standards.

Two styles of frozen raw breaded shrimp are commonly available. "Regular breaded" are frozen raw breaded shrimp containing a minimum of 50 percent of shrimp material. "Lightly breaded" contain a minimum of 65 percent of shrimp material.

Two types of breaded shrimp are marketed: "Breaded Fantail Shrimp" and "Breaded Round Shrimp." Both types are available in three forms which vary in the amount of tail fin and shell segments retained.

Breaded shrimp are graded on a number of factors that affect the quality of the product. The standards are set by the National Marine Fisheries Service, taking into account consumer needs and industry capabilities. In the frozen breaded state, the product is checked for uniformity, condition of coating, damaged breaded shrimp, and extraneous material. Cooked samples are rated for flavor and odor.

"U.S. Grade A" indicates the frozen product scores at least 85 points, based on a numerical scoring system of 100 for a perfect product. When cooked, the product has a good flavor and odor.

"U.S. Grade B" indicates the frozen breaded shrimp score at least 70 points, based on the assigned scoring system. Frozen raw breaded shrimp that fail to meet the requirements of "U.S. Grade B" are graded "Substandard."

Fish Portions and Fish Sticks

Fish portions[3] and fish sticks are generally made of cod, haddock, whiting, or pollock. The prepared products come in frozen, raw, or partially-cooked forms. They are processed in a variety of sizes and shapes for different markets.

Portions and stocks are machine-cut from large, solidly-frozen blocks of fish fillets. The cut pieces are dipped in batter and coated with breading. Most fish sticks and some portions are then partially cooked, rapidly frozen, and packaged. They take only a few minutes to prepare.

Fish portions range in weight from 1 ½ to more than 5 ounces and come in a variety of shapes. One 8- or 10-ounce package usually serves two persons. Raw breaded fish portions are at least ⅜ inch thick and contain at least 75 percent fish. Partially-cooked fish portions are at least ⅜ inch thick and contain at least 65 percent fish.

---

[2]*Food Fish Facts* No. 54, NOAA.
[3]*Food Fish Facts* No. 53, NOAA.

Fried fish sticks are 3 to 4 inches long and weigh up to 1½ ounces. They are at least ⅜ inch thick and contain at least 60 percent fish. An 8-ounce package will usually serve two persons.

Portions and sticks are graded on a number of factors that affect the quality of the products. The standards are set by the National Marine Fisheries Service, taking into account consumer needs and industry capabilities. In the frozen state, the portions and sticks are checked for condition of package, ease of separation, broken or damaged pieces, and uniformity of weight and size. Cooked samples are checked for color, coating, defects, blemishes, flavor, and odor.

"U.S. Grade A" indicates frozen fish portions or fish sticks that possess good flavor and odor for the species and rate a score of at least 85 points, based on a numerical scoring system of 100 for a perfect product.

"U.S. Grade B" indicates frozen fish portions or fish sticks that rate a score of at least 70 points on the assigned scoring system. Portions and sticks failing to meet the requirements of "U.S. Grade B" are graded "Substandard."

QUESTIONS

1. Define:

   Dressed fish   Steak (fish)
   Butterfly fillet   Crustaceans
   Drawn fish   Mollusks
   Round fish

2. Which grade of fish is most appropriate for fish chowder?
3. Give examples of fish products required to bear federal inspection marks.
4. Which variety of tuna would you expect when labeled "white meat" tuna?
5. Which crab is the most economical purchase: Blue or Dungeness?
6. Indicate the purchase unit of the following:

   Fresh lobster   Blue crabs
   Live oysters   Dungeness crab
   Soft-shell crab   Green shrimp

7. Describe the quality of determinants of fresh fish, crabs and lobster, clams and oysters.
8. How could an operator determine that his or her raw breaded fish portions yield 70 percent raw flesh?
9. Distinguish between the following kinds of shrimp: Whole shrimp, Frozen raw breaded shrimp, and Lightly breaded shrimp.
10. What is the difference in the percent fish between raw breaded fish portions and partially cooked fish portions?
11. List the factors for which frozen fish are graded.
12. On a scale of 1 to 100, U.S. Grade A indicates how many points (minimum)?

Other Popular Species and Shellfish

Species	Other Names	Where Caught	Market Forms
Butterfish		Northeastern U.S.	Whole, dressed; smoked
Catfish	Fidler, Blue Channel	Pond raised commercially, Great Lakes, other U.S. lakes, rivers, ponds, creeks, Brazil	Whole, dressed; fresh, frozen
Lake Trout	Togue	Cold water lakes of North America	Whole, drawn, fillets; steaks; fresh, frozen
Mackerel	Atlantic Blue	New England, Norway	Whole; fresh, frozen
Spanish	American	South Atlantic, Gulf	Whole, drawn, fillets; steaks; fresh, frozen
King	Cero, Kingfish	South Atlantic, Gulf, Pacific Coast	Drawn, steaks, fillets; fresh, frozen
Mullet	Striped, White	South Atlantic and Gulf, Mexico	Whole; fillets; fresh, frozen, smoked, salted Mullet dip
Rainbow Trout		Northwestern U.S. (commercial fish farms), Denmark, Japan	Dressed, boned, boned and breaded; fresh, frozen
Sablefish	Black Cod	Pacific Coast	Whole, steaks, fillets, kippered, smoked
Salmon	Red	Pacific Coast, Alaska	
Sockeye	Spring, King	Pacific Coast, Alaska	
Chinook	Silversides, Coho	North Pacific	Dressed, steaks, fillets; fresh, frozen,
Silver	Humpback	Pacific Coast	smoked canned
Pink	Fall	Pacific Coast	
Chub		North Atlantic	
Atlantic			
Sea Herring	Atlantic or Pacific Herring	New England, Middle Atlantic, North Pacific, Iceland, Denmark, Norway, Germany, England, Scotland, Holland, Sweden (virtually worldwide)	Whole, chunks; fresh, salted, pickled, smoked (sardines)
Shad	Buck, Roe or White Shad	Coastal rivers from Maine to Florida, Washington to California	Whole, drawn, fillets, boned; fresh, frozen, smoked, canned. Shad roe: fresh, frozen, canned
Smelt	Whitebait, Surf Smelt, Grunion, Eulachon or Columbia River Smelt, Silverside, Jacksmelt, Bay Smelt	North Atlantic, Pacific Coast, Columbia River, and bays from Mexico to Canada, Great Lakes	Whole, dressed, breaded, pre-cooked; fresh, frozen
Tuna	Albacore, Yellowfin, Skipjack, Blue Fin, Little	Atlantic and Pacific Coasts, Worldwide	Canned, drawn, smoked
Whitefish		Great Lakes, Canada	Whole, drawn, dressed, fillets; frozen, fresh, smoked

Species	Other Names	Where Found	Market Forms
Yellow Perch	Lake Perch, Ringed Perch, Pacific Perch	Great Lakes, Canada; Pacific Coast	Whole, drawn, dressed fillets; butterfly fillets; fresh and frozen
Clams			
Butter		Pacific Coast, Alaska	Live in shell; Shucked, fresh and frozen; Frozen breaded, raw and cooked; Canned
Hard	Hard Shell, Cherry-stones, Quahog	New England, Middle and South Atlantic	
Little Neck		Pacific Coast, Alaska	
Razor		Pacific Coast, Alaska	
Soft	Soft Shell, Skimmer	New England, Middle Atlantic, Pacific	
Surf		Middle Atlantic, Pacific	
*Geoduck	King Clam, Gweduc, Gwee Duk, Gooey-Duck	Washington's Puget Sound, South of Anacortes and in Hood Canal	
*Ocean Quahog	Mahogany and Black Quahog, Mahogany Clam	New England Coast	
Crabs			
Blue		Middle and South Atlantic, Gulf	Live in shell; Fresh or frozen: Cooked meat, sections, claws; Specialties: Frozen breaded, raw or cooked (cakes, patties, devilled, stuffed, etc.); Canned
Dungeness		Pacific Coast, Alaska	
King		Alaska	
Stone		Florida	
Snow	Tanner, Queen	Pacific Coast, Alaska; New England Coast from Maine to Cape Hatteras, North Carolina	
*Jonah			
*Red	Deep Sea Red Crab	New England and Middle Atlantic Coast	
Lobsters			
Northern	Maine Americana	New England, Canada	Live in shell; Fresh or frozen: Cooked meat, cooked whole, tails raw; Canned
Rock		South Africa, Australia, Europe, Australia, North America, South America, Japan, Africa	
Spiny	California Spiny	California Coast, Mexico	
Mussels	Bay Mussels	New England and Middle Atlantic	Live in shell, frozen in sauces, canned
Oysters			
Eastern		New England, Middle and South Atlantic, Gulf	Live in shell; shucked, fresh, frozen; frozen breaded raw or fried, canned, smoked
Pacific	Japanese	Pacific Coast, Japan, Korea	
Olympia	Western	Pacific Coast	
Scallops			
Bay		Middle and South Atlantic, New England, Gulf	Fresh or frozen: Shucked; Frozen breaded, raw or cooked; Specialties
Calico		South Atlantic	
Sea	Alaska Scallops	New England, Alaska, Canada	
Shrimp	Prawn	Worldwide. In U.S.: South Atlantic, Gulf, Alaska, Maine	Fresh or frozen: Raw, headless; Peeled (also de-veined), raw or cooked; Frozen breaded, raw or fried; Cooked whole; Canned; Packaged: split-in-the-shell
*Rock		Mexico, Florida	
Squid	Inkfish, Bone Squid, Sea Arrow, Calamari, Calamary, Flying Squid, Taw Taw	Atlantic, Gulf and Southern California	Frozen; canned

*Available on a regional basis

Piscatorial Primer

	Form	Definition	Preparation	Best Ways to Cook
	FIN FISH: **Whole or round,** **fresh**	Whole fish, just as it comes from the water.	Remove scales and entrails. Head, fins and tail may be removed. Cut into serving size pieces or cook whole.	Bake, poach, broil, fry, steam
	Drawn, **fresh or frozen**	Whole fish, eviscerated.	Scale. Head, fins and tail may be removed. Cut into servings or cook whole.	Bake, poach, broil, fry, steam
	Dressed or **pan-dressed,** **fresh or frozen**	Ready to cook.	Cut into steaks or fillets, if you wish.	Bake, poach, broil, fry, steam
	Steaks, **fresh or frozen**	Cross-section cuts of large fish.	None	Bake, poach, broil, fry, steam
	Fillets, **fresh or frozen**	Meaty sides of the fish.	None	Bake, poach, broil, fry, steam
	Butterfly fillets, **fresh or frozen**	Two single fillets held together by a small piece of skin.	None	Bake, poach, broil, fry, steam
	Breaded fillets, **frozen raw or** **cooked**	Fillet with seasoned crumb coating.	None	Oven finish, deep fry
	Breaded portions, **frozen raw or** **cooked**	Uniform, serving portions. Cut from frozen blocks or fillets. Seasoned crumb coating.	None	Oven finish, deep fry

	Product	Description	Preparation	Cooking
	Fish sticks and bite-size pieces, frozen raw or cooked	Uniformly cut from frozen fillet blocks. Seasoned crumb coating.	None	Oven finish, deep fry
	SHRIMP: Green, headless, fresh or frozen	Raw, in-shell shrimps.	Remove shell and black sand vein in back either before or after cooking.	Boil, bake or broil
	Peeled and deveined, fresh or frozen	Shrimp from which shell and black sand vein have been removed.	None	Boil, bake, broil or sauté
	Cooked, peeled and deveined, fresh or frozen		None	Already cooked
	Deveined, frozen raw or cooked breaded— also extruded	Peeled shrimp from which black sand vein has been removed and which has been breaded. Extruded product formed from shrimp pieces and breaded.	None	Deep fry or oven finish
	OYSTERS/CLAMS/ MUSSELS: Shucked, fresh or frozen	Removed from shell.	Wash out sand and bits of shell if frozen, thaw before cooking.	Steam, bake, sauté
	LOBSTER: Tail, fresh or frozen	Meat from tail of lobster. Usually sold in shell.	Before cooking, remove thin undershell to reduce curling.	Bake, broil, or simmer
	Live	Whole lobster.	For details refer to a seafood cookbook.	Boil, broil
	CRAB: See page 6 for types and market forms.		For details on various types refer to a seafood cookbook.	Depends on market form; refer to cookbook or, if frozen breaded, to package directions.

EXHIBITS

Fish (market forms):
Round (whole): As it comes from the water
Drawn: Eviscerated
Dressed: Eviscerated, head, tail, and fins off
Filets: ½ the fish removed from head, tail, fins, and skin
Sticks: Blocks of fish meat of uniform size
Steaks: Cross-section of one fish cut from a dressed fish with the skin off.

Item	State	Unit	Portion Size	No. of Portions
Salmon	Canned	16 oz (13 oz)*	3 oz	4.3
Salmon	Canned	64 oz (50 oz)*	3 oz	16.7
Sardines, Maine	Canned	12 oz (10 oz)*	3 oz	1.2
Sardines, Pacific	Canned	15 oz (11.5 oz)*	3 oz	3.8
Tuna	Canned	7 oz (6 oz)*	3 oz	2.0
Tuna	Canned	66½ oz (58 oz)*	3 oz	19.3
Filets	Fr; Frz	1 lb	3 oz	3.4
Steaks	Fr; Frz	1 lb	3 oz	3.1
Dressed	Fr; Frz	1 lb	3 oz	2.4
Drawn	Fr; Frz	1 lb	3 oz	1.7
Whole	Fr; Frz	1 lb	3 oz	1.4
Portions, Breaded	Frz	1 lb	2 oz	8
Portions, Breaded	Frz	1 lb	3 oz	5.3
Portions, Unbreaded	Frz	1 lb	2 oz	8
Portions, Unbreaded	Frz	1 lb	3 oz	5.3
Crabmeat	Fr; Frz	1 lb	3 oz	5.2
Lobster Meat	Fr; Frz	1 lb	3 oz	4.8
Scallops	Fr; Frz	1 lb	3 oz	3.4
Shrimp, Cooked	Fr; Frz	1 lb	3 oz	5.3
Shrimp, Raw/Shell	Fr; Frz	1 lb	3 oz	2.7
Shrimp, Raw/Peeled	Fr; Frz	1 lb	3 oz	3.3
Shrimp, Breaded	Fr; Frz	1 lb	3 oz	4.5

Inspection of Fish and Fish Products
The inspection of fish is a voluntary program. It is not used by all companies processing fish.
Any fish, fresh or processed, that bears the inspection mark, has been "packed under continuous inspection of the U.S. Department of Commerce."
The product is inspected for wholesomeness and truthful labeling.

A Fish Specification	
Product	Fish Sticks
Species	Cod
Breading	20% maximum by weight
Size	1 oz. portions
Pack	4 boxes of 64 portions
Condition	Cooked, frozen, U.S. Grade A

10
POULTRY AND EGGS

INTRODUCTION

Grading of poultry includes the determination of class, quality, quantity, condition, or any combination of these factors. USDA grades are required for both consumer and procurement for ready-to-cook poultry. While the original grading and inspection services were on a voluntary basis prior to 1970, the Wholesome Poultry Products Act requires that each state have its own inspection system that is equal to the federal programs.

This chapter includes specifications for chickens, ducks, guineas, turkeys, and even rabbits. Poultry food products and poultry parts, today very popular, are listed with specifications also. Official inspection marks are required on all shipping containers. Examples of labels bearing inspection and grade marks are shown in this chapter.

Shell eggs are purchased according to grade and size. Consumer and procurement grades include the most economical use of eggs for each group. A table indicating yields expected from whole eggs and dried egg products is a valuable resource. The reader should distinguish between the USDA Acceptance Service and other federal stamps and grades. Storage conditions for shell eggs is indicated.

POULTRY GRADES

U.S. Consumer Grades for Ready-to-Cook Poultry

U.S. Grade A. A lot of ready-to-cook poultry or parts consisting of one or more ready-to-cook carcasses, or parts of the same kind and class, each of which conforms to the requirements for A Quality, may be designated as U.S. Grade A.

U.S. Grade B. A lot of ready-to-cook poultry or parts consisting of one or more ready-to-cook carcasses, or parts of the same kind and class, each of which conforms to the requirements for B Quality or better, may be designated as U.S. Grade B.

U.S. Grade C. A lot of ready-to-cook poultry or parts consisting of one or more ready-to-cook carcasses, or parts of the same kind and class, each of which conforms to the requirements for C Quality or better, may be designated as U.S. Grade C.

U.S. Procurement Grades for Ready-To-Cook Poultry

The U.S. Procurement Grades for ready-to-cook poultry are applicable to carcasses of ready-to-cook poultry of the kinds and classes when graded, as a lot, by a grader on the basis of an examination of each carcass in the lot, or each carcass in a representative sample thereof.

U.S. Procurement Grade I. Any lot of ready-to-cook poultry composed of one or more carcasses of the same kind and class may be designated and identified as U.S. Procurement Grade I when:

1. Ninety percent or more of the carcasses in such lot meet the requirements of A Quality, with these exceptions:
    a. Fat covering and conformation may be as described in the manual for B Quality.
    b. Trimming of skin and flesh to remove defects is permitted to the extent that not more than one-third of the flesh is exposed on any part, and the meat yield of any part is not appreciably affected.
    c. Discoloration of the skin and flesh may be as described in the manual for B Quality.
    d. One or both drumsticks may be removed if the part is severed at the joint.
    e. The back may be trimmed in an area not wider than the base of the tail and extending to the area between the hip joints.
    f. The wings or parts of wings may be removed if severed at a joint.
2. The balance of the carcasses meet the same requirements, except they may have only a moderate covering of flesh.

U.S. Procurement Grade II. Any lot of ready-to-cook poultry of the same kind and class which fails to meet the requirements of U.S. Procurement Grade I may be designated and identified as U.S. Procurement Grade II provided that:

1. Trimming of flesh from any part does not exceed 10 percent of the meat.
2. Portions of a carcass weighing not less than one-half of the whole carcass may be included, if the portion approximates in percentage the meat-to-bone yield of the whole carcass.

Voluntary Programs

For many years the USDA has offered the poultry industry official grading and inspection services on a voluntary basis. These services have been carried on under authority of Congressional Acts which have provided that fees shall be charged users of the service to cover costs.

Mandatory Program

Under the Poultry Products Inspection Act, enacted August 28, 1957, USDA provides compulsory federal inspection of poultry and poultry products that are shipped in interstate or foreign commerce. The Wholesome Poultry Products Act, enacted August 18, 1968, amended the law to strengthen it and to open the way for vastly improved state poultry inspection systems. Each state was given from August, 1968, two years (or three if progress is being made) to develop its own inspection system that is equal to the federal inspection programs.

Administration of mandatory federal inspection is assigned to the Meat and Poultry Inspection Program of USDA's Consumer and Marketing Service. All poultry slaughtered for human food which is destined for sale in commerce must be processed and handled in accordance with the Act and its regulations. Federal inspection service performed under the Act, except for overtime and holiday work, is paid for by the government.

Poultry grading service is available to the industry on two bases: *fee* and *resident* or *continuous grading*.

Fee grading is performed on the basis of request from applicants for the grading of a particular lot or carload of poultry. Requests for this type of service are usually made irregularly, and the charges for the service are based on the time consumed in performing the service. Most of the fee grading work is done at the terminal markets where impartial certification of quality or condition is desired. However, some service is rendered to shippers and processors on a fee basis, as required primarily in fulfilling purchase contract specifications.

Resident or *continuous grading* is performed by graders who are stationed in the applicant's processing plant, and are available at all times to perform grading service at the plant. Most of the resident grading is performed in processing plants at shipping points within the more concentrated areas of production, although some processors and distributors at terminal markets or major distribution centers also use resident or continuous grading service. The costs of resident grading service include an amount equal to the salary of the grader, plus an additional charge, based on the volume of product handled in the plant, to cover supervisory and administrative costs.

Grading generally involves the sorting of products according to quality and size, but it also includes the determination of the class and condition of products. For poultry, grading may be for determining class, quality, quantity, condition, or any combination of these factors.

Grading for quality can be accomplished by examining a representative sample of the lot of poultry to be graded. Only ready-to-cook poultry that is first inspected for wholesomeness, and then is graded on an individual-bird basis, may be individually marked with an official grade mark. Dressed poultry may not have individual grade labels applied.

Resident grading service is provided on the basis of written application on forms supplied by the Poultry Division of the Consumer and Marketing Service. The applicant agrees to comply with the regulations governing grading and agrees to pay the full cost of the service requested. The government and cooperating agencies, in turn, agree to provide an adequate number of graders to perform the service. The conditions under which the service is performed are specified in the application and the regulations. The cost per pound for this service is generally very little more than in plants not using the grading service, but instead employing their own graders.

Inspection

Inspection refers to the condition of poultry and its healthfulness and fitness for food. It is not concerned with the quality or grade of poultry. The inspection mark on poultry or poultry products means that they have been examined during processing by a veterinarian or by qualified inspectors under the supervision of a veterinarian. Plants that apply for inspection service and are approved are known as official plants.

Voluntary Inspection Service

The voluntary inspection service is provided for under the authority of the Agricultural Marketing Act of 1946. The cost of services rendered on this basis is paid for by the applicant for the service.

Processors who desire inspection for squab, game birds, and rabbits may apply for inspection under the voluntary program. These items are not covered under the mandatory program. The requirements for the plant, operating procedures, inspection procedures, and packaging and labeling are the same for the voluntary program as those outlined for the mandatory program. Grading service is conducted on the basis of cooperative agreements between the Consumer and Marketing Service and various state agencies.

TYPES OF POULTRY

Chickens

Rock Cornish Game Hen or Cornish Game Hen. A Rock Cornish game hen or Cornish game hen is a young immature chicken (usually 5 to 7 weeks of age), weighing not more than 2 lb. ready-to-cook weight, which was prepared from a Cornish chicken, or the progeny of a Cornish chicken crossed with another breed of chicken.

Broiler or Fryer. A broiler or fryer is a young chicken (usually 9 to 12 weeks of age), of either sex, that is tender-meated, with soft, pliable, smooth-textured skin and flexible breastbone cartilage.

Roaster. A roaster is a young chicken (usually 3 to 5 months of age), of either sex, that is tender-meated, with soft, pliable, smooth-textured skin, and breastbone cartilage that may be somewhat less flexible than that of a broiler or fryer.

Capon. A capon is a surgically unsexed male chicken (usually under 8 months of age) that is tender-meated, with soft, pliable, smooth-textured skin.

Stag.   A stag is a male chicken (usually under 10 months of age) with coarse skin, a somewhat toughened and darkend flesh, and a considerable hardening of the breast-bone cartilage. Stags show a condition of fleshing and a degree of maturity intermediate between that of a roaster and a cock or rooster.

Hen or Stewing Chicken or Fowl.   A hen, or stewing chicken or fowl, is a mature, female chicken (usually more than 10 months of age) with meat less tender than that of a roaster, and a nonflexible breastbone tip.

Cock or Rooster.   A cock or rooster is a mature male chicken with coarse skin, toughened and darkened meat, and a hardened breastbone tip.

Ducks

Broiler Duckling or Fryer Duckling.   A broiler duckling or fryer duckling is a young duck (usually under 8 weeks of age), of either sex, that is tender-meated and has a soft bill and soft windpipe.

Roaster Duckling.   A roaster duckling is a young duck (usually under 16 weeks of age), of either sex, that is tender-meated and has a bill that is not completely hardened and a windpipe that is easily dented.

Mature Duck or Old Duck.   A mature duck or an old duck is a duck (usually over 6 months of age), of either sex, with toughened flesh, hardened bill, and hardened windpipe.

Geese

Young Goose.   A young goose may be of either sex, is tender-meated, and has a windpipe that is easily dented.

Mature Goose or Old Goose.   A mature goose or old goose may be of either sex and has toughened flesh and hardened windpipe.

Guineas

Young Guinea.   A young guinea may be of either sex, is tender-meated, and has a flexible breastbone cartilage.

Mature Guinea or Old Guinea.   A mature guinea or an old guinea may be of either sex, has toughened flesh, and a hardened breastbone.

Pigeons

Squab. A squab is a young, immature pigeon of either sex and is extra tender-meated.

Pigeon. A pigeon is a mature pigeon of either sex, with coarse skin and toughened flesh.

Each class of poultry has one or more distinctive characteristics which enable the grader to properly classify an individual bird, or a lot of poultry. The list of characteristics is not all-inclusive. A lot of poultry containing two or more classes would be described as a "mixed class."

The degree of maturity as used as a guide in cooking and the names given to the classes are such that they are readily recognized. Processing into ready-to-cook poultry eliminates many of the definite indications which are seen in live and dressed poultry. Various indications which may be seen in live, dressed, and ready-to-cook poultry are listed on the following pages.

Rabbits

Fryer or Young Rabbit. A fryer or young rabbit is a young, domestic rabbit carcass, weighing not less than 1½ lb., and rarely more than 3½ lb., processed from a rabbit usually less than 12 weeks of age. The flesh of a fryer or young rabbit is tender and fine-grained and of a bright, pearly pink color.

Roaster or Mature Rabbit. A roaster or mature rabbit is a mature or old domestic rabbit carcass of any weight, but usually over 4 lb. processed from a rabbit usually 8 months of age or older. The flesh of a roaster or mature rabbit is more firm and coarse-grained, the muscle fiber is slightly darker in color and less tender, and the fat may be more creamy in color than that of a fryer or young rabbit.

Carcasses found to be unsound, unwholesome, or unfit for food shall not be included in any of the quality designations specified.

To be of A Quality, the rabbit carcass:

1. Is short, thick, well-founded, and full-fleshed.
2. Has a broad back, broad hips, broad deep-fleshed shoulders, and firm muscle texture.
3. Has a fair quantity of interior fat in the crotch and over the inner walls of the carcass, and a moderate amount of interior fat around the kidneys.
4. Is free of evidence of incomplete bleeding, such as more than occasional slight coagulation in a vein. Is free from any evidence of reddening of the flesh due to fluid in the connective tissues.

5. Is free from all foreign material (including, but not being limited to, hair, dirt, and bone particles) and from crushed bones caused by removing the head or the feet.

6. Is free from broken bones, flesh bruises, defects, and deformities. Ends of leg bones may be broken due to removing the feet.

Turkey

Fryer-Roaster Turkey. A fryer-roaster turkey is a young, immature turkey (usually under 16 weeks of age), of either sex, that is tender-meated with soft, pliable, smooth-textured skin and flexible breastbone cartilage.

Young Hen Turkey. A young hen turkey is a young, female turkey (usually 5 to 7 months of age) that is tender-meated, with soft-pliable, smooth-textured skin, and breastbone cartilage that is somewhat less flexible than in a fryer-roaster turkey.

Young Tom Turkey. A young tom turkey is a young, male turkey (usually 5 to 7 months of age) that is tender-meated, with soft, pliable smooth-textured skin, and breastbone cartilage that is somewhat less flexible than a fryer-roaster turkey.

Yearling Hen Turkey. A yearling hen turkey is a fully matured, female turkey (usually under 15 months of age) that is reasonably tender-meated with reasonably smooth-textured skin.

Yearling Tom Turkey. A yearling tom turkey is a fully matured, male turkey (usually under 15 months of age) that is reasonably tender-meated, with reasonably smooth-textured skin.

Mature Turkey or Old Turkey (Hen or Tom). A mature or old turkey is an old turkey of either sex (usually in excess of 15 months of age), with a coarse skin and toughened flesh.

(For labeling purposes, the designation of sex within the class name is optional, and the three classes of young turkeys may be grouped and designated as ''young turkeys.'')

DRESSED POULTRY

''Dressed Poultry'' refers to poultry slaughtered for human food, with head, feet, and viscera intact, and from which the blood and feathers have been removed. While the U.S. standards of quality apply to dressed poultry, and the USDA poultry grading regulations provide for the grading of dressed poultry, this product is practically non-existent on today's poultry market.

The individual carcasses of dressed poultry may not be officially identified with the grade mark. Under certain conditions the grade mark may be applied to shipping containers of dressed poultry. No part other than wing tips may be removed from dressed poultry.

The determination of whether dressed poultry carcasses are unwholesome or unsound is based only on external characteristics. The following conditions would exclude a dressed poultry carcass from a quality designation:

1. Decomposition (slippery or slimy condition, putrid or sour odor, greenish cast over the back and between thigh and rib).
2. Emaciation.
3. Bruises or mangling in excess of that permitted in C quality.
4. External evidence of disease, such as abnormally dark flesh or skin, external tumors, and abdominal accumulations.
5. Dirty head, carcass, feet, or vent; bloody head or carcass; green vent; feathers on the carcass; feed in the crop.

READY-TO-COOK POULTRY

The great majority of ready-to-cook birds are graded in processing plants following evisceration. Ready-to-cook poultry must have been inspected for wholesomeness in accordance with the regulations of the USDA before it can be officially graded. Relatively few birds are graded at points other than processing plants, and these birds must be in a form which makes it possible to examine the entire carcass. (For example, frozen poultry cannot be graded initially at a terminal market because the carcasses are not entirely visible.)

Ready-to-cook poultry, parts, or poultry products which are unsound or unwholesome are not eligible to be graded. Decomposition (slimy or slippery condition of the skin, or putrid or sour odor) would exclude ready-to-cook products from a grade.

In addition, ready-to-cook birds showing any of the following conditions cannot be graded. Such birds will be sent back for further processing, if grading is done at the processing plant.

1. Protruding pinfeathers.
2. Bruises requiring trimming.
3. Lungs or sex organs incompletely removed.
4. Parts of the trachea.
5. Vestigial feathers.
6. Feathers.
7. Extraneous material of any type inside or outside of carcass (for example, fecal material, blood, etc.).

EXPOSED FLESH—GRADE A

Carcass Weight		Maximum Aggregate Area Permitted	
Minimum	Maximum	Breast & Legs	Elsewhere
None	1 lb. 8 oz.	None	3/4 in.
Over 1 lb. 8 oz.	6 lb.	None	1-1/2 in.
Over 6 lb.	16 lb.	None	2 in.
Over 16 lb.	None	None	3 in.

DISCOLORED FLESH—GRADE A

Carcass Weight		Maximum Aggregate Area Permitted		
Minimum	Maximum	Breast & Legs	Elsewhere	Parts
None	1 lb. 8 oz.	1/2 in.	1 in.	1/4 in.
Over 1 lb. 8 oz.	6 lb.	1 in.	2 in.	1/4 in.
Over 6 lb.	16 lb.	1-1/2 in.	2-1/2 in.	1/2 in.
Over 16 lb.	None	2 in.	3 in.	1/2 in.

POULTRY PARTS

Poultry parts have become increasingly popular with the consumer. Some people prefer all white meat, and the all-breast pack serves this need. For those who prefer all dark meat, drumsticks, thighs, or whole-leg packs serve the purpose. Parts are versatile. They are especially popular in specialty dishes and are ideal for barbecuing.

A ready-to-cook carcass that has a defect may be graded after the defective portion has been removed, and the fact that a portion of the carcass has been removed will not be considered in determining the quality of the balance of the carcass if the remaining portion of the carcass is to be disjointed and packed as parts in the official plant where graded.

In 1969, specific grade standards were established for parts, and provision was made for parts after they have been cut from the carcass, providing the class is known, the parts are not misshapen and have nearly the same appearance as they had prior to cutting from the carcass. Specific requirements for parts are set forth in the preceding ''Fleshing'' categories for Grade A and Grade B ready-to-cook poultry.

The USDA standards of quality are applicable to poultry parts cut in the manner described in the following paragraphs, or in some other manner when approved by the Administrator. In addition, grade standards have been established for A, B, and C Quality poultry backs, depending upon the manner in which they are cut.

"Breasts" are separated from the back at the shoulder joint, and by a cut running backward and downward from that point along the junction of the vertebral and sternal ribs. The ribs may be removed from the breast, and the breast may be cut along the breastbone to make two approximately equal halves; or the wishbone portion (as described under "wishbone" in this section) may be removed before cutting the remainder along the breastbone to make three parts. Pieces cut in this manner may be substituted for light or heavier pieces for exact weight-making purposes, and the package may contain two or more of such parts without affecting the appropriateness of its labeling as "chicken breasts." Neck skin is not included.

"Breast with ribs" are separated from the back at the junction of the vertebral ribs and back. Breasts with ribs may be cut along the breastbone to make approximately two halves; or the wishbone portion (as described under "wishbone" in this section) may be removed before cutting the remainder along the breastbone to make three parts. Pieces cut in this manner may be substituted for light or heavier pieces for exact weight-making purposes, and the package may contain two or more of such parts without affecting the appropriateness of its labeling as "breast with ribs." Neck skin is not included.

"Wishbones" (Pulley bones) with covering muscle and skin tissue are severed from the breast approximately half-way between the end of the wishbone (hypocledium) and front point of the breastbone (cranial process of the sternal crest) to a point where the wishbone joins the shoulder. Neck skin is not included.

"Legs" include the whole leg, i.e., the thigh and the drumstick, whether jointed or disjointed. Back skin is not included. Pelvic meat may be attached to the thigh, but shall not include the pelvic bones.

"Wings" include the entire wing, with all muscle and skin tissue intact, except that the wing tip may be removed.

"Drumsticks" are separated from the thigh by a cut through the knee joint (femorotibial and patellar joint) and from the hock (tarsal joint).

"Thighs" are disjointed at the hip joint and may include the pelvic meat, but shall not include the pelvic bones. Back skin is not included.

"Halves" are prepared by making a full-length back and breast split of the carcass, so as to produce approximately equal right and left sides.

"Quarters" are prepared by splitting the carcass (as specified under "halves" in this section) with the resulting halves cut crosswise at almost right angles to the backbone to form quarters.

"Backs" include the pelvic bones and all the vertebrae posterior to the shoulder joint. The meat may not be peeled from the pelvic bones. The vertebral ribs and/or scapula may be removed or included. Skin shall be substantially intact.

A Quality backs shall meet all applicable provisions pertaining to parts, and shall include the meat contained on the ilium (oyster), pelvic meat and skin, and vertebral ribs and scapula with meat and skin.

B Quality backs shall meet all applicable provisions pertaining to parts, and shall include either the meat contained on the ilium (oyster), and meat and skin from the pelvic bones, or the vertebral ribs and scapula with meat and skin.

C Quality backs shall include the meat and skin from the pelvic bones, except that the meat contained on the ilium (oyster) may be removed. The vertebral ribs and scapula with meat and skin may also be removed, but the remaining portion must have the skin substantially intact.

POULTRY FOOD PRODUCTS

In the past few years, numerous frozen poultry pies and dinners have appeared on the market. Recently, other poultry food products (such as specialty dishes containing poultry, raw and cooked poultry rolls, and roasts) have become available to the consumer.

A standard for Grade A poultry roasts is shown below. This is the first grade standard for a poultry food product.

Poultry Roast—A Quality

The standard of quality contained in this section is applicable to raw poultry products labeled in accordance with the poultry inspection regulations as ready-to-cook "Rolls," "Roasts," "Bars," or "Logs," or with words of similar import.

1. The deboned poultry meat used in the preparation of the product shall be from young poultry of A Quality with respect to fleshing and fat covering.

2. All tendons, cartilage, large blood vessels, blood clots, and discolorations shall be trimmed from the meat.

3. All pinfeathers, bruises, hair, discolorations, and blemishes shall be removed from the skin, and where necessary, excess fat shall be removed from the skin covering the crop area or other areas.

4. Seventy-five percent or more of the outer surface of the product shall be covered with skin, whether attached to the meat or used as a wrap. The skin shall not appreciably overlap at any point. Product packaged in an oven-ready container need have only the entire exposed surface of the roast covered with skin. The combined weight of the skin and fat used to cover the outer surface and that used as a binder shall not exceed 15 percent of the total net weight of the product.

5. The product shall be fabricated in such a manner that each slice remains substantially intact (does not separate into more than three parts) when sliced warm after cooking. This may be accomplished by use of large pieces of poultry or by use of approved binders.

6. Seasoning or flavor enhancers, if used, shall be uniformly distributed.

7. Packaging shall be neat and attractive.

8. Product shall be practically free of weepage after packaging and/or freezing, and, if frozen, shall have a bright, desirable color.

Boneless Poultry Breasts and Thighs—A Quality

The standards of quality contained in this section are applicable to raw poultry products labeled as ready-to-cook boneless poultry breasts or thighs, or as ready-to-cook boneless poultry breast fillets or thigh fillets, or with words of similar import.

1. The breast or thigh shall be cut as specified.
2. Prior to deboning, the breast or thigh shall meet the A Quality requirements for ready-to-cook poultry parts, as specified.
3. The bone or bones shall be removed in a neat manner, without undue mutilation of adjacent muscle.

Official Identification Marks for Ready-to-Cook Poultry

The official, circular inspection mark is required on immediate containers and shipping containers for poultry that is inspected under the Poultry Products Inspection Act.

The grade mark must be one of the forms and designs illustrated and must be printed with light-colored letters on a dark field.

Any wing tag, metal clip, insert label, or other label which bears either the inspection mark, grade mark, or both, must also show either the plant number or the firm name and address.

Wing tags and metal clips, bearing the grade mark, that are to be applied to poultry that is not consumer-packaged must show the class of the product. The class name can be the appropriate individual class, or the classes can be grouped according to the following system:

Name	*Poultry to Be Packed Thereunder*
Young poultry	Young birds of any kind
Mature poultry	Any mature or old bird of any kind
Young chicken	Roasters and other young chickens
Stewing chicken	Fowl, baking hen, chicken hen
Young turkey	Young hen, young tom, and fryer-roaster turkeys
Yearling turkey	Yearling hen turkey, yearling tom turkey
Duckling	Broiler duckling, roaster duckling
Mature Duck	Old duck

Indicating the *kind,* such as chicken, turkey, or duck without the qualifying term "young," or "mature," or "old," or the class name, is not permitted.

Examples of wing tags are shown. When both marks are shown on a tag, they must both appear on the same side of the tag. Both marks may appear on each side of the tag. Wing tags of shield design may not be used for showing the inspection mark only, but may be used to show both marks, or the grade mark singly.

FORMS OF OFFICIAL IDENTIFICATION FOR READY-TO-COOK POULTRY

Inspection Mark

Grade Mark

Federal—State Graded

Grade Mark

EXAMPLES OF LABELS BEARING INSPECTION AND GRADE MARKS

WING TAGS

METAL WING CLIPS

Grade Mark for Fryers, Broilers, Stewing Chickens, Turkeys, Ducks, Geese, Guineas

In the case of multiple-bird ice pack, when the grade mark appears on a tag, or clip, without the inspection mark, the inspection mark must be printed on the giblet wrapper and packed with the bird. If the tag or clip does not show the plant number, then the plant number must be shown on the giblet wrapper.

Poultry Products

All percentages of poultry—chicken, turkey or other kinds of poultry—are on cooked, deboned basis unless otherwise indicated. When standard indicates poultry meat, skin, and fat, the skin and fat are in proportions normal to poultry.

Baby Food. High Poultry Dinner: At least 18¾ percent poultry meat, skin, fat, and giblets. Poultry with Broth: At least 43 percent poultry meat, skin, fat, and giblets.

Beans and Rice with Poultry. At least 6 percent poultry meat.

Breaded Poultry. No more than 30 percent breading.

Cabbage Stuffed with Poultry. At least 8 percent poultry meat.

Canned Boned Poultry. Boned (kind), Solid Pack: At least 95 percent poultry meat, skin, and fat. Boned (kind): At least 90 percent poultry meat, skin, and fat. Boned (kind) with Broth: At least 80 percent poultry meat, skin, and fat. Boned (kind) with Specified Percentage of Broth: At least 50 percent poultry meat, skin and fat.

Cannelloni with Poultry. At least 7 percent poultry meat.

Chicken Cordon Bleu. At least 60 percent boneless chicken breast (raw basis), 5 percent ham, and either Swiss, Gruyere, or Mozzarella cheese. (If breaded, no more than 30 percent breading.)

Creamed Poultry. At least 20 percent poultry meat. Product must contain some cream.

Egg Roll with Poultry. At least 2 percent poultry meat.

Entree. Poultry or Poultry Food Product and One Vegetable: At least 37½ percent poultry meat or poultry food product. Poultry or Poultry Food Product with Gravy or Sauce and One Vegetable: At least 22 percent poultry meat.

Poultry a la Kiev. Must be breast meat (may have attached skin) stuffed with butter and chives.

Poultry a la King. At least 20 percent poultry meat.

Poultry Almondine. At least 50 percent poultry meat.

Poultry Barbecue. At least 40 percent poultry meat.

Poultry Blintz Filling. At least 40 percent poultry meat.

Poultry Brunswick Stew. At least 12 percent poultry meat. Must contain corn.

Poultry Burgers. Must be 100 percent poultry meat, with skin and fat.

Poultry Burgundy. At least 50 percent poultry, enough wine to characterize the product.

Poultry Cacciatore. At least 20 percent poultry meat, or 40 percent with bone.

Poultry Casserole. At least 18 percent poultry meat.

Poultry Chili. At least 28 percent poultry meat.

Poultry Chili with Beans. At least 17 percent poultry meat.

Poultry Chop Suey. At least 4 percent poultry meat. Chop Suey with Poultry: At least 2 percent poultry meat.

Poultry Chow Mein (without noodles). At least 4 percent poultry meat.

Poultry Croquettes. At least 25 percent poultry meat.

Poultry Croquettes with Macaroni and Cheese. At least 29 percent croquettes.

Poultry Dinners (a frozen product). At least 18 percent poultry meat, figured on total meal minus appetizer, bread, and dessert.

Poultry Empanadillo. At least 25 percent poultry meat including skin and fat (raw basis).

Poultry Fricassee. At least 20 percent poultry meat.

Poultry Fricasee of Wings. At least 40 percent poultry wings (cooked basis, with bone).

Poultry Hash. At least 30 percent poultry meat.

Poultry Lasagna. At least 8 percent poultry meat (raw basis).

Poultry Livers with Rice and Gravy. At least 30 percent livers in poultry and gravy portion, or 17½ percent in total product.

Poultry Paella. At least 35 percent poultry meat or 35 percent poultry meat and other meat (cooked basis); no more than 35 percent cooked rice; must contain seafood.

Poultry Pies. At least 14 percent poultry meat.

Poultry Ravioli. At least 2 percent poultry meat.

Poultry Roll. No more than 3 percent binding agents, such as gelatin, in the cooked product; no more than 2 percent natural cooked-out juices. Poultry Roll with Natural Juices: Contains more than 2 percent natural cooked-out juices. Poultry Roll with Broth: Contains more than 2 percent poultry broth in addition to natural cooked-out juices. Poultry Roll with Gelatin: Gelatin exceeds 3 percent of cooked product.

Poultry Salad. At least 25 percent poultry meat (with normal amounts of skin and fat).

Poultry Scallopini. At least 35 percent poultry meat.

Poultry Soup. Ready-to-Eat: At least 2 percent poultry meat. Condensed: At least 4 percent poultry meat.

Poultry Stew. At least 12 percent poultry meat.

Poultry Stroganoff. At least 30 percent poultry meat and at least 10 percent sour cream, or a "gourmet" combination of at least 7½ percent sour cream and 5 percent wine.

Poultry Tamales. At least 6 percent poultry meat.

Poultry Tetrazzini. At lest 15 percent poultry meat.

Poultry Wellington. At least 50 percent boneless poultry breast, spread with a liver or similar pate coating, and covered in not more than 30 percent pastry.

Poultry with Gravy. At least 35 percent poultry meat. Gravy with Poultry: At least 15 percent poultry meat.

Poultry with Noodles or Dumplings. At least 15 percent poultry meat, or 30 percent with bone. Noodles or Dumplings with Poultry: At least 6 percent poultry meat.

Poultry with Noodles Au Gratin. At least 18 percent poultry meat.

Poultry with Vegetables. At least 15 percent poultry meat.

Stuffed Cabbage with Poultry. At least 8 percent poultry meat.

Sauce with Poultry or Poultry Sauce. At least 6 percent poultry meat.

EGGS

Consumer Grades

Size is determined by weight per dozen, in the shell. Since eggs are generally packed in 30-doz., corrugated fiber cases, the buyer is concerned with case weight, as well as per-dozen weight. Two or more cases of 30-doz. eggs are known as a lot. When purchased by the lot, the lot is allowed to have a maximum of 3.3 percent of its eggs in the next lower weight range. Case weights, indicated below, include the 4½ lb. weight of the standard, corrugated fiber case and the filler flats used to separate the individual eggs, and layers of eggs.

Size	Per Dozen	Per 30-Doz. Case
Jumbo	30 oz.	56 lb.
Extra Large	27 oz.	50½ lb.
Large	24 oz.	45 lb.
Medium	21 oz.	39½ lb.
Small	18 oz.	34 lb.
Peewee	15 oz.	28 lb.

Large and Medium eggs are most frequently used for fried, poached, hard-cooked, or soft-cooked eggs. If fresh eggs are to be used in cooking scrambled eggs, baked goods, etc., then the buyer will be concerned with comparative price per dozen. Using the price of Large eggs as a base, Medium eggs are a better buy when Medium eggs are 12 percent cheaper than Large eggs. Small eggs are a better buy than Large eggs when 24 percent cheaper than Large eggs, or 12 percent cheaper than Medium eggs.

The Consumer Grades for shell eggs are U.S. Grade AA, U.S. Grade A, and U.S. Grade B. The grade is shown inside the USDA shield on the case. The size is sometimes included in that shield, also. The quality standard for individual cases within a lot are lower than the quality standards for the lot as a whole. The quality standards for eggs at the grading point (time and place) is higher than at the point of receipt. This has to be so because eggs deteriorate in quality as they age. The grade of the individual eggs within the case or lot may be of the next lower grade (except in the case of U.S. Grade B) to the extent of a specified percentage.

U.S. Grade AA

Clean, unbroken, and practically normal shells; practically regular air cell, no more than ⅛ in. deep, and practically regular in shape; clear and firm white; yolk practically free from defects with outline slightly defined. No less than 85 percent U.S. Grade AA at point of origin, and no less than 80 percent U.S. Grade AA at destination. Individual cases to be no less than 75 percent U.S. Grade AA, and no more than 15 percent U.S. Grade A and 10 percent U.S. Grade B at point of origin, and no less than 70 percent U.S. Grade AA, but no more than 20 percent U.S. Grade A and 10 percent U.S. Grade B at destination.

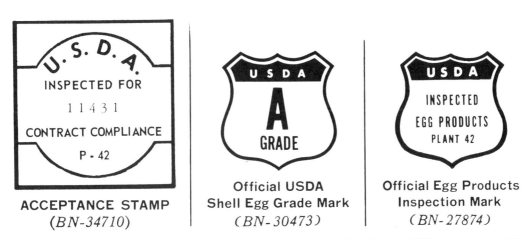

ACCEPTANCE STAMP
(BN-34710)

**Official USDA
Shell Egg Grade Mark**
(BN-30473)

**Official Egg Products
Inspection Mark**
(BN-27874)

When poultry and eggs are bought on the basis of contract specifications, a USDA grader carefully examines each delivery to see that it meets the specifications of the buyer. An acceptance stamp is applied to each container found to meet contract requirements. The grader then seals the container to prevent tampering or opening prior to delivery.

U.S. Grade A

Clean, unbroken, and practically normal shells, practically regular air cell, 3/16 in. or less in depth; clear and reasonably firm white; yolk outline fairly well defined and practically free from defects. No less than 85 percent U.S. Grade A at point of origin, and no less than 80 percent U.S. Grade A at destination. Individual cases to be no less than 75 percent U.S. Grade A, and no more than 25 percent U.S. Grade B at point of origin, and no less than 70 percent U.S. Grade A, and no more than 30 percent U.S. Grade B at destination.

U.S. Grade B

Clean to slightly stained shells, which may be slightly abnormal in shape; air cell may be free or bubbly, but not more than 3/8 in. in depth; the white must be clear, but may be slightly weak; yolk may be slightly enlarged, and have a well-defined outline. No less than 85 percent U.S. Grade B at point of origin, and no less than 80 percent U.S. Grade B at destination. Individual cases to be no less than 75 percent U.S. Grade B at point of origin, and no less than 70 percent U.S. Grade B at destination. No eggs that are less than Grade B can be included.

Procurement Grades

The Procurement Grades are used mostly by large egg processors, repackers, and other middlemen. An individual foodservice operation would not use the Procurement Grades, especially since these grades include a Grade C which, by federal law, may not be used by foodservices. The Procurement Grades provide that the individual cases contain not more than 10 percent less than U.S. Grade A eggs in the entire lot: below

Egg Grade Marks

U.S. Grade B, there may be up to 3 percent Checks, 0.3 percent Dirties, Leakers and Loss, of which the Loss cannot contain more than 0.15 percent at point of origin and 0.2 percent at destination of blood spots and meat.

Grade I

Not less than 85 percent U.S. Grade AA and U.S. Grade A at origin, nor less than 80 percent U.S. Grade AA and U.S. Grade A at destination. Origin allowed up to 15 percent U.S. Grade B, but not more than 5 percent U.S. Grade C[1], Dirty, Leaker or Loss; destination allowed up to 20 percent U.S. Grade B, but not more than 5 percent U.S. Grade C, Dirty, Leaker or Loss.

---

[1]Grade C: Shell is clean to moderately stained, unbroken, and may be abnormally shaped; air cell may be free, or bubbly, and more than ⅜ in. in depth; the white may be watery or weak, and small blood clots or spots may appear; the yolk may be flat and enlarged, with visible germ development, no blood, outline plainly visible, and may have other serious defects.

Grade II

Not less than 65 percent at origin and 60 percent at destination of U.S. Grade AA and U.S. Grade A, with up to 35 percent U.S. Grade B and no more than 10 percent U.S. Grade C, Dirty, Check or Loss at origin, and up to 40 percent U.S. Grade B, but no more than 10 percent U.S. Grade C, Dirty, Check or Loss at destination.

How to Buy Shell Eggs

Specify the grade and size. U.S. Grade AA is best for visual appearance, as in fried eggs; U.S. Grade A is fine for hard-cooked and soft-cooked. Medium or Large size is best for those uses. U.S. Grade A eggs should be used for omelets and souffles; size is not important in this case. U.S. Grade B eggs are well-suited for general use, such as mixed-in for cooking or baking. Buy Medium size for these uses, unless Large or Small are better in price according to the formula stated earlier. Eggs should be delivered within 2 to 3 days of grading and kept at a temperature of no more than 42°F in an area where they cannot absorb strong odors from other foods. U.S. Grade AA eggs will remain U.S. Grade AA for 10 days when held at 42°F.

Estimated conversion factors for yields of liquid eggs and dried eggs and the moisture content of dried eggs, by types of product, 1961[1]

Egg products	Liquid yield from 30 dozen shell eggs	Yield from one dozen shell eggs		Requirements for one pound of dried egg products		Yield of dried egg product from		Approximate moisture content of egg product[2]
		Liquid egg	Dried egg	Liquid egg	Shell eggs	100 pounds of liquid egg	30 dozen shell eggs	
	POUNDS	POUNDS	POUNDS	POUNDS	POUNDS	POUNDS	POUNDS	PERCENT
Whole eggs	39.50	1.317	0.343	3.84	2.92	26.04	10.29	2-3
Albumen (flake)	22.55	.752	.099	7.58	10.10	13.19	2.97	12-14
Albumen (spray)	22.55	.752	.096	7.84	10.42	12.76	2.88	5-8
Yolk	16.95	.565	.257	2.20	3.89	45.45	7.70	3.5-5

1. The conversion factors were taken from table 16, page 36, *The Egg Products Industry of the United States*, Kansas Agricultural Experiment Station Bulletin 466, N. Cent. Reg. Res. Pub. No. 154.
2. Conversion factors were based on an average of the moisture content shown. It is recognized that moisture content may have ranged as high as 5% in some packs of dried whole egg.

Acceptance Service

Foodservice operators may have eggs graded to their own specifications by federal graders. The inspection service which does this at the point of origin is the USDA Acceptance Service. In order to use this service, the operator must provide the purveyor with notice of inspection as a requirement, and provide both the purveyor and the grader with the specifications. Eggs so graded will have their cases on the invoices stamped with the USDA Acceptance Service Stamp. The cases may also bear the federal stamps, and a grade letter designation.

A fresh egg is one that has been stored 29 days or less. Eggs that are held in storage for 30 or more days are called ''storage eggs.'' Storage eggs must be held at a temperature of 29°F to 31°F, with a humidity of 90° to 92°. Storage eggs are sometimes oiled to prevent CO_2 loss; sometimes CO_2 is injected.

Factors relating to shell eggs

U.S. weight classes, consumer grades	Minimum net weight per		Minimum quantity of product approximating the amount in one dozen eggs						
	Case [30 doz.]	Dozen	Liquid or frozen			Dried			
			Whole	Yolk	Albumen	Whole	Yolk	Albumen	
	POUNDS	OUNCES	POUNDS	POUNDS	POUNDS	POUNDS	POUNDS	POUNDS	POUNDS
Shell eggs:									
Jumbo	56.0	30	1.88	1.64	0.71	0.93	0.42	0.32	0.12
Extra large	50.5	27	1.69	1.48	0.64	0.84	0.38	0.29	0.11
Large	45.0	24	1.50	1.32	0.57	0.75	0.34	0.26	0.10
Medium	39.5	21	1.31	1.16	0.50	0.66	0.30	0.23	0.09
Small	34.0	18	1.12	1.00	0.43	0.57	0.26	0.20	0.08
Peewee	28.0	15	0.94	0.80	0.35	0.47	0.21	0.16	0.06
Average weight									
Sold at retail	47.0[1]	25	1.57[1]	1.38	0.60	0.78	0.35	0.27	0.10

1. The approximate weight of eggs sold at retail is 1.57 pounds per dozen.

QUESTIONS

1. List the specifications of poultry you would purchase for the following items in a college foodservice.
   Sliced chicken sandwich_____
   Chicken a la King_____
   Baked chicken breast_____
2. What is the difference between fee grading and resident or continuous grading of poultry?
3. In which way does poultry inspection differ from inspection of beef?
4. What is the principal difference between a Grade A and a Grade C turkey?
5. In judging of poultry, the shape of a normally developed bird will be ____ or ____.
6. In the consumer purchasing of poultry, name the various parts that should have been removed.
7. What is the quality grade of poultry found in a Chicken Pot Pie?
8. What kinds of poultry may the consumer expect when purchasing a stewing chicken?
9. What will the age of rabbits marked "fryer" usually be?
10. What is the difference between the grade marks and inspection marks used in identifying poultry?
11. List the different sizes in which eggs are graded. Explain how size is determined.
12. Specify the most appropriate grade to be used in the following egg dishes.
    Fried egg_____
    Cheese souffle_____
    Chocolate cake_____
13. What is the advantage to the operator of using the USDA Acceptance Service?
14. How many cases of whole shell eggs should be purchased to yield 39 pounds of egg yolks?

EXHIBIT

A Poultry Specification	
Product	Turkey, boneless roll
Weight	8#–10# each
Detail	All white meat. No seasoning or preservatives
Condition	Frozen. U.S. inspection stamp applied

11

MEAT

INTRODUCTION

There is no single item in the foodservice budget as large or as important as meat. Of food purchases alone, meat may range from 30 percent of total food expenditures for an institution to 70 percent of food expenditures for a steak and chop house. Meat purchases may range from as much as 20 percent of all operating expenditure for the institutional foodservice to 40 percent for the commercial establishment. There is no way to overemphasize the importance of the proper purchasing and receiving of meat.

The purchase of the proper cut for the use intended is of paramount importance in the purchase of meat. Later on in this section you will note that each cut of meat is accompanied by cooking suggestions. As a general rule of thumb, one should buy the higher grades of meat for the dry methods of cooking (broiling, roasting), as such cuts have adequate marbling (fat) to retain the moist, juicy texture expected when eaten.

The lower grades of meat, which are not as well marbled, are good for the moist heat methods of cooking (braising, boiling, stewing) as the slow, moist cooking breaks down the tough meat fibers to an acceptable level for comfortable chewing. Thus, it is wise to purchase USDA Choice for roasts and steaks, but wasteful to use USDA Choice grades of meat for stews and pot roasts.

Control of costs is achieved through accurate records. Cooking loss cards, percentage of portions served, inventory/order/receiving records will aid in curtailing runaway costs. Costs are reduced by ordering in mass with infrequent deliveries. Weighing each delivery and comparing with specifications will reduce costs.

Meat specifications serve to notify the operator and employee product purpose, as well as provide the purveyor with exactly what the purchaser expects. A meat specification should include: class of animal, quality grade, yield grade, weight range, state of refrigeration, and fat limitations.

There are specific standards which a processor is required to follow regarding refrigeration, packaging, and labeling. One should check if these are met; if they are not, the meat can deteriorate more quickly than what is considered normal.

Names of meat cuts will often identify what area of the carcass the cut came from. Curing is a process of imparting flavor and preserving meat. Tables are given of ingredients and purpose for curing. Vacuum packing cured meats aids in eliminating deterioration.

COMPOSITION AND STRUCTURE

The meat we eat is the muscle of the animal. Muscles are of two types with two respective functions. The involuntary muscles are the smooth muscles of the blood vessels and digestive tract which do their jobs automatically and virtually continuously. These muscles are lacking in interspersed fat and are, therefore, very tough. The voluntary muscles are composed of many tiny fibers joined together by connective tissues in a fashion which is analogous to the wire cables used in building bridges. This type of formation is called striated. Muscles are composed of cells of sizes and shapes which vary according to the feed, age, sex, and type of animal.

The connective tissue cells are joined together into bundles by two types of connective tissue. White connective tissue, called collagen, is found in all the muscles of the animal; it is dominant in the more tender cuts of meat. Yellow connective tissue, called elastin, is predominant in the muscles which carry the heaviest load of constant strain and work.

The white connective tissue breaks up and becomes moist in cooking, whereas the yellow connective tissue requires mechanical means of tenderizing such as pounding, cubing, or grinding. The younger and less exercised an animal is, the less yellow connective tissue it will have and the more tender its meat will be.

FAT AND MARBLING

Of all the factors that go into the measurement of the quality of meat, fat is the most important. The amount, the distribution, and the condition of an animal's fat are essential ingredients in the mix of cost, cutability, and palatability of meats. The total amount of fat may range from as little as 5 percent on a very lean animal to as much as 35 percent on a very fat animal. The fat on the outside of an animal's muscles is called cover. The fat that lies between the bundles of muscle fibers is called marbling. The amount of marbling in the meat and between the connective tissues is a very important factor in meat since it creates the chewability looked for in cooked meat.

Meat in the United States is usually well marbled because the animals are finished on specialized grain feeds which convert rapidly to fat. This is in marked contrast to South American or Spanish meat which is usually raised only on grazing grasses and is, therefore, less fatty and much tougher to chew.

Fat accounts for much of the flavor of meat because a fat subcomponent, esters, imparts and enhances the typical ''meat'' flavors. The type of feed, again, reflects in the type of fat and the eventual flavor of the meat (thus, the regional preference for ''corn-fed'' beef, for example).

The more fat on an animal, the less lean. This factor means that the more fat an animal has in ratio to its lean, the higher the cost of that lean. Prime Beef, for example, is very well marbled and has a thick fat cover and thus costs much more than Choice, Good, or the lesser grades of meat.

The positive nutritive value of meat is in the lean tissue and not in the fat. The food value of a pound of lean is the same whether it is from costly Prime or from inexpensive Commercial. As mentioned earlier, the means of cooking has much to do with the chewability; therefore, the smart operator will buy according to need.

Prime meat should be purchased only for the "carriage trade" business of expensive steak and chop operations where the finest quality is called for and paid for by a clientele that can afford it. It is wasteful and foolish to use Prime meat in noncommercial applications.

PIGMENTS, EXTRACTS, AND WATER

The color of meat depends on the animal's age at slaughter. The older an animal is, the more red pigment (myoglobin) is found in the meat. The range of color varies with the type of animal as well as the use of the particular muscles. Heavily exercised muscles, such as the muscles of the legs, and the involuntary muscles tend to be darker.

The connective tissue of meat contains extracts that contribute to the flavor of the meat. These extracts are water soluble; thus the meat that is cooked by the moist-heat method is less flavorful than meat cooked by dry-heat methods. The stock made of boiled meats is especially flavorful because it contains so much of these extracts.

The amount of water in meat increases as the percentage of fat decreases. Because meat may contain more than 60 percent water, the longer meat is cooked and the higher the temperature at which it is cooked, the greater the water loss and, therefore, the more "shrinkage" or loss of weight that occurs. Since fat is desirable, meat which is firm, as opposed to soft, is of preferred quality.

AGING OR DISPENSING

Aged meat is meat which has had the fibers broken down through material processes. Meat contains many fermenting agents called enzymes. These enzymes break down the cell structures of the lean and the connective tissue and so make the meat easier to chew. By storing meat at a controlled temperature and humidity, for a controlled period of time, the aging or ripening process will increase the tenderness and flavor of the meat. Generally speaking, it is not economical to age meat more than two weeks as water loss and discoloration may cause losses of 15 to 20 percent of the meat.

Beef may be aged as much as 45 days if held at 34°F and 88 percent humidity with at least 10 CFM air circulation. Lamb and mutton may be aged up to 10 days, but pork and veal are never aged.

All meat should be held at a temperature between 34° and 40°F for at least 4 days after slaughter. This period of time will allow the enzymes to combat the rigor mortis, or postslaughter hardening, to a point where the meat has softened and is no longer considered "green."

Refrigeration

Fresh meat is best stored at a temperature of 32° to 34°F and a humidity of no less than 80 percent in a well-ventilated refrigerator. The meat should be allowed to "breathe," which means that it should be covered with material no more dense than a loose-net treated cheesecloth.

A temperature of 32°F is the ambient state of liquid. It takes 160 BTU's to change a temperature from 32°F, the *frozen state of water,* to 32°F, the *liquid state of water.* The higher the temperature and the longer the fresh storage of meat, the greater the amount of weight which will be lost through evaporation, and the greater the amount of meat which will have to be trimmed off and, therefore, lost. A very important part of meat purchasing is keeping loss, due to storage time, to a minimum. Because of this potential for loss, it is often the wisest purchasing decision to specify delivery of fabricated meat in the frozen state.

Freezing

When meat is frozen, the water in the meat expands. This is analogous to the expansion of tap water when frozen into ice cubes. If meat is frozen slowly, then the water in the meat will expand enough to form ice crystals, and the result will be broken cell walls in the meat. For this reason, it is important that meat be frozen very quickly in order to prevent formation of destructive ice crystals. Meat should be frozen at temperatures of at least −25°F in an atmosphere with air circulating at 40 CFM. The center of the meat should be 0°F in a maximum of four hours. Do not accept frozen meat from a purveyor unless you are certain that this procedure has been followed.

When meat is frozen, a certain amount of evaporation takes place. This drying of the surface is commonly known as "freezer burn." Freezer burn may be prevented by wrapping the meat so that it is as airtight as possible before freezing. Many meat purveyors freeze their meats in vacuum (totally air free) bags. Some of these bags can be used to cook the meat in, saving the operator steps in handling and cutting down on pot washing.

Tempering

Tempering is the process of defrosting frozen foods. Frozen meat must be tempered under refrigeration only. If meat is tempered at room temperature (or any temperature between 50°F and 140°F), then an ideal medium for the growth of harmful bacteria will exist. It generally takes about 24 hours to completely defrost an 8-lb. roast at 34°F to 40°F, 72 hours for a 24-lb. roast. Never, never put any kind of meat in a sink of water for any reason.

Meat may be roasted or potted from the frozen state only if done so at a carefully controlled low temperature. Many tests have shown that the difference in yield of roasts cooked at 250°F as opposed to 350°F may be as great as 10 percent.

HOW MUCH TO ORDER?

To know how much meat to order, an operator needs to know how much is used. Knowing how much to use means knowing both how much is used per serving and how many servings are needed.

The question of how much meat to use per serving is a matter of operational philosophy and type of institution. Our society places a large psychological value on meat. Nutritional adequacy calls for only 56 grams of protein per adult per day. If given their preference, people want as much meat as possible. This fact can be traced to the close correlation between our image of success and the meat we eat.

By far, the most popular meat in the United States is beef. In order to make a menu popular, the mix of meat dishes should take this preference into consideration. The means of keeping the cost of meat on the menu down are varied.

1. Balance the menu entree offerings with popular, less expensive, extender items when offering the more expensive, solid entrees. A clientele that likes a relatively expensive, solid entree, like sauerbraten, may well choose a less expensive option such as stew or goulash.
2. Never buy a better grade of meat than needed for the use intended.
3. Buy meat on tight specifications. It is a costly mistake to pay for fat which is not needed or to fail to pay for fat when it is needed.
4. Cook meat at the proper temperature. Cooking losses increase in proportion to the rise in oven temperature. A study, summarized below, of roasts cooked to identical internal temperatures shows just how great cooking loss may be.

Knowing how much meat to order means keeping accurate records. The first record needed is a file of Cooking Loss Cards. This record needs to be computed only once for each menu item, as the loss should always be about the same for the same grade and cut of meat.

Well-done	125°C	225°C
Ribs of Beef	23.0 percent	37.5 percent
Chuck of Beef	33.8 percent	34.6 percent
Rump of Beef	27.4 percent	29.8 percent
Half-ham of Pork	26.8 percent	36.1 percent
Leg of Lamb	16.4 percent	27.3 percent
Rare	125°	225°
Ribs of Beef	7.1 percent	20.2 percent
Chuck of Beef	11.6 percent	21.4 percent

COOKING LOSS

ITEM _____

PORTION SIZE _____

PORTION COST FACTOR _____

COOKED _____ HOURS _____ MINUTES AT _____ DEGREES

_____ HOURS _____ MINUTES AT _____ DEGREES

BREAKDOWN	NO.	WEIGHT		RATIO TO TOTAL WEIGHT	VALUE PER POUND	TOTAL VALUE	READY TO EAT VALUE PER		READY TO EAT PORTION		COST FACTOR PER	
		LBS.	OZ.				LB.	OZ.	SIZE	VALUE	LB.	PORTION
ORIGINAL WEIGHT												
LOSS IN TRIMMING												
TRIMMED WEIGHT												
LOSS IN COOKING												
COOKED WEIGHT												
BONES AND TRIM												
LOSS IN SLICING												
SALABLE MEAT												
REMARKS												

$$\frac{\text{COST FACTOR}}{\text{PER LB. OR PORTION}} = \frac{\text{READY TO EAT VALUE PER LB. OR PORTION}}{\text{PURCHASE PRICE PER LB.}}$$

To find ready to eat value of cuts at a new market price, multiply new price per lb. by the cost factor.

With the usable after-cooking weight as a base, one may calculate the number of portions per cooked pound and then the number of raw pounds needed for a given number of cooked portions by determining a multiplier. The multiplier is simply the result of the following operation:

$$\frac{\text{raw pounds}}{\text{cooked pounds}} \times \frac{\text{cooked pounds}}{\text{portion weight}}$$

The second necessary record is a card that records the number of portions used in the past. The percentage of items used, *in the same menu combination,* will stay within a narrow percentage range. Although the customer count in an individual operation may vary greatly from day to day, the percentage of the customers who favor a particular entree will remain very close to the same. Seasons of the year may have some bearing upon the ratio but, again, the ratio will remain true within that particular season. Keeping such a record for a few months will be sufficient to start using it as an ordering guide; keeping the record over the years will help identify unpopular menu combinations, changing taste trends, and need for menu change.

The third record needed is some type of inventory/order/receiving record. Consideration should be given to the needs of the institution, i.e., volume, refrigeration and freezing capacity, management time, and purchasing plan (butchering vs. fabricated and portion controlled product). These methods are:

1. Operations that have a standing menu (restaurants, hotels) or a short cycle menu of 7 or 10 days will probably find a "par-stock" or a "minimum-maximum stock" inventory system best.
    a. Par-Stock. Under this system, the operator determines a stock level which will cover the institution's needs for the period of the ordering cycle. For purposes of example, we will call it one week. If the maximum weekly need for Item No. 137 Ground Beef is 100 lb., then the par-stock is 100 lb. Each week the Ground Beef order will be the difference between the on-hand inventory and 100 lb. Thus, if the current inventory is 30 lb., the order will be for 70 lb., etc.
    b. Minimum-Maximum Stock. In this method the operator determines the maximum amount of the item which may be needed in the ordering cycle and the minimum quality which must be kept in inventory to prevent running out. This system is very good for operations which tend to have a week-to-week fluctuation, not setting a pattern. Whenever the inventory falls to the minimum level, an order is placed to bring the stock back up to a maximum. Again, using the 100 lb. of Ground Beef as a maximum inventory, then a minimum inventory of say, 20 lb., may be determined. Whenever the inventory falls to 20 lb., an automatic reorder of 80 lb. is placed.
2. Operations which have a cyclical menu of some length (3 to 6 weeks), or operations which have high volume and/or limited refrigerated storage space often find it most convenient to order on an as-needed basis. The drawbacks of this system are twofold. The first is that, unlike the "par-stock" and "minimum-maximum stock" systems, management must review the stock and menu needs at regular intervals instead of placing standing orders or leaving the ordering in clerical hands. The second drawback is that there is no reserve stock to call upon in an emergency situation.

The advantages of this system are that no inventory is being carried on the books, and there is no excess stock in the house and, therefore, no chance of spoilage.

Simply stated, the procedure is to estimate, from the production history cards, the number of portions (converted to raw pounds) that are needed, and then order just that quantity.

HOW MUCH TO PAY?

High quality and high price do not necessarily go hand-in-hand any more than do low quality and low price. When buying meat, the buyer must be aware of certain things.

1. It costs the purveyor money to make deliveries. The larger the order and the less frequent the deliveries, the more likely it is that the price will be lower.
2. Excessive "fill-in" orders, unclear specifications, and unreasonable demands put upon a purveyor will result in higher prices.

3. If you deal with a purveyor who has an inefficient plant operation, the cost of such inefficiency will be passed on to you either in price, poor trim, or improperly cared-for product.

4. Each grade of meat has a range of tolerance, thus there *is* such a thing as "high" Choice and "low" Choice meat. Beware of the purveyor who always claims his meat is "high" choice; appreciate the purveyor who tells you when the meat is "low," "middle range," or "high" in the grade.

5. Beware of the "special" or the "lowball" price. Chances are that the meat is too fresh or has been either aged too long or aged improperly.

6. Receiving controls must be *very tight*. Each piece of meat must be weighed and measured against the specifications. A simple ruler and the pictures later in this section are excellent receiving tools.

7. Storage temperatures must be exact and storage time as brief as possible. Meat shrinks due to evaporation during storage.

8. The buyer and the receiver must have complete loyalty to the operation. A system of checks and balances must be established in order to assure a high degree of honesty. Dishonesty takes many forms and is often difficult to uncover.

9. Meat buying must be conducted either on a bid basis or on a contract. Base contract prices should be arrived at by using one of the various USDA market reports or on the "Yellow Sheet" which is published by the National Provisioner.

HOW MUCH TO CHARGE?

What an operator must charge for meat entrees is contingent both upon what the cost per portion is and upon the financial goals of the operation. The method for arriving at the charge is the same for all types of operation, but the goals may be very different.

A public establishment such as a hotel or restaurant is in business to make a profit. Here the price charged will have to contribute to a profit mixture. If the total profit from operations must be, for example, 12 percent, then every item must contribute to the profit to a degree of 12 percent. Some price-balancing may be done, but the average gain must be 12 percent over *all* costs involved. If the food cost of the operation is 40 percent of expenditures, then each item will have to sell at 2.5 times (100% ÷ 40%) its cost plus 12 percent.

Schools and colleges generally must run foodservice operations on a no profit-no loss basis. In this case, the price of food must be the amount which contributes to breaking even. Using the above example (40 percent food cost), the food in these institutions would be priced 2.5 times the raw cost.

Some institutions, such as industrial feeding operations and hospital employee cafeterias, operate on company subsidies in order to keep food charges low. The idea is to provide eating facilities for the employees which are close to the job. Prices in this situation are based either on what ceiling top management wants on food prices or on the amount of subsidy.

In the first case, the cost of raw food bears no relationship to the price charged. In the second case, it is necessary to estimate the total operating costs, subtract the subsidy, and charge prices for food which contribute proportionately to that expense figure. For example, if the total operating costs are $100,000, the food cost $40,000, and the subsidy $30,000, then the pricing calculation is as follows:

$$\begin{array}{r} \$100{,}000 \text{—operating costs} \\ \underline{30{,}000 \text{—subsidy}} \\ 70{,}000 \text{—income needed} \\ \div\, 40{,}000 \text{—food cost} \end{array}$$

$$= 1.75 \times \text{raw food cost} = \text{price to be charged.}$$

What is The Cost?

The steps to computing the cost per portion are as follows:

1. Compute the raw ready-to-cash weight. (Meat either purchased that way *or* see Yield Test Card.)
2. Cook, trim, and carve the meat. Subtract the combined weight of the carved *portions* from the cooked weight.
3. Divide the total raw cost by the total weight of the carved portions. For example,

100 lb. Inside Round – R.T.C. at $1.24 = 124.00
76 lb. Carved Weight

$$\begin{array}{r} 1.63 \times \\ \hline 76\overline{)124.00} \\ \underline{76} \\ 480 \\ \underline{456} \\ 240 \\ \underline{228} \\ 120 \end{array}$$

Cost per saleable pound $1.63
6 oz. Portion Weight
$1.63 ÷ 16 oz. = $.1078 per oz. × 6 = .612 per portion

or

76 lb. × 16 oz. = 1216 oz. ÷ 6 = 202.7 portions

$$\begin{array}{r} .6117 \text{ or } .612 \text{ per portion} \\ \hline 202.7\overline{)124.00000} \\ \underline{121.62} \\ 2380 \\ \underline{2027} \\ 3530 \\ \underline{2027} \\ 15030 \end{array}$$

The preceding calculation should be made for every menu item served. The carved weight percentage (76 percent in the above example) can be used to quickly recalculate the cost per portion when the raw product cost changes or portion size is changed. A comparison of the cost per portion on various cuts of meat will quickly reveal the most economical cut of meat to use for any given menu item.

WRITING MEAT SPECIFICATIONS

Purpose

The purpose of written specifications for meat and meat products is dual. The first purpose is to give the operator and employees knowledge of which product should be used for what purpose. The second purpose is to tell the purveyor *exactly* what the expected product is. It is not possible *honestly* to take quotations on a meat item if the purveyor and the operator do not agree on the *exact* definition of the meat item.

Once written, a copy of the operation's specifications must be sent, for reference, to every purveyor that the operation buys from. The operator must insist that deliveries meet the *exact* specifications set. Any variance from these standards is dishonest, costly to the operation, and, therefore, forbidden.

What Must be Included:

The properly written meat specification should include the operation's exact requirements regarding:

1. Class of Animal
2. USDA Grade and Division of Grade
3. USDA Yield Grade
4. Acceptable Weight Range
5. State of Refrigeration
6. Fat Limitations

What are the IMPS?

IMPS, the Institutional Meat Purchase Specifications, are the official USDA requirements for the inspection, packaging, packing, and delivering of specific meats and meat products, and for the certification of those products by USDA meat graders. The IMPS are the most widely known and accepted meat specifications in our country. Formally, the IMPS are applied with the use of the Meat Acceptance Service of the USDA. In operations too small to use the Meat Acceptance Service, the IMPS can still be used as long as the person receiving the meat knows how to translate the written specification to the physical object.

What is *The Meat Buyers' Guide?*

The Meat Buyers' Guide contains the meat specifications agreed upon by the National Association of Meat Purveyors (NAMP), the largest and most powerful of all wholesale meat purveyor associations. The publication, *The Meat Buyers' Guide to Standardized Meat Cuts,* was written as a means of simplifying the IMPS and to give pictoral definition to the most common meat cuts. There is no better set of meat specifications anywhere in the country than the *IMPS* and *Meat Buyers' Guide.* Since the *Meat Buyers' Guide* is illustrated with photographs which show the proper dimensions of the cut product, they are the specifications that should be used by all operators. Every meat purveyor knows the MBG specifications and, therefore, should have no difficulty in delivering products that meet the MBG specifications. IMPS and MBG have replaced the prevalent regional names for the various meat cuts.

INSTITUTIONAL MEAT PURCHASE SPECIFICATIONS— GENERAL REQUIREMENTS

Beef Specifications

USDA Grade.   To be specified by purchaser. The purchaser must specify either (1) a quality grade, or (2) a combination of quality grade and yield grade. Yield grades 1 through 5 are applicable to all quality grades. However, those yield grades indicated by an "X" are in the largest supply.

USDA GRADES

Quality	Yield[1]				
	1	2	3	4	5
U.S. Prime			x	x	x
U.S. Choice		x	x	x	x
U.S. Good		x	x		
U.S. Standard	x	x	x		
U.S. Commercial		x	x	x	x
U.S. Utility		x	x	x	
U.S. Cutter		x	x		
U.S. Canner		x	x		

1. The yield grades reflect differences in yields of boneless, closely trimmed retail cuts. Yield grade 1 represents the highest yield of cuts and yield grade 5, the lowest.

Division of Quality Grade.   To be specified by purchaser (not applicable to yield grade). Note: If the upper half or lower half of a quality grade is desired, it must be so specified, otherwise the full range of the grade is acceptable.

Weight Range.   To be specified by purchaser. Range A, B, C, D, or E, or actual weight range in pounds (8/10, 20/24, etc.).

State of Refrigeration.   To be specified by purchaser. (1) chilled, or (2) frozen.

Fat Limitations.   Carcasses, sides, or quarters (not applicable if yield grade is specified). Except when yield grade is specified by the purchaser, the thickness of external fat measured at the thinnest point over the rib or loin eye must not exceed that indicated for each quality grade in the following schedule:

MAXIMUM THICKNESS OF FAT AT THINNEST POINT OVER RIBEYE

Grade	Weight Range A & B	Weight Range C, D, & E
U.S. Prime	⅞ in.	1¼ in.
U.S. Choice	⅝ in.	1 in.
U.S. Good	⅜ in.	¾ in.
U.S. Standard	¼ in.	⅜ in.
U.S. Commercial	⅝ in.	⅞ in.
U.S. Utility	¼ in.	½ in.
U.S. Cutter or Canner	⅛ in.	¼ in.

In addition, carcasses, sides, or quarters are not acceptable if, because of an uneven distribution of external fat or large deposits of kidney and pelvic fat, they are wasty in relation to the maximum permitted thickness of fat over the ribeye.

Fat Limitations.   Wholesale and fabricated cuts: To be specified by purchaser (not applicable if yield grade is specified). Except when yield grade is specified, for all wholesale and fabricated beef products—except those for which definite fat limitations are indicated in the detailed specifications—the purchaser must specify one of the following maximum average thicknesses of surface fat:

1. 1 in. (1¼ in. maximum at any point except for seam fat)
2. ¾ in. (1 in. maximum at any point except for seam fat)
3. ½ in. (¾ in. maximum at any point except for seam fat)
4. ¼ in. (½ in. maximum at any point except for seam fat)

Defatting must be done by smoothly removing the fat by following the contour of the underlying muscle surface. Beveling of edges only is not acceptable.

Note: When string tying is required, roasts must be made firm and compact and held intact by individual loops of strong twine uniformly spaced at approx. 2-in. intervals girthwise. In addition, some roasts may require string tying lengthwise. In lieu of string tying, it is permissible to enclose roasts in a stretchable netting, provided it complies with the Regulations Governing the Meat Inspection of the USDA. Purchasers may specify that roasts be string tied when this requirement is not specified in the detailed roast item specifications.

Material. Beef products described must be derived from sound, well-dressed, split and quartered beef carcasses or from sound, well-trimmed, primal cuts from such carcasses. The beef must be prepared and handled in accordance with good commercial practice and must meet the type, grade, style of cut, weight range, and state of refrigeration specified.

Beef cuts which have been excessively trimmed in order to meet specified weights, or which are substandard according to the specifications for any reason, are excluded. The beef must be of good color normal to the grade, be practically free of residue remaining from sawing the meat and bones, and free of blood clots, scores, odor foreign to strictly fresh beef (e.g., kerosene, putrid, stale, rancid, chemicals, etc.), mutilations (other than slight), ragged edges, superficial appendages, blemishes, discoloration, (e.g., green, black, blue, etc.), deterioration, damage, or mishandling. The spinal cord must be completely removed, and the beef also must be free from bruises, evidence of freezing or defrosting, and must be in excellent condition to the time of delivery. Stag and bull beef are not acceptable.

Portion-cut items described herein must be prepared from fresh-chilled carcasses or bone-in cuts which are in excellent condition, and they must be of the applicable kind and of the U.S. grade or selection specified. The meat must show no evidence of off-condition, including but not restricted to off-odor, slightly sticky, gassy, rancid, sour, discolored, and evidence of defrosting or mishandling. Also, the portion-cut items must be free of blood clots, scores (other than slight), ragged edges, bruises, and spinal cord, and must be practically free of bone and meat dust. Portion-cut items supplied must be in compliance with applicable requirements specified herein and with other requirements specified by the purchaser.

COMPARISON OF YIELDS* OF RETAIL CUTS AND RETAIL VALUES BETWEEN USDA YIELD GRADE 2 AND YIELD GRADE 4 CARCASSES

Closely Trimmed Retail Cuts	Percent Carcass Weight USDA 2	Percent Carcass Weight USDA 4	Price per Pound**	Retail Value in Dollars per cwt. USDA 2	Retail Value in Dollars per cwt. USDA 4
Rump, boneless	3.5	3.1	$1.68	$5.88	$5.21
Inside round	4.5	3.7	1.81	8.15	6.70
Outside round	4.6	4.2	1.75	8.05	7.35
Round tip	2.6	2.4	1.77	4.60	4.25
Sirloin	8.7	7.9	1.69	14.71	13.35
Short loin	5.2	5.0	1.94	10.09	9.70
Rib, short cut (7 in.)	6.2	6.0	1.59	9.86	9.54
Blade chuck	9.4	8.4	.93	8.75	7.80
Chuck, arm, boneless	6.1	5.5	1.32	8.05	7.26
Brisket, boneless	2.3	1.9	1.48	3.41	2.81
Flank steak	.5	.5	2.01	1.01	1.01
Lean trim	11.3	9.3	1.21	13.67	11.25
Ground beef	12.2	10.0	1.01	12.30	10.10
Fat	12.7	22.9	.02	.25	.46
Bone	9.9	8.9	.01	.10	.09
Kidney	.3	.3	.66	.20	.20
TOTAL	100.0	100.0		$109.08	$97.08

Difference in retail value per cwt. between Yield Grade 2 and 4—$12.00

* Cuts trimmed to ½ inch of fat.

** Average retail prices for Choice beef for October 1973 (including sale priced items) as furnished by a large number of selected retailers throughout the country.

Portion Weight or Thickness of Steaks, Chops, Cutlets

Purchasers must specify *either* the portion weight or thickness desired—*not both*. However, in order to control uniformity of portion sizes, the weight range of the trimmed meat cut from which the portions are to be produced may also be specified.

Portion Weight.   If portion weight is specified, the actual portion weights desired (3 oz., 6 oz., 12 oz., etc.) must be indicated.

Weight Tolerances.   Unless otherwise specified by the purchaser, dependent upon the portion weight specified, the following tolerances over and under the weight specified will be permitted.

Weight Specified	Tolerances (Over and Under)
less than 6 oz.	1/4 oz.
6 oz. but less than 12 oz.	1/2 oz.
12 oz. but less than 18 oz.	3/4 oz.
18 oz. or more	1 oz.

Example: When 8-oz. steaks are specified, individual steaks weighing 7½ to 8½ oz. are applicable.

Thickness.   If thickness is specified, the actual thickness desired must be indicated. (Cubed steaks, ground beef patties, and cubed cutlets excepted.)

Thickness Tolerance.   Unless otherwise specified by the purchaser, dependent upon the thickness specified, the following tolerances over and under the thickness specified will be permitted:

Thickness Specified	Tolerances (Over and Under)
1 in. or less	3/16 in.
More than 1 in.	1/4 in.

Example: When 1¼ in. steaks are specified, individual steaks measuring 1 to 1½ in. are acceptable.

Weight Range for Roasts

Purchasers must specify the actual weight range (4–6, 8–10, 17–19, etc.) desired. If purchasers want roasts further reduced in size, this must also be specified.

Surface Fat

Steaks.   Unless otherwise specified by the purchaser, or unless definite fat limitations are indicated in the detailed item specifications, on surfaces where fat is present, the fat must not exceed an average of ½ in. in thickness, and the thickness at any point must be not more than ¾ in.

Chops, Cutlets, and Filets.   Unless otherwise specified by the purchaser, surface fat, where present, must not exceed an average of ¼ in. in thickness, and the thickness at any one point must be not more than ⅜ in.

Roasts.   The purchaser must specify the maximum average surface fat thickness desired, unless definite fat limitations are indicated in the detailed item specifications. The maximum average surface fat thickness (seam fat excepted) for ¾ in. is 1 in. maximum at any one point; and for ½ in. is ¾ in. maximum at any one point.

Note: Defatting must be done by smoothly removing the fat by following the contour of the underlying muscle surface. Beveling of the edges only is not acceptable. In determining the average thickness of surface fat or the thickness of fat at any one point on steaks and roasts which have an evident, natural depression into the lean, only the fat above the portion of the depression which is more than ¾ in. in width will be considered.

Inspection

All meats, prepared meats, meat food products, and meat by-products (as defined in Rules and Regulations of the Department of Agriculture Governing the Grading and Certification of Meats, Prepared Meats, and Meat Products) covered by these specifications must originate from animals which were slaughtered or from product items which were manufactured or processed in establishments regularly operated under the supervision of the Meat and Poultry Inspection Program (MPIP) of the Consumer and Marketing Service (C&MS) of the United States Department of Agriculture (USDA) or under any other system of meat inspection approved by the Consumer and Marketing Service of the USDA.

Ordering Data

The purchaser will requisition product items by specifying the item number, name, and the desired options such as grade or selection, weight range, formula, state of refrigeration, etc., indicated in each specification, and products must be offered for delivery on such basis by the contractor, subject to official examination, acceptance, and certification by USDA meat graders or other designated personnel. The examination, acceptance, and certification of products by the USDA shall be in accordance with USDA Meat Grading instructions. (Copies of Meat Grading instructions may be obtained from the local Meat Grading Branch Main Station Office.)

Certification

In connection with the issuance of meat grade certificates, one or more kinds of official USDA meat grade certificates will be involved depending on whether the product is for delivery chilled or frozen.

Products for Delivery Chilled

When products are to be delivered chilled, an official final certificate will be issued by the responsible USDA meat grader to cover all factors and details of the products.

Products for Delivery Frozen

When products are to be delivered frozen, the responsible USDA meat grader will issue an official preliminary certificate, identified as such, to cover all factors and details of the chilled product prior to freezing. The responsible USDA meat grader will issue an official final certificate covering all factors and details of the frozen product prior to loading for delivery.

Disposition of Certificates

The original and up to two extra copies of all preliminary and final certificates are available to the contractor. The purchaser may request the contractor to supply copies of all final certificates.

The cost of the examination, acceptance, and certification shall be paid by the contractor.

Time Limitation

Products prepared for delivery under a purchase order shall not be offered to USDA meat graders for examination and acceptance more than 72 hours before shipment.

State of Refrigeration

The detailed specifications for the various products indicate two different states of refrigeration. These are defined as follows:

Chilled

Chilled products are those which, promptly after preparation and in accordance with good commercial practice, are thoroughly chilled (but not frozen or defrosted) to an internal temperature of not higher than 50°F. They must be held in suitable temperatures (32° to 38°F) and must be in excellent condition to the time of delivery.

Frozen

Products to be delivered frozen must be promptly and thoroughly frozen in suitable and reasonably uniform temperatures not higher than 0°F. Products thus frozen must be maintained and delivered in a solidly frozen state. The products must show no evidence of defrosting, refreezing, freezerburn, contamination, or mishandling.

When the state of refrigeration is not specified in the purchase order, the product must be maintained and delivered chilled.

Packaging and Packing

Packaging

1. All carcass meat and wholesale cuts that are normally wrapped in commercial practice must be completely and properly packaged in suitable material (crinkled paper bags, grease and moisture-resistant paper, suitable plastic or metal foil covering, stockinettes, etc.) to insure sanitary delivery.

2. Fabricated and boneless cuts (including units of diced and ground meat); cured, smoked, and dried meat; and edible by-products that are normally wrapped in commercial practice must be separately and closely packaged with suitable grease and moisture-resistant paper or suitable plastic or metal foil covering, etc.

3. Portion-control products must be suitably packaged in accordance with good commercial practice and, unless otherwise specified in the purchase order, such packages must contain not more than 25 pounds net weight.

4. Unless otherwise specified in the purchase order, products such as frankfurters, sliced bacon, sliced dried beef, linked or bulk pork or breakfast sausage, etc., must be suitably packaged and placed in immediate containers of the kind conventionally used for such products as illustrated in the following:

   a. Frankfurters and linked sausage—One-pound retail-type individual packages packed not more than 10 pounds per unit in the outer container, or layer packed 1 link deep with parchment or waxed paper separators between layers in a 5- to 10-pound container.

   b. Sliced bacon—One-pound retail-type individual packages such as folded or sleeve-type cartons, cello covering, or flat hotel-style packets snugly packed in a substantial outer container not to exceed 50 pounds net packed weight.

   c. Sliced dried beef—Either ¼-pound, ½-pound, or 1-pound retail-type individual packages, snugly packed not more than 10 pounds net weight per outer container, or bulk or layer packed in a substantial inside-waxed or plastic or waxed paper-lined container not to exceed 10 pounds net packed weight.

   d. Bulk pork or breakfast sausage—One-pound retail-type individual packages such as cello rolls, plastic bags, waxed paper cups, or folded or sleeve-type cartons, packed not more than 10 pounds net weight per container, or in waxed or plastic coated paper tubs of either 5 or 10 pounds net weight.

5. It is the contractor's responsibility to assure that products to be frozen are suitably wrapped and packaged in a material which is grease and moisture resistant and which will also prevent freezer deterioration.

Packing

Unless otherwise specified in the purchase order, products customarily packed in shipping containers must not be packed in excess of 100 pounds, net weight, except that portion-control products are limited to units weighing not more than 25 pounds. Containers must be of a size and shape normally used and adapted to the product being packed. The shipping containers must be made from material which will impart no odor, flavor, or color to the product and must be packed to full capacity without slack-filling or overfilling.

Immediate containers used for packaging which meet the packing requirements may be used as shipping containers. Otherwise, immediate containers must be placed in a master container meeting the packing requirements except that part or whole shipments of not more than 5 packaged units may be shipped in their immediate containers.

Chilled products must be packed in wirebound wooden boxes or in fiberboard boxes. Products to be frozen must be packed in fiberboard boxes. Fiberboard used in making these boxes shall be as described in Federal Specification PPP-F-320 and must comply with the requirements listed below.

Products that are normally bulk packed (spareribs, oxtails, tongues, etc.) or those that are normally moist or subject to dripping moisture must be packed in either wax-resin impregnated fiberboard boxes or in boxes which are protected by one or both of the following methods:

1. Appropriate moisture-proof plastic or wax coated on the inside (not applicable to wirebound wood boxes). The quantity of wax applied to the interior must be sufficient to be visible when lightly scraped with the fingernail.
2. Completely lined on the inside (sides, ends, top, and bottom) with suitably waxed kraft or parchment paper or with appropriate moisture-proof plastic liners.

Cured products in pickle may be either put in plastic bags and then packed into fiberboard boxes of the type specified for use with products subject to dripping moisture or they may be packed directly into fiber, wooden, or metal drums. Drum interiors shall be suitably protected by a wax or plastic coating or lined with a plastic bag liner. When used, plastic bags and plastic bag liners must be securely closed. Drums shall have full opening tops with lock rim closures which permit sealing by USDA and opening and reclosure by the purchaser.

Unless otherwise specified in the purchase order, in lieu of the aforementioned shipping containers, new or reconditioned wooden slack barrels or fiber drums may be used for packing full ribs, oven-prepared ribs, roast-ready ribs, strip loins, lamb backs and similar cuts to be delivered in the fresh state. The wooden slack barrels must be protected from absorption and leakage by an inside lining of plastic or crinkled kraft paper. The fiber drums must be protected from absorption and leakage by a wax or plastic inside coating or by an inside lining of plastic or crinkled kraft paper. After packing, the barrels or drums must be properly headed and covered.

Closure

Fiberboard boxes shall be securely closed using one or more of the following methods:

1. Strapping—Boxes may be strapped with one of the following:
   a. Flat steel straps, at least ¼ inch in width, that are protected with an enameled or rust-resistant coating.

    b. Pressure-sensitive adhesive, filament reinforced tape at least 0.5 inch in width.

    c. Non-metallic strapping at least ⅜ inch wide by 0.015 inch thick, or at least ¼ inch wide by 0.027 inch thick.

    d. Substantial round or twist-tie galvanized, steel wire.

Containers with a net weight of more than 25 pounds must be strapped by placing one strap, wire, or tape girthwise at the approximate center around the top, sides, and bottom of the container and by a second strap, wire, or tape centrally located around the top, ends, and bottom of the container at a right angle to the first. For containers with a net weight of 25 pounds or less, the second strap may be omitted.

2. Stapling—Staples shall be sufficient in number and shall be properly distributed to insure a secure closure and to prevent lifting of edges and corners of outer flaps.

3. Gluing—The top and bottom flaps shall be firmly glued together over a sufficient area to insure a secure closure and to prevent lifting of edges and corners of outer flaps.

Note: USDA maintains the right to have the packing and closure materials determined by appropriate test procedures.

REQUIREMENTS FOR FIBERBOARD[1]

Weight of Product	State of Refrigeration of Product		
	Chilled	Frozen	
		Weather Resistant	Wax-Resin Impregnated
More than 25 pounds	200 p.s.i.	275 p.s.i.	200 p.s.i.
25 pounds or less	175 p.s.i.	175 p.s.i.	175 p.s.i.

1. Dry board bursting strength of fiberboard used in making boxes for products to be delivered either chilled or frozen.

Sealing

When individual products are not stamped, the immediate or shipping containers in which the products are packed must be sealed in accordance with USDA meat grading instructions.

Note: If a tape or strap specified for sealing also qualifies as a strapping material under "Closure," it may be used as both a strap and the seal.

Marking

Containers Packed to More Than 25 Pounds Net Weight

1. The following markings must be legibly and conspicuously stenciled or printed on one end of the container in letters and numbers not less than ½-inch high:

    a. Upper left hand corner. The true name of the product and the code identification of these specifications (IMPS), together with the product item number (Roast Ready Ribs, IMPS No. 109; Bologna, IMPS No. 801, etc.).

b. Upper right hand corner. The date of examination and acceptance by the USDA meat grader (month, day, and year).

c. Lower left hand corner. The grade or selection of product (U.S. Prime, U.S. Choice, etc.; or Slection No. 1, Selection No. 2, as applicable).

d. Lower right hand corner. The number of pieces or packages of product in the container and the net weight of the product. (This information may be applied with a felt tip pen, crayon, or pencil.)

2. The following markings must be stenciled or printed on the top or side of the container in letters and numbers not less than ½-inch high:

a. The name and address of the contractor.

b. The name and address of the supplier if other than the contractor.

c. The name and address of the consignee (not applicable to stockpiled products).

In addition to the above markings, when the product is prepared for stockpiling (not prepared under a purchase order) it shall have any deviations from specification requirements and all applicable options such as weight range, formula, portion-size, etc., stenciled or printed on the lower left hand corner of the same end on which the other markings appear.

Note: When lack of space precludes listing all the information required on the lower left hand corner of the end, it may be stenciled or printed on the opposite end or on a side panel.

The marking material must be flat, waterfast, nonsmearing (take-on fiber), and black in color.

Containers Packed to 25 Pounds or Less Net Weight

In lieu of stenciling, such containers may have a printed or typewritten label firmly attached by adhesive material on one end of the container which legibly and conspicuously bears the markings indicated above.

Examination for Condition of Containers

Definitions and procedures contained in the United States Standards for Conditions of Food Containers shall apply for lots containing 50 or more shipping containers or 300 or more primary containers. (Copies of the Standard may be obtained from the Livestock Division, C&MS, USDA, Washington, D.C. 20250.)

In lots that include less than 50 shipping containers or less than 300 primary containers, the containers shall be examined individually and all defective containers must be replaced or corrected, as applicable.

Examination for condition of containers shall be made in conjunction with the final examination and acceptance of the product. However, at the option of the contractor, on product to be delivered frozen, such an examination also may be made in conjunction with the preliminary examination and acceptance.

Condition of Product at Time of Delivery

Refrigerated trucks must be used when necessary to protect products during transport and these trucks must be clean and free from foreign odors. At destination, all products will be re-examined by the consignee for cleanliness and soundness.

Special Notice

Contractors furnishing products under these specifications are expected to furnish such assistance as may be necessary to expedite the grading, examination, and acceptance of these products. These specifications will be strictly enforced by the using agencies. The consignee may, by purchasing acceptable products in the open market, immediately replace any products which are not delivered or which he rejects. In such case, any increase in cost of these products will be charged against the defaulting contractor.

Waivers and Amendments to Specifications Requirements

Waivers of a few specification requirements may be made provided: (1) the change can be indicated clearly and precisely, (2) there is agreement between purchaser and contractor on the changes, and (3) the purchaser furnishes the USDA meat grader who is to perform the examination and acceptance of the product with a written statement indicating the precise nature of the changes.

Examples of waivers that may be made include:

1. Substitution of weight ranges for those specified.
2. Substitution of grade of meat specified.
3. Modification of fat content in ground or diced meat.
4. Slight variations in trim or style of cutting.
5. Slight variations in sausage formulas.

Changes involving extensive rephrasing of specification requirements must be considered as an amendment to the specification and may be placed in effect only after such changes have been submitted and approved by the Standardization Branch, Livestock Division, C&MS, United States Department of Agriculture.

Institution Inspection

Final acceptance of all products will be by the consignee at the point of delivery. Products that are not appropriately identified with the "USDA Accepted As Specified" stamp will be rejected. Products that are appropriately identified with that stamp but which have other obvious, major deviations from specification requirements also will be rejected. Products appropriately identified with the "USDA Accepted As Specified" stamp but which, in the opinion of the consignee, have minor deviations

Beef: Yield of wholesale cuts from the carcass and yield of boneless meat from wholesale cuts

Carcass and wholesale cuts	Yield of bone-in wholesale cuts		Yield of boneless meat from wholesale cuts[1]	
	Prime, Choice, and Good	Canner and Cutter	Prime, Choice, and Good	Canner and Cutter
	PERCENT	PERCENT	PERCENT	PERCENT
Carcass, whole	100.0	100.0	66.0	73.0
Forequarter	51.5	52.0	69.0	72.5
Rib	9.5	8.5	65.0	71.0
Chuck, square cut	26.5	28.5	73.5	76.0
Plate	8.5	7.5	63.5	74.0
Brisket	4.0	4.0	58.5	64.0
Foreshank	3.0	3.5	58.0	53.5
Hindquarter	48.5	48.0	63.0	73.0
Rump	5.5	6.0	63.0	65.5
Round, rump and shank off	14.0	16.0	79.5	87.0
Shank	3.0	3.5	46.0	44.5
Sirloin	9.0	10.0	72.5	76.0
Short loin	7.0	6.5	70.5	71.0
Flank	6.0	4.5	49.0	75.0
Kidney knob	4.0	1.5	—	—

1. All cuts trimmed of fat exceeding that amount normally left on retail cuts (1/4 in. to 1/2 in.).

from the specification requirements which do not materially affect the usability of the product may be tentatively accepted subject to verification of such deviations by local USDA meat grading personnel. Disposition of products with such verified minor deviations will be at the option of the consignee. All deviations from the specifications noted at the point of delivery must be reported promptly to local USDA meat grading personnel who are instructed to investigate all such reports without delay.

Beef, cured, corned, pickled, dried or dehydrated: Relation between procurement and carcass weights

Product	Factors for determining equivalent carcass weight
Boneless beef:	
Cured, corned, or pickled:[1]	
Brisket, or corned beef unspecified	1.08
Plate, or family beef	1.31
Dried or chipped beef, sliced or unsliced	2.08
Dehydrated beef	3.00

1. Based on 20% gain in pickling brisket from fresh weight, and 10% gain in pickling plate.

Beef: Conversion factors for determining equivalent carcass weight of boneless wholesale cuts and for converting boneless wholesale cuts to equivalent bone-in cuts of various U.S. grades.

Carcass and wholesale cuts	Factors for converting boneless wholesale cuts to equivalent carcass weight		Factors for converting boneless wholesale cuts to equivalent bone-in cuts	
	Prime, Choice, and Good	Canner and Cutter	Prime, Choice, and Good	Canner and Cutter
Carcass, whole	1.52	1.37	1.52	1.37
Forequarter	1.60	1.36	1.45	1.38
Rib	1.49	1.33	1.55	1.41
Chuck, square cut	1.69	1.42	1.37	1.32
Plate	1.46	1.38	1.58	1.36
Brisket	1.35	1.21	1.71	1.56
Foreshank	1.34	1.00	1.73	1.88
Hindquarter	1.44	1.37	1.60	1.37
Rump	1.44	1.23	1.60	1.52
Round, rump and shank off	1.84	1.63	1.26	1.15
Shank	1.06	.84	2.17	2.25
Sirloin	1.67	1.42	1.38	1.32
Short loin	1.63	1.33	1.42	1.41
Flank	1.12	1.41	2.05	1.33

BONE STRUCTURE IMPORTANT IN MEAT IDENTIFICATION

The names of meat cuts frequently are related to the bone structure. Ribs, for instance, provide the names of rib roast, rib steak, and rib chops. Other cuts named for bones include arm and blade roasts and pot-roasts, arm and blade steaks and chops, short ribs, back bones, neck bones, spareribs, riblets, breasts of veal and lamb, T-bone steaks and wedge bone, flat bone and pin bone sirloin steaks.

Bones show the location of retail cuts and also are a clue to a cut's tenderness. The supporting muscles along the back bone are generally more tender than those in the shoulders, legs, breasts, and flanks. Consequently, the meat along the back bone is considered the most tender.

Bones in the four kinds of meat are almost identical in appearance. Their common and technical names are given in the box below. Note that with minor exceptions, bones in the four meats carry the same names.

The seven bone groups are about the only ones the average shopper needs to know. Most other bones are removed before the cuts are sold. Upon learning to recognize the bones that identify the seven groups of retail cuts, it becomes surprisingly easy to call by name a large number of retail cuts in the food store.

Breast Cuts (Brisket, Short Plate)

Bones in the breast are shown clearly in the diagram. They are: (a) breast bone, (b) ribs, and (c) rib cartilages. Shaded areas in the chart show the relative location of com-

Common Names of Bones	No.	Technical Names of Bones
Neck bone	1	Cervical vertebrae—1 to 7
Atlas	1a	First cervical vertebra
		Thoracic vertebrae—1 to 13 (up to 15 in pork)
Back bone	2	Lumbar vertebrae—1 to 6 (7 in lamb and pork)
		Sacral vertebrae—1 to 5 (4 in lamb and pork)
Button	2a	Cartilage of spinous process
Feather bone	2b	Spinous process
Finger bone	2c	Transverse process
Chine bone	2d	Body of vertebra
Slip joint	3	Sacro-iliac diathrosis
Tail bone	4	Caudal (coccygeal) vertebrae—2 to 6 (varies in different carcasses)
Blade bone	5	Scapula
Arm bone	6	Humerus
Fore shank bone(s)	7	Ulna and radius
		Removed from beef and veal
Fore foot bone(s)	7a	Pork—Carpal, metacarpal and phalangeal bones, dew claws and toes
(lower shank)		Lamb—Carpal and metacarpal bones
Elbow bone	8	Olecranon process
Breast bone	9	Sternum—sternebrae 1 to 7 (6 in pork)
Rib cartilages	10	Costal cartilages
Ribs	11	Ribs
Pelvic bone	12	Pelvis
Hip bone	12a	Ilium
Rump (aitch) bone	12b	Ischium
Leg (round) bone	13	Femur
Knee cap	14	Patella
Stifle joint	15	Femro-tibial articulation
Hind shank bone(s)	16	Tibia (includes fibula in pork)
Hock bones	16a	Parts of tibia and fibular tarsal bones
		Removed from beef and veal
Hind foot bones	16b	Pork—Tarsal, metatarsal and phalangeal bones, dew claws and toes
(lower shank)		Lamb—Metatarsal and 1st phalangeal bones

parable cuts of the four meats. Also shown are several retail cuts from the breast areas of beef, veal, pork and lamb. The main features to observe are:

1. Similarity in general contour of fresh beef boneless brisket, veal breast, lamb breast, and pork spareribs.
2. Similarity of bones in veal and lamb breasts and pork spareribs.
3. Characteristic alternating layers of lean and fat that are particularly noticeable in sliced bacon, plate beef, and lamb riblets.

BONES IDENTIFY SEVEN GROUPS OF RETAIL CUTS

Shoulder Arm Cuts	Arm Bone		
Shoulder Blade Cuts (Cross Sections of Blade Bone)	Blade Bone (near neck)	Blade Bone (center cuts)	Blade Bone (near rib)
Rib Cuts	Back Bone and Rib Bone		
Short Loin Cuts	Back Bone (T-Shape) T-Bone		
Hip (Sirloin) Cuts (Cross Sections of Hip Bone)	Pin Bone (near short loin)	Flat Bone* (center cuts)	Wedge Bone† (near round)
Leg or Round Cuts	Leg or Round Bone		
Breast, or Brisket Cuts	Breast and Rib Bones		

*Formerly part of "double bone" but today the back bone is usually removed leaving only the "flat bone" (sometimes called "pin bone") in the sirloin steak.

†On one side of sirloin steak, this bone may be wedge shaped while on the other side the same bone may be round.

4. Comparatively thick layers of lean in the beef boneless fresh brisket, beef short ribs, and veal brisket pieces.
5. Diaphragm or "skirt" in lamb breast and pork spareribs and absence of skirt in veal breast indicating its removal.

Shoulder Blade Cuts

Since part or all of back bone (b) and rib bone (c) in the diagram may have been removed by the packer or retailer, the most important identifying bone in shoulder blade cuts is blade bone (a). (The shoulder is known as the chuck in beef.) It may resemble a reversed 7, or it may be almost flat like the one in the beef blade steak (flat bone).

In the bone charts, note the triangular shape of the blade bone and location of the "ridge" on this bone which forms the 7. The short 7 is near the neck while the long 7 is in the center and the flat bone is adjacent to the rib. Most of the meat in blade cuts is

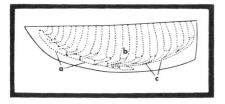

Breast Cuts
(Brisket, Short Plate)

BEEF
Brisket and Short Plate

PORK
Spareribs, Bacon Side (Belly)

VEAL
Breast

LAMB
Breast

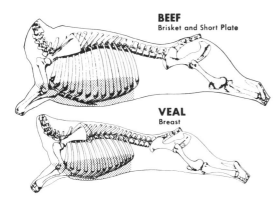

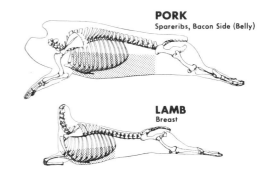

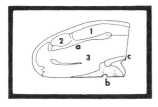

Shoulder Blade Cuts

BEEF
Blade Steaks and Pot-roasts

PORK
Blade Steaks: Boston Butt Roast

VEAL
Blade Steaks and Roast

LAMB
Blade Chops

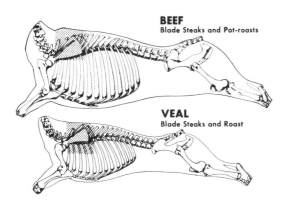

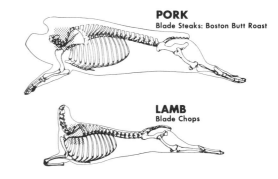

more tender than that in arm cuts, and the cuts near the rib are more tender than those near the neck.

When the blade chuck is boned, several cuts can be made. The three most common are: (1) boneless top blade steak, (2) mock tender, and (3) boneless eye roast.

Shoulder (Chuck) Arm Cuts

Bones in shoulder arm cuts include (a) arm bone and (b) cross sections of rib bones as shown. In the photograph, the main features to observe and compare are:

1. Similarity in bone and muscle structure as well as shape of beef arm steak (full cut), veal and pork arm steaks and lamb arm chop. Also note differences in sizes of the respective cuts.
2. Lack of rib bones in beef and pork arm steaks consistent with modern cutting methods.
3. Boneless beef shoulder steaks and pot-roasts from section (1) in diagram. Beef chuck short ribs include rib bones (b). Beef chuck cross rib pot-roast includes both section (1) and rib bones (b).
4. The somewhat similar appearance of cuts from the arm or leg since both may contain a round bone; as well as the wide difference in muscle structure.

Rib (Hotel Rack) Cuts

Identifying bones in retail cuts from the rib are shown in the diagram. They are (a) rib bone and the back bone which consists of (b1) feather bone, and (b2) chine bone. The chine bone is usually removed from steaks and chops. Even when all of the bones are removed, cuts from the rib are comparatively easy to recognize by the appearance of the rib eye (1) which is part of the tender muscle (longissimus dorsi) that lies along the back bone in the rib and loin.

In the photograph, similarity in appearance of the beef rib steak, veal rib chop, lamb rib chop and pork rib chop will be noted. The pork butterfly chop is made from two boneless rib chops (or loin chops) hinged together. Canadian style bacon is made from the rib eye of the rib and the loin eye of the loin.

Loin (Short Loin) Cuts

With one exception, bone-in cuts from the loin (short loin) contain only the back bone. The exception is one top loin steak which may include part of the 13th rib. The back bone consists of three parts as indicated. They are (a) spine bone, (b) chine bone, and (c) finger bone (stem of T-bone).

The three muscles in the short loin are (1) top loin or loin eye (also part of the longissimus dorsi muscle), (2) tenderloin, and (3) flank meat. Pork loin chops contain very little flank meat. Porterhouse and T-bone steaks also are being sold in more and more stores without the flank portion.

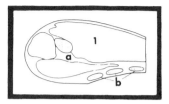

Shoulder (Chuck)
Arm Cuts

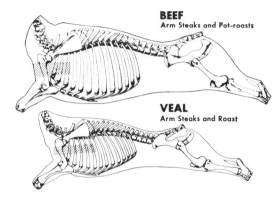

BEEF
Arm Steaks and Pot-roasts

VEAL
Arm Steaks and Roast

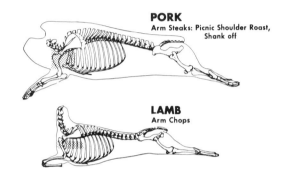

PORK
Arm Steaks: Picnic Shoulder Roast,
Shank off

LAMB
Arm Chops

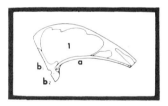

Rib (Hotel Rack) Cuts

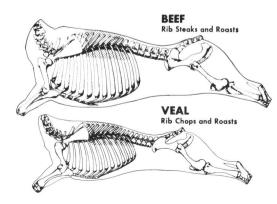

BEEF
Rib Steaks and Roasts

VEAL
Rib Chops and Roasts

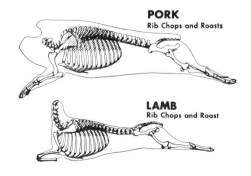

PORK
Rib Chops and Roasts

LAMB
Rib Chops and Roast

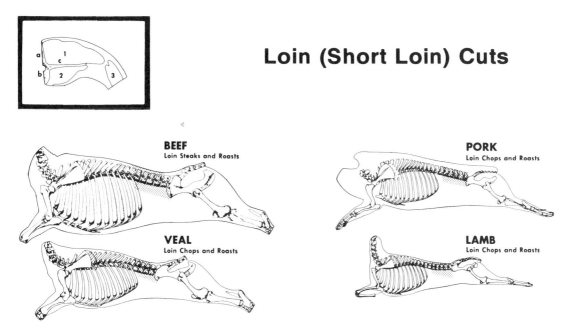

Loin (Short Loin) Cuts

BEEF
Loin Steaks and Roasts

PORK
Loin Chops and Roasts

VEAL
Loin Chops and Roasts

LAMB
Loin Chops and Roasts

Similarity of muscle and bone structure in beef porterhouse steak to veal, pork, and lamb loin chops is shown clearly. Beef top loin steak has been known by several names including New York cut, Kansas City steak, strip steak, and sirloin steak (hotel style). The tenderloin is a long tapering muscle that extends the full length of the loin (short loin and sirloin). The thick end of the tenderloin is in the sirloin.

Leg, Round, and Ham Cuts

Only a cross-section of the leg bone is found in center cut steaks from the leg, round and ham. This bone (a) in the diagram appears in all of the full cut steaks in the photograph. Note the oval shape of the steaks and separating lines of connective tissue and fat between muscles.

The four muscles in the leg are important in meat identification. As numbered in the diagram, they are:

1. Tip (knuckle, sirloin tip, top sirloin, face, or veiny)
2. Top (inside) round or leg
3. Bottom (outside) round or leg
4. Eye of round or leg

Cuts (3) and (4) frequently are left together and sold as bottom round or outside round.

In the photograph, a beef round steak is divided into top round, bottom round, and eye of round. The tip is a separate cut in beef, but it is part of the steaks in other meats.

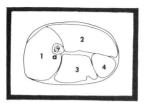

Leg, Round and Ham Cuts

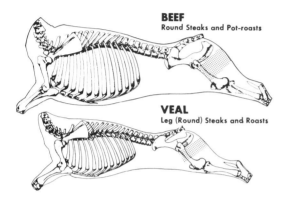

BEEF
Round Steaks and Pot-roasts

VEAL
Leg (Round) Steaks and Roasts

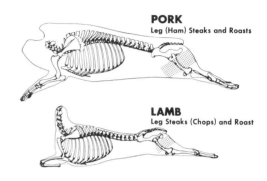

PORK
Leg (Ham) Steaks and Roasts

LAMB
Leg Steaks (Chops) and Roast

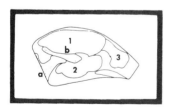

Sirloin (Hip) Cuts

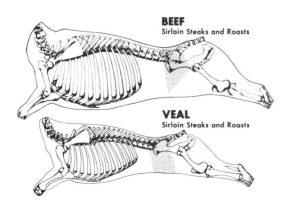

BEEF
Sirloin Steaks and Roasts

VEAL
Sirloin Steaks and Roasts

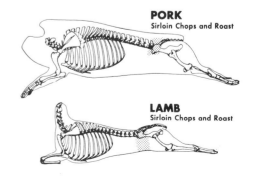

PORK
Sirloin Chops and Roast

LAMB
Sirloin Chops and Roast

Sirloin (Hip) Cuts

The two bones in cuts from the sirloin are illustrated. They are (a) back bone and (b) hip bone. Frequently, the back bone is removed leaving only the hip bone in steaks and chops. It can be seen from the chart that the hip bone in nearly every sirloin steak or chop varies in shape. Slices nearest the round (leg section) contain a wedge-shaped bone. Just ahead of these are one or two steaks with a round or oval-shaped bone. Flat bone sirloin steaks and chops contain the widest section of hip bone. Pin bone steaks and chops contain the tip (front end) of the hip bone. For all practical purposes, it is necessary to remember only the name "sirloin."

The muscles include (1) top sirloin, (2) tenderloin, and (3) sirloin tip. The latter is designated by the figure 1 in the beef chart. When hindquarters of beef are broken into cuts in the retail market, the tip is usually removed in one piece. It is known by several names including tip, sirloin tip, top sirloin and bottom sirloin, knuckle, face rump, and veiny.

BEEF

Grade

Carcasses, Sides, or Quarters. The purchaser must specify a quality grade and a yield grade.

Cuts and Roasts. The purchaser must specify a quality grade, and may also specify a yield grade.

Portion Cuts and Diced Beef. The purchaser must specify a quality grade.

USDA GRADES

Quality Grades	Yield Grades[1]				
	1	2	3	4	5
U.S. Prime			X	X	X
U.S. Choice		X	X	X	
U.S. Good		X	X		
U.S. Standard	X	X	X		
U.S. Commercial		X	X	X	X
U.S. Utility		X	X	X	
U.S. Cutter		X	X		
U.S. Canner		X	X		

[1]The yield grades reflect differences in yields of boneless, close trimmed, retail cuts. As such, they also reflect differences in the overall fatness of carcasses and cuts. Yield Grade 1 represents the highest yield of retail cuts and the least amount of fat trim. Yield Grade 5 represents the lowest yield of retail cuts and the highest amount of fat trim. If desired, Bullock beef may be specified by the purchaser.

Ground Beef. The purchaser must specify a quality grade for Item Nos. 137 and 1137. However, a quality grade shall not be specified for other ground beef items. The upper half or lower half may be specified, otherwise the full range of the grade is acceptable.

When yield grade is specified for forequarters or forequarter cuts, any such item may not be derived from a carcass or side which was yield graded after the removal of more than minor amount of kidney and pelvic fat.

Yield grades 1 through 5 are applicable to all quality grades. However, those yield grades indicated by an "X" are in the largest supply.

Weight Range or Size

Carcasses, Sides, Quarters, and Cuts. See weight ranges.

Roasts. See weight range table. If desired, purchasers may specify that roasts be further reduced in size.

Ground Beef Patties. Either the individual patty weight or the number of patties per pound must be specified.

Ground Beef Patty Weight Tolerances. For patties with a specified weight of 3 oz. or less, a tolerance of +2 patties from the projected number in a 10-lb. unit will be permitted. For patients with diets having a specified weight of more than 3 oz., a tolerance of +1 patty from the projected number in a 10-lb. unit will be permitted. (When patties are specified by a number per pound, this shall be converted to patty weight to determine tolerances, i.e., 6 to the pound = 2.67 oz.) For example,

Specified Size		Number Per 10-Pound Unit	Tolerances (Over and Under)
Weight	No. Per Lb.		
1.6 oz.	10	100	2
2.0 oz.	8	80	2
3.2 oz.	5	50	1
4.0 oz.	4	40	1

Example: When 2 oz. patties are specified, 10-lb. units containing 78 to 82 patties are acceptable.

Portion Cut Items. Either the portion weight or thickness desired—not both—must be specified. If weight is specified, see the weight range tables. If thickness is specified, the actual thickness desired must be indicated. (Not applicable to cubed steaks.) Also, in order to control uniformity of portion sizes, the weight range of the IMPS cut from which the portions are to be produced may also be specified. In this case, the fat thickness of the referenced IMPS cut should be the fat thickness specified for the portion cut.

Portion Cut Weight Tolerances. If portion weight is specified, the following tolerances will be permitted:

Weight Specified	Tolerances (Over and Under)
Less than 6 oz.	¼ oz.
6 oz. but less than 12 oz.	½ oz.
12 oz. but less than 18 oz.	¾ oz.
18 oz. or more	1 oz.

Example: When 8 oz. steaks are specified, individual steaks weighing 7½ to 8½ oz. are acceptable.

Portion Cut Tolerances. If thickness is specified, the following tolerances will be permitted.

Thickness Specified	Tolerances (Over and Under)
1 in. or less	³⁄₁₆ in.
More than 1 in.	¼ in.

Example: When 1¼ in. steaks are specified, individual steaks measuring 1 to 1½ in. are acceptable.

Fat Limitations

Cuts and Roasts. Except when yield grade is specified, the purchaser must specify one of the following maximum average thicknesses of surface fat, unless definite fat limitations are indicated in the detailed specifications.

Maximum Average Thickness	Maximum at Any One Point
1 in.	1¼ in.
¾ in.	1 in.
½ in.	¾ in.
¼ in.	½ in.

Note: When average fat thicknesses are specified in item descriptions, the appropriate ''Maximum at Any One Point'' limitations shall apply.

Steaks. Unless otherwise specified by the purchaser, or unless definite fat limitations are indicated in the detailed item specifications, on surfaces where fat is present, the fat must not exceed ½ in. in thickness, and the thickness at any one point must be not more than ¾ in.

Chops, Cutlets, and Filets.   Unless otherwise specified by the purchaser, surface fat, where present, must not exceed an average of ¼ in. in thickness, and the thickness at any one point must not be more than ⅜ in.

Note: Defatting must be done by smoothly removing the fat by following the countour of the underlying muscle surface. Beveling of the edges only is not acceptable. In determining the average thickness of fat at any one point on steaks and roasts, which have an evident, natural depression of the lean, only the fat above the portion of the depression which is more than ¾ in. in width will be considered.

State of Refrigeration

Chilled or Frozen.

Tying

When tying is required, roasts must be made firm and compact, and held intact by individual loops of strong twine, uniformly spaced at approximately 2-in. intervals girthwise. In addition, some roasts may require tying lengthwise. In lieu of string tying, it is permissible to enclose roasts in stretchable netting, or by any other equivalent method. Purchasers may specify that roasts be tied, when this requirement is not specified in the detailed item specification.

Aged Beef

The purchaser may specify aged beef. Unless otherwise specified, bone-in cuts may be dry aged, or aged in plastic bags. Boneless cuts must be aged in plastic bags. Meat which is dry aged must be trimmed to remove meat which is dry and discolored, and/or which has an odor foreign to fresh beef. When examining beef for compliance with these specifications, USDA meat graders will take into consideration the deviation of color from that of fresh-chilled meat that is normal for aged meat.

Material

Beef products described in these specifications must be derived from beef carcasses or wholesale cuts. Cuts that have been excessively trimmed in order to meet specified weights, or that do not meet the specification requirements for any reason, are excluded. The beef shall be of good color normal to the grade; be practically free of bruises, blood clots, bone dust, ragged edges, and discoloration. The spinal cord, thymus glands, and heart fat must be removed. Except as otherwise provided herein, the meat shall show no evidence of freezing or defrosting. Also, the product shall show no evidence of mishandling, and shall be in excellent condition to the time of delivery.

Portion-cut items to be delivered frozen may be produced from frozen meat cuts which have been previously accepted in the fresh-chilled state, provided such cuts are in excellent condition, and in their original shape. Products thus produced shall be packaged, packed, and promptly returned to the freezer.

PRIMAL (WHOLESALE) CUTS AND BONE STRUCTURE OF BEEF

Chuck, Sq. Cut Chuck, Blade Half Chuck, Blade Portion Chuck, Arm Half	Rib, Regular 10" × 10" Ribs 3 × 4 Short Ribs	Short Loin Regular 10" Short Loin 3 × 4 Tenderloin	Sirloin Bl Top Sirloin Bottom Sirloin Half Tip Tenderloin	Round Rump Shank Half Tip
CHUCK	**RIB**	**(SHORT LOIN) LOIN (SIRLOIN)**		**ROUND**

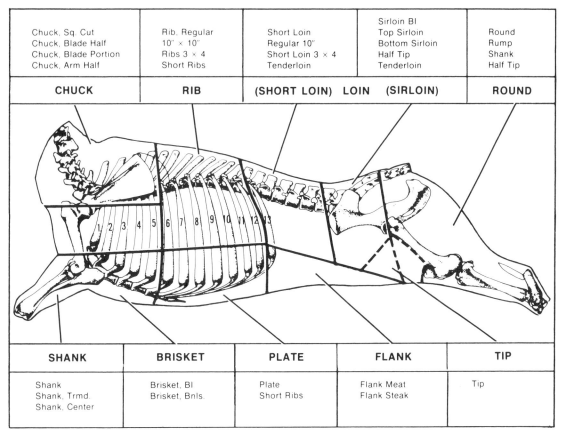

SHANK	**BRISKET**	**PLATE**	**FLANK**	**TIP**
Shank Shank, Trmd. Shank, Center	Brisket, Bl Brisket, Bnls.	Plate Short Ribs	Flank Meat Flank Steak	Tip

National Live Stock and Meat Board.

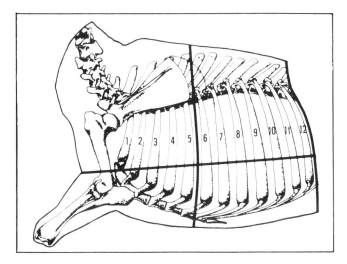

COUNTING RIBS IN A BEEF FOREQUARTER

In this manual, the method used to count ribs in the beef forequarter is to start at the front (chuck) and count toward the rear (1 to 12). The primal chuck contains five ribs (1–5). The primal rib contains seven ribs (6–12).

Some retailers reverse the counting process in the primal rib. They number ribs 6–12 instead by starting at the loin end, and numbering 1–7 from rear to front.

INDEX OF PRODUCTS AND WEIGHT RANGE TABLE

Item No.	Product	Range A Pounds	Range B Pounds	Range C Pounds	Range D Pounds
100	Carcass	500-600	600-700	700-800	800-up
101	Side	250-300	300-350	350-400	400-up
102	Forequarter	131-157	157-183	183-210	210-up
102A	Forequarter, Boneless	104-125	125-146	146-168	168-up
103	Rib, Primal	24-28	28-33	33-38	38-up
107	Rib, Oven-Prepared	17-19	19-23	23-26	26-up
108	Rib, Oven-Prepared, Boneless & Tied	13-16	16-19	19-22	22-up
109	Rib, Roast-Ready	14-16	16-19	19-22	22-up
109A	Rib, Roast-Ready, Special	14-16	16-19	19-22	22-up
109B	Blade Meat	Over-3			
110	Rib, Roast-Ready, Boneless & Tied	11-13	13-16	16-19	19-up
111	Spencer Roll	10-12	12-15	15-17	17-up
112	Ribeye Roll	5-6	6-8	8-10	10-up
112A	Ribeye Roll, Lip-On	6-7	7-9	9-11	11-up
113	Square-Cut Chuck	66-79	79-93	93-106	106-up
114	Shoulder Clod	13-15	15-18	18-21	21-up
114A	Shoulder Clod Roast	Under-15	15-18	18-21	21-up
115	Square-Cut Chuck, Boneless	54-65	65-77	77-88	88-up
116	Square-Cut Chuck, Boneless, Clod Out	40-48	48-57	57-65	65-up
116A	Chuck Roll	13-15	15-18	18-21	21-up
117	Foreshank	7-8	8-10	10-12	12-up
118	Brisket	12-14	14-17	17-20	20-up
119	Brisket, Boneless, Deckle On	9-10	10-12	12-14	14-up
120	Brisket, Boneless, Deckle Off	6-8	8-10	10-12	12-up
121	Short Plate	20-27	27-31	31-35	35-up
121A	Short Plate, Boneless	16-23	23-27	27-31	31-up
122	Full Plate	28-37	37-44	44-51	51-up
122A	Full Plate, Boneless	21-27	27-29	29-32	32-up
123	Short Ribs	2-3	3-4	4-5	5-up
123A	Short Ribs, Short Plate	Amount as Specified			
123B	Short Ribs, Special	Amount as Specified			
125	Armbone Chuck	77-88	88-103	103-118	118-up
126	Armbone Chuck, Boneless	59-70	70-82	82-90	90-up
126A	Armbone Chuck, Boneless, Clod Out	46-57	57-69	69-77	77-up
127	Cross-Cut Chuck	86-103	103-120	120-138	138-up
128	Cross-Cut Chuck, Boneless	68-81	81-95	95-109	109-up
132	Triangle	107-129	129-150	150-172	172-up
133	Triangle, Boneless	83-101	101-117	117-134	134-up
134	Beef Bones	Amount as Specified			
135	Diced Beef	Amount as Specified			
135A	Beef for Stewing	Amount as Specified			
136	Ground Beef, Regular	Amount as Specified			
136A	Ground Beef, Regular, TVP Added	Amount as Specified			
137	Ground Beef, Special	Amount as Specified			

NOTE: The weight ranges of cuts as shown in these tables do not necessarily reflect any relation to the carcass weight ranges. Studies have shown that all carcasses within a given weight range will not produce cuts that are uniform in weight. Therefore, in ordering cuts, purchasing officials should specify the weight range(s) desired without regard to the carcass weights shown in the various ranges.

INDEX OF PRODUCTS AND WEIGHT RANGE TABLE—Continued

Item No.	Product	Range A Pounds	Range B Pounds	Range C Pounds	Range D Pounds
155	Hindquarter	119-143	143-167	167-190	190-up
155A	Hindquarter, Boneless	90-108	108-126	126-143	143-up
158	Round, Primal	59-71	71-83	83-95	95-up
159	Round, Boneless	44-53	53-62	62-71	71-up
160	Round, Shank Off, Partially Boneless	47-57	57-67	67-76	76-up
161	Round, Shank Off, Boneless	44-53	53-62	62-71	71-up
163	Round, Shank Off, 3-Way, Boneless	41-50	50-58	58-66	66-up
164	Round, Rump & Shank Off	40-48	48-56	56-64	64-up
165	Round, Rump & Shank Off, Boneless	35-43	43-50	50-57	57-up
165A	Round, Rump & Shank Off, Boneless, Special	38-46	46-54	54-60	60-up
165B	Round, Rump & Shank Off, Boneless, Tied, Special	38-46	46-54	54-60	60-up
166	Round, Rump & Shank Off, Boneless, Tied	35-43	43-50	50-57	57-up
166A	Round, Rump Partially Removed, Shank Off	44-52	52-61	61-70	70-up
167	Knuckle	8-9	9-11	11-13	13-up
167A	Knuckle, Trimmed	8-9	9-11	11-13	13-up
168	Top (Inside) Round	14-17	17-20	20-23	23-up
170	Bottom (Gooseneck) Round	18-21	21-25	25-29	29-up
170A	Bottom (Gooseneck) Round, Heel Out	17-20	20-24	24-28	28-up
171	Bottom (Gooseneck) Round, Untrimmed	18-21	21-25	25-29	29-up
171A	Bottom (Gooseneck) Round, Untrimmed, Heel Out	17-20	20-24	24-28	28-up
171B	Outside Round	8-10	10-13	13-16	16-up
171C	Eye of Round	Under-3	3-5	5-up	
172	Full Loin, Trimmed	35-42	42-50	50-57	57-up
173	Short Loin	17-21	21-25	25-28	28-up
174	Short Loin, Short Cut	14-19	19-23	23-26	26-up
175	Strip Loin	11-13	13-16	16-19	19-up
176	Strip Loin, Boneless	8-10	10-12	12-14	14-up
177	Strip Loin, Intermediate	10-12	12-14	14-16	16-up
178	Strip Loin, Intermediate, Boneless	8-9	9-11	11-13	13-up
179	Strip Loin, Short Cut	8-10	10-12	12-14	14-up
180	Strip Loin, Short Cut, Boneless	7-8	8-10	10-12	12-up
181	Sirloin	16-19	19-24	24-28	28-up
182	Sirloin Butt, Boneless	11-14	14-16	16-19	19-up
183	Sirloin Butt, Trimmed	9-10	10-13	13-15	15-up
184	Top Sirloin Butt	6-7	7-9	9-11	11-up
185	Bottom Sirloin Butt	4-5	5-6	6-7	7-up
185A	Bottom Sirloin, Flap	1-3	3-up		
185B	Bottom Sirloin, Ball Tip	1.5-3	3-up		
185C	Bottom Sirloin, Triangle	1.5-3	3-up		
185D	Bottom Sirloin, Triangle, Defatted	1.5-3	3-up		
186	Bottom Sirloin Butt, Trimmed	2-3	3-4	4-5	5-up
189	Full Tenderloin	4-5	5-6	6-7	7-up
189A	Full Tenderloin, Defatted	3-4	4-5	5-6	6-up
190	Full Tenderloin, Special	2-3	3-4	4-up	
190A	Full Tenderloin, Skinned	2-3	3-4	4-up	
191	Butt Tenderloin	1-2	2-3	3-4	4-up
192	Short Tenderloin	2-3	3-4	4-up	
193	Flank Steak	Under-1	1-2	2-up	

INDEX OF PORTION-CUT PRODUCTS AND WEIGHT RANGE TABLE

Item No.	Product	\ Portion Size \ 3 ozs.	4 ozs.	6 ozs.	8 ozs.	10 ozs.	12 ozs.	14 ozs.	16 ozs.	18 ozs.	20 ozs.	24 ozs.
1100	Cubed Steaks	X	X	X	X							
1101	Cubed Steaks, Special	X	X	X	X							
1102	Braising Steaks, Swiss		X	X	X							
1103	Rib Steaks				X	X	X	X	X			
1103A	Rib Steaks, Boneless		X	X	X	X	X					
1112	Rib Eye Roll Steaks		X	X	X	X	X					
1112A	Rib Eye Roll, Lip-On, Steaks		X	X	X	X	X					
1136	Ground Beef Patties, Regular	Size as Specified										
1136A	Ground Beef Patties, Regular, TVP Added	Size as Specified										
1137	Ground Beef Patties, Special	Size as Specified										
1167	Knuckle Steaks	X	X	X	X	X						
1168	Top (Inside) Round Steaks	X	X	X	X	X	X					
1170	Bottom (Gooseneck) Round Steaks	X	X	X	X	X	X	X	X	X	X	X
1173	Porterhouse Steaks						X	X				
1173A	Porterhouse Steaks, Intermediate					X	X	X	X	X	X	X
1173B	Porterhouse Steaks, Short Cut					X	X	X	X	X	X	X
1174	T-Bone Steaks				X	X	X	X	X	X	X	X
1174A	T-Bone Steaks, Intermediate				X	X	X	X	X	X	X	X
1174B	T-Bone Steaks, Short Cut				X	X	X	X	X	X	X	X
1177	Strip Loin Steaks, Bone-In, Intermediate			X	X	X	X	X	X	X	X	
1178	Strip Loin Steaks, Boneless, Intermediate				X	X	X	X	X	X	X	X
1179	Strip Loin Steaks, Bone-In, Short Cut				X	X	X	X	X	X	X	X
1179A	Strip Loin Steaks, Bone-In, Extra Short Cut				X	X	X	X	X	X	X	X
1179B	Strip Loin Steaks, Bone-In, Special				X	X	X	X	X	X	X	X
1180	Strip Loin Steaks, Boneless, Short Cut			X	X	X	X	X	X	X	X	
1180A	Strip Loin Steaks, Boneless, Extra Short Cut		X	X	X	X	X	X	X	X		
1180B	Strip Loin Steaks, Boneless, Special			X	X	X	X	X	X	X	X	
1184	Top Sirloin Butt Steaks		X	X	X	X	X	X	X	X	X	X
1184A	Top Sirloin Butt Steaks, Semi-Center Cut		X	X	X	X	X	X	X			
1184B	Top Sirloin Butt Steaks, Center Cut		X	X	X	X	X	X	X			
1189	Tenderloin Steaks		X	X	X	X	X	X				
1189A	Tenderloin Steaks, Defatted	X	X	X	X	X	X	X				
1190	Tenderloin Steaks, Special	X	X	X	X	X	X	X				
1190A	Tenderloin Steaks, Skinned	X	X	X	X	X	X	X				

NOTE: Because it is impractical to list all portion weights that purchasers may desire, those identified by the letter "X" are suggested only. Other portion weights may be specified if desired.

Cutting Steaks

Unless otherwise specified in the individual item specification, steaks must be cut in full slices, in a straight line reasonably perpendicular to the outer surface, and at an approximate right angle to the length of the meat cut from which steaks are produced. Butterfly steaks are not acceptable.

Boning

Boning shall be accomplished with sufficient care to allow each cut to retain its identity, and to avoid objectionable scores in the meat.

LAMB

Grade

Carcasses, Saddles and Cuts. The purchaser shall specify a quality grade and may also specify a yield grade, except that when surface fat thickness is included in the item description, yield grade shall not be specified.

Roasts. The purchaser shall specify a quality grade, and may also specify a yield grade.

Portion Cuts and Lamb for Stewing. The purchaser shall specify a quality grade.

Ground Lamb. The purchaser shall specify a quality grade.

Yield grades 1 through 5 are applicable to all quality grades. However, those yield grades indicated by an "X" are in the largest supply.

USDA GRADES

Quality Grades	Yield Grades[1]				
	1	2	3	4	5
U.S. Prime[2]			X	X	X
U.S. Choice		X	X	X	
U.S. Good	X	X	X		
U.S. Utility	X	X			
U.S. Cull	X	X			

[1]The yield grades reflect differences in yields of boneless, closely trimmed, retail cuts. As such, they also reflect differences in the overall fatness of carcasses and cuts. Yield grade 1 represents the highest yield of retail cuts and the least amount of fat trim. Yield grade 5 represents the lowest yield of retail cuts and the highest amount of fat trim.

[2]Prime does not apply to mutton.

Class

A—Lamb
B—Yearling Mutton
C—Mutton

Weight Range

Ground Lamb Patty Weight Tolerances.   For patties with a specified weight of 3 oz. or less, a tolerance of plus/minus 2 patties from the projected number in a 10-lb. unit will be permitted. For patties with a specified weight of more than 3 oz., a tolerance of plus/minus 1 patty from the projected number in a 10-lb. unit will be permitted. (When patties are specified by a number per pound, this shall be converted to patty weight to determine tolerances, e.g., 6 to the lb. = 2.67 oz.) For example, see the second table on p. 465.

Lamb: Yield of boneless meat from carcass and wholesale cuts of various U.S. grades, and conversion factors for determining carcass weight equivalent of boneless meat and bone-in cuts

Wholesale cuts	Percent of carcass weight	Percent of boneless meat[1]		Factors for determining equivalent carcass weight[3]
		Average above Cull[2]	Cull	
Boneless meat, all cuts:				
Average above Cull	—	—	—	1.39
Cull	—	—	—	1.60
Bone-in cuts:				
Carcass, whole[4]	100.0	72.0	62.5	1.00
Foresaddle, whole	50.0	67.9	58.5	.94
Breast, including shank	14.0	67.0	57.7	.93
Chuck	25.0	73.2	63.0	1.02
Hotel rack	11.0	72.7	62.6	1.01
Hindsaddle, whole	50.0	76.1	65.5	1.06
Leg	33.0	78.8	67.9	1.10
Loin, including flank and kidney	17.0	81.1	69.8	1.13

1. Commercial boning practice.
2. U.S. grades for lamb are Prime, Choice, Good, Utility, and Cull.
3. Edible offal items are excluded when converting to carcass weight. These include brains, casings, heart, liver, stomach or tripe, and tongue.
4. Pluck out.

Portion Cut Items.   Either the portion weight or thickness desired—not both—must be specified. If weight is specified, see the weight range table. If thickness is specified, the actual thickness desired must be indicated. Also, in order to control uniformity of portion sizes, the weight range of the IMPS cut from which the portions are to be produced may also be specified. In this case, the fat thickness of the IMPS cut should be approximately the same as the fat thickness specified for the portion cut.

INDEX OF PRODUCTS AND WEIGHT RANGE TABLE

Item No.	Product	Range 1 Pounds	Range 2 Pounds
701	Beef Liver	Under 13	13–16
702	Beef Liver, Sliced (Frozen)	Under 13	13–16
703	Beef Liver, Portion-Cut (Frozen)	5-to-the-pound	4-to-the-pound
704	Calf Liver	Under 6½	6½–8½
705	Calf Liver, Sliced (Frozen)	Under 6½	6½–8½
707	Veal Liver	Under 3	3–5
708	Veal Liver, Sliced (Frozen)	Under 3	3–5
710	Pork Liver	Under 5	
713	Lamb Liver	Under 1½	
716	Beef Tongue	3–5	
720	Beef Heart	3–5	

Note: Because it is impractical to list all weight ranges for edible by-products that purchasers may desire, those included in this table are suggested only. Other weight ranges may be ordered if desired.

Specified Size Weight	Number Per 10-lb. unit No. per pound	Tolerances (Over and Under)	
1.6 oz.	10	100	2
2.0 oz.	8	80	2
3.2 oz.	5	50	1
4.0 oz.	4	40	1

Example: When 2 oz. patties are specified, 10-lb. units containing 78 to 82 patties are acceptable.

Portion Cut Weight Tolerances. If portion weight is specified, the following tolerances will be permitted:

Weight Specified	Tolerances (Over and Under)
less than 6 oz.	¼ oz.
6 oz. or more	½ oz.

Example: When 4 oz. chops are specified, individual chops weighing 3¾ to 4¼ oz. are acceptable.

Portion Cut Thickness Tolerances. If thickness is specified, the following tolerances will be permitted:

Thickness Specified	Tolerances (Over and Under)
1 in. or less	
More than 1 in.	¼ in.

Example: When 1 ¼ in. chops are specified, individual chops measuring from 1 to 1 ½ in. are acceptable.

Fat Limitations

Chops. Unless otherwise specified by the purchaser, surface fat, where present, must not exceed an average of ¼ in. thickness, and the thickness at any one point must not be more than ⅜ in.

State of Refrigeration

Chilled or Frozen.

Tying

When tying is required, roasts must be made firm and compact, and held intact by individual loops of strong twine, uniformly spaced at approximately 2-in. intervals girthwise. In addition, some roasts may require tying lengthwise. In lieu of string, it is permissible to enclose roasts in a stretchable netting, or by any other equivalent method.

Purchasers may specify that roasts be tied, when this requirement is not specified in the detailed roast item specification.

Material

Unless otherwise specified, the wholesale and fabricated cuts described in these specifications are double cuts. Single cuts are produced by cutting lengthwise centrally through the backbone. Cuts that have been excessively trimmed in order to meet specified weights, or that do not meet the specification requirements for any reason, are not acceptable. The meat shall be of good color, normal to the class, be practically free of bruises, blood clots, bone dust, ragged edges, and discoloration. Except as otherwise provided herein, the meat shall show no evidence of mishandling and shall be in excellent condition to the time of delivery.

Cutting Chops

Unless otherwise specified in the individual item specification, chops shall be cut in full slices in a straight line, reasonably perpendicular to the outer surface, and at an approximate right angle to the length of the meat cut from which chops are produced.

Boning

Boning shall be accomplished with sufficient care to allow each cut to retain its identity, and to avoid objectionable scores in the meat.

EDIBLE BY-PRODUCTS—LAMB

Material

The edible by-products described herein shall show no evidence of freezing or defrosting, and must be in excellent condition up to the time of delivery.

All livers shall be trimmed free of ragged edges, and the gall bladder shall be removed. Whole livers shall have the heavy connective tissue, the large blood vessel, and ducts lying along the liver wall trimmed even with the surface.

Livers to be sliced shall have the heavy connective tissue, the large blood vessel, and ducts lying along the liver wall removed and excluded. Type B beef and calf livers shall have the outer connective tissue (capsula fibrosa), or "skin," removed and excluded, except for small pieces remaining on the edges and in the crease of the small (caudate) lobe. Veal livers shall not be skinned. The liver may be molded, frozen, tempered (but not thawed), and/or pressed before slicing. Slices which are broken are not acceptable. Liver slices shall be practically free from liver sawdust. As specified, they may be either (1) reassembled in natural sequence, or (2) layer-packed with plastic, parchment, or waxed paper separators between layers. After slicing, the liver slices shall be promptly packaged and solidly frozen.

Livers to be portion-cut must be prepared as described for livers to be sliced, except that the small (caudate) lobe and the "skin" must be removed and excluded. Portion-cut liver shall be layer packed only.

Note: Because it is impractical to list all weight ranges for edible by-products that purchasers may desire, those included in this table are suggested only. Other weight ranges may be ordered if desired.

Ordering Data: To be Specified by the Purchaser

Selection.   Selection No. 1 or Selection No. 2.

State of Refrigeration (not applicable to sliced or portion-cut liver).   Chilled or Frozen.

INDEX OF PRODUCTS AND WEIGHT RANGE TABLE

Item No.	Product	Range A Lamb Pounds	Range A Mutton Pounds	Range B Lamb Pounds	Range B Mutton Pounds	Range C Lamb Pounds	Range C Mutton Pounds	Range D Lamb Pounds	Range D Mutton Pounds
200	Carcass	30–41	55–75	41–53	75–95	53–65	95–115	65–75	115–130
202	Foresaddle	15–21	28–38	21–27	38–48	27–33	48–58	33–38	58–65
203	Bracelet (Double)	5–6	8–11	6–8	11–14	8–10	14–17	10–12	17–19
204	Rib Rack (Double)	3–5	6–8	5–6	8–10	6–7	10–13	7–8	13–14
205	Chucks and Plates (Double)	12–16	22–30	16–21	30–38	21–26	38–46	26–30	46–52
206	Chucks (Double)	11–14	19–26	14–19	26–33	19–23	33–40	23–27	40–46
207	Square-Cut Shoulders (Double)	8–10	14–19	10–13	19–24	13–16	24–29	16–19	29–33
208	Square-Cut Shoulder, Boneless	3–4	6–8	4–6	8–10	6–7	10–12	7–8	12–16
209	Breast, Flank On	4–6	8–11	6–7	11–13	7–9	13–16	9–11	16–18
209A	Breast, Flank Off	3–5	7–10	5–6	10–12	6–8	12–16	8–10	16–18
210	Foreshank	1–1.5	2–3	1.5–2	3–4	2–2.5	4–5	2.5–3	5–6
230	Hindsaddle	15–21	28–38	21–27	38–48	27–33	48–58	33–38	58–65
231	Loin (Double)	5–6	8–11	6–8	11–14	8–10	14–17	10–12	17–20
232	Loin, Trimmed (Double)	3–4	6–8	4–5	8–10	5–7	10–12	7–8	12–15
233	Leg (Double)	11–14	19–26	14–19	26–33	19–23	33–40	23–27	40–46
233A	Leg, Lower Shank Off (Single)	5–7	9–12	7–9	12–15	9–12	15–19	12–Up	19–Up
233B	Leg, Lower Shank Off, Boneless	4–6	8–11	6–8	11–13	8–11	13–17	11–Up	17–Up
233C	Leg, Shank Off (Single)	5–7	8–10	7–9	10–12	9–12	12–15	12–Up	15–Up
233D	Leg, Shank Off, Boneless	4–6	7–9	6–8	9–11	8–11	11–14	11–Up	14–Up
233E	Hindshank, Heel Attached	Under 1	1–1.5	1–2	1.5–3	2–Up	3–Up		
234	Leg, Oven-Prepared	4–6	8–10	6–8	10–13	8–9	13–16	9–11	16–18
234A	Leg, Oven-Prepared, Boneless, & Tied								
235	Back	9–12	17–23	12–16	23–29	16–20	29–35	20–23	35–39
236	Back, Trimmed	6–8	11–15	8–11	15–19	11–13	19–23	13–15	23–26
237	Hindsaddle, Long Cut	20–27	36–49	27–34	49–62	34–42	62–75	42–49	75–85
238	Hindsaddle, Long Cut, Trimmed	17–23	33–41	23–29	41–52	29–36	52–63	36–41	63–72

Note: When single chucks, backs, etc., are specified, their respective weights must be one-half of that prescribed for double cuts in the table. The weight range of cuts shown in the above table do not necessarily reflect any relation to the carcass weight ranges. Studies have shown that all carcasses within a given weight range will not produce cuts that are uniform in weight. Therefore, in ordering cuts, purchasing officials should specify the weight range(s) desired without regard to the carcass weights shown in the various ranges.

INDEX OF PORTION-CUT PRODUCTS AND WEIGHT RANGE TABLE

Item No.	Product	Portion Size							
		3 ozs.	4 ozs.	5 ozs.	6 ozs.	7 ozs.	8 ozs.	9 ozs.	10 ozs.
1204	Rib Chops....................	X	X	X	X	X	X	X	X
1204A	Rib Chops, Frenched.........	X	X	X	X	X	X		
1207	Shoulder Chops..............		X	X	X	X	X		
1232	Loin Chops..................		X	X	X	X	X	X	X
1295	Lamb for Stewing[1].........	Amount As Specified							
1296	Ground Lamb[1]..............	Amount as Specified							
1296A	Ground Lamb Patties.........	Size As Specified							

Note: Because it is impractical to list all portion weights that purchasers may desire, those identified by the letter "X" are suggested only. Other portion weights may be specified if desired.

[1] May also be prepared from yearling mutton or mutton as specified, in which case the appropriate name—Ground yearling mutton, etc.—shall apply.

Style of Packaging (applicable only to sliced livers).   Reassembled in natural sequence, or layer packed.

Descriptions of Selections

Selection No. 1 Liver. Selection No. 1 livers shall be compact, thick, short, plump, and shall be practically free from blemishes. However, livers with cuts or scores not exceeding 1 in. in any dimension, or livers with small sections removed and excluded are acceptable, provided such defects do not interfere with making satisfactory, intact slices. Selection No. 1 livers shall possess a bright, uniform color typical of the species.

Selection No. 2 Liver.   Selection No. 2 livers shall be at least moderately compact, thick, short, plump, and shall be practically free from blemishes. However, livers with cuts or scores not exceeding 2 in. in any dimension, or livers with up to approximately ⅓ of the liver removed are acceptable, provided such defects do not interfere with making satisfactory, intact slices. Selection No. 2 livers shall possess a bright, uniform color typical of the species.

Weight Range (in Pounds)

Range 1: under 1½; Range 2: none.

VEAL AND CALF

When single fores, hotel racks, chucks and plates, square-cut chucks, hinds, loins, backs, legs, etc., are specified, their respective weight shall be ½ of that prescribed for double (i.e., in pairs) cuts.

The weights of the various wholesale, fabricated, and boneless cuts are usually produced from carcasses of corresponding weight range groups. It should not be expected that all carcasses having weight within one of the indicated weight ranges will always produce cuts within the weight ranges shown. Nor should it be expected that cuts of the weights shown in each weight range will always originate from carcasses in the indicated weight range. Therefore, in ordering cuts, purchasing officials should order the specific weight range(s) desired, without regard to the carcass weights shown in the various ranges. Because it is impractical to list all weights that purchasers may desire, those identified are suggested only. Other weight ranges may be ordered, if desired.

Grade

U.S. Prime, U.S. Choice, U.S. Good, U.S. Standard, U.S. Utility, and U.S. Cull.

Class

> A—Veal
> B—Calf

Weight Range

> Range 1, Range 2, or Range 3.

State of Refrigeration

> 1. Chilled
> 2. Frozen

Veal and calf: Yield of wholesale cuts from the carcass and yield of boneless meat from wholesale cuts

Carcass and wholesale cuts	Yield of bone-in cuts		Yield of boneless meat from wholesale cuts[1]	
	Choice and Good	Standard, Utility, and Cull	Choice and Good	Standard, Utility, and Cull
	Percent	*Percent*	*Percent*	*Percent*
Carcass, whole	100.0	100.0	68.5	69.5
Foresaddle	48.6	49.7	70.4	69.3
Chuck	26.1	27.6	73.5	72.8
Breast	14.3	14.3	62.8	62.6
Hotel rack, 7 rib	8.2	7.8	73.8	69.3
Hindsaddle	51.4	50.3	66.6	70.1
Leg, includes sirloin	36.4	38.8	72.8	73.5
Loin	7.0	6.4	73.3	69.8
Flank	4.8	3.4	53.4	68.5
Kidney knob	3.2	1.7	—	—

1. All cuts trimmed of fat exceeding that amount normally left on retail cuts (1/4" to 1/2").

Veal and calf: Conversion factors for determining equivalent carcass weight of bone-in cuts and for converting boneless meat to the equivalent bone-in cuts of various U.S. grades

Carcass and wholesale cuts	Factors for converting bone-in cuts to equivalent carcass weight		Factors for converting boneless wholesale cuts to equivalent bone-in cuts	
	Choice and Good	Standard, Utility, and Cull	Choice and Good	Standard, Utility, and Cull
Carcass, whole	1.00	1.00	1.46	1.44
Foresaddle	1.03	.99	1.42	1.45
Chuck	1.07	1.04	1.36	1.38
Breast	.92	.89	1.59	1.62
Hotel rack, 7 rib	1.08	.99	1.35	1.45
Hindsaddle	.97	1.00	1.51	1.44
Leg, includes sirloin	1.06	1.05	1.38	1.37
Loin	1.07	.99	1.36	1.45
Flank	.78	.97	1.87	1.48

Material

The veal and calf product items described herein must be derived from sound, well-dressed, unsplit veal or calf carcasses without the hide and caul fat; from sound, split-sides; or from sound, well-trimmed, wholesale market cuts derived from such car-casses. Unless otherwise specified, the wholesale and fabricated cuts are double cuts. Single cuts are produced by splitting, or sawing and cutting through the median section of the long axis of the spinal processes, and related attachments of flesh and bone join-ing the pair of such cuts.

Veal or calf cuts that have been excessively trimmed in order to meet specified weights, or that are substandard according to the specifications for any reason are excluded. The veal and calf must be free from any objectionable odors, blood clots, scores and mutilations (other than slight), discoloration, ragged edges, superficial appendages, blemishes, deterioration, damage, or signs of mishandling. The veal and calf also must be free from bruises, evidence of freezing or defrosting, and must be in excellent condition up to the time of delivery.

In ordering the various veal or calf portion-cut items covered by these specifica-tions, purchasers must specify: (1) the grade and class; (2) thickness *or* portion weight (chops), or actual weight range in pounds (roasts); and (3) state of refrigeration desired. Also, when ordering chops, purchasers may specify the weight range of the trimmed meat cut from which the portions are to be produced.

Veal and Calf Portion-Cut Chops, Steaks and Cutlets. Unless otherwise speci-fied in the individual item specifications, chops, cutlets, and steaks must be cut in full slices, in a straight line reasonably perpendicular to the outer surface, and at an approximate right angle to the length of the meat cut from which chops, cutlets, or steaks are produced.

Tying

When string tying is required, roasts may be made firm and compact and held intact by individual loops of strong twine, uniformly spaced at approximately 2 in. intervals girthwise. In addition, some roasts may require string tying lengthwise. In lieu of string tying, it is permissible to enclose roasts in a stretchable netting, provided it com-plies with the Regulations Governing the Meat Inspection of the U.S. Department of Agriculture. Purchasers may specify that roasts be string-tied, when this requirement is not specified in the detailed roast item specification.

EDIBLE BY-PRODUCTS—VEAL AND CALF

Note: Because it is impractical to list all weight ranges for edible by-products that pur-chasers may desire, those included are suggested only. Other weight ranges may be ordered if desired.

Ordering Data: To be Specified by the Purchaser

Selection.   Selection No. 1, Selection No. 2.

Style (applicable only to calf livers).   Regular or Skinned.

Weight Range.   See weight range table.

State of Refrigeration (not applicable to sliced or portion-cut liver.   Chilled or Frozen.

Style of Packaging (applicable only to sliced livers).   Reassembled in natural sequence, or layer packed.

Description of Selections

Selection No. 1 Liver.   Selection No. 1 livers shall be compact, thick, short, plump, and shall be practically free from blemishes. However, livers with cuts or scores not exceeding 1 in. in any dimension, or livers with small sections removed and excluded are acceptable, provided such defects do not interfere with making satisfactory, intact slices. Selection No. 1 livers shall possess a bright, uniform color typical of the species.

Selection No. 2 Liver.   Selection No. 2 livers shall be at least moderately compact, thick, short, plump, and shall be practically free from blemishes. However, livers with cuts or scores not exceeding 2 in. in any dimension, or livers with up to approximately ⅓ of the liver removed are acceptable, provided such defects do not interfere with making satisfactory, intact slices. Selection No. 2 livers shall possess a bright, uniform color typical of the species.

Material

The edible by-products described herein shall show no evidence of freezing or defrosting, and must be in excellent condition to the time of delivery.

All livers shall be trimmed free of ragged edges and the gall bladder shall be removed. Whole livers shall have the heavy connective tissue, the large blood vessel, and ducts lying along the liver wall trimmed even with the surface.

Livers to be sliced shall have the heavy connective tissue, the large blood vessel, and ducts lying along the liver wall removed and excluded. Type B beef and calf livers shall have the outer connective tissue (capsula fibrosa), or ''skin,'' removed, and excluded, except for small pieces remaining on the edges and in the crease of the small (caudate) lobe. Veal livers shall not be skinned. The liver may be molded, frozen, tempered (but not thawed), and/or pressed before slicing. Slices which are broken are not acceptable. Liver slices shall be practically free from liver sawdust. As specified, they may be either: (1) reassembled in natural sequence, or (2) layer-packed with plastic or parchment, or have waxed paper separators between layers. After slicing, the liver slices must be packaged and solidly frozen promptly.

Livers to be portion-cut must be prepared as described for livers to be sliced, except that the small (caudate) lobe and the "skin" must be removed and excluded. Portion-cut liver shall be layer-packed only.

Weight Range (in Pounds)

Calf Liver.   Range 1: under 6½; Range 2: 6½ to 8½. The color of calf liver may range from tan to light brown, with reddish shades predominating.

Calf Liver, Sliced, Frozen.   Range 1: under 6½; Range 2: 6½ to 8½. Sliced calf liver must be prepared from Calf Liver (above). Liver slices shall be approximately ⅜ to ½ in. thick.

Veal Liver.   Range 1: under 3. The color of veal liver may range from light reddish tan to tan.

Veal Liver, Sliced, Frozen.   Range 1: under 3. Sliced veal liver must be prepared from Veal Liver (above). Liver slices shall be approximately ⅜ to ½ in. thick.

PORK

Grade

Carcasses.   U.S. No. 1, U.S. No. 2, U.S. No. 3, U.S. No. 4, and U.S. Utility.

Wholesale and Fabricated Cut Selections. See Description of Selection Section.   Selection No. 1 and Selection No. 2. (Not applicable to spareribs, tenderloins, hocks, feet, trimmings, ground items, and neckbones.)

Weight Range or Size

Ground Pork Patty Weight Tolerances.   For patties with a specified weight of 3 oz. or less, a tolerance of 2 patties from the projected number in a 10-lb. unit will be permitted. For patties with a specified weight of more than 3 oz., a tolerance of 1 patty from the projected number in a 10-lb. unit will be permitted. (When patties are specified by a number per pound, this shall be converted to patty weight to determine tolerances, i.e., 6 to the lb. = 2.67 oz.) For example,

Specified Size		Number Per 10-pound	Tolerance
Weight	No. Per Lb.	Unit	(Over and Under)
1.6 oz.	10	100	2
2.0 oz.	8	80	2
3.2 oz.	5	50	1
4.0 oz.	4	40	1

Example: When 2-oz. patties are specified, 10-lb. units, having 78–82 patties are acceptable.

Portion Cut Items.   Either the portion weight or thickness desired—not both—must be specified. If weight is to be specified, see the weight range table. If thickness is to be specified, the actual thickness desired must be indicated. (Not applicable to cubed filets.) Also, in order to control uniformity of portion sizes, the weight range of the IMPS cut from which the portions are to be produced may be specified. In this case, the fat thickness of the IMPS cut should be approximately the same as the fat thickness specified for the portion cut.

Portion Cut Weight Tolerances.   If portion weight is specified, the following tolerances will be permitted:

Weight Specified	Tolerances (Over and Under)
Less than 6 oz.	¼ oz.
6 oz. or more	½ oz.

Example: When 4-oz. chops are specified, individual chops weighing 3 ¾ to 4 ¼ oz. are acceptable.

Portion Cut Thickness Tolerances.   If thickness is specified, the following tolerances will be permitted:

Thickness Specified	Tolerances (Over and Under)
1 inch or less	3/16 inch
More than 1 inch	1/4 inch

Example: When 1 ¼ in. chops are specified, individual chops measuring 1 to 1 ½ in. are acceptable.

Description of Selection

Selection No. 1. Hams, shoulder, shoulder picnics, loins, and Boston butts of Selection No. 1 are meaty, based on a composite evaluation of thickness of muscling and quantity of intermuscular and external fat. To meet the minimum requirements for meatiness, cuts usually are at least moderately thick and plump throughout; have at least moderately thick muscling, and not more than a small amount of intermuscular fat, nor more than a small amount of external fat on the unskinned portions of skinned hams and shoulders.

The bones must not be ossified to a degree that cartilage is not in evidence in the pelvic, spinal, and scapular sections of the pork cuts. The split chine bone, spinous processes, and cross-cut sections of bones must be porous and not appreciably brittle or flinty. The color of the bones must be in the range from red to deep pink. The exterior surfaces of the rib bones must show at least some redness. The lean must be at least slightly firm; possess a bright, reasonably uniform color (slightly two-toned is permissible), ranging from light pink to light red; and have a fine smooth texture. In addition, hams must have at the minimum two traces of marbling, and shoulders, shoulder picnics, loins and Boston butts must have at least a slight amount of marbling.

Selection No. 1 bellies must indicate a slightly high ratio of lean to fat, and have a uniform distribution of fat and lean layers. They may vary in thickness from slightly thick to moderately thick, and must be moderately uniform in thickness, moderately long in relation to width, and may show a slight amount of marbling.

The exterior fat on the fresh pork cuts must be at least slightly firm, white, and reasonably uniform in distribution. The skin must be thin, smooth and pliable. The pork cuts must be free from bruises, dislocated or enlarged joints or other malformation, or odor foreign to fresh pork. They must be practically free from scores, miscut, abrasions, hook marks, blemishes, hair roots, or other defects.

Selection No. 2. Hams, shoulders, shoulder picnics, loins, and Boston butts of Selection No. 2 have a moderate degree of meatiness, based on a composite evaluation of thickness of muscling and quantity of intermuscular and external fat. Although various combinations of thickness of muscling and quantities of intermuscular and external fat will meet the minimum requirements for meatiness, cuts usually are at least slightly thick and plump throughout, with slightly thick muscling and a slightly high to high amount of intermuscular fat, with a somewhat high to high amount of external fat on the unskinned portions of skinned hams and shoulders.

The bones must not be ossified to a degree that cartilage is not in evidence in the pelvic, spinal, and scapular sections of the pork cuts. The split chine bone, spinous processes, and cross-cut sections of bones must be porous and not appreciably brittle or flinty. The color of the bones must be in the range from red to deep pink. The exterior surfaces of the rib bones must show at least some redness. The lean meat must indicate at the minimum a slight degree of firmness, possess a bright, reasonably uniform color (slightly two-toned is permissible), ranging from light pink to light red, and have a fine, smooth texture. In addition, hams must have some traces of marbling, and shoulders, shoulder picnics, loins, and Boston butts must have at least a slight amount of marbling.

Selection No. 2 bellies must indicate a slightly low to moderately low ratio of lean to fat, except that bellies with a higher ratio of lean to fat, although not eligible for Selection No. 1 because of thickness, uniformity, or length-width proportions, may be included, provided they meet those requirements for Selection No. 2. They usually are moderately thick or thick, and usually have moderately thick fat deposits between the layers of lean. They may be uneven in thickness; may be slightly short in relation to width, and may have a slight amount of marbling.

The exterior fat on the fresh pork cuts must be at the minimum slightly firm, white, and fairly uniform in distribution. The skin must be thin, smooth, and pliable. The pork cuts must be free from bruises, dislocated or enlarged joints or other malformation, or odor foreign to fresh pork. However, pork cuts with slight scores, abrasions, hook marks, or other cuts, which do not interfere with the making of satisfactory slices, will be acceptable. Pork cuts showing only a slight amount of hair roots, or which are only slightly miscut, or misshapen, may be included.

Tying

When tying is required, roasts must be made firm and compact, and held intact by individual loops of strong twine uniformly spaced at approximately 2-in. intervals girthwise. In addition, some roasts may require tying lengthwise. In lieu of string tying, it is permissible to enclose roasts in a stretched netting, or by any other equivalent method. Purchasers may specify that roasts be tied, when this requirement is not specified in the detailed roast item specification.

Material

Items with coarse-textured dark meat, or other characteristics indicating that they were produced from aged sows, stags, or boars, are not acceptable. Cuts that have been excessively trimmed in order to meet specified weights, or that do not meet the specification requirements for any reason are not acceptable. Except as otherwise provided herein, the meat shall show no evidence of freezing or defrosting. Also, the product shall show no evidence of mishandling, and shall be in excellent condition to the time of delivery.

Portion-cut items to be delivered frozen may be produced from frozen cuts which have been previously accepted in the fresh-chilled state, provided such cuts are in excellent condition, and in their original shape. Products thus produced shall be packaged, packed, and promptly returned to the freezer.

Cutting Chops

Unless otherwise specified in the individual item specification, steaks and chops shall be cut in full slices, in a straight line reasonably perpendicular to the outer surface, and at an approximate right angle to the length of the cut from which they are produced.

Pork: Yield of boneless meat from carcass and wholesale cuts of pork, and conversion factors for determining weight of pork excluding lard

Carcass and wholesale cuts	Approximate percent of		Percent of boneless skinless meat, fresh	Factors for determining equivalent weight of pork excluding lard[1]			
	Live weight	Pork, excluding lard		Fresh or frozen	Cured	Smoked	Ready-to-eat
Total pork excluding lard[2, 3]	57.9	100.0	83.0	1.00	—	—	—
Packer-dressed carcass	69.1	—	—	.82	—	—	—
Shipper-dressed carcass	76.1	—	—	.74	—	—	—
Boneless skinless meat, all cuts	—	—	—	1.20	—	—	—
Hams:[4]							
Skinned, bone in	13.2	22.8	85.0	1.02	.94	1.02	1.15
Skinless, boneless	—	—	100.0	1.20	1.10	1.20	1.35
Shoulders:[5]							
Skinned, bone in	—	—	86.9	1.04	.98	1.06	—
Skinless, boneless	—	—	100.0	1.20	1.13	1.22	—
Picnics:[4]							
Skinned, bone in	6.1	10.5	81.9	.98	.90	.98	1.10
Skinless, boneless	—	—	100.0	1.20	1.10	1.20	1.35
Butts, skinless:							
Bone in (Boston)	4.8	8.3	93.3	1.12	1.08	1.17	1.31
Boneless	—	—	100.0	1.20	1.15	1.25	1.40[6]
Loins:							
Bone in	10.0	17.3	78.3	.94	.88	1.04	—
Semiboneless	—	—	87.0	1.04	.98	1.16	—
Boneless	—	—	100.0	1.20	1.13	1.33	—
Bellies:							
Bacon, slab, skin on	11.5	19.9	91.8	1.10	1.10	1.22	—
Bacon, sliced, skin off	—	—	100.0	1.20	1.20	1.33	—
Jowls (bacon squares)	1.8	3.1	88.0	1.06	1.06	1.12	—
Spareribs	1.5	2.6	58.0	.70	.67	.73	—

1. Edible offal items are excluded when converting to weight of pork excluding lard. These include brains, casings, heart, kidneys, liver, stomach or tripe, sweetbreads and tongue.
2. Pork excluding lard is computed by deducting the weight of fats rendered into lard or pork fat from the shipper-style carcass. Shipper-style carcass is computed by adding 7% to packer-style carcass, the 7% to include 4.5% head, 2.25% leaf fat, and 0.25% kidney, or the items normally on the shipper-style carcass.
3. 1954-63 average yield for federally inspected slaughter.
4. Skinned hams or picnics have about 50% of the skin removed. Skinless cuts have all of the skin removed.
5. Shoulder is picnic, butt, and plate, before cutting.
6. This factor may also be used for Capicola butts.

Boning

Boning shall be accomplished with sufficient care to allow each cut to retain its identity, and to avoid objectionable scores in the meat.

SMOKED AND CURED PORK

Description of Selections

Selection No. 1. Hams, shoulders, shoulder picnics, loins, and Canadian-style bacon of Selection No. 1 are meaty as a result of a combination of thick muscling and a minimum of intermuscular and external fat. The cuts are thick and plump throughout, with at least moderately thick muscling and have not more than a small amount of

Pork: Yield and Conversion Factors (Cont.)

Carcass and wholesale cuts	Aproximate percent of		Percent of boneless skinless meat, fresh	Factors for determining equivalent weight of pork excluding lard[1]			
	Live weight	Pork, excluding lard		Fresh or frozen	Cured	Smoked	Ready-to-eat
Feet, front[7]	1.0	1.7	10.0	.12	.10	—	—
Tails.	.1	.2	20.0	.24	.23	—	—
Neckbones	1.0	1.7	37.4	.45	.43	.45	—
Trimmings, lean	2.7	4.7	87.2	1.05	—	—	—
Fat backs and plates, not rendered[8]	2.9	5.0	88.3	1.06	1.04	1.12	—
Head, snout, and cheek meat	.7	1.2	87.2	1.05	—	—	—
Snouts, ears, and lips	.6	1.0	10.0	.12	.12	—	—
Other cuts or items:							
Canadian-style bacon	—	—	100.0	1.20	1.15	1.41	—
Tenderloins	—	—	100.0	1.20	1.15	1.41	—
Briskets[9]	—	—	91.8	1.10	1.10	1.22	—
Hocks and knuckles	—	—	25.0	.30	.29	.30	—
Salt pork	—	—	90.0	1.08	1.08	—	—
Pork, dehydrated	—	—	—	—	2.18	—	—

7. Because of gambrel damage hind feet usually go to tankage.
8. Fat backs and plates amount to approximately 9% of live weight. During the three-year period 1947-49, however, only 2.9% were sold as such and the balance rendered into lard. The amount rendered and hence, the percentage of pork excluding lard represented by these items, will vary from month to month, and year to year, depending upon the price of lard and fat back or salt pork.
9. Brisket is shoulder end of belly.

intermuscular fat. The lean meat must be firm and must possess a bright, reasonably uniform cured color (slightly two-toned permissible), and a fine, smooth texture. Selection No. 1 slab bacon must be slightly thick and moderately uniform in thickness, and be moderately long in relation to width. The bacon (slab or sliced) must indicate a moderately high ratio of lean to fat, and a uniform distribution of fat to lean layers. The exterior fat on Selection No. 1 pork cuts must be firm, white (except for the cured or well-penetrated smoke color), and reasonably uniform in distribution. The skin must be thin, smooth, and pliable. The pork cuts must be free from bruises, broken bones, dislocated or enlarged joints, or other malformation, odor, or flavor foreign to meat, and practically free from scores, miscuts, abrasions, hook marks, blemishes, hair roots, or other defects.

Selection No. 2.   Hams, shoulders, shoulder picnics, loins, and Canadian-style bacon of Selection No. 2 lack meatiness, either because of thin muscling or thick intermuscular and external fat, or a combination of characteristics intermediate in both respects. The cuts are slightly thick and plump throughout, with slightly thick muscling. They have a slightly high to high amount of intermuscular fat. The lean meat must be firm and must possess a bright, reasonably uniform cured color (slightly two-toned permissible), and a fine, smooth texture. Selection No. 2 slab bacon must be not more than moderately thick, but it may be uneven in thickness, and slightly short in relation to width. The bacon (slab or sliced) may indicate a moderately low ratio of lean to fat, and have rather thick fat deposits between layers of lean. The exterior fat on Selection No. 2 pork cuts must be firm, white (except for the cured or well-penetrated smoke color), and fairly uniform in distribution. The skin must be at least moderately thin, smooth and pliable. Pork cuts, otherwise eligible for Selection No. 1 or Selection No. 2, but which have slight scores, abrasions, hook marks, or cuts not exceeding ½ in. in depth or more than 2 sq. in. in area on the surface of the pork cuts used for slicing, but which do not interfere with the making of satisfactory slices, will be acceptable. Pork cuts showing only a slight amount of hair roots, or which are only slightly miscut or misshaped may be included; however, pork cuts which have broken bones, dislocated or enlarged joints, or other malformation, bruises, abrasions, or odor, or flavor foreign to meat are not acceptable.

INDEX OF PRODUCTS AND WEIGHT RANGE TABLE

Item No.	Product	Range A Pounds	Range B Pounds	Range C Pounds
400	Carcass	120–150	150–180	180–210
401	Ham, Regular	10–14	14–17	17–20
401A	Ham, Regular, Short Shank	10–14	14–17	17–20
402	Ham, Skinned	10–14	14–17	17–20
402A	Ham, Skinned, Short Shank	10–14	14–17	17–20
402B	Ham, Boned and Tied	6–8	8–10	10–12
403	Shoulder	8–12	12–16	16–20
404	Shoulder, Skinned	8–12	12–16	16–20
405	Shoulder Picnic	4–6	6–8	8–12
406	Boston Butt	4–8	8–12	
406A	Boston Butt, Boned and Tied	4–6	6–8	
407	Shoulder Butt, Boneless	1½–3	3–5	
408	Belly	10–12	12–14	14–16
409	Belly, Skinless	10–12	12–14	14–16
410	Loin	10–14	14–17	17–20
411	Loin, Bladeless	10–14	14–17	17–20
412	Loin, Center Cut	4–6	6–8	8–10
413	Loin, Boneless	6–8	8–10	10–12
413A	Loin, Boned and Tied	6–8	8–10	10–12
414	Canadian Back	3–4	4–5	5–6
415	Tenderloin	¼–½	½–¾	¾–1
416	Spareribs	1½–3	3–5	5–up
416A	Spareribs, Breast Off	1–2½	2½–4	4–up
417	Shoulder Hock	½–1	1½	1½–2½
418	Trimmings (90% Lean)	Amount as specified		
419	Trimmings (80% Lean)	Amount as specified		
420	Front Feet	¾–1½		
421	Neck Bones	¾–1	1–2	
422	Back Ribs	Under 1½	1½–3	3–up
423	Country Style Ribs	1–2	2–3	3–up

Note: The weight ranges of cuts as shown in the above table do not necessarily reflect any relation to the carcass weight ranges. Also cuts derived from another cut do not necessarily reflect any relation to the basic cut. Therefore, in ordering cuts, purchasing officials should specify the weight range(s) desired without regard to the carcass or basic cut weight shown in the various ranges.

INDEX OF PORTION-CUT PRODUCTS AND WEIGHT RANGE TABLE

Item No.	Product	Portion Size				
		3 ozs.	4 ozs.	5 ozs.	6 ozs.	8 ozs.
1400	Filets	X	X	X	X	X
1406	Boston Butt Steaks, Bone-In		X	X	X	X
1407	Shoulder Butt Steaks, Bnls.	X	X	X	X	X
1410	Chops, Regular	X	X	X	X	
1410A	Chops, with Pocket			X	X	X
1410B	Rib Chops, with Pocket			X	X	X
1411	Chops, Bladeless	X	X	X	X	X
1412	Chops, Center Cut	X	X	X	X	X
1412A	Chops, Center Cut, Special	X	X	X	X	X
1412B	Chops, Center Cut, Boneless	X	X	X	X	X
1413	Chops, Boneless	X	X	X	X	X
1495	Pork for Chop Suey	Amount as Specified				
1496	Ground Pork	Amount as Specified				
1496A	Ground Pork Patties	Size as specified				

Note: Because it is impractical to list all portion weights that purchasers may desire, the portion weights identified by the letter "X" are suggested only. Other portion weights may be ordered if desired.

State of Refrigeration

Chilled or Frozen.

Processing

Curing. In accordance with the regulations of the applicable meat inspection agency, all product items covered by these specifications must be mildly and thoroughly, but not excessively, cured, by an acceptable and recognized conventional method which will impart the typical, well-cured texture, cohesion, flavor, aroma soundness, and appearance (including a bright, stable, cured color) to the finished product.

Smoking. In accordance with the regulations of the applicable meat inspection agency, all smoked products covered by these specifications must be smoked for a sufficient time, and with temperatures as necessary to appropriately dry the product, and to impart a uniform, bright, well-penetrated smoke color, and the characteristic aroma, flavor, firmness, bright sheen, and appearance of a well-smoked product. Any encrusted salt, extraneous matter, and smokehouse residue—other than the normal smoke color—must be closely removed (no washing), such as careful light brushing or

**RELATIONSHIP BETWEEN AVERAGE THICKNESS OF BACKFAT,
CARCASS LENGTH OR WEIGHT, AND GRADE FOR CARCASSES
WITH MUSCLING TYPICAL OF THEIR DEGREE OF FATNESS.**

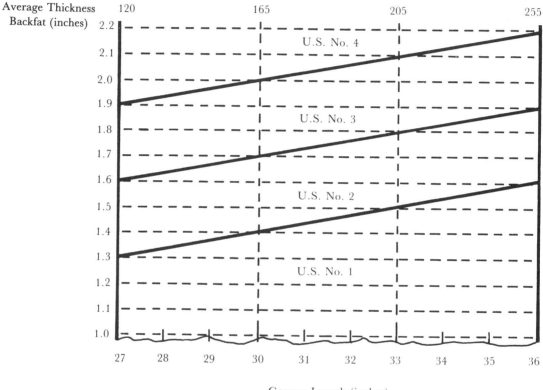

Hot Carcass Weight (pounds)

Carcass Length (inches)

wiping, without damage to the product. Stockinettes, strings, and similar hanging devices must be completely removed, and excluded, prior to wrapping, packing, and delivery of product.

Cooking. In accordance with the regulations of the applicable meat inspection agency, all product items covered by these specifications requiring cooking must be cooked by one of the following means as specified for the product item:

1. Dry Heat. Dry-heat fully cooked, smoked meat items should be smoked and cooked simultaneously without undue interruption, by an acceptable conventional method or means, for sufficient time to impart a uniform, bright, well-penetrated smoke color, and characteristic aroma and flavor to the product, and with tempera-

tures as necessary to reflect the typical, fully-cooked characteristics in the finished product. The smoking and cooking procedure must be conducted in a fairly continuous manner, to appropriately dry the product without undue rendering of fat, undercooking, overcooking, or other damage. The fully-cooked items must be handled as necessary to remove rendered surface fat and extraneous matter.

2. Moist Heat. The cured pork items should be fully-cooked with moist (hot water, or hot water and steam) heat, in temperatures and for the time necessary to impart the typical, fully-cooked characteristics to the finished product. After cooking, the fully-cooked products must be lightly showered with tepid water to remove surface meat juices, jelly, or albumin, and then trimmed lightly and smoothly to conform them to the specification requirements.

Finished Product Characteristics

The finished product as delivered must be sound and in excellent condition. The product must reflect appropriate selection, style, shape, weight range, curing, skinning, boning, defatting, smoking, cooking, packaging, packing, and state of refrigeration (as applicable). In addition, the product must meet other factors of conformance, without evidence of faulty workmanship and handling. The color of the lean meat must be fairly uniform and stable, characteristic of well-cured product, without evidence of greening, streaking, or other discoloration, (a slightly two-toned or iridescent color is permissible). The lean meat must possess a fine, smooth-texture, and be tender, cohesive, firm, or only slightly resilient, but not unduly hard.

Smoked products must have an acceptable flavor and aroma and a fairly uniform, bright, well-penetrated smoked color, and must be free from extraneous material, including encrusted salt and smokehouse residue (except the natural smoke color). The smoked product must be fairly dry on the exterior and the interior (including a well-sealed butt on hams not smoked in artificial casings), but not excessively dried or scorched. It must not have more than a very slight amount of dripping or exuding moisture upon appreciable careful hand pressure, although not such as will damage the product. Cooked products must be thoroughly cooked, and practically free from air holes, pockets of moisture, rendered fat, gelatinous matter, ragged edges, surface strings (except closely tied necessary stitching), and extraneous matter, and must be free from fermented, or other odor or flavor foreign to meat, rancidity, mold, or other deterioration or damage.

Tying

When string tying is required, roasts must be made firm and compact, and held intact by individual loops of strong twine, uniformly spaced at approximately 2-in. intervals girthwise. In addition, some roasts may require string tying lengthwise. In lieu of string, it is permissible to enclose roasts in a stretchable netting, provided it complies with the Regulation Governing the Meat Inspection of the USDA. Purchasers may specify that roasts be string-tied, when this requirement is not included in the detailed items specification.

Material

The curved and otherwise processed pork cuts described in these specifications must be derived from sound, well-trimmed wholesale market and fabricated cuts. The pork must show no evidence of freezer burn, mishandling, rancidity, or other detrimental blemish. Pork cuts which have been excessively trimmed in order to make specified weights, or which, for any reason, are substandard with these specifications must be excluded. They must be in excellent condition to the time of delivery.

Cross Reference Table:
Fresh to Cured or Smoked

401 = 501
403 = 515 = 516
405 = 525
410 = 545
411 = 546
414 = 550
416 = 558 = 559
417 = 560 = 561
420 = 563

TECHNIQUES OF CURING[1]

Dry Curing

The object of the curing process is to uniformly distribute the curing ingredients throughout the meat. Of the principal methods in use, the oldest is that of dry curing. In this procedure, the mixture of dry curing ingredients is spread on, or more correctly, rubbed into the surface of the piece of meat to be cured and the meat held under refrigeration until the salt and other materials penetrate to the center.

Penetration rate is dependent on time and temperature. The higher the temperature, the more rapid the penetration. However, temperatures much above 40°F will encourage spoilage bacteria and usually result in souring before the cure fully penetrates. Most recommendations give a time-weight relationship for curing. In some recent research at Iowa State University with country cured hams, it was found that it required a minimum of 40 days for salt concentration in the center of hams to approach the 1 percent level regardless of weight. At the same time, the salt concentration in the outer layer of the ham was 5 to 7 percent. Penetration of salt from the skin side of the meat is considerably slower than from the lean side. In fact, both skin and fat make relatively effective barriers for cure penetration.

In the case of dry cured meats the curing mixture is applied to the surface in one, two, or three 5-day intervals by a rubbing process. The amount applied is dependent upon final salt concentrations required. Usually a dry cured product will use upwards of 3 percent salt based on original green weight.

[1]The author thanks Koch Supplies, Inc. for use of this material from *Meat Curing Principles and Practices,* 1975.

In dry curing mixtures, the addition of the ascorbates or phosphates is not recommended. Usually the curing mixture consists of salt, sugar, and nitrate. While nitrite could be added, the curing time is sufficient for nitrate to be broken down to nitrite by bacterial action.

After rubbing with the cure, the products are stacked on shelves or in boxes and held for the prescribed curing time, usually at a temperature of 36 to 40°F. When curing is completed, large pieces, such as hams and shoulders, are held under refrigeration for an additional 30 days to allow the salt concentration to equalize. Following salt equalization, the products are then smoked and aged as desired.

Since most dry cured hams and shoulders are often eaten without sufficient cooking to destroy trichinae, the USDA prescribes rather rigid procedures for handling. Check with your state or federal meat inspector as to exact procedures that may be used.

Dry curing is sometimes used in conjunction with brine injection for some specialty products. In this procedure the product is usually pumped with not more than 10 percent of a fairly strong brine. The balance of the curing ingredients are then applied as a dry rub and the product handled much like dry cured.

Brine Soaking

In terms of historic use, this procedure closely followed dry curing and was used commercially for many years. In brine soaking, the product is placed in a brine solution for an appropriate period of time until the brine penetrates the entire piece. Again, this procedure involves a race against spoilage development and has severe limitations for large pieces, principally because of the relatively slow brine penetrations.

Brine soaking is still used commercially for small items such as tongues, corned beef, etc. Brine strength is variable depending on the desired saltiness of the finished product. With this method there is a tendency to want to reuse brine. This is not a wise practice for several reasons. First of all, the strength of the brine is reduced since some of the curing agents have been incorporated into the meat. Also, the brine at this point has been diluted with meat juices. Finally, the brine has become contaminated with bacteria, something that is absolutely unavoidable.

Brine Injection

Since one of the critical factors involved in curing is the uniform incorporation of the curing ingredients into the meat itself, it would seem logical to assume that forcing the brine directly into the meat would be an advantage. Without brine injection, rapid curing would be unknown.

Stitch or Spray Pumping

With this procedure the brine is pumped into the meat with a needle that has a number of holes along its length. Sometimes gangs of needles are employed. Usually the injections are made at several sites as close together as possible.

Artery Pumping

In artery pumping, the brine is injected through the femoral artery and follows the arterial system throughout the ham. Proponents of artery pumping ignore the fact that the arterial system in a ham is not uniform in its distribution. The distribution may be sufficient to allow immediate smoking. However, most plants hold at least 24 hours to be safe. Holding in a curing cooler 5 to 7 days·after pumping will greatly improve uniformity of cure distribution.

Artery pumping has a disadvantage in that it is a relatively slow procedure and has a high labor requirement. It would not be recommended for an operator who produces more than 400 hams per day.

In order to get a successful job of artery pumping it requires careful workmanship during slaughter, cutting and subsequent handling to insure that the arteries are intact. You will find that hams purchased from most packers will have anywhere from 25 to 50 percent damaged arteries. This is particularly true if hams are 4 to 5 days old before they are pumped. Damage here is largely due to drying of the arteries. Under certain conditions freezing can also cause damage to arteries.

Machine Pumping

The advent of relatively low cost, continuous brine injection machines offer the processor an opportunity for rapid processing of hams, bellies and other cured meat items. The principle used is similar to spray pumping with the exception that the needles inject the brine at hundreds of points. The pressure of the brine forces relatively uniform brine distribution throughout the meat.

It should be remembered that brine localizes in the lean. Overpumping is not a good procedure. The brine forms pockets in the seams between the muscle areas. The result will be the formation of open seams in the finished ham.

The multiple needle injection process provides a simple answer to the curing or injection of a number of other products. These include beef roasts, poultry products, corned beef, and tongues.

One question that often arises is whether or not visible marks or holes are left by the injector in the finished product. There is no evidence of this being a particular problem. The holes will normally close during processing and cooking.

Care should be taken where brine is recirculated to make periodic checks for dilution and contamination. When the brine shows evidence of accumulation of meat juices, it should be discarded and replaced with fresh brine. The best procedure to follow would be to pump the tank down to the last few inches, discard the balance and start with fresh brine.

Quality Control

The need for adequate quality control procedures cannot be overemphasized. Too often processors look on quality control as a necessary but often unwanted cost. In effect, however, it is one of the best insurances of profit a processor can institute in his operation.

A majority of the problems arising in processed meat can be traced to microbiological activity. Bacteria, yeasts, and molds are all enemies of cured meat. They surround us everywhere and cannot be eliminated, but their deleterious effects can be greatly reduced. Nothing beats a good sanitation program. It reduces initial microbiological loads on product and processing surfaces.

All fresh meat destined for curing should be handled with extreme care. These products should be processed as soon as possible after cutting and if held at all they should be held at coolers as near to the initial freezing point of meat (28°F) as possible. Certainly temperatures of over 36°F should be avoided for storage. Generally the product is allowed to warm up to 40 to 45°F for the actual pumping process but it should not be held at this temperature prior to pumping for any length of time.

Where longer precuring storage periods are required, freezer storage should be used. Here temperatures should be 0°F or below and the product should reach these temperatures as soon as possible. Since meat develops rancidity in the freezer, storage periods should be held to a minimum. Pork, because of its softer fat becomes rancid the quickest; storage periods of over 6 months are not recommended. Frozen products should be thawed quickly but where large units are involved, care should be taken not to allow surface spoilage to develop during thawing.

During the smoking and cooking period for cured meats much of the surface bacteria growth is destroyed. Therefore after this heat processing, recontamination should be avoided. This comes principally from processing surfaces. The shelf life of cured meats can be greatly extended by avoiding as much recontamination as possible.

Every processor should institute a program of periodic checks for bacterial contamination on processing surfaces before operation, during operation and after clean up. These bacteria counts can give an indication of where problem areas lie and will help pinpoint principal contamination sources.

Vacuum packaging can also extend shelf life of cured meats. The vacuum package discourages the growth of most of the common spoilage organisms. In addition, it reduces the availability of oxygen to the surface of the cured meat thus helping eliminate that source of cured meat color deterioration.

Cured meats are not good candidates for freezer storage. First of all, oxidative rancidity of the fat will continue to develop in the freezer. Thus, frozen cured meats will develop rancidity and also lose flavor in the freezer. Second, freezing produces some very characteristic texture changes in lean products such as cured hams. If you intend to build inventories, it is better to build them with fresh rather than cured product.

Quality control should also extend to curing procedures. Poorly trimmed cuts result in dissatisfied customers. Every attempt should be made to maintain uniform cutting techniques. Standards should be set for surface fat trim and in boneless products, internal fat. Personnel should be instructed in the proper application of these standards.

One of the most frequent complaints in hams is the problem of bruises. Of course, careful preslaughter handling can reduce this problem. If it is present, bruises can be noticed on the meat surface and should be trimmed out there and then even if it means reducing the cut to trimmings. This is far better than having it returned with a credit claim by the customer.

Internal bruises in hams are a more serious problem since they are not visible from the outside. Usually these are the result of improper shackling placing a strain on the joints prior to the time the hog is completely bled out. Often blood splashes or pinpoint blood spots are observed. These are usually the result of preslaughter stress or high voltages when the pig is electrically stunned. This needs careful attention.

Bacon has some physical characteristics that need further care in insuring maximum yields. A lot of sliced bacon is consigned to ends and pieces as a result of misshapen bellies due to careless hanging. Slanted ends and deep folds usually cannot be completely eliminated by the belly press.

Proper hanging of hams to insure uniform smoke distribution and an acceptable shape is likewise important. A lot of boneless hams are left with pockets in the interior as a result of careless insertion into the stockinette or the casing.

Finally, good record keeping is a must. If you keep detailed records of your processing procedures, it is easy to spot problems when they arise. Too often a processor will have no record of what was done when the product turned out satisfactorily and thus when something goes amiss, it is difficult to pinpoint problem causes. Remember that the best profit producers in the meat industry are those plants that have the best quality control.

SAUSAGE[2]

The word *sausage* is derived from the Latin "salus," meaning salted or preserved meat. While sausage was originally made of pork, during the last 700 years it has been made of mixed meats of all kinds, seasoned with spices gathered from around the world.

Modern sausage was developed mainly in the Germanic countries and in Italy. There the people, with their flair for the poetry of flavors, realized how enticing meat could be made by the skillful blending of different kinds of meats with various spices, and by curing and aging.

The warm Italian climate encouraged the development of the so-called "dry sausage." It was preserved with an abundance of salt and pungent spices, such as pepper and garlic, then thoroughly dried, generally without smoking. Treated in this way, the sausage could be kept for long periods, and stored against months of meat scarcity. Many a delectable sausage today bears the name of an Italian City, Milano, Romano, Genoa, Bologna.

In Germany, the much cooler climate and the cooler storage cellars accounted for the development of fresh and cooked sausage. These are the predecessors of our domestic sausage today; included are frying sausages, "bratenwurst," many styles of liver sausage, head cheese, blood sausage, and various cooked, smoked sausages. Of all of these, the wiener and frankfurter, the "hot dog," has become the most popular sausage in the United States.

---

[2]Substantial portions of the material appear in *Sausage and Smoked Meats,* 1966, a publication of Oscar Mayer Co. Reprinted with permission.

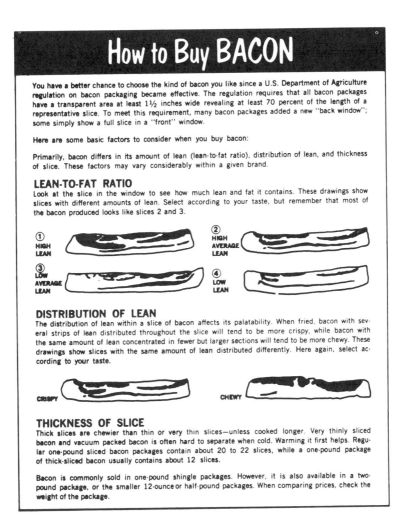

How to Buy BACON

You have a better chance to choose the kind of bacon you like since a U.S. Department of Agriculture regulation on bacon packaging became effective. The regulation requires that all bacon packages have a transparent area at least 1½ inches wide revealing at least 70 percent of the length of a representative slice. To meet this requirement, many bacon packages added a new "back window"; some simply show a full slice in a "front" window.

Here are some basic factors to consider when you buy bacon:

Primarily, bacon differs in its amount of lean (lean-to-fat ratio), distribution of lean, and thickness of slice. These factors may vary considerably within a given brand.

LEAN-TO-FAT RATIO
Look at the slice in the window to see how much lean and fat it contains. These drawings show slices with different amounts of lean. Select according to your taste, but remember that most of the bacon produced looks like slices 2 and 3.

① HIGH LEAN
② HIGH AVERAGE LEAN
③ LOW AVERAGE LEAN
④ LOW LEAN

DISTRIBUTION OF LEAN
The distribution of lean within a slice of bacon affects its palatability. When fried, bacon with several strips of lean distributed throughout the slice will tend to be more crispy, while bacon with the same amount of lean concentrated in fewer but larger sections will tend to be more chewy. These drawings show slices with the same amount of lean distributed differently. Here again, select according to your taste.

CRISPY
CHEWY

THICKNESS OF SLICE
Thick slices are chewier than thin or very thin slices—unless cooked longer. Very thinly sliced bacon and vacuum packed bacon is often hard to separate when cold. Warming it first helps. Regular one-pound sliced bacon packages contain about 20 to 22 slices, while a one-pound package of thick-sliced bacon usually contains about 12 slices.

Bacon is commonly sold in one-pound shingle packages. However, it is also available in a two-pound package, or the smaller 12-ounce or half-pound packages. When comparing prices, check the weight of the package.

A Pinch of Spice

One of the secrets of sausage flavor is the delicate blending of pure spices with fine meats. The old "wurstmacher" measured out spices with a well-trained eye and an experienced hand. Today's exacting formulas call for precise quantities and strict quality to assure uniformity. This is not easy to acquire. Mere weight or volume measures are not enough.

Spice control is so essential in maintaining a uniform flavor standard that sausage processors often maintain a special spice department. They begin by analyzing the basic materials even before purchase. Samples of natural spices and essential oils, as the liquid spice extracts are called, are tested thoroughly in the flavor laboratory.

Spice blends are prepared from basic spice materials in a centralized production unit. Blending spices in large lots—sometimes as much as 500-lb. batches—permits consistent seasoning of sausages even though they are made in different plants.

INDEX OF PRODUCT AND WEIGHT RANGE FOR WHOLESALE AND FABRICATED CUTS (POUNDS)

Item No.	Product	4-6	6-8	8-10	10-12	12-14	14-16	16-18	18-20
500	Ham, Regular (Cured)				x	x	x	x	x
501	Ham, Regular (Cured and Smoked)				x	x	x	x	x
502	Ham, Skinned (Cured)				x	x	x	x	x
503	Ham, Skinned (Cured and Smoked)				x	x	x	x	x
504	Ham, Sknls. (Cured and Smoked) Partially Boned			x	x	x	x	x	
505	Ham, Sknls. (Cured and Smoked) Completely Boneless			x	x	x	x	x	
505A	Ham, Sknls, Boned, Rolled, and Tied (Cured and Smoked)			x	x	x	x	x	
506	Ham, Sknd. (Cured and Smoked) Fully-Cooked, Dry Heat			x	x	x	x	x	
507	Ham, Bnls., Sknls. (Cured and Smoked) Fully-Cooked, Dry Heat		x	x	x	x	x		
508	Ham, Bnls., Sknls. (Cured) Pressed, Full-Cooked, Moist Heat			x	x	x			
509	Ham, Bnls., Sknls. (Cured and Smoked) Pressed, Fully-Cooked Moist Heat		x	x	x	x			
515	Shoulder, Regular (Cured)			x	x	x	x		
516	Shoulder, Regular (Cured and Smoked)			x	x	x	x	x	x
517	Shoulder, Skinned (Cured)			x	x	x	x	x	x
518	Shoulder, Skinned (Cured and Smoked)			x	x	x	x	x	
525	Shoulder, Picnic (Cured)	x	x	x	x	x	x	x	

No.	Item	Specifications / Sizes
526	Shoulder, Picnic (Cured and Smoked)	x x x
527	Shoulder, Picnic (Cured and Smoked) Boneless, Skinless, Rolled, and Tied	x x
530	Shoulder Butt, Boneless (Cured and Smoked)	x
535	Belly, Skin-On (Cured)	x x x x
536	Bacon, Slab (Cured and Smoked) Skin-On	x x x
537	Bacon, Slab (Cured and Smoked) Sknls	x x x
539	Bacon, Sliced (Cured and Smoked) Sknls	x x x x — Number of slices per pound (18–22; 22–26; 26–30; 28–32, or as specified
541	Bacon, Sliced (Cured and Smoked) End Pieces	5- and 10-pound containers, as specified
545	Loin, Regular (Cured and Smoked)	x x x
546	Loin, Bladeless (Cured and Smoked)	x x x
550	Canadian Style Bacon (Cured and Smoked)	3–5; 5–9 pounds
551	Canadian Style Bacon (Cured and Smoked) Sliced	x — 5- and 10-pound containers, as specified
555	Jowl Butts, Cellar Trim (Cured)	1 to 2½; 2½ to 4 pounds
556	Jowl Squares (Cured and Smoked)	¾ to 2; 2 to 3 pounds
558	Spareribs (Cured)	3 pounds or less; 3–5; 5 pounds or more
559	Spareribs (Cured and Smoked)	3 pounds or less; 3–5; 5 pounds or more
560	Hocks, Shoulder (Cured)	½ to 1; 1 to 1½; 1½ to 2½ pounds
561	Hocks, Shoulder (Cured and Smoked)	½ to 1; 1 to 1½; 1½ to 2½ pounds
562	Fatback (Cured)	x x
563	Feet, Front (Cured)	¾ to 1½ pounds

A Whiff of Smoke

Smoking began as a very ordinary procedure, but today it is a technical, processing plant operation. Not all processed meat products are smoked, nor are all of them cured. However, with few exceptions, meats to be smoked must first be cured.

After the curing process is complete, meats and processed products are routed to the smokehouse on a conveyor system, or on a "smoking tree" assembly. Production employees transfer the meat to the smokehouse interior where the penetrating effect of time and temperature-controlled smoke determine the final flavor and appearance.

In "rotary" smokehouses, 6 or 7 stories high, meat products hung on racks circulate through the smoke chambers on a moving frame resembling a ferris wheel. The products travel first in an upward direction and then downward for a thorough exposure to the permeating smoke. It requires almost 1½ hours for 1 rack to complete a rotation. Hams and bacon sides usually are smoked in the large "rotary" houses.

In "stationary" smokehouses, meats are hung on standing frames or "trees," rather than on the rotating racks. These houses are smaller, have less capacity, but require much less floor space and are easier to clean and maintain than the multi-story rotary smokehouses. They are used for smoking smaller sausages and specialties.

Hardwood sawdust, selected for its pleasant smoke aroma, is fed by stokers into a combustion chamber, and the resulting clouds of smoke are funneled into the smokehouse area. Large fans keep the air circulating so that the smoke reaches every corner of the smokehouse.

Smoking times vary according to product, some requiring 4 hours of smoke, and others requiring 24 hours. Temperature control is critical. Internal temperature of a pork product to be labelled "fully cooked" must reach at least 137°F, according to federal inspection regulations. Any trichinae would be destroyed at this temperature. Actually, many smoked meat products are processed to temperatures of 148°F or higher to develop flavor and firmness. Other products which are to be cooked by the consumer may not require as high a temperature, but these products also depend on precise temperature controls to assure unique flavor qualities.

Smoking is said to give processed meat products their "second helping" of flavor, but according to research specialists, you don't taste the smoke—you smell it!

Hang It Up To Dry

One of the most interesting and exacting processes in sausage-making is drying. The practice probably originated centuries before Christ near the Mediterranean Sea as one of the earliest methods of preserving foods. Many names of dry sausages are taken from the city of origin, as each community developed its own particular style. There were differences in the kinds of meat and casing used, methods of chopping meat, seasonings, even in the wrapping of twine around the sausage for hanging to dry. Dried sausage may or may not be smoked after curing.

Sausage drying rooms have carefully controlled humidity, temperature, and air circulation. The drying process must be exact to produce even drying throughout the sausage, without too hard a crust and internal "soft" spots. The air is continuously washed and re-dried to eliminate air-borne spores and molds that could produce undesirable characteristics in the salami.

Drying may begin in the smokehouse, and some semi-dry sausages are processed entirely by smoking. Lebanon Bologna, for example, is smoked for as long as two weeks to develop its texture and flavor.

The distinctive tangy flavor typical of most dry sausages as well as the semi-dry varieties results from a bacterial fermentation. In addition to traditional methods, pure starter cultures have been developed to control and speed fermentation.

Dry and semi-dry sausages usually are eaten cold, although they have not been fully cooked in processing. There are various precautions taken to insure wholesomeness in this type of sausage. Either controlled refrigeration or controlled curing are effective treatments in destroying trichinae, as is heating to 137°F.

Although controlled freezing is an approved method of destroying trichinae, meats to be used in dry sausage are not generally certified this way. Frozen pork is not considered desirable for dry sausage-making.

Federal requirements for the refrigeration methods are specific for minimum temperatures and time in relation to the size of the meat pieces, to assure necessary penetration of freezing temperatures. For example, meat pieces requiring 20 days at 5°F need only 10 days at −10°F and 6 days at −20°F.

What's In a Name?

Sausages are usually classified according to processing procedures after stuffing. Although there are differences among sausages within a group, these differences are due primarily to meat combinations and seasonings used, and not to basic processing procedures. Also, they are basically alike, as far as preparation procedures and typical serving uses, are concerned.

The major sausage classifications, as recognized by the American Meat Institute and National Livestock and Meat Board, are:

- Fresh Sausage
- Uncooked, Smoked Sausage
- Cooked, Smoked Sausage
- Cooked Sausage
- Cooked Meat Specialties
- Dry and Semi-Dry Sausage

Fresh Sausage

As the name suggests, fresh sausage is made of meats that have not been cured—generally, selected cuts of fresh pork and sometimes beef. It is the most perishable of all sausage products. Its taste, texture, tenderness and color are directly related to the ratio of fat to lean.

Makers of quality fresh sausage use "trimmings" from primal cuts; that is, the pork loin, ham, or shoulders. As with other sausage products, the spice formulation will vary with the meat processor. Expert wurstmachers say the product should be seasoned delicately, with a view toward enhancing the natural meat flavors, not masking them.

Fresh sausage must always be kept under refrigeration. It must be cooked thoroughly before serving, and is usually fried or grilled. Pork sausage and bratwurst are popular varieties in this classification.

Uncooked, Smoked Sausage

This class of sausage has all the characteristics of fresh sausage, with one major difference: it is smoked, producing a different flavor and color. Sometimes it contains fresh meat. These sausages, too, must be cooked thoroughly before serving. Smoked pork sausage and Kielbasa are two of the few examples of uncooked, smoked sausage.

Cooked, Smoked Sausage

Sausage in this category, usually made from cured meats, is chopped or ground, seasoned, stuffed into casings, smoked, and cooked. The use of cured meats contributes to flavor, color, and preservation of the product.

Cooked, smoked sausage comes in all shapes and sizes—short, thin, long, chubby—and is the largest and most popular of all the categories. The "skinless" varieties have been stripped of their casings after cooking. Wieners and Smokie Links are included in this grouping.

Within this category there are two basic classes: fine-cut sausage (such as wieners and bologna) and course-cut sausage (such as Berliner or New England).

Cooked Meat Specialties

As the name implies, the primary difference between this classification and cooked sausage is that specialty items, such as meat loaves, head cheese, souse, and scrapple, are included.

These prepared meat products are cooked or baked, and always ready to serve.

Cooked Sausage

Cooked sausage is usually prepared from fresh, uncured meats, although occasionally cured meats are used. Often variety meat or organ meat, such as liver, is included so that sausages in this classification may be especially nutritious. In many instances, the product is smoked; however, the essential difference between this class and cooked, smoked sausage is that the smoking is done after cooking has been completed. This product is always ready to serve.

Liver sausage is the most popular variety in this class, and has enjoyed increasing consumer acceptance in recent years.

Dry, Semi-dry Sausage

All dry sausages are characterized by a bacterial fermentation. This intentional encouragement of a lactic acid bacteria growth is useful as a meat preservative, as well as producing the typical, tangy flavor.

The meat ingredients, after being mixed with spices and curing materials, are generally held for several days in a curing cooler. Afterward, the meat is stuffed into casings, and is started on a carefully-controlled, air-drying process. Some dry sausage is given a light preliminary smoke, but the key production step is the relatively long, continuous, air-drying process.

Principal dry sausage products are salamis and cervelats. Salamis are coarsely cut; cervelats, finely cut—with few exceptions. They may be smoked, unsmoked, or cooked. Italian and French dry sausages are rarely smoked; other varieties usually are.

Dry sausage requires more production time than other types of sausage, and results in a concentrated form of meat. Medium-dry sausage is about 70 percent its ''green'' weight when sold. Less-dry and fully-dried sausage range from 60 to 80 percent of original weight at completion. Logically, many varieties in this group are more expensive per pound than ones in other classifications.

Semi-dry sausages are usually heated in the smoke house to cook the product fully and partially dry it. Semi-dry sausages are semi-soft sausages, with good keeping qualities due to their lactic acid fermentation.

Although dry and semi-dry sausages originally were produced in the winter for use in the summer, and were considered summer sausage, the term ''summer sausage'' now refers to semi-dry sausages, especially Thuringer Cervelat.

Smoked Meats

Cuts of fresh meat, usually pork, may be cured with salt or brine, and then smoked to give a distinctive flavor and aroma. Current smoking techniques result in a product which is considerably less dry than the smoked products of the last century. The original drying-out in smoking meat contributed greatly to its keeping qualities. Modern refrigeration facilities have reduced the need for this effect of smoking, and methods have been developed which emphasize flavor and aroma rather than drying.

Kitchen preparation of today's fully cooked hams is quite different from the cooking methods necessary for heavily salted, slowly smoked hams which need to be simmered in water to reduce the salt content, and then slowly baked to an internal temperature of 160°F.

Fully cooked hams are heated in the oven without simmering to serving temperature (130°F) in about half the baking time required for the cook-before-eating type ham. This is a time-saving factor of considerable importance.

INDEX OF PRODUCTS AND WEIGHT RANGE TABLE

Item No.	Product	Weight Range 1	Weight Range 2	Weight Range 3
600	Spencer Roll, Corned	Under 15	15–22	22-Up
601	Brisket, Boneless, Deckle off, Corned	Under 9	9–12	12-Up
602	Knuckle, Corned	Under 8	8–15	15-Up
603	Knuckle, Dried	Under 5	5–8	8-Up
604	Inside Round, Corned	Under 14	14–20	20-Up
605	Inside Round, Dried	Under 9	9–12	12-Up
606	Outside Round, Corned	Under 11	11–18	18-Up
607	Outside Round, Dried	Under 8	8–14	14-Up
608	Gooseneck Round, Corned	Under 16	16–27	27-Up
609	Rump Butt, Corned	Under 8	8–12	12-Up
613	Tongue, Cured	3–5		
614	Tongue, Smoked	3–5		
617	Process Dried Beef	Under 8	8–14	14-Up
618	Sliced Process Dried Beef			
619	Sliced Dried Beef			
620	Sliced Dried Beef, Ends and Pieces	¼-pound, ½-pound, 1-pound individual packages, or bulk or layer packed.		

Curing and smoking meat inhibit the development of bacterial growth, thus increasing the refrigerated storage life of the product. However, the smoke residues have no effect on mold growth.

Curing produces chemical changes in meat pigments; these are stabilized during the heat of smoking. This accounts for the characteristic deep pink color of the lean muscle of bacon, ham, and other smoked meats.

QUESTIONS

1. Define:

marbling
collagen
aging
IMP
bracelet shoulder clod
dry curing
elastin

cover
par stock
longissimus dorsi
hotel rack
rapid curing
sausage

2. What grade of meat would one purchase for roasting?

3. Explain why two grades of meat, good and cutter, have the same nutritive value.
4. What is state of refrigeration? Give examples and reasons for specifying each.
5. What are the allowable weight deviations in an 18 oz. steak?
6. Write specifications for Ribeye Roll, then order for 20 servings.
7. Why in lamb carcass specifications does one specify surface fat thickness or yield grade, but not both?
8. What is not allowed in ground meats? How often may it be mixed?
9. Why is meat aged?
10. What should a buyer look for in a cured meat product?
11. Why are there such rigid standards for curing?
12. What state of refrigeration would be specified for corned beef?

EXHIBITS

Indicators to Assist in Determining What's Contained in a Meat Product

1. The name as indicated on the label and the standard for the product.

2. Ingredients as indicated on the label. Percent labeling is helpful.

3. Written statement by an official of the company certifying the weight of the cooked or uncooked lean meat and fat contained in the product.

4. Laboratory analysis indicating to what extent the meat/meat alternate requirement is met.

5. Inspection by the *USDA Acceptance Service* to insure that meat products meet desired specifications.

The ingredients, as indicated on the label, are monitored by APHIS.

The information contained in a certified written statement or in a separate "handout" is *not* checked by Aphis.

Each purchaser should, therefore, have a satisfactory method to ascertain that the product does, in fact, contain what is purported.

Most effective methods are:

1. Independent laboratory analysis.

2. USDA - Acceptance Service

Animal	Prime	Choice	Good	Standard	Commercial	Utility	Cutter	Canner
Steer, Heifer, Bullock	Yes	Yes	Yes	Yes	Yes	Yes	Yes	Yes
Cow	No	Yes	Yes	Yes	Yes	Yes	Yes	Yes
Bull, Stag	No	Yes	Yes	Yes	Yes	Yes	Yes	Yes
Veal	Yes	Yes	Yes	Yes	Yes	Yes	Yes	Yes
Calf	Yes	Yes	Yes	Yes	Yes	Yes	Yes	Yes

	Prime	Choice	Good	Utility	Cull			
Lamb, Yearling Mutton	Yes	Yes	Yes	Yes	Yes			
Mutton	No	Yes	Yes	Yes	Yes			

	U.S. No. 1	U.S. No. 2	U.S. No. 3	U.S. No. 4	U.S. Utility	Medium	Cull	
Barrow, Gilts	Yes	Yes	Yes	Yes	Yes	No	No	
Sows	Yes	Yes	Yes	No	No	Yes	Yes	

Equivalents: Steer = Barrow   Heifer = Gilt
Cow = Sow   Bull = Boar
Stag = Stag

How do American beef cattle grade out? 4% Prime, 60% Choice, 25% Good, 11% less than Good.

A Meat Specification	
Product	Ground Beef, regular
IMPS/MBG No.	136
Weight	10 pound container
Detail	Max. 30% fat. Ground through ¾" plate, then ⅛" plate, thoroughly blended.
Condition	Frozen. Marked with U.S. inspection stamp

12

MISCELLANEOUS GROCERIES

INTRODUCTION

Miscellaneous groceries require a sizeable amount of time for procurement. Many of these goods are regulated only by trade names rather than federal regulations. In selecting products from this group, the same basic purchasing principles prevail. The buyer needs accurate knowledge as to the final use that will be made of the product to be purchased; and information as to the products that are available, their description, and the range of quality offered for selection.

Coffee has a short storage life because the oils are easily oxidized and turn disagreeable. It is usually a blend of several varieties of coffee, and ground to regular grind, drip grind, or fine grind. Other coffee forms are decaffeinated coffee, freeze-dried coffee, frozen coffee, and soluble coffee.

Tea varies in relation to altitude, soil, and climate. Green tea, Oolong tea, and Black tea are the three types of tea.

Fats and oils are used shortenings which are commonly plastic. They act to shorten the gluten strands. Solid fats are usually of an animal origin, while liquid fats are of a vegetable origin. It is important to specify oils for frying with a high smoking point.

Honey is liquid sugar prepared from flowers. It is used as a substitute for sugar in baking and can be found in a comb or extracted.

Jams and jellies may contain spice, vinegar, pectin, sodium citrate, sodium benzoate, mint flavoring, cinnamon flavoring, anti-foaming agents, sugar, invert sugar syrup, and honey.

Juices may be sweetened or unsweetened but should closely resemble the fruit they originated from in regard to taste and smell. There are canned, concentrated, and dehydrated juices. Only orange and grapefruit juices are federally graded in the dehydrated stage.

Kosher foods, described in the Rules of Kashruth, mean food that is fit. There are three types: (1) food that is fit all the time, (2) food that requires some preparation, and (3) food that is not fit.

Cured pickles or fresh pack pickles are determined by the pickling process. A kosher style dill pickle in the United States indicates a highly seasoned pickle. One can find pickles in many different forms, such as dill, sour, sweet, and whole, sliced, chopped, etc.

Peanut Butter is scored on color, consistency, absence of defects, flavor, and aroma. Water, insoluble inorganic residue, and salt are all quality factors of peanut butter.

Spices and herbs are found in seeds, whole or ground. Grinding allows for a shorter cooking time because the essential oils are more exposed. They should be inspected for quality and tasted for ''strength of flavor'' usage. A list is given of spices and their common available forms.

There are two types of flavorings and extracts. Imitation flavorings are synthetic chemical compounds which resemble the natural flavors. Natural extracts are the oils from the fruits and nuts.

Inspection of nuts is not mandatory, but is provided by the USDA at cost to the nut packagers. Price and shell appearance are not always reliable factors for selection. The packager of graded nuts is obligated to make sure the nuts meet the standards. Some nuts such as cashew and macadamia nuts require the shell to be removed, although the shell does retain some of the freshness.

BEVERAGES

Coffee

Coffee[1] is difficult to keep. The oils and other constituents that provide its flavor and fragrance are easily dissipated or, if exposed to air, are quickly oxidized to substances yielding disagreeable odors and tastes. In contrast, coffee is a rare treat when made from freshly roasted and ground beans in an atmosphere where the air is still full of the rich aroma released by roasting, grinding, and brewing.

By the time most roasted and ground coffee reaches the consumer, even when protected in vacuum-packed containers, much of its aroma and flavor have been lost. Once the container is opened, the loss speeds up. It can be retarded, but not stopped, by keeping the coffee container tightly closed and stored in a cool place. Coffee should be purchased in amounts small enough to be quickly used.

The coffee beans that the foodservice operator buys are the product of roasting and, usually, grinding. Coffee is usually a blend of more than one coffee. Some of the important varieties are:

- Armenia—full bodied (Colombia)
- Aukola—light, sweet (Sumatra)
- Blue Mountain—full bodied (Jamaica)
- Bogota—full bodied (Colombia)

---

[1]USDA.

- Cootepec—full bodied (Mexico)
- Excelso—full bodied (Colombia)
- Giradot—full bodied (Colombia)
- Java—mild, good quality (Java)
- Liberica—somewhat acrid (Venezuela)
- Mandhelling—light, sweet (Sumatra)
- Manizule—full bodied (Colombia)
- Marciabo—light, rich (Venezuela)
- Medellin—full bodied (Colombia)
- Mocha—full bodied, rich (Arabia)
- Oaxaca—low quality (Mexico)
- Rio—low quality (Mexico)
- Robusta—somewhat acrid (Kenya)
- Sevilla—full bodied (Colombia)
- Santo—somewhat acrid, high quality (Brazil)

It is possible to brew coffee from roasted whole beans, but this would take hours and the beverage would not taste very good.[2] It is also possible to make a beverage from pulverized coffee. Single cup vending machines, which are scientifically designed to use such coffee, can produce a good beverage from a very fine grind, but institutional and home-type brewing equipment are not designed for pulverized coffee, and its use in such equipment would result in a very bitter tasting brew. Consequently, beans for normal use should *not* be ground to a powder. This means that some intermediate grind size is required. To achieve this end there must be a method for accurately measuring sizes of particles. Such a method permits grinding to a desired degree of fineness and consistently provides the same balance of particle sizes.

Food operators should know whether their suppliers are actually making measurements of grinds, and whether consistency of grind is being provided.

Any grind contains particles of many sizes. Samples differ only in the proportion of each size of particles they contain. These proportions are measured by shaking the sample through a set of graded screens. A drip (or urn) grind, for example, should contain about 7 percent of particles that will be held back by a 14 mesh screen, 73 percent that will be held back by a 28 mesh screen, and 20 percent that will pass through a 28 mesh screen.

Any day-to-day or periodic variations in the consistency of the grind supplied can result in an inconsistent beverage. As the percentage of large particles increases, the brewed coffee will be weaker. As the fine particles increase, the resultant brew may become bitter.

	Regular	**Drip**	**Fine**
14 mesh screen	33 percent	7 percent	None
28 mesh screen	55 percent	73 percent	70 percent
Pan	12 percent	20 percent	30 percent

[2]*Facts About Coffee,* The Coffee Brewing Center, New York, N.Y.

A cautionary note should be added here on the use of coffee grinders on location. These grinders can and do vary in the type of grind they produce. This lack of control in the grind will be directly reflected in the beverage quality.

Accumulation of rancid oils and other materials in the grinder will offset the fine flavor of fresh coffee as well. Coffee that is ground in a roasting plant will be uniform day after day and will not adversely affect the quality of your beverage.

There are no federal grades for coffee, but there are grades maintained by the New York Coffee and Sugar Exchange. The grades limit the number of defects allowed in the coffee; the more defects the lower the grade.

Some things to look for include:

1. Coloring. The coffee might be dyed. The color should be even throughout the bean.
2. Additives. Cereals and beans may have been ground into the coffee.
3. Glazing. Adding of materials in the roasting to improve color. This adds weight but does not improve quality.

A specification for coffee should include: (1) roast, (2) grind, (3) percentage of types desired in blend, and (4) packaging. Since few foodservice operators have the purchasing power to specify the types, it is suggested that several brands be ordered ''in the bean'' and sent to the Coffee Brewing Center for quality evaluation. Customer testing must be part of the cost/quality evaluation.

Decaffeinated Coffee. This product is an instant coffee from which 97 to 99 percent of caffeine has been removed. It is packaged in various sized jars and individual packets.

Freeze-Dried Coffee. This product is the result of freezing brewed coffee and then drying it in a vacuum without going through a liquid state. It has a higher quality and better aroma than soluble coffee.

Factors for obtaining equivalents of green coffee beans and leaf tea from specified products

Product	Description	Factors
Coffee, green, bag[1]	Standard bag of 60 kilograms, number of pounds	132.276
Coffee, parchment	The green coffee bean contained in the parchment skin	.80
Coffee, roasted	Green coffee roasted to any degree and includes ground coffee	1.19
Coffee, soluble, pure (instant)	The water-soluble solids derived from roasted coffee	3.00
Coffee, decaffeinated	Green, roasted or soluble coffee from which caffein has been extracted:	
	Green	1.00
	Roasted	1.19
	Soluble (instant)	3.00
Tea, soluble (instant)	3 lb. of leaf tea yields 1 lb. of soluble tea	3.00

1. All coffee in the naked bean form before roasting.

Frozen Coffee. This is a concentrate coffee resulting from the partial extraction of the liquid from brewed coffee. It is smooth, high quality, but lacks aroma.

Soluble Coffee. This powdered product is a result of vacuum drying brewed coffee. Often called "instant" coffee, it is of good quality but usually lacks aroma.

Cocoa

Breakfast cocoa is the product resulting from roasting, grinding, and defatting the nibs of the cocoa bean. Breakfast cocoa must have 22 percent cocoa butter but may have as much as 35 percent. The higher the cocoa butter content, the richer the product. Dutch process breakfast cocoa has been treated to make it richer and more easily soluble.

Hot Chocolate. This beverage is made from chocolate liquor, liquid or dried, which may contain up to 50 percent cocoa butter.

Tea

Tea varies in quality according to the altitude at which it is grown (the higher the better), the soil, and climate. There are three types of tea and many classes within those types. Quality and cost of tea can be affected by the amount of hand work that is done in the drying (fermenting) and rolling processes.

Green tea is fired to stop fermentation shortly after it is picked. Green tea is classed as Basket Fired and Pan Fired when it is Japan Green. China Green is classed as Gunpowder, Imperial, Young Hyson, and Hyson. The Basket Fired variety is best as it is the result of a hand process which treats the tea gently. The best of the China Greens is Gunpowder, followed by Young Hyson, Hyson, and Imperial.

Oolong tea is allowed to oxidize for a few hours before it is fired.

Black tea oxidizes for many hours before it is fired. There are two kinds of black tea: China, and those from Sri Lank, India, Java, and Sumatra. The Tea Council of the U.S. grades black teas by Leaf Grades or Broken-Leaf Grades. These are O.P. [Orange Pekoe], a pale tea; P.E.K. [Pekoe], a medium colored tea; S.O.U. [Souchong], a pale tea; B.O.P. [Broken Orange Pekoe], a heavily colored tea; B.P. [Broken Pekoe], a pale tea; B.P.S. [Broken Pekoe Souchong], lighter than B.P.; F.N.G.S. [Fannings], a heavily colored tea; D. [Dust], strong. Teas are often marketed by the name of the area in which they were grown. North China Congous is a strong, full-bodied tea; South China Congous is a light tea; Darjeeling is generally thought to be the finest, most delicate tea; Dovars is a gentle tea; Assam is strong; Trarancore is another fine delicate tea, as is Ceylon Black. Sumatra and Java Black are heavier than Darjeeling, but lighter than the stronger teas.

Postum

This coffee-substitute product is free of caffeine. It is packaged in various sized jars and individual packets.

FATS AND OILS

Shortenings[3] are edible fats used to shorten baked goods. A baked mixture of flour and water would be tough without the addition of proper amounts of fat or oil. Fats produce tenderness by surrounding particles of starch and strands of gluten. In this way the strands of gluten are kept short; hence, the name "shortening."

Although oils, butter, margarine, and lard may all be used as shortening agents, the products that have come to be known as shortenings are the vegetable fats or animal and vegetable mixtures that are plastic. This means they are soft and creamy and may be easily molded or shaped.

Shortening as a food product is an American invention, growing out of the cotton-raising industry. The first shortenings, prepared by a blending of hard fats (edible tallows) and soft fats (cottonseed oil), were called *compounds*. They were conceived and marketed as substitutes for lard. In the beginning, the American meatpackers literally controlled the shortening industry, for they controlled the supply of hard animal fat which was an essential ingredient.

Solid fats are usually of animal origin and are composed of considerable amounts of saturated fatty acids which contain as many hydrogen atoms as the carbon chain can hold. Fats of vegetable origin are usually liquid oils, and the unsaturated fatty acids are predominant. These may be mono-unsaturated with one reactive unsaturated linkage (double bond) which has two hydrogens missing; or poly-unsaturated with two or more reactive unsaturated linkages (double bonds) with four, six, eight, or more hydrogens missing. (*Food, The 1959 Yearbook of Agriculture,* pp. 76–77, contains an excellent discussion on structure.)

Introduction of the hydrogenation process in about 1910 made the manufacturer of vegetable shortening independent. The hydrogenation process adds hydrogen to the unsaturated fatty acids, reducing their degree of unsaturation and transforming them to the corresponding saturated fatty acids. This changes the liquid oil to a plastic fat, and makes any blending with an animal fat unnecessary.

Since about 1933, further changes in the method of manufacturing hydrogenated shortenings have involved the addition of mono- and di-glycerides. The superior emulsifying properties of fats so treated cause a fine dispersion of the fat in the dough or cake and allow a higher ratio of sugar to flour.

These shortenings are described as "high ratio" or emulsified. They have become popular for use in cakes, sweet yeast doughs, and similar products. The shortenings have a lowered smoke point and are less desirable for frying.

For a long period of time there was an approximate parity in price between compound shortening and lard, but high production and undesirable qualities in lard caused a decrease in its price. Until recently, the lack of uniformity of lard and some of its properties such as odor, flavor, grainy texture, low smoke point, and susceptibility to rancidity have resulted in a greatly reduced usage of lard. Many years of research by

---

[3]USDA.

government and industrial laboratories have improved its quality, uniformity, and functional properties.

Shortenings of the all-vegetable-oil variety have always commanded a price above the compound shortenings. Retail prices of vegetable oils are even higher than hydrogenated shortenings.

In recent years, shortening products containing lard or lard and beef fat blends have been refined, stiffened by hydrogenation, fortified with an antioxidant, deodorized, and in some cases superglycerinated to make them comparable to all-vegetable hydrogenated shortenings.

Commonly used food fats are complicated mixtures which do not have a sharp melting point but solidify over a wide temperature range. This fact is demonstrated when oils cloud on refrigeration. Many vegetable oils are ''winterized'' to prevent this, particularly salad oils. The process of winterizing an oil consists of chilling it to a temperature of 40 to 45°F and removing the precipitated solid crystals by filtration. The resulting oil remains clear at ordinary refrigerator temperatures.

The first recognizable deterioration in fats, such as lard, oils, and shortening, is the development of rancidity. This is an oxidative change which in vegetable oils is inhibited by naturally occurring antioxidants. Since animal fats do not contain natural antioxidants to protect them, it is necessary to add chemical agents to delay the onset of rancidity. The U.S. Department of Agriculture has approved and specified the amount permitted for about a dozen antioxidants that may be used in animal fats.

Shortenings, whether of vegetable origin or mixtures, keep well at room temperature.

Only shortenings containing animal fats are inspected by USDA. A system of continuous inspection has been developed with the federal inspectors placed in each plant to supervise the handling at every step. Inspection is concerned with facilities, equipment, sanitation, source and quality of raw materials, acceptable manufacturing practices, laboratory testing, and labeling. Only edible fats from U.S. inspected and passed carcasses may be used in animal fat shortenings.

As previously stated, shortenings with emulsifiers have a low smoke point. When fats or oils are heated to a high temperature, decomposition occurs, and finally a point is reached at which visible fumes are given off. This is the smoke point. The fumes have an unpleasant odor and are irritating to the nose and eyes.

Food fried in smoking fats is likely to have an unpleasant flavor, and the fat will become rancid faster than fat which has not been heated to smoke temperatures.

An ideal fat for frying food is one that has a fairly high smoke point. Most cooking oils and all hydrogenated shortenings (without emulsifiers) have high smoke points. Smoke points vary for lards. Butter, margarine, and shortenings with emulsifiers have low smoke points and do not make good frying fats. Repeated use of a fat lowers the smoke point. Foods absorb more fat, which is undesirable, when they are cooked in a fat with a low smoke point.

Although fried foods are generally cooked at 375°F, or less, it is important to specify a frying oil with a smoking point of no less than 426°F. Hydrogenated vegetable shortenings, peanut oil, and soybean oils meet this standard.

Products Prepared From Fats and Oils[4]

A wide variety of products based on edible fats and oils is offered the consuming public. Shortening, margarines, butter, salad and cooking oils, and other specialty salad dressings are some of the widely available products that are either based entirely on fats and oils or contain fat or oil as a principal ingredient. Many of these products are also sold in commercial quantities to food processors, bakeries, restaurants, and institutions.

Salad and Cooking Oils.   Salad and cooking oils are prepared from vegetable oils that are usually refined, bleached, deodorized, and sometimes lightly hydrogenated. Cottonseed, corn, and soybean are the principal oils sold in this form, although peanut, safflower, and olive oils are also used. Due to the presence of substantial quantities of linolenic acid naturally occurring in soybean oil, it is frequently desirable to lightly hydrogenate this oil when it is to be used as a salad and cooking oil.

The fatty acid composition and iodine value of the principal vegetable oils used for food purposes in the United States are given in the accompanying table.

TYPICAL FATTY ACID COMPOSITION AND IODINE VALUE OF SOME VEGETABLE OILS

| Vegetable Oil | % of Total Fatty Acids | | | | |
| | Unsaturated Fatty Acids | | | Saturated Fatty Acids | Iodine Value |
	Oleic	Linoleic	Linolenic		
Soybean oil	24	54	7	15	132
Cottonseed oil	22	52	tr	26	110
Corn oil	29	56	tr-1	15	126
Peanut oil	49	30	tr	21	95
Olive oil	73	12	tr	15	85
Safflower oil	14	75	tr-1	10	144

Margarine.   Margarines are fatty foods prepared by blending fats and oils with other ingredients such as milk solids, salt, flavoring materials, and Vitamins A and D. By federal regulation, margarine must contain at least 80 percent fat. The fats used in margarines may be of either animal or vegetable origin although vegetable oils are by far the most widely used.

The fats may be prepared from single hydrogenated fats, from two or more hydrogenated fats, or from a blend of hydrogenated fat and an unhydrogenated oil. Many manufacturers of margarines are now producing these products with substantially higher levels of polyunsaturated fatty acids, in response to medical research findings which suggest the advisability of higher levels of these fatty acids in the diet. These

---

[4]*Food Fats and Oils,* Technical Committee of Shortening and Edible Oils, Inc., Institute of Shortening and Edible Oils, Inc., Washington, D.C. 20006, 1968.

margarines contain fats having 22 to 60 percent polyunsaturated fatty acids and iodine values ranging from 92 to 130. In contrast, regular margarines contain 10 to 20 percent polyunsaturated fatty acids and have iodine values from 78 to 90. Some medical workers have referred to these products high in polyunsaturated fatty acids as ''special'' margarines because, in addition to their use in normal diets, they are also suitable for use in special diets where an increased level of linoleic acid is desired.

Included here is a table that gives the range in fatty acid composition and iodine value for the various types of margarine products made from vegetable oils.

FATTY ACID COMPOSITION AND IODINE VALUE OF FAT AND OILS IN MARGARINE PRODUCTS

Type Margarine	% of Total Fatty Acids			Saturated Fatty Acids	Iodine Value
	Unsaturated Fatty Acids				
	Monoenoic	Dienoic	Trienoic		
Vegetable margarine —regular	42 to 63	10 to 20	0 to 0.5	16 to 25	78 to 90
Vegetable margarine —special	20 to 57	22 to 60	0 to 0.5	13 to 30	92 to 130

Corn Oil. This refined oil from corn germ is used in salad oils and for deep frying. It has a high smoking point.

Cottonseed Oil. This refined oil from cottonseed is used in making margarine, salad oils, and vegetable cooking fats. It has a high smoking point.

Hydrogenated Fats. These vegetable oils, usually cottonseed oil solidified by hydrogen, are used as shortening. Smoking point is 440 to 460°F.

Lard. Lard is melted pig fat. The best is from the abdomen or around the kidneys. The highest grade is kettle-rendered, leaf lard. It is used for frying and baking, and should be firm when cold. Kettle-Rendered Lard: From back and leaf fat. Prime Stream Lard: From fats taken when preparing cuts for market.

Olive Oil. Types of olive oil include:

- Virgin Olive Oil. Taken from ripe olives under low pressure.
- Second Grade Olive Oil. Most olive oil. Taken under pressure from remaining pulp after first press.
- Third Grade Olive Oil. Press cake remaining from second pressing is reheated in water and then pressed.
- Bleached Olive Oil. Dark oil bleached to resemble better grade oils.

- Cloudy Olive Oil. May become thick and white when stored in refrigerator. Will melt if kept at room temperature.
- French Olive Oil. Best. Fruity taste and golden color.

These are used in mayonnaise, salad dressings, batters, marinades, and for frying foods.

Grade A. Color: Typical greenish to light yellow color. Free Fatty Acid Content: Not more than 1.4 percent calculated as oleic acid. Defects: Entirely free from cloudiness at 60°F due to stearin, and from sediment. Odor: Has a typical olive oil odor and is practically free from off-odors of any kind. Flavor: Has a typical olive oil flavor and is practically free from off-flavors of any kind.

Grade B. Color: Typical greenish to light yellow color. Free Fatty Acid Content: Between 1.4 and 2.5 percent, calculated as oleic acid. Defects: Reasonably free from cloudiness at 60°F due to stearin, and from sediment; and no water or other liquid immiscible with the olive oil is present. Odor: Has a typical olive oil odor and is reasonably free from off-odors of any kind. Flavor: Has a typical olive oil flavor and is reasonably free from off-flavors of any kind.

Minimum score for Grade A "Fancy" is 90; Grade B "Choice" is 80; Grade C "Standard" is 70; and Grade D "Substandard" is less than 70. Buy Grade B.

Peanut Oil. This oil is taken from peanuts and used in cooking and salad dressings.

Suet. This fat is taken from around the kidneys and loins of sheep and bullocks. It is bought in lumps or shreds, and used in mincemeat, steamed puddings, stuffings, and suet-crust pastry. Store it in air-tight containers in the refrigerator.

HONEY

Honey is liquid sugar prepared from flow nectar. It may be used as a substitute for sugar in baking and as a preserve. It is packaged in 1 lb., 5 lb., 6/3 lb., 6/4 lb., and 6/5 lb. packages.

Comb Honey and Comb-Section Honey: U.S. Fancy: Comb

Has no uncapped cells except in row attached to wood section; is attached to 75 percent of adjacent area of wood section if outside row of cells is empty, or attached to 50 percent if the outside row is filled with honey; does not project beyond the edge of the wood section; does not have dry holes; not more than 2½ in. of through holes, and is free from cells of pollen. Cappings: Dry and free from weeping and damage and have a uniformly even appearance except in the row attached to the wood section. Color: Conform to the requirements in the official color chart. Honey: Uniform in color, and free from damage, and objectionable flavors and odors. Wood Section: Free from excessive propolis and/or pronounced stains; is smooth and new in appearance, of white to light buff basswood, and does not contain excess knots and/or streaks. Net weight: 12 oz. or more.

Shallow-Frame Comb Honey: U.S. Fancy: Comb

Produced in shallow frame, spaced 1⅜ in. from center to center, which will give a comb thickness of at least 1 in.; is drawn out on foundation which is light in color and is thin enough to produce a comb that is comparable in texture with the comb in comb-section honey; is well built out; has never contained brood; has no dry holes; has no un-capped cells except empty cells in the row attached to the frame and 150 uncapped cells filled with well-ripened honey in the adjoining row; and is free from cells of pollen. Cappings: Not broken or damaged; and have a uniformly even appearance. Color: Conforms to requirements for comb-section honey in the official color chart. Honey: Uniform in color and free from damage and objectionable flavors or odors.

Wrapped Cut-Comb Honey: U.S. Fancy: Comb

Drawn out on foundation that is light in color and is thin enough to produce a comb comparable in texture with the comb in comb-section honey; has no uncapped cells ex-cept on the cut edges; has never contained brood; has no dry holes; and is free from cells of pollen. Cappings: Free from weeping and damage and have a uniformly even appearance. Color: Conforms to the requirements for comb-section honey in the offi-cial color charts. Honey: Uniform in color throughout the comb, and free from damage and objectionable flavors and odors. Wrapper: Transparent, clean, and sealed to pre-vent leakage. Minimum net weight: 12 oz., unless otherwise specified.

Chunk or Bulk Comb Honey: U.S. Fancy

Packed in tin. Consists of not less than 50 percent, by volume, of honey, unless other-wise specified. Comb: Drawn out on foundation that is light in color and is thin enough to produce a comb that is comparable in texture with the comb in comb-section honey; has no more than one uncapped cell per sq. in. of comb surface; has never contained brood; has no dry holes; and is free from cells of pollen. Cappings: Free from damage and have a uniform even appearance. Color: Conforms to the requirements for U.S. Fancy comb-section honey in the official color chart, except that any amount of watery cappings is permitted. Honey: Uniform in color throughout the comb and the color shall not be darker than the next darker color classification of the extracted honey used to make up the total weight and is free from damage and objectionable flavors and odors. Weight: Made up with U.S. Fancy extracted honey.

Extracted Honey

Grade B: Contains not less than 81.4 percent soluble solids. Flavor: Has a reasonably good, normal flavor and aroma for the floral sources, and is practically free from cara-melized flavor, and is free from objectionable flavor due to any cause except the floral source. Defects: May have defects which do not materially affect the appearance or edibility of the product and shall be at least as free from defects as honey that has been strained through a standard No. 50 sieve, at a temperature of not over 130°F. Clarity: May have air bubbles, pollen grains, or other finely divided particles of suspended material which do not materially affect the appearance of the product.

Comb Honey Grades

- Comb-section Honey
  U.S. Fancy comb-section honey
  U.S. No. 1 comb-section honey
  U.S. No. 1 mixed color comb-section honey
  U.S. No. 2 comb-section honey
  Unclassified comb-section honey
- Grades for Shallow-Frame Comb Honey
  U.S. Fancy shallow-frame comb honey
  U.S. No. 1 shallow-frame comb honey
  Unclassified shallow-frame comb honey
- Grades for Wrapped Cut-Comb Honey
  U.S. Fancy wrapped cut-comb honey
  U.S. No. 1 wrapped cut-comb honey
  Unclassified wrapped cut-comb honey
- Grades for Chunk or Bulk Comb Honey
  U.S. Fancy chunk or bulk comb honey—packed in tin
  U.S. No. 1 chunk or bulk comb honey—packed in tin
  Unclassified chunk or bulk comb honey—packed in tin
  U.S. Fancy chunk or bulk comb honey—packed in glass
  U.S. No. 2 chunk or bulk comb honey—packed in glass
  Unclassified chunk or bulk comb honey—packed in glass

Minimum score for canned extracted honey Grade A ''Fancy'' is 90; Grade B ''Choice'' is 80; Grade C ''Standard'' is 70; Grade D ''Substandard'' is less than 70. Net weight should be not less than 95 percent capacity of the container. Buy: U.S. Fancy Comb, U.S. Fancy Shallow-Frame Comb, U.S. Fancy Wrapped Cut-Comb, U.S. Fancy Chunk or Bulk Comb, and U.S. Grade B Extracted Honey.

JAMS AND JELLIES

The jellies for which definitions and standards of identity are prescribed are the jellied foods each of which is made from a mixture composed of not less than 45 parts by weight of one or any combination of 2, 3, 4, or 5 of the fruit juice ingredients, to each

55 parts by weight of one of the optional saccharine ingredients. Such mixture may also contain one or more of the following optional ingredients:

1. Spice.
2. A vinegar, lemon juice, lime juice, citric acid, lactic acid, malic acid, tartaric acid, fumaric acid, or any combination of two or more of these, in a quantity that reasonably compensates for deficiency, if any, of the natural acidity of the fruit juice ingredient.
3. Pectin, in a quantity that reasonably compensates for deficiency, if any, of the natural pectin content of the fruit juice ingredient.
4. Sodium citrate, sodium potassium tartrate, or any combination of these, in a quantity the proportion of which is not more than 3 oz. avoirdupois to each 100 lb. of the saccharine ingredient used.
5. Sodium benzoate or benzoic acid, or any combination of these, in a quantity reasonably necessary as a preservative.
6. Mint flavoring and harmless artificial green coloring, in case the fruit juice ingredient or combination of fruit juice ingredients is extracted from apple, crab apple, pineapple, or 2 or all of such fruits.
7. Cinnamon flavoring, other than artificial flavoring, and harmless artificial red coloring, in case the fruit juice ingredient or combination of fruit juice ingredients is extracted from apple or crab apple, or both such fruits.
8. The antifoaming agents, butter, oleomargarine, lard, corn oil, coconut oil, cottonseed oil, mono- and diglycerides of fat-forming fatty acids, in a quantity not greater than reasonably required to inhibit foaming.

Such mixture is concentrated by heat to such point that the soluble solids content of the finished jelly is not less than 65 percent, as determined by the method prescribed in "Official Methods of Analysis of the Association of Official Agricultural Chemists."[5]

Any requirements of this section with respect to the weight of any fruit juice ingredient, whether concentrated, unconcentrated, or diluted, means the weight determined by the following method: Determine the percent of soluble solids in such fruit juice ingredient by the method for soluble solids; multiply the percent so found by the weight of such fruit juice ingredient; divide the result by 100; subtract from the quotient the weight of any added sugar or other added solids; and multiply the remainder by the factor for such fruit juice ingredient. The result is the weight of the fruit juice ingredient.

Each of the fruit juice ingredients referred to is the filtered or strained liquid extracted, with or without the application of heat and with or without the addition of

---

[5]"Solids by means of a Refractometer—Official" in *Official Methods of Analysis of the Association of Official Agricultural Chemists,* Seventh Edition, p. 495.

water, from one of the following, mature, properly prepared fruits which are fresh, frozen and/or canned:

Name of Fruit	Factor
Apple	7.5
Apricot	7.0
Blackberry (other than dewberry)	10.0
Black Raspberry	9.0
Cherry	7.0
Crab Apple	6.5
Cranberry	9.5
Damson, Damson Plum	7.0
Dewberry (other than boysenberry, loganberry, and youngberry)	10.0
Fig	5.5
Gooseberry	12.0
Grape	7.0
Grapefruit	11.0
Greengage, Greengage Plum	7.0
Guava	13.0
Loganberry	9.5
Orange	8.0
Peach	8.5
Pineapple	7.0
Plum (other than damson, greengage, and prune)	7.0
Pomegranate	5.5
Prickly Pear	5.5
Quince	7.5
Raspberry, Red Raspberry	9.5
Red Currant, Currant (other than black currant)	9.5
Strawberry	12.5
Youngberry	10.0

In any combination of 2, 3, 4, or 5 of such fruit juice ingredients, the weight of each is not less than $1/5$ of the weight of the combination. Each such fruit juice ingredient in any such combination is an optional ingredient.

The optional saccharine ingredients are:

1. Sugar.
2. Invert sugar syrup.
3. Any combination composed of optional saccharine ingredients (1) and (2).
4. Any combination composed of dextrose and optional saccharine ingredients (1), (2), or (3).
5. Any combination composed of corn syrup, dried corn syrup, glucose syrup, dried glucose syrup, or any 2 or more of the foregoing, with optional saccharine ingredient (1), (2), (3), or (4), in which the weight of the solids of corn syrup, dried corn

syrup, glucose syrup, dried glucose syrup, or the sum of the weights of the solids of corn syrup, dried corn syrup, glucose syrup, and dried glucose syrup, in case 2 or more of these are used, does not exceed ¼ of the total weight of the solids of the combined saccharine ingredients.

6. Honey.

7. Any combination composed of honey and optional saccharine ingredient (1), (2), or (3), in which the weight of the solids of each component except honey is not less than ¹⁄₁₀ of the weight of the solids of such combination, and the weight of honey solids is not less than ⅖ of the weight of the solids of such combination.

Fruit Jelly

Grade A.   Consistency: Has a tendency to slightly firm texture and retains a compact shape without excessive "weeping." Color: Characteristic of the fruit jelly ingredient or ingredients, and the fruit jelly has a sparkling luster or may not be more than slightly cloudy, and is free from any dullness of color. Flavor: Has a good distinct flavor characteristic of the fruit ingredients after preserving and is free from any caramelized or objectionable flavor of any kind.

Grade B.   Consistency: May lack firmness, but is not syrupy; may be more than slightly firm, but is not tough or rubbery. Color: Characteristic of the fruit jelly ingredients; and the fruit jelly may be slightly cloudy and have a slight dullness of color. Flavor: Has a reasonably good flavor characteristic of the fruit ingredients after preserving and may have a slightly caramelized flavor, but is free from any bitter flavor or objectionable or off-flavor of any kind.

Substandard.   Fails to meet requirements.

Minimum score for canned fruit jelly and fruit preserve (or jam) Grade A "Fancy" is 85; Grade B "Choice" is 70; and Substandard Grade is less than 70. Net weight should not be less than 90 percent capacity of the container.

Fruit Preserves/Jams

The preserves or jams for which definitions and standard of identity are prescribed are the viscous or semi-solid foods, each of which is made from a mixture composed of not less than 45 parts by weight of one of the fruit ingredients specified, to each 55 parts by weight of one of the optional saccharine ingredients specified. Such mixture may also contain one or more of the following optional ingredients:

1. Spice.
2. A vinegar, lemon juice, lime juice, citric acid, lactic acid, malic acid, tartaric acid, fumaric acid, or any combination of 2 or more of these in a quantity that reasonably compensates for deficiency, if any, of the natural acidity of the fruit ingredient.

3. Pectin, in a quantity that reasonably compensates for deficiency, if any, of the natural pectin content of the fruit ingredient.

4. Sodium citrate, sodium potassium tartrate, or any combination of these, in a quantity the proportion of which is not more than 3 oz. avoirdupois to each 100 lb. of the saccharine ingredient used.

5. Sodium benzoate, or benzoic acid, or any combination of these, in a quantity reasonably necessary as a preservative.

6. The antifoaming agents, butter, oleomargarine, lard, corn oil, coconut oil, cottonseed oil, mono- and dyglycerides of fat-forming fatty acids; in a quantity not greater than reasonably required to inhibit foaming.

Such mixture, with or without added water, is concentrated by heat to such point that the soluble solids content of the finished preserve is not less than 68 percent of the fruit ingredient. The soluble solids content is determined by the method prescribed in ''Official Methods of Analysis of the Association of Official Agricultural Chemists,'' except that no correction is made for water insoluble solids.

Grade A.   Consistency: Fruit or fruit particles are dispersed uniformly throughout the product; the product is a tender gel, or may have no more than a very slight tendency to flow, except that a slightly less viscous consistency may be present when the fruit is chiefly in the form of whole or almost whole units; in the following kinds, the product does not have a macerated or pureed appearance, but in appearance and eating quality consists of whole units or pieces of fruit particles as indicated for the respective kinds, either singly or in combination with any other kind: Apricot—halves, pieces, or combination thereof. Cherry—whole, almost whole, or pieces of pitted cherries, or combinations thereof. Gooseberry— whole, almost whole, or combinations thereof. Peach—slices, pieces, or combinations thereof. Pineapple—crushed pieces, small pieces, or combinations thereof. Strawberry—whole or almost whole berries or combinations thereof. Color: Bright, practically uniform throughout, and characteristic of the variety of the fruit ingredients; the product is free from dullness of color due to any cause. Defects: Type I—Applicable defects do not exceed the allowance for Grade A as specified, and any defects do not materially affect the appearance or edibility of the product. Type II (and any kinds with a macerated or pureed appearance, whether of Type I or II)—Defects do not materially affect the edibility or appearance of the product. Flavor: Has a good and distinct flavor characteristic of the applicable kinds of fruit ingredients.

Orange Marmalade

Grade A.   Color: Has a practically uniform, bright color, characteristic of properly prepared and processed orange marmalade for the respective kind; the product is practically free from green-colored peel; and the product is free from dullness of color due to any cause. Consistency and Character: Product is a firm but tender gel and may have no more than a very slight tendency to flow: contains a substantial, but not excessive, amount of peel; the peel is evenly distributed; the peel is tender; in "sliced" style, the thin strips of peel are predominantly of strips approximately $\frac{1}{32}$ in. to $\frac{1}{16}$ in. in width; and in "chopped" style, the small pieces of peel are reasonably uniform in size. Defects: Not more than 1 seed or portion of seed, and not more than 6 pieces of blemished peel, may be present on an average for each 16 oz. net weight; and in a single container, the appearance and eating quality of the product is not materially affected by the presence of seeds, portions of seeds, blemished peel, objectionable material, harmless, extraneous material or any other defects. Flavor and Odor: Has a good and distinct flavor and aroma characteristic of properly processed orange marmalade; the flavor is neither excessively tart nor excessively sweet; and the product is free from any caramelized flavor or objectionable flavor or odor of any kind.

Fruit Butters

This smooth, semi-solid food is made from a mixture of not less than 5 parts of 1 or any combination of 2, 3, 4, or 5 of the optional fruit ingredients to each of 2 parts of an optional saccharine ingredient, except a saccharine ingredient is not needed when fruit juice of at least one-half the weight of the optional ingredient is used. Mixtures may be seasoned with spice, flavoring, vinegar, lemon or lime juice, or citric, lactic, malic, or tartaric acid, and contain fruit juice, or sorbic acid, sodium sorbate, or potassium sorbate so long as the total of the last 3 ingredients does not exceed 0.1 percent of the finished food. Soluble solids content may not be less than 43 percent.

The optional fruit ingredients are prepared by cooking one of the following fresh, frozen, canned, and/or dried mature fruits, with or without added water, and screening out skins, seeds, pits, and cores: apple, apricot, grape, peach, pear, plum, prune, or quince. Optional saccharine ingredients are sugar, invert sugar syrup, brown sugar, invert brown sugar syrup, honey, dextrose, and one of the above-mentioned ingredients (except honey) and any combination of corn syrup, dried corn syrup, glucose syrup, or dried glucose syrup with one of the above mentioned ingredients (except honey). When the fruit butter is made from one fruit ingredient, the name is "Butter" preceded by the name of the fruit. When the fruit butter is made from more than one fruit ingredient, the name is "Butter preceded by "Mixed Fruit" or the names of the fruits in the order of predominance of the weight of the fruit ingredients used.

JUICES

Canned juices may be sweetened or unsweetened. The product should taste and look very much like the fresh product, allowing for some difference due to processing. The usual federal grades are U.S. Grade A (90 points); U.S. Grade C (80 points), and Substandard (less than 80 points). Purchase of U.S. Grade A is recommended.

Concentrate juices may or may not be purchased frozen. Both have grading levels of 90 and 80 points; U.S. Grade A and U.S. Grade C for canned, and U.S. Grade A and U.S. Grade B for frozen. The water/juice ratios for reconstitution vary from 2:1 to 18:1, an important factor in specifying for bids.

Only orange and grapefruit juices have federal grades in the dehydrated state, although some other dehydrated juices are marketed. The federal grades are U.S. Grade A (90) and U.S. Grade B (80); buy the former.

APPLE JUICE

CANNED |7/1/71   52.301|

Grades:	"A" or "FANCY"	"B" or "CHOICE"	"SUBSTAN- DARD"
Minimum Score:	90	80	Less than 80

Syrup	Specific Gravity [Brix]
"A" Classification	not less than 11.5
"B" Classification	not less than 10.5

FROZEN CONCENTRATED |5/15/75   52.6321|

Grades:	"A" or "FANCY"	"B" or "CHOICE"	"SUBSTAN- DARD"
Minimum Score:	90	80	Less than 80

Dilution Factor	Minimum Brix Value of Concentrate
1 plus 1	22.9
2 plus 1	33.0
3 plus 1	42.2
4 plus 1	50.8
5 plus 1	58.8
6 plus 1	66.3
7 plus 1	73.3

Apple Juice, Canned

Grade A. Color: Bright and typical of freshly pressed juice; may vary from characteristic light non-amber shades to medium amber shades. Style I, Clear, is sparkling clear and transparent, and Style II, Cloudy, may range from a slight translucent appearance to a definitely hazy appearance. Defects: May have a slight amount of sediment or residue of an amorphous nature; may not have more than a trace of dark specks or of sediment or residue of a non-amorphous nature, and shall be free from particles of seed, coarse particles of pulp, or other defects. Flavor: Has a fine, distinct, fruity flavor that is free from astringent flavors, flavors due to overripe apples, oxidation, caramelization, ground or musty flavors, or any other undesirable flavor, and shall meet the following requirements: Brix—Not less than 11.5°. Acid—Not less than 0.25g nor more than 0.70g, calculated as malic acid, per 100 ml. of juice.

Grape Juice

GRAPE JUICE

JUICE GRAPES:
FRESH |7/20/39   51.4290|
Grades: U.S. No. 1 Juice Grapes; U.S. No. 1 Mixed Juice Grapes; U.S.
No. 2 Juice Grapes; U.S. No. 2 Mixed Juice Grapes

CANNED |5/14/51 52.1341|			
Grades:	"A" or "FANCY"	"B" or "CHOICE"	"D" or "SUB-STANDARD"
Minimum Score:	85	70	Less than 70

Syrup	Specific Gravity (Brix Measurements)
Grade A Unsweetened	15.0°
Sweetened	17.0°
Grade B Unsweetened	14.0°
Sweetened	16.0°

FROZEN CONCENTRATED SWEETENED |11/1/57 52.2451|			
Grades:	"A" or "FANCY"	"B" or "CHOICE"	"SUB-STANDARD"
Minimum Score:	85	70	Less than 70

Dilution Factor	Brix Value
1 plus 1	24.8°
1 plus 2	35.5°
1 plus 3	45.4°
1 plus 4	54.5°
1 plus 5	62.8°
1 plus 6	70.7°

Grapefruit Juice, Canned

Grade A.   Color: Bright, typical color of freshly extracted juice. It may be pale yellow to very slightly amber (if pink, clearly distinguishable). Defects: Not more than 10 percent free and suspended pulp, and no seeds, or seed particle, or other defects that more than slightly affect the appearance of the product. Flavor: "Good Flavor" substantially typical of freshly extracted grapefruit juice, may be only slightly affected by the process and complies with limits.

Grapefruit Juice, Dehydrated

Grade A.   Color: The color is bright and typical of fresh grapefruit juice. Defects: Appearance and drinking quality of the juice is not affected by defects. Flavor: Flavor is a fine, distinct grapefruit juice flavor, typical of properly processed, canned grapefruit juice; is definitely free from off-flavors; and the reconstituted juice meets the following requirements: recoverable oil not less than 0.011 nor more than 0.017 ml. per 100 ml. Acid—not less than 0.85 gram per 100 grams. Brix-acid ratio for the respective styles: Style I (unsweetened)—not less than 8 to 1 or more than 14 to 1; Style II (sweetened)—not less than 11 to 1 or more than 14 to 1.

Grapefruit Juice and Orange Juice, Canned

Grade A. Color: Juice mixture has a yellow orange color that is bright and typical of freshly extracted juice of oranges and either white-fleshed grapefruit or red- or pink-fleshed grapefruit, and is free from flavors due to scorching, oxidation, caramelization, or other causes. Defects: Juice may not contain more than 12 percent free and suspended pulp, and that any other defects present may no more than slightly detract from the appearance or drinking quality. Flavor: Refrigerated juice or juice not subjected to high temperatures prior to refrigerating must have flavor that is fine, distinct, and substantially typical of freshly extracted grapefruit juice and orange juice which is free from off-flavors and off-odors of any kind. Canned juice or juice that has been subjected to high temperature: Fine, distinct grapefruit juice and orange juice flavor which is free from off-flavors and off-odors of any kind; and the flavor of all juices may be affected only slightly by the process, the packaging or storage conditions, and the juice complies with the analytical limits.

Minimum score for frozen concentrated blended grapefruit and orange juice Grade A "Fancy" is 85; Grade B "Choice" is 70; and Substandard Grade is less than 70.

Lemonade

Minimum score for frozen concentrate lemonade Grade A "Fancy" is 85; Grade B "Choice" is 70; and Substandard Grade is less than 70. All syrups should have a Brix measurement of 10.5° or more.

Lemon Juice, Canned

Grade A. Color: Color is bright and typical of fresh, properly processed lemon juice that is practically free of browning caused by scorching, oxidation, storage, storage combinations, or any other causes. Defects: There may be present: small seeds or portions thereof that are of such size that they could pass through round perforations not exceeding ⅛ in. in diameter, provided such seeds or portions do not affect the appearance or drinking quality of the juice; not more than 13 percent, by volume, of fine centrifuged pulp calculated; no coagulated pulp; and the juice does not contain peel, core, seeds, seed particles, or other defects that detract from the appearance or utility. Flavor: Product has the distinct flavor of properly prepared, freshly extracted, canned lemon juice that is free of any trace of terpenic, oxidized, scorched, or caramelized flavors, and is free of any other abnormal flavors. In addition, there are not less than 5.0 grams or more than 7.0 grams of acid per 100 ml. of juice.

Minimum score for canned lemon juice Grade A ''Fancy'' is 90; Grade C ''Standard'' is 80; and Substandard Grade is less than 80. Minimum score for concentrated lemon juice for manufacturing Grade A ''Fancy'' is 85; Grade C ''Standard'' is 70; and Substandard Grade is less than 70.

Limeade—Concentrate, Frozen

Grade A. Color: A good, light, characteristic color that reflects the appearance of the limeade prepared from freshly expressed lime juice; or, if artificially colored, possesses a bright attractive light green color typical of artificially colored limeade. Defects: There may be present not more than an average of one seed or portion of seed for each quart of prepared limeade; and the appearance and drinking quality of the limeade is not materially affected by the presence of seeds, portions of seeds, objectionable material, harmless extraneous material, any other defects not specifically mentioned, or any combination thereof. Flavor: Fine, distinct, and substantially typical flavor of limeade prepared from freshly expressed lime juice, which flavor is free from terpenic, oxidized, rancid, or other off-flavors. To score in this classification, the limeade shall test not less than 10.5° Brix; shall contain not less than 0.7 gram of acid per 100 ml. of the limeade; may not contain more than 0.025 ml. or less than 0.008 ml. of recoverable oil per 100 ml. of the limeade; and the Brix-acid ratio shall not exceed 18:1.

Minimum score for limeade frozen concentrate Grade A ''Fancy'' is 85; Grade B ''Choice'' is 70; and Substandard Grade is less than 70. Syrups should have a Brix measurement of 10.5° or more.

Orange Juice

Orange juice is the unfermented juice obtained from mature oranges of the species Citrus sinensis. Seeds (except embryonic seeds and small fragments of seeds that cannot be separated by good manufacturing practice) and excess pulp are removed. The juice may be chilled, but it is not frozen. The name ''orange juice'' may be preceded on the label by the varietal name of the oranges used, and if the oranges grew in a single state, the name of such state may be included in the name, as for example, ''California Valencia orange juice.''

Minimum score for pasteurized orange juice Grade A ''Fancy'' is 90; Grade B ''Choice'' is 80; and Substandard Grade is less than 80. Grade A syrup without sweetener should have a Brix measurement of 11°; Grade B, 10.5°.

Orange Juice, Canned

Grade A. Color: Bright yellow to yellow orange color. As compared with USDA Orange Juice Color Standards may be scored as follows:

Equal to or better than USDA OJ 2	40 points
Equal to or better than USDA OJ 3	39 points
Equal to or better than USDA OJ 4	38 points

| Equal to or better than USDA OJ 5 | 37 points |
| Equal to or better than USDA OJ 6 | 36 points |

Defects: There may be present not more than 0.035 percent of recoverable oil, and juice does not contain particles of membrane, core, or skin, seeds or seed particles, or other defects that affect appearance more than slightly. Flavor: Fine, distinct, canned orange juice flavor, definitely free from traces of scorching, caramelization, oxidation, or terpene; is free from off-flavors of any kind; and meets the following requirements: without sweetener: possesses a minimum of 10.5° Brix; a minimum acid per 100 grams of 0.70 grams, in California or Arizona oranges (0.60 grams outside of California or Arizona), and a maximum of 1.40 grams wherever grown; possesses a minimum Brix-acid ratio of 10.5 to 1 if Brix is less than 11.5° (9.5 to 1 if Brix is more than 11.5°), and a maximum of 20.5 to 1 in either case. With sweetener—Brix and acid same as unsweetened. Brix-acid ratio minimum of 12.5 to 1 if Brix less than 15° and a maximum of 20.5 to 1 in either case.

Minimum score for canned orange juice Grade A "Fancy" is 90; Grade C "Standard" is 80; and Substandard Grade is less than 80. Grade A syrup and Grade C syrup with sweetener should have a Brix measurement of 10.5°. Grade C syrup without sweetener should have a Brix measurement of 10.0°.

Orange Juice, From Concentrate

Concentrated orange juice contains not less than 11.8 percent orange juice soluble solids. When concentrated to a dilution ratio of 3 plus 1, it is named "canned concentrated orange juice" or "canned orange juice concentrate." The name of the food when concentrated to a dilution ratio greater than 3 plus 1 is "canned concentrated orange juice, __ plus 1" or "canned orange juice concentrate, __ plus 1," the blank being filled in with the whole number showing the dilution ratio; for example, "canned orange juice concentrate, 4 plus 1." However, where the label bears directions for making one quart of the reconstituted article (or multiples of a quart), the blank in the name may be filled in with a mixed number; for example, "canned orange juice concentrate, 4⅓ plus 1." For containers larger than one pint, the dilution ratio in the name may be replaced by the concentration of orange juice soluble solids in degrees Brix; for example, a 62° Brix concentrate in 1 gallon cans may be named on the label "canned concentrated orange juice, 62° Brix." If the food does not purport to be canned concentrated orange juice, the word "canned" may be omitted from the name.

U.S. Grade A (or U.S. Fancy) shows no coagulation, no material separation, has a very good color, is practically free from defects, possesses a very good flavor, and scores not less than 90 points. The Brix measurement should be 11.5:1 to 18:1 (except in California and Arizona where it should be 12.5:1 to 20.5:1). The Brix-acid ratio should be 12.5:1 to 20.5:1.

Orange Juice—Concentrated, Frozen

Grade A.   Color: Very good color is bright yellow to yellow orange, typical of richly colored fresh juice. As compared with USDA OJ color standards, is scored as follows:

Equal to or better than USDA OJ 2	40 points
Equal to or better than USDA OJ 3	39 points
Much better than USDA OJ 4	38 points
Equal to or slightly better than USDA OJ 4	37 points
Equal to or better than USDA OJ 5	36 points

Defects: Any combination of small seeds or portions that could pass readily through round holes ⅛ in. (3.2 mm) diameter, discolored specks, white flakes, harmless extraneous material, and similar defects: juice sacs, membrane, core, and peel may no more than slightly detract from appearance or drinking quality. Recoverable oil per 100 milliliters of reconstituted juice is not more than 0.035. Flavor: Very good flavor, is fine, distinct, and similar to fresh orange juice. Irrespective of style or area of production, it has a maximum Brix value to acid ratio of 19.5 to 1. The following minimums are applicable to style and area; Without Sweetener—California and Arizona 11.5 to 1, other areas 12.5 to 1. With sweetener—California and Arizona 12 to 1, other areas 13 to 1.

Minimum score for concentrated and concentrated frozen orange juice Grade A "Fancy" is 90; Grade B "Choice" is 80; and Substandard Grade is less than 70. Syrup without sweetener in the concentrate should have a Brix measurement of 11.8°. Minimum score for concentrated orange juice for manufacturing Grade A "Fancy" is 90; Grade C "Standard" is 80; and Substandard Grade is less than 80.

Orange Juice—Dehydrated

Grade A. Color: Very good yellow to yellow orange color that is bright and typical of fresh orange juice. Defects: Appearance and drinking quality of the juice are not affected by defects. Flavor: Fine, distinct orange juice flavor typical of properly processed, canned orange juice, which is definitely free from terpenic, caramelized, oxidized, rancid, or off-flavors. Ratio of the Brix to acid must range from 12:1 to 18:1; and the recoverable oil content should range from 0.011 to 0.017 ml. per 100 ml. of the reconstituted juice.

Minimum score for dehydrated orange juice Grade A "Fancy" is 85; Grade B "Choice" is 70; and Substandard Grade is less than 70.

Pineapple Juice, Canned

Grade A. Color: Has a bright, typical color, characteristic of canned pineapple juice made from freshly pressed pineapple juice from properly matured and ripened pineapple, which pineapple juice has been properly processed. Defects: Does not contain specks or other objectionable particles that affect the appearance or palatability of the juice, and the canned pineapple juice may contain not less than 5 percent or more than 26 percent finely divided "insoluble solids." Flavor: Fine, distinct, canned pineapple juice flavor, characteristic of canned pineapple juice made from properly matured and ripened pineapple, which is free from any caramelized flavor. Must meet the following requirements: Not less than 12° Brix; not more than 1.10 grams of acid per 100 milliliters of juice; and not less than a 12 to 1 Brix-acid ratio.

Minimum score for canned pineapple juice Grade A "Fancy" is 85; Grade C "Standard" is 70; and Substandard Grade is less than 70. Grade A syrup should have a Brix measurement of not less than 12°; Grade C, not less than 10.5°.

Tangerine Juice

TANGERINE JUICE

CANNED [7/1/69	52.2071]		
Grades:	"A" or "FANCY"	"C" or "STANDARD"	"D" or "SUB-STANDARD"
Minimum Score:	85	70	Less than 70

Syrup	Specific Gravity (Brix Measurements)
"A" classification	
Regular	10.5°
Sweet	12.5°
"B" Classification	
Regular	10.0°
Sweet	12.5°

CONCENTRATED TANGERINE JUICE FOR MANUFACTURING [10/31/55   52.2931]

Grades:	"A" or "FANCY"	"C" or "STANDARD"	"STANDARD"
Minimum Score:	85	70	Less than 70

Dilution Factor	Brix Value
1 plus 3	38° to 41°
1 plus 4	46° to 49°
1 plus 5	53.3° to 56.3°
1 plus 6	60.3° to 63.3°

Tangerine Juice, Canned

Grade A. Defects: Not more than 7 percent free and suspended pulp and not more than 0.025 percent by volume of recoverable oil; no seeds or seed particles or other defects that more than slightly affect the appearance of the product. Flavor: Fine, distinct, canned tangerine juice flavor, free from traces of scorching, caramelization, oxidation, or terpene; Brix not less than 10.5°. Grade A sweet, 12.5°. Acid not less than 0.65 gram or more than 1.35 grams; Grade A sweet, 0.65 gram, not more than 1.35 grams. Brix-acid ratio—not less than 10.5 to 1 or more than 19 to 1; Grade A sweet, 11.5 to 1, not more than 19 to 1 provided that when the Brix is 16° or more, the Brix-acid ratio may be less than 11.5 to 1.

Tomato Juice, Canned

Grade A. Color: Typical color of canned tomato juice, made from well-ripened red tomatoes, which has been properly prepared and processed. Consistency: Tomato juice flows readily and has a normal amount of insoluble tomato solids in suspension, with little tendency for such solids to settle out. Defects: Any defects present do not more than slightly affect the appearance or drinking quality of the product. Flavor: Has a distinct flavor and odor characteristic of good quality tomatoes and is not adversely affected by stems, leaves, crushed seeds, cores, immature tomatoes, or the effects of improper trimming or processing.

Tomato Juice, Concentrated

Grade A.   Color: Typical color of canned tomato juice, made from well-ripened red tomatoes, which has been properly prepared and processed. Consistency: The reconstituted tomato juice flows readily and has a normal amount of insoluble tomato solids in suspension, with little tendency for such solids to settle out. Defects: Defects present in the reconstituted juice do not more than slightly affect the appearance or drinking quality of the juice. Flavor: Distinct flavor and odor characteristic of good quality tomatoes. The flavor of the reconstituted juice may not be adversely affected by stems, leaves, crushed seeds, cores, immature tomatoes, or the effects of improper trimming or processing.

Grade C.   Color: Typical color of canned tomato juice. Consistency: The reconstituted tomato juice flows readily and has a normal amount of insoluble tomato solids in suspension, without a marked tendency for such solids to settle out. Defects: Defects present in the reconstituted juice may be noticeable, but are not so large, numerous, or of such contrasting color as to seriously affect the appearance or drinking quality of the juice. Flavor: Has a characteristic canned tomato juice flavor which may be affected adversely, but not seriously so, by stems, leaves, crushed seeds, cores, immature tomatoes, or the effects of improper trimming or processing.

Minimum score for canned and concentrated tomato juice Grade A "Fancy" is 85; Grade C "Standard" is 70; and Substandard Grade is less than 70.

Fruit and vegetable juice powders: Factors relating to farm and processed weights

Items	Approximate percentage solids content of juice	Yield of juice as a percentage of raw material	Factors for converting to —	
			Processed weight from farm weight	Equivalent farm weight from processed weight
	PERCENT	PERCENT		
Apple	14	75	0.107	9
Citrus:				
Grapefruit	11	49	.055	18
Lemon	9	40	.037	27
Orange	13	55	.072	14
Grape	17	75	.130	8
Pineapple[1]	15	58	.089	11
Prune	32	74	.250	4
Tomato	6-1/4	70	.044	23

1. Assuming juice is only product. In practice, however, juice is made only from edible grade peels, cores, trimmings, and sortouts.

Fruit juices and concentrates: Factors relating to farm and processed weights[1]

Item and specification	Approximate brix	Equivalent farm weight per gallon	Gallons per unit of farm weight		Net weight per gallon
	DEGREES	POUNDS	BOX[2]	TON	POUNDS
Apple:					
Single strength	13	12	—	170	8.7
Frozen 3 to 1 concentrate	45	47	—	43	10.0
Citrus fruits:[3]					
Orange					
Single strength juice	12	16	5.7	126	8.7
Frozen concentrate	42	60	1.5	34	9.9
Grapefruit					
Single strength juice	10	18	4.6	108	8.7
Frozen concentrate	40	76	1.1	26	9.8
Lemon					
Single strength juice	*	26	2.9	76	—
Non-frozen concentrate	*	148	0.5	13.5	—
Concentrate for lemonade	*	18	4.2	110	—
Grape:					
Single strength	16	11	—	175	8.9
Frozen concentrate	50	40	—	50	10.3
Pineapple:					
Single strength	14	15	—	133	8.8
4 to 1 concentrate	61	75	—	27	10.8
3 to 1 concentrate	50	60	—	33	10.3
Prune (from fresh prunes):					
Single strength	31	13	—	155	9.4
One & one-half to 1 concentrate	73	32	—	62	10.9

1. For additional information on concentration of fruit juices, see *Calculations of Volume and Weight Reduction in the Concentration of Fruit Juices*, Agricultural Research Service, U.S. Department of Agriculture, ARS 74-7, June 1956.
2. Oranges, 90 pounds; grapefruit, 85 pounds; lemons, 76 pounds.
3. Orange and grapefruit products based on Florida yields; lemons on California.
* Lemon product yields are based on a standard ton containing 36.5 pounds of anhydrous citric acid.

KOSHER PRODUCTS

A press release from Schreiber Caterers, of Brooklyn, specialists in Glatt kosher meat, poultry, and fish, and home-style meals, so clearly explains kosher food, that we are glad to reproduce it.

Put very simply, ''kosher'' or ''kasher'' means ''fit.'' ''Kosher'' is also the popular name for the Jewish Kashruth (pronounced as spelled) dietary laws, which are the discipline of the Jewish faith set forth in the Bible.

''Glatt'' kosher means that the meat used satisfies even the strictest of kosher standards.

The laws of Kashruth are concerned with the fitness of food for the Jewish table. However, in the traditional Jewish interpretation of the Bible, spiritual, not physical, health is the sole reason for their observance. The Kashruth laws as part of Judaism help to keep the Jewish people aware of their obligations to God, to their fellow man, and to themselves.

Jewish dietary laws divide all food into three classifications:

1. Those which are inherently kosher (par-ve) and may be eaten in their natural state: grains, fruit, vegetables, tea, coffee, and so on.
2. Those which require some form of processing to be kosher, such as meat and poultry.
3. Those which are inherently not kosher: pork products, shellfish, and fish without scales and fins. Kosher meat may come only from cloven-hooved creatures, such as cows, sheep, and goats—animals that graze and chew their cud. Only those fish that have fins and scales are permitted, such as halibut, sole, cod, tuna, and salmon.

It is not enough, however, for an animal to belong to the right family. It must be completely healthy and even then, some parts are not considered kosher. It must be quickly and painlessly slaughtered by an ordained "Shochet," and thoroughly cleaned (koshered) by soaking in water for half an hour, then salted, and left to stand for one hour to drain off the prohibited blood, and then completely rinsed—in preparation for cooking—to remove the salt which has soaked up the blood.

According to the rules, meat and milk products must not be cooked together, nor is one permitted to eat meat or meat products with milk or milk products. For example, butter may not be given with bread that is served with meat, nor is cream allowed with coffee served at the end of a meat meal.

No product that is processed should be considered kosher unless so certified by a reliable rabbinical authority whose name or insignia appears on the sealed package. Such an insignia is the Ⓤ which is the copyrighted symbol of the Union of Orthodox Jewish Congregations of America, who certify to the kosher nature of the product by the use of the Ⓤ symbol.[6]

It is, therefore, important that in serving a kosher food package, it should be sealed, served, and presented to the user that way.

LEGUMES, DRIED (BEANS, LENTILS, PEAS)

Quality Factors

If you do not find packages of beans, peas, or lentils marked with federal or state grades, you can be your own grader in a way by looking for the same factors a federal grader considers.

Brightness of Color: Beans, peas, and lentils should have a bright uniform color. Loss of color usually indicates long storage, lack of freshness, and a product that will take longer to cook. Eating quality, however, is not affected. Uniformity of Size: Look for beans, peas, or lentils of uniform size. Mixed sizes will result in uneven cooking,

---

[6]Union of Orthodox Jewish Congregations of American, Harold M. Jacobs, President, 116 E. 27th St., New York, N.Y. 10016—212-725-3415.

since smaller beans cook faster than larger ones. Visible Defects: Cracked seed coats, foreign material, and pinholes caused by insect damage are signs of a low quality product. Grades to Buy: U.S. No. 1 for dry whole or split peas, lentils, and black-eyed peas (beans). U.S. No. 1 Choice Handpicked, or Handpicked for Great Northern, pinto, and pea beans. U.S. Extra No. 1 for lima beans, large or small. Instead of the federal grade on beans, you might find a state grade which is based on quality factors similar to those for federal grades.

Beans

Beans undergo rather extensive processing before reaching the consumer. They are delivered to huge processing plants where they are cleaned to remove pods, stems, and other debris. Special machines separate debris by weight (gravity) and then screen the beans by size. Discolored beans are removed by machines equipped with photo-sensitive electric eyes.

Black Beans (or black turtle soup beans). They are used in thick soups and in Oriental and Mediterranean dishes.

Black-eyed Peas (also called black-eyed beans or cowpeas). These beans are small, oval-shaped, and creamish white with a black spot on one side. They are used primarily as a main dish vegetable. Black-eyed peas *are* beans. There is no difference in the product, but different names are used in some regions of the country.

Garbanzo Beans. Known as chick-peas, these beans are nut-flavored and commonly pickled in vinegar and oil for salads. They can also be used in the unpickled form as a main dish vegetable. Similar beans are cranberry and yellow-eyed beans.

Great Northern Beans. Larger than but similar to pea beans, these beans are used in soups, salads, casserole dishes, and home-baked beans.

Kidney Beans. These beans are large, red, and kidney shaped. They are popular for chili concarne, and add zest to salads and many Mexican dishes.

Lima Beans. Not widely known as dry beans, lima beans make an excellent main dish vegetable and can be used in casseroles. They are broad and flat. Lima beans come in different sizes, but the size does not affect the quality.

Navy Beans. This is a broad term which includes Great Northern, pea, flat small white, and small white beans.

Pea Beans. Small, oval, and white, pea beans are a favorite for home-baked beans, soups, and casseroles. They hold their shape even when cooked tender.

Pinto Beans. These beans are of the same species as the kidney and red beans. Beige-colored and speckled, they are used mainly in salads and chili.

Red and Pink Beans.   Pink beans have a more delicate flavor than red beans. Both are used in many Mexican dishes and chili. They are related to the kidney bean.

Lentils

Types of lentils are Chilean, Giant, and Russian. Sizes are Jumbo and Regular.

Peas

Green Dry Peas.   This type of dry pea has a more distinct flavor than yellow dry peas. Green dry peas enjoy their greatest popularity in the United States, England, and North European countries, and are gaining in popularity in Japan.

Yellow Dry Peas.   This type of dry pea has a less pronounced flavor than other types of peas but is in popular demand in the southern and eastern parts of the country. They are also preferred in eastern Canada, the Caribbean, and South America.

Dry Split Peas.   These peas have had their skins removed, and they are mainly used for split pea soup. Dry split peas also combine well with many different foods. How do split peas get split? Specially grown whole peas are dried, and their skins removed by a special machine. A second machine then breaks the peas in half.

Dry Whole Peas.   These peas are used in making soups, casseroles, puddings, vegetable side dishes, dips, and hors d'oeuvres.

NUTS[7]

Grade standards[8] have been established for a number of kinds of nuts by the Consumer and Marketing Service of the U.S. Department of Agriculture. Use of standards is not compulsory, nor are packers of nuts required to mark containers with grade designations. However, if a package of nuts is so marked, the packer is legally obligated to make the contents meet requirements of the grade specified. Hence, a grademark on a container is a reliable indicator of the quality. The upper grades provided in each of the existing standards are listed in an accompanying table.

Inspection service is made available at cost to the nut packing industry by the Consumer and Marketing Service and cooperating state departments of agriculture. Government inspectors will, upon request, determine and certify the quality and grade of a specific lot of nuts.

Some packers of nuts have contracted with USDA's Inspection Service to have "continuous inspection" at their plants. Inspectors are present in such plants at all

---

[7]The author thanks Blue Goose, Inc., for allowing the use of substantial material from *The Buying Guide for Fresh Fruits, Vegetables, Herbs, and Nuts,* sixth revised edition (Fullerton, CA: Blue Goose, Inc., 1976).
[8]USDA.

U.S. GRADE STANDARDS FOR NUTS

Kind of Nut	Grade	Description of Quality
In-shell		
Almonds	U.S. No. 1	Best quality.
Brazils	U.S. No. 1	Best quality.
English walnuts	U.S. No. 1	Best quality.
Filberts	U.S. No. 1	Best quality.
Pecans	U.S. No. 1	Best quality.
Mixed nuts (almonds, brazils, filberts, pecans, and English walnuts)	U.S. Extra Fancy	Best quality and largest sizes
	U.S. Fancy	At least 10 percent but not over 40 percent of each kind in the mixture.
Shelled, raw		
Almonds	U.S. Fancy	Best quality.
	U.S. Extra No. 1	Almonds the best—permits a few doubles and broken.
	U.S. No. 1	Very good quality—permits more doubles and broken.
English walnuts	U.S. No. 1	Best quality.
Pecans	U.S. No. 1	Best quality.
Peanut butter	U.S. Grade A	Best quality.

times. A packer agrees to place high-quality nuts in his packages in return for the privilege of printing the U.S. Department of Agriculture quality shield or the statement ''USDA Inspected'' on his containers. This shield indicates the best quality grade, and the ''USDA Inspected'' indicates a very good quality.

Selection of nuts deserves care. Like the cover of a book, the shell of a nut may be deceiving. Fully developed shells can contain defective or poorly developed kernels even though the shells may be bleached or dyed and waxed to improve their appearance.

Price alone is not a reliable basis for judging quality of either shelled, unshelled, or roasted nuts. Price tags may be governed by kind, size, form of nutmeats, a name, or other factors rather than the actual quantity and quality of the nut kernels.

The best aid to the shopper is a statement on the label which shows that the nuts are of a certain U.S. grade, or they have been subjected to USDA inspection, or both.

When nuts are ungraded or do not carry the inspection mark or USDA shield, you will especially need to look for other signs of quality.

Nuts with clean, bright shells are likely to contain good kernels. Shells that are dull, dirty, or stained, and those that are cracked or broken are sometimes indicative of defective kernels inside. More important is weight of individual nuts in proportion to their size. The heavier the nut, the meatier the kernel.

Chestnuts can be deceiving in appearance, but there are a few criteria that may guide shoppers. Heavy weight is the best single indication of a sound, fresh kernel.

Shells should be somewhat glossy and should be pliable under pressure from the fingers. They should also be free from mold.

As a rule, broken kernels or "pieces" are less expensive than whole kernels or "halves" of the same kind of nuts. The smaller pieces are just as well or better suited for a great many uses.

Exposed flesh of broken or chopped nutmeats should be light colored and look fresh, though color will vary somewhat with the kind of nut. Yellowish, oily appearance indicates aging with probable stale flavor or possible early stages of rancidity.

Color of the skin covering the nutmeat may also vary with the age and kind of nut. Although lighter color is generally considered preferable, this is largely a matter of appearance.

Large amounts of powdery material and "chaff" or "meal" in a package may be due to poor screening before packing. However, plastic bags sometimes create static electricity and attract particles which give an exaggerated impression of the amount of meal present.

Almonds

Scientists consider the almond as a stone fruit, much like the peach, but because most of us know and use only the seed (stone) of this fruit, it is generally accepted as a nut.

The almond is ellipsoid in shape with a soft, yellowish-tan shell. The kernels are eaten unprocessed, used in cooking, and ground to make almond nut butter. The two principal varieties introduced to California in 1938 for commercial production are the Harpareil and the Jordanolo, both having large nuts and smooth, soft shells.

Almonds in the Shell: U.S. No. 1.   Similar in shape and degree of hardness of the shells, and bitter almonds are not mixed with sweet almonds; are free from loose, foreign material; have shells that are clean, fairly bright, fairly uniform in color, and free from damage due to discoloration, adhering hulls, broken shells, or other means; and have kernels that are well dried, free from decay, rancidity, and damage caused by insects, mold, gum, shriveling, discoloration, or other means; and are not less than 28/64 in. in thickness. Grades: U.S. Fancy; U.S. No. 1 Mixed; U.S. No. 2; U.S. No. 2 Mixed.

Almonds, Shelled: U.S. Fancy.   Similar varietal characteristics which are whole, clean, and well dried, and which are free from decay, rancidity, insect injury, foreign material, doubles (shells containing 2 kernels), split or broken kernels, injury caused by chipped and scratched kernels, and damage caused by any means. Grades: U.S. Fancy; U.S. Extra No. 1; U.S. No. 1; U.S. Select Sheller Run; U.S. Standard Sheller Run; U.S. No. 1 Whole and Broken; U.S. No. 1 Pieces

Beechnuts

Because they are so small, beechnuts are not easy to harvest and are infrequently used as a commercial crop. There are no beechnut orchards in the United States, but the trees grow wild throughout the eastern part of the country.

Brazil Nuts

These nuts grow wild exclusively in South America's dense forests. They are never cultivated! Trees often grow to a height of 150 feet.

The nuts, as you know them, are really the seeds of the fruit. The round fruit, similar in appearance to a coconut, is 4 to 6 inches in diameter, has a brittle crust, and a tough, woody shell on the inside. This "pod" may contain 12 to 30 or more nuts. When the pods ripen and fall to the ground, the hard shell has to be broken open to free the nuts inside. The closely-packed nuts are three-sided, a size and shape very similar to sections of an orange. Thus, the unusual three-angled shape. The rough shells generally measure 1 ½ to 2 inches in length. The nut meats (kernels) are white, solid, and quite oily. Those not used for eating are broken up and crushed for making oil. Brazilnuts are also called "cream nuts" and "paranuts."

After the small nuts are extracted from the large pod, it is then necessary for the commercial enterprise to place the small nuts (in shells) in dehydrating ovens until the moisture content has been reduced to 10 to 12 percent. After this, the nuts are put through a massive commercial brushing process to brighten the rough, brown skin. Many commercial distributors additionally color the shells with a light-brown dye.

Brazil Nuts in the Shell: U.S. No. 1 Grade. Well-cured whole Brazil nuts which are free from loose, foreign material and meet one of the size classifications below. The shells are clean and free from damage caused by splits, breaks, punctures, oil stain, mold, or other means, and contain kernels which are reasonably well developed, free from rancidity, mold, decay, and damage caused by insects, discoloration, or other means.

Carob

Also known as St. John's bread, the carob can be eaten plain soon after harvesting, but it becomes brittle and acid after storage. Milled carob is used for baking as a filler.

Cashew

This nut is the fruit of a tropical American tree believed to have originated in Brazil, now propagated in practically all hot, humid countries. It is of the same family as the mango and pistachio. The trees, spreading evergreens which grow to a height of 40 feet, bear clusters of pear-shaped fruit called "cashew apples." The apples are juicy and soft, eaten as a fruit in the countries where they are grown.

The kernel of the cashew nut is protected by a double shell, the cavity between the inner and outer shell being filled by a phenolic oily liquid known as cashew nut-shell oil, principally used in making phenolic resins, noted for their anti-friction properties, and also made into a flexible material that is alkali resistant. But the inner shell and kernel retain a certain amount of this oily liquid and thus must be roasted to dissipate the substance, otherwise the kernel would severely burn the mouth and lips of anyone attempting to bite into a fresh nut. The oily substances decompose by heat and the roasted nut can be eaten without the slightest danger.

The cashew kernel is contained in a soft, thick, cellular shell, is kidney-shaped, and about an inch in length. The kernel is of fine texture and has a delicate and distinct flavor.

By weight, the ratio of edible kernel gained from the cashew nut is approximately one pound of kernels from four pounds of nut-in-shell.

Chestnuts

The chestnut belongs to the same tree family as the beech, although chestnuts and beechnuts are very dissimilar. Chestnuts have been called the greatest tree-food crop of the world, for in southern Europe, China, and Japan, chestnuts are widely grown for their food value.

The nuts are eaten fresh, boiled, or roasted, and some are made into flour. In some parts of Europe, chestnuts are fed to animals and poultry. The nuts of the chestnut tree are a beautiful brown color, and they grow within a green burr covered with bristles.

Magnificent chestnut forests once stood in America and were prized by the pioneers, but between 1900 and 1940 a blight destroyed most of the native chestnut trees.

Practically all supplies of chestnuts originate in Europe, imported through eastern ports of the United States. While distribution through the United States is wide, greatest consumer interest in this nut is concentrated along the eastern seaboard.

Chinquapins

This is a small chestnut tree or bush that bears nuts. Its burrs are like those of the chestnut, but generally only one small nut is contained in each burr. The single nut is shaped somewhat like a child's top. The shell is smooth and glossy and very dark brown. The kernel is fine-grained and sweet to the taste. Chinquapins grow east of the Mississippi River and throughout the South. A type of Chinquapin, sometimes called a Golden Chestnut, is grown in the Far West.

Filberts

Filberts are round or oblong, and they are eaten plain. They are in season in September. They come in 5 lb. cartons and 100 lb. bags.

Filberts in the Shell: U.S. No. 1 Grade. The shells are well formed; clean and bright; free from broken or split shells, and kernels filling less than ¼ the capacity of the shell, and free from damage caused by stains, adhering husks, or other means. The kernels are reasonably well developed; not badly misshapen; free from rancidity, decay, mold, and insect injury; and free from damage caused by shriveling, discoloration, or other means.

Hazelnuts (Filberts)

The nut of the Hazel tree or shrub sometimes grow wild in pastures and along fence rows. While these wild bushes have nuts that are good to eat, the production is usually small and the shells very hard.

The brown nuts are round or oval, with a flat end showing where they were fastened to the tree. The orchard dirt is generally washed from the surface and the nuts are placed in bins where pots of sulphur are ignited under the storage areas, the fumes rising through the mass of nuts and bleaching them to an amber color. The nut meats are sweet and firm.

Hickory Nut

The hickory nut is also known as kingnut, mocker nut, pig nut, shagbark, and water hickory. It is round to oblong in shape.

Lotus Seed

Also known as rattle nut and water nut, the lotus nut has a less delicate flavor, but firmer, than macadamia nuts. Available canned or dried.

Macadamia Nuts

This is the generic and common name for the edible seeds of two closely-related silk-oak trees native to Queensland and New South Wales. Other names for the delicately-flavored, rich kernel are Queensland Nut and Australia Nut.

The hard-shelled, shiny-round nuts, covered by thick husks, are produced on racemes 6 to 8 inches long. The husks split open and release the nuts when the latter are fully ripe. The kernels, used almost exclusively as dessert nuts, bring high prices in food-specialty markets. Macadamia nuts are seldom sold in-shell, for the shell is about one inch in diameter, about ⅛ inch thick, and very difficult to crack. The flavor of the kernel resembles the Brazil nut, but it is milder and more delicate.

Mixed Nuts in the Shell

Mixed nuts in the shell that meet the requirements of a U.S. grade are required to conform to the applicable mixture, sizes, and grades set forth in one of the following grades: U.S. Extra Fancy, U.S. Commercial, or U.S. Select.

Peanuts

Botanically, the peanut belongs to the same group of plants as the bean and pea, but it possesses the character of maturing its fruit (nut) beneath the surface of the soil, rather than above ground. Peanuts have the softest shells of any of the nuts. From our research, apparently little world trade is carried on in peanuts.

The peanut is known under the names of goober, goober pea, ground pea, and ground nut. To be precise, the peanut is a pea, rather than a nut, the term ''nut'' having been added because of its flavor and oil. The oil that can be pressed out of crushed peanuts is used as a cooking oil, and for making margarine, peanut butter, and other products where vegetable oil is required.

There are two general types: bunch nuts and vine or trailing nuts. Spanish and Valencia are bunch types, others falling in the other category.

Shelled Runner Type: U.S. No. 1 Runner. Have similar varietal characteristics; are whole; are free from foreign material, damage, and minor defects due to discoloration, sprouts, and dirt, and will not pass through a screen having $^{16}/_{64}$ in. by ¾ in. openings. Grades: U.S. No. 1 Runner; U.S. Runner Splits; U.S. No. 2 Runner.

Shelled Spanish Type: U.S. No. 1 Spanish. Whole and free from foreign material, damage, and minor defects, and will not pass through a screen having $^{15}/_{64}$ in. by ¾ in. openings. Also known as goober, groundnut, and monkey nut. In season in November. Eaten plain and used in cooking. Size: 85 lb. bag roasted. Grades: U.S. No. 1 Spanish, U.S. Spanish Splits, U.S. No. 2 Spanish.

Cleaned Virginia Type: U.S. Jumbo Hand Picked. Peanuts which are mature, dry and free from loose peanut kernels, dirt, or other foreign material, fully developed shells that contain almost no kernels (pops), peanuts that have very soft and/or very thin ends (paper ends), and from damage caused by cracked or broken shells, discoloration, or other means. The kernels are free from damage. The peanuts may not pass

GRADES

U.S. Extra Fancy

Species of Nut	Allowable Mixture		Minimum Size	Minimum Grade
	Minimum Percent	Maximum Percent		
Almonds	10	40	28/64 in.	U.S. No. 1
Brazils	10	40	Large	U.S. No. 1
Filberts	10	40	Long type varieties 44/64 in. Round type varieties 49/64 in.	U.S. No. 1
Pecans	10	40	Extra Large	U.S. No. 1
Walnuts	10	40	Large	U.S. No. 1

§51.3522 U.S. Fancy

Species of Nut	Allowable Mixture		Minimum Size	Minimum Grade
	Minimum Percent	Maximum Percent		
Almonds	10	40	28/64 in.	U.S. No. 1
Brazils	10	40	Medium	U.S. No. 1
Filberts	10	40	Long type varieties 44/64 in. Round type varieties 49/64 in.	U.S. No. 1
Pecans	10	40	Large	U.S. No. 1
Walnuts	10	40	Medium	U.S. No. 1

§51.3523 U.S. Commercial or U.S. Select

(Cont.)

GRADES [Cont.]

Species of Nut	Allowable Mixture Minimum Percent	Maximum Percent	Minimum Size	Minimum Grade
Almonds	5	40	28/64 in.	U.S. No. 1
Brazils	5	40	Medium	U.S. No. 1
Filberts	5	40	Long type varieties 34/64 in. Round type varieties 45/64 in.	U.S. No. 1
Pecans	5	40	Medium	(a) External quality: U.S. No. 1. (b) Internal quality: 75 percent U.S. No. 1 quality with not more than 10 percent seriously damaged kernels, including therein not more than 6 percent which are rancid, moldy, decayed, or damaged by insects.
Walnuts	5	40	Baby	(a) External quality: 85 percent U.S. No. 1 quality. (b) Internal quality: 85 percent U.S. No. 1 quality, except that the lot need only meet the requirements for U.S. No. 2 grade for kernel color; with not more than 8 percent seriously damaged kernels, including therein not more than 5 percent which are damaged by insects.

through a screen having $^{37}/_{64}$ in. by 3 in. perforations and shall not average more than 176 count per lb. Grades: U.S. Jumbo Hand Picked; U.S. Fancy Hand Picked.

Shelled Virginia Type: U.S. Extra Large Virginia. Kernels of similar varietal characteristics that are whole, and free from foreign material, damage due to rancidity, decay, mold, or insects, and minor defects due to discoloration, sprouts, and dirt, and which will not pass through a screen having $^{20}/_{64}$ in. by 1 in. openings. There may not be more than 512 peanuts per lb. Grades: U.S. Extra Large Virginia; U.S. Medium Virginia; U.S. Virginia Splits; U.S. No. 1 Virginia; U.S. No. 2 Virginia.

Pecan

Most popular native nut. Hardshell or soft shell; small, medium, and large. In season in November and December. Sizes: SHELLED—3 oz. can, 8 oz. can, 5 lb. box, 25 lb. box, 50 lb box, 180 lb. bushel; UNSHELLED—25 lb. box, 50 lb. box, 140 lb. bag, 175 lb. bushel.

Pecans grow in clusters, their thin husks frequently split when the nuts are ripe. The shell is smooth, light brown in color, round in shape (some varieties) but mostly oval. Direct from the tree, the color of the pecan is a dull but rather light brown, but they are always polished before placed in commercial sale. Some suppliers dye the shells a color indicative to consumer acceptance in their areas of distribution.

Hard-shell or soft-shell, the pecan is the most popular native nut. Sizes: small, medium, or large. Shelled—3 oz. can, 8 oz..can, 5 lb. box, 25 lb. box, 50 lb. box, 180 lb. bushel. Unshelled—25 lb. box, 50 lb. box, 140 lb. bag, 175 lb. bushel.

Shelled grades include U.S. No. 1 Halves, U.S. No. 1 Halves and Pieces, U.S. No. 1 Pieces, U.S. Commercial Halves, U.S. Commercial Halves and Pieces, U.S. Commercial Pieces.

Size Classification	Number of Nuts per Pound	Minimum Weight of the 10 Smallest Nuts in a 100-Nut Sample
Oversize	55 or less	In each classification, the
Extra large	56 to 63	10 smallest nuts per
Large	64 to 77	100 *must* weigh at least
Medium	78 to 95	7 percent of the total
Small	96 to 120	weight of the 100-nut sample.

PECANS—CROSS SECTION ILLUSTRATION

1. WELL DEVELOPED

Lower limit. Kernels having less meat content than these are not considered well developed.

2. FAIRLY WELL DEVELOPED

Lower limit for U.S. No. 1 grade. Kernels having less meat content than these are not considered fairly well developed and are classed as damaged.

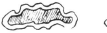  

3. POORLY DEVELOPED

Lower limit, damaged, but not seriously damaged. Kernels having less meat content than these are considered undeveloped and are classed as seriously damaged.

Pecans in the Shell: Size Classification.   Specified in connection with the grade. U.S. No. 1 or U.S. Commercial.

Kernel Color Classification

1. Light. Outer surface is mostly golden color or lighter, with not more than 25 percent darker than golden, none of which is darker than light brown.
2. Light Amber. More than 25 percent of outer surface is light brown, with not more than 25 percent darker than light brown, none of which is darker than medium brown.
3. Amber. More than 25 percent of outer surface is medium brown, with not over 25 percent darker than medium brown, none of which is darker than dark brown.
4. Dark Amber. Over 25 percent of outer surface is dark brown, with not over 25 percent darker than dark brown. *Grade No. 1:* Free from loose hulls, empty broken shells and other foreign material. Shells are fairly uniform in color and free from damage; but 5 percent damaged shells, including not over 2 percent seriously damaged shells, are allowed. Kernels are free from damage; but 12 percent damaged kernels, including not over 7 percent seriously damaged, and 8 percent discolored kernels are allowed.

Pinenuts

These are the edible nuts produced by the nut pine tree, the edible seed borne in the pine cone of certain pine trees.

The pinenuts grown in the United States are usually small as an orange seed, never much bigger than twice that size. They are also known as Indian nut, pignolia, and pinon. They are used in Levantine and barbecue dishes.

Size Classifications for Halves:	Number of Halves per Pound:
Mammoth	250 or less
Junior mammoth	251–300
Jumbo	301–350
Extra Large	351–450
Large	451–550
Medium	551–650
Small (topper)	651–750
Midget	751 or more

Pilinuts

These are a tropical nut growing on trees that thrive in the Philippines. There are no established commercial varieties propagated. The shell is thick and hard.

Pistachio

Like almonds, pistachio nuts are the seed of a fruit and are sometimes mistakenly called ''green almonds,'' although they are not the shape nor the color of an almond. The pistachio is the stone or seed of the fruit of the pistachio tree, which is an evergreen that grows in tropical climates. The red fruit, generally about ½ inch long, grows in bunches. Inside are the seeds or kernels we call pistachio nuts. The nuts have a double shell. The outside shell is red and is removed before the nuts are sent to market. The inside shell is thin, smooth, and brittle, and may be one of several colors.

The natural color of the shell known to consumers is a grayish-white. It may be found in the market with this color, but more frequently it is dyed red, simulating the slight skin over the nut. The long, greenish seed is used as flavoring in cooking, candies, and ice cream.

Since the consumer finds it difficult to crack open a pistachio nut to eat the kernel, foreign processors run the nuts through crude equipment that cracks most of the shells under a stone wheel. Pistachios come in 25 and 27 lb. tins.

Walnuts

In referring to "walnuts," most people consider the rough-shelled, golden English walnut as the entire walnut family; however, Black walnuts, hickory nuts, and butternuts should also be included.

Black Walnuts. They have not gained the popularity of the English walnut since their thick, green husks do not split open easily—and the dark shells of these nuts have numerous rough ridges and do not split into halves, as do English walnuts. The delicious nut meat is difficult to free from the husk. They are extremely tasty, and high in oil content.

Butternuts. Also known as white walnuts, they have been growing wild in the northeastern states for many years. While some people confuse this type of walnut with the black walnut, there is a vast difference between the two, both in flavor and thickness of the shell. Butternuts are about ½ inch in diameter, about 2 inches long, sweet flavored, almost smooth shell, thin, and easily broken. Many of the varieties found growing wild in New England have a sticky, furry, difficult-to-crack husk.

English Walnuts. The nuts are washed and polished in a water-bleach solution to lighten the color of the shell, dried, and sorted according to size: large, medium, and babies. Most walnuts are dried by mechanical dehydration, for moisture is the biggest enemy of the nut. Prior to packing, vacuum machines automatically lift out nuts partially filled.

The shell of the English walnut is somewhat rough, a golden-tan color, generally oval in shape, and it splits easily into halves. Five varieties are grown commercially in the United States, included under the term "soft shelled," as opposed to the black or hard-shelled walnuts. Different varieties are distinguishable only by shape and/or shell structure, some varieties being perfectly round.

Nature provides one of the best protections to quality by giving the walnut the hard, outer shell. It is advisable not to crack walnuts until you are ready to use them. The kernels of cracked walnuts should be placed in a tightly closed jar in the refrigerator to protect the quality.

The inside of the kernel is white, clear, and clean. If the kernel is rubbery, you can be sure it's past its prime. If the color of the inside kernel is a dingy gray, that means oiliness and possibly rancid kernels. Color of the kernel depends upon the amount of sunshine the walnut receives prior to harvest. The darker kernels merely received more sunshine, and many prefer the darker kernels, for they are generally richer and more flavorful.

Hickorynuts.   Another kind of walnut, the hickory tree is found growing principally in the central and northeastern parts of the United States.

Despite the lack of large, commercial production, there are several varieties of this nut—the pignut is bitter, but the meat of the shagbark, sometimes called shellbark, is sweet and excellent eating.

Walnut, Black.   Also known as American walnut, the black walnut has a hard shell which is hard to crack. Sizes: 50 lb. bushel, 100 lb. bag.

Walnut, English.   Round to slightly elongated shape, medium light to hard shell, and small to large. Fresh nuts deteriorate a few months after harvesting but are good

Grade	Tolerances for Grade Defects			
	Total Defects	**Serious Damage**	**Very Serious Damage**	**Shell and Foreign Material**
U.S. No. 1	*Percent* 5	*Percent* 2 (included in 5 percent total defects)	*Percent* 1 (included in 2 percent serious damage)	*Percent* 0.05 (included in 1 per-cent very serious damage)
U.S. Commercial	8	4 (included in 8 percent total defects)	2 (included in 4 percent serious damage)	0.05 (included in 2 per-cent very serious damage)

Color Classification	Tolerances for Color			
	Darker than Extra Light[1]	**Darker than Light[1]**	**Darker than Light Amber[1]**	**Darker than Amber[1]**
Extra light	15 percent	2 percent (included in 15 percent darker than extra light)		
Light	—	15 percent	2 percent (included in 15 percent darker than light)	
Light amber	—	—	15 percent	2 percent (included in 15 percent darker than light amber)
Amber	—	—	—	10 percent

1. See illustration of this term on color chart.

Size Classification	Tolerances for Size				
	Smaller than three-fourths halves	**Will not pass through 24/64 in. round hole**	**Pass through 24/64 in. hole**	**Pass through 16/64 in. hole**	**Pass through 8/64 in. hole**
Halves	5 percent	—	—	1 percent (included in 5 percent)	—
Pieces and Halves[1]	—	—	18 percent	3 percent (included in 18 percent)	1 percent (included in 3 percent)
Pieces	—	—	25 percent	5 percent (included in 25 percent)	1 percent (included in 5 percent)
Small pieces[2]	—	10 percent	—	—	2 percent

1. No part of any tolerance shall be used to reduce the percentage of halves required or specified in a lot of "pieces and halves."
2. The tolerances of 10 percent and 2 percent for "small pieces" classification shall apply, respectively, to any smaller maximum or any larger minimum sizes specified.

before this time. Meats are high in oil but quickly oxidize when exposed to air. In season in December. Sizes: 3 oz. can, 8 oz. can, 5 lb. carton, 25 lb. carton.

Walnuts, Shelled.   U.S. No. 1: Portions of kernels that are well dried, clean, and free from shell, foreign material, insect injury, decay, rancidity, and damage due to shriveling, mold, and discoloration. Tolerances for defects: See Table. Color: See Table. Size: See Table. U.S. Commercial: Same as U.S. No. 1 except for increased tolerances. Color may not be darker than "amber." Tolerance for Defects: See Table. Color: See Table. Size: See Table. Unclassified: No grade applied.

OLIVES

Olives, Green

Grade A: Color: Whole, pitted, stuffed, and halved—Practically uniform, bright, yellow green to green exterior, a light-colored flesh, and not over 5 percent may vary from the typical color, provided that, when applicable, the garnish and stuffing shall have a good color characteristic of the product used. Sliced—Have at least reasonably good color, and when garnish is added, it shall be of a good characteristic color. Size: Not more than a ⅛ in. variation in diameter; and in 90 percent that are most uniform in diameter, the largest diameter does not exceed the smallest diameter by over ¹⁄₁₆ in. Defects: Practically free from defects, and the defects may no more than slightly affect the appearance or edibility; packing medium is practically free of detached bits of stuffing; the appearance is not materially affected by insignificant blemishes; and the defects do not exceed the allowances. Character: Have a uniform tender texture; and are practically free of slip skins.

Olives, Ripe, Canned

Grade A: Flavor: Ripe type—distinctive, nut-like flavor characteristic of properly prepared and processed ripe olives which are free from objectionable flavors. Green type—Distinctive, sweet, and mellow flavor characteristic of properly prepared and processed green ripe olives; and which are free from objectionable flavors. Color: Ripe type (whole, pitted, halved, and quartered)—Have a practically uniform black color or dark rich brown color. Not less than 90 percent, by count, have a color no lighter than that produced by spinning the Munsell color discs in the following combinations: 3½ percent Red (5R 4/14), 3½ percent Yellow (2.5Y 8/12), and 93 percent Black (N/1 Glossy). Ripe type (sliced, chopped or minced)—Normal and typical of olives of at least reasonably good color. Green ripe type—Normal and practically uniform in such normal color for the type. Size: Variation in diameters is not over ⅛ in.; and of all the olives, in 90 percent, by count, that are most uniform in diameter, the largest diameter does not exceed the smallest diameter by more than ¹⁄₁₆ in. Defects: Practically free from any defects, and the defects present may not more than slightly affect the appearance or edibility; the appearance is not materially affected with insignificant blemishes; and in whole, pitted, halved, and quartered styles there may be present, per 100 whole

OLIVES

GREEN [9/8/67 52.5444]

Grades:	"A" or "FANCY"	"B" or "CHOICE"	"C" or "STANDARD"	"SUB-STANDARD"
Minimum Score:	90	80	70	Less than 70

	NET WEIGHT OZ.	NET WEIGHT METRIC	DRAINED WEIGHT OZ. Whole	DRAINED WEIGHT OZ. Pitted and Stuffed	DRAINED WEIGHT METRIC Whole	DRAINED WEIGHT METRIC Pitted and Stuffed
Subpetite; Petite						
1/2 pt.			5-1/2		155.9 g	113.4 g
1 pt.			11		311.8 g	255.2 g
1 qt.			22		623.7 g	510.3 g
1 gal.			88		2.5 kg	—
Small; Select Standard; Medium						
1/2 pt.			5	3-3/4	141.8 g	106.3 g
1 pt.			10	8	283.5 g	226.8 g
1 qt.			21	17	595.4 g	482.0 g
1 gal.			88	—	2.5 kg	—
Large; Extra Large; Mixed Sizes						
1/2 pt.			5	4	141.8 g	113.4 g
1 pt.			10	8-1/2	283.5 g	241.0 g
1 qt.			21	18	595.4 g	510.3 g
1 gal.			88	—	2.5 kg	—
Mammoth						
1/2 pt.			4-3/4	4	134.7 g	113.4 g
1 pt.			10	8-1/2	283.5 g	241.0 g
1 qt.			21	18	595.4 g	510.3 g
1 gal.			88	—	2.5 kg	—
Giant; Jumbo; Colossal						
1/2 pt.			4-1/2	3-3/4	127.6 g	106.3 g
1 pt.			9-1/2	8	269.3 g	226.8 g
1 qt.			20-1/2	17	581.2 g	482.0 g
1 gal.			86	—	2.4 kg	—
Super Colossal						
1/2 pt.			4-1/2	3-1/2	127.6 g	99.2 g
1 pt.			9	7-1/2	255.2 g	212.6 g
1 qt.			19	16-1/2	538.6 g	467.8 g
1 gal.			86	—	2.4 kg	—

CANNED RIPE OLIVES [9/1/71 52.375]

Grades:	"A" or "FANCY"	"B" or "CHOICE"	"C" or "STANDARD"	"SUB-STANDARD"
Minimum Score:	90	80	70	Less than 70

	NET WEIGHT OZ.	NET WEIGHT METRIC	DRAINED WEIGHT OZ.	DRAINED WEIGHT METRIC
Halves and Sliced				
4.4 oz.			2-1/4	63.8 g
1 pt.			7-1/2	212.6 g
1 qt.			15	425.2 g
1 gal.			72	2.0 kg
Chopped or Minced				
4.4 oz.			4-1/2	127.6 g
1 pt.			15-1/2	439.4 g
1 qt.			31	878.8 g
1 gal.			122	3.5 kg
Broken Pitted				
1 pt.			7-1/2	212.6 g
1 qt.			15	425.2 g
1 gal.			72	2.0 kg

	DRAINED WEIGHT OZ.		DRAINED WEIGHT METRIC	
Sliced				
8Z Tall	3-3/4		106.3 g	
No. 300	6-1/2		184.3 g	
No. 10	55		1.6 kg	
Broken Pitted				
No. 10	55		1.6 kg	
Small, Select, Standard, and Medium				
8Z Tall	4-1/2	3-1/4	127.6 g	92.1 g
No. 1 Tall	9	7	255.2 g	198.4 g
No. 300	7-3/4	6	219.7 g	170.1 g
No. 10	66	–	1.9 kg	–
Large, Extra Large				
8Z Tall	4-1/2	3-1/2	127.6 g	99.2 g
No. 1 Tall	9	7-1/2	255.2 g	212.6 g
No. 300	7-3/4	6	219.7 g	170.1 g
No. 10	66	–	1.9 kg	–
Mammoth				
8Z Tall	4-1/2	3-1/2	127.6 g	99.2 g
No. 1 Tall	9	7-1/2	255.2 g	212.6 g
No. 300	7-1/2	6	212.6 g	170.1 g
No. 10	66	–	1.9 kg	–
Giant, Jumbo, Colossal				
8Z Tall	4	3-1/4	113.4 g	92.1 g
No. 1 Tall	8-1/2	7	241.0 g	198.4 g
No. 300	7-1/4	5-3/4	205.5 g	163.0 g
No. 10	64	–	1.8 kg	–
Super Colossal or Special Super Colossal				
8Z Tall	4	3-1/4	113.4 g	92.1 g
No. 1 Tall	8	6-1/2	226.8 g	184.3 g
No. 300	7-1/4	5-1/2	205.5 g	155.9 g
No. 10	64	–	1.8 kg	–

CANNED OLIVES

	NET WEIGHT OZ.	NET WEIGHT METRIC	DRAINED WEIGHT OZ. Whole	Pitted	DRAINED WEIGHT METRIC Whole	Pitted
Family						
8Z Tall			4-1/2	3-1/2	127.6 g	99.2 g
No. 1 Tall			9	7-1/2	255.2 g	212.6 g
No. 300			7-3/4	6	219.7 g	170.1 g
No. 10			66	–	1.9 kg	–
King						
8Z Tall			4	3-1/4	113.4 g	92.1 g
No. 1 Tall			8-1/2	6-1/2	241.0 g	184.3 g
No. 300			7-1/4	5-3/4	205.5 g	163.0 g
No. 10			64	–	1.8 kg	–
Royal						
8Z Tall			4	3	113.4 g	85.05 g
No. 1 Tall			8	6-1/2	226.8 g	184.3 g
No. 300			7-1/4	5-1/2	205.5 g	155.9 g
No. 10			64	–	1.8 kg	–
Other Blends and Mixed Sizes						
8Z Tall			4-1/2	3-1/2	127.6 g	99.2 g
No. 1 Tall			9	7-1/2	255.2 g	212.6 g
No. 300						
No. 10			66	–	1.9 kg	–
Halved and Quartered						
8Z Tall			3-3/4		106.3 g	
No. 300			6-1/2		184.3 g	
No. 10			55		1.6 kg	
Chopped or Minced						
No. 10			100		2.8 kg	

or pitted olives per 200 units in halved style, or per 9 oz. in quarter style, not more than 1 piece of harmless, extraneous material not more than 1 pit in pitted style and not more than 3 stems, of which not more than 1 may be a major stem; not more than 10 percent may have minor and major blemishes; minor, major, or serious wrinkles; and there may be mutilated olives, provided that not over 5 percent have major blemishes or wrinkles; and not over 2 percent may be mutilated, or 1 olive may be mutilated if there are less than 50 olives in the container. Sliced, chopped, or minced olives—May not be more than slightly affected in appearance or edibility by defects. Character: Have a characteristic fleshy texture, and at least 95 percent are practically uniform in texture, and are tender but not soft.

PEANUT BUTTER

Scoring Factors

Color—Refers to the color hue and color intensity of overall mass, regardless of texture and variety. Grade A color is rich and typical and is no less brown than USDA Color 1 or no more brown than USDA Color 4,[9] and is without any tinge of a dull, grey, or other abnormal cast. Grade B color is typical and may be slightly dull and/or may have a slight grey cast; may be lighter brown in color than USDA Color 1 but is not excessively pale as indicative of insufficient roasting; or, such typical color may be more brown than USDA Color 4 but is not excessively brown as indicative of excessive roasting.

Consistency—Refers to spreadability and degree of oil separation, if any. Consistency is determined at a product temperature of not less than 70°F, nor more than 80°F, without mixing the product in the stabilized type, and after reasonable mixing of the product in the nonstabilized type. Grade A peanut butter spreads easily; shall not be thin nor more than slightly stiff; and, (1) in *stabilized* type, there is no noticeable oil separation, or (2) in *nonstabilized* type, there is no more than slight mixing required to disperse any separated oil. Grade B peanut butter is spreadable; may be moderately, but not excessively, thin or stiff; and, (1) in *stabilized* type, there may be no more than slightly noticeable oil separation, or (2) in the *nonstabilized* type, there may be no excessive oil separation that causes noticeable dryness or that requires more than moderate mixing to disperse the oil.

Absence of Defects—The presence of dark particles and any other defects does not, in Grade A more than slightly, in Grade B materially, affect appearance or eating quality; and there may be present, in Grade A, not more than 8, in Grade B not more than 20 milligrams of water-insoluble inorganic residue per 100 grams, provided that such residue does not affect the edibility or wholesomeness of the product. (Particles of dark skins not considered defects in specialty pack made from unblanched peanuts.)

Flavor and Aroma—Grade A peanut butter has a flavor and aroma typical of freshly roasted and freshly ground peanuts and of properly proportioned and blended

[9]Plastic Color Standards, Information available from USDA.

ingredients, free from staleness, free from rancidity, and free from objectionable flavors and objectionable odors of any kind. There may be not less than 1.0 percent, nor more than 1.8 percent, by weight, of salt in the finished peanut butter. Grade B has a flavor and aroma typical of properly prepared peanut butter, which may be lacking good flavor and good aroma, but is free of objectionable flavors and objectionable aromas of any kind. There may be not less than 0.5 percent, not more than 2.5 percent, by weight, of salt in the finished peanut butter. (Salt requirements waived in unsalted specialty packs.)

Water-Insoluble Inorganic Residue and Salt—The water-soluble inorganic residue and salt in peanut butter is determined in accordance with the latest official method outlined in the Official Methods of Analysis of the Association of Official Analytical Chemists or any other method that gives equivalent results. Minimum score for canned peanut butter Grade A "Fancy" is 90; Grade B "Choice" is 80; and Substandard Grade is less than 80.

PICKLES

Pickles[10] are a product of natural fermentation—either of the vegetable or food ingredients or of the liquid surrounding them. This fermentation process, carefully controlled by the amount of salt used, the temperature, herbs, spices, and other factors, develops the flavor, color, aroma, and texture desired for the particular kind of pickles.

Because of the way they are made they are called either "cured pickles" or "fresh pack pickles." Each has its own characteristics of flavor and texture.

Cured pickles have been slightly fermented in a salt brine for several months. They are then de-salted and washed. The pickling process is completed in a vinegar solution, also a fermentation product, and seasoned to give the flavor characteristics desired. The curing process imparts subtle flavor changes and produces edible acids in the pickles themselves. They are usually crisp, dark green, and somewhat translucent.

Fresh-pack pickles are relatively new in the market. In this process the cucumbers are packed directly into the containers, and covered with a pickling solution containing vinegars, other acids, flavorings, and other suitable ingredients to give the desired characteristics to the pickles. The containers are then sealed and pasteurized with heat to preserve them. Fresh-pack pickles have not been fermented, and they retain something of the flavor of fresh cucumbers. They are usually a light yellow-green color and are not usually as salty or as acid as the cured type. "Fresh-pack" is often shown on the label.

For cured pickles, the selected cucumbers are put in a salt water bath in vats, where controlled fermentation takes place. The salt is added gradually, according to an exact formula and it penetrates the pickles slowly, evenly, and thoroughly.

After weeks and even months of such curing, the cucumbers are called "brine stock." The brine stock may then be removed from the salting station to the finishing plant, according to the plant's schedule. Cucumbers for fresh pack are hauled directly to the packing plant since they must be processed within a few hours.

---

[10]USDA.

The kinds of pickles you can buy are almost as infinite as the kinds of cooking that exist. You may sometimes be confused by the number of different styles, colors, and shapes that fill the shelves. However, all cucumber pickles are related to one or another of an easily-remembered handful of basic kinds. Here are some typical variations.

Dill Pickles

Dill pickles are flavored primarily with dill, an aromatic herb, which may be supplemented by various mixed spices. They come in three variations. Genuine dill pickles are prepared entirely by a lengthy process of natural fermentation with the various herbs. Processed dill pickles are started as regular brine stock, and finished later in a dill solution; they possess somewhat better keeping qualities than the genuine dill pickles. Between these sometimes you may find an "overnight dill" pickle. This is a quickly fermented variation of the genuine dill pickles produced by stopping the fermentation after only a day or two through placing the pickles in cold storage. These pickles retain some of the flavor of the fresh cucumber, along with the dill flavor. Like the genuine dills, they are commonly sold in bulk.

The label may indicate that many of these dills are "kosher" or "kosher-style" pickles. The term "kosher" has religious significance in accord with Hebrew law. However, in the United States it also has come to mean that these pickles are more highly spiced, including onion and garlic flavors. Most dill pickles are large or medium in size. They may have been cut into strips, slices, cubes, or in any manner.

Sour Pickles

Sour pickles are brine stock pickles which have been finished in vinegar with spices. While normally packed whole, they may be cut in strips, slices, or in any manner. There are a number of different styles. Sour mixed pickles are produced by combining sour cucumber pickles with the other sour pickled vegetables such as cauliflower, onions, peppers, all cut into small convenient pieces. Sour relish or piccalilli includes finely chopped sour pickles, sometimes packed alone and sometimes with other finely chopped sour cured vegetables. Chow chow is similar to sour mixed pickles except for the addition of a mustard sauce flavored with spices such as yellow and brown mustard seed, turmeric, garlic, cinnamon, cloves, ginger, nutmeg, cayenne, and black and white pepper.

Sweet Pickles

Sweet pickles start as sour pickles from which the vinegar has been drained. They are finished in sweet, spicy liquids which are added from time to time until the desired degree of sweetness is attained. A lengthy aging process follows. Sweet pickles are available in many variations such as the following: sliced sweet pickles, chips, or wafers (plain sweet pickles cut crosswise into discs); candied chips (extra sweet, sliced sweet pickles); sweet dill pickles (made from genuine or processed dill pickles instead of sour pickles and frequently cut lengthwise as well as crosswise); mixed sweet pickles (sweet pickles combined with other sweet pickled vegetables, such as cauliflower, onions, sweet pepper, and green tomatoes); and sweet relish or piccalilli (finely chopped sweet pickles sometimes combined with other finely chopped sweet pickled vegetables).

Some of the pickles that are classified as cured type are also available in the fresh type pack.

Among them are fresh-packed dill pickles, fresh-packed sweet pickles and mild sweet pickles, fresh-packed sweet relish and mild sweet relish, fresh-packed sweetened dill pickles, and fresh-packed sweetened dill relish.

Pickles belong to a larger family of foods with many of the same characteristics and which add interest and zest to your meals. Many other fruits and vegetables are pickled commercially or by homemakers. Some you may find are: peach, pear, crabapple, watermelon rind, beet, onion, okra, peppers, tomatoes (ripe or green), and green beans.

You may also find a variety of relishes such as: pepper-onion, tomato apple-chutney, tomato-pear chutney, horseradish, and corn relish.

Grade A

Color: Typical of properly prepared, and preserved, or processed pickles; shall be free from ripe cucumbers or other off-color vegetable ingredients; and possess the following characteristics by type: Cured type—Skin color ranges from a translucent light green to dark green; practically free from bleached areas. Not more than 10 percent may vary markedly from typical color. In mixed pickles, chow-chow pickles, and pickle relish, all of the pickle ingredients possess a good, practically uniform, typical color for the respective ingredients. Fresh-Pack type—Skin color ranges from opaque yellow green to green; not more than 15 percent vary from typical color. In pickle relish, all of the pickle ingredients possess a good, reasonably uniform, typical color for the respective ingredient. Size: Units are practically uniform in size; may vary moderately in size but not to the extent that overall appearance is materially affected. Small odd size units in the top of the container, added to insure well-filled containers shall not be deemed as detracting from Grade A. Defects: Possesses no more than a trace of grit, not seriously affecting edibility; and other defects individually or collectively do not materially affect appearance or edibility. Texture: Cucumber and other vegetable ingredient(s) are firm and crisp, practically free from units with large objectionable seeds, detached seeds and tough skins, and in cured pickles, there may be present not more than 5 percent that are shriveled, soft, or slippery (very slight shriveling permitted in sweet pickles); 5 percent by count of whole units with hollow centers; and 10 percent of count of whole, sliced, or cut units with chalky white areas. In the fresh-pack type, not more than 10 percent are shriveled, soft, or flabby; and not more than 15 percent are whole units with hollow centers.

Minimum score for canned pickles Grade A "Fancy" is 90; Grade B "Extra Standard" is 80; and Substandard Grade is less than 80. Net weight should not be less than 90 percent of container.

SPICES AND HERBS[11]

Spices are easy to get to know, in part because most of them have distinctive flavor and aroma, but also because they come in just a few basic forms. Spices, herbs, and seeds are marketed whole or ground. Dehydrated vegetable seasonings are sold usually in a chopped or minced form, and as ground powders, and salts. Blends are combinations of spices, herbs, seeds, dehydrated vegetable seasonings, and salt.

The form in which the chef will use whole, ground, or blended spices, or seasoning salts will depend on the recipe. The flavor of spices, herbs, and seeds is derived largely from essential oils that are contained within their microscopic cell walls. In whole spices, the cell walls are intact. This means that they may be cooked for longer periods of time to release their full flavor.

In grinding spices, many cell walls are broken and the oils are more exposed; hence, their flavor is released more readily than the whole spice.

Spices are added to foods early in the cooking process to give them ample time to mature to a desirable blending and delicate suspension. Whole spices require longer periods of time to produce their ultimate flavor, while ground spices require shorter time.

Whole spices are usually put in a small cheesecloth or muslin bag so that they may be removed easily when the desired level of flavor has been reached. The bag also prevents pieces of the whole spice from remaining in the finished dish. Ground spices are added directly to the food. Regardless of which form of spice is used, the dish should be tasted before it goes to the customer to see if last-minute spice correction is required.

Seasoning salts are usually added at the very end of the cooking, either just before or after the food is removed from the fire.

With this knowledge, the chef is ready to work with the actual spices. First, examine them visually. Some have a distinctive color and shape, like bay leaf, allspice, rosemary, and cloves. Then smell them. Some spices are not aromatic, but others definitely are, and once sniffed, the aroma of ground cinnamon, pepper, nutmeg, or clove will tend to be remembered.

Tasting and chewing the spice itself comes next. Remember that spices are natural products, not chemicals. They do not affect the chemistry of cooking. Spices may be added to any recipe without fear that they will change the time of cooking or the relationship and behavior of the other ingredients.

In tasting spices, chew them or keep them on the tongue until the flavor develops. The last way, incidentally, is especially good since it permits development of the full flavor of the spice and makes the cook aware of how much flavor potential is in that spice. Chefs who learn to know spices in this way usually do not use a "heavy hand." They know the flavor power of various spices.

---

[11]The American Spice Trade Association, *Food Service Seasoning Guide*, Empire State Building, N.Y., N.Y. $1.25 per copy plus $.35 postage.

Commonly Available Spice Products

Included is a list of the commonly available spices from institutional supply houses. The name of the "true spice," herb, seed, or dehydrated vegetable seasoning is given in the left column, while the next two columns indicate if the spice is usually available in whole or ground form. The spice blend section gives only a sampling of the blends that are available. Many spice blends are sold only regionally so it is best to check with your supplier to see what is in stock. Also, new spice blends are being introduced frequently, and it is almost impossible to keep up with all of them.

SYRUPS

Corn Syrup

Made from corn flour and used as a table syrup or sweetening agent. Clear white to amber color. Used in baking and is served hot on waffles. Specify: 30 percent glucose, 30 percent dextrin, 20 percent maltose, 5 percent ash, and 15 percent maximum moisture.

Refiner's Syrup: Grade A or Fancy

Has a flavor characteristic of refiner's syrup of fancy quality; contains no sediment; is free of foreign matter; has a Brix solids content of not less than 72 percent when corrected to 20°C (68°F); has a ratio of total sugars to Brix solids of at least 92 percent; has a ratio of sulfated ash to Brix solids of not more than 3 percent; and has a color no darker than RS Color Standard No. 1.

Grade B "Choice" refiner's syrup should also have a Brix solids content of not less than 72 percent when corrected to 20°C (68°F). Grade C "Extra Standard" and Grade D "Standard" should have a Brix solids content of not less than 70 percent when corrected to 20°C (68°F).

Maple Syrup: Grade AA

Sap from maple tree species boiled down to a syrup and used on waffles and pancakes and to flavor cakes, pudding, candy, and ice cream. Color: No darker than light amber as represented by the color standards of the USDA. Clarity: No cloudier than light amber cloudy standard as represented by the standards of the USDA for cloudiness. Weight: Not less than 11 lb. per gal. of 231 cu. in. at 68°F corresponding to 65.46° Brix or 35.27° Baume. Flavor: Has a characteristic maple flavor; is clean, and free from fermentation, damage caused by scorching, buddiness, and any objectionable flavor or odor.

In table maple syrup, there are Grades AA and Fancy. Grades A and B are unclassified. In maple syrup for reprocessing, there are Grades AA and Fancy. Grades A, B, and C are unclassified.

Spice	Forms Available	
Allspice	Whole Allspice	Ground Allspice
Anise	Anise Seed	Ground Anise
Basil	Basil Leaves	
Bay Leaves	Bay Leaves	Ground Bay Leaves
Caraway	Caraway Seed	Ground Caraway Seed
Cardamom	Whole Cardamom	Ground Cardamom Seed
Celery	Celery Seed	Ground Celery Seed
Chervil	Chervil Leaves	
Chives	Chopped (Dehydrated or Freeze-dried)	
Cinnamon	Stick Cinnamon	Ground Cinnamon
Cloves	Whole Cloves	Ground Cloves
Cumin	Cumin Seed	Ground Cumin Seed
Dill	Dill Seed	Ground Dill Seed
Dill Weed	Dill Weed	
Fennel	Fennel Seed	Ground Fennel Seed
Garlic		Instant Minced Garlic Instant Garlic Powder
Ginger	Whole Ginger	Ground Ginger
Mace	Whole Mace	Ground Mace
Marjoram	Marjoram Leaves	Ground Marjoram
Mustard	Mustard Seed	Powdered Mustard
Nutmeg	Whole Nutmeg	Ground Nutmeg
Onion		Instant Minced Onion (or Chopped Onion) Instant Onion Powder (or Granulated Onion)
Oregano	Oregano Leaves	Ground Oregano
Paprika		Ground Paprika
Black Pepper	Whole Black Pepper	Ground Black Pepper, Coarse Ground Black Pepper
Red Pepper	Whole Red Pepper	Crushed Red Pepper Ground Red Pepper Ground Cayenne
White Pepper	Whole White Pepper	Ground White Pepper
Poppy	Poppy Seed	
Rosemary	Rosemary Leaves	Ground Rosemary
Saffron	Saffron	
Sage	Sage Leaves	Rubbed Sage, Ground Sage
Savory	Savory Leaves	Ground Savory
Sesame	Sesame Seed	
Shallots		Chopped (Freeze-dried)
Tarragon	Tarragon Leaves	
Thyme	Thyme Leaves	Ground Thyme
Turmeric		Ground Turmeric

Spice Blends

Apple Pie Spice	Curry Powder	Onion Salt
Barbecue Spice	Garlic Salt	Poultry Seasoning
Celery Salt	Herb Seasoning	Pumpkin Pie Spice
Chili Powder	Italian Seasoning	Seasoned or Flavor
Cinnamon Sugar	Mixed Pickling Spice	Salt
		Shrimp Spice or
		Crab Boil

Dehydrated Flakes

Celery Flakes	Mixed Vegetable	Parsley Flakes
Mint Flakes	Flakes	Sweet Pepper Flakes
	Onion Flakes	

Sugarcane Molasses: Grade A

Syrup taken from sugar during refinement. Flavor: Has a flavor and odor characteristic of first centrifugal molasses of fancy quality. Brix, Sugar, Ash, and Sulfites: Refer to table. Color: Bright and typical of molasses properly prepared and processed from sound, well-matured sugarcane, and is no darker than USDA permanent, glass color standard No. 1 for sugarcane molasses. Defects: Appearance and edibility are not affected by the presence of harmless extraneous material which may be in suspension or deposited as sediment in the container.

Minimum score for canned sugarcane molasses Grade A ''Fancy'' is 90; Grade B ''Choice'' is 80; Grade C ''Standard'' is 70; and Substandard Grade is less than 70. Net weight should be as full as practicable.

Sugarcane Syrup: Grade A

Made by evaporation of sugarcane without removing any sugar. Color: Bright and typical of syrup properly prepared and processed from sound, well-matured sugarcane and is no darker than USDA permanent, glass color standard No. 1 for sugarcane syrup. Flavor: Has a good, characteristic flavor and is free from objectionable flavors of any kind. Defects: Appearance and edibility are not affected by the presence of harmless extraneous matter of other material. Clarity: May contain not more than a trace of finely divided particles of suspended material which does not affect the appearance or edibility of the product.

Minimum score for canned sugarcane syrup Grade A ''Fancy'' is 90; Grade B ''Choice'' is 80; Grade C ''Standard'' is 70; and Substandard Grade is less than 70.

MISCELLANEOUS

Almond Paste. Also known as Marzipan. Made from ground almonds, sugar, and eggs. Used in baking.

SUGARCANE MOLASSES

CANNED [11/16/59   52.3651]

Grades:	"A" or "FANCY"	"B" or "CHOICE"	"C" or "STAN-DARD"	"SUB-STAN-DARD"
Minimum Score:	90	80	70	Less than 70

NET WEIGHT: As full as practicable

REQUIRED MINIMUM BRIX SOLIDS AND TOTAL SUGAR AND MAXIMUM ASH AND TOTAL SULFITES

Grade Designation	Brix Solids [percent] [minimum]		Total Sugar [percent] [minimum]	
	Average from All Containers	Limit for Individual Container	Average from All Containers	Limit for Individual Containers
Grade A	79.0	78.5	63.5	63.0
Grade B	79.0	78.5	61.5	61.0
Grade C	79.0	78.5	58.0	57.0
Sstd.	Under 79.0	—	Under 58.0	—

Grade Designation	Ash [percent] [maximum]		Total Sulfites [ppm] [maximum]
	Average from All Containers	Limit for Individual Container	Average from All Containers
Grade A	5.00	5.25	200
Grade B	7.00	7.50	250
Grade C	9.00	10.00	250
Sstd.	Over 9.00	—	Over 250

Anchovy Paste.   Mixture of pounded anchovies, vinegar, water, and spices. Pack: Case of 24/2 oz. containers.

Annona.   The tropical fruits cherimoza, soursop, custard apple, and bullock's heart. Canned. Imported. No grades.

Apple Butter.   Buy: Grade A: lusterous, uniform color; moderately reddish brown or dark brown, no separation of liquid 2 minutes after mounding; practically free from defects; good and distinct flavor and aroma.

Apple Butter, Canned.   (See also Fruit Butters.) Jam or sauce made by stewing apples in cider or water, with added flavoring and sugar. Minimum score for canned apple butter Grade A "Fancy" is 85; Grade C "Standard" is 70; and Substandard Grade is less than 70. Net weight should be not less than 90 percent capacity of container.

Applesauce, Canned. (See also Chapter 4.) Buy: Grade A: Color: Natural color is typical of the variety or varieties used; may range from white that may be slightly translucent to light golden. Artificially colored is bright and distinct but not saturated. All types are free from tinges of pink or gray and from discoloration due to oxidation, scorching, or other causes. Consistency: After stirring and emptying on a dry flat surface, forms a moderately mounded mass, and at the end of 2 minutes there is not more than a slight separation of liquor. Finish: Apple particles are evenly divided; product is granular but not lumpy, pasty, or "salvy," and the apple particles are not hard. Absence of Defects: Number, size, and color of defects do not materially affect the appearance or eating quality of product. Flavor: Distinct, desirable, characteristic normal flavor and odor, and free from objectionable odors of any kind, including but not limited to those caused by oxidation, fermentation, and caramelization.

Minimum score for canned applesauce Grade A "Fancy" is 90; Grade B "Choice" is 80; and Substandard Grade is less than 80. Net weight should not be less than 90 percent of capacity of container; except in the case of glass containers having a total capacity of 6½ fluid oz. or less, the fill is not less than 85 percent.

Arrowroot. Used for thickening sauces, making pudding, etc., and flavoring biscuits. Made from the root of tropical plants. Types: (1) Arum maculatum: Portland arrowroot; (2) Brazilian: cassava; (3) British: a potato farina; (4) East India: curcuma; (5) Tacca: tacca pinnatifida; and (6) Tulema: Indian. Excellent for bake shop use. Buy by the (expensive!) pound.

Asperge. Asparagus spears. U.S. products subject to grading as detailed in Chapter 5 under Asparagus, Canned. The white asparagus is often an ungraded import.

Baking Powder. Raising agent used in baking. Mixture of sodium bicarbonate, an acid substance, and a starchy base such as flour. When a mixture containing baking powder is wetted and heated, at least 12 percent carbon dioxide must be given off. Types: (1) Tartrate—contains cream of tartar. Quick acting. (2) Phosphate—contains sodium acid phosphate or calcium acid phosphate. Quick acting. (3) S.A.S. Phosphate—contains calcium acid phosphate and sodium aluminum phosphate. Slow acting. Double-action. (4) Combinations of above. Sizes: 1 lb. package, 5 lb. package, 10 lb. package.

Baking Soda. Sodium Bicarbonate. Used in baking, cooking, and general cleaning. Sizes: 12 oz. package, 1 lb. package, 5 lb. package, 10 lb. package.

Beans. See Legumes, Dried.

Beef Extract. Made of beef juice and other soluble parts of beef meat. Used in sauces, stews, soups, etc. Very strong. Packs: 24/1 lb., 10 lb., 25 lb.

Benzoate of Soda. Food preservative. Benzoic acid dissolved in water and sodium carbonate. Illegal in some states.

Boletus (cepes). A French mushroom. Market forms, dried or canned. Imported.

Bouquet Garni. Herbs held together in cheesecloth. Used in sauces, stews, soups, and stock. Consists of a few basil sprigs, 1 bay leaf, 1 celery rib top, 1 kernel garlic, 1 marjoram sprig, 3 parsley branches, 1 tarragon leaf, a few thyme sprigs.

Bouillon Cubes. Used to intensify flavor of soups and sauces. Beef flavor or chicken flavor. Usually contain salt. Quantity of beef or chicken flavor varies; buy according to flavor percentage. Packaged in tins of 12, 50, and 100 cubes.

Braben (fiddlehead). A fern. Fresh. Canned.

Bread Crumbs. Crumbs of bread, fresh or browned, used in puddings, as a topping, or as a coating for foods before frying. Usually purchase in 10 lb. or 25 lb. cartons.

Cantharellus (chanterelles). A mushroom. Canned. Imported.

Capers. Flower buds of a plant grown in the Mediterranean area. Pickled in salt and vinegar. Used as sauce flavoring, seasoning, and a condiment. Sizes: 2 oz., 4 oz., 6½ oz., 9 oz., pint, ½ gal., gal.

Carottes. Very small Belgian or French carrots. Some at 350 + per No. 10 can. Domestic product graded according to Carrots, Canned in Chapter 5.

Cassia Buds. Dried flower bud of Cinnamemum cassia. Used in mincemeat, stewed fruits, and in pickling.

Catsup, Tomato. Spiced sauce with tomatoes as the main ingredient. Sizes: 8 oz. bottle, 12 oz. bottle, 14 oz. bottle, No. 10 can, 1 gal. can.

Buy: Grades A and B: Color: Color is typical of tomato catsup made from well-ripened, red tomatoes which has been properly prepared and processed. Such color contains as much or more red than produced by spinning that specified Munsell cdn discs in the following combination: 65 percent of the area of Disc 1; 21 percent of the area of Disc 2; 14 percent of the area of either Disc 3 or 4, or 7 percent of the area of Disc 3 and 7 percent of the area of Disc 4, whichever most nearly matches the reflectance of the tomato catsup. Consistency: Tomato catsup shows not more than a slight separation of free liquid when poured on a flat grading tray; is not excessively stiff; and flows not more than 9 centimeters in 30 seconds at 20 degrees Centigrade in the Bostwich Consistometer. Defects: Any defects present do not more than slightly affect the appearance or eating quality. Flavor: Good, distinct flavor characteristic of good quality ingredients. Such flavor is free from scorching or any objectionable flavor of any kind.

Minimum score for canned tomato catsup Grade A ''Fancy'' is 85; Grade B ''Extra Standard'' is 85; Grade C ''Standard'' is 70; and Substandard Grade is less than 70. The net weight should be not less than 90 percent fill of the container. To be Grade A, the catsup must have 33 percent solids.

This device measures the flowing quality of catsup. High quality catsup should not be too thick or too thin. This is one of several devices used by USDA fruit and vegetable inspectors to help them enforce the standards for grades of processed fruits and vegetables.

Chagote. A South American squash.

Chestnuts (Marrons). Marrons au sirop—Whole or pieces, used in sweet foods, Marron entiers au naturel—Whole, in water, for use as a vegetable or in stuffing. Puree de marrons au naturel—Unsweetened puree used with other vegetables. Creme de marrons—Sweetened puree.

Chili Sauce, Canned. Tomato sauce flavored with onions, red chili peppers, spices, sugar, and vinegar. Sizes: 8 oz. bottle, 12 oz. bottle, 14 oz. bottle, No. 10 can, 1 gal. can.

    Buy: Grade A: Color: Color of the chili sauce is bright; the color of the tomato ingredient is predominant and characteristic of properly prepared, well-ripened, properly processed tomatoes, and the added seasoning ingredients do not materially detract from the appearance of the product. Consistency: Chili sauce is heavy-bodied and when emptied from the container to a flat surface forms a moderately mounded mass and shows not more than a slight separation of free liquid at the edges of the mass. Character: Product does not have a finely communited appearance, and the onion, celery, pickle relish, and other similar ingredients are tender, reasonably firm, and crisp in texture. Defects: Do not more than slightly affect the appearance or eating quality of the product. Flavor: A good, distinct flavor characteristic of chili sauce properly prepared from good quality ingredients, and free from scorching or any objectionable flavor of any kind.

Minimum score for canned chili sauce Grade A ''Fancy'' is 85; Grade C ''Standard'' is 70; and Substandard Grade is less than 70. Net weight should not be less than 90 percent of volume of container.

Chocolate Liquor. (See also Cocoa.)   Bitter—Ground, roasted cocoa beans. 45 to 50 percent cocoa butter. Generally 10 lb. cakes. In small cakes is called Premium Chocolate. Sweet—Bitter chocolate liquor with sugar added. Generally 10 lb. cakes. Milk Chocolate—Sweet chocolate with a minimum of 12 percent whole milk solids.

Chocolate Syrup.   Sweet syrup made with cocoa or chocolate, corn syrup, salt, sugar, and vanilla. Pack: Usually 6/No.10 or in gallons.

Chutney.   Indian condiment made with fruits, spices, sugar, and vinegar. Served with cold meat. Packed in quarts.

Coconut. (See also Chapter 4.)   Fruit of the coconut palm. Shredded or grated and used in confectionery and baking. Available chip, sliced, shred, thread, or dessicated; sweetened or unsweetened; domestic or imported. Packs: 4 oz., 8 oz., 10 oz., 1 lb., 5 lb., 10 lb.

Cranberry Sauce.   Minimum score for canned cranberry sauce Grade A ''Fancy'' is 85; Grade C ''Standard'' is 70; and Grade D ''Substandard'' is less than 70. Net weight should not be less than 90 percent of capacity of container.

Cream of Tartar.   Acid salt used in baking powders and self-rising flour. Used in icings. Found in wine vats. Packs: Oz., lb.

Dressings

- Salad dressing. An emulsified, semisolid food prepared from edible vegetable oils, acidifying ingredients, and 1 or more egg-containing ingredients, and a cooked starchy paste prepared with food grade starches. May be seasoned or flavored with 1 or more of the following ingredients: salt, sugar, mustard, paprika, other spice or spice oil, except that no turmeric or saffron is used and no spice oil or spice extract is used which imparts to the salad dressing a color simulating the color imparted by egg yolk. Contains not less than 30 percent by weight of vegetable salad oil and not less than 4 percent by weight of liquid egg yolk.

- Mayonnaise. An emulsified, semisolid food prepared from edible vegetable oil, acidfying ingredients, and 1 or more of egg yolk-containing ingredients, and flavored with salt, sugar, spices, and any suitable harmless food flavoring other than imitations. Contains not less than 65 percent by weight of vegetable oil.
- Sandwich spread. A preparation made from either mayonnaise or salad dressing base usually with the addition of pickle relish and may or may not contain cooked starch paste.
- Refrigerated dressing. An emulsified, semisolid food of a perishable nature which requires refrigerated temperatures at all times. May contain ingredients such as blue cheese, Roquefort cheese, sour cream, pickle relish in combination with mayonnaise and salad dressing.
- Spoon-type. All other emulsified, semisolid types prepared with either a mayonnaise or salad dressing base in combination with other suitable food grade ingredients.
- French dressing. A separable, liquid food or emulsified, viscous, fluid food prepared from vegetable oil, vinegar or a mixture of vinegar, and optional acidifying ingredient citric acid. May be seasoned or flavored with 1 or more of the following ingredients: salt, sugar, mustard, paprika, spice or spice oils, monosodium glutamate, and any suitable harmless food seasoning other than imitations, tomato paste or tomato puree, emulsifying ingredients. Contains not less than 35 percent by weight of vegetable oil.
- Oil and vinegar. A separable, clear, liquid food meeting the requirements of a French type dressing, not emulsified or containing paprika, tomato paste, or tomato puree. Includes Italian garlic, herb and spice liquid dressing.
- Cheese. An emulsified, pourable, French dressing with cheese and egg yolk added.
- Low calorie and dietetic. A separable, liquid food which may or may not be emulsified. Contains selected ingredients and is normally a product having low caloric content.
- Pourable-type. All other separable, liquid food containing selected ingredients which may or may not be emulsified with a French type dressing base.

File Gumbo.   Powdered sassafras leaves. Used in soups. Pack: Oz.; lb.

Fines Herbes.   1 spray chervil, 1 chive, 1 leek, 1 tsp. marjoram, 1 small onion, 2 parsley sprays, and 2 scallions mixed together. Used in stuffings, butter sauce for fish, and omelets.

Flavorings and Extracts

- Imitation. Synthetic chemical compounds which approximate the natural flavors extracted as oils from fruits and nuts. Available in oz., pints, quarts, gallons. Natural: The oils extracted from fruits and nuts (bark, leaves, sap, roots too) and emulsified (oil) or mixed with alcohol or water. Strength: Specify either 5:100 or 8:100 ratio of natural oil to the solvent (alcohol, water).

- Lemon. Natural: 90 percent terpenes; 5 percent aldehyde, 5 percent alcohol esters. Pure: 5 percent lemon oil, 80 percent ethyl alcohol.
- Vanilla. Pure: Specify Mexican, Bourbon, or Tahiti beans in that order of quality. Federal standards demand 10 g. soluble matter per 100 cc in extract. Pure vanilla is the best buy. Imitation: An artificial vanilla made from the oil of cloves. Other extracts and flavorings available include: almond, walnut, maple, clove, cinnamon, anise, tonka, peppermint, mint, spearmint, wintergreen, cheng, banana, orange, strawberry, raspberry, pineapple.

Flour. (See Dry Cereals, Grains, and Flours.)

Fonds D'Artichauts.   Artichoke bottoms. Imported. Various can sizes. Not graded.

Gelatin.   Transparent, tasteless, hard substance from animal connective tissue. Various flavors with sugar added. Sizes: 6/4½ lb.; 2/20 lb.; 50 lb. packages of 12, 40 and 50 to a case (1 lb. each), 60 sheets per lb., 1 lb. packages of ¼ oz. individual envelopes.

Gum Tragacanth.   Gum from the tragacanth plant used in ice cream powders and for thickening jellies, creams, pastes, and icing. Primarily used in foodservice to coat culinary show pieces. Pack: By the pound, thin pieces.

Kitchen Bouquet.   Seasoning and coloring for sauces and gravies. Blend of 13 vegetables, herbs, and spices. Pack: 12/quarts; 4/1 gallon.

Marshmallows.   A soft, white, spongy candy, covered with powdered sugar and made from corn syrup, sugar, starch, and gelatin. Pack: 12 oz., 1 lb.

Mincemeat.   Preserve used as a filling for tarts, pies, and in puddings. Made from dried fruits, sugar, spices, suet, peeled and cooked lean beef. Pack: Usually 6/No. 10.

Monosodium Glutamate.   A wheat salt used to enhance meat, soups, stock, fish, cheese dishes, and poultry. Pack: 1 lb. can, 10 lb. can, 100 lb. drum.

Morels.   A French mushroom. Canned, Imported.

Noodles, Chinese.   Pasta strings made from wheat and rice flour and served in soup, meat sauces, or fried. Pack: 6/No. 10 (64 oz.)

Popcorn.   Type of Indian corn whose kernels pop open when heated. Pack: Usually 24/1 lb.

Potato Chips.   Peeled potatoes cut into strips and deep fried. Some are prepared out of processed "paste." Pack: Various package sizes of quarts, 12 oz., 1 lb., 3 lb., 4 lb., 5 lb.

Purslane.   Green, leafy plant for salads, mostly, fresh.

Raisins, Processed

- Muscat raisins. Grade A: Have similar varietal characteristics; have a good, typical color with not more than 10 percent, by weight, of raisins that may be dark, reddish brown berries in Soda-dipped Unseeded or Seeded (Valencia) raisins; have a good characteristic flavor; show development characteristic of raisins prepared from well-matured grapes; contain not more than 18 percent, by weight, of moisture, except that Seeded or Soda-dipped Seeded raisins may contain not more than 19 percent, by weight, of moisture and meet the requirements for absence of defects. Grades include Grade A "Fancy," Grade B "Choice," and Substandard Grade.
- Layer (or cluster) muscat raisins. Grade A: Have similar varietal characteristics; have a good typical color; have a good characteristic flavor; are uniformly cured and show development characteristic of raisins prepared from well-matured grapes; contain not more than 23 percent, by weight, of moisture; not less than 30 percent, by weight, of the raisins, exclusive of stems and branches, are 3-Crown size or larger, and meet the requirements for absence of defects. Grades include Grade A "Fancy," Grade B "Choice," and Substandard Grade.
- Sultana Raisins. Grade A: Have similar varietal characteristics; have a good, typical color; have a good characteristic flavor; show development characteristic of raisins prepared from well-matured grapes; contain not more than 18 percent, by weight, of moisture, and meet the requirements for absence of defects. Grades include Grade A "Fancy," Grade B "Choice," Grade C "Standard," and Substandard Grade.
- Thompson seedless raisins. Grade A: Have similar varietal characteristics; have a good typical color in Unbleached and Soda-dipped raisins; have a good characteristic flavor; show development characteristics of raisins prepared from well-matured grapes with not less than 80 percent, by weight, of raisins that are well matured or reasonably well matured raisins; and not more than 1 percent, by weight, of select and mixed size raisins, and 2 percent, by weight, of small (midget) size raisins may have substandard development; contain not more than 18 percent, by weight, of moisture, and meet the requirements for absence of defects. Grades include Grade A "Fancy," Grade B "Choice," Grade C "Standard," and Substandard Grade.
- Zante Currant Raisins. Grade A: Have similar varietal characteristics; have a good typical color; have a good characteristic flavor; show development characteristics of raisins prepared from well-matured grapes; have not less than 75 percent, by weight, of raisins that are well-matured or reasonably well-matured; contain not more than 20 percent, by weight, of moisture; and meet the additional requirements.

Relish, Pickle.   Chopped pickles, peppers, etc., with slightly sweet seasoning. Specify: minimum 60 percent immature cucumbers; minimum 25 percent cauliflower; or minimum 10 percent tomatoes; 3 to 5 percent onions; cured in brine; then cured in vinegar. Chopped fine and preserved in 15° Baume Vinegar/Sugar liquor. Pack: 4/1 gal. 6/No. 10.

Sago. Starchy, grain-like substance taken from the pith of the sago palm, used to thicken milk puddings, soups, and fruit molds.

Salsifis. Peeled oyster plant used in garnish work. Imported. Canned. Specify: Firm, crisp, well shaped.

Salt Smoke. Mixture of salt, propylene glycol, hardwood tar fractions, and tricalcium phosphate. Used in barbecued meats and barbecue sauce.

Sauerkraut, Canned. Buy: Grade A: Color: Possesses a light, practically uniform, typical white to light cream general appearance, characteristic of properly prepared and properly processed canned kraut equal to or better than kraut model No. 1. Cut: With respect to shredded kraut, the shreds are uniform in thickness, and the appearance of the product is not more than slightly affected by the presence of short or irregular cut pieces; and with respect to chopped kraut, the pieces are uniform in size, and the presence of pieces marked by smaller or larger than the predominant size of pieces does not more than slightly affect the appearance. Defects: Minor defects may be present that do not materially affect the appearance or eating quality, and major defects may be present that do not more than slightly affect the appearance or eating quality. Character: Kraut is crisp and firm. Flavor: Possesses a good characteristic kraut flavor which is free from off-flavors and odors of any kind.

SAUERKRAUT

BULK [5/24/67   52.3451]

Grades:	"A" or "FIRST QUALITY"	"C" or "SECOND QUALITY"	"SUB-STANDARD"
Minimum Score:	85	70	Less than 70

CANNED [5/13/63   52.2951]

Grades:	"A" or "FANCY"	"B" or "EXTRA STAN-DARD"	"C" or "STAN-DARD"	"SUB-STAN-DARD"
Minimum Score:	90	80	70	Less than 70
	NET WEIGHT OZ.	NET WEIGHT METRIC	DRAINED WEIGHT OZ.	DRAINED WEIGHT METRIC
No. 8Z Tall	8.2	232.5 g	6.7	189.9 g
No. 303	16.0	453.6 g	13.2	374.2 g
No. 2½	28.3	802.3 g	23.0	652.0 g
No. 10	104.0	2.9 kg	80.0	2.3 kg

Soy Sauce. Dark brown, pungent sauce made from fermented soy beans. Used as a seasoning and flavoring agent. Genuine soy sauce is a fermented product and is not legal in the United States. Pack: 24/3 oz.; 24/5 oz.; gallons.

Sugars. Sugar is almost pure sucrose when made by evaporating and crystallizing sugarcane or sugar beets. Corn sugar, made by the hydrolysis of the starch of corn, is dextrose. Glucose is dextrose in syrup form. Cellulose is crystallized dextrose.

Sugar's fineness is indicated by the number of "x's," with x being the most coarse and 10x being the most fine.

- Brown sugar (also called "Soft"). A mixture of granulated sugar and molasses. Grades are 1 through 15 and 15 being the darkest color. Buy No. 8 to No. 10 for light brown and No. 11 to No. 15 for dark brown.
- Confectioner sugar. xxxx (4x). Has 3 percent starch added. For icing. (6x also.)
- Fine granulated (also Beng). For baking; dissolves quickly.
- Molasses. Uncrystallized sugar. (See Syrups.)
- Powdered sugar. xx (2x).

Sugar Packaging: Granulated available in 100 lb., 50 lb., 25 lb., 10 lb., 5 lb., 2 lb., 1 lb. containers, as well as cases of 1000 to 3000 individual packets of ⅙ oz. and ¼ oz. each. Powdered and brown sugars usually purchased in cases of 24/1 lb. boxes.

Tomato Paste. The degree of concentration is not considered a factor of quality for the purposes of the standards, but the following designations of concentration may be used in connection with the standards for the applicable natural tomato soluble solids group:

1. Extra heavy concentration: 39.3 percent or more.
2. Heavy concentration: 32 percent or more, but less than 39.3 percent.
3. Medium concentration: 28 percent or more, but less than 32 percent.
4. Light concentration: 24 percent or more, but less than 28 percent.

Texture is the degree of fineness or coarseness of the product. Texture is classified when the product is diluted with water to between 8 and 9 percent, inclusive, of natural tomato soluble solids.

"Fine" texture means a smooth, uniform finish.

"Coarse" texture means a coarse, slightly granular finish.

Buy: Grade A: Color: Bright, typical red tomato paste color. Such color, when the product is diluted and observed, is as red as or more red than that produced by spinning the specified Munsell color discs in the following combinations or is an equivalent of such composite color: 65 percent of the area of Disc 1; 21 percent of the area of Disc 2; and 14 percent of the area of Disc 3 or Disc 4, or 7 percent of the area of Disc 3 and 7 percent of the area of Disc 4, whichever most nearly matches the appearance of the diluted sample. Defects: Any defects present do not more than slightly affect the appearance or usability of the product.

Minimum score for canned tomato paste Grade A "Fancy" is 90; Grade C "Standard" is 80; and Substandard Grade is less than 80. Net weight should be as full as practicable.

Tomato Puree (Pulp), Canned. Grade A: Color: Bright, typical, red tomato puree color. Such color, when the product is of the proper concentration and observed, is as red as or more red than that produced by spinning the specified Munsell color discs in the following combinations, or is an equivalent of such composite color: 65 percent of the area of Disc 1; 21 percent of the area of Disc 2; and 14 percent of the area of either Disc 3 or Disc 4, or 7 percent of the area of Disc 3 and Disc 4, whichever most nearly matches the appearance of the sample. Defects: Any defects present do not more than slightly affect the appearance or usability of the product.

Minimum score for canned tomato puree (pulp) Grade A "Fancy" is 90; Grade C "Standard" is 80; and Substandard Grade is less than 80. Net weight should be as full as practicable.

Tomato Sauce, Canned. Buy: Grade A: Color: Color is typical of tomato sauce made from well-ripened red tomatoes and which has been properly prepared and processed. Such color contains as much or more red than that produced by spinning the specified Munsell color discs in the following combinations: 65 percent of the area of Disc 1; 21 percent of the area of Disc 2; 14 percent of the area of Disc 3 or of Disc 4, or 7 percent of the area of Disc 3 and Disc 4, whichever most nearly matches the reflectance of the tomato sauce. Consistency: Tomato sauce shows not more than a slight separation of free liquid when poured on a flat grading tray; is not excessively stiff, and flows not more than 14 centimeters in 30 seconds at 20°C. in the Bostwich Consistometer. Defects: Any defects present may be noticeable but are not so large, so numerous, or of such contrasting color as to seriously affect the appearance or eating quality. Flavor: Good, distinct flavor characteristic of good quality ingredients. Such flavor is free from scorching or any objectionable flavor of any kind.

Minimum score for canned tomato sauce Grade A "Fancy" is 85; Grade C "Standard" is 70; and Substandard Grade is less than 70. Net weight should be not less than 90 percent of capacity of the container.

Truffles. A mushroom-like fungus. Black truffles are best. Available only from France; fresh in late winter, canned year round; ⅞ oz. upwards. Market forms: whole (extra or brushed), peelings, puree, paste.

Vanilla Extract. See Flavorings and Extracts.

Vinegar. Diluted, impure acetic acid made from apples, beer, sugar, etc., and is used for pickling, preserving, sousing, and marinating. Pack: 5 gal. kit or jug, 10 gal. kit, 15 gal. keg, 30 gal. half-bushel, 50 gal. bushel. Specify: Clear, bright, free from sediment and floating particles, sterilized, 4 percent minimum and 5 percent maximum acetic acid.

Waxy Maize Starch.   A starch made from corn. Thickening power equal in hot food and cold food. Has a clear finish. Used in frozen goods because of its stability. Trade names: Colflo, Clearjel, Purity 69. Highly recommended replacement for cornstarch but not as good as arrowroot.

Worcestershire Sauce.   Thin, dark, spicy sauce with a piquant flavor. Added to stews, soups, etc. Specify: Wood ripened minimum of 60 days; 20 percent minimum solids. Pack: 12 and 24/5 oz.; gallons.

Yeast.   See table.

Relation between yeast solids of specified types of yeast and yeast products

Product	Factors for Converting to —	
	Compressed Yeast	**Dry Active Yeast**
Compressed yeast	1.00	0.305
Dry active yeast[1]	3.17	1.00

1. The functional relation between dry and compressed yeast differs from the weight relation. It requires about 40-45% of the weight of compressed yeast to give an equivalent activity of dried yeast. These factors are based upon the following average moisture levels: Compressed yeast, 70.5%; dry active yeast, 8.0%; nutritional yeast, 4.5%.

QUESTIONS

1. Define and give an example of each:

kernel	salad dressing
texture	mayonnaise
grind sizes	color
additives	glazing
pack	shortening
basket fired	plastic
saturated fat	unsaturated fat
high ratio	winterized
comb honey	kosher
breakfast cocoa	hot chocolate

2. What factors affect the quality of tea?
3. Define lard and give reasons why it is not commonly used nowadays.
4. What are the indications of smoking fats?
5. What are the differences in Grade A and Grade B fruit jelly?
6. What does "canned concentrate orange juice 4 plus 1" mean?
7. What is the size variation on large ripe olives?
8. List differences between fresh-pack and cured pickles.
9. Why are some nuts shelled before appearing on the market?

EXHIBIT

Cereals, Mixes, and Bakery Products			
	Unit	Portion Size (Cooked)	No. of Portions
Corn Grits	1 lb.	¾ c.	16.4
Macaroni	1 lb.	¾ c.	12.0
Noodles	1 lb.	¾ c.	10.7
Rice	1 lb.	¾ c.	11.3
Rolled Oats	1 lb.	¾ c.	15.3
Spaghetti	1 lb.	¾ c.	12.1
Bran Flakes	14 oz.	1¼ oz.	11.2
Corn Flakes	12 oz.	1 oz.	12.0
Cake Mixes	5 lb.	6 sq. in.	75–100
Frosting Mix	5 lb.	6 sq. in.	125–130
Biscuit	5 lb.	2 in.	100
Raisin Bread	2 lb.	1 slice	36
Rye Bread	1½ lb.	1 slice	28
White Bread	1½ lb.	⅝ in. slice	24

13

MAJOR EQUIPMENT

INTRODUCTION

Considerations for buying commercial cooking equipment involves a lot of time, research, and careful selection. The author recommends looking at the newest specialized equipment because of improvement of equipment performance and changes in preparation techniques. Specific recommendations are given for purchasing cooking and baking equipment. A checklist for writing food service equipment specifications is included.

Dry storage equipment, nonfood storage equipment, hoods or canopies, sinks, tables, and standard pieces of equipment are listed with specific considerations and recommendations. Methods of preparation are discussed relating to certain pieces of equipment. Photographic examples are given of numerous pieces of equipment.

The standard sizes, materials, and unique features presented give you information by which to initiate the investigation of equipment needed for an efficient and smooth running operation.

WHAT TO CONSIDER BEFORE BUYING COMMERCIAL COOKING EQUIPMENT

Whether you are selecting an individual piece of cooking equipment or choosing an entire complement of cooking units for a complete kitchen installation, you should heed certain caution signs and follow a number of guideposts.

Improper equipment selected unwisely is a burden to smooth food preparation procedure and is a costly burden to management. Good equipment wisely selected for specific cooking applications can help to upgrade your menu, speed your food preparation, and reduce your operating costs.

Equipment purchased is cared for and used for a period of many years. It is therefore prudent to select the equipment that will serve you profitably rather than become a costly hindrance. Observe the following caution signs:

1. Beware of Claims. Do not be misled by sales presentations with claims of doubtful value that are unsupported by facts.
2. Do Not Overlook Economic Factors. What are the costs? Equipment cost, installation cost, operating cost, service, and maintenance cost. Weigh fact against fancy.
3. Keep an Open Mind. Too much progress is being made today in improving equipment performance and too many changes are being made in foods and cooking techniques for you to fail to look at the newest specialized equipment, as well as to fail to look for changes in food preparation.

Consider these guideposts:

1. Whom will you serve?
2. What will you serve?
3. How many will you serve?
4. Where will you serve?
5. When will you serve?

COOKING AND BAKING EQUIPMENT

Types of cooking and baking equipment to be used will, of course, depend primarily on type of fuel available. New and improved refrigeration, food preparation, cooking, and sanitation devices are constantly being developed. Many of these make possible better food products and also minimize food waste and labor. Careful study needs to be given the selection of equipment to make sure that each device will do the job expected of it and to make certain that it will be economical in the long run.

It is recommended that cooking, baking, and mechanical equipment be approved by and carry the following seals:

• NSF—National Safety Foundation.
• UL—Underwriters Laboratory. All electrical equipment should carry this seal.
• AGA—American Gas Association.
• NEMA—National Equipment Manufacturers Association.

The following is a checklist for persons writing foodservice equipment specifications:[1]

1. Is the specification free of any possibilities of misunderstanding? Is the language used to describe details similar to that which is used in "the trade"? (Writing the spec-

---

[1] Arthur Avery, "Writing Specs," *Food Management* (March 1978). Reproduced by permission.

ification with the manufacturer's "spec sheet" for reference will usually take care of this.)

2. Is everything important to you included in the specification? If a six-inch fence around the griddle will be necessary to you when you use the griddle, it should be in the specification.

3. Is the specification free of all frivolous requirements? Nothing should be included in the specification that is not important to you. Anything that is different from the usual manufacturer's specification sheet should be reviewed several times for necessity. As a general rule, it will cost much more and, in many cases, manufacturers of quality equipment will not bid on the equipment since they have not tested the modification and they will not want their brand name on something they have not tested.

4. Are all construction details uniform so that several parts of similar purpose and design are described in identical terms?

5. Are gauges, finishes, and compositions of materials described using approved standard terms (such as 302 corrosion resistant steel, 12 gauge metal thickness, and No. 4 finish)?

6. Is the design well balanced? Is the frame adequate to support the top you have specified? Will the feet be adequate for the weight they will carry and compatible with the floor on which they will rest? Are the hinges adequate for the size and weight of door? Will the drawer slide carry the drawer weight plus contents? Has a table with an adequate heavy gauge top been properly balanced with lightweight side panels?

7. Are greater quality, more expensive metal, heavier gauge, or finer finish being used that the anticipated use of the equipment warrants? While an oven front may be specified to be made of corrosion resistant steel, it may be possible to use enameled cheaper steels for the sides and back of the oven if they won't be subjected to corrosion. Also, a kitchen table carrying heavy loads of food materials or equipment may warrant a 12 gauge table top while one used to prepare sandwiches or salad could use 14 to 16 gauge.

8. Does the specification cover who will provide, or will not provide, the associated equipment (facets, valves and traps for sinks, electrical connections for work tables and similar equipment)?

9. Is the dealer to install the equipment? If so, how much responsibility does he have for preparing the location of the equipment and bringing in utilities and drains? Are all electrical, water, steam, and gas connections specified as to size, material, construction, and other details?

10. Is workmanship defined?

11. Where the successful bidder is to install the equipment, is he required to submit proposed installation and hook-up plans for approval?

12. Is it specified that construction details, particularly those which relate to water and drains, conform to local regulations? Be sure that nothing in the construction will violate OSHA regulations.

13. While it is difficult to enforce sometimes, it is desirable to require that the manufacturing be done by workers experienced in fabrication of the specified type of equipment for foodservice. Then, if you have forgotten any details in the specification, they will be covered by "good commercial practice."

14. It is important to remember that even the best of equipment must be maintained

and repaired. Thus, provisions should be made in the equipment design for easy access to the part on which repairs or adjustments will have to be made.

15.   If the specification is being written to encourage a number of bidders, it should be written loosely enough so that a number of manufacturers can comply with the specification details. If a number of manufacturers or their dealers bid, it means that competition should lower the price. However, if the specification is written tightly so that only one piece of equipment can comply with all of the details, there is no competition and the price may be high.

DRY STORAGE EQUIPMENT

Shelving.   Wood or metal, supported by uprights, not more than 48 inches apart, 7 feet 6 inches maximum practical height; 1 inch vertical adjustment of shelf supports convenient for arranging shelving to accommodate inventory. Allow 1 inch minimum clearance from all walls for cleaning and air circulation. Brace well against tipping. Standard shelving available, 12 inches, 18 inches, or 24 inches deep. Provide 36 inches vertical clearance under shelving where portable platforms, cans, and dollies may be located. Aisle space, 30 inches minimum for access to shelving only; 42 inches minimum for movement of portable platforms.

Adjustable shelves should be provided for broken case lots and pallets (dunnage platforms) for case quantities.

A substantial portion of the storage room should be left free of shelves in order to provide dunnage platforms in sections sized for adequate storage and sized for convenient movement (on casters). The dunnage should be so designed that there is free movement of air underneath. It saves labor to use canned goods directly from the cases in which they are received.

Current trends are mobilized, adjustable metal shelves. They are very versatile and may be used in other areas, refrigerated or work, when not needed in dry storage area.

**CAN AND CARTON MEASUREMENTS FOR
ESTIMATING SHELF CAPACITY**

Size Can	Approx. Diameter of Can (Inches)	Clear Height Per Tier (Inches)	Cans Per Carton (Number)	Size of Carton (Inches)
No. 10	6 ¼	7 ½	6	19 × 12 ¾ × 7 ¾
No. 2	3 ½	5	24	14 ½ × 10 ¾ × 10
No. 2 ½	4	5	24	17 × 12 ¾ × 10 ¼
No. 3 (Cylinder)	4 ¼	7 ½	12	17 ½ × 13 ½ × 7 ¾

Portable Platforms (Dollies, pallets, skids). In small sections approximately 24 inch by 36 inch; constructed of heavy-gauge steel tubing or wood slats; caster mounting desirable. To be used under bottom shelf or in center of room if space is sufficient.

Floor Storage Containers (50 or 100 lb. size). Available aluminum, stainless steel, or galvanized iron, with vermin-tight covers; coved corners desirable. Available with or without casters or may be used on dollies.

Grocers' Scoops. Corrosion-resistant material; 1 to 1½ lb. capacity.

Thermometers, Wall Type. Temperature range, minus 20°F to plus 120°F in 2° scale divisions; 12 inch minimum overall length.

Hand Trucks. Frame approximately 48 inches high; at least 14 inches wide; bottom angle nose at least 14 inches by 7 inches; rubber-tired wheels. Optional features, curved brace bars for handling round containers; glides for going up and down steps; handles, brakes. Truck may also be used in the Receiving Area. Bumpers optional.

Casters for Mobile Equipment. Stationary, swivel, locking, ball bearing swivel axle, brake type, stem and plate construction, caster sized to each piece of equipment, taking into account such requirements as load capacities, overall height and transportation involved; rubber-tired, special casters to meet specific requirements can be purchased. Generally, no caster smaller than 5 inches should be used in food services. Casters capable of static load, minimum of 250 lbs. per caster. Lifetime lubrication. Bumpers optional.

NONFOOD STORAGE EQUIPMENT

Cabinets. Metal or wood; 36 inches by 24 inches by 72 inches high; locker type; fixed bottom, 4 intermediate shelves; hinged doors.

Shelving. Wood or metal; supported by upright, not more than 48 inches apart; 7 feet 6 inches maximum practical height; 1 inch vertical adjustment convenient for arranging shelving to accommodate inventory; 1 inch minimum clearance from all walls for air circulation; brace well against tipping. Standard shelving available. Portable metal shelving recommended.

HOODS OR CANOPIES

Should be provided over all cooking and baking equipment. Hoods are used for the removal of heat, grease, moisture, and steam. Sizing and height from the heat source are important. Canopies should usually have about a 2 inch overhang for each food above the equipment. The usual clearance of the canopy is 5 feet above equipment and a minimum of 6 feet 3 inches where workers pass under. To work properly, canopies should be at least 2 feet from the bottom edge to the top, and one outlet should be provided for every 6 to 8 linear feet of canopy. In some instances a ventilator or backshelf hood is now preferred. These units sit about 18 to 22 inches above equipment and give the strongest pull of air where it is most needed. They may vary from 200 cfm to a high of 350 cfm per lineal foot of appliance. The National Fire Protective Association recommends that all hoods be equipped with grease filters or be provided with a fire extinguishing system that meets their No. 96 Standard. Filters should not be installed less than 3½ feet above an open flame and not less than 4½ feet above charcoal flames. Filters should be easily removable and of a size easily sent through the dishwasher.

Canopy hoods should be integrally constructed with smooth surfaces, free of crevices, trim, or other projections. Suitable drains should be provided for condensation and grease troughs not less than 1¼ by 1¼ inch, and should permit easy cleaning. Baffles, dampers, and turning vanes should be easily removable and cleanable. An automatic device should be provided to close dampers and vents when temperatures go over 360° to 400°F. Hoods should be rigidly supported to equipment, wall, or ceiling. Marine-type or sealed-in vapor-proof lights should be installed as required for proper illumination.

SINKS

Cooks' Vegetable Preparation, and Pot Washing. Stainless steel; welded seamless construction; sanitary inside corners (coved); integral rims, splashboards, and drainboards that slope toward sink for draining. Bottom sloped to drain through removable stainless steel strainers into waste; exterior-operated lever waste control desirable. Mixing faucet with swing-spouts located for filling each compartment. Mount entire fixture on sanitary metal legs or concealed wall hangers.

Cooks' Sink. Installed in cooks' table or near ranges; inside measurements, approximately 15 inches by 15 inches by 8 inches to 12 inches deep. Long swing-spout mixing faucet mounted 24 inches above range top or over steam jacketed kettles also desirable.

Vegetable Preparation Sink. Two or more compartments; each compartment approximately 20 inches by 20 inches by 12 inches to 14 inches deep, inside measurements. Front rim 34 inches to 38 inches above floor. Two drainboards, at least 24 inches long, draining into sink. Waste disposer needed under this sink. Second sink 22 inches by 24 inches and 12 inches deep.

Pot Sink. Two or three compartments as required by local and state regulations; each compartment not smaller than 24 inches wide, 24 inches front-to-back; 12 inches to 16 inches deep, inside measurements. Sink bottom at least 24 inches above floor; front rim 36 inches to 40 inches above floor. Splashboard on rear, 10 inches to 15 inches high, turned back 2 inches on top and sides to conceal water supply pipe; high faucet mounting, 20 inch minimum clearance under faucet to sink bottom. Thermostatically-controlled booster heater or auxiliary heating cycle such as side-arm heater for maintaining 180°F water in final sanitizing compartment. Two drainboards at least 24 inches long, draining into sink. Grease overflow compartments and food waste disposers optional accessories. To clear 18 inches by 25 inches bun pans it is suggested that faucet mounting be 6 inches higher and splashboard height increased correspondingly.

Hand Lavatory. Stainless steel, vitreous china, or acid-resisting porcelain enamel on cast iron; standard size, mixing faucet with foot-operated control valves; stops and trap. Provide soap dispensers and towel dispensers or automatic hand dryers.

TABLES

Bakers', Cooks', and Vegetable Preparation. 34 inch to 36 inch working height; 24 inch to 30 inch width if used on one side only, 42 inches to 48 inches wide if used from both sides; center overhead shelf if double service type. If table use requires cutlery, provide drawer, approximately 20 inches by 20 inches by 5 inches deep. Space under table top may be enclosed storage cabinet, lower metal shelf between table legs, or open to floor for storing portable bins, trucks, etc. Mount tables on tubular legs with sanitary adjustable feet or on casters with brakes. Consult local authorities for approval before ordering wood top tables.

Bakers' Table. 3 inch thick laminated maple strip top, stainless steel top, or 1½ inch thick polished marble top. Base open for storing portable bins, overhead rack.

Cooks' Table. 14 gauge stainless steel or 12 gauge stainless steel if working surface is 12 feet or more, or laminated maple strip top, one or two drawers. Overhead utensil rack optional; approximately 7 feet 6 inches above floor. Lower shelf, 18 gauge stainless steel for storage cabinet.

Vegetable Preparation Table. Stainless steel or laminated maple strip top; two drawers; removable cutting board, lower shelf, or storage cabinet.

Utility Trucks. For all purpose use in kitchen. Stainless steel or aluminum, approximately 38 inches long, 22 inches wide, 36 inches high; two or three decks; rubber-tired ball-bearing wheels; rubber bumpers; two rigid and two swivel wheels preferable, or four swivel wheels if desired.

TILTING BRAISING OR FRYING PANS

The tilting braising or frying pan is an idea originally imported from Europe but now offered by American manufacturers. It is being used in American foodservice production to cook everything from fish to meat to egg foo yong. Its usefulness is based on the large cooking surface with its wide range of even temperatures, resulting from higher power input, that is now possible. Adequate insulation on front of equipment keeps working temperatures comfortable. It can be mounted on casters for use in more than one location. Ingredients can be cooked from the raw stage to completion in the tilting pan.

Units are all equipped with pouring lips and self-locking tilt mechanism for easy removal of stews, sauces, and gravies, as well as fat used in frying and braising. Models are 36 inches in height to make operation easy. A counter-top model comes in these 3 dimensions: 24⅝ in. deep by 24⅝ in. wide; 24⅝ in. deep by 31⅝ in. wide; 24⅝ in. deep by 51⅝ in. wide.

The tilting fry skillet saves time and physical strain. *Courtesy of Crown-X, Inc.*

BROILERS

A good working definition of the broiler confines it to equipment for cooking food by great heat (usually direct) or by radiant heat. In another definition, broiling is said to be the process of cooking a piece of meat in its own juices without using the fat (as in frying.) The faster the cooking, the better, in terms of maximum juiciness retained and minimum shrinkage.

Broilers are classified by one expert in these three general types: (1) horizontal or overhead broilers, such as electric, conventional gas, or infra-red type; (2) char or underfired broilers; and (3) specialty broilers.

These can all be characterized as having highly radiant heat sources, over 1000°F; high grid or rack temperatures, up to 1200°F when preheated, and high ambient (broiling area) temperatures of 600° to 1200°F with the grid preheated in a raised position.

How well a broiler can sustain these conditions under load; how much flexibility and control is available for different products; and degrees of doneness and finish are important operating features.

Two basics of broiler selection that the individual operator must determine are: (1) quantity and kind of broiled food to be served, and (2) available floor space.

When shopping for broilers, you should look for:

1. Proper concentration and direction of radiant heat to assure efficiency and low operating cost.

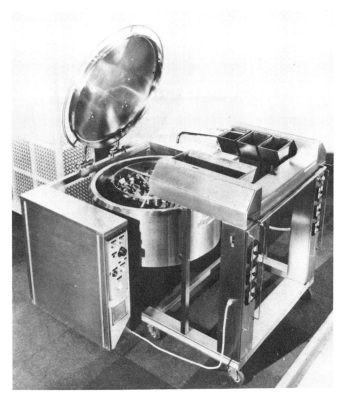

Semi-automatic sauce maker with automatic ingredient dispenser.
Courtesy of Crown-X, Inc.

2. Warp resistant heating units with radiant ceramic or alloy materials.
3. Broiler linings of reflective materials that promise long service.
4. Units that heat to broiling temperatures in about 10 minutes or infra-red broilers that require only 30 seconds to preheat.
5. Variable temperature controls.
6. Separate switches or turn-offs.
7. Flues adequate to remove smoke, odors, and combustion products.
8. Air drafts designed so they do not affect flames or cook foods.
9. Bodies of 16 gauge or better sheet steel, rigidly enforced with sturdy angle support.
10. Rugged, sturdy grids easy to adjust over distances 1½ to 8 inches from heat source.
11. Easily pulled out grids with safety stop locks.
12. All parts and areas accessible for easy cleaning and servicing. Broilers are often set in a battery with other broilers or pieces of equipment and placed under and attached to special hoods. Broilers do require servicing and if the unit must be freed from the ventilation system and pulled out of the battery, much high cost labor is expended. Particularly in these set-ups, accessibility for service repaid from the front is essential.

13. Arrangements for catching grease and drawing it into receptacle for easy disposal.
14. Charcoal broiler beds of heavy construction.
15. Loading and unloading away from heat zone.

CUTTERS OR CHOPPERS

Electric; table type; revolving bowl, 15 inch to 20 inch diameter; safety device; bowl and knife guard readily removable for cleaning. Attachments may be obtained.

Food choppers or grinders may operate as an attachment on another motor-driven piece of equipment but for heavy work independent equipment is preferred. Important selection points are the manner in which the chopper cuts, safety and sanitary factors. Plates from ⅛ to ½ inch are available. Usually a feed pan and wooden stomper are furnished with the machine. The cylinder may be horizontal or at a slant to provide gravity flow.

Recommend approval by NSF and UL.

The vertical cutter-mixer reduces hours of hand work to minutes. *Courtesy of Hobart Corp.*

FRYERS

Fryers are of four types:

1. Conventional restaurant-types ranging from a small 11 by 11 inch kettle to a 24 by 24 inch size with corresponding fat capacities of 15 to 130 lbs. Models may be free standing or built-in fryers in single or multiple units.

2. Pressure fryers, equipped with tightly sealed lid permitting moisture given off in cooking process to build up steam pressure within kettle; this retains moisture within fried product though coating continues crisp.

3. Semi-automatic, high production model turns out continuous portion batches via conveyor. Each batch is discharged as it is cooked while other batches continue to cook.

4. Automatic fryers that completely control the frying cycle from the time the operator pushes the time button. When button is pushed, a cycle is set in motion that automatically lowers basket into frying fat, fries food to serving state, then raises baskets to drain position. One 14¾ by 23⁵⁄₁₆ by 13 fryer has an output of 300 2-ounce servings of prebalanced french fries per hour; other models offer output of 480 and 600 2 ounce servings per hour. A kettle 15 inches wide by 17 inches deep turns out 6 breaded pounds of fried chicken every 8 minutes or 2½ pounds of fried shrimp in 3 minutes.

Also available are counter models at small end of size range. They are excellent where space is limited or as auxiliary fryers.

When looking at fryers to purchase, check out the following points and be sure they meet your specifications:

temperature control	design
speed of recovery	usable dimensions
economical use of fat	signal light, timers
flavor protection	type (counter, free-standing, or built-in)
ease and safety of use	drain facilities
cleaning ease	basket construction
sturdiness	

WHAT HAPPENS AS YOU FRY?[2]

When fresh oil is heated in a deep fat fryer and the frying operation begins, three general chemical reactions occur simultaneously.

1. Hydrolysis. This is the reaction of the oil with moisture wherein the fatty acids are separated from the glycerol-forming free fatty acids. This change, when analyzed, is expressed as the percentage of free fatty acids.

A fresh oil will have a free fatty acids level of about 0.05 percent or less, but during the course of frying this value may go as high as 5 percent, if the oil is badly abused and

---

[2]*Frying Facts From Kraft,* Kraft Foods, Chicago, Illinois.

broken down. Usually a value of 1 percent free fatty acids is considered maximum for most frying operations.

The smoke point of a fresh oil is usually in excess of 425°F, but as the free fatty acids rise, the smoke point correspondingly goes down so that at 0.8 percent free fatty acids, the smoke point is about 325°F.

Metals containing copper will cause an appreciable increase in the percentage of free fatty acids. Drip-back from the exhaust system will also cause increases in fatty acids.

2. Oxidation. Frying oils have a bland flavor, but upon heating and frying become less bland and develop burned, scorched, or off-flavors through abuse.

During the frying operation, the surface of the oil is protected by a blanket of steam arising from the foods being fried. During slack periods, air comes in contact with the surface of the oil causing deterioration of the oil by oxidation. Reducing the temperature of the oil to 150° to 200°F when it is not being used will reduce the rate of oxidation.

Aeration of the oil by allowing a pump to pull air or allowing the oil to cascade from one area to another results in rapid oxidation. It is best to have the oil enter the fryer or holding tank near the bottom to minimize the aeration. Holding tanks should be designed, if possible, to be vertical with a small surface area rather than horizontal or flat with a large surface area. Light catalyzes the development of off-flavors in oil and should be excluded wherever practical.

3. Polymerization. The union of two or more molecules of oil to form a larger molecule is known as polymerization. Thermal polymers cannot be detected by odor or flavor as can oxidative polymers. The decrease in iodine number, a measure of unsaturation or double bond, is an indication of polymer formation.

Polymer formations are visible on frying equipment that is not properly cleaned. This polymerized material should be removed at frequent intervals and the proper technique used in filtering the oil to remove as many of these polymers as possible.

DOUGHNUT FRYERS

Doughnut kettles turn out doughnuts that are fried uniformly since heat is distributed evenly throughout the fat. The frying process can be automated with an adjustable thermostat which can be set to the proper frying temperatures.

In one model, a special light indicates when proper temperature has been reached. Thermostat maintains this temperature automatically for as long as the kettle is turned on. Batches can be turned out continuously with no delay.

A portable doughnut machine that turns out 16 doz. doughnuts per hour takes only 16 inches of counter space. Two fry screens and a detachable drain tray simplify continuous production; new batch can be frying while previous batch drains.

Another compact portable counter top model automatically fries, ices, and/or glazes both yeast-raised and cake doughnuts in one continuous operation at the rate of 40 doz. per hour. It measures 49 inches wide by 25 inches high by 25 inches deep.

Three important pieces of equipment in any professional kitchen are shown here: the automated roll-through steam cooker (right), the automated fryer (left), and the rotivator (center). *Courtesy of Crown-X, Inc.*

GRIDDLES AND GRILLS

In any discussion of griddles and grills the first challenge is to define your terms. Generally the griddle is described as a flat top appliance, usually heated from beneath by gas or electricity, ranging from 7 inches wide by 14 inches deep up to 60 inches wide by 24 inches deep.

The grill is a cooking unit similar to a griddle except that where food cooks on top of a griddle, the grill has two heated surfaces. Food is placed between the two surfaces and cooked simultaneously from top and bottom in a grill.

Some facts to investigate when considering a griddle include:

1. Type of metal, shape, position of drainage run.
2. Drainage run should be positioned so that scrapings can be moved out of the way as rapidly as possible with minimum motion and effort.
3. Rate of heat introduction, retention, and recovery adequate for speedy production.
4. Ease of cleaning.
5. Minimum maintenance.

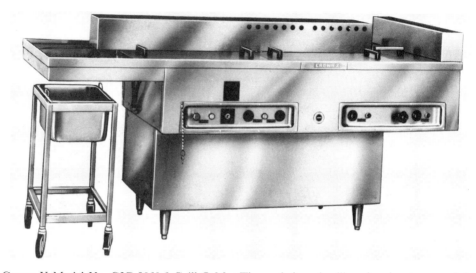

Crown-X Model No. CJG-5060-3 Grill-O-Mat The oval shaped grill surface has two parallel heated surfaces. The loading end surface is also heated. A turning device is at one end of the appliance and on the opposite end is the loading space and discharge chute for cooked food products. The design of the frying surfaces assures the continual circulation of the cooking oil. The Grill-O-Mat can be used for low oil-level, as well as for high oil-level frying (deep frying). The Grill-O-Mat is the ideal appliance for cooking all types of large volume Fast-Food-Orders. For example, Meat, Fish, Meat Balls, French Fries, Home Fries. The unit operates by a continuous-rotating technique, with a frying capacity of 300–600 pieces per hour. After food products are placed manually between the transport bars; the conveying over the cooking surfaces, the turning of the pieces and the emptying into the discharge chute of the ready to serve cooked food, takes place automatically.

MIXERS

Heavy duty, bench, or floor model. Sizes available and most commonly used are 20 quart, 30 quart, and 60 quart models with extra bowls as specified. The size should be in keeping with the capacity of related equipment. Large mixers should be purchased with bowl dollies, adapters, and, if possible, with an electric bowl raiser and timer. Other desirable attachments to include are an oil dropper, bowl splash cover extension rim, pouring chutes, vegetable slicer with grater or shredder plates, dicer, meat and food chopper, beater, whip, and dough hook.

Important selection points are ease of cleaning and sanitary use, satisfactory performance, desirability, compactness of space requirements, appearance, and ease of operation and maintenance. Sealed-in motor advisable. Large mixers should be fastened to the floor. Mobility is frequently desirable for small mixers.

Recommend approval by NSF and UL.

A mixer with dial timer: high quality mixers have been known to give as many as 40 years of service. *Courtesy of Hobart Corp.*

OVENS

Standard heavy duty ovens are engineered for use with 18 by 26 inch pans. Pie, cake, bread, muffin, and similar pans should be of sizes to fit in multiples within the 18 by 26 inch dimension.

Restaurant range-type ovens are generally intended for use with a 20 by 21 inch pan size base. Ovens that don't list capacities on that base, or show usable baking area or maximum pan size, should be checked. Oven size is not necessarily the same thing as baking area.

Range and general purpose ovens are of one-pan (18 by 26 inch) capacity.

Deck or peel ovens are of two-pan (side by side) capacity. These ovens are direct fired with items baked on the hearth or with indirect, recirculating heating systems—sized from 1 bun pan to 70 per oven. They may be roasting or baking, with roasting deck 12 to 15 inches high and baking deck 4 to 8 inches high. These ovens are most often made up of 3 or 4 decks. Each deck may be separately heated.

Oven purchasers should look for:

1. Design that permits easy and thorough cleaning. If ceramic material is used, it should be non-absorbent and sufficiently hard so it will escape injury during cleaning.
2. Wiring or manifolds concealed.
3. Easy access to all parts.
4. All-welded construction of structural steel for durable rigid frames.
5. Outside bodies of 16 to 18 gauge metal attached to solid frame support with durable finishes.
6. Inner linings of 18 gauge rustproof sheet metal, reinforced to prevent buckling.

**THE NUMBER OF ROAST PANS WHICH MAY BE PLACED
ON OVEN DECK OR PAN**

Pan Sizes (Inches)	Deck Ovens (Inches)				Heavy Duty Range Ovens (Inches)			Restaurant Range Ovens (Inches)			
	33 by 22	42 by 32	37 by 54	56 by 54	26 by 28	26¼ by 29	24 by 28	24 by 22	26¼ by 22	26 by 22½	23 by 26
17¾ by 25¾	1	2	4	6	1	1	1	0	1	1	1
20⅞ by 17⅜	1	2	4	6	1	1	1	1	1	1	1
21⅝ by 18½	1	2	4	6	1	1	1	1	1	1	1
16 by 20	2	4	5	8	1	1	1	1	1	1	1
18 by 24	1	2	4	6	1	1	1	1	1	1	1
23 by 12⅝	1	3	6	8	2	2	2	1	1	2	2
24 1/16 by 14 1/16	1	3	4	7	1	2	1	1	1	1	1
21 13/16 by 19 13/16	1	2	2	4	1	1	1	1	1	1	1
22⅛ by 20⅛	1	2	2	4	1	1	1	1	1	1	1
19¾ by 10⅞	3	5	7	12	2	2	2	2	2	2	2
20 by 11⅛	2	5	7	11	2	2	2	2	2	2	2

Various combinations of pans will in some cases increase capacity of a deck. Shelves in range and deck ovens increase capacity if of sufficient height. Dimensions for pans are maximum overall dimensions.

7. Fronts all one-piece construction.
8. At least 4 inches of nonsagging, rodent proof, spun fiber glass or other equally efficient insulation on all sides.
9. Walls surrounding insulation tightly sealed to prevent entrance of moisture.
10. Devices around doors to minimize heat loss. Handles that stay cool to the touch.
11. Sturdy doors, preferably containing windows so contents can be viewed without opening door.
12. Doors that can easily hold 150 pounds in weight, counter-balanced for easy opening and closing and to prevent slamming. Hinges of the heavy duty type.
13. Doors that open level with bottom of oven or deck.
14. Durable heating units made of warp proof alloys.
15. Thermostatic control precise between 150° and 550°F.
16. Signal lights to indicate when oven is on, timers, and outside indicating thermometers.
17. Chambers vented, dampered, and with battling required to direct the heat.
18. System to conduct vapor out, preventing its flow back as condensate.
19. Controls in front, easily accessible to workers.

20. Where necessary, decks valved individually for steam delivered in even distribution. Traps and drains to prevent water from being blown into oven.
21. Capacity to heat to 450°F in 20 minutes plus good recovery ability and equally good cooling ability.
22. Height of top and bottom decks suitable for comfortable loading and unloading.

Revolving Ovens

Revolving tray ovens, a prime factor in cost control wherever they are used, are characterized by their use of flat trays suspended between two revolving spiders and rotating in an arrangement similar to a ferris wheel or merry-go-round. This entire assembly is housed inside a chamber that is usually porcelain or stainless. The food is loaded on the trays as they appear opposite the door opening. Provision is made to prevent the escape of a blast of hot air when the door is opened for loading and unloading.

Unique characteristics of this oven are:

1. Increased capacity for baking and roasting.
2. Several basic menu items can be cooked simultaneously in one piece of equipment.
3. Oven construction includes vent systems which assure needed moisture retention in completed products.
4. Menu variety can be extended through introduction of casseroles, easily turned out in this equipment.
5. Revolving tray ovens offer a working surface at normal working heights when pans are properly racked for loading and unloading. A bakery cart used to unload items of all kinds from the revolving tray oven markedly reduces the lifting required.
6. Fuel use decreases as oven load decreases so minimum load is economically feasible.

ROTATING OVEN CAPACITY

No. Trays	Tray Size	2½ lb. Chickens	25-lb. Ribs or 25-lb. Turkeys	15-in. Pizza Per Hr.	9 in. Cakes 9 in. Pies	18-by 26-in. Bun Pans
4	30 by 18	80	8	80	24	4
4	60 by 18	160	16	160	48	8
4	60 by 26	240	24	280	72	12
5	60 by 23	300	30	350	75	10
4	96 by 26	400	40	440	112	20
5	96 by 23	460	50	550	130	15

The above capacities are approx. per oven load. Capacities for 8- and 12-inch pizzas are proportionately larger.

Factors to check out when purchasing revolving ovens include:

1. Sound construction.
2. Trays perfectly stabilized with adequate facilities for leveling; trays should be firm, sway proof, tip proof at all stages of revolution.
3. Maximum of automatic controls.
4. Tray constructed to carry load.
5. Tray position indicator.
6. Adequate motor.
7. Temperature of exterior.
8. Right kind of insulation.
9. Cleaning ease; access door and easily removed parts.
10. Most oven capacity of least space.
11. Exterior finish.
12. Opening properly located, easy to operate.
13. Maximum flexibility in heat-up, cool-down time.
14. Emergency hand-drive for quick unloading in case of power failure.
15. Automatic and instantaneous motor shut-off, alarm bell, and momentary push button release or equivalent controls to prevent damage to oven caused by careless loading of trays.
16. Fuel capacity sufficient to bring oven temperature from normal room temperature to baking or roasting temperature speedily—in indirect-fired units, a temperature increase of about 5 or 6 degrees per minute; in semi-direct or direct-fired units, about 8 to 10 degrees per minute.

Convection Ovens

There are four types of convection ovens.

1. Convection ovens where forced air circulation within the oven is accomplished by means of a motor-driven fan. The rapid air circulation insures even temperature distribution to all parts of the oven and fast heat transfer to the food products.

Some models are practically airtight. Therefore, during roasting, when a pan of water is placed in the oven, moisture is drawn off the pan and the air inside the oven becomes saturated. Thus, with 100 percent humidity in the air, very little moisture is drawn from the food.

2. Thermionic ovens are highly efficient electric directional bake or roast ovens with power blower and duct system that provides for low velocity, high volume air movement.

3. Muffle ovens are a combination of a standard oven and a forced convection oven designed to perform with the speed and efficiency of forced air convection or operate as a standard oven; oven preheats quietly without fan; with a flick of a switch, it becomes a convection oven.

The roll-in convection ovens reduces travel time. *Courtesy of Crown-X, Inc.*

These ovens are available in three basic compartment heights: 7¼ inch, 12¼ inch, and 16¼ inch. Ovens are sectional type; sections are 60 inches wide by 36 inches deep and are designed for stacking in any combination of heights. Forced air convection sections may be added to existing ovens to a maximum of three sections in height.

In models which are indirectly heated, the oven chamber is sealed when both oven door and damper are closed. The moisture retained in the sealed oven chamber provides an ideal roasting climate and is an ideal baking climate for all except a few baked items.

4. The single roll-in rack convection oven, with heating element and fan housed outside the cooking area. Baffles placed on two sides of oven increase air movement created by the fan. Controlled air movement directed from two sides of the oven is designed to equalize velocity of hot air. Especially designed graduated openings in baffles on two sides of oven (with smallest openings closest to source of heat) are responsible for even distribution of heat.

Dual temperature controls permit two different types of food to be cooked at the same time at two different temperatures. Steam injection controls oven moisture content, speeds heat-up of frozen foods. Steam may also be used to clean the oven when the cooking process is completed.

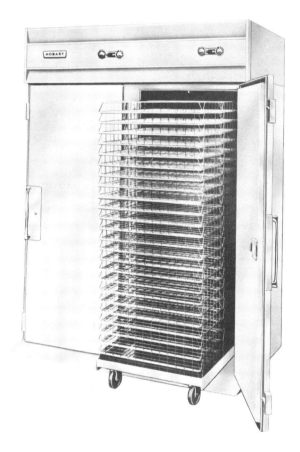

From the roll-in convection cabinet to the roll-in heated cabinet, not a pan need be touched. *Courtesy of Cres-Cor.*

Taking the following preliminary steps will assure the selection of the convection oven that will perform best in your operation:

1. Estimating amount of space available for oven.
2. Careful analysis of production requirements set by the menu so oven capacity will match needs.
3. Investigation of all equipment available to do job.
4. Ordering equipment of proper fuel requirements (gas type or voltage.)
5. Correct installation of equipment and thorough understanding of its operation by all personnel scheduled to use it.

Microwave Ovens

Models of microwave ovens vary to fill the requirements outlined on the preceding pages. These are:

1. Single cavity microwave oven—on counter, at waitress stations, in kitchen near food supply; small portable units also available for poolside or similar locations or

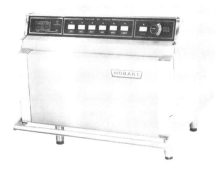

The microwave oven with dial timer provides extremely fast cooking. *Courtesy of Hobart Corp.*

for truck operation using portable generator for power. Can deliver from 650 to 1300 watts depending on model.

2. High wattage output, usually 2-magnetron oven for reconstituting bulk items for steam table supply, heavy-duty defrosting, multiplate and multi-container supply and increased production at point of service.

To insure successful experience with a microwave installation, foodservice operations should look for these qualities in microwave ovens:

1. Easy access to filter.
2. Separate power circuit.
3. Regulated supply of power.
4. Ease of maintenance.
5. Timer system with choice of controls, dial or pushbutton.
6. Provisions for cooling.
7. Easy-set timer.
8. Safety provisions.
9. Signal system.

RANGES

Ranges come in two basic styles: "heavy duty" and "restauraunt" or "cafe."

Heavy duty ranges designed to meet heavy production requirements may have solid hot top, a set of open top burners, or a solid griddle. Underneath this top there is usually an oven although there may be only a skeleton range having shelves or a storage cabinet.

Restaurant or cafe ranges are suggested for smaller establishments with short order menus or for intermittent use in diet kitchens, churches, etc. They are not built to stand up to continuing heavy production requirements.

Guidelines for selecting a range include:

1. Production capacity.
2. Reliable temperature controls.
3. Warp-free tops.
4. Ease of dismantling and assembling.

5. Coved corners.
6. Flat top easily kept clean.
7. Accessibility of moving parts for minor repairs without disturbing line up or battery of ranges.
8. Environmental comfort.

A super heavy duty range has recently been developed to combine efficient, fast cooking, and easy maintenance plus environmental temperatures with production capacity to meet the stiffest demands for food production.

Range sections vary from 39 to 37 inches in width and from 34 to 42 inches in depth. Extensions, commonly half as wide as a range section, may be installed either between two sections or at either side of the range section for extra hot top, open top or fry top space.

SLICERS

Complete with attachments, electric, table, or pedestal type available. Gravity or mechanical feed; safety device; stainless steel, aluminum, or chip-proof porcelain enamel finish. Small size approximately 6 inch cutting capacity. Large size approximately 9 inch cutting capacity. The vertical blade type is less desirable for slicing foods that crumble or fold as they are sliced. The angle blade type is preferred. The diameter of the knives vary 10 to 11⅞ inches. The diameter of the knife limits the size or diameter of the material slices to approximately one-half of its diameter. Knives should be of high quality steel, taking a keen edge, and holding it. The slicer should be equipped with sharpening stones that are easy to use on the machine. Knives should be well guarded. Select a model easy to take apart for thorough cleaning. Some slicers have self-contained portion seals to weigh portions as they are sliced and others have counters that count the portions as they are sliced.

Recommend approval by NSF and UL.

The non-automated food slicer is a standard piece of equipment. *Courtesy of Hobart Corp.*

STEAM KETTLES

A steam-jacketed kettle is described as two stainless steel hemispheres or bowls, one sealed inside the other with about 2 inches of space in between for the steam.

Steam is made up of tiny molecules of water vapor which are very hot. When the steam comes into the jacket, the molecules touch the inside bowl and condense, or turn back into water. When this happens, the great heat of the molecule goes into the metal and is transferred into whatever is being cooked. The water dips down inside and runs off through the outlet valve, sometimes called the condensate line.

To get a specific temperature, the steam inlet valve is opened—all the way to bring quantities of water to a boil quickly—or only partly for simmering.

Steam-jacketed kettles differ from model to model in depth of kettle; steam-jacketing (either full or ⅔ jacketed); mounting-pedestal, legs, or wall; whether tilting or stationary, method of steam supply, whether direct connected or self-generating; and aluminum or stainless steel.

TYPES OF STEAM-JACKETED KETTLES

Capacity	Jacket Height		Mounting		
1 qt.	½	TT			
4 qt.	½	TT			
5 qt.	½	TT			
6 qt.	½	TT			
8 qt.	½	TT			
10 qt.	½	TT		T	
20 qt.	½	TT		T	
10 gal.	⅔	F		T	
20 gal.	⅔ FULL	F	W	T	TW
25 gal.	FULL	F			
30 gal.	⅔ FULL	F		T	
40 gal.	⅔ FULL	F	W	T	TW
50 gal.	FULL	F		T	
60 gal.	⅔ FULL	F	W	T	TW
80 gal.	⅔ FULL	F	W	T	TW
100 gal.	⅔ FULL	F	W		TW
125 gal.	⅔ FULL	F			
150 gal.	⅔ FULL	F			
200 gal.	⅔	F			

F = Floor Mounted
W = Wall Mounted
T = Tilting
TW = Tilting Wall Mounted
TT = Tilting Table Mounted

Self-contained gas or electric steam generator or direct connection to steam line. Use direct steam connection only if 15 pounds per square inch minimum pressure is available during the entire school year. Where used provide pressure-reducing valve. Meter device for measuring water or internal measuring mark.

Installation: Kettles set for easy draw-off of food and drip into grated drain in floor or table; height convenient for workers.

Types include:

1. Deep kettles, fully or ⅔ jacketed—best for soups, puddings, pie fillings.
2. Shallow kettles, always full jacketed—suitable for braising and browning meats, stews. Prevents crushing of under layers of food as in deep type.
3. Trunion or tilting kettles mounted on trunions with tilting device and pouring lip for easy unloading; either power-driven or manual mechanism; self-locking devices to secure kettle in any position.

Recommend approval by NSF and either UL or AGA.

The size of available kettles ranges from the 10 to 20 quart table model to the 20 to 200 gallon floor or wall models. The capacity needed in a specific kitchen depends on the kinds of foods to be cooked, the volume, and the speed of turnover.

Selection of kettle size must also be guided by the ability of workers to handle food in masses required to fill kettles of the sizes being considered. Mechanical mixers now available with some kettles increase the amount of food which can be easily handled.

One suggested rule of thumb for estimating size of kettles needed allows about 8 pounds of meat or vegetables or about 4 pounds of poultry for each gallon of kettle capacity. These figures take shrinkage into account and leave a reasonable level below the brim of the kettle.

SCALES FOR SYSTEMS CONTROL

Essential considerations in scale selection include:

1. Accuracy.
2. Speed and ease in using.
3. Easy reading.
4. Durability.
5. Compactness.
6. Attractive and easy-to-clean design and finish.
7. Decisions as to whether large number of small scales strategically placed will increase efficiency.
8. Springs of sturdy construction.
9. Space required by scale.
10. Dial position.

11. Protection for pendulum mechanism when scale is not in use.
12. Need for portability.
13. Clean definition for figures and graduations.

Some special points to keep in mind when deciding on scales:

1. Time required for adjustment of beams and counterweights.
2. Relation of scales to mixer equipment (i.e., kitchens using 60 to 80 quart mixers should have a formula scale that will weigh quickly and accurately from ½ ounce to 50 pounds).
3. Where floors are uneven, adjustments needed for stability; one floor-type dial scale has wheels that counteract unevenness.

Types of scales found in food service operations range from:

1. Floor scales.
2. Suspended platform scales.
3. Overhead track scales.
4. Built-ins.
5. Portion scales.
6. Count or table scales.
7. Dough or bakers' scales.
8. Balancing scales.
9. Portion and bench scales, standing and heavy duty.
10. Scales capacity ranges from 50 to 6000 pounds in one line, with other manufacturers listing 5 to 10 pound portion scales as well as $\frac{1}{10}$ plus or minus $\frac{1}{1000}$ pound for spices.
11. Space requirements and capacities of several scales will help in making estimates of areas needed for scale placement.

Portion Scale: capacity 32 ounces by ¼ ounce; diameter 6½ by 9¼ inches high; platform 5½ inches square.
Some of the developments which assure quick and accurate scale reading.:

1. Scale dials that may be installed in any one of eight positions.
2. Balance indicator.
3. Use of china marking pencil to mark dial for predetermined portion weight; place plate on platform, rotate dial to zero, then uniform servings can be weighed to exact requirements.
4. Adjustable rotating dial that allows the weighing of each ingredient of a batch to start at zero thus eliminating the errors that are possible when separate calculations are required.
5. Reading chart magnified and optically projected on mirror set behind protective glass shield. Figures and graduations appear bright and bold even in brightly lighted room.

Bench Type Counter Scale:

Capacity lb. & oz.	Platform Dimensions
30 by 1	10 ½ by 13 ½ in.
50 by 2	10 ½ by 13 ½
100 by 8	10 ½ by 13 ½

Platform Scale—36 inches high:

Capacity lb. & oz.	Platform Dimensions
60 by 2	10 ½ by 14 ½ in.
100 by 1 lb.	10 ½ by 14 ½
100 by 2	10 ½ by 14 ½
200 by 4	10 ½ by 14 ½
300 by 1 lb.	10 ½ by 14 ½
50 by 1	13 by 19
100 by 2	13 by 19
200 by 4	13 by 19
300 by 1 lb.	13 by 19

Bakers Dough Scales:

Capacity	Beam	Size
8 lb.	1 lb. × ¼ oz.	10 × 19
8 lb.	1 × ¼	12 × 22
16 lb.	2 × ¼	12 × 22

STEAM COOKERS

There are two types of steam cooker most commonly specified. The large compartment steam cooker steams at a pressure of 5 pounds, 225°F; has six 2½ inch or four 4 inch pans; is made in semi-automatic and fully automatic styles. It can be used for cooking vegetables, meats, poultry, fish, cereal products, eggs, fruit and starch products.

The high-pressure steam cooker, a smaller unit, cooks more quickly than the 5 pound pressure steam cooker. It cooks at 250°F (15 psi). It is used for frequent cycling of food, for blanching, and for reheating previously prepared food. These cookers may hold three 12 by 20 by 2½ inch pans or two 12 by 20 by 4 inch pans.

One of these speed cookers has a perforated plate designed to send steam jets onto frozen food to defrost it and heat it quickly. Longer heating for other food items is also possible since this unit is cycled for pressure.

The importance of good construction underlies this purchasing check list:

1. Heavy duty gaskets.
2. Adequate safety devices.
3. Accurate pressure gauges.

High pressure steamers let food retain more vitamins and reduce cooking time by 50 percent or more from that needed by conventional steamer. *Courtesy of Hobart Corp.*

4. Compartments fabricated to form one piece body and entire interior of stainless steel.
5. Shelves removable without use of tools.

Some models also offer automatic controls such as timers mounted in door arms for each compartment. In these models, when food in the compartment is done, a bell rings to notify the user. In other models, steam automatically shuts off and all steam and condensate is exhausted from the compartment when cooking cycle is completed.

CONVEYOR TOASTERS

For heavy and continuous toast production, conveyor models utilizing either gas or electricity are available.

In one conveyor model, the bread or buns to be toasted go into toasting baskets at the loading position, next are carried up through a pretoasting chamber, then down through the toasting chamber where degree of color can be thermostatically controlled. When toast is crisped to desired standard, basket containing it turns over to drop toast automatically into tray for piping hot service.

REFRIGERATORS

Reach-In. Institutional type; minimum size 25 cubic foot aluminum, stainless steel, or procelain enamel interiors and exteriors; vermin-proof insulation; hinged or sliding doors with rotproof gaskets and plated or stainless steel hardware. Interior fitted with door-operated electric lights, adjustable plated wire shelves or non-corrodible slides for

The reach-in refrigerator is a fundamental piece of foodservice equipment. *Courtesy of Hobart Corp.*

The prefabricated walk-in refrigerator saves expensive remodeling costs by providing built-in insulation and inexpensive installation. *Courtesy of Hobart Corp.*

trays. Blower type cooling unit connected to self-contained or remote refrigeration equipment. Optional features: doors on both sides for pass-through; locking hardware. Approximately ¼ to ⅓ cubic foot per meal served. Consider reach-in-walk-in combination when total capacity exceeds 60 cubic feet. Consider pass-through type between kitchen and serving areas for approximately 30–40 cubic foot and 40–60 cubic foot capacities.

Recommend approval by NSF and either UL or AGA.

Walk-In. Sectional commercial type or built-in as part of building contract. May be several separate rooms with varying temperature and humidity conditions. Vermin-proof insulation on walls, floor, ceiling; interior stainless steel or glazed tile preferable; Portland cement plaster acceptable. Doors on heavy hinges with compression-type gaskets; door latches with integral keyed lock and interior safety latch, which can be opened from inside. Half-height reach-in doors also available; arrange for opening into kitchen area. Interior shelving, wood, or metal, portable type desirable. Blower-type refrigeration coils connected to remote refrigeration equipment. Service and maintenance features important as part of purchase contract.

Frozen Food Storage Cabinet.   Commercial; upright type is preferable; 1 fixed freezing shelf; other shelves adjustable and/or removable for maximum storage.

Size depends on local needs such as location of school, food purchasing practices, frequency of delivery, use of central storage, etc. One cubic foot stores approximately 30 to 35 pounds.

Refrigerator Thermometers.   Refrigerator-freezer. Remote reading type or one designed to hook on shelf or partition; temperature range of at least minus 40° to plus 60°F in 2°-scale divisions; red-liquid-filled magnifying-glass tube for easy reading; rust-proof scale and frame; scale encased. One for each reach-in refrigerator and frozen food cabinet.

For large-quantity service, the roll-in refrigerator rack and banquet serving unit are especially useful. *Courtesy of Cres-Cor.*

This hospital/nursing home tray assembly line shows powerized conveyor, hot and cold stations and transportation equipment. *Courtesy of Crimsco, Inc.*

Single-pen Recording. Designed to record temperatures continuously 7-day revolution chart graduated from at least minus 40° to plus 70°F. In low-scale divisions; mercury-actuated thermal system with temperature-compensated smooth capillary; rectangular aluminum dust-proof case; lock in door to prevent tampering. One for each walk-in refrigerator.

CRYOGENIC FREEZING[3]

The word cryogenics comes from the Greek cryo (kyros), meaning ''very cold,'' and genic (genes) meaning ''to become to produce.'' It is appropriate that cryogenics, ''to become or produce very cold'' refers to the coldest area in nature—and the lower limits

---

[3]Cres-Cor Bulletin CX–272–R.

of absolute zero (−460°F). The freezing process using a liquid gas, as a direct contact refrigerant, is referred to as cryogenic freezing.

Freezing foods with liquid nitrogen grew out of the U.S. Government Space Program Research. It was soon recognized by the scientists and engineers that the most efficient use of liquid nitrogen, as a direct contact refrigerant, was in a totally isolated cryogenic environment.

In recent years, the liquid nitrogen and carbon dioxide food freezing process has grown from a relatively unknown method of freezing to a widely accepted procedure in the food processing industry, and in foodservice. Today, over 1,000 items are frozen commercially using the cryogenic freezing process.

The incredible speed of the cryogenic freezing process is a result of the extremely low temperature (−320°F, −196°C for liquid nitrogen LN_2) (−110°F, −79°C for liquid carbon dioxide LCO_2). Because of this high-speed freezing, the produce experiences none of the deterioration that is normally associated with the mechanical chilling and freezing process.

Principal of Operation

The food produce to be processed (chilled, chilled and frozen, frozen, and sub-cooled) is portioned or panned, and loaded onto the shelves of the Crown-X Mobile Chil-Frez Rack. The mobile rack is positioned in the Super Chil-Frez Cryogenic Cabinet. Liquid nitrogen (LN_2) or liquid carbon dioxide (LCO_2) flows from the outside storage tank through the cabinet temperature controlled solenoid valve to two liquid gas injection

The waste pulper reduces garbage to 20 percent of its original volume.
Courtesy of Hobart Corp.

HOW CAN THE CROWN-X SUPER CHIL-FREZ FIT INTO YOUR SYSTEM?

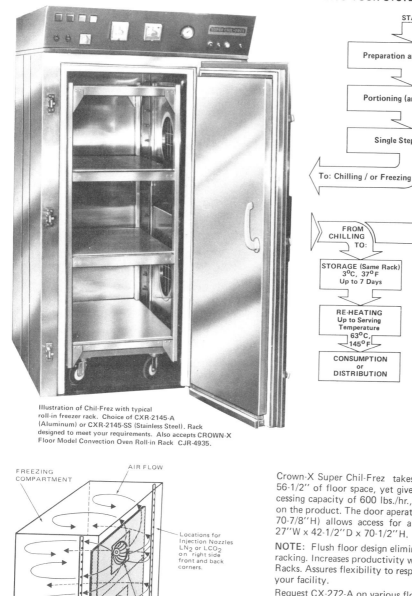

Illustration of Chil-Frez with typical roll-in freezer rack. Choice of CXR-2145-A (Aluminum) or CXR-2145-SS (Stainless Steel). Rack designed to meet your requirements. Also accepts CROWN-X Floor Model Convection Oven Roll-in Rack CJR-4935.

START

Preparation and production

Portioning (and packaging)

Single Step Loading

To: Chilling / or Freezing

FROM CHILLING TO:	FROM FREEZING TO:
STORAGE (Same Rack) $3^{o}C$, $37^{o}F$ Up to 7 Days	STORAGE (Same Rack) $-18^{o}C$, $0^{o}F$ For Several Months
RE-HEATING Up to Serving Temperature $63^{o}C$, $145^{o}F$	TEMPERING $3^{o}C$, $37^{o}F$
CONSUMPTION or DISTRIBUTION	RE-HEATING Up to Serving Temperature $63^{o}C$, $145^{o}F$
	CONSUMPTION or DISTRIBUTION

FREEZING COMPARTMENT

AIR FLOW

Locations for Injection Nozzles LN_2 or LCO_2 on right side front and back corners.

Two Shockproof PVC CIRCULATING FANS. Belt driven by 3 Hp. Motor, 1200 RPM, 220-240 or 440-480 Volts, 3 phase. Motor is mounted on top of the cabinet.

Crown-X Super Chil-Frez takes up only 47-1/4'' x 56-1/2'' of floor space, yet gives outstanding processing capacity of 600 lbs./hr., or more depending on the product. The door aperature of (27-1/2''W x 70-7/8''H) allows access for a rack measuring 27''W x 42-1/2''D x 70-1/2''H.

NOTE: Flush floor design eliminates racking and unracking. Increases productivity with the use of Mobile Racks. Assures flexibility to respond to the needs of your facility.

Request CX-272-A on various floor mounting arrangements and general installation instructions.

CX-SCF-2145-N (Liquid Nitrogen) Standard Model with Single Door -320° F, -196° C.
CX-SCF-2145-D (Carbon Dioxide) Model with Single Door -110° F, -79° C.

FastRack
Warewashing Systems

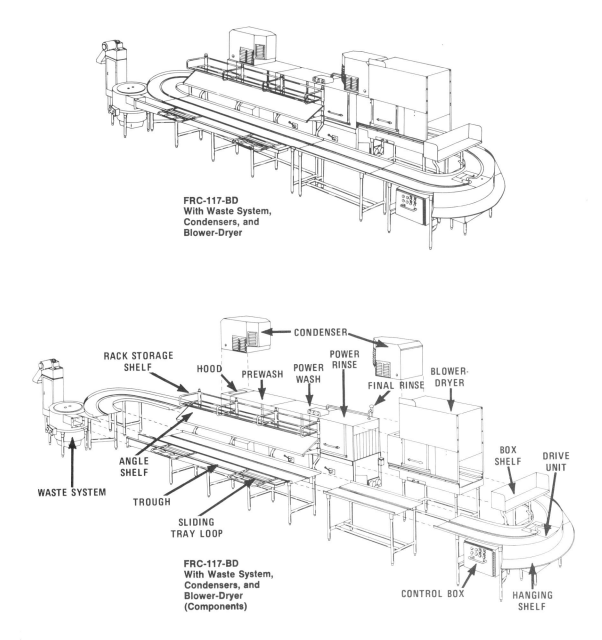

FRC-117-BD
With Waste System,
Condensers, and
Blower-Dryer

FRC-117-BD
With Waste System,
Condensers, and
Blower-Dryer
(Components)

Courtesy: Hobart Corp.

manifolds. The injection manifolds equipped with sufficient and suitably sized nozzles are vertically mounted down both front and back corners on one side wall where the fans also are located. They are positioned in such a way as to feed refrigerant in the direction of the stream of gas being circulated by the fans. A temperature controller actuates an electric solenoid valve which controls the flow of liquid refrigerant from the supply source to the injection manifolds and nozzles.

The constant circulation of the vaporized refrigerant improves the uniformity of thermal refrigerating transfer between the food product and the refrigerant.

Slight over pressure in the Cryogenic Cabinet, created by the expanding refrigerant gas, is vented through a vent port located in the top of the cabinet.

ELECTRONIC EQUIPMENT[4]

The development of low-cost computer electronics—in some cases so small they have virtually disappeared into the machines they run—has spawned a rapidly growing field of restaurant business controls.

Over two dozen manufacturers offer a wide spectrum of devices to replace mechanical cash registers. The equipment they offer ranges from low cost stand-alone registers that are the size of a small typewriter (and which, say ECR suppliers, do more, yet cost less than mechanicals) to huge master-to-satellite computer networks spanning the whole nation. And there are a variety of designs in between.

Tighter control over meals served and cash collected, elimination of waiter/cashier arithmetic errors, speed-up of the order-taking process, and reduction in inventory shrinkage are among the major reasons why more and more chain operators, as well as independent restaurateurs, are turning to electronic control systems at their point of sale and service.

Electronic point-of-sale devices fall into two broad categories: stand-alone electronic cash registers and master-to-satellite data terminal systems. Within this latter category, the master control unit can either be an off-the-counter minicomputer or it can be a microprocessor built into the cabinet of the countertop register. (It should be noted that while some stand-alone manufacturers prefer to refer to themselves as electronic cash register (ECR) suppliers and some master-to-satellite vendors consider themselves electronic point-of-sale (EPOS) suppliers, in fact electronic cash registers are point-of-sale devices.)

Advances in technology in recent years have to some extent blurred the distinctions between standard-alones and master-to-satellite systems. Advanced stand-alone registers can be hard-wired together to allow a store manager to automatically consolidate sales and management reports of individual registers. With early stand-alone designs such reports had to be consolidated manually, or stored on a tape and run through a computer. By the same token, advanced master-to-satellite systems have incorporated microprocessors into the "slave" terminals, thus giving them a great deal of "stand-alone" capacity from the master control unit.

---

[4]"Cashing in on Electronic Controls—Part 2: Electronic Cash Registers for Point–of–Sale Control," *Restaurant Business* (Bill Communications, Inc., 1978), pp. 92–96.

The proliferation of price levels and processing powers of electronic cash registers offers important profit and benefit potentials for the restaurant operator. But it also makes a final equipment choice from the ocean of alternatives difficult. To a great extent, the old adage, "You get what you pay for," holds true for today's ECR and EPOS market. The type of cost controls (food, liquor, labor) and management reports (menu item sales mix, inventory depletion, waitress productivity, etc.) a restaurant operator wants will dictate the price of the electronic control system he needs.

One of the simplest ways to examine the benefits currently available, and to estimate future developments, is to follow hypothetical customer activity as it flows through a foodservice establishment and interacts with electronic controls.

The area of restaurant/customer interaction that generally comes first, whether it's fast food, fine food, cafeteria, or coffee shop, is order entry. The extended, preset keyboards of both stand-alones and master-to-satellite systems are ideally suited to the fast-moving, limited inventory situation of fast food and specialty restaurants.

Although up to 200 keys are offered, much over 100 becomes counterproductive as the operator's search for the correct key in a large field will slow entry. Many preset keyboards feature an alternate menu operation which, when actuated, can electronically change the whole system to a second set of prices and accumulating totals. Thus, a terminal, or even stand-alone register, can track the contents of two complete menus (with split-coded key tops or a keyboard overlay) or two price rates on one menu.

Future developments in this area may well include scanners reading premarked food wraps similar to the UPC (universal product code) system and OCR (optical code reader) wanding currently being initiated in the supermarket and general merchandise retailing industries. One manufacturer has under development a stand-alone scanning ECR, so this capability may not necessarily be limited to master-to-satellite computer-based systems.

Other restaurant types with more extensive food selection also use presets in combination with a price look-up (PLU) file for numbered entrees or complete dinners. Sophisticated system-type form readers will also automatically enter the contents of a preprinted form marked by the waiter.

In addition to pure merchandise information, the electronic terminal will often accept a numeric sign-on or coded key to identify a particular employee with each transaction. Check tracking capabilities also assign an ID number to each customer tab so that with a previous balance/balance forward key it can be added to, credited, or recalled later.

Once the information has been introduced into the system, it is processed and transferred. With stand-alone registers, the order is normally handled manually, via guest check or receipt slip printed by the ECR. Stand-alones in the $1,500 to $2,500 range have the power to drive a remote slip printer for this purpose with four characters of alpha-numeric information. Also, codes can often be printed on the receipt tape to specify condiments, sizes, or extras.

More extensive receipt generation is available at the higher end of the market, including remotely driven kitchen printers and CRT displays with full itemization for preparation of the food.

Direct transmission of the order is possible with communicating stand-alone ECRs and master-to-satellite control systems. In this way, for example, an order rung into a precheck register can be balance forwarded to a cashier station. Or, a drink purchased at a bar location can be added, electronically, to the final bill. With equipment of this type, the guest check merely serves as a deluxe customer receipt as the table, waiter, and totals are all identified electronically.

At the cashier point, all entries are automatically totalled and taxed, by either electronic collection or ring-in from the guest check. Advanced stand-alone, alternate tax (useful when eat-in and take-out meals have differing tax status), auto discount, and check endorsement/validation are common features. Most equipment can interface to coin and beverage dispensers for control in these areas, also.

Future developments in this area, particularly for communicating terminals may well include credit card, and even check number scanners for instantaneous credit authorization. With an EFT (electronic funds transfer) system in operation, accounts could be paid automatically. An interesting sidelight is that one current stand-alone design incorporates a self-contained negative credit file for up to 4,080 bad check or account numbers. It will halt operation if an existing bad number is entered.

Other cashier capabilities available at virtually all cost levels are extra customer display, tracking of payments by media (i.e., cash, check, charge, credit cards, etc.), totals for two separate cashiers or more, and optional two-drawer operation.

For a manager with a communicating stand-alone ECR system, it is simply a matter of stepping up to a register and requesting a consolidated report. The electronics will then collect and total reports in each category from all registers on the system. With expanded keyboards or PLU files, the sales will be broken down by individual menu items.

In a master-to-satellite system, a special manager terminal usually allows the polling for information already stored at the central processor or in each terminal's microprocessor. In addition to sales movement by menu item, menu explosion power will break this down even more to individual ingredients.

Both master-to-satellite systems and some high-power stand-alone equipment provide productivity information, such as sales per hour, thanks to an internal "real time" clock. And, with controls that offer a check tracking feature, a nightly report of all customer tabs will indicate if any remain unpaid—with the corresponding number of the waiter responsible. This feature goes a long way to eliminating walk-outs.

Among the key concerns to keep in mind is that cash control is not merely a tool for today, but an investment in the future of electronics. Locations that foresee expansion should, therefore, consider master-to-satellite systems or stand-alone equipment that can be upgraded and expanded as their needs—and the existing technology—progress, without overbuying for the present.

Day-in day-out reliability may not have the mystique of powerful electronic features but it is equally important. Find out what the Mean Time Between Failure is of the equipment you are considering.

Warranty and maintenance provisions should also be carefully examined. For example, a 90-day warranty is considered the industry standard, but parts and labor guarantees of up to one year are offered by some suppliers. Check also whether the maintenance figures quoted are for hours that coincide with your operation—beyond 9 to 5 is usually extra.

FUNCTION-ROOM FURNITURE

Function-room furniture is the term for equipment used in rooms where public functions are held. Function-room furniture is essential equipment for hotels, motels, clubs, restaurants, and those institutions that host to business functions, social affairs, recreational gatherings, or community events.[5]

General Features

1. Strength and durability. Watch for the weakest link such as mechanical folding devices that are easily broken, or strong components which may depend on a weak hinge or spring. Safety of guests is a foremost consideration. Simple and effective folding devices minimize the possibility of failure by complicated locking devices and human error. Frequency of use means frequency of cleaning. Parts that rest on the floor must be made to withstand and facilitate frequent scrubbings, waxings, and vacuuming.

2. Ease of handling. Folding or knock-down equipment should be simple to set up. Equipment that is light in weight may not be the most durable. There are a variety of carriers such as dollies and trucks which are designed to aid in handling.

3. Ease of storage. Equipment should be able to be stacked so that one piece does not mar the next, and in a manner which prevents vulnerable parts from protruding. In choosing dollies or trucks, check to see that they are designed to handle the particular piece of equipment in your particular setting.

4. Flexibility. It may be advisable to buy a piece of function-room furniture which serves two or more purposes in order to avoid extra handling or storage. Examples include a knockdown cabaret table that allows for different-sized tops to be used interchangeably with the same column and base, enabling it to fill many different needs; one dual height folding platform serves two different levels, many different purposes, can save up to 50 percent on initial outlay, and an additional 50 percent on handling costs and storage space.

Folding Tables

Folding tables come with various shaped tops: oblong, round, serpentine, oval, quarter-round, half-round, and trapezoid.

Serpentine tables are shaped like an arc making part of an open circle. When butted in reverse directions, they make an S-shaped set up. Using serpentines only, one can make round, half-round, S-shaped, horse-shoe shaped, and many other graceful buffet or head table set ups. Used together with oblongs, they round off rectangular buffets, make half-round projections, U-shaped arrangements, open ovals, and many other buffet, gift, and head table combinations.

Quarter-round end tables make a rounded corner for two tables placed at right angles. Half-round end tables round out a rectangular end and also serve as a raised center for a half-round buffet.

---

[5]*Guide to Function Room Furniture,* reprinted by permission of King Arthur Incorporated.

Some folding tables, rather simple in shape, have, however, been used effectively for many different purposes over a number of years. Such a table is the schoolroom table. Normally 18 inches wide, it also comes 15 inches wide, so that two can be connected side-by-side to make either a 30 inch or a 36 inch wide banquet table. They are used singly as meeting room tables where persons sit at one side facing the speaker. They are also used singly against a wall for display purposes.

The rules of thumb for estimating seating capacity at tables are:

1. For oblong tables, divide the room area (sq. ft.) by 8.
2. For round tables, divide the room area (sq. ft.) by 10.

This figure allows for chair room and aisle service. It does not allow for problems caused by location of columns, service doors, and unique room shapes. It is useful for a quick, general approximation.

QUESTIONS

1. Briefly explain eight of the rules for writing foodservice equipment specifications.
2. What does return on investment really mean to the operator when considering purchasing some equipment?
3. How is the consumption factor for fuel oil determined?
4. Discuss some reasons for excessive fuel use of equipment and ways to reduce usage.
5. Compare single phase and three phase electrical systems.
6. List five points to consider when purchasing a broiler.
7. What is the difference between a griddle and a grill?
8. What are the advantages of a convection oven over a rotating oven?
9. Describe the mechanism for heating in a steam-jacketed kettle.
10. Write a specification for a scale to be used for weighing in meat.
11. What are the advantages an electronic cash register can provide to a foodservice operator?

14

TABLEWARE AND TEXTILES

INTRODUCTION

Proper selection of linens, carpeting, and tableware are discussed in this chapter. As with food, important considerations are quality and cost. However, another fact in selection of these materials is that of durability.

Durability in linens is measured by the length of time a particular item is in use. The type of weave, construction of the fabric, use, and weight are factors affecting durability.

Man-made fibers are discussed in detail in this chapter. Since the amount of cotton grown in the United States is controlled, man has been forced to develop fibers to support domestic and commercial necessities. Some of these fibers include rayon, nylon, polyester, triacetate, and alefin. The advantages of these fibers to cotton generally are explained by their absorbancy, abrasion resistance, resilience, strength, and economical factors.

Considerations are given to both appearance and service when choosing carpet quality. Basic factors by which to judge the quality include pile density, pile height, and weight of the yarn. Other factors to consider before making a choice are described in various tables throughout the chapter. The amount of food-traffic a carpet receives is probably the biggest indication affecting its durability. Extra heavy traffic will require a carpet to be as much as 70 to 90 ounces of pile yarn per square yard.

The chapter concludes with a brief discussion of dish, glass, and flatware selection. The process used to make dishes is explained. Note that in addition to the various compositions of china stoneware, pottery, and terra cotta that the vitrification temperatures also vary.

The biggest difference in price of stainless steel flatware comes in the manufacturing process. The grading process produces different thicknesses of stainless steel and a stronger utensil. Good stainless steel will be at least 12 gauge.

LINEN[1]

There is a growing tendency toward laundry managers having a greater voice in the selection of linens. After all, in the final analysis, the laundry manager is held responsible for the normal life expectancy of those articles which pass through his or her laundry. The laundry manager is in a position to furnish actual, not merely theoretical, technical knowledge on the linens most suited for a particular institution.

However, in order that proper recommendations be submitted to the purchasing department, the laundry manager should have a working knowledge of textiles. This does not necessitate being an expert on the matter, but merely understanding the fundamental principles as to what is the proper composition of linens and bedding for institutional use.

In selecting the proper linens, the three most important features to look for are durability, laundry costs, and purchase price. From these three features the true cost of an item can be determined.

The original cost is a minor factor in determining the actual cost of an article during its period of service. The cost per use is obtained by adding the original cost of the article to the total laundry cost during its life expectancy, divided by the life expectancy, or the total number of launderings that might be expected for the item.

Therefore, the following Cost Per Use formula is of invaluable use in determining the difference between operating efficiency and a profit, or incompetency and a loss.

$$\text{Cost Per Use} = \frac{\text{Wt} \times \text{Ldr Cost/lb} \times \text{Life Exp.} + \text{Orig. Cost}}{\text{Life Exp.}}$$

For example, a tablecloth or bedsheet weighing 1.4 lbs. which has a life expectancy of 250 launderings and costs $3.50 when new, is processed in a laundry which figures that their laundry cost is $.10 per pound. Cost Per Use is derived in the following manner:

$$\text{Cost Per Use} = \frac{(1.4)(.10)(250) + 3.50}{250} = \frac{35 + 3.50}{250} = \frac{38.50}{250} = .1542$$

It is quite evident from the above Cost Per Use formula that the original purchase price plays a relatively insignificant part in arriving at the true cost of an item. In the above formula you will note that the institution had invested $35.00 in the laundering of the item during a period of 250 uses. The investment of the original cost of $3.50 is rather insignificant when compared to the investment of $35.00 spent on this item to process it through the laundry 250 times. It is the number of launderings an article can sustain through normal processing which is the most important factor in determining the true cost an item or its Cost Per Use. The finesse in purchasing linen, therefore, is to be able to closely approximate the probable additional uses you might obtain from an item, weighed against its cost to launder and, lastly, its purchase price.

---

[1]The author thanks the National Association of Laundry Managers and the H.B. Baker Linen Co. for permission to use some of their materials in this chapter.

Construction and Types of Weaves

The durability of a fabric is contingent on construction of the material. Construction of a woven piece of textile is the interlacing of yarns woven at right angles to each other. The lengthwise yarns are called the *warp*. The crosswise threads are referred to as *filling* or *weft*. The lengthwise sides or edges of a fabric are called the *selvages*.

There are three types of weaves, but you are confronted with only two basic weaves, namely plain and twill. The plain weave is the common weave method. It is accomplished by alternately interlacing the warp and filling threads, one warp over and one warp under the filling throughout the construction of the fabric. Both muslin and percale, for example, are made from plain weaves. The twill weave forms diagonal lines on the face of the cloth. Each warp yarn does not interlock with each filling yarn. Instead it interlaces with only the second, third, or fourth filling yarn, floating over and

THREE BASIC FABRIC TYPES

woven	*knitted*	*texturized woven*
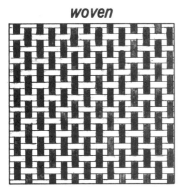	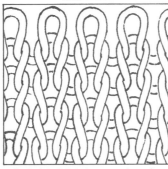	

In woven fabrics, produced on looms, vertical threads called warp yarns and horizontal threads called filling yarns are interlaced at right angles. There are three basic types of woven fabric:

In knitted fabrics, produced on knitting machines, rows of yarn are interlooped in stitches. Vertical stitches are called wales and horizontal stitches are called courses. There are three basic knits:

Two way texturized fabrics woven of 100% Dacron polyester use continuous filament yarns that have been permanently heat set into a coil shape.

Plain weave Twill weave Satin weave

Single knit Double knit Warp knit

Polyester yarn Twisting process Heat-setting

In general, woven fabrics are:
1. tailorable (hold details like creases)
2. durable (high abrasion resistance)
3. crisp and neat (good shape retention)

In general, knitted fabrics are:
1. drapable (fabric folds are soft)
2. wrinkle resistant (good recovery)
3. stretchable (springy, elastic)

In general these luxurious fabrics offer the best qualities of both knitted and woven fabrics:
1. move-with-the-body comfort
2. long lasting washability (also dry cleanable)
3. excellent drape and hand (plus tailorability)

Burlington Industries.

under the remainder. This creates the illusion of a diagonal weave. Twill weaves are frequently used in heavier cloths, sheets, and work cloths.

The number of threads that are interlaced together in a square inch constitute "a thread count." For example, the most commonly used sheet in a hotel or a hospital is approximately 180 threads per square inch. It is made from approximately 94 threads per inch running in the warp (lengthwise direction), and 86 threads per inch in the fill, with a total of 180 threads per square inch. The weight of the average 180 thread count sheet is approximately 3.6 ounces per square yard.

The weight of a fabric is specified in one of two forms: either ounces per square yard or yards per pound. When the weight is specified in yards per pound, it is important that the width of the fabric is defined. Naturally, the wider width fabrics will weigh more per lineal yard than the narrow width fabrics of similar construction.

In addition to thread count and weight of a fabric, it is necessary to be aware of the item's tensil strength, which will give a good indication of its potential durability. The tensil strength is determined in laboratory conditions under controlled temperature and humidity. It is the number of pounds required to break a strip of fabric, or any other piece of textile, one inch in width and three inches long.

Another important guide in predetermining the possible durability of an item is an abrasion test, which measures the degree to which a fabric resists surface wear. Institutional linens, including apparel, are very often subjected to more surface wear than strain. The abrasion test itself determines how many rubs the material will withstand under certain circumstances until the yarn weakens.

Textile Fibers

For many years cotton has long been the staple fiber from which most textiles have been woven. Physically, cotton is stronger when wet, a characteristic which lends itself to the repeated launderings it must have in order to be kept clean. However, it soils easily, has little elasticity, and musses readily. Prolonged boiling has little or no effect on cotton, nor does fairly strong alkaline solutions, particularly those used in commercial launderings processing. Another characteristic of cotton is that dry temperatures of 320°F will cause some deterioration, while at 400°F, care must be exercised to prevent scorching.

Since 1970 there has been a rapid transition from textiles made from fibers which nature provides, such as cotton and wool, to textiles produced from man-made fibers.

There are numerous valid reasons which account for the switch from natural to synthetic fibers. One of the prime reasons is supply, which of course, is directly related to cost. The supply of man-made fibers is limitless compared to cotton, which can be grown only in certain parts of the world, and even then, is dependent upon favorable weather conditions. Also, the amount of cotton grown in the United States is controlled to a great degree by government subsidies. This accounts partially for the fact that it is probable that the cost of cotton will continue to increase. This means the price differential between man-made fibers and cotton will continue to widen.

During the 1970s the cost of cotton soared from $.26 per pound to as high as $1.00 per pound. During 1976 the cost of cotton settled at $.75 to $.80 per pound. Man-made polyester, on the other hand, has declined from $1.25 in 1960 to $.36 per pound in 1971. In 1976 the price of polyester fluctuated between $.55 to $.60 per pound. Cotton is no longer "King," at least not in the United States.

The first man-made fiber commercially produced in the United States was rayon in 1910. Rayon is produced from cellulose, the fiberous substance of all forms of plant life.

The next synthetic fiber of dramatic impact was nylon, produced and commercially manufactured in 1939.

There are nineteen various types of synthetic fibers made from plentiful, low cost, basic raw materials such as coal, air, water, petroleum, limestone, peanuts, and corn. During 1970 and 1971, there was a change, almost overnight, of napery and sheets made from all cotton to those made from blended fibers consisting of 50 percent polyester and 50 percent cotton.

Man-made fibers can be engineered to exhibit special qualities and characteristics for specific end purposes. A fabric may be made from one type of man-made fiber, or may be a blend of fibers, either natural or man made, to provide a variety of characteristics.

Under the Textile Fiber Products Identification Act the Federal Trade Commission has assigned nineteen generic names to the various types of man-made fibers according to the chemical composition of the forming substances:

Acetate	Acrylic
Anidex	Azlon
Glass	Listrile
Metallic	Modacrylic
Nylon	Nytril
Olefin	Polyester
Rayon	Rubber
Saran	Spandex
Triacetate	Vinal
Pinyon	

Acetate, rayon, and triacetate are derived from cellulose, the fiber substance in plant life. The fibers generally are absorbant, easy to dye, luxurious, economical and have a hard luster.

Most other man-made fibers are made by combining all materials, such as nitrogen, oxygen, hydrogen, and carbon.

Selected fiber-forming ingredients are combined to form long-chain polymers from which fibers are made. The fibers generally have the following characteristics: thermoplastic (able to be molded or shaped into desired forms with the application of high temperatures); abrasion resistant (able to withstand surface wear and rubbing); relatively non-absorbant; resilient (fibers spring back when crushed); strong; and resistant to sunlight, mildew, and moths.

In 1940, the United States Mill consumption of man-made fibers accounted for 10 percent of all major fibers used. The amount of man-made fibers consumed totalled 28 percent in 1960 to 65 percent in 1972 of all major fibers used in the United States Mill consumption.

COTTON PRICE CURVE

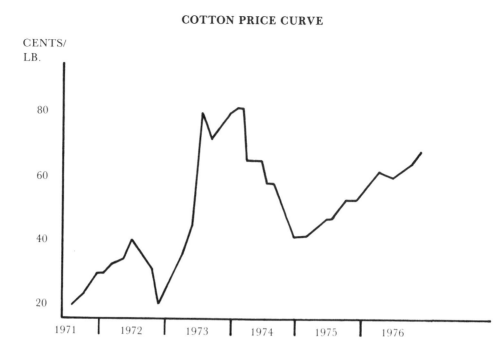

POLYESTER PRICE CURVE

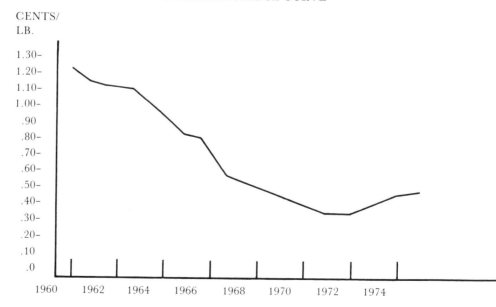

Flame Retardant Fabrics

Fire retardant fabrics are gradually being legislated into institutions on both federal and state levels. The first legislation was the Flammable Fabrics Act, 1953, which established Consumer Standard 191-53. This legislation was so lenient that approximately 99 percent of all apparel fabric passed. Even some writing paper would pass.

In 1967, the 1953 Act was amended to include all interior furnishings as well as apparel. In 1972, the Consumer Product Act was enacted. This act created the CPSC-Consumer Product Safety Commission which was given the authority to set standards, stop shipments, order recalls, seize goods, etc.

In June, 1973, all mattresses and mattress pads were covered by Federal Flammability Standards FF-4-72. This was followed by Federal Flammability Standard FF-3-71, regulating children's sleepwear in sizes 0-6X, effective July, 1973. Sizes 7-14 came under FF-5-74 on May, 1975.

Fabric choices available on the market for possible use in children's sleepwear are numerous. Some of them were available before the standards were imposed, but most of them have been developed specifically to meet or exceed the standards. As is true in most new developments, one or more desirable properties are traded off to obtain a new, more desirable property as is the case with most flame resistant fabrics.

Most flame retardant fibers are modified acrylic or modacrylic fibers containing built-in fire retardants.

Verel® is one of the earlier modacrylic fibers to be used in flame retardant fabrics. Unfortunately, it is very susceptible to high wet and dry heat shrinkage. Verel® cannot tolerate the high temperatures used in an institutional laundry.

Sef® is a new modified acrylic or modacrylic fiber, but modifications make it not as temperature sensitive as Verel®. The improved dimensional heat stability allows fabrics containing Sef® to be laundered in a more conventional institutional type laundry process. However, Sef® cannot tolerate the high temperatures of a flat work ironer.

Sef®, like Verel®, is highly toxic. In fact it is the gas or smoke given off from the fabric when exposed to a flame that smothers the oxygen feeding the flame and thus extinguishes the fire.

In recent years polymerization technology has progressed to the point that fibers of the same chemical composition, such as modacrylics, can be formed having very different physical properties.

Leavil® is one of these new fibers with self-extinguishing properties. It is a form of polyvinyl chloride or vinyon fiber that possesses improved thermodimensional stability over earlier fibers of this composition.

Leavil® displays excessive shrinkage in 100 percent Leavil® fabrics laundered under institutional conditions. Therefore, Leavil® has been blended with a low level polyester content blend to stabilize shrinkage and impart added strength.

The Kohjin Company of Japan has introduced a flame resistant fiber called Cordelan®. This fiber is self-extinguishing and does not melt-drip in a fire. Further, the manufacturer claims that it does not produce toxic fumes on combustion and is capable of being processed in the usual types of institutional launderings. However, to add stability and strength several manufacturers are blending low levels of polyester.

Polyester fabrics can be topically treated with a fire retardant chemical which can incorporate into the fabric a durable flame resistant finish. The resultant fabrics are not adversely affected by normal hospital launderings although repeated steam autoclaving does have an adverse affect on the FR (flame retardant) durability of "tris" treated fabrics. "Tris" is the FR chemical used in treating polyester fabrics to render them durably flame resistant. Flame resistant polyester fabrics will melt and drip in a flame, but to a lesser extent than untreated polyester fabrics.

Recently the Environmental Protection Fund filed a petition with the Consumer Product Safety Commission alleging that "tris" was both a possible nerve poison and a possible carcinogen. The National Cancer Institute has also indicated that "tris" may be a potent cancer-causing agent. This has caused the manufacturing industry to switch away from the use of "tris" in sleepwear fabrics. Several alternate flame retardant chemical additives are being evaluated as substitutes.

Exactly how these new finishes will hold up to institutional type laundering is not presently known.

Nomex® is self-extinguishing and a type of nylon that does not melt and drip in a flame. It was initially developed for high performance military and industrial end-uses. The Veterans Administration hospitals have been using pajamas made from lightweight Nomex® fabric for a number of years and report excellent wear life for these garments (up to 1,500 launderings).

Whereas all other flame retardant fabrics have proven to be a problem one way or another in an institutional laundry, Nomex® is the one fiber that has proven foolproof. It can be washed and dried, even commercially, without any adverse effects.

The long-wearing qualities of Nomex®, plus its self-extinguishing characteristic, has prompted its use in sheets, pillow cases, thermal cellular blankets, mattress pads, cubical curtains, and pillows.

Indications of Durability

Although high thread count generally indicates durability, many materials of high thread count can be quite fragile and those with a low thread count can be extremely durable. The factors contributing to this condition can be related to the length of the fibers, the size of the yarn, and the tightness of the twist. What will happen after repeated washings? What are the factors that effect the launderability of materials? They are, first, color fastness, and second, shrinkage and resistance to shrinkage.

When considering color fastness there are two basic types of dying processes—vat and naphthol. For the colors generally used in hospitals, vat-dyed fabrics are desirable. Vat-dyed refers to a classification of chemical dyes that are superior to all others and which will best withstand the effects of laundry washing, auto-claving, and other color destroying agents. Vat-dyeing may be done in three ways: (1) dyeing in the piece, (2) dyeing the yarns before weaving, and (3) making printed materials. In printing, the dyes are applied to one side with the result of achieving the same on both sides in the finished piece.

White fabrics are obtained by bleaching. Bleaching agents will weaken fabrics if too much is used or if it is allowed to remain in the fabric too long. Laundry bleaching, if it is not carefully done, can be the greatest cause of fabric deterioration. This is thoroughly explained in another portion of this book.

Shrinkage

A fabric from which shrinkage has been removed is described as being fully "pre-shrunk." Sanforizing is a process that pre-shrinks material before it is manufactured into the finished goods. It is a mechanical process employing only pure water spray, steam, and heat which shrinks the cloth after it has been woven. A residual shrinkage of 1 percent is still permissible and accepted as normal.

Fabrics that are not pre-shrunk are referred to as regular finish and will shrink in varying degrees. Lightweight fabrics such as sheeting, twills, and print cloths may have a shrinkage of up to 7 percent in the warp (length) and up to 3 percent in the fill (width). In this same weight class, the unbleached fabrics will shrink slightly more in both directions. On heavier materials, such as ducks, shrinkage up to 10 percent in the warp and 4 percent in the fill is not unusual.

Durability Test

A tensile-strength test merely shows the ability of a material to resist breakage by tension. It is measured in terms of pounds per inch. Each piece of fabric has a tensile-breaking strength of so many pounds per inch in both the warp and the fill. If used for comparison, the results of these tests are valid only if they are conducted under scientifically controlled conditions. Changes in temperature, humidity, and similar external factors can cause wide variations in results, therefore, tests should be conducted under standard conditions.

An abrasion test measures the degree to which a fabric resists surface wear. Institutional apparel is very often subjected to more surface wear than strain. An employee in the dietary department comes in contact with abrasive surfaces, such as delivery carts, beds, trays, table edges, etc. The abrasion test itself merely determines how many rubs a material will withstand under certain conditions before the yarn weakens.

Tablecloths and Napkins

Tablecloths and napkins of the best quality are made of cotton damask, two layers thick, weighing 10 ounces or more per square yard. They will have about 200 threads per square inch and shrink less than 10 percent. Combed cotton, broadcloth, and momie cloth are also commonly used. The trend in recent years has been to the use of synthetic fibers due to their resistance to wrinkles and ease of care. Some of these synthetic fibers resist absorption of spills. That may please the restaurant owner but highly displease the customer.

Tablecloths and napkins should be ordered pre-shrunk. If ordering to the cut size, remember that shrinkage will reduce tablecloth dimensions as much as four inches (a 72 × 72 cut becomes a 69 × 69 cloth) and napkins by as much as two inches. Specify a 64 pound or greater seam strength, nonfading fast colors, a breaking strength appropriate to the type of material, and a weight of at least 4 ounces per square yard on single thickness materials.

Terry Towels

Terry towels are intricate in their construction in that they have two warps instead of one. One of the warps is used with the filling to make the underweave. The other warp is used to make the pile or terry loops. The pile, or loops, of a terry towel hide the under threads so that it is necessary to dig right down to the underweave to determine the closeness of construction and inherent staying power of a bath towel or hand towel.

There is no strength in the terry warp yarns of a bath towel. In nontechnical language, the loop yarns are simply twined in and out and around the basic fabric formed by the ground warp and filling yarn to make an absorbent drying surface.

From the very nature of the weave of a terry towel it is easier to conceal poor quality yarns than in a sheet, or other fabric, where the construction is more readily examined. Consequently, do not be too ready to judge a bath towel merely by weight. The heavy bath towel made of short coarse cotton may easily weigh considerably more than the towel constructed of finer yarn, yet not wear half as long.

A well balanced bath towel must have a high tensil strength which is derived only from ground yarns, in that the terry yarns do not add to the tensil strength of a towel. Further a towel should have good absorbency, which is obtained in the terry yarn.

Most manufacturers are now producing terry towels and washcloths which incorporate a polyester/cotton blend yarn in the ground, that is, the yarns running under the terry that lie under the all cotton terry loops. The terry or loop warp yarn remain all cotton and, therefore, there is no loss of absorbency. The ground warp yarns are a blend of 65 percent polyester and 35 percent cotton or 35 percent polyester and 65 percent cotton; the ground filling yarns are usually all cotton. Some manufacturers, however, have also incorporated a 35 percent polyester and 65 percent cotton blend ground fill yarn to match the 35/65 ground warp.

The terry towels with the blend ground yarns are much stronger than similar constructed towels using the all cotton warp yarn. In fact, the towel manufactured with the polyester/cotton blend ground yarn is stronger after approximately 50 launderings than when new, as is the case with the polyester/cotton blend sheets and pillow cases.

The first signs of wear in the bath towel usually comes at the side selvages. This wear is usually the result of the abrasion on the selvages during the process of tumble drying. Therefore, the bath and hand towels should have double reinforced side selvages. The side selvages are turned and hemmed to form two thicknesses of fabric on both sides and thus eliminate the fraying of the edges which might appear after just a few washings. The washcloth is very vulnerable to the fraying of the edges in that they are dried along with other terry items. As the dried terry washcloths continue to be tumbled there is an extreme amount of abrasion on the side selvages, which results in the breaking down of the whipped yarns used to finish the edges of the wash cloths. It is for this reason that the hemmed double thickness, four-sided washcloths are now being made to withstand this extra abrasion.

COMMON COMPONENTS OF CARPET CONSTRUCTION[2]

Carpet Yarns

Pile or surface yarns are upstanding yarns which form the wearing surface of the carpet. They are the only yarns we see and walk upon. The pile yarns may be cut, looped, or a combination of both. As a convenient measure of construction, the amount of pile yarn in a carpet refers to the weight of yarn forming the wear layer, plus the weight of yarn "roots" buried in the body of the carpet. The buried weight of yarn is significant in the case of Wilton weaves and when the yarn is woven through the back.

Though loosely applied to all carpets, two terms that are properly asssociated with woven fabrics are *warp yarns* and *weft yarns*.

Warp yarns (lengthwise yarns) refer to those backing yarns which run lengthwise through the carpet. There are two types of warp-backing yarns used in weaving carpet: *chain* and *stuffer yarns*.

Weft yarns (crosswise yarns) are those backing yarns which run through the carpet in a crosswise direction. Combined with the warp yarns, weft yarns (also called "shots") bind the pile yarns together in a woven fabric.

Carpet Quality

When we think of carpet quality, we must consider both appearance quality and service quality. *Appearance quality* takes into account the styling design, which includes such factors as surface pattern, texture, color, and such. *Service quality* is concerned with the ability of the carpet to retain its original "look" by resisting soiling, crushing, wear, color change, tuft pull-out, and the like.

Although a discussion of appearance quality is beyond the scope of this book, it is recommended that no carpet purchase be based solely on appearance quality; purchase should be compatible with the desired service quality.

A number of rules-of-thumb have been suggested for anticipating the service quality of commercial carpeting. Yet, none of these "guesstimates" are completely accurate because many variables are involved and it is difficult to reduce these variables to measurable qualities. Some common basic factors by which experienced carpet personnel judge the quality of any carpet are: (1) pile density, (2) pile height, and (3) weight of the yarn.

---

[2]The author thanks the American Hotel and Motel Association for the use of this material from their publication, "The Selection and Maintenance of Commercial Carpet."

Pile Density

The weight of pile yarn per unit volume is a relative measure of pile density. The denser the pile, or the more tufts per square inch of a specific yarn size, the less weight each tuft must bear. With weight more evenly distributed, there will be less flexing within the pile. This is one factor in obtaining greater crush resistance. Likewise, in a dense pile each tuft is closer to the surrounding tufts, so the support provided is of a collective nature. Also, the more support, the less flexing action. Therefore, carpets of denser piles give greater compression resistance and longer wear.

Because pile density is difficult to measure accurately, it is commonly calculated from the following construction features: (1) tufts per square inch, (2) pitch, (3) rows or wires, (4) weight of pile yarn, (5) pile height, and (6) yarn size.

Tufts.   An alternate method of judging closeness of pile construction is to rely on the number of tufts per square inch. This technique is preferred for tufted and knitted carpets, and can also be meaningful when applied to all the weaves. For the woven carpets, the number of tufts per square inch is related to the pitch and rows per inch.

Pitch.   This is the number of warp (lengthwise) lines in a 27-inch width of carpet. When we speak of ''189 pitch'' or ''216 pitch,'' we mean 189 or 216 lines of yarn running through each 27-inch width.

Pitch is indicative of the closeness of a weave crosswise of the fabric. Consequently, the higher the pitch, the finer the weave. Pitch will vary in accordance with the type of weave and the various grades within each weave. A standard pitch for Wilton is 256, and for Axminster, 189.

The term *pitch* does not have any real significance for tufted or knitted carpets because their constructions differ so radically from woven carpets. In a tufted carpet, the only warp yarn is the stitching which runs the length of the carpet. Therefore, the number of needles per widthwise inch or the space between needles (gauge) parallels the term *pitch.* Knitted carpets have no continuous warp lines that can be used as a measure of pitch. Flocked carpets, consisting of individual, upright fibers held in a latex sizing, have no lengthwise or crosswise yarns.

Rows, Wire per Inch.   Rows or wire per inch are the number of weft shots, or crosswise units, measured per inch along the length of a carpet. It is literally the number of pile tufts per inch lengthwise of the carpet. As with pitch, the number of rows or wires per inch are indicative of the closeness of the weave. The number will differ among the different grades of the same weave. For example, it may vary from as low as 4 in an economy fabric (such as a low density Axminster) to as high as 13 in a densely woven, highgrade Wilton.

Three inches are marked off on the back of the piece of carpet, and the number of weft shots counted. The result is divided by three, to give the number per inch. Thus, 17 rows in 3 inches of a certain Axminster gives it a designation of 5⅔ rows per inch. The number of wires or rows on the back usually is an indication of the rows of yarn on the face. Axminsters' weft shots are described in ''rows''; that of Wiltons, or Velvets, in ''wires.''

Tufted carpets and knitted carpets have no weft or crosswise yarns; however, it is possible to measure the number of tufts or loops per inch lengthwise for each type of carpet. In tufteds, the number of stitches per lengthwise inch is roughly equivalent to rows in woven carpets. Because of their unique construction, flocked carpets have no tufts that can be used as a visual measure of density.

Weight of Pile Yarn.   The total weight of pile yarn per unit surface area (ounces per square yard) is probably the most important factor in wear life. When considered together with pile height, it can give a fairly good measure of service quality. The weight of pile yarn per unit surface area is dependent upon carpet construction, the yarn count or weight of the yarn, and the pile height.

Pile Height

Pile height is the thickness of the wear layer. It is measured from the top of the pile to the top of the back. It does not include the thickness of the backing. If all other factors are equal, particularly pile density, a carpet with a higher pile will give longer service wear. The pile heights vary in carpets whose surfaces are textured, high-low looped, and in combinations of cut and loop construction. In these carpet designs, therefore, the average maximum pile height is used to measure pile thickness.

Weight of the Yarn (Yarn Size, Yarn Count)

The weight or thickness of a single strand of yarn is also a factor of quality. Carpets require yarns of special thickness. Two examples of systems used to express yarn count are the *woolen count,* or actual number of yards per ounce, and *denier,* or number of grams per 9,000 meters.

ADDITIONAL FACTORS

Many other factors influence service quality besides those already described. A few of the more important ones are as follows: (1) ply, (2) fiber type and quality, (3) surface construction, (4) body construction, (5) backing, (6) dyes, and (7) padding. These factors vary considerably according to the weave and the specific piece of goods under consideration.

Ply

Ply is the number of strands of single yarns twisted to form one pile yarn. The final yarn is designated as 1-ply, 2-ply, 3-ply, 4-ply, and so forth. Ply by itself, however, is not an index of quality. The weight or size of the yarns twisted into the ply must always be considered.

Fiber Type and Quality

Fibers differ considerably in many respects, such as abrasion resistance, twist retention, compression resistance, resilience, soil resistance, stain resistance, wet cleanability, and static generation. The physical properties are also influenced by the fiber denier or thickness. See the section ''Carpet Fibers'' for more details.

Surface Construction

Cut-pile, twist or straight yarn, loop or round-wire, and combinations of each, influence crush resistance, resilience, cleanability and texture retention.

In general, round-wire or loop construction is more functional than cut-pile, but is more difficult to clean. The round-wire gives fuzzier details of design while cut-pile produces a ''luxury'' effect and sharp design detail.

Body Construction

The form of carpet construction has a bearing on the maximum attainable pile density, tuft retention, and dimensional stability. The choice of designs, textures, and use of colors is limited by the type of loom used to make the carpet. The fibers for the body of the carpet are also important, since they affect service life regarding shrinkage, dimensional stability, mildew resistance, and insect resistance.

Backing Yarns

Backing yarns are made of various fibers. As a general rule, the stronger the fiber, the longer the life of the carpet. The backing yarns are particularly important in providing the necessary strength to prevent tearing when heavy objects, such as furniture, are moved across the carpet surface. By adding more fibers to the back of the carpeting, the life of the carpet is prolonged. Additional heavy yarn running the length of the carpet is the common method of increasing the amount of backing fibers. These are called *stuffers*. Some of the fibers used as backing yarns are:

- Jute. Jute comes from the sisal plant that grows in India and the Philippines. It is spun into a strong and durable yarn that adds strength, weight, and stiffness to carpet backing. A woven jute burlap is generally used as the backing fabric for tufted carpets.
- Kraftcord. This tightly twisted yarn is made from wood pulp. It has the advantages of uniform diameter and availability, for it is produced from American wood pulp.
- Cotton. Used in a chain stitch, cotton fiber has surprising strength. It is also used as a stuffer to lend bulk and durability to carpet backings.
- Rayon. Heavy strands of rayon are woven into a tough, durable backing.
- Wool. Wool is the most expensive backing material. In quality carpetings like Chenilles, wool is used to add performance and value.

For woven carpets, backing yarns and pile yarns are woven together to form the carpet. But for tufted and flocked carpets, a separate sheet of backing is needed. Called the *prime backing,* this most frequently consists of a 10 oz. jute sheet.

Certain synthetic materials may also serve as backings. Woven polypropylene strips (recently put on the market) are now being used in tufted carpet construction. New forms of nonwoven polypropylene backings are in the final testing stages and should soon be available for commercial use. A new kind of backing, based on urethane foam reinforced with nylon scrim, should soon be on the market.

When polypropylene serves as a backing, some sort of adhesive may be needed to bind the yarns of the tufted carpet in place. Synthetic materials are of special value in carpet backings because they are not susceptible to shrinkage or mildew. Furthermore, they are proof against wicking, which occurs when stains absorbed on the back of the carpet seep through to the surface of the carpet.

Of side interest to the commercial carpeting field is the use of powdered polyethylene as a backing material for tufted carpets. Although powdered polyethylene has been used in Europe for more than ten years, it was only introduced in the United States in 1960. The biggest user of powdered polyethylene in this country is the automobile industry. They now use powdered polyethylene instead of rubber and styrene latices for automobile carpet backing because it offers these advantages:

1. The carpet coating operation is faster.
2. Equipment coating costs are lower.
3. The finished carpet can be molded to fit the contour of the floor, eliminating cutting and sewing operations.

Currently, producers of powdered polyethylene are developing smaller-sized comestic carpets which could be sold in the domestic carpet market.

Reinforced Backing. Reinforced backing can be a woven-mesh fabric, tightly woven burlap, or similar fabric. Scrim backing is a woven mesh fabric that is laminated to the regular carpet backing and usually impregnated with a latex compound coating. It is primarily used on tufted carpets, but it is also found on woven and knitted carpets. Scrim backing cloth may have a weight range from 4 to 12 ounces a square yard, plus the additional weight of the adhesive used to bind it to the fabric.

The use of a double jute back for tufted carpets has increased considerably in the last few years. Tufted carpet is made by stitching yarn into a sheet of jute, 10 oz. per square yard, and then back-coating with latex to bind the yarns in place. While the cement is still wet, a second jute sheet of equal weight is bonded to the latex.

Some purposes served by scrim backing are:

1. It increases the carpet's ''dimensional stability''—the ability to resist stretching and shrinking.
2. It counteracts excessive humidity effect on carpet (swelling and buckling).
3. It gives the carpet greater ''hand'' or ''feel'' (more body).
4. It strengthens the carpet by further securing the tufts in place.
5. It prevents the corners from curling up in rugs.

Dyeing Methods

There are a variety of methods used to dye carpet fibers. However, no matter which method is used, the quality of the dyes and the mode of application should result in satisfactory colorfastness to light and to wet cleaning procedures.

- Raw-Stock Dyeing. The wool is dyed in bulk before it is spun. This assures uniform color throughout a large batch.
- Skein Dyeing. Yarn (skeins of it) is dyed after spinning, but before weaving.
- Solution Dyeing. Man-made fibers are dyed in liquid form, before becoming solid threads. In this method, the dyes become part of the yarn.
- Package Dyeing. Spun and wound yarn is placed on large perforated forms. The dye is forced through perforations to ''soak'' the yarn with color.
- Piece Dyeing. After the carpet is woven, the whole piece of goods is dyed.
- Print Dyeing. After the carpet is woven, the pattern is screen-printed with premetalized dyes in up to six colors. Deep penetration of the pile is achieved by an electromagnetic technique.

As the technology of dyeing synthetic fibers has advanced, the number of special effects that can be achieved in the different methods of dyeing has increased. Of special interest are the color alternatives made possible in skein dyeing and piece dyeing yarns for tufted carpets. Take the case of acrylic carpet fibers. When two different acrylic yarn components are plied together, skein dyeing offers three alternatives for color and effect in the same bath operation: (1) color-on-white, in which only one of the yarn components is dyed; (2) tone-on-tone, in which the dye is distributed in different intensities on each yarn component; and (3) two-color or cross-dye effects, in which each yarn component is dyed a different color in the same bath.

Similar techniques can be applied in piece dyeing nylon and acrylics to create decorative two-color effects. In fact, when nylon is used, three-color or three-way crossed dye effects can be imparted to the material in one dye bath.

Two notable novelty methods of dyeing are space-dyeing and resist-printing. For space-dyeing yarns, a special machine applies two or more colors to the yarn at predetermined intervals prior to tufting. To make resist-printed carpet, a dye-resist agent is printed on tufted carpet prior to piece dyeing.

An important breakthrough in dyeing tufted carpets has been achieved by a printing technique that uses pre-metalized dyes. This new method provides a deeper penetration of the dye and a better definition of pattern on tufted carpets than was possible with the older method of drum-printing. In the new technique, plain tufted carpets are silk-screened with a pre-metalized dye in a shallow trough. An electromagnetic charge, applied under the carpet, rapidly drives the dye deep into the pile. It is possible by this process to print-dye piles up to 1¼ inches in height. The carpet is continuously processed through a series of printing troughs in each of which a different color is applied by silkscreen to build up a final pattern containing up to six colors. The carpet is then cured to set the dyes, after which it is washed and dried.

The new printed tufted carpet may become a serious competitor of Wilton and Axminster carpets. With deep dye-penetration and good definition of pattern, printed tufted carpets are now equal in appearance to Wilton or Axminster carpets. Also, the new dyeing process has a relatively low cost and tufted carpets are inherently more economical to produce than woven fabrics.

Padding and Underlays

The term *carpet padding* includes all of the following: padding, underlay, lining, cushion, and pads. Although the use of an underlay or pad beneath the pile floor covering is not a substitute for carpet quality, it serves a number of useful functions:

1. It provides extra insulation against extremes of cold or heat.
2. It adds extra sound-absorbing qualities.
3. It lengthens the life of the carpet.
4. It improves underfoot comfort.
5. It cushions the shock of walking.
6. It absorbs crushing forces on pile.

The conventional hair-type underlays are made of felted cattle hair. They may have a waffle design to provide a skid-proof surface and improve resiliency; and sometimes they are reinforced with backings of jute fiber (often referred to as India fiber) or with burlap center interliners. Where burlap reinforcing is used, the hair is punched through burlap fabric and then compressed to a uniform thickness. Starch sizing or adhesive of sufficient quantity is sometimes used to provide a strong bond between the fibers and the burlap core.

Before construction of the underlay, the hairs and fibers to be used are cleaned, washed, and sterilized. Many manufacturers also permanently mothproof the underlay to protect it against the larvae of moths and carpet beetles.

The conventional hair-type underlays are sold in all standard widths, i.e., 27 in., 36 in., 54 in., 6 ft., 9 ft., and 12 ft. Special widths can be made to specification. They are available in weights of 32, 40, 48, 54, and 86 ounces per square yard.

Some underlays made of hair or of hair and jute are coated with rubber on one or both sides to hold the fibers together securely and to provide additional cushioning. In some instances, the underlay has an animal hair waffle top and a jute back reinforced with a designed rubberized application. The rubberized cushions are available in all standard widths and range in weight from 32 to 56 ounces per square yard.

Cushions made of hair and sponge rubber are also available. In making these combination cushions, animal hairs and jute fibers are punched through burlap backing and bound to the burlap by a synthetic latex; then the fiber side of the felt is bonded to a foam rubber coating. A typical construction of 44 oz. per square yard combination carpet cushion consists of: 25.0 oz. of fibers, 4.5 oz. of burlap backing, 4.5 oz. of latex sizing, and 10.0 oz. of foam rubber.

Foam and sponge rubber cushions (see the discussion on bonded rubber cushioning) are made as flat sheets, with or without perforations. The cushion backs have different designs (e.g., waffle, ripple, grid and V-shaped ribs).

A carpet-laying problem associated with "low-slip" rubber pads is the difficulty encountered in stretching the carpet across the pad during the installation operation. Therefore, a scrim or burlap fabric is usually bonded to the rubber padding. When laid with the fabric side up, these underlays permit a taut and even stretch of the carpet.

Sponge and foam rubber cushions are available in widths of 36 in., 54 in., 6 ft., and 9 ft., and in thickness from 3/16 in. to 7/16 in. The weights of high-density rubber cushions range from 38 to 75 ounces per square yard.

Evaluation of Underlays

Underlays of different material will vary in their effectiveness. Felted pads of jute or hair have two defects—they may mat down in time, and they may develop mildew, especially if their fibers (primarily animal and vegetable) get too wet during shampooing. Nevertheless, hair-type pads are highly desired for their impact resistance and lack of color transfer to rugs. When properly cleaned, sterilized, and treated, hair-type pads are suitable for use on all grade levels and on conventional radiant heated floors.

Although more expensive, sponge and foam rubber retain their resilience much longer than hair pads and permit a variety of improved construction designs. They

CARPET PADDING AND UNDERLAYS

Type of Installation	Where to Use	Recommended Cushion Weight* (oz./sq. yd.)
Maximum Luxury Areas	Executive Suites, Conference Rooms, Banquet Halls, Luxury Homes.	over 56
Extra-Heavy Traffic Areas	Corridors, Lobbies, Schools, Exhibition Halls, Shops, Clubs, Restaurants, Libraries, Theatres.	56
Medium-Heavy Traffic Areas	Offices, Reception Rooms, Hotels, Motels, Clinics, Beauty Parlors, Banks, Churches, Temples.	50
Normal Traffic Areas	Living Rooms, Bedrooms, Dens, Family Rooms, Hallways.	40
Light Traffic Areas	Guest Rooms, Summer Homes.	32

*Depending on the construction, there may be some overlapping weight ranges.

have high resistance to humidity and vermin, and they are nonallergenic. Rubber cushionings are suitable for use on all grade levels, but some of the denser grades are not recommended on radiant heated floors.

When purchasing any type of carpet underlay, check to see that the cushion is suitable for the existing type of installation. It is wise to obtain a guarantee from the manufacturer on this matter, as well as a guarantee that the padding is free from holes, tears, lumps, wrinkles, tackiness, or other apparent defects which might impair its serviceability. (See *IRC Carpet Underlay Report,* Institutional Research Council, Inc., 221 West 57th Street, New York, N.Y. 10019.)

Before installing the underlay, make sure the area is dry and clean. Installations should be made with as few seams as possible, and where joints are necessary, edges should be butted together.

Bonded Rubber Cushioning

Rubber cushioning bonded to carpet is available in different forms. One kind of rubber cushioning, prepared and manufactured prior to application of the rug or carpet, is bonded to the carpet in strip form by means of an adhesive. This type of cushioning can either be sponge rubber or latex foam. In this case, the lamination process is generally done by a company other than the carpet manufacturer. This type of custom work makes it possible to obtain any form of carpet construction with a bonded rubber cushioning back.

The other general class of rubber cushioning is manufactured and cured in place on the back of the carpet or rug in seamless widths.

Rubber cushioning is a general term describing all elastomeric materials. We should go further than this definition and distinguish between sponge rubber and latex foam, often referred to as simply sponge and foam.

Foam and Sponge.   Both latex foam and sponge rubber are filled with air cells. Sponge, having a thicker cell wall, is usually heavier than foam. In addition, sponge is more often made from a solid, whereas foam is usually made from a liquid mix. Sponge rubber is made only by a few rubber companies. Carpet must be sent to these plants where the sponge is laminated to the finished carpet. Sponge can now be made in widths only up to 6 feet.

Two kinds of foam are made. The first is a separate sheet which is laminated to the carpet in much the same manner as sponge. The other form of latex foam is applied in a continuous process to the back of the carpet as a liquid. The coated carpet is then heated, causing the liquid to foam in place and become cured. The heavier the mix density, the longer it takes for finished carpet to pass through the oven to foam and cure. For example, 56 ounce foam moves through an oven at the rate of 67 feet per minute. The 38 to 40 ounce foam moves at 94 feet per minute.

In its natural state, latex foam is cream-colored. If desired, it can be colored without impairment of its performance. Unlike sponge rubber, latex foam can be made by the mill, usually in a 3/16 inch thickness and in widths up to 15 feet on a continuous seamless basis.

The quality of rubber cushioning can generally be estimated from its density, expressed as ounces or pounds per square yard. The danger in complete acceptance of density as the sole measure of quality is keyed to the fact that density can be adjusted by the use of "fillers" in latex. Some filler is normally used in the mix, whether foam is made separately for lamination, or foamed in place on the carpet. Filler is usually Fuller's earth or clay. Unfortunately, it is virtually impossible to tell how much filler has been added by looking at the foam. To obtain a true estimate of the filler content, it is necessary to burn the foam sample and analyze the ash for inert ingredients. Inexpensive foam can be made easily by adding more clay to the mix. However, excessive amounts of filler tend to speed foam decomposition and have other unpleasant effects on wearing.

Density Requirement.   In a recent federal specification (DDD-C-95 dated April 16, 1965), approved by the General Services Administration, rubber cushioning is required to meet the following requirements:

1. Cushioning shall average not less than 3/16 inch in thickness.
2. The weight per square yard shall not be less than 3.50 pounds (56 oz.) nor more than 4.25 pounds (68 oz.).
3. The compressibility (weight required to compress 1 square inch to 75 percent of its original thickness) shall be not less than 5 pounds nor more than 9 pounds.
4. The compression set shall be not more than 15 percent after being compressed 50 percent of its original thickness for 22 hours at a temperature of 158°F.
5. Cushioning foamed in place and cured on the carpet should tear before pulling free from the carpet after being stored at 90°F for 96 hours. Laminated cushioning attached to the carpet by an adhesive should have a minimum strip strength of 2.0 pounds per inch of width.
6. The cushion should not deteriorate; i.e., become sticky or crack when bent back on itself, after being subjected to accelerated aging conditions.

The government's minimum requirement of 56 ounces per square yard is believed, by some, to be much higher than necessary. Among more reputable producers, 38 to 40 ounces are now being used for commercial qualities. According to a representative[3] of a latex company, when a producer goes as low as 32 ounces, wearing problems can be expected. A minimum of 38 ounces has been suggested as being sufficient to be labeled high-density foam.

New Products

There are several new types of cushioning. Vinyl foam is made from a combination of solids and liquids. While it will be the specified 3/16 inch thickness, it is expected to be lighter than the so-called high density foam. It is claimed that vinyl foam does not decompose. This, along with other inherent advantages, may make vinyl foam a satisfactory replacement for rubber.

[3]C. Wells Moore, Southern Latex Co., in an article by Ed McCabe appearing in *Home Furnishings Daily* (Friday, June 11, 1965).

The molded rubber back is another new type of backing. In this process, which can be done by the carpet mill, liquid rubber is first coated on the carpet back; then the rubber is rolled out with an embossed roller to give it a non-skid, designed surface.

Carpet Fibers

Synthetic fibers have become very important in the carpet industry. The original development of synthetics made a number of new fiber types available for carpet use. Since their introduction, these synthetic fibers have been vastly improved and their use has steadily increased. In 1964, man-made fibers accounted for approximately 70 percent of broadloom surface fiber consumption. Wool, which was for a long time the single most important fiber in terms of poundage used, was surpassed by nylon in 1964.

Other synthetic fibers besides nylon may also increase in use, and there is every indication that new fibers may be created and marketed. Acrylic and modacrylic fibers, being used more and more, may equal or possibly exceed wool for carpet use. The con-

GENERIC NAMES AND DEFINITIONS OF MANUFACTURED FIBERS

Generic Name	Definition	Examples
	A manufactured fiber in which the fiber-forming substance is any long chain synthetic . . .	
Rayon	A manufactured fiber composed of regenerated cellulose in which the substituents have not replaced 15% of the hydrogens of the hydroxyl groups.	Avisco Avisco Super L
Nylon	Polyamide having reoccurring amide groups as an integral part of the polymer chain.	Nylon Nylon 6, 6
Acrylic	Polymer composed of at leat 85% by weight of Acrylonitrile units.	Acrilan Creslan, Orlon Zefran Zefkrome
Modacrylic	Polymer composed of less than 85% but at least 35% by weight of Acrylonitrile units.	Dynel Verel
Olefins	Any long chain synthetic polymer composed of at least 85% by weight of ethylene, propylene or other Olefin units.	Herculon Polycrest
Polyester	Polymer composed of at least 85% by weight of an ester of Dihydric alcohol and terephthalic acid.	Dacron Vicron
Saran	Polymer composed of at least 80% by weight of vinylidene chloride units.	
Vinal	Polymer composed of at least 50% by weight of vinyl alcohol units and in which the total of the vinyl alcohol units and any one or more of the various Acetal units is at least 85% by weight of the fiber.	

Federal Trade Commission—Textile Fiber Products Identification Act March 3, 1960.

MAJOR FIBER PRODUCERS

Manufacturer	Fiber Type	Reg. Trade Name
Allied Chemical Corp.	Continuous filament nylon	Caprolan, A.C.E. Nylon
American Cyanamid Co.	Acrylic staple	Creslan
American Enka Corp.	Continuous filament nylon Nylon staple	Enkaloft
American Viscose Corp.	Rayon staple Rayon filament	Avisco Avicron
The Chemstrand Corp.	Acrylic staple Continuous filament nylon	Acrilan Cumuloft
Courtaulds (Alabama) Inc.	Rayon staple Rayon staple (solution dyed) Cross-linked rayon staple Cross-linked rayon staple	Coloray Corval Topel
The Dow Chemical Co.	Acrylic staple	Zefran
E. I. duPont deNemours & Co.	Acrylic staple Continuous filament nylon Nylon staple	Orlon Nylon 501, Antron
Eastman Chemical Products, Inc.	Modacrylic staple	Verel
Firestone Synthetic Fibers Co.	Continuous filament nylon	Nyloft
Hercules Powder Co.	Continuous filament olefin Olefin staple	Herculon
National Plastics Products Co.	Continuous filament olefin	Vectra
Union Carbide Corp.	Modacrylic staple	Dynel
U.S. Rubber Co.	Continuous filament olefin	Polycrest

COMPARATIVE BEHAVIOR OF CARPET-TYPE FIBERS

Factor	Wool	Nylon	Acrylic	Modacrylic	Polypropylene
Wear Life	High	Extra High	High	High	Extra High
Texture Retention	High	Medium	Medium	Medium	Low-Medium
Compression Resistance	Medium	Medium	Medium	Medium	Low
Resilience	High	Medium	High	Medium	Medium
Soil Resistance	High	Medium	High	High	High
Stain Resistance	Medium	High	High	High	High
Wet Cleanability	High	High	High	High	High
Static Generation	Medium	High	Medium	Medium	Low
Cost	Medium	Medium	Medium	Medium	Medium

EXAMPLES OF TYPICAL COMMERCIAL CARPETS

Type of Carpet: Traffic Level:	Velvet Heavy Traffic	Wilton Heavy Traffic	Axminster Medium Traffic	Knitted Heavy Traffic	Tufted Heavy Traffic
Description	Single-level loop pile, woven through back	Single-level loop pile, woven through back	Single-level cut pile, pattern	Single-level loop pile	Single-level loop pile
Tufts/Sq. in.	60	53	47	36	60
Pitch	216	180	189	—	—
Row or Wire	8	8	7⅓	—	—
Shots	2	2	3	—	—
Frame	—	3	—	—	—
Pile Weight (Oz./Sq. yd.)	42	54	26	37	42
Total Weight (Oz./Sq. yd.)	60	75	56	58	80
Pile Height, inches:					
Minimum	0.200	0.250	0.200	0.230	0.250
Maximum	0.250	0.300	0.310	0.290	0.300
Material of Construction:					
Pile	Wool	Wool	Wool	Wool	Wool
Chain	Cotton or rayon	Cotton or rayon	Cotton or rayon	Cotton, rayon or nylon	—
Filling	Cotton or jute	Cotton or jute	Jute or kraftcord	Jute or kraftcord	—
Stuffer	Cotton, jute or kraftcord	Cotton, jute or kraftcord	Cotton or rayon	—	—
Backing	—	—	—	—	Jute or cotton (Min. 10 oz./sq. yd.)
Back Coating, Oz./Sq. yd.	8	None required	6	14	Clear latex Min. 4 oz./sq. yd.
Backing Reinforcement	—	—	—	—	—
Tuft Bind, Oz. (Force required to pull a tuft or loop loose)	80	50	16	32	100

sumption of polypropylene, though still small compared to that of other synthetic fibers, could increase significantly within the coming years.

Although there are no statistics to indicate the exact ratio of fibers used in the commercial field, there is growing evidence that the use of synthetics is following the same pattern seen for the entire industry. Large instutional users are turning more and more to synthetic fibers which offer greater uniformity, longer wear life, and brighter colors.

The face yarns presently used in significant quantity for commercial carpet are made of nylon, wool, and acrylics. Other available materials include polypropylene, rayon, acetate, and cotton.

Guide to Commercial Carpet Grades

There is no absolutely sure and simple method for predicting the service quality of a carpet. A number of helpful guides do exist, however, which can be used to advantage by purchasing agents.

An up-to-date master classification of commercial carpets was researched and put together by the General Services Administration of the United States government, working in cooperation with the American Carpet Institute, Inc. On April 16, 1965, this comprehensive work was incorporated in Federal Specification DDD-C-95, entitled ''Carpets and Rugs, Wool, Nylon, Acrylic, Modacrylic.'' For any serious purchaser of commercial carpets, reading of this specification is a must. The specification may be purchased for 15¢ from the United States Government Printing Office, Washington, D.C. 20402.

Given in the specification are requirements for the common carpet fibers, chain, filling and stuffer yarns, backing material, backing reinforcement, attached rubber cushioning, and back coating. The specification also presents requirements for color fastness and various physical requirements and tolerances. A wide variety of construction types are described, including, Axminster, Velvet, Wilton, Tufted, Knitted, and Modified carpet constructions. Some helpful information which can be used as a guide in selecting carpets appears in the specification notes. This section is reproduced in its entirety since it could be helpful to the casual reader.

As a guide in the selection of the quality of carpeting to be used in the various areas of use, the following suggestions are offered. It should be kept in mind that each installation must be judged carefully as to the peculiar traffic conditions expected. In some areas, it might be advisable to use a heavier, better grade due to the peculiar wear factors in these situations. As a basis for estimating probable carpet performance in use, the levels of traffic experienced can be broken down as follows:

- Light. Bedrooms, dressing rooms, some dining rooms in private homes.
- Medium. Living and dining rooms in private homes, private offices, motel and hotel bedrooms.
- Heavy. Commercial type installations in office buildings, public rooms, hotel lobbies, stairways, and stores.

Carpets having wool, acrylic, or modacrylic pile yarn in the range of approximately 20 ounces per square yard or more should be satisfactory for light traffic areas. Fabrics of 25 ounces per square yard or more of pile yarn should be satisfactory for medium traffic areas. Those having 36 ounces per square yard or more of pile yarn should be satisfactory for heavy traffic. Carpets having 100 percent nylon pile yarn in weights of 20 ounces per square yard or more should be satisfactory for medium traffic. Those having 28 ounces per square yard or more should be satisfactory for heavy traffic.[4]

Pile Density

A number of years ago, the American Hotel and Motel Association recognized the importance of pile density and pile height in estimating the relative wearing qualities of pile floor coverings. It was proposed that wearing qualities of different carpets would be judged by comparing *the pile density squared times pile height* (D^2H).

The density factor took into account pitch, rows or wires per inch, and pile yarn weight. The relationship was expressed by the formula:

$$D = 2RPB$$

where

D is the density of the pile
R is the number of rows per inch lengthwise
P is the number of rows or pitch widthwise
B is the weight of the pile yarn in grains per inch.

All things being equal, a fabric with twice the pile height of another should be twice as durable. Furthermore, if the pile heights were the same and the density of one fabric twice that of another, *then the denser fabric should have approximately four times the durability.*

Suggested Carpet Specification

We have previously indicated that durability and service quality depend to a large degree on the pile density of a carpet. This in turn is largely determined by two factors: weight of yarn in the pile, and height of the pile.

Since both of these factors can be evaluated by analysis (total weight of pile yarn as *ounces per square yard of carpet,* and pile height as *thousandths* of an inch) it is possible to set up specification requirements which, if met, will result in adequate levels of pile density.

In developing the minimum requirements of this specification, a round-wire, all-wool velvet carpet was used as the reference level of performance, under commercial conditions of average heavy traffic. The density factors were set on the basis of ounce weight and pile height for this type of carpeting.

Requirements are presented for two levels of traffic conditions, illustrating the necessary variation in pile yarn weight and pile height for average heavy traffic and average medium traffic. For an explanation of these terms, see the section on ''Classification of Traffic.''

---

[4]Federal Specification DDD-C-95.

The specification takes into account the differences in service quality attributable to carpet construction. Grade limits are set according to the method of carpet manufacture. It is believed that the minimum requirements for other construction types gives durability qualities comparable to the round-wire velvet used as the reference level of performance.

The specification requirements will assure satisfactory service life, provided that the carpet construction conforms to accepted commercial practice and the materials of construction are of good quality. As a guide to acceptable carpet construction, we cite

MINIMUM SPECIFICATION REQUIREMENTS BASED ON PILE DENSITY FOR WOOL OR ACRYLIC CARPETS

	Average Heavy Traffic[1]		Average Medium Traffic[1]	
	Minimum Weight per Square Yard (ounces)	Average Pile Height (inches)	Minimum Weight per Square Yard (ounces)	Average Pile Height (inches)
Axminster Carpet..............	36	0.200–0.310	28	0.200–0.310
Knitted Carpet...............	42	0.250–0.300	36	0.200–0.250
Tufted Carpet................	42	0.250–0.300	36	0.200–0.250
Velvet Carpet:				
woven through the back.......	42	0.200–0.250	32	0.175–0.230
not woven through the back....	36	0.200–0.250	28	0.175–0.230
"Twist"...................	—	—	42	—
Wilton Carpet................	42	0.200–0.250	34	0.200–0.250

[1]See "Classification of Commercial Traffic."

MINIMUM SPECIFICATION REQUIREMENTS BASED ON PILE DENSITY FOR NYLON OR POLYPROPYLENE CARPETS

	Average Heavy Traffic[1]		Average Medium Traffic[1]	
	Minimum Weight per Square Yard (ounces)	Average Pile Height (inches)	Minimum Weight per Square Yard (ounces)	Average Pile Height (inches)
Tufted Carpet................	28	0.190–0.290	22	0.190–0.290
Velvet Carpet................ woven through the back	28	0.210–0.290	22	0.210–0.290
Loomed Carpet[2]..............	16	max. 0.150	—	—

[1]See "Classification of Commercial Traffic."
[2]Sponge-bonded, high density nylon pile.

typical examples of commercial carpets for each type of construction in the preceeding table. The recommended ounce weights and pile heights for woven, tufted, and knitted carpets are also summarized in accompanying tables.

Classification of Traffic

Foot-traffic conditions vary with the type, size, and location of the commercial area involved. Generally the type and location of the commercial area determine whether a particular space will be subjected to *heavy* or *medium* traffic.

For example, the lobbies, public rooms, corridors, and stairways in a hotel will normally receive heavy traffic, but the hotel guest rooms usually encounter medium traffic. Also, a large department store will have heavy traffic conditions throughout the aisles and selling areas while a small shop selling women's apparel will very likely get medium traffic. A classification of different building areas, according to the extent of traffic that may be expected, is given in the next table. There are other carpetable commercial areas not included in the table. Consultation with commercial carpet specialists will help determine the traffic conditions.

Stairways Installations

Carpeting on stairs wears out much faster than on level areas. Particularly hard wear occurs at the leading edge of the steps. For this reason, it is especially important to use a very good pad under the carpet on the stairs, regardless of the quality of the padding you use elsewhere. Cut-pile construction is sometimes preferred, since it shows less "grin" at the rounded stair edges.

Heavy wear can be distributed over more of the carpet if, at the time of installation, an extra foot or so of carpeting is folded under one or two of the risers at the top of the flight. Thereafter, the whole carpet can be shifted downward an inch or two—preferably before wear becomes noticeable. There will be some expense at each shifting. This, too, is a job best left to a professional, but the practice of shifting will help make a stair carpet last as long as the same carpet used on the floor area.

Extra-Heavy Traffic Conditions

It should be noted that the commercial carpet recommendations given here are *minimum* specification for *average* heavy and medium foot traffic conditions. Yet, traffic conditions in some commercial areas are often substantially higher than the average. As a result, these areas demand carpets with yarn-weight requirements higher than the minimums specified for normal heavy traffic use and luxurious effect.

For example, large motion picture theaters and department stores in major metropolitan centers use carpets containing as much as 70 to 90 ounces of pile yarn per square yard because of the extra-heavy traffic they encounter.

It is not unusual for theaters, stores, offices, and other commercial areas subjected to *heavier-than-average* traffic to use carpets with 50 to 60 ounces pile yarn per square yard.

Consultations with commercial carpet specialists can help determine whether a particular area would require carpeting with specifications above the yarn weights recommended for average heavy traffic conditions.

Key Points for Purchasers

In *Contract—The Trade Magazine of Space Planning and Furnishing,* several valuable suggestions were offered to potential carpet purchasers. These are reprinted below with the publisher's permission.

As with any other basic building material, wise and careful advance planning in the selection of carpet for a public area offers many advantages. It will provide sufficient time to choose the correct grade of carpet and most desirable styling. It will expedite delivery and installation of the carpets to conform with the over-all building schedule. Possibly the most important advantage is that advance planning will enable the architect and builder to design a building or interior with carpet in mind. This will not only help prevent installation problems, but can also produce substantial construction economies.

Here are some key points to consider in specifying carpet:

1. Consult with commercial-carpet specialists as early as possible. In the case of a new building, call in the carpet specialists when construction plans are still in the "drawing board" stage.

2. If the building specifications call for carpet, consider the use of economical sub-flooring materials such as plywood. Significant savings can be realized.

3. Plan the acoustical design of a building or interior with carpet in mind. Other sound-conditioning treatments may be unnecessary or minimal.

4. Anticipate the carpet installation when designing the interiors of a building. Carpets are made in widths of 27 inch, 36 inch, 54 inch, 9 foot, 12 foot, 15 foot, and 18 foot. Planning room dimensions and modules with these widths in mind will hold carpet wastage to a minimum.

5. Carpet pile heights vary. Plan door sizes so that they will swing freely over the carpet and padding specified.

6. Take full advantage of the extensive knowledge and background offered by the commercial-carpet specialists consulted in selecting and specifying the grade and styling of carpet that will provide the best possible service within the proposed budget.

7. Different areas within the same interior are often subjected to varying conditions of traffic and soiling. Stairways, for example, usually receive considerably more traffic and wear than floors. For these areas, consider purchasing carpets of heavier grades than those used for the less-trafficked spaces. Carpets of varying grades, but identical styling and appearance, are available from most manufacturers. (An alternate suggestion is to purchase additional carpet for replacement in these extra-heavy traffic areas.)

8. Consider local soiling conditions when selecting the color and design of the carpet. Just as in clothing, light colors will tend to show soil more than darker tones. Medium shades, tweed stylings, and multi-color patterns tend to camouflage soil best.

9. The anticipated direction of traffic-flow across a public space would be considered when planning placements of seams in a wall-to-wall carpet installation. The commercial-carpet specialist and the experienced carpet installer are the best sources of advice on seam placement.

10. Take advantage of the styling services offered by carpet manufacturers' design studios. The artists and technical experts employed by the mills can furnish invaluable assistance in the selection of a design, color, and texture that will be coordinated with the other furnishings and over-all decor of an interior.

11. Take a thorough look at all of the stock commercial-carpet lines offered by the manfacturers. Besides providing a wide assortment of grades and stylings, they are available for quick delivery for any size installation.

12. If you allow enough "lead-time" in selecting the carpet, and the size of the public space is 200 square yards or more, consider the custom-design services offered by most manufacturers of commercial-grade carpets.

13. Make certain that the carpet selected is permanently "mothproofed." All carpets made today by major American manufacturers are mothproofed for the life of the carpet, even after repeated shampooings.

14. Consult the commercial-carpet specialist and the carpet installer for recommendations on the correct padding and proper installation method required. Always specify the best installation job possible. A poorly executed installation can be not only unsatisfactory, but costly.[5]

BUILDING AREAS CLASSIFIED BY EXPECTED FOOT TRAFFIC

Applications	Average Heavy Traffic	Average Medium Traffic
Office Buildings	Reception areas, aisles, open work areas, stairways and elevators	Executive offices
Banks/Stores	Entranceways, lobbies, stairways, elevators, aisles and selling areas*	Executive offices, semi-private office areas, aisles and selling areas*
Churches/Funeral Homes		Entranceways, stairways, aisles, areas under seats or benches, chapel and altar
Restaurants/Clubs	Dining areas, bars and grill	
Schools	Corridors, classrooms, libraries and stairways	Administrative offices and faculty lounges
Transportation: planes, trains, railroads, ships	Aisles, dining areas and lounges	Staterooms and compartments
Hotels/Motels/ Hospitals/Libraries	Lobbies, stairways, elevators, corridors, public rooms, meeting and banquet rooms, wards	Guest rooms, executive offices, staff lounges, private rooms and waiting rooms
Professional Offices		Reception areas and consultation rooms of doctors, dentists, lawyers, etc.
Theatres/Bowling Alleys	Lobbies, stairways, lounges and aisles	

*Dependent on size and volume of customers.

[5]The author thanks the American Hotel and Motel Association for use of material from their publication, "Contract—The Trade Magazine of Space Planning and Furnishing."

TABLEWARE

Dishes

Dishes are made of ceramics or glass or, in the case of Pyroceram, both. Dishes are also made of a plastic, malamine.

The ceramics are made into a dense, relatively nonporous mass by a baking process of clay. The process is called *vitrification*. The ceramics are (1) China, which is a high quality clay that may contain some ground bone or calcium phosphate which is vitrified at 2250°F or above; (2) Stoneware, which is made of clay not as fine as used for China, and vitrified at about 2200°F; (3) Pottery, which is made of even less refined clay and is baked but not vitrified at a temperature of about 1500°F; and (4) Terra Cotta, which is baked at about 1000°F.

Glass dishes are made of a glass which is manufactured from boric oxide, soda, and silica (sand). Pyroceram is made of metals, silica, and clay.

Malamine dishes are made by casting or pressing heat-softened plastic into dish shape.

The process of manufacturing china is illustrated in an accompanying figure. The clay-formed plate is called a bisque. The bisque is vitrified and then cleaned. At this point, a decoration may be applied as well as a glaze. The bisque is then baked (or fried) again at a temperature slightly less than 2200°F. Some final decorating in materials such as silver and gold that would melt at the vitrifying temperatures may be done after the final firing. This is called over-glazing.

The glaze is a type of glass that adds a shine and toughness to the china. The glaze should be even over the surface of the dish. When the glaze has worn through, after perhaps as many as 750 uses, the china should be discarded. It is important that the glaze allows water to "sheet" freely from its surface.

Decorations may be applied to the bisque by hand or may be stenciled or decaled onto the plate. The china must be baked separately for each color used in decoration so the more colors added, the more manufacturing expense. Having a custom pattern, with good dish-handling procedures, should add only a fraction of a cent to the cost-per-use of china, but it will require placement of large orders and delivery lead time of about six months.

For foodservice use, china must be strong. The addition of aluminum oxide to the clay, in place of the ground quartz usually used, will make the china as much as twice as tough and increase chip resistance many times over. Such china is said to have an alumna body. Toughness is also increased by having a thicker body, thicker base (well), and rolled or scalloped edges. The china should be able to take rapid temperature changes and impacts to the body and edge. The glaze should withstand moisture and sharp knives.

There are no standard sizes for dishes. Each manufacturer has its own sizes, and frequently not all those sizes in all the patterns carried.

China grades are as follows:

- Selects ⎫
- Firsts ⎬ Rum of the Kiln
- Seconds
- Thirds
- Culls or dumps

Glasses

As mentioned earlier, glass is made by fusing sand (silica) in combination with soda and lime. Addition of metals to this mixture will add strength and beauty. Thus, good crystal has 24 percent lead. There is one line of very competitively priced glassware available today which is extremely difficult to break.

Glassware is usually very fragile. It may be made stronger by addition of metals or compounds, by being cooled slowly, by being reheated and recooled (causing the surfaces to shrink and gain tensile strength), and by shaping in other than straight or flared shapes or by being made thicker.

Standard glass sizes are illustrated.

Flatware

Due to the skyrocketing prices of silver, stainless steel flatware is in use in most restaurants and institutions. Stainless steel flatware may cost as little as 10 to 50 percent as much as silverplate and 3 to 15 percent as much as sterling silver. It is not difficult to understand the wide acceptance of stainless steel on raw cost alone, but it is even easier to understand when one considers the necessity of burnishing and periodic replating of silverplate.

Much stainless steel flatware is punched out of sheets of stainless steel. The biggest part of the spread in price in stainless steel flatware comes in the manufacturing process. That which is not punched out is made from stainless steel which has been formed to different thicknesses by rollers. This process, known as grading, produces a stronger utensil which is higher priced. Good stainless steel flatware will be at least 12 gauge.

The best stainless steel flatware is manufactured from 18-8 chrome nickel. Next would be 17-7 chrome nickel. There are other chrome alloys which are known by their numbers, 301, 302, 410, 430, with the higher number representing more chrome in the alloy. The chrome content determines the lightness and brightness of the color, which is a positive factor that has to be weighed against the ease with which chrome rusts and pits.

The finish given stainless steel equipment is usually No. 4. Stainless steel flatware is usually given the brighter and more reflective No. 2B or No. 7 finish.

The important considerations with teaspoons are the strength of the neck. Hollow handle knives give better balance but must be welded to the blade. The weld point is usually susceptible to rust and may be hard to sanitize. Forks, especially, should not

HOW CHINA IS MADE

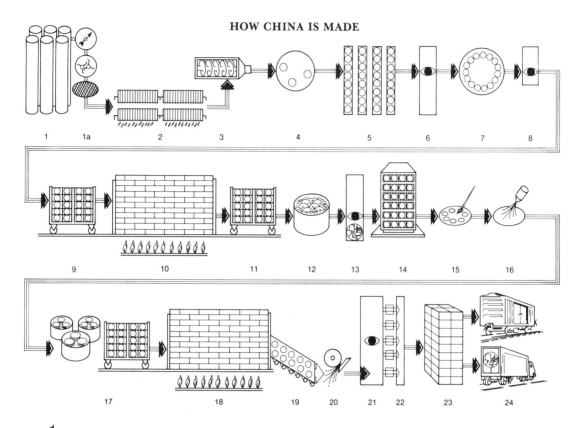

1   1a   2   3   4   5   6   7   8

9   10   11   12   13   14   15   16

17   18   19   20   21   22   23   24

1 RAW MATERIAL STORAGE   Finely pulverized inorganic raw materials are pneumatically unloaded from railroad cars and stored in large concrete silos.

1a BODY BATCHING   Raw materials are automatically weighed and mixed with water to specific formulas by a programmed system that is unique in the industry. Oversize particles and magnetic impurities are removed by fine screening and magnetic separators. The resultant body slurry, or "slip," is stored in large holding tanks under constant agitation.

2 FILTER PRESSING   The body slip is pumped under high pressure into filter presses where the excess water is removed forming square filter cakes having the required moisture content.

3 VACUUM PUG MILLING   Filter press cakes are fed into pug mills which further homogenize the clay, removing included air and moisture to improve the workability. The mills extrude "pugs" of required cross section and length for the ware forming operations.

4 JIGGERING   This is the basic forming operation. Slices from the clay pugs are formed into various shapes . . . cups, saucers and plates . . .by automatic or semi-automatic machines using rotational or pressure forming techniques on plaster molds. Guiding these delicate operations are the deft hands of highly skilled artisans who blend the traditions of the past with the newest technology of today.

5 MOLD RELEASE DRYING   Approximately one half of the forming moisture is removed in these controlled heat dryers, allowing the ware to release evenly and without distortion from the molds. Molds are returned to the jigger for the next forming cycle.

6 INSPECTION   As ware is removed from the molds, it is carefully inspected and any imperfectly formed pieces are discarded. Syracuse China's Quality Assurance Laboratory has developed specific tests and standards which the ware must meet at each inspection stage in the manufacturing process. Experienced inspectors, their keen eyes trained by years of exposure to the art of china manufacturing, make swift, professional decisions with uncanny accuracy.

7 FINISHING   This stage of the craft is performed by individuals possessing not only manual dexterity, but also a well-honed sense of taste and judgment. Edges of plates and rims of cups are smoothed and rounded. Cup handles are attached and where necessary surfaces are lightly damp sponged to remove blemishes.

8 INSPECTION   To eliminate any ware not conforming to quality standards, another inspection is made at this point. Once again, each inspector's decisions are the result of years of professional experience and a precise knowledge of quality control standards. Imperfect ware is thrown out.

PREPARATION FOR FIRING   Since the product becomes fully vitrified and non-absorbent during the "bisque" or first firing, a thin layer of refractory parting agent must be applied to each piece of ware stacked for bisque firing to prevent fusion of one piece to another.

9 KILN CAR LOADING   The stacked ware is loaded on the bisque kiln car shelves for maximum utilization of the available space.

10 BISQUE KILN FIRING   To fully vitrify the body into a strong, sanitary, non-porous product, about 50 hours is required for the ware to transit through the tunnel kilns during which time the temperature reaches a peak of 2250°F, subsequently cooling back to room temperature.

11 KILN CAR LOADING   The cooled bisque ware is removed from the kiln cars and forwarded to the bisque cleaning area.

12 BISQUE CLEANING   To thoroughly remove the firing parting agent and smooth the surface to facilitate subsequent decorating steps, the ware is passed through vibratory barrel finishers or tube tumblers where abrasive media scours the ware. The removed powder is flushed away with water.

13 INSPECTION   This inspection selects out all ware that fails to meet quality standards. All accepted ware is back-stamped with the familiar Syracuse China logo at this time.

14 BISQUE WAREHOUSING   The accepted bisque china is recorded into the computer inventory and placed in storage until ordered out by decorating department schedules.

15 DECORATING   Here a wide variety of underglaze and overglaze decorating techniques are employed using both machine and highly skilled manual applications of many specially compounded ceramic colors. A fully equipped decal printing plant . . . first in the entire industry to develop a successful multi-color underglaze decal . . . serves this department. Part of Syracuse China's rich heritage of decorating excellence is due to the talents of the artists and craftsmen who infuse each piece with a true element of handcraftsmanship; skills such as these, nurtured and developed over long years, are precious commodities which contribute to Syracuse China's design leadership.

16 GLAZING   A glaze slurry or "slip" coating of carefully controlled thickness is applied to the ware by spray or dip methods. This glaze—actually a high quality crystal—is compounded to fuse at glost kiln temperatures to form a hard, durable, glassy-smooth, transparent, continuous coating over the entire surface of the ware, allowing the underglaze decorations to show through in their true colors.

17 GLOST KILN PLACING   The glaze coated ware is supported on special ceramic pins in fire clay box-like saggers or open racks for passage through the glost kilns.

18 GLOST KILN FIRING   Glost firing takes place in tunnel kilns similar to those used for bisque firing with about 30 hours being required to reach the peak temperature of 2140°F and subsequent cooling. A small percentage of glazed ware is returned to the decorating department for the application of overglaze gold lines or special decals.

19 GLOST KILN CAR UNLOADING Saggers and racks of fired ware are unloaded from the cars, the ware removed and placed on conveyors.

20 PIN GRINDING   The three small marks left on the underside of the flatware by the support pins are removed in this operation. Gold decorations are burnished to bring up their full color and luster. Each craftsman exhibits the surehanded control and refined judgment of a master jeweler as the ware is given its finishing touches.

21 INSPECTION AND SORTING The moment of truth for each piece of Syracuse China. The inspectors at this final stage are true connoisseurs of the state of the art in chinamaking; people whose valued judgment enables Syracuse China to offer consistently fine quality. Final inspection is made, defective ware thrown out and first quality ware sorted by shape, size and decorations.

22 PACKAGING   To reduce handling and warehousing problems for our customers, and provide them with the advantages of transparent packaging, Syracuse China has introduced a rugged, transparent sleeve packaging concept called ChinaPak™, which is smaller and lighter than the traditional carton it replaces for many of our chinaware items.

23 GLOST WAREHOUSE   Packaged china is stored until disbursed by the order-service and shipping department. Computerized inventory control keeps stock at proper levels of availability.

24 SHIPPING   To the North, East, South, and West, Syracuse China is shipped by the best, fastest and safest carriers possible.

Courtesy: Syracuse China

Bar Service

Minimum quantities and assortment required for service of 50 to 75 guests during a two hour rush period.

No. 48—2 oz. Lined Whiskey Jigger
1 oz. Capacity Line
For "good measure"... or serving straight.

No. 225—9 oz. Hi-Ball
For all liquor highballs mixed with water, soda or ginger ale—good, too, for fizzes, daisies, rickeys, sangarees, spritzers and swizzles.

No. 226—11 oz. Collins
Made for Tom or John Collins, plus many soft drinks.

No. 227—7¼ oz. New Fashioned
Besides New Fashioneds, this is fine for aperitifs, crustas, on-the-rocks, smashes and toddies.

No. 1178—10 oz. Heat Treated
Beer Glass
An appropriate glass for all beers, ales, porter and stout.

No. 3770—4½ oz. Cocktail Glass
This is the glass for a multitude of cocktails—from ever-popular Manhattans and Martinis to Side Cars and Stingers.

No. 3775—4½ oz. Sour
For all sours, whether made with whiskey, rum, brandy, vodka or gin.

No. 8491—1 oz. Dutch Cordial
That special service for all the delightful sips called cordials (liqueurs)—from Benedictine to Drambuie and Anisette to Triple Sec.

No. 3792—2 oz. Lined Brandy—
1 oz. Line
Specially for brandy... can be used with liqueurs, cordials, etc.

No. 3788—3 oz. Sherry
Try this also with "sipping" liqueurs, cordials, etc.

No. 3765—8½ oz. Wine
Proper for serving a wide variety of red and white table wines or fortified wines, such as port or muscatel.

No. 3773—5½ oz. Champagne
Whether imported or domestic, white or pink, champagne and all sparkling wines belong in a champagne glass. Fine also for a frozen daiquiri.

Libbey Glass, Division of Owens, Illinois.

have any rough edges. Rough edges, scratches, and manufacturing defects of all kinds should not be accepted.

Silverplated flatware is used where elegance and class are a must. Silverplated flatware is manufactured by coating a basically copper and nickel "blank" with silver through electrolysis. The points of greatest wear, the spoon bowl back and fork tines, for example, should have an undercoating or inlay of silver to prevent wearing through.

Silverplate is purchased by the weight of the silver in a gross of teaspoons and the weight of the blank. The silver weight will vary from 2½ ounces to 8 ounces per gross and the blank weight from 9 to 11 pounds per gross.

HOTEL AND RESTAURANT TABLEWARE COST AND AMORTIZATION WORK SHEET

This work sheet affords a simple and fast method to aid the food-service operator in establishing cost of flatware for original installation and future replacement cost as well as cost per meal.

Pattern Name __Chateau_____ Line __Oneida Deluxe Stainless Steel_____

Place Setting Consists of: 2 Teaspoons, 2 Forks, 1 Soup Spoon, ⅓ Iced Teas, ⅓ Oyster Forks, 1 Knife

	With H. H. Knife $9.13	
Cost Per Place Setting	With 1-Pc Knife $7.21	

1. Number of seats		200
2. Number of place settings (1.5 × number of seats) (1-pc kn)		300
3. Number of place settings × cost per place setting		2163.00
4. Cost for 1 years replacement @ 25% orig. install. cost		540.75
*5. *Total numbers 3 & 4 to get total 1st year cost*		2703.75
6. Average number of meals served daily		800
7. Number of annual business days		360
8. Number of meals served per year *(Multiply #6 × #7)*		288000
9. *Divide dollar total (#5) by yearly meals served (#8) to get cost per meal served for 1st year*		.009¢
10. Cost for 1 years replacement @ 25% original installation cost (Same as #4)		540.75
11. Number of meals served per year (Same as #8)		288000
12. *Divide dollar total (#10) by number of meals served (#11) to get cost per meal served for 2nd year*		.0018¢

Third, Fourth, Fifth and ensuing years - Same as #12

*When using these computations, with an existing food-service operation, there may be a trade-in value or tax write off figure on in-use flatware. If so, simply subtract such value from #5 to arrive at true 1st year investment.

Oneida Ltd. Silversmiths, Oneida, N.Y. 13421.

TABLEWARE FACTS

1. Women are among the most valued patrons of the majority of good restaurants and, much more so than men, they are very conscious of all table arrangements. Some of the rules which you would do well to keep in mind when setting tables follow. They are the same things that most women are well aware of when they set their own tables at home.

2. First of all, in any table arrangement, place settings should be directly opposite each other unless there is an odd number. Allow a minimum of eighteen inches for each setting because nothing is more uncomfortable and ungracious than being crowded while eating.

3. All flatware, china and napkins should be in a straight line, one inch from the edge of the table, and you should use only the pieces required by the food actually being served. Do not use more than six pieces at a time, except in the instance where the cocktail fork is used. If the menu calls for more, then put the dessert pieces on the table at the time that course is served.

4. Pieces are placed in the order in which they are used, with the forks on the left, knives, spoons and cocktail forks on the right. Be sure the cutting edge of the knife is turned in toward the plate. Except in the case of a formal dinner when the napkin is placed on the service plate, the napkin goes to the left of the fork. It may be folded into square, oblong or triangle shape but more elaborate and tricky folds are not in especially good taste.

5. The water glass should be placed above the knife, and if other glasses are used, they go to the right of the water glass. Be sure that salt and pepper shakers are available so that it isn't necessary to interrupt the meal to pass them constantly. Make certain, too, that centerpieces are low enough so that diners can see each other across the table. If candles are on the table, they must be lit, and they should be a proper length so that the flame is out of the line of vision.

Hotel/Restaurant Division, Oneida Ltd. Silversmiths, Oneida, N.Y. 13421

SUGGESTED REQUIREMENTS FOR YOUR GUIDANCE

The following table is based on normal operation and is divided into 3 types of feeding operations:

Requirements per seat:	Hotel dining rooms	Average good restaurant or coffee shop	Smaller operation
Teaspoon	5	4	4
Dessert or Soup Spoon	2	2	2
Tablespoon	¼	¼	—
Iced Drink Spoon	1½	1½	1
A. D. Coffee Spoon	2	—	—
Bouillon Spoon	2	2	2
Restaurant Fork	3	3	3
Salad or Pastry Fork	1½	1½	—
Cocktail or Oyster Fork	1½	1½	1½
Dinner Knife	2	2	2
B & B Knife/Butter Spreader	1½	1	—

SILVERPLATED TABLEWARE

Follow these simple steps that insure sparkling silverware service and satisfied customers

1. *Washing* Silverware should be pre-soaked immediately following its removal from the table. Be sure that it is not allowed to remain in the water too long before it is washed in hot water and a good non-abrasive soap or detergent. Use extreme caution in selecting your cleaning agent, making absolutely sure there are no abrasive qualities in it which might damage your silverware. *A word of caution*—It is in the pre-soaking that improper use of detergent or compound causes discoloration and corroding of stainless knife blades. This is particularly true if an aluminum pan is used. Except when de-tarnishing, use a plastic or stainless steel pan for pre-soaking.

2. *Rinsing* The clean silverware should be rinsed in water of at least 180°. This is an important step and do not spare the amount of water used. A wetting agent may be added to the rinse to prevent minerals in water from staining your silverware. Again, make sure this wetting agent contains no chemicals harmful to silver. Should you have very hard water, a softener is recommended.

3. *Handling* When specialized silver washing equipment is not available, excellent results are achieved by a silver handling system. Perforated cylinders in a portable rack—suitable for sink or dishwasher use—make it possible to wash, transport and dispense silver with a minimum of handling. The tableware should be sorted into cylinders, eating side down, to prevent hand contamination after the cleansing operation. The cylinder should be made of nylon or stainless steel.

4. *De-tarnishing* A most important step in proper silver care is proper de-tarnishing, particularly prior to burnishing. There are a number of commercial preparations on the market to do this job. They are a convenient, efficient way to de-tarnish silverplate. Consult with a reputable detergent manufacturer as to his recommendations. In every case the *directions should be followed carefully;* and in *no case* should the items remain in the solution for more than *one* minute. The reason for this is that all de-tarnishing agents contain some chlorides which can harm silver when over concentrated, or over exposed. A less convenient, but effective, and inexpensive de-tarnishing solution can be made by placing 1 tablespoon each of salt and baking soda in 1 gallon of boiling water in a clean aluminum vessel; or one lined with aluminum foil. *It is imperative that knives with stainless blades be removed* from the de-tarnishing solution *within 30 seconds.* The de-tarnishing action tends to discolor or corrode stainless steel if left in for a longer time.

5. *Burnishing* There are fine burnishing machines on the market, manufactured in sizes to fit any operation. The dollars invested in this piece of equipment pay excellent dividends in sparkling, customer-pleasing flatware; plus increased wear due to the hardening and scratch-removing action of the burnishing process. As with any other piece of fine equipment—keep it clean and follow the manufacturer's instructions. Your burnisher will then give you many years of sparkling flatware; a luster which can be achieved by no other means. *Sparkling silverplate brings your customers back again and again!*

6. *Storage* Provide adequate space, preferably away from tarnishing effects of the kitchen. Make sure that the silverware is clean when you store it. Store your silverplate in tarnish-resistant cabinets. When stored under such conditions, it will be clean whenever you use it.

Hotel/Restaurant Division, Oneida Ltd. Silversmiths, Oneida, N.Y. 13421

QUESTIONS

1. Define the following terms:

   tensil strength
   thread count
   Verel®
   Sef®
   Leavil®
   polyester
   "tris"
   Nomex®
   sanforizing
   chain and stuffer yarns
   shots
   pitch ply
   malamine
   vitrification
   stoneware
   pottery
   china
   terra cotta

2. In order of priority, list the three most important features in the selection of proper linens.
3. Of what significance is the cost per use of a tablecloth to an operator?
4. Distinguish between warp and weft.
5. Give examples of fabrics used in a food service operation where the abrasion test would be important.
6. What characteristics do fabrics made of acetate, rayon, and tri-acetate have in common?
7. When looking for flame-retardant fibers, what information should be included on the labels?
8. What are the advantages of vat-dyed fabrics?
9. Write a specification for use when purchasing a tablecloth.
10. What are the differences between woven, knitted, and texturized woven fabrics?
11. A carpet's service quality generally refers to what characteristics?
12. Discuss the basic factors experienced buyers will use to determine the quality of a carpet.
13. What is the significance of the backing material in carpet selection?
14. In carpeting a hospital cafeteria, what would the recommended padding weight (oz./sq. yd.) be? What material would you select for padding?
15. Distinguish between foam and sponge.
16. How can the buyer determine the amount of filler content in a foam sample?

17. Give examples of carpet-type fibers which are of high quality when considering: wear life, resilience, soil resistance, wet cleanability.
18. Discuss five key points to consider when purchasing carpeting for a new area.
19. How is glass made?
20. What are the specifications of a high quality stainless steel flatware? What about silverplate?

15

SMALLWARES

INTRODUCTION

Small equipment is used to portion, transfer, and cook in. Materials are discussed in relation to what is the best conductor, has the lightest weight, and is the strongest. A mass of equipment is described and there are some comparison examples given for aid in recognizing utensils.

The smallwares, hand utensils, and equipment, are relatively inexpensive when considered individually, but taken as a whole, they account for a substantial investment in the foodservice operation.

Smallwares see the most constant use of all kitchen equipment. Unlike fixed equipment, they are constantly being banged around, dropped, and subjected to abuse. Improper selection of these items can result in unhappy employees, frequent replacement of equipment, and reduced efficiency of production.

For example, scoops or dishers with a weak mechanism soon make releasing dished food nearly impossible: employees either lose time or switch to the wrong size (but functioning) scoop. Selection of knives manufactured of a metal which does not "hold an edge" long may result in loss of time as well as employee injuries. Selection of aluminum pots for preparing tomato sauces will certainly result in an acrid sauce as well as a short life for the pot due to the way that high ph foods "eat" aluminum.

The considerations given to the purchase of smallwares should be:

1. What is the frequency of use? The strongest, most durable piece should be selected for frequently used items. Infrequently used items may be of lesser quality.
2. Safety. Knives without blade guards, for example, impose an unneeded kitchen hazard.
3. Sanitation. Select equipment which has easy to clean surfaces. Look for the National Sanitation Foundation (NSF) sticker as a guarantee of easy-cleaning design.
4. Ease of use. Pick the equipment that is easiest to handle. Why create unnecessary labor?

Aluminum is a good material for pots and pans because of its good thermal conduction properties, but it has disadvantages in that it corrodes fairly easily and is damaged by alkaline cleaning compounds. Aluminum pots and pans are generally manufactured in light, medium, and heavy weight cast-aluminum, whereas utensils are made of sheet aluminum. Because their equipment damages easily, you should assure that aluminum smallwares are made of anodized aluminum. Aluminum is inexpensive when compared to stainless steel or copper.

Cast-iron is inexpensive and heavy. Little cast-iron is selected for commercial use because of its tendency to rust, break when dropped, and heavy weight.

Copper has the best thermal conduction properties of the metals used for kitchen equipment, but it is also the most expensive material. Before purchasing copper utensils you should consider the ease with which it scratches, dents, and forms a green rust. If desired, copper's conduction can be obtained at lower cost by purchasing pots and pans with copper bottoms or copper cores covered with stainless steel.

Stainless steel is often the material of choice because it is pretty and durable. The choice of stainless steel in hand tools is usually wise but not so wise in pots and pans. Stainless steel is a poor thermal conductor, expensive, and heavy as compared to aluminum. It does clean relatively easily and is resistent to corrosion.

Sheet steel is an inexpensive material commonly used for baking and roasting pans. As with cast-iron, sheet steel rusts easily.

Tin is often used for pie tins (though the trend is to disposable aluminum) and for coating sheet steel, cast steel, and copper utensils such as mixing bowls. Tin is rust resistent but wears through quickly.

Plastics that can withstand 300°F and take virtually as much abuse as metals have been available in commercial equipment since the early 1970s. Relatively expensive, they are finding increasing acceptance due to their very light weight and optical transparency.

Enameled porcelain utensils have virtually disappeared from the commercial kitchen due to the ease with which they crack, chip, and scratch. It cleans easily and is inexpensive, but is not recommended by this author.

Knowledge of smallwares terminology is important in purchasing. The unaware buyer might need a china cap but order a collander, need a meat turner and get a spatula. The listing that follows should clarify matters.

CUTTING IMPLEMENTS

- Boning Knife. A short, thin knife with a pointed blade used to remove bone from raw meat with minimal waste. It may be either stiff or flexible. Popular lengths run 6 to 8 inches.
- Butcher's Steel. A round steel rod, approximately 1½ feet long with a wooden handle, used to maintain an edge on a knife. It does not sharpen the edge but merely straightens it and breaks off the burrs after sharpening. It is magnetized to remove burrs.
- Clam Knife. A short, flat bladed, round-tipped knife used to open clams.

- Cleaver. An extra wide, carbon steel, heavy, square blade knife used to chop bones.
- French Knife. The most used piece of equipment. Near the handle, the blade is wide and generally a bolster is present; the blade tapers to a point. It is used for slicing, chopping, mincing, and dicing. The most popular blade lengths are 8, 10, and 12 inches.
- Ham Slicer. A narrow, long, flexible carbon steel blade about 12 inches long, so named because it is used to slice ham.
- Hand Meat Saw. A thin, fine-toothed blade, attached to a bow-shaped metal frame with a wooden handle, used to saw through bone structure of edible animals. Hand meat saws are available in two or three sizes.
- Paring Knife (vegetable knife). A short, pointed blade knife, 2 ½ to 3 ⅓ inches long, used for paring fruits and vegetables. Point is used to remove eyes and blemishes in the fruits and vegetables.
- Pastry Wheel. A round, stainless steel disc with a cutting edge and mounted handle used to cut all types of pastry.
- Pie and Cake Knives. An offset knife with a wide, flat blade tapered to a point, shaped like a wedge of cake or pie, and used to cut and serve pies and cakes without breaking the pieces.
- Potato or Vegetable Peeler. A cutting tool with a metal blade attached to a metal handle. The blade is in the form of a loop, with sharpened edges, formed over a pin or axis attached to the handle. The blade will shift from side to side, so peeling may be done in two different directions.
- Oyster Knife. A short, slightly thin, dull-edged knife, with a tapered point. It is used to open oysters.
- Roast Beef Slicer. A round nosed, long blade knife (14 inches) used to slice any size beef roast.

Small knives (top to bottom): steak knife, steak knife—alternate design, 3-inch paring knife, poultry paring knife, spreader, and spatula. (*"Courtesy of Wear-Ever Food Service Equipment."*)

Utility knives (top to bottom): 5-inch utility slicer, 6-inch utility slicer, 8-inch utility slicer, 9-inch utility/bread slicer, and 10-inch utility/bread slicer. (*"Courtesy of Wear-Ever Food Service Equipment."*)

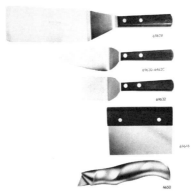

Utensils (top to bottom): turner, pie and cake server, all-purpose server, dough cutter, and carton knife. (*"Courtesy of Wear-Ever Food Service Equipment."*)

Butcher knives (top to bottom): 8-inch butcher knife, 10-inch butcher knife, 10-inch scimitar (curved steak knife), 12-inch scimitar, and cleaver. (*"Courtesy of Wear-Ever Food Service Equipment."*)

Meat knives (top to bottom): 12-inch beef slicer, 12-inch beef slicer with serrated edge, 14-inch beef slicer, 14-inch beef slicer with serrated edge, and 10-inch ham slicer. (*"Courtesy of Wear-Ever Food Service Equipment."*)

Boning knives (top to bottom): 5-inch narrow boning knife, 6-inch wide boning knife, 6-inch narrow boning knife, and 6-inch curved boning knife. (*"Courtesy of Wear-Ever Food Service Equipment."*)

Larger knives (top to bottom): 8-inch French knife, 10-inch French knife, 12-inch French knife, and steel (for sharpening). (*"Courtesy of Wear-Ever Food Service Equipment."*)

FOOD HANDLING IMPLEMENTS

- Food Tongs. Spring-type metal consisting of two limbs shaped like a U with a saw-tooth grip on each end. They are used to pick up and serve foods without using the hands.
- Hot-Cake or Meat Turner. A wide, flat, offset chisel-edged blade with a wooden handle. It is used to slip under and turn hot cakes, hamburgers, and so forth while grilling, broiling, etc.
- Kitchen Fork. A large, two pronged fork used for holding meat while slicing, turning roasts, and broiling steaks.

STIRRING, SERVING, SCRAPING, AND SPREADING IMPLEMENTS

- Ladle. A stainless steel cup, solid or perforated, attached to a long handle used to stir, mix, and dip. It is also used to serve sauces, dressing, and other liquids when portion control is desired. Ladles are available in many sizes. The following relates ladle size to the approximate weight of the portion in ounces.

Ladle Size	Approx. Weight of Portion
¼ cup	2 ounces
½ cup	4 ounces
¾ cup	6 ounces
1 cup	8 ounces

- Melon Ball or Parisienne Scoop. A stainless steel blade formed into a round half-ball cut attached to a handle. It is used for cutting various fruits and vegetables into small balls.
- Pierced Kitchen Spoon. A large stainless steel spoon, pierced with holes so liquid will run off, used to serve small cut vegetables (for example, diced carrots, peas, or corn).
- Plastic Scraper. A flexible piece of plastic approximately 4 inches wide and 6 inches long, used to scrape down bowls when mixing batters so that all ingredients will be incorporated into the mixture.
- Scraper or Dough Cutter. A wide, rectangular metal blade, mounted with a wooden handle, used for scraping meat blocks and cutting doughs.
- Skimmer. A flat, stainless steel perforated disc connected to a long handle. It is used to skim grease or food particles from soups, stocks, or sauces.
- Slotted Kitchen Spoon. A large stainless steel spoon with three to four slots cut into the base of the spoon so the liquid will drain off. It is used to serve large, cut vegetables or whole items without its liquid.
- Solid Kitchen Spoon. A large stainless steel spoon, holding about 3 ounces, used to perform the task of folding, stirring, and serving.

- Spatula or Palette Knife (the names are used interchangeably). A broad, flexible, flat or offset blade knife with round nose used for mixing, spreading, and sometimes scraping. It comes in lengths from 3⅓ to 12 inches and is semi-flexible to highly flexible. It is used mostly for spreading icing on cakes.
- Wood or Metal Paddles. They come in various lengths and sizes and are used to stir foods in deep pots or steam kettles.

Two-quart transfer ladle. (*"Courtesy of Wear-Ever Food Service Equipment."*)

Two-quart dipper. (*"Courtesy of Wear-Ever Food Service Equipment."*)

Paddle. (*"Courtesy of Wear-Ever Food Service Equipment."*)

FOOD PREPARATION IMPLEMENTS

- Box Grater. A metal box with various sized grids used to rub or wear food into small particles.
- China Cap. A pointed, extra strong strainer, shaped like a Chinaman's cap. It has a long handle and hook for hanging on side of pots and is used to strain gravies, soups, sauces, and other liquids or semi-liquids.
- Colander. A bowl-shaped strainer with loop handles, usually made from stainless steel. It is perforated to allow liquids to run off and is used in washing cooked spaghetti and other pastas.
- Strainer. A perforated metal bowl with a fairly long handle and hook for placing across pots. It is used to strain and drain all types of foods.
- Wire Whips. There are two kinds that are in popular use in the commercial kitchen. French whips are fairly steady; piano whips are more delicate and flexible. Each serves its purpose, depending on the consistency of the item being whipped. Whips are constructed of wire loops with ends brought together to form a handle. They are used for whipping eggs, cream, gravies, sauces, etc.

Sieve. (*"Courtesy of Wear-Ever Food Service Equipment."*)

Colander. (*"Courtesy of Wear-Ever Food Service Equipment."*)

Strainer. (*"Courtesy of Wear-Ever Food Service Equipment."*)

Wooden roller (to use with china cap). (*"Courtesy of Wear-Ever Food Service Equipment."*)

China cap (to use with wooden roller). (*"Courtesy of Wear-Ever Food Service Equipment."*)

BAKING IMPLEMENTS

- Bench Brush. A long, thin brush with long black or white bristles set in vulcanized rubber with a wooden handle. A bench brush is used to brush excess flour from the bench when working with pastry doughs.
- Flour Sifter. A round metal container varying in height and diameter, with a sieve or screen stretched across the bottom. A device, such as paddle wheel, is installed to help work the material being sifted through the sieve. The purpose of the sifting is to make products light and fluffy.
- Pastry Bag. Cone-shaped cloth bag made of duck (water repellent cloth) or other materials used to decorate cakes with icing, plank steaks with duchess potatoes, short cakes with whipped topping, etc.
- Pastry Brush. Similar to a paint brush. A narrow shaped implement made of bristles or other material fixed to a plastic, metal, or wooden handle. They are

used to brush on icing or egg wash (a mixture of egg and milk) when working with certain types of pastry.

- Pastry Tubes. A metal canister with metal tips with various shaped openings used to decorate cakes, canapes, cookies, etc.
- Peel. A fairly long, flat, narrow piece of wood with a handle at one end. It is shaped like a paddle, and it is used to place pizzas in the oven and to remove them.
- Pie and Cake Marker. A round, heavy wire disc with guide bars for accurate marking of pies or cakes prior to cutting. They come in various diameters and portion sizes.
- Rolling pin. A roller, made of wood, teflon, or other materials, ranging in size from 10½ to 25 inches. Handles are attached on each side of the roller. The rolling pin is used to roll pie dough, sweet dough, biscuit dough, etc.

MEASURING DEVICES

Most recipes are given in weight, however, some are given in measures. The common measures used are: teaspoon, tablespoon, cup, pint, quart, and gallon. Their common abbreviations usually found in recipes is given. Also included is the relationships of the various measures and weights to each other, an aid in converting from one measure to another.

Abbreviations for Recipes

Tsp.	Teaspoon
Tbsp.	Tablespoon
Pt.	Pint
Qt.	Quart
Gal.	Gallon
Oz.	Ounce
Lb.	Pound
Bch.	Bunch

Equivalents of Measures

1 Pinch	½ Teaspoon (Approx.)
3 Teaspoons	1 Tablespoon
16 Tablespoons	1 Cup
1 Cup	½ Pint
2 Cups	1 Pint
2 Pints	1 Quart
4 Quarts	1 Gallon
16 Ounces	1 Pound
1 Pound (water)	1 Fluid Pint
2 Pounds (water)	1 Fluid Quart

For example, if 2½ pounds of water is called for, this may be measured at 1 fluid quart and 1 cup. (Two pounds of water is equivalent to 1 fluid quart. A fluid pint is equivalent to 1 pound of water, but since 1 pint is also equivalent to 2 cups, ½ pound of water would be equivalent to 1 cup of water.) Occasionally a recipe will call for a ''pinch'' of some ingredient. This would be roughly equivalent to ½ of a teaspoon.

- Measures. Metal cups, round, with a slight lip for easy pouring. They have a side handle and are accurately graduated in quarters. They are available in gallons, half-gallons, quarts, and pints. They are used to measure liquids and some dry ingredients.
- Measuring Cup Set. A set consists of one-quarter, one-third, one-half, and one cup measures. These aluminum cups are used to measure liquids and some dry ingredients.
- Scoops (ice cream). A metal bowl of known capacity with an extended handle and thumb-operated level to release the item it holds. Scoops are used to serve food and also to control the portion. The various sizes of scoops or dippers are designated by numbers. The following tables relate the numbers to their approximate capacity in ounces, and the scoop numbers to the approximate content of each scoop size in cups or tablespoons. The numbers which identify scoops or dippers indicate the number of scoopfuls required to make 1 quart. Scoops or dippers are used for portioning muffin batter, meat patties, potatoes, rice, bread dressing, croquette mixtures, some vegetables and salads, etc.

Scoop. (*''Courtesy of Wear-Ever Food Service Equipment.''*)

SCOOP OR DIPPER SIZES AND APPROX. WEIGHTS

Scoop or Dipper No.	Approximate Weight
8	5 ozs.
10	4 ozs.
12	3 ozs.
16	2 to 2½ ozs.
20	1⅔ ozs.
24	1½ ozs.
30	1¼ ozs.
40	1 oz.

SCOOP OR DIPPER SIZES AND APPROX. MEASURES

Scoop or Dipper No.	Level Measure	Scoop or Dipper No.	Level Measure
8	½ Cup	20	3⅕ Tbsp.
10	⅖ Cup	24	2⅔ Tbsp.
12	⅓ Cup	30	2⅕ Tbsp.
16	¼ Cup	40	1⅗ Tbsp.

COOKING UTENSILS

- Bain Marie. A stainless steel food storage container which is round and has high walls. They are available in many sizes from 1¼ quarts to 11 quarts. Also a pan for holding hot water into which other pans, containing food, etc., are put for heating.
- Bake Pan. A rectangular, aluminum pan with straight or sloped medium-high walls and loop handles. Bake pans are used for baking apples, macaroni, and certain meat and vegetable items.
- Braiser. A shallow-walled, large round pot. It has a large surface that comes in contact with the heat for quicker heating, has loop handles for easy lifting, and is very heavy to resist warping under high heat. It is used for braising, stewing, and searing meats. Braisers are available in sizes from 15 to 28 quarts.
- Double Boiler. Consists of two containers. The bottom part resembles a stock pot and holds the boiling water; the upper section is suspended in the boiling water, thus preventing contact with direct heat. A double boiler is used to prepare items that will scorch quickly if they come in contact with direct heat. Items such as cream pie filling, pudding, etc., are prepared in a double boiler. Double boilers are available in sizes ranging from 8 to 40 quarts.
- Frying or Saute Pan. A round, sloped, shallow-walled pan with a long handle and a hole in the end for easy hanging. They are generally made of aluminum and range from 7 to 16 inches in the top diameter. Frying or saute pans are used to saute vegetables and some meat items.
- Hand Meat Tenderizer: A solid, square block of cast aluminum attached to a wooden handle. The aluminum block is cast with two chopping grids—one coarse, the other fine. It is used to pound and break the muscle fibers of tough cuts of meat, therefore making the meat more tender.
- Iron Skillet. Made of thick, heavy iron. They hold heat well and are used for pan broiling and frying such items as chicken, pork chops, veal cutlets. Iron skillets are available in many sizes, with a top diameter of 6½ to 15¼ inches.
- Roasting Pan. A generally large, rectangular, medium to high-walled metal pan. Roasting pans can be purchased with or without covers and come in various sizes to fit any size oven. They are used for roasting beef, pork, veal, etc.
- Sauce Pan. A pan similar to the sauce pot, but smaller, shallower, and much lighter. It has only a single long handle with a hole in the end for easy hanging. It is used the same as a sauce pot but for smaller amounts.

- Sauce Pot. A fairly large, round, slightly deep pot with loop handles for easy lifting. It is used for cooking on top of the range when stirring and whipping is necessary.
- Sheet Pan. A very shallow, rectangular, metal pan used for baking cookies, sweet cakes, and sheet pies. Sheet pans are available in various sizes.
- Skewer. A pin of wood or metal used to hold foods together or in shape while broiling or sauteing them.
- Steel Skillet. Made of steel, light weight with sloping walls. They are used for frying eggs, potatoes, omelets, etc. Steel skillets are available in various sizes, with a top diameter of 6½ to 15⅞ inches.
- Stock Pot. A large round, high-walled pot made of either heavy or light metal. It has loop handles for easy lifting and, in some cases, is equipped with a faucet for drawing off contents. It is used for boiling and simmering items, such as turkeys, bones for stock, ham, and some vegetables. Size range from 2½ gallons to 40 gallons.

Sauce pot. (*"Courtesy of Wear-Ever Food Service Equipment."*)

Stock pot. (*"Courtesy of Wear-Ever Food Service Equipment."*)

Brazier. (*"Courtesy of Wear-Ever Food Service Equipment."*)

Sheet pan. (*"Courtesy of Wear-Ever Food Service Equipment."*)

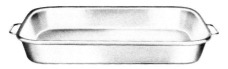

Bake pan. (*"Courtesy of Wear-Ever Food Service Equipment."*)

Fry pan. (*"Courtesy of Wear-Ever Food Service Equipment."*)

QUESTIONS

1. List reasons why hand tools have a short life.
2. Discuss material construction selection for a 2-inch full pan.
3. Discuss the differences between an oyster knife, palm knife, paring knife, and boring knife.

16

ENERGY

INTRODUCTION

This chapter explains some of the basic tools of financial analysis which are useful to operators in the economic evaluation of energy conservation opportunities. It is important that operators be able to quantify factors which ultimately affect the amount of profit attained. These factors include first cost, annual operating cost, annual fuel savings, projected fuel prices, and estimated lifetime.

Additional considerations that need be looked at along with first-level measures of performance are second-level measures of performance. These are discussed in the chapter and are those which incorporate an allowance for the time value of money, seen as a discount factor. Three of several second-level measures included are benefit/cost analysis, time to recoup capital investment, and internal rate of return. Examples of how to evaluate a capital investment explain the necessity for this type of calculation.

Guidelines are given for ensuring efficient systems. The most important factor for an efficient operation is keeping all parts of the system clean on a regularly scheduled basis. Annual energy consumption should be logged on a monthly basis to follow usage and notice potential problems.

A listing of publications to help build energy conservation systems is also included.

ENERGY FINANCIAL EVALUATION PROCEDURES[1]

Energy conservation opportunities (ECO's) which generate benefits greater than costs sacrificing product quality are generally profitable and therefore attractive. Those which require little more than operational changes that can be made at negligible cost clearly fall into this category. Many ECO's, however, require an initial capital outlay

---

[1]*Energy Conservation Program Guide for Industry and Commerce,* National Bureau of Standards Handbook 115, September 1974, pp. 5-1 to 5-5.

which must be amortized by the energy savings generated over their expected lifetime. Many ECO's that might have been unprofitable or merely marginal investments before the price of fuels and electricity began their rapid increase are now economically justifiable. The purpose of this section is to review some of the basic tools of financial analysis which may be useful in the economic evaluation of such ECO's.

Sound, consistent economic criteria for evaluating energy conservation opportunities are quite important. Before any investment is undertaken, some quantitative measure of profitability is desirable so that the investment's expected return can be compared with that for alternate investment opportunities. Because true economic cost includes opportunity costs of foregone investments, ECO's should be considered to be profitable only when their expected rate of return is greater than that which could be realized from alternative investment opportunities, whether in energy conservation or elsewhere.

In reality, investment decisions are generally based on more than simple rates of return. Factors such as risk, cash flow, taxation schedules, preference between long- and short-term investments, and others should be considered as well. Since these factors may vary greatly among firms they will not be considered directly here. The outcome of any economic evaluation may be considerably affected by them, however, so they should not be overlooked in actual applications but used in conjunction with the measurement criteria presented here.

FIRST-LEVEL MEASURES OF PERFORMANCE

While many energy conservation opportunities may be found during a close examination of plant and operations, some can be quickly rejected because of a low or negative return on investment. First-level measures of performance can be useful in screening out such ECO's without the application of more sensitive second-level measures. In general, however, first-level measurements should not be used for justifying major investments for energy conservation projects since these measures do not reflect the time value of money. Because first-level measurements, such as "payback period" and "return on investments," are often referenced and useful for screening candidate investments, it is desirable to show how they are computed and why they are not complete.

The information needed to calculate these performances measures is as follows:

- First Cost, *FC*
- Annual Operating Cost (if any due to investment), *AOC*
- Annual Fuel Savings, *AFS*
- Projected Fuel Price, *PFP*
- Estimated Lifetime, *EL*

First cost is the estimated dollar cost of labor and materials required to implement the scheme. The other four items determine the annual benefit stream. (Salvage value of the investment is disregarded here.)

Projected fuel price represents an average fuel price during the estimated lifetime of the investment. The use of current fuel prices will result in lower total savings than can be reasonably expected, inducing a bias against energy conservation investments.

At this point, the net annual saving is defined for application in forthcoming equations and discussion:

$$\text{Net Annual Savings, } S = (AFS \times PFP) - \text{AOC}$$

Payback period (PP) is defined as the first cost divided by the net annual savings, or

$$PP = \frac{FC}{(AFS \times PFP) - AOC} \text{ or } \frac{FC}{S}$$

The payback period is then compared to the expected lifetime of the investment in order to make some rough judgment as to its potential for recoupment. A payback period of less than one-half the lifetime of an investment would generally be considered profitable where the lifetime is ten years or less.

The payback period as a measure of performance gives rise to problems, however. For instance, dollars saved in future years are credited the same as dollars saved in current years and comparisons between alternative investment opportunities of different lifetimes cannot be made.

Return on Investment (ROI) is somewhat superior to the above because it takes into account the depletion of the investment over its economic life by providing for renewal through a depreciation charge. Using a straight line depreciation charge (DC) where:

$$DC = \frac{FC}{EL}$$

the percent return on investment can be calculated using

$$ROI, \ \%/yr = \frac{S - DC}{FC} \times 100\%$$

ROI has the advantage of putting investments with different life expectancies on a comparable basis. It is frequently used in the financial analysis of potential investments because of its simplicity of calculation. Where the rate of return appears small, however (say less than 20 percent), second-level measurements are called for.

SECOND-LEVEL MEASURES OF PERFORMANCE

Second-level measures of performance are those which incorporate an allowance for the time value of money, generally in the form of a discount factor. Because of alternative investment opportunities, a dollar held today is worth more than a dollar held in some future time period. The internal rate of return on the best available investment alternative is generally considered to be the appropriate discount rate for evaluating new investment opportunities, unless this rate is below the true borrowing rate when a new investment needs to be financed. In this case, the discount rate must be at least as high as the borrowing rate.

While appropriate discount rates may differ widely in different industries and even among firms within the same industry, corporate discount rates usually run between 10 to 20 percent or higher. This, again, is equivalent to saying that such a return can be realized elsewhere and thus for a new investment to be justified it must yield a return somewhat greater than this. It should be noted that profits generated by energy savings are generally taxed at the same rate as profits earned elsewhere within or outside of the firm, affirming the need for an equivalent discount rate for energy saving projects.

Several second-level measurements for evaluating ECO's are available. The following will be presented and discussed: (1) benefit/cost analysis, (2) time to recoup capital investment, and (3) internal rate of return.

Benefit/cost analysis requires the direct comparison of the present value benefits (savings) generated by a given investment with its costs. Generally this is formulated in terms of a benefit/cost ratio (B/C). A ratio greater than unity implies that the expected net benefits (properly discounted and summed over the lifetime of the investment) will exceed the initial costs and therefore such an investment is profitable. Likewise, a benefit/cost ratio less than unity implies that such an investment is not profitable. As an absolute measure of the profitability of an investment this is generally considered superior to all others.

The stream of benefits, or net savings (S), when constant in each time period, can be expressed in terms of present value (PV) by using a discount rate (D) and summing the benefits over the expected lifetime (EL) of the project. The present value can be easily estimated using the present worth factors (PWF) in the accompanying Table. By finding the appropriate factor (PWF) for the discount rate (D) and expected lifetime (EL) of the investment and multiplying the factor (PWF) by the net annual savings (S), the present value (PV) of the future savings can be determined. If this present value is greater than the first cost of the investment, the project is profitable.

Time to recoup capital investment, or the "breakeven" period, is similar in concept to the payback period (PP) discussed earlier, except that the breakeven period takes discount rates into consideration. Again, the chief disadvantage of such a measurement is that investments of unequal lifetimes cannot be compared. However, this measurement of performance is often useful to financial planners and budget analysts.

The breakeven period (BP) can be quickly approximated using the present worth factors table. Locate in the column for the appropriate discount rate (D) the present worth factor (PWF) on either side of the payback period (PP) calculated as shown previously. The breakeven period (BP) will be between two years; interpolation will allow a closer approximation.

The Internal Rate of Return (IRR) is defined as that discount rate, (D), which reduces the stream of net returns associated with the investment to a present value of zero. While in general the IRR is not always a good measurement of economic performance, IRR will give good results when evaluating a project which has a fixed first cost followed by a stream of positive net benefits.

PRESENT WORTH FACTORS (PWF)

Lifetime (EL)	Discount Rate (D)				
	5%	10%	15%	20%	25%
1	0.952	0.909	0.870	0.833	0.800
2	1.859	1.736	1.626	1.528	1.440
3	2.723	2.487	2.283	2.106	1.952
4	3.546	3.170	2.855	2.589	2.362
5	4.329	3.791	3.352	2.991	2.689
6	5.076	4.355	3.784	3.326	2.951
7	5.786	4.868	4.160	3.605	3.161
8	6.463	5.335	4.487	3.837	3.329
9	7.108	5.759	4.772	4.031	3.463
10	7.722	6.145	5.019	4.192	3.571
11	8.306	6.495	5.234	4.327	3.656
12	8.863	6.814	5.421	4.439	3.725
13	9.394	7.103	5.583	4.533	3.780
14	9.899	7.367	5.724	4.611	3.824
15	10.380	7.606	5.847	4.675	3.859
16	10.838	7.824	5.954	4.730	3.887
17	11.274	8.022	6.047	4.775	3.910
18	11.690	8.201	6.128	4.812	3.928
19	12.085	8.365	6.198	4.843	3.942
20	12.462	8.514	6.259	4.870	3.954
21	12.821	8.649	6.312	4.891	3.963
22	13.163	8.772	6.359	4.909	3.970
23	13.489	8.883	6.399	4.925	3.976
24	13.799	8.985	6.434	4.937	3.981
25	14.094	9.077	6.464	4.948	3.985

Unfortunately, the calculation of *IRR* is not a straightforward exercise but requires an iterative approach converging on the solution. Many computerized financial analysis programs can estimate this quite easily. While the *IRR* does not require that a discount rate be used in its determination (we are solving for the discount rate), it will be explicitly compared to the appropriate discount rate for the firm in justifying the investment. *IRR,* like the benefit/cost ratio, is useful when comparing the expected rates of return for alternative investments.

EXAMPLE OF CALCULATION

Management is considering a capital investment in its manufacturing process for energy conservation purposes which will cost $100,000 to design and install but will involve no new recurring costs. This project is expected to save an average of 27,500 MBtu of natural gas per year for the next ten years. The projected average cost of this fuel during the time period is assumed to be $1.00 per MBtu. Assuming that management feels that a 20 percent discount rate is appropriate, will this be a profitable investment?

First Cost (FC) = \$100,000
Annual Fuel Savings (AFS) = 27,500 MBtu/yr
Projected Fuel Price (PFP) = \$1.00/MBtu
Net Annual Savings (S) = $(AFS \times PFP)$
$$- AOC$$
$$= 27{,}500 \text{ MBtu/yr}$$
$$\times 1.00 \text{ \$/MBtu} - 0$$
$$= \$27{,}500 \text{ per yr}$$

First-Level Measures of Performance

Payback Period (No Discounting)

$$PP = \frac{FC}{S} = \frac{\$100{,}000}{\$27{,}500/\text{yr}} = 3.6 \text{ yr}$$

Return on Investment

$$DC = \frac{FC}{EL} = \frac{\$100{,}000}{10 \text{ yr}} = \$10{,}000 \text{ per yr}$$

$$ROI, \frac{\%}{\text{yr}} = \frac{S - DC}{FC} \times 100\% =$$

$$\frac{(\$27{,}500 \text{ \$/yr} - \$10{,}000 \text{ \$/yr})}{\$100{,}000} \times 100\%$$

$$= 17.5\% \text{ per year}$$

Using return on investment (ROI) as an approximation of the profitability of this project, we see that even after an allowance for depreciation this appears to be an attractive investment. Second-level measurements of performance are needed, however, if we wish to incorporate the time value of money into the analysis.

Second-Level Measures of Performance

Benefit/Cost Analysis

In order to formulate a benefit/cost ratio we must find the present value of the future savings.

Using the present worth factor (PWF) from the previous table for 20 percent discount rate (D) and ten-year lifetime (EL) we find that the present value (PV) of the net annual savings (S) is

$$PV = S \times PWF = \$27{,}500 \times 4.192 = \$115{,}280$$

.

This will result in a benefit/cost ratio (*B/C*) equal to

$$B/C = \frac{PV}{FC} = \frac{\$115,280}{\$100,000} \text{ or } 1.15$$

Now it becomes apparent that this is a profitable investment even when the time value of money is considered.

Time to Recoup Investment

This can be quickly approximated by using the previous table and the payback period (*PP*) estimated earlier as 3.6 years. In the 20 percent discount rate column, one can find that the present worth factor closest to 3.6 is 3.605 which indicates that the investment will be entirely recouped in about seven years when taking the time value of money into consideration. While this is considerably longer than the payback period without discounting, it provides a much better indication of the profitability of this investment because it includes the cost of foregone investment opportunities. If the proper discount rate has been used any investment which is recouped in a period less than its lifetime should be considered profitable.

In the following equation,

$$PWF = \frac{1 - (1 + D)^{-EL}}{D}$$

D is discount rate expressed as a fraction and *EL* is the expected lifetime of the project in years.

MARGINAL ANALYSIS

Typical of many investments are those energy conservation opportunities whose rates of return decrease as the levels of investment increase. An example is the application of insulation, where each additional increment generates less savings than the last. In considering such investment, one may wish to estimate the optimal level of application, in the sense that no other level will generate greater net savings (savings minus costs).

The following equality will be useful in estimating such an optimal investment size for any given *ECO* with variable application levels:

$$MS = MC$$

where:

MS = marginal savings, the present value savings generated by the last increment of the project, and

MC = marginal cost, the present value cost of this last increment.

This can be shown to hold true by referring to the accompanying figure. The upper part of the figure shows total cost (*TC*) and total savings (*TS*) is a function of

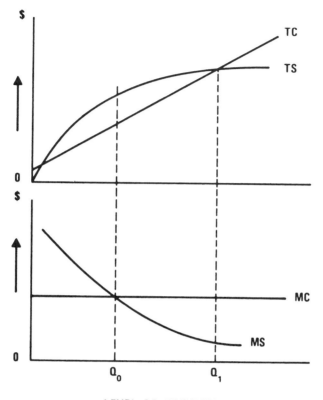

**Determination of Optimal
Investment Size Based on the Marginal Savings —
Marginal Cost Relationship.**

investment size. While any level of investment between Q and Q_1 is profitable (since $TS > TC$), the most profitable level is at that point where the distance between TS and TC is maximized, at Q_0. This occurs when the slope (or rate of change) of the TC and TS functions are equal. Directly below this point, on the lower diagram, we see that $MS = MC$.

That this point, Q_0 is indeed the optimal level of investment can be shown as follows. At any investment level less than Q_0, further profit can be earned by expanding investment since the additional savings generated are greater than their cost. At any point beyond Q_0, however, increased savings are not covered by their costs and thus profits will be decreased by adding investment beyond point Q_0. This leaves only that point where $MS = MC$ as the true optimal investment level.

It should be noted that the use of marginal analysis not only will aid in determining the point at which adding investment ceases to be profitable, it may also be used in the reverse sense. That is, marginal analysis may also indicate that by reducing the level of investment in a proposed project that appears to be unprofitable to the point where $MS = MC$, the project may indeed be made profitable.

For a more comprehensive discussion of marginal analysis techniques and application, consult any basic economics text, such as D. S. Watson's *Price Theory and Its Use* (Houghton-Mifflin Company, 1963) and P. A. Samuelson's *Economics* (McGraw-Hill, 1973).

FANS, PUMPS, AND MOTORS

Fans

1. Check for excessive noise and vibration. Determine cause and correct as necessary.
2. Keep fan blades clean.
3. Inspect and lubricate bearings regularly.
4. Inspect drive belts. Adjust or replace as necessary to insure proper operation. Proper tensioning of belts is critical.
5. Inspect inlet and discharge screens on fans. They should be kept free of dirt and debris at all times.
6. Inspect fans for normal operation.

Pumps

1. Check for packing wear which can cause excessive leakage. Repack to avoid excessive water wastage and shaft erosion.
2. Inspect bearings and drive belts for wear and binding. Adjust, repair, or replace as necessary.

Motors

1. Check alignment of motor to equipment driven. Align and tighten as necessary.
2. Check for loose connection and bad contacts on a regular basis. Correct as necessary.
3. Keep motors clean.
4. Eliminate excessive vibrations.
5. Lubricate motor and drive bearings on a regular basis. This will help reduce friction and excessive torque which can result in overheating and power losses.
6. Replace worn bearings.
7. Tighten belts and pulleys to eliminate excessive losses.
8. Check for overheating. It could be an indication of a functional problem or lack of adequate ventilation.
9. Balance three-phase power sources to motors. An imbalance can create inefficient motor operation and use of more energy.
10. Check for overvoltage or low voltage condition on motors. Correct as necessary.

Air Handling Equipment

1. Inspect ductwork for air leakage. Seal all leaks by taping or caulking.
2. Inspect ductwork insulation. Repair or replace as necessary.
3. Utilize ductwork access openings to check for any obstructions such as loose hanging insulation (in lined ducts), loose turning vanes and accessories, and closed fire dampers. Adjust, repair, or replace as necessary.
4. Inspect damper blades and linkages. Clean, oil, and adjust them on a regular basis.
5. Inspect air valves in dual duct mixing boxes to insure full seating and minimum air leakage.
6. Inspect mixing dampers for proper operation. Adjust as necessary.
7. Clean or replace air filters on a regular basis.
8. Inspect air heating, cooling, and dehumidification coils for cleanliness. Coils can be kept clean by using a mixture of detergent and water in a high pressure (500 psig) portable cleaning unit.
9. Inspect for leakage around coils or out of the casing. Seal all leaks.
10. Inspect all room air outlets and inlets (diffusers, registers, and grilles). They should be kept clean and free of all dirt and obstructions. Clean and remove obstructions as necessary.
11. Inspect air washers, and evaporative air cooling equipment for proper operation. Clean damper blades and linkages if so equipped. Inspect nozzles and clean as necessary.
12. If electronic air cleaners are installed, check them regularly for excessive accumulations on the ionizing and grounding plate section. Replace filter media if necessary. Follow manufacturer's written instructions whenever adjustment or maintenance is required.
13. Inspect humidifier/dehumidifier air dampers, fan parts, spray chamber, diffuser, controls, strainer, and eliminator. All must be kept free of dirt, lint, and other foreign particles. Clean eliminator wheel by directing a high pressure stream of water between blades.
14. Adjust all VAV (variable air volume) boxes so they operate precisely. This will prevent overheating or overcooling, both of which waste energy.

Refrigeration Equipment

Circuit Controls

1. Inspect moisture-liquid indicator on a regular basis. If the color of the refrigerant indicates "wet," it means there is moisture in the system. This is a particularly critical problem because it can cause improper operation or costly damage. A competent mechanic should be called in to perform necessary adjustments and repairs immediately. Also, if there are bubbles in the refrigerant flow as seen through the moisture-liquid indicator, it may indicate that the system is low in

refrigerant. Call in a mechanic to add refrigerant if necessary and to inspect equipment for possible refrigerant leakage.

2. Use a leak detector to check for refrigerant and oil leaks around shaft seal, sight glasses, valve bonnets, flanges, flare connections, relief valve on the condenser assembly, and at pipe joints to equipment, valves, and instrumentation.

3. Inspect equipment for any visual changes such as oil spots on connections or on the floor under equipment.

4. Inspect the liquid line leaving the strainer. If it feels cooler than the liquid line entering the strainer, it is clogged. If it is very badly clogged, sweat or frost may be visible at the strainer outlet. Clean as required.

5. Observe the noise made by the system. Any unusual sounds could indicate a problem. Determine cause and correct.

6. Establish what normal operating pressures and temperatures for the system should be. Check all gauges frequently to ensure that design conditions are being met. Increased system pressure may be due to dirty condensers, which will decrease system efficiency. High discharge temperatures often are caused by defective or broken compressor valves.

7. Inspect tension and alignment of all belts and adjust as necessary.

8. Where applicable, lubricate motor bearings and all moving parts according to manufacturer's recommendations.

9. Inspect insulation on suction and liquid lines. Repair as necessary.

Compressor

1. Look for unusual compressor operation such as continuous running or frequent stopping and starting, either of which may indicate inefficient operation. Determine the cause and, if necessary, correct.

2. Observe the noise made by the compressor. If it seems to be excessively noisy, it may be a sign of a loose drive coupling or excessive vibration. Tighten compressor and motor on the base. If noise persists, call a competent mechanic.

3. Check all compressor joints for leakage. Seal as necessary.

4. Inspect the purge for air and water leaks. Seal as necessary.

5. Inspect instrumentation frequently to ensure that operating oil pressure and temperature agree with manufacturer's specifications.

Air-Cooled Condenser

1. Keep fan belt drive and motor properly aligned and lubricated.

2. Inspect refrigeration piping connections to the condenser coil for tightness. Repair all leaks.

3. Keep condenser coil face clean to permit proper air flow.

4. Determine if hot air is being bypassed from the fan outlet to the coil inlet. If so, correct the problem.

Evaporative Condenser

1. Inspect piping joints and seal all leaks.
2. Remove all dirt from the coil surface by washing it down with high velocity water jets or a nylon brush.
3. Inspect air inlet screen, spray nozzle or water distribution holes, and pump screen. Clean as necessary.
4. Use water treatment techniques if local water supply leaves surface deposits on the coil.
5. Follow guidelines for fan and pump maintenance.

Watercooled Condenser

1. Clean condenser shell and tubes by swabbing with a suitable brush and flushing out with clean water. Chemical cleaning also is possible, although it is suggested that a water treatment company be consulted first.

Chillers

1. Chillers must be kept clean. Inspect on a regular basis. Clean as necessary.
2. Inspect for evidence of clogging. A qualified mechanic should be called in to service equipment in accordance with manufacturer's specifications.

Absorption Equipment

1. Clean strainer and seal tank on a regular basis.
2. Lubricate flow valves on a regular basis.
3. Follow manufacturer's instructions for proper maintenance.

Self-Contained Units (Windows, Through-the-Wall Units, Heat Pump, etc.)

1. Clean evaporator and condenser coils.
2. Keep air intake louvres, filters, and controls clean.
3. Keep air flow from units unrestricted.
4. Caulk openings between unit and windows or wall frames.
5. Check voltage. Full power voltage is essential for proper operation.
6. Follow applicable guidelines suggested for compressor, air-cooled condenser and fans.

Heating Equipment

Boilers (General)

1. Inspect boilers for scale deposits, accumulation of sediment, or boiler compounds on water side surfaces. Rear portion of the boiler must be checked because it is the

area most susceptible to formation of scale. (Scale reduces the efficiency of the boiler.) It is far better to operate one boiler at 90 percent capacity than two at 45 percent capacity each. The more boilers used, the greater the heat loss.

2. Clean mineral or corrosion build-up on gas burners.

Boilers (Fuel Oil)

1. Check and repair oil leaks at pump glands, valves, or relief valves.
2. Inspect oil line strainers. Replace if dirty.
3. Inspect oil heaters to ensure that oil temperatures are being maintained according to manufacturer's or oil supplier's recommendations.

Boilers (Coal Fired)

1. Inspect coal-fired stokers, grates, and controls for efficient operation. If ashes contain an excessive amount of unburned coal, it's probably a sign of inefficient operation.

Boilers (Electric)

1. Inspect electrical contacts and working parts of relays and maintain in good working order.
2. Check heater elements for cleanliness. Replace as necessary.
3. Check controls for proper operation. Adjust as necessary.

Central Furnaces, Make-up Air Heaters, and Unit Heaters

1. All heat exchanger surfaces should be kept clean. Check air-to-fuel ratio and adjust as necessary.
2. Inspect burner couplings and linkages. Tighten and adjust as necessary.
3. Inspect casing for air leaks and seal as necessary.
4. Inspect insulation and repair or replace as necessary.
5. Follow guidelines suggested for fan and motor maintenance.

Radiators, Convectors, Baseboard and Finned Tube Units

1. Inspect for obstructions in front of the unit and remove whenever possible. Air movement in and out of convector unit must be unrestricted.
2. Air will sometimes collect in the high points of hydronic units. It must be vented to enable hot water to circulate freely throughout the system. Otherwise, the units will short cycle (go on and off quickly), wasting fuel.
3. Heat transfer surfaces of radiators, convectors, baseboard and finned-tube units must be kept clean for efficient operation.

Electric Heating

1. Keep heat transfer surfaces of all electric heating units clean and unobstructed.
2. Keep air movement in and out of the units unobstructed.
3. Inspect heating elements, controls and, as applicable, fans on a periodic basis to ensure proper functioning.
4. As appropriate, check reflectors on infrared heaters for proper beam direction and cleanliness.
5. Determine if electric heating equipment is operating at rated voltage as necessary.
6. Check controls for proper operation.

Hot and Chilled Water Piping

1. Inspect all controls. Test them for proper operation. Adjust, repair, or replace as necessary. Also check for leakage at joints.
2. Check flow measurement instrumentation for accuracy. Adjust, repair, or replace as necessary.
3. Inspect insulation of hot and chilled water pipes. Repair or replace as necessary. Be certain to replace any insulation damaged by water. Determine source of water leakage and correct.
4. Inspect strainers. Clean regularly.
5. Inspect heating and cooling heat exchangers. Large temperature differences may be an indication of air binding, clogged strainers, or excessive amounts of scale. Determine cause of condition and correct.
6. Inspect vents and remove all clogs. Clogged vents retard efficient air elimination and reduce efficiency of the system.

Steam Piping

1. Inspect insulation of all mains, risers and branches, economizers, and condensate receiver tanks. Repair or replace as necessary.
2. Check automatic temperature-control system and related control valves and accessory equipment to ensure that they are regulating the system properly in the various zones—in terms of building heating needs, not system capacity.
3. Inspect zone shut-off valves. All should be operable so steam going into unoccupied spaces can be shut off.
4. Inspect steam traps. Their failure to operate correctly can have a significant impact on the overall efficiency and energy consumption of the system. Several different tests can be utilized to determine operations.
5. Listen to the trap to determine if it is opening and closing when it should be.
6. Feel the pipe on the downstream side of the trap. If it is excessively hot, the trap probably is passing steam. This can be caused by dirt in the trap, valve off stem, excessive steam pressure, or worn trap parts (especially valve and seats). If it is moderately hot (as hot as a hot water pipe, for example) it probably is passing condensate, which it should do. If it's cold, the trap is not working at all.
7. Check back pressure on downstream side.
8. Measure temperature of return lines with a surface pyrometer. Measure temperature drop across the trap. Lack of drop indicates steam blow-through. Excessive

drop indicates that the trap is not passing condensate. Adjust, repair, or replace all faulty traps.

9. Inspect all pressure-reducing and regulating valves and related equipment. Adjust, repair, or replace as necessary.

10. Inspect condensate tank vents. Plumes of steam are an indication of one or more defective traps. Determine which traps are defective and adjust, repair, or replace as necessary.

11. Check accuracy of recording pressure gauges and thermometers.

12. Inspect pump for satisfactory operation, looking particularly for leakage at the packing glands.

13. Correct sluggish or uneven circulation of steam. It usually is caused by inadequate drainage, improper venting, inadequate piping, or faulty traps and other accessory equipment.

14. Correct any excessive noise which may occur in the system to provide more efficient heating and to prevent fittings from being ruptured by water hammer.

15. Check vacuum return system for leaks. Air drawn into the system causes unnecessary pump operation, induces corrosion and causes the entire system to be less efficient.

Pneumatic Air Compressor for Controls

1. Inspect all connections for air leaks using a soap solution. Seal as necessary.

2. Note operation. If compressor seems to run excessively, it could be a sign of pressure loss at the controls or somewhere in the piping system. Determine cause and correct.

3. Inspect air pressure in supply tank and pressure regulator adjustment in supply line for proper limits.

4. Check belt tension and alignment.

5. Inspect air compressor intake filter pads and clean or replace as necessary.

6. Lubricate electric motor bearings according to manufacturer's recommendations.

7. Descale system at least once per year and set "PH" level to minimize scale build-up.

PUBLICATIONS TO HELP BUILD ENERGY CONSERVATION SYSTEMS

The following list of publications is based on a search carried out on behalf of *Institutions*[2] by the Department of Energy's Technical Information Center. Publications concerning energy conservation in the food industry were the basis of the search. The list details all publications included in the Technical Information Center's data banks through December, 1977. All ERDA- and NEA-authored documents are available, at a cost, from the Department of Energy. Other publications may be obtained at libraries.

---

[2]*Institutions/VFM,* March 1, 1978.

Identification of Major Areas of Energy Utilization in the Food Processing/Foodservice Industry. Dwyer, S. J. III; Unklesbay, K.; Unklesbay, N.; Dunlap, C. Missouri University, Columbia. January 1977.

Energy Conservation in the Meat Processing Industry, Phase I. Henrickson, R. L.; Ferguson, E. J. Oklahoma State University, Stillwater. Dec. 31, 1976.

Industrial Energy Conservation. Harvey, D. G. Energy Research and Development Administration, Washington, D.C. 1977.

Analysis of the Energy Potential of Solar-Thermal Energy to Provide Industrial Process Heat, Vol. I, II, III. Intertechnology Corp., Warrenton, Va. Feb. 7, 1977.

A Study of Energy-Conservation Potential in the Meat Packing Industry. Johns-Manville Corp., Denver. November 1976.

A Study of Energy-Conservative Potential in the Baking Industry. Johns-Manville Corp., Denver. November 1976.

Case Studies of Successful Systems for Industrial Waste Heat Recovery. Leidy, B. National Bureau of Standards, Federal Energy Administration, University of Pittsburgh. February 1977.

Energy Use in Industry. Newton, G. E. H. Pergamon Press, Inc. 1976.

Energy and Food: Energy Used in Production, Processing, Delivery and Marketing of Selected Food Items. Pierotti, A.; Keeler, A. G.; Fritsch, A. Center for Science in the Public Interest, Washington, D.C. 1977.

Study of Energy-Conservation Potential in the California Canning Industry. Electric and Gas Industries Assn., San Francisco. December 1976.

Analysis of Federally Funded Demonstration Projects, Vol. III. Baer, W.; Conover, C. J.; Cook, C.; Fleischauer, P.; Goeller, B. Rand Corp., Santa Monica, Calif. April 1976.

Energy-Conservation Program at Ralston Purina. Bossman, G. A. Ralston Purina Co., St. Louis. 1976.

Energy Conservation in Fruit Dehydrators Utilizing Recirculation of Exhaust Air and Heat Recovery Exchangers. Groh, J. E. Arizona University, Tucson. November 1976.

Voluntary Industrial Energy Conservation. Department of Commerce. Federal Energy Administration, Washington, D.C. 1976.

Energy and Food. Battelle Memorial Institute, Columbus, Ohio. 1976.

Engineering for Food Production. Mosaic. 1976.

Energy Use in the Food System. Booz, Allen and Hamilton, Inc., Bethesda, Md. May 1976.

Energy Conservation in the Food System: A Publications List. Booz, Allen and Hamilton, Inc., Bethesda, Md. May 1976.

Food-Related Energy Requirements. Hirst, E. Oak Ridge (Tenn.) National Laboratory. *Science Magazine,* April 12, 1974.

Energy Conservation, Part III, Industry. Hundemann, A. S. National Technical Information Service, Springfield, Va.

Conservation Response: Strategies for the Design and Operation of Energy-Using Systems. Dumas, L. J. D. C. Heath and Co., Lexington, Mass. 1976.

Application of Solar Energy in the Food Processing Industry. Proctor, D.; White, R. F. Commonwealth Scientific and Industrial Research Organization, East Melbourne, Australia. 1975.

Energy Consumption: Fuel Utilization and Conservation in Industry. Reding, J. T.; Shepherd, B. P. Dow Chemical Co., Freeport, Texas. September 1975.

Guide to Energy Conservation for Food Service. Federal Energy Administration, Washington, D.C. October 1975.

Energy: The Case for Conservation. Hayes, D. Worldwatch Institute, Washington, D.C. 1976.

U.S. Industrial Outlook with Projections to 1980. U.S. Department of Commerce, Washington, D.C. 1974.

Energy Use in the U.S. Food System. Steinhart, J. S.; Steinhart, C. E. University of Wisconsin, Madison, and Committee on Interior and Insular Affairs, Washington, D.C. 1975.

Industrial Energy Study of Selected Food Industries. Development Planning and Research Associates, Manhattan, Kan. July 1974.

Maintenance Tips that will Help Conserve Energy and Improve Your Food Service Operation. American Gas Assn., Inc., Arlington, Va.

Food Service Operator's Guide to Saving Natural Gas and Money. East Ohio Gas Co., Cleveland. May 1974.

Key Employees Save Money and Energy. East Ohio Gas Co., Cleveland.

Meet These Energy-Saving Good Neighbors. East Ohio Gas Co., Cleveland. 1976.

Energy-Conserving Systems in Restaurants. Energy Research and Development Administration, Washington, D.C.

Cooking—Food Service. Northeast Utilities Service Co., Hartford, Conn. July 16, 1975.

Change Your Cooking Habits. East Ohio Gas Co., Cleveland.

For the Energy-Conscious Chef: Recipes of Oil Workers. American Petroleum Institute, Washington, D.C.

A Practical Guide to Energy Management—Electric Food Service Facilities. The Electrification Council, New York, N.Y.

Energy Management and Energy Conservation Practices for the Foodservice Industry. Midwest Research Institute, Chicago. February 1977.

Information on Barbecue Machines, Braising Pans, Broilers, Fryers, Griddles and Grills, Ovens, Ranges, Steam Kettles, Scales, Steam Cookers, and Toasters is reprinted from *The Complete Book of Cooking Equipment,* 1st ed. by Jule Wilkinson by permission of Cahners Publishing Co.

The author wishes to express appreciation to the Utah State Board of Education for permission to use detailed specification information from their publications.

QUESTIONS

1. Define the following terms:

ECO	*PP*
ROI	Life Cycle Cost
EUI	*UL*

2. Briefly discuss the information needed in order to calculate performance measures.
3. What are the first- and second-level measures of performance?
4. In first-level measures of performance, what are the advantages of *ROI* as compared to *PP*?
5. Briefly define Internal Rate of Return and explain its usefulness.
6. In relation to marginal analysis, define *MS* and *MC*.
7. How would you explain a high utility bill when you were only in town for two of four weeks?

17

CHEMICALS

INTRODUCTION

Physical forms of cleaning are force, colloids, and dissolution. Emulsification chemical forms are chelation, ionization, peptization, saponification, and sequestration. Alkalines, brown soap, buffers, chlorinated TSP, oxalic acid, phosphoric acid, soda ash, sodium orthosilicate, and tetra-sodium pyrophosphate are some cleaning agents listed.

If warewashing is done by hand, the cleaning agent should have a pH between 7–10. Cleaning agents should be selected according to need if warewashing is done by machine.

Soap is the salt of a fatty acid. It is composed of either animal or vegetable oils and either sodium or potassium hydroxides.

Sodium hydroxide is the most caustic soda, followed by sodium orthosilicate. Both are hard on human skin. Sodiums sesquisilicate and metasilicate have a pH slightly above 11 and are not always preferred for handware washing.

Water is the best known solvent, but the surface tension of the water may inhibit it from doing a good job. Surface tension is the cohesiveness exerted by the water molecules for each other. A wetting agent reduces the surface tension.

Relatively little soil could be suspended if not for the long-chain soap molecule that is soluble in water because it is equipped with an alkaline head but still attractive to oils, solvents, and other hydrocarbons. The only thing that keeps soap soluble is the alkaline head.

There are two factors to be considered in cleaning utensils and equipment. They are composition of soil and water hardness. Since foodservice utensils usually contain fat, protein, and carbohydrates, an alkali cleaner should be used. When lime deposits appear, an acid cleaner should be used.

Sanitizing is done with heat or chemicals. Chemically sanitizing requires that the utensil be clean first.

Insecticides for pest control are found as oil solutions, water emulsions, water suspensions, baits, powders, and dusts. A residual spray requires an insect to come in contact with the treated surface. A space spray has a better effect on flying insects.

The actions used to remove soil are physical, chemical or a combination of both. Physical action may mean:

1. Force. The pressure used in a dishwashing machine or the application of a brush is mechanical force.
2. Colloids. These are substances put into cleaning agents which attract soil and collide with one another to penetrate and remove soil.
3. Dissolution. Water will break the surface tension of some matter like sugars and dissolve the matter from the surface it is clinging to. Heat makes many materials soften or even liquify and be removed easier. Organic solvents such as alcohol, naphthaline, carbon tetrachloride, and acetone dissolve other materials.
4. Emulsification. When we get oils and fats to mix in solution with other liquids, we have an emulsified solution. Cleaning agents with emulsifiers in them help remove fats and oils.

Chemical action may mean:

1. Chelation. Chelating agents pick up soil and salts such as lime and hold onto them for rinsing without returning them to the object that was soiled.
2. Ionization. The electrical charge of a molecule is half positive and half negative; such is called an ion. An anionic (negative charge) cleaning agent will attract to the cationic (positive charge) in soil to remove the soil. A cationic agent attracts to bacteria, making a good disinfectant. A non-ionic agent does not separate its charges easily.
3. Peptization. Proteins changed in chemical structure are said to be peptized. Thus, changed they become suspended in the liquid solution as collides and wash away.
4. Saponification. When an alkaline material combines with an oil or fat to form a soap, the materials have saponified.
5. Sequestration. A sequestering agent such as a phosphate collects and holds soils and salts away from the surface of the soiled object.

TYPES OF CLEANING AGENTS AND CLEANING PROBLEMS AND SOME APPLICATIONS

Alkalines. High pH (7 to 14) compounds that saponify fats and oils. Works by reducing water's surface tension. Corrodes aluminum.

Brown soap. A high pH soap used for tough cleaning jobs.

Buffers. Agents added to alkalines to reduce corrosion of aluminum, bronze, brass.

Chlorinated TSP. Trisodium phosphate with chlorine. A good cleaner, but corrosive.

Glycerine. A substance added to soap to give smoothness.

Oxalic acid. A bleach.

Phosphoric acid. A descaling agent.

Soap. A detergent made of a salt and an alkalai.

Soda ash. Corrosive detergent which may leave deposits.

Sodium bicarbonate. A poor low alkaline detergent often used as a buffer.

Sodium carbonate. See Soda ash.

Sodium hexameta-phosphate. An efficient chealting agent used to condition water.

Sodium hydroxide (Lye). Very high pH, highly caustic and corrosive. Hydrolyzes proteins and saponifies grease.

Sodium metasilicate. High pH silicate which peptizes, saponifies and emulsifies. Inhibits corrosion.

Sodium orthosilicate. High pH alkaline silicate which sucks up moisture. Corrosive.

Sodium sesquisilicate. High pH alkaline which absorbs moisture on solid metals. Corrosive.

Sodium tetra-phosphate. A chealting agent used to condition water.

Sodium tri-polyphosphate. A chealting agent used to condition water.

Tetra-sodium pyrophosphate. A chealting agent used to condition water.

Tetra-sodium salt of ethylenediamine tetra-acetic acid. An efficient sequestering agent used to condition water.

Tri-sodium phosphate (TSP). Corrosive and likely to leave deposits but a good cleaner which rinses well. pH of 10.5 to 12.

Hand Washing.   Pick a soap, liquid, or solid with a pH of 7 to 10 with an additive that destroys bacteria.

Warewashing by Hand.   Pick a cleaning agent with a pH no higher than 11 as a higher pH is too caustic for human skin contact. High pH products will corrode aluminum pots and pans; it is better to soak such ware in a lower pH solution than to expose them to a high pH for shorter time.

Machine Warewashing.   Pick a cleaning agent that answers the specific problem. If the water is hard, then you will want water softening agents in the solution. You want agents that are nontoxic and noncorrosive which will saponify grease, peptize proteins, and chealt or sequester soils from the ware. If the interior surfaces of the warewashing machine are shiny, then it is possible that the water is "hungry," meaning too soft and needs to have some hard salts added. If there is a film on glasses it may be a result of beer or milk proteins interacting with hard water salts (beerstone and milkstone) such as calcium or magnesium so you need agents that attack those salts, peptize proteins, and sequester.

Floor Cleaning.   Pick materials that sequester and rinse well but do not corrode adjacent painted or metal surfaces. A mild abrasive to aid in physical action is acceptable but the product should not produce heavy suds or foam. Wax strippers should dissolve and chealt but not mar the floor. Floor polishes should have 12 to 16 percent solids depending on the amount of traffic.[1]

SOAP

Soap is made from a fatty acid and a strong alkali, through saponification. It is approximately fourteen parts fatty acid and one part caustic soda. When particles of compounds containing calcium, magnesium, chlorides, carbonates, and sulphate types, are present in water and soap is added, the tendency is for the soap particles to break down into its fatty acid and alkali state. The fatty acid portion and the hardness chemicals have a strong affinity for each other and they combine to form insoluble compounds which you know as "lime soaps." The alkali portion of the soap compound is so small that when liberated by this breakdown is insufficient to maintain sufficient akalinity to overcome the action of the hardness particles.

Chemically, soap is the salt of a fatty acid. It is made from a combination of either animal or vegetable oils mixed with either sodium hydroxide or potassium hydroxide. Approximately one pound of the caustic soda, or the hydroxide, is needed to saponify (change into soap) fourteen pounds of either animal or vegetable oils. The processes of making soap seem very simple, but actually they are a scientifically controlled series of processes.

The oils are heated and the selected hydroxide is added, then it is brought to a boil for a prescribed length of time to insure complete saponification. The combining of a weak acid and a strong alkali produces a mildly alkaline product. (Tallow base soaps have a pH of about 10.2 or 10.4). After soap is formed, ordinary salt is added. As the salt travels down to the bottom of the soap kettle it takes with it all the impurities and the glycerides. The latter is drawn off and distilled into pure glycerine. The impurities are allowed to settle in the bottom of the soap kettle. To insure a good product, a kettle of soap may be salted several times.

While the soap is still in its molten state, it is pumped out of the kettle from a point above the sediment line and either goes to a dryer or into large flasks and is allowed to cool; it is then ground into a powder. Soap flakes are made by running the liquid soap over water cooled rolls, much the same as a cylinder type flat work ironer, and the thin layer applied to the rolls is peeled off as flakes. The products resulting are either 88 percent flakes or 92 percent powdered soaps; the remaining 12 percent or 8 percent is allowable moisture content.

Built soaps, or soap powders, are mixtures of pure soap, and one or a combination of alkalies. The most modern method for making a built soap is to pump the molten soap to the top of a "spray tower," a cylindrical tower which may be several stories high, containing baffle plates and into which hot air is pumped at strategic locations. The liquid soap combines with measured quantities of alkalies at the top of the tower, and as it descends through the maze of hot air currents and baffle plates it becomes

---

[1]The author expresses his gratitude to the National Laundry Managers Association for granting permission to reprint some materials from their certification manual.

cooled and forms little beads of homogenized soap and alkali, which fall to the bottom and are packed in bags, barrels, or boxes.

The other method for making built soap is by mechanical mixing of powdered soap and the dry powdered alkalies. This is considered as good a mix as any other type. Some complain, by saying that the specific gravity of some alkalies causes them to settle at the top or bottom of the container in which they are packed, as a result of vibration from handling in transporting. However, in most cases the mixture remains uniform in spite of opinions to the contrary.

Being a product of saponification, it is reasonable to assume that soap will not further saponify any oils that might be encountered in the soil content of fabrics.

Chemistry of Soap

Soap will "ionize," which means that it will disassociate in solution back to its fatty acid and alkaline parts and vice versa. Generally, there is a slight excess of hydroxides released which are advantageous in the washing solution.

Soap "hydrolizes" in a solution, which means that it combines with other things that are present to form other compounds. We know that it will readily combine with calcium and magnesium, present in hard water.

Soap will "emulsify," in that it will surround the loosened soil particles and hold them in suspension so that they are carried away when the solution is dumped.

Soap forms a true solution, also an emulsion, in that it readily dissolves and distributes itself throughout the entire bath. It also forms a colloidal suspension.

Alkalies

Sodium hydroxide (caustic soda, sodium hydrate, lye, or NaOH). The strongest available alkali. It should be kept in a closed container to prevent absorption of moisture and carbon dioxide which form sodium carbonate. Starting at 76 percent Na_2O (which compares with 98 percent caustic soda) it may be purchased in a descending number of percentages. It has no buffer value.

Sodium Orthosilicate (ortho). A combination of silica and caustic soda and next to caustic soda in strength. Has very little buffering ability but some colloidal properties. (Both sodium hydroxide and orthosilicate are termed *caustic,* a term used meaning anything that will attack the skin. This condition is the one objection to their use, but safety is assured if handled carefully.)

Sodium sesquisilicate (sesqui). A compound between orthosilicate and metasilicate in strength. Having the properties of silicated compounds and a buffer range between 11.1 and 11.6 pH.

Sodium metasilicate (meta). The oldest type of the known silicates. Buffering value of the amount of alkali required will take care of average variations of soil without too great variations in the pH. Because of the latter, this alkali has gained considerable favor. It is an effective detergent, good soap builder, and in ordinary concentrations not caustic enough to be harmful. It has great colloidal activity.

Tri-sodium phosphate (tri-sodium). Before the days of mechanical water softening tri-sodium was favored by a great many because of its ability to produce satisfactory work under average hard water conditions. It is found in a number of proprietory alkalies because of its effectiveness in hard water. Some have given it the property of suspending and removing iron—this has not been proven by tests. So be sure by removing any iron present at the source of water supply.

Sodium carbonate (soda ash, ash). Is an alkali of moderate strength and a considerable quantity must be used to attain satisfactory pH values. The soil, etc., breaks down the carbonates and the total alkalinity is so great in most cases rinsing becomes a problem. However, it is used as a basic chemical in the manufacture of many detergent compounds and is in a large number of proprietory alkalies.

Sodium sesquicarbonate (modified soda). Is one of the weaker alkalies and is made from approximately a 50–50 mixture of sodium carbonate and sodium bicarbonate. Modified soda has a high buffer value and shows lower pH values. It is necessary to control the amounts used within the degree of a reasonable alkalinity.

The following tables show some comparisons of the values of the various alkalies mentioned in different respects. For example, it will be seen that the alkali having the highest alkalinity is the poorest in soil suspending, etc.

ALKALINITY TABLE

Soda	Percent Alkali Na$_2$O	Percent Active Alkali as Na$_2$O	Characteristic Buffer Range in Suds Bath pH
Caustic soda	76	76	Above pH 12.0
Orthosilicate	60.8	57.0–59.0	10.5 to 12.0
Sesquisilicate	55.5	55	11.1–11.6
Metasilicate	50.4	47.0–49.0	10.8–11.4
Tri-sod-phosphate	24.5	8.2	10.3–10.6
Sodium carbonate	56	28	10.0–10.4
Sodium sesquicarbonate	41–44	11. –13.5	9.0–10

WATER SOFTENING TABLE

Alkali	Number of Drops of Standard Soap Solution to Make Suds in 25 c.c. of .1% Solution of Each Alkali Water Average 8.6 g.p.g.
Trisodium phosphate	3
Sodium metasilicate	5
Sodium sesquisilicate	7
Sodium orthosilicate	8
Caustic soda	11
Soda ash	14
Sodium sesquicarbonate	19

This demonstrates the ability of tri-sodium phosphates to form compounds that are soluble to some extent, and the same holds true for some types of silicates. It may be that the silicates do not combine as readily as other alkalies with magnesium and calcium forming compounds having soap destroying properties.

Soil Suspending Properties	*Effect on Greases and Oils*
1. Sodium metasilicate	1. Sodium metasilicate
2. Sodium sesquisilicate	2. Sodium sesquisilicate
3. Trisodium phosphate	3. Trisodium phosphate
4. Sodium orthosilicate	4. Sodium orthosilicate
5. Soda ash	5. Caustic soda
6. Sodium sesquicarbonate	6. Soda ash
7. Caustic soda	7. Sodium sesquicarbonate

Note that the first four alkalies are in the same order for soil suspending and their effect on oil and greases, both very important detergent factors in establishing the right type of alkali to use.

Also, caustic soda shows so poorly in both these comparisons yet it is the number one alkali in the neutralization of acids and in quantity of suds produced in comparison with any of the other alkalies.

As stated before, metasilicate seems to have the best properties. It leads in wetting out as well as the two instances above and is no lower than fourth in any comparison.

DETERGENCY PROCESS

Water, the Best of All Solvents

There is no solvent known to chemistry that will dissolve as many different substances as water. Dry cleaners know it well. They have to use water to supplement the solvent power of their drycleaning solvents to supplement the solvent power of water.

We Can Improve Its Solvent Power

The value of water in laundering is further enhanced by the fact that we have learned how to *improve* upon its natural solvent power.

We add soap and alkaline detergents to water to make it "wetter" and to enable it to dissolve, emulsify, and suspend soil that would normally be insoluble in water. We add bleach to water to enable it to dissolve insoluble stains. A great deal of chemistry consists of various steps toward increasing the solvent power of water.

That is where complications arise. Almost every effort we make involves a soap of some sort. Unfortunately, water and soap don't always get along too well together. Why? Again, indirectly because water is such an excellent solvent. Even without any help, water dissolves very substantial quantities of minerals.

The heaviest natural concentration of minerals occurs in the Dead Sea which contains about 30 oz./gal. (22.7 percent) or 227,000 parts per million of dissolved minerals. Great Salt Lake in Utah is a little less highly concentrated, with about 25 oz./gal. (19 percent) or 190,600 ppm of dissolved minerals. The mineral concentration in ocean water is substantially lower—about 4⅔ oz./gal. (3.5 percent) or 35,207 ppm.

Most of the inland water with which you are likely to come into contact has a total dissolved mineral content of around 300 to 400 ppm. In a very few areas of the United States, the total mineral content of the water runs as high as 1,800 to 2,000 ppm.

As a rule, the portion of the total dissolved mineral content in water that directly interferes with cleaning is the hardness.

What Is Water Hardness?

Water hardness consists of those dissolved minerals that are capable of entering into chemical reaction with soap and alkaline detergents to precipitate insoluble compounds.

Most of the soaps and alkaline detergents used for laundering are sodium compounds. They would still be soluble and useful as detergent, though, if they were converted to potassium (potash) compounds. They become insoluble, however, when they are converted to calcium compounds, magnesium compounds, iron compounds, aluminum compounds, or manganese compounds.

The most common hardness salts are the salts of calcium magnesium, aluminum, and manganese. Salts of sodium and potassium may, under some circumstances, indirectly interfere with soap-and-builder detergency, but not as hardness salts.

Anti-Detergent Forces in Water

To remove soil, obviously the first step must be to get hold of it. This sounds simple enough, but it is sometimes quite an achievement to bring our laundering solvent (water) into intimate contact with soil.

This detergent job of bringing soil and water together into more or less stable mixtures such as solutions, emulsions, dispersions, and/or suspensions of soil in water is usually complicated rather seriously by the existence in water (and other liquids) of some powerful and antagonistic molecular forces.

These physical forces normally tend to prevent water from mixing readily with the solid and liquid substances that ordinarily constitute the soil. The most familiar of such physical forces in water is known as surface tension.

Surface Tension and Wetting Agents

Surface tension is brought about by the fact that the molecules of a liquid exert a strong pull toward one another. The molecules on the surface of the liquid are pulled inward by the other molecules in the liquid, and inasmuch as there is no corresponding pull from outside, the liquid tends to pull itself together. We call that cohesive inter-molecular force in liquids *surface tension*.

Surface tension causes water to form spherical drops because a sphere represents the minimum of exposed surface area. A drop of water placed on a greasy, waxy, or other water-repellent surface will tend to remain pulled up away from the surface, so that only a small portion of the drop actually touches the surface.

When the drop is touched by soap or other wetting agent, however, it flattens out and begins to "wet" the surface. The wetting agent makes the water "wetter," causes it to spread out and form more intimate contact with the surface, and often enables it to penetrate the surface.

A *wetting agent,* then, is a compound that will reduce surface tension. A wetting agent is also a penetrant or penetrating agent. It makes water more penetrating by making it "wetter."

INTERFACIAL TENSIONS

There is molecular force in liquids that is of considerable detergent importance. It is called interfacial tensions or sometimes interfacial surface tension.

Interfacial tension and surface tension are related, but they manifest themselves in different ways. Surface tension exists at the surface of a liquid—where the liquid is exposed to the atmosphere.

Interfacial tension, on the other hand, exists at those points in a liquid at which it is exposed either to other liquids or to solids.

It is important to understand, though, that these physical forces or tensions in water have nothing to do with the hardness or softness of water. Surface tension and interfacial tension exist in the same degree in both hard and soft water.

It happens that soap is a combination water softener, wetting agent, emulsifier, and dispersant, but that is only coincidence.

When soap is used in hard water, some of it has to react to precipitate the hardness elements and thus soften the water. The rest of the soap remaining in solution can then go on to function as a wetting agent, emulsifier, and dispersant—in fundamentally the same manner in which synthetic surface active compounds function in either hard or soft water.

SURFACTANTS

Surfactants are groups of compounds which act on the surface of a liquid to lower the surface tension so as to bring about a more intimate mingling between liquids or liquids and solids.

Detergents

A detergent is any substance that cleanses. Under these terms then, water itself, is a detergent. However, in a more strict classification, detergents are those substances which, when added to a liquid (water, in laundering), affect to lesser or greater degrees the removal of soil. This implies that all detergents are not equally effective as cleansing agents.

Surface active agents (surfactants), which may or may not have detergency properties, are most commonly classified according to the charge of the comprising ion which acts on the surface or interfacial tension to promote detersive action. One characteristic common to detergents, regardless of their ionic classification, is that they are comprised of one portion which is oil-loving or lipophilic. The detergent, or surfactant, is also comprised of a portion which is water-loving (hydrophilic) or less lipophilic which gives it solubility in an aqueous medium.

Anionic

This class of detergent is characterized by a negatively charged portion which is largely responsible for the detergent properties. Tallow, or true soap, is a good example of an anionic detergent. Below, you will note that one portion has a positive + charge and the other portion a negative – charge. It is the activity or alignment in the solution of this negatively charged portion which is responsible for the detersive action.

$$0$$
$$(C_{17}H_{35}C - 0)^- \qquad (Na)+$$

Chemists know that adding specified amounts of soap to water will enable water to dissolve measurable amounts of such water-insoluble hydrocarbons as benzene, oil, gasoline, etc. This process is known as solubilization. The insoluble hydrocarbons are solubilized by soap so that instead of forming a distinct layer over the surface of water, they will actually dissolve to form clear solutions.

In our efforts to understand how soap can accomplish this solubilizing function, it may help to visualize the molecular structure of soap and of its chemical parent—fatty acid. Let's assume, for instance, that the soap we are talking about is sodium sterate which is derived from stearic acid—an important constituent of tallow fatty acid.

H H H H H H H H H H H H H H H H H H 0
HC-C-C-C-C-C-C-C-C-C-C-C-C-C-C-C-C-C-0H + NaOH =
H H H H H H H H H H H H H H H H H H H

H H H H H H H H H H H H H H H H H H 0
HC-C-C-C-C-C-C-C-C-C-C-C-C-C-C-C-C-C-0Na + H0H
H H H H H H H H H H H H H H H H H H H

There is very little difference in molecular structure between the soap and the fatty acid from which it was derived. The fatty acid molecule is headed up, so to speak, with a hydrogen atom (H), which is replaced with a sodium atom (Na) when the fatty acid is converted to soap.

Small Head—Long Tail

The outstanding feature of both molecules is, of course, the long hydrocarbon chain, consisting, in this case, of a chain of seventeen carbon atoms to which are attached a total of thirty-five hydrogen atoms. This long hydrocarbon chain is characteristic of a number of organic compounds and is ordinarily associated with solubility in hydrocarbon solvents such as benzene, gasoline, drycleaning solvents, oils, etc.

In fatty acid, this long hydrocarbon chain dominates the behavior of the entire molecule, making fatty acid behave as a hydrocarbon. It is soluble in hydrocarbons and insoluble in water.

When the hydrogen atom at the end of the fatty acid molecule is replaced with a sodium atom and the fatty acid is converted to soap, the tail ceases to wag the dog and we have a soap that is soluble in water but largely insoluble in hydrocarbon solvents—even though the soap molecule retains the long hydrocarbon chain.

Hydrocarbon Chain Seeks Oil

Physical chemists sometimes refer to the hydrocarbon chain as the oil-loving end of the soap molecule. Although it has become part of a water-soluble soap, this long hydrocarbon chain still shows quite a strong affinity for hydrocarbons such as benzene, drycleaning solvents, oils, etc.

Nevertheless, so long as the hydrocarbon chain is attached to a sodium atom, the soap is soluble in water. The closest approach that the hydrocarbon chain on the soap molecule can make toward association with other hydrocarbons is to gravitate toward them whenever such insoluble hydrocarbons as solvents, oils, etc., are added to water in which soap is dissolved.

Oil-Water Coupler

Inasmuch as the entire soap molecule is actually dissolved in the water, this gravitation of the hydrocarbon chain toward oil that is added to the water tends to pull the oil into films around each cluster of soap molecules. This clustering of soap molecules is, of course, what is often referred to in physical chemistry as *micelle formation*. If the amount of oil so added to a soap solution in water is not too great, the tendency of soap micelles is to solubilize the oil and bring it into solution in the water.

Probably the actual amount of real solubilizing accomplished by soap in a laundry washwheel is relatively slight. If soap were capable of actually solubilizing all of the soil found on a load of clothes, the dump waters from the break onward in the formula would be fairly clear solutions.

Solubilizing, Emulsifying, Suspending

We can visualize soap detergency as consisting of a number of steps, starting with solubilizing. Obviously, if a soap solution can solubilize a little oily matter from the soil, it will become a different kind of solution—a solution of oil-and-soap in water.

Thereby, our soap-in-water solution becomes a better solvent because the oil in that solution has considerable solvent power for other oil matter. Even though solubilized oil may not be able to pull much additional oily matter actually into solution with itself, it does become a type of coupling agent between the soap solution and other oily matter, thus enabling the soap solution to attract elements in the soil that are normally more soluble in oil or solvents than in water.

Emulsifying Soil with Soil

We call this process emulsifying. It is a process of attracting materials that cannot be made completely soluble in water. Some soil elements can often be held by the attraction of their potential solubility in some portion of the soil that is already dissolved in the water.

Undoubtedly, a great deal of the soil that is loosened by alkali and soap is emulsified. The rest of the soil is probably suspended, since it is so heavy that it probably cannot be actually emulsified and certainly not truly dissolved.

The important thing to remember, though, is that relatively little soil could be suspended in the washwheel at all if it were not for that peculiar-shaped, peculiar-acting, long-chain soap molecule that is soluble in water because it is equipped with an alkaline head but still attractive to oils, solvents, and other hydrocarbons because of its hydrocarbon-chain tail. Moreover, soap can perform its solubilizing, emulsifying, and suspending functions only if it retains its complete solubility in water.

What Keeps Soap Soluble?

The only thing that accounts for soap solubility in water is that little bit of alkali tacked onto the end of a long hydrocarbon chain. Our problem, then, in keeping the soap soluble under all conditions is a problem of keeping the alkaline head attached to the hydrocarbon tail.

Structurally, the soap molecule is quite lopsided in the direction of its fatty portion which accounts for more than 90 percent of its weight.

The following table lists the pH of the common basic alkalies and the amount of sodium oxide which is in active form. The data also includes the silicon dioxide content of the commonly used basic silicates.

The data shows that caustic soda (sodium hydroxide) contains appreciably more sodium oxide than any of the other alkalies listed. It also shows that the sodium oxide in the silicated alkalies is active almost to the extent of that contained in caustic soda so that practically all of the alkalinity in the silicated alkalies, as well as that in caustic soda, is effective in building detergency and in preventing the breakdown of soaps.

Because caustic soda contains so much active sodium oxide, one might be led to believe that it is the best of the alkaline builders. The study of the ion action of the various alkalies shows that certain ones are excellent emulsifiers and possess fine colloidal activity in general, whereas the hydroxyl ion (OH) of caustic soda does not exhibit these properties.

Type of Alkali	Percent Active Sodium Oxide	Percent Silicon Dioxide	pH (0.01N)
Sodium hydroxide	76.0	0.0	12.4
Sodium orthosilicate (anhydrous)	59.0	28.0	11.6
Sodium sesquisilicate (anhydrous)	55.0	36.0	11.57
Sodium metasilicate (anhydrous)	49.0	45.0	11.55
Sodium metasilicate (pentahydrate)	28.0	28.0	11.55
Sodium carbonate	29.0	0.0	10.2

Colloidal Effect of Silicated Alkalies

Colloidal activity can be described as violent molecular motion. This motion, when applied in the laundry, bombards soil masses, breaks them into tiny particles, and then bounces the particles around in the detergent liquor so the soil doesn't redeposit in fabrics. In this way soil is removed, suspended, and carried away efficiently.

Silicated alkalies are colloidal in nature, whereas other laundry alkalies have little or no colloidal cleaning action. To understand the advantage the colloid provides, it is necessary to consider the whole procedure. Soap is highly colloidal, but even small amounts of calcium or magnesium salts take the life out of soap. This effect of hardness salts on soap, however, is reduced by silicated alkalies. Therefore, a combination of silicated alkali and soap protects against overbalance, soap breakdown, and soil redeposition. As carryovers and rinses dilute the detergency, silicates remain colloidally active, continuing to suspend soil as an aid to rinsing.

Silicates and Wetting

An important attribute of a good detergent is its ability to wet out the fabric. Silicate solutions generally possess lower surface tensions, greater "wetability," than do solutions made up of equivalent amounts of other alkalies. The wetability makes it possible for the liquid (detergent solution) to come between the soil and the surface and thus break the bond between them. For this reason it is advantageous to use the wetting out solution in the break operation or even in the flush. Frequently, a flush is used to eliminate large amounts of loose soil such as fine particles of metal or other inert matter.

Silicates and Emulsification

Removal of all soil classifications requires emulsification. The soils common to food-service surfaces contain varying amounts of greases and oils which may or may not be of the saponifiable (vegetable or animal) type. These greases and oils do not saponify under ordinary conditions and the addition of an emulsifier is necessary to lift the mineral greases and so prevent the formation of a gummy residual film embodying fine particles of inert soil. Even some saponifiable oils are more readily removed by emulsification than by saponification. The silicates help emulsify severe impregnations of greasy soil better than nonsilicate builders because they have such good soil dispersing action.

Hardness and Silicates

Because silicates protect soap against water hardness, less soap is required to overcome water hardness and generate and hold a good suds when they are used. This means that not only is soap saved when a silicated alkali is used as a builder, but also that soil redeposition problems resulting from the interaction of soap and hard water are minimized. The use of a silicated alkali, therefore, produces better quality work as well as lower costs.

Saponification

This is the process of combining fatty acids with an alkali or alkaline salt to form a soap. Since various fatty acids are present in linens and garments, soap is formed in the wash-wheel by the reaction between these soils and the alkali builder. The use of an alkali containing a large sodium oxide content may not necessarily assure greatest saponification efficiency, however. Because of the power of the silicates to peptize (break up) greases and oils into finer particles, thus increasing the extent of saponification, they have proved themselves superior detergents.

The alkalies must also maintain a saponified detergent system. If the soap is broken down by the soils present, its ability to suspend and deflocculate the soil and wet the fabric and soil is greatly impaired. Visually, soap breakdown is noted by a fall in the suds level and is accompanied by soil redeposition. Redeposited soil is the most difficult type to remove because the fabric is wetted and in a slightly swollen condition, which causes deeper penetration of the redeposited soil. It is, therefore, extremely important that a slight excess of alkali be used at the sudsing.

The Buffering Effect of Silicates

The ability of a solution to resist changes in pH is due to a property known as *buffering*. A buffered alkaline solution will maintain a fairly constant pH despite the addition of a given amount of acid. Silicates release their alkali ions as needed, so are said to be highly buffered. In the detergency process they serve to buffer the detergent liquors and maintain the pH at the necessary level for peak efficiency, preventing redeposition of soil. This is important because the requirements of the washing process necessitate the control of the pH at a specific level for each step in the cleaning operation.

SUMMARY OF ALKALIES AND ALKALINE SALTS

1. Hydroxide of alkaline metals or bases—most common are KOH, NaOH, slacked lime CA (OH)$_2$ is insoluble, NH$_4$OH (weak) Al (OH)$_3$ textile finish, Mg(OH)$_2$ milk of magnesium. Some of these alkaline salts such as KOH and NaO$_4$ will degrade cotton cellulose under certain conditions.
2. Alkaline Salts
   * Soda ash—carbonates, silicates, phosphates.
   * These salts are partially neutralized alkalies.
   * Most soil salts are sodium salts.
   * Table salt is an example of an alkali that is completely neutralized. NaOH +HCl = NaCl +HOH
   * Soda Ash—strong alkali NaOH and H$_2$CO$_3$—alkaline salt.
   * Trisodium phosphate strong alkali and weak acid.
   * Buffered action
     a. Better control of pH
     b. Milder alkalinity, alkalinity released as needed
   * Alkaline soap builders
     a. Loosen soil
     b. Pre-soften water save soap but not as efficient as sequestrants
     c. Fortify soap—pH of above 10.0 needed
3. Chlorine
   * Kills most all types of bacteria.
   * Not affected by water hardness.
   * Affected by presence of organic matter.
   * Corrosive to utensils if left in contact with the utensils for prolonged periods of time.
   * Irritating to skin when used in higher concentrations than are recommended.
   * Effectiveness is decreased as the solution becomes more alkaline.
4. Iodine
   * Kills most all types of bacteria.
   * Not affected by water hardness.
   * Noncorrosive to utensils.
   * Nonirritating to the skin.
   * Affected by presence of organic matter.
   * Effectiveness is decreased as the solution becomes more alkaline.
   * Should not be used in water over 120°F.
5. Quats or Quaternary Ammonium Compounds
   * Noncorrosive.
   * Active in alkaline or acid solutions.
   * May be selective in the type of bacteria it will kill.
   * Affected by the presence of organic matter
   * Affected by hard water and washing solution residues
   * Has a longer residue effect

Recommended Concentration, Times, and Temperatures of Exposure

Chlorine temperature of 75° or higher:

Dipping or submersion	50–100 ppm for 2 min.
Circulating	100–200 ppm for 2–3 min.
Spraying or fogging	200–300 ppm for 2–3 min.

Iodine Temperature 75–100°F

Dipping or submersion	12½ ppm for 2 min.
Circulating	12½ ppm to 25 ppm for 2–3 min.
Spraying or fogging	25 ppm for 2–3 min.

Quaternary ammonium compounds temperature of 75° or higher:

Dipping or submersion	50–100 ppm for 2 min.
Circulating	100–200 ppm for 2–3 min.
Spraying or fogging	200–300 ppm for 2–3 min.

CHEMICAL CONTROL OF INSECTS[2]

Control measures must be continual and on a routine maintenance basis. One cannot expect to eliminate an existing infestation and have the premises remain insect-free for an indefinite period of time. Insects may (and most probably will) reappear, no matter how good the sanitation and housekeeping. Proper sanitation and housekeeping reduce the likelihood of infestation and they make control measures much more effective when infestation does occur.

Insecticides, that is, materials used for insect control, may be purchased in concentrated form or at ready-to-use strength. They are available in various formulations, such as oil solutions, water emulsions, water suspensions, baits, and dry powders or dusts. There are situations in which any of these might properly be used in or around a foodservice establishment, but most commonly, oil solution or water emulsion sprays will be utilized.

Some of the situations for which oil-based sprays are required or preferred are:

1. Where water might cause an electrical short circuit.
2. Where water might cause shrinkage of fabrics.
3. Where wallpapers, etc., may be stained or spotted.
4. Where water applications will not dry quickly enough to avoid mildew.
5. When the insecticide is oil soluble.

Some of the situations for which water-based sprays are required or preferred are:

1. Where the use of any oil spray creates a fire hazard, as about hot ovens or pilot flames.

---

[2]The author thanks the National Restaurant Association for use of this material from their technical bulletin ''Pest Prevention.''

2. Where oil solutions would cause damage to such materials as rubber or asphalt tile.
3. Where the odor of oil is objectionable.
4. Where the insecticide is water miscible or soluble.

Insecticidal sprays are designated as residual sprays, contact sprays, and space sprays, based upon their characteristics and method of application.

A residual spray is one which is applied to a surface, as a wall or floor, so that a deposit is left to kill insects that get on it later. The water or oil which is used to carry the insecticide evaporates away, leaving the insecticide as a very thin layer over the treated surface. The surface being treated should be uniformly wet with the spray, but not so heavily that applications on a wall will run.

Contact sprays are those which must hit the insect in order to kill it. They are usually applied to a concentration of insects, as a cluster of roaches in a corner or a crack. They only kill the insects that are wet with the spray.

Space sprays are a special kind of contact spray. Both kill on contacting the insect, but the contact spray is sprayed at the insects as coarse droplets which fall quickly, while the space spray is discharged into the air as fine droplets to form a fog which drifts about in the air for several minutes or more. Space sprays are more effective against flying insects than crawling insects. Contact and space sprays usually kill the insects more quickly than do the residual sprays.

Insecticidal dusts generally contain in dry form the same toxic agents as are found in the various sprays. There are situations in which it may be preferable to use a dry dust rather than a spray. Generally speaking, more skill and care is required in utilizing dusts, and such applications might best be left to your professional pest control operator.

Baits are combinations of an attractive food such as sugar with an insecticide. They are seldom used but may be used effectively to control hard to reach ant and roach infestations and to reduce outdoor fly populations. Since their attractant is usually a food item, foodservice operators must use and store them with special care.

Control of Flies, Mosquitoes and Gnats

Foodservice operators can do their own space spraying for controlling such flying insects. The most convenient method is through the use of one of the industrial aerosol "bombs" designed for this purpose. Or, they can utilize a space sprayer and one of the non-toxic space sprays, such as those made of pyrethram or pyrethrum plus an activator. The aerosol "bombs," sprayers, and space spray can be purchased from a pest control operator. The location and elimination of fly breeding is best performed by a pest control operator.

Control of Roaches and Ants

Your pest control contractor can advise you on what insecticides are approved for use to control roaches, ants, and other crawling insects in foodservice establishments. In difficult cases it is best to depend on a pest control operator to accomplish the required treatment.

Control of Pantry Pests

This can best be achieved by removing and destroying any infested food materials from the shelves. Preventive sanitation measures are the best control agent.

Details Concerning the Control of Other Insect Pests

Consult your professional pest control operator for advice on pests not listed and discussed above.

Immunity to Insecticides

An insecticide that is effective against one type of insect may be ineffective against another type. Adding to the complexity and ever-changing nature of the control problem is the fact that insects acquire a strong resistance or immunity to insecticides which were formerly most effective against them. Flies and mosquitoes, for example, have developed an immunity to DDT and related chemicals. In many areas the German Roach has become immune to chlordane and can no longer be controlled with this insecticide, which was formerly so very effective against them. Fleas, bedbugs, ticks, and others have also developed such resistance to chemicals which formerly were good control agents against them. This immunity of insects to materials formerly effective in controlling them is increasing both in the number of insect species involved and in geographical areas affected.

QUESTIONS

1. Define and give examples of:

ionization	residual insecticide
sequestration	hydrolize
colloids	contact spray
''hungry'' water	peptization
beerstone	space spray
solvent	saponification
glycerine	built soap
interfacial tension	time soaps
emulsification	surface tension
sanitize	dissolution
chelation	

2. Why is a cleaning agent with a high pH effective? Give some examples.
3. What is milkstone and how is it remedied?
4. Does soap form a solution or colloidal dispersion?
5. What type of insecticides would be best for ants and flies?
6. What are some of the characteristics of soap in the cleaning process?

BIBLIOGRAPHY

"All About Meat." *Food Service,* December 1964, pp. 4–56.

The Almanac. Westminster, MD: Edward E. Judge & Sons, Inc., 1969–72, 1974–75, 1977.

"Agricultural Prices and Parity." *Major Statistical Series of The U.S. Department of Agriculture,* vol. 1, no. 365 (Government Printing Office, October 1970): 1–44.

"Agricultural Production and Efficiency." *Major Statistical Series of the U.S. Department of Agriculture,* vol. 2, no. 365 (Government Printing Office, April 1970): 1–39.

American Hospital Association. *Food Service Manual for Health Care Institutions.* Chicago: American Hospital Association, 1972.

Andersen, Alex L. *Dry Bean Production in the Lake and Northeastern States,* no. 285, August 1965, pp. 1–13.

"April Highlights." *Dairy Products,* 31 May 1974, pp. 2–14.

"August Highlights." *Dairy Products,* 30 September 1974, pp. 2–14.

Avery, Arthur. "Writing Specs." *Food Management,* March 1978.

Bakery, May 1977; June 1977.

Base Plans in U.S. Milk Markets: Development, Status, and Potential, no. 957, June 1972, pp. 1–35.

Basic Fish Cookery, USDI Test Kitchen Series 2, 1948.

Beau, Francis N. *Quantity Food Purchasing Guide.* Boston: Cahners Books International, Inc., 1974.

Berkeley, Bernard. *The Selection and Maintenance of Commercial Carpet,* 1967, pp. 2–10, 19, 26–32.

Berry, Harold A. *Purchasing Guide, vol. 23.* Waterford, CT: Prentice-Hall, Inc., 1970.

Bolton, Ralph A. *Systems Contracting: A New Purchasing Technique, 1966.* American Medical Association, 1966.

Bowes, Clifford D. *Complete Guide to Profitable Meat Management, Vol. 1, Meat Department Management.* Boston: Cahners Books International, Inc., 1971.

Breads, Cakes, and Pies In Family Meals, no. 186, December 1971, pp. 1–30.

Brosington, Clayton F., Jr. "Marketing Research Report." *Hotel and Restaurant Meat Purveyors: Improved Methods and Facilities for Supplying Frozen Portion-Controlled Meat,* April 1971, pp. 1–44.

Bulletin CX-272-R. Cleveland: Cres-Cor, Inc.

Buying Beef For the Eating-Out Business. Chicago: Armour and Company.

The Buying Guide for Fresh Fruits, Vegetables, Herbs, and Nuts. sixth revised ed., Fullerton, CA: Blue Goose, Inc., 1976.

Buying, Handling and Using Fresh Fruits. Chicago: National Restaurant Association, 1973.

Canned Fruit and Vegetables. Chicago: American Hospital Association, 1958.

"Capabilities of U.S. and Mexican Production Areas." *Supplying U.S. Markets with Fresh Winter Produce,* no. 154, September 1971, pp. 1–25.

"Cashing in on Electronic Controls—Part 2." *Restaurant Business,* 1978.

"Cashing in on Pork." *National Live Stock and Meat Board,* September 1971, pp. 3–78.

Castille, M.A., Dawson, E.H., and Thompson, E.R. "The Vegetable Round Up—From Buying to Cooking." *U.S. Department of Agriculture Yearbook 1969* (Government Printing Office, 1969): 174–195.

Certification Manual. National Association of Institutional Laundry Managers, 1969.

Checklist of U.S. Standards for Farm Products. rev. ed. AMS-210, January 1963 (Marketing Information Division, AMS, U.S. Dept. of Agriculture).

Cheese in Family Meals. Washington, DC: USDA Home and Garden Bulletin No. 112, 1966.

Cleaning Agents Standards. New York: Institutional Research Council.

Committee on Preparation Factors, National Cooperative Meat Investigations. *Meat and Meat Cookery.* Chicago: National Livestock and Meat Board, 1942.

Companion, October 1977.

Container Net Weights. Washington, DC: United Fresh Fruit and Vegetable Association, 1976.

Conversion Factors and Weight and Measures. Washington, DC: U.S. Department of Agriculture/Economic Research Service, May 1952.

Cooking for Profit, August 1973, pp. 5–50.

Cost of Dry Whole Milk Packaged for Household Use. Washington, DC: U.S. Department of Agriculture, September 1973.

Crawford, Hollie, and McDowell, Milton. *Mathematics for Food Service/Lodging.* Boston: CBI Publishing Co., Inc., 1971.

Dahl, Crete. *Food and Menu Dictionary.* Boston: CBI Publishing Co., Inc., 1972.

"December Highlights." *Dairy Products.* 30 January 1975, pp. 2–11.

Directory of Meat and Poultry Inspection Program Establishments and Officials. Washington, DC: U.S. Department of Agriculture, 1974.

Dowst, Somerby R. *Basic for Buyers: A Practical Guide to Better Purchasing.* Boston: CBI Publishing Co., Inc., 1971.

Dry Beans, Peas, Lentils . . . Modern Cookery. rev. ed. USDA Leaflet 326, 1957.

Dyer, Dewey A. *So You Want to Start a Restaurant?* Boston: CBI Publishing Co., Inc., 1971.

Econometric Models of Cash and Future Prices of Shell Eggs. no. 1502, August 1974, pp. 1–32.

Economic Week. Citibank, N.A.

Effects of Alternative Marketing Margins for Beef and Pork. Washington, DC: U.S. Department of Agriculture, 1973.

Egg Grading Manual. Washington, DC: U.S. Department of Agriculture, 1972.

The Egg Product Industry: Structure, Practices and Costs, no. 917, February 1971, pp. 1–44.

Eggs in Family Meals—A Guide for Consumers. Washington, DC: USDA Home and Garden Bulletin No. 103, 1965.

Energy Conservation Program Guide for Industry and Commerce. National Bureau of Standards Handbook 115, September 1974.

Escoffier, Auguste, and Gilbert, Phileas. *Larousse Gastronomique.* New York: Crown Publishers, Inc., 1961.

Eshbach, Charles E. *Food Service Management: A Consideration of Selected Problem Areas in the Management of Foodservice Operations.* Boston: CBI Publishing Co., Inc., 1974.

Eshbach, Charles E. *Food Service Trends.* Boston: CBI Publishing Co., Inc., 1974.

Facts and Pointers on Marketing Fresh Tomatoes. Washington, DC: United Fresh Fruit and Vegetable Association, 1972.

"February Highlights." *Dairy Products,* 31 March 1975, pp. 2–12.

Federal and State Standards for the Composition of Milk Products (and Certain Non-Milk Fat Products). Washington, DC: U.S. Department of Agriculture, 1974.

Feldman, Julian. *Church Purchasing Procedures.* Englewood Cliffs, NJ: Prentice-Hall, Inc., 1964.

Fish Cookery for One Hundred. USDI Test Kitchen Series 1, 1950.

Fish Recipes for School Lunches. rev. ed. USDI Test Kitchen Series 5, 1959.

Fish and Wildlife Circular 214. Washington, DC: Department of the Interior.

Food and Beverage Cost Control Manual. Boston, MA: Sheraton Hotel Corp.

Food Buying Guide for Type A School Lunches. Washington, DC: USDA Program Aid 270, 1964.

Food Consumption of Households in the North Central Region, Seasons and Year 1965–66, September 1972, pp. 1–214.

Food Fish Facts, no. 50, 51, 53, 54. Chicago: National Marine Fisheries Service.

Food for Fitness: A Daily Food Guide. rev. ed. Washington, DC: USDA Leaflet 424, 1964.

Food for Groups of Young Children Cared for During the Day. U.S. Children's Bureau Pub. no. 386 (1960).

Food Management Magazine, March 1978, pp. 66, 68.

Food Purchasing Guide. Chicago: American Hospital Association, 1966.

Food Purchasing Guide for Group Feeding, June 1965, October 1976. U.S. Department of Agriculture.

Food Service Seasoning Guide. New York: The American Spice Trade Association.

Foods Your Children Need. U.S. Children's Bureau Unnumbered, 1958.

"Foreign Trade, Production and Consumption of Agriculture Products." *Major Statistical Series of the U.S. Department of Agriculture,* vol. 2, no. 365, April 1972, pp. 1–29.

Fresh and Frozen Fish Buying Manual. USDI Circular 20, 1954.

Gardner, Jerry D. *Contract Foodservice/Vending.* Boston: CBI Publishing Co., Inc., 1973.

Gillian, Margiet. *The Master Food Purchasing Guide.* Chicago: The American Hospital Association, 1953.

Glassware for the Food Service Industry. Toledo: Libby Glass, 1979.

A Glossary of Spices. New York: American Spice Trade Association, 1966.

Goldbeck, Nikki, and Goldbeck, David. *The Supermarket Handbook.* New York: Harper & Row, Pub., Inc., 1973.

Grading America's Food. Washington, DC: U.S. Department of Agriculture, Consumer and Marketing Service, 1970.

Green Vegetables for Good Eating. rev. ed. Washington, DC: USDA Home and Garden Bulletin No. 41, 1964.

"Gross and Net Form Income." *Major Statistical Series of the U.S. Department of Agriculture,* vol. 3, no. 365, September 1969, pp. 1–17.

A Guide for Planning and Equipping School Lunchrooms. USDA Program Aid 292, 1956.

Guide to Function Room Furniture. Pennsauken, NJ: King Arthur, Inc., AIA File 28-A.

Haines, Robert G. *Food Preparation for Hotels, Restaurants and Cafeterias.* Chicago: American Technical Society, 1973.

Handbook Agricultural Charts. Washington, DC: U.S. Department of Agriculture, 1974.

Handbook of Food Preparation. Washington, DC: American Home Economics Association, 1964.

"Helping the Consumer Choose." *NOAA Magazine,* January 1975.

Hertzson, David, ed. *Food and Beverage Purchasing.* New York: ITT Educational Services, Inc., 1971.

Hodges, Henry. *The Modern Science of Purchasing.* New York: Harper, 1961.

Home Canning of Fruits and Vegetables. rev. ed. Washington, DC: USDA Home and Garden Bulletin No. 8, 1964.

Home Canning of Meat. rev. ed. Washington, DC: USDA Home and Garden Bulletin No. 6, 1958.

''Home Economics.'' Washington, DC: Government Printing Office, April 1972.

Home Freezing of Fruits and Vegetables. Washington, DC: Agriculture Research Service, November 1971.

Home Freezing of Poultry. rev. ed. Washington, DC: USDA Home and Garden Bulletin No. 70, 1964.

Household Weights and Measures. National Bureau of Standards, Misc. Publication 234, November 15, 1960.

''How to Buy Beef Roasts.'' Washington, DC: U.S. Department of Agriculture, January 1968, pp. 3–15.

''How to Buy Beef Steaks,'' Washington, DC: U.S. Department of Agriculture, February 1973, pp. 3–15.

''How to Buy Canned and Frozen Vegetables.'' Washington, DC: U.S. Department of Agriculture, January 1975, pp. 3–23.

''How to Buy Fresh Fruits.'' Washington, DC: U.S. Department of Agriculture, October 1967, pp. 3–21.

''How to Buy Fresh Vegetables.'' Washington, DC: U.S. Department of Agriculture, December 1967, pp. 3–23.

''How to Buy Meat for Your Freezer.'' Washington, DC: U.S. Department of Agriculture, July 1974, pp. 3–27.

How to Cook Clams. USDI Test Kitchen Series 8, 1953.

How to Cook Crabs. USDI Test Kitchen Series 10, 1956.

How to Cook Lobster. USDI Test Kitchen Series 11, 1957.

How to Cook Oysters. USDI Test Kitchen Series 3, 1953.

How to Cook Scallops. USDI Test Kitchen Series 13, 1959.

How to Cook Shrimp. USDI Test Kitchen Series 7, 1952.

''How to Eye and Buy Seafoods.'' Washington, DC: U.S. Department of Commerce, 1970, pp. 3–19.

''How to Use USDA Grades in Buying Food.'' Washington, DC: Government Printing Office, 1967.

The Impact of Dairy Imports on the U.S. Dairy Industry, no. 278, January 1975, pp. 1–77.

Institutional Textile Manual. H. N. Baker Linen Company, 1977, pp. 1–9, 52–55.

Institutions/VFM. March, 1978.

Johnson, Hugh. *The World Atlas of Wine.* England: Mitchell Beazley Publishers, Ltd. 1971.

''July Highlights.'' *Dairy Products,* August 30, 1974, pp. 2–14.

''June Highlights.'' *Dairy Products,* July 30, 1974, pp. 2–18.

Kahrl, W.L. *Foodservice on a Budget for Schools, Senior Citizens, Colleges, Nursing Homes, Hospitals, Industrial and Correctional Institutions.* Boston: CBI Publishing Co., Inc., 1974.

Kerr, R.G. ''Savvy with Seafood.'' *U.S. Department of Agriculture Yearbook 1969.* Washington, DC: U.S. Government Printing Office, 1969, pp. 127–130.

''Knowing What's Good for You.'' Campbell Soup Company, pp. 1–21.

Kotschevar, Lendal H. *Management by Menu.* Chicago: National Institute for the Foodservice Industry, 1975.

Kotschevar, Lendal H. *Quantity Food Purchasing.* New York: John Wiley & Sons, Inc., 1975.

Kotschevar, Lendal H. *Standards, Principles, and Techniques in Quantity Food Production.* Boston: Cahners Books International, Inc., 1974.

Kramer, Amilhud. *Food and the Consumer.* Westport, CT: Avi Publishing Company, Inc., 1973.

Kramlich, W.E., et al. *Processed Meats.* Westport, CT: Avi Publishing Company, Inc., 1973.

The Lab Notebook. Decatur, IL: ADM Foods, September 1977, October 1977.

Lamb Cutting and Purchasing Manual. Denver: American Sheep Products Council, 1957.

Lamb, How to Cut Today's New Lamb for Greater Sales and Profits. Chicago: National Livestock and Meat Board, 1971.

"Land Values and Farm Finance." *Major Statistical Series of the U.S. Department of Agriculture,* vol. 6, no. 365, April 1971, pp. 1–35.

Lausanne, Edita. *The Great Book of Wine.* New York: A & W Publishers, Inc., 1970.

Lennartson, Roy W. "What Grades Mean, Food." *The Yearbook of Agriculture, 1959.* Washington, DC: Supt. of Documents, pp. 344–352.

Lessons on Meat. Chicago: National Livestock and Meat Board, 1964.

Levie, Albert. *The Meat Handbook.* Westport, CT: Avi Publishing Company, Inc., 1967.

Lews, Bernard L. *Food Service Seasoning Guide.* New York: American Spice Trade Association, 1969.

Lifquist, Rosalind C., and BeTate, Edith. *Planning Food for Institutions.* Washington, DC: U.S. Department of Agriculture, 1951.

Livestock and Meat Statistics. Washington, DC: U.S. Department of Agriculture, 1973.

Maizel, Bruno. *Food and Beverage Purchasing.* New York: ITT Educational Services, Inc., 1961.

Manning, Thorner. *Quality Control in Food Service.* Westport, CT: Avi Publishing Company, Inc., 1976.

"March Highlights." *Dairy Products,* 30 April 1974, pp. 2–14.

"Market Disease of Stone Fruit: Cherries, Peaches, Nectarines, Apricots and Plums." Washington, DC: U.S. Department of Agriculture, 1972.

"Market Diseases of Tomatoes, Peppers and Eggplants." Washington, DC: U.S. Department of Agriculture, 1968.

"Market News." *Major Statistical Series of the U.S. Department of Agriculture,* vol. 10, no. 365, 1972, pp. 1–42.

Martin, Ruth. *International Directory of Food and Cooking.* New York: Hasting House, 1974.

"May Highlights." *Dairy Products,* 1 July 1974, pp. 2–14.

Meat Buyers Guide to Portion Control Meat Cuts. Chicago: National Association of Meat Purveyors, 1967.

Meat Buyers Guide to Standardized Meat Cuts. Chicago: National Association Of Meat Purveyors, 1961.

Meat Curing Principles and Modern Practice. Koch Supplies, Inc., 1973, pp. 18–24, 28–30.

Meat Curing Principles and Practices. Koch Supplies, Inc., 1976.

Meat Evaluation Handbook. Chicago: National Livestock and Meat Board, 1969.

"Meat Facts." *American Meat Institute.* July 1974, pp. 2–22.

Meat for Thrifty Meals. rev. ed. Washington, DC: USDA Home and Garden Bulletin No. 27, 1963.

"Merchandising Beef Loins." Chicago: National Livestock and Meat Board, pp. 3–32.

"Merchandising Beef Ribs." Chicago: National Livestock and Meat Board, pp. 3–36.

"Merchandising Beef Rounds." Chicago: National Livestock and Meat Board, pp. 3–24.

Merrill, Anabel L., and Watt, Bernice K. *Energy Value of Foods . . . Basic and Deviation.* Washington, DC: United States Department of Agriculture, 1973.

Milk Ordinance and Code. 1953 Recommendations of the Public Health Service, 3rd Printing. Washington, DC: Department of Health, Education and Welfare.

Miller, A.R., D.V.M. "To Assure Good Clean Meat, Food." *The Yearbook of Agriculture 1959.* Washington, DC: Government Printing Office, 1959, pp. 340–343. (Yearbook Separate No. 2970).

NOAA Magazine. Department of Commerce, January 1975, pp. 59–60.

Nelson, John, and Trout, Malcomb. *Judging Dairy Products,* 4th ed. Milwaukee: Olsen Publishing Co., 1964.

Newer Knowledge of Cheese. Rosemont, IL: National Dairy Council, 1948.

Newer Knowledge of Milk. Chicago: National Dairy Council, 1965.

"November Highlights." *Dairy Products,* 31 December 1974, pp. 2–11.

Nutrition and Healthy Growth. U.S. Children's Bureau Pub. No. 352, 1955.

Nutrition and Technical Services Staff. *Food Buying Guide for Type A School Lunches.* Washington, DC: Food and Nutrition Service, 1972.

Nutrition Up to Date . . . Up to You. rev. ed. Reprint from USDA Home and Garden Bulletin No. 1, Family Fare, Separate 1, 1960.

Nutritive Value of Foods. rev. ed. Washington, DC: USDA Home and Garden Bulletin No. 72, 1964.

"Nutritive Value of Fruits and Vegetables." Washington, DC: United Fresh Fruit and Vegetable Association, pp. 1–12.

Official Grain Standards of the United States, rev., SRA-AMS 177, Grain Division, AMS, U.S. Department of Agriculture, Washington, DC: Government Printing Office, 1961.

"The Official United States Standards for Grain." Washington, DC: Government Printing Office, 1974, pp. 11–96.

101 Meat Cuts . . . A Guide to Meat Selection and Care. Chicago: National Livestock and Meat Board.

"Operating Budgets for Food Service Establishments." *Food Management,* Leaflet 12, pp. 2–10.

Past Prevention (Technical Bulletin No. 190). Chicago: National Restaurant Association, pp. 11–12.

Peddersen, Raymond B. *SPECS: The Comprehensive Foodservice Purchasing and Specification Manual.* Boston: CBI Publishing Co., Inc., 1977.

Planning the School Foodservice Facilities Equipment Specifications. Salt Lake City: Utah State Board of Education, 1967.

"Plant Hardiness Zone Map." Washington, DC: United States Department of Agriculture, 1972.

"Popular Publications for the Farmer, Suburbanite, Homemaker Consumer." Washington, DC: U.S. Department of Agriculture, November 1973, pp. 1–18.

"Pork in the Foodservice Industry." *Pork Industry Committee,* pp. 2–47.

Potatoes in Popular Ways. USDA Home and Garden Bulletin No. 55, 1957.

Poultry Grading Manual. Washington, DC: U.S. Department of Agriculture, 1971.

Poultry Products Inspection Act, 71 Stat. 441, 21 U.S.C. 451–469.

Price—Quantity Relationships for Selected Retail Cuts of Pork. Washington, DC: U.S. Department of Agriculture.

"Production of Manufactured Dairy Products 1973." *Manufactured Dairy Products,* June 20, 1974, pp. 2–63.

"Protection Through Inspection." Washington, DC: U.S. Department of Commerce, May 1974, pp. 1–8.

"Publications Food and Nutrition Service." Washington, DC: U.S. Department of Agriculture, May 1974, pp. 3–18.

Purchases and Stores: School, Business, Management Handbook Number 5. New York: The University of the State of New York, 1964.

Putman, D.A., Northeastern Region, et. al. *Beef Cattle Breeds.* February 1975, pp. 1–33.

Quantity Recipes for Type A School Lunches (card file). USDA Program Aid 631.

Rainbird, George. *The Wine Handbook.* London: Michael Joseph Ltd., 1963, pp. 16–20, 36–38.

Recipes for Quantity Service. USDA Home Economics Research Report No. 5, 1958.

Reginald, Sister Mary. *Manual of Specifications for Canned Fruit and Vegetables.* Chicago: American Hospital Association, 1958.

Reitz, L. P., and Lebsock, K. L. *Distribution of the Varieties and Classes of Wheat in the United States in 1969.* Washington, DC: U.S. Department of Agriculture, 1972.

Rice in the United States: Varieties and Production. No. 289, June 1973, pp. 1–154.

Rietz, C. A., and Wanderstock, J. J. *A Guide to the Selection, Combination, and Cooking of Foods,* vol. 2. Westport, Connecticut: Avi Publishing Co., Inc., 1965.

Reitz, Carl A. *A Guide to the Selection, Combination and Cooking of Foods, Vol. 1, Selection and Combination of Foods.* Westport, Connecticut: Avi Publishing Company, Inc., 1961.

Robards, Terry. *Wine Cellar Journal.* New York: Quadrangle/The N.Y. Times Book Co., 1974.

Rodgers, Richard K. "Procurement Programmed for Profit." *Foodservice Magazine,* February 1974, pp. 44–51.

Root Vegetables in Everyday Meals. USDA Home and Garden Bulletin No. 33, 1961.

Rust, Robert E., and Olson, Dennis G. *Meat Curing Principles and Modern Practice.* Kansas City, MO: Koch Supplies, Inc., 1973.

"Salad Dressing, Mayonnaise, and Related Products 1969." Washington, DC: United States Department of Commerce, November 1970, pp. 1–12.

The Sale of Wine in Restaurants. San Francisco, CA: The Wine Institute, 1976.

Sanders, G. B. *Cheese Varieties and Descriptions.* Agr. Handbook No. 54, Washington, DC: Government Printing Office, 1953.

Schoonmaker, Frank. *Almanac of Wine.* New York: Hastings House Publishers, 1975.

Schoonmaker, Frank. *Encyclopedia of Wine.* New York: Hastings House Publishers, 1975.

The Seafood Game. Chicago: National Fisheries Institute, Inc.

Selected Research Abstracts of Published and Unpublished Reports Pertaining to the Food Service Industry. Washington, DC: U.S. Department of Agriculture, 1970.

Selection and Care of Fresh Fruits and Vegetables—A Consumer's Guide. United Fresh Fruit and Vegetable Association, 1971.

"A Selective List with Descriptive Annotations." *New Technical Books,* vol. 59, no. 8, reviews 1051–1247, October 1974, pp. 291–388.

"September Highlights." *Dairy Products,* 31 October 1974, pp. 2–16.

Ser-Vo-Tel Institute. *Foodservice Vocabulary.* Boston: CBI Publishing Co., Inc., 1974.

"Shelf Life of Food." *Food Technology,* August 1974.

Shopper's Guide to U.S. Grades for Food. rev. ed. Washington, DC: USDA Home and Garden Bulletin no. 58, 1964.

"Solids by Means of a Refractometer—Official." *Official Methods of Analysis of the Association of Official Agricultural Chemists,* seventh ed., p. 495.

Sunkist Fresh Citrus Quantity Serving Handbook. Los Angeles, CA: Sunkist Growers, 1963.

Szathmary, Louis. "Fish—Food for Gourmets." *The Cornell Hotel and Restaurant Administration Quarterly,* 1965, pp. 1–13.

Todoroff, Alexander. *Food Buying Today.* Chicago: The Grocery Trade Publishing House, 1934.

Tomatoes on Your Table. rev. USDA Leaflet 278, 1964.

"Trouble Shooting Hints" (chart). *Tableware Survival Kit.* Corning, NY: Corning Glass Works.

United States Standards for Fruits and Vegetables.

Units of Weight and Measure (United States Customary and Metric), Definitions and Tables of Equivalents. National Bureau of Standards, Misc. Publication 233. Washington, DC: Government Printing Office, 1960.

"USDA Standards for Food and Farm Products." Washington, DC: U.S. Department of Agriculture, November 1974, pp. 1–15.

U.S. Department of Agriculture. *Better Marketing for Beef with a New USDA Grading System,* (AMS-471). Washington, DC: Government Printing Office.

U.S. Department of Agriculture. *Consumer and Marketing Service.* Washington, DC: Government Printing Office, 1971.

U.S. Department of Agriculture. *Federal and State Standards for the Composition of Milk Products,* Agr. Handbook No. 51. Washington, DC: U.S. Government Printing Office, May 1971.

U.S. Department of Agriculture. "Food Purchasing Guide for Group Feeding." Agriculture Handbook No. 281, Washington, DC: Government Printing Office, 1965.

U.S. Department of Agriculture. "Home Freezing of Poultry." Washington, DC: U.S. Department of Agriculture, February 1970, pp. 2–24.

U.S. Department of Agriculture, Marketing Economics Division. *Market Structure of the Food Industries.* Washington, DC: Government Printing Office, 1972.

U.S. Department of Agriculture. *Meat and Poultry Standards for You.* Home and Garden Bulletin No. 171, Washington, DC: Government Printing Office, 1969.

U.S. Department of Agriculture. "Meat Poultry." Washington, DC: U.S. Department of Agriculture, October 1969, pp. 1–3.

U.S. Department of Agriculture. *Poultry Grading Manual.* Agriculture Handbook No. 31. Washington, DC: Government Printing Office, 1971.

U.S. Department of Agriculture. *Poultry Products Inspection Regulations.* vol. 37, no. 95, part II of Federal Register. Washington, DC: Government Printing Office, 16 May 1972.

U.S. Department of Agriculture. *Regulations Governing the Grading and Inspection of Poultry and Edible Products Thereof and U.S. Classes, Standards, and Grades with Respect Thereto,* 7CFR, part 70. Washington, DC: Government Printing Office, 30 June 1975 and 1 July 1971.

U.S. Department of Agriculture. *Regulations Governing the Grading of Shell Eggs and U.S. Standards, Grades and Weight Classes for Shell Eggs.* 7CFR, part 56. Washington, DC: Agricultural Marketing Service, Poultry Division, 1 July 1971.

U.S. Department of Agriculture. *Regulations Governing the Inspection of Eggs and Egg Products.* 7CFR, part 59, Washington, DC: Government Printing Office, 30 June 1975.

U.S. Department of Agriculture. *Shopper's Guide.* Washington, DC: Government Printing Office, 1974.

U.S. Department of Agriculture. *Standards for Butter.* Washington, DC: Government Printing Office, 1960.

U.S. Department of Agriculture. *Standards for Frozen Desserts.* Washington, DC: Government Printing Office, 1968.

U.S. Department of Agriculture. *USDA Grade Marks and the Foods on Which They are Used.* AMS-242. Washington, DC: Agricultural Marketing Service.

U.S. Department of Agriculture. *The Yearbook of Agriculture 1959.* Washington, DC: Government Printing Office, 1959.

U.S. Supply Service Standard Stock Catalogue. General Services Administration.

Wanderstock, J. J. "Meat Purchasing." *The Cornell Hotel & Restaurant Administration Quarterly,* vol. 11, no. 3, 1970, pp. 60–64.

Washington Food Report. Fair Lawn, NJ: American Institute of Food Distribution.

Watt, Bernice K., and Merrill, Annabel L. *Composition of Foods.* Washington, DC: U.S. Department of Agriculture, 1963.

Wenzel, George L. *How to Build Volume.* Austin: George Wenzel, Sr., 1971.

Wenzel, George, Sr. *Wenzel's Menu Maker.* 2nd ed. Boston: CBI Publishing Co., Inc., 1979.

West, B. B., Wood, L., and Shugart, G. *Food Service in Institutions.* 5th ed. New York: John Wiley & Sons, Inc., 1970.

"Wildlife and Fisheries." *Code of Federal Regulations,* part 261, 1972, pp. 1–5.

"Wildlife and Fisheries." *Code of Federal Regulations,* part 262, 1973, pp. 1–3.

"Wildlife and Fisheries." *Code of Federal Regulations,* part 263, 1972, pp. 1–30.

"Wildlife and Fisheries." *Code of Federal Regulations,* part 264, 1972, pp. 1–5.

"Wildlife and Fisheries." *Code of Federal Regulations,* part 265, 1972, pp. 1–2.

"Wildlife and Fisheries." *Code of Federal Regulations,* part 266, 1972, pp. 1–5.

"Wildlife and Fisheries." *Code of Federal Regulations,* part 267, 1972, pp. 1–5.

"Wildlife and Fisheries." *Code of Federal Regulations,* part 268, 1972, pp. 1-4.

"Wildlife and Fisheries." *Code of Federal Regulations,* part 269, 1972, pp. 1-4.

"Wildlife and Fisheries." *Code of Federal Regulations,* part 270, 1972, pp. 1-5.

"Wildlife and Fisheries." *Code of Federal Regulations,* part 271, 1972, pp. 1-3.

"Wildlife and Fisheries." *Code of Federal Regulations,* part 272, 1972, pp. 1-5.

"Wildlife and Fisheries." *Code of Federal Regulations,* part 273, 1972, pp. 1-3.

"Wildlife and Fisheries." *Code of Federal Regulations,* part 274, 1972, pp. 1-3.

"Wildlife and Fisheries." *Code of Federal Regulations,* part 275, 1973, pp. 1-3.

"Wildlife and Fisheries." *Code of Federal Regulations,* part 276, 1972, pp. 1-5.

"Wildlife and Fisheries." *Code of Federal Regulations,* part 277, 1972, pp. 1-4.

"Wildlife and Fisheries." *Code of Federal Regulations,* part 279, 1972, pp. 1-3.

Wilkinson, Jule. *The Complete Book of Cooking Equipment.* Boston: CBI Publishing Co., Inc., 1972.

Wilkinson, Jule. *The Components of Communication.* Chicago: Cahners Books International, Inc., 1968.

Wilkinson, Jule. *The Finishing Kitchen.* Chicago: Medalist Publication, 1969.

Wood, Adeline. *Quantity Food Buying Guides,* parts I and II. New York: Ahrens, 1957.

"The World Food Situation." Washington, DC: U.S. Department of Agriculture, October 1974, pp. 1-5.

World Foodservice Markets Encyclopedia. Chicago, IL: International Foodservice Manufacturers Association.

Wrisley, Albert L., Buck, Ernest M., and Eshbach, Charles E. *Purchasing Beef for Food Service Establishments.* Amherst: University of Massachusetts.

Zaccarelli, Brother Herman E., *Purchasing Techniques for Hospital Food Services.* North Easton, MA: The International Food Research and Educational Center, 1972.

Zaccarelli, Brother Herman E., and Maggiore, Josephine. *Nursing Home Menu Planning, Food Purchasing, and Management.* Boston: CBI Publishing Co., Inc., 1972.

INDEX